A DICTIONARY OF
RELIGIOUS EDUCATION

A DICTIONARY OF
RELIGIOUS
EDUCATION

EDITED BY
JOHN M. SUTCLIFFE

SCM PRESS LTD
in association with
The Christian Education Movement

334 01968 0

First published 1984
by SCM Press Ltd
26–30 Tottenham Road, London N1
in association with
The Christian Education Movement
2 Chester House, Pages Lane, London N10

Phototypeset by Input Typesetting Ltd
and printed in Great Britain by
Richard Clay (The Chaucer Press) Ltd
Bungay, Suffolk

PREFACE

This *Dictionary* is concerned with religious education in every continent, and as practised in many different faiths. It takes account of new developments throughout the world, with a special focus on areas like Australia, North America and Western and Scandinavian Europe, where RE research and teaching have moved on apace. However, because of the complexity of the questions involved, it has had to be rooted in one specific field of practice, and therefore provides more information about British religious education than about any other area.

The *Dictionary* concentrates on methods of teaching rather than the content of what is taught – there are adequate accounts of that elsewhere. Entries fall into four main categories: descriptions of the major religious teaching traditions and of religious education in school; summaries of the philosophical, theological, sociological and psychological understandings of religious education; outlines of curriculum and teaching methods; and notes on some of the resources for the teaching of religious education. A common assumption of the contributors, which perhaps needs to be stressed to those comparatively unfamiliar with the scope of the subject, is that religious education in its various forms is a lively and enterprising discipline and activity.

Religious education is continually developing. For example, in the period leading up to the production of the *Dictionary* there has been a new interest in spirituality, in the use of art and computers in religious education, in the relation of religious education to the personal and social development of pupils and in more general life skills, humanities and pastoral programmes. None of this could have been foreseen even five years beforehand. That this is the case and that computers and video are increasingly used in religious education reflects something of the dynamism of the subject and commitment of innumerable teachers.

The range of contributors to the *Dictionary* is itself testimony to the geographical and intellectual diversity represented. The journey from British humanism to Indian Jainism is long in every sense. For all this diversity contributors have been united in showing extraordinary interest in the project, and I am grateful for their encouragement and friendship. Religious education is capable of developing its own international multi-cultural fellowship.

Faith communities have an historic interest in teaching. In world terms they constitute the major source of modern religious education. Some, like parts of the Muslim community, have continued to use long established methods. Others have developed new approaches in the light of recent psychological, educational and theological insights. In parts of the world church, for instance, there have been renewed emphases on experience within the community of faith, the Bible as a theological resource and catalyst, and on social and international issues as being jointly central to the church's educational task. Developments of a different kind, often based on locally evolving expressions of the conscientization process, have taken place in Latin and South America. From some of these significant contributions have been made to national life, as in Nicaragua.

Since the 1960s, however, religious education in schools and religious education in faith communities have to some extent developed independently. This *Dictionary* acknowledges the roots of religious education in the faith communities, but in concentrating on religious education in schools it points to the distinctiveness of the subject.

Certain names recur. The works of Jean Piaget and Ronald Goldman are mentioned repeatedly. In general, however, I have been cautious about names, partly because developments in religious education are often due to corporate rather than to individual activity, and partly because individual contributors clearly have adopted opposing views about mentioning individuals. The name of Paulo Freire, for instance, is scarcely mentioned in the text, though in some places those who have been inspired by his work have collectively changed the whole direction of religious teaching and sometimes of social policy. An index of those mentioned in the text will be found on page 375.

In planning this *Dictionary* I acknowledge with gratitude the assistance of Dr John Hull, Paul King, Brenda Lealman, Gwen Palmer and Dr Derek Webster who formed an initial planning group. I express my gratitude to my former secretary, Phyl Cheswright, who coped with the three thousand letters involved, and to Ros Bacon and Linda Foster of SCM Press whose care and attention to detail have been exemplary. I wish also to thank Philip Lee-Woolf for considerable editorial assistance, and my family for living with the project for longer than they anticipated.

It is a matter of particular satisfaction to me that this publication represents very congenial collaboration between the Christian Education Movement and SCM Press.

JOHN M. SUTCLIFFE

CONTRIBUTORS

Colin Alves, *Deputy Secretary, General Synod Board of Education.* **History of RE in England; Objectives in RE**

David Anderson, *Head of Religious Studies, Herts College of Higher Education.* **Literature**

D. R. Ap-Thomas, *Senior Lecturer in Hebrew and Biblical Studies, University College of North Wales, Bangor.* **Hebrew: Study of in RE**

Tosh Arai, *Secretary for Study and Renewal Centres, World Council of Churches.* **Asia**

Elvira Romera de Arcaute, *Publishing Secretary, United Council of Christian Education.* **Latin/South America**

J. W. Ashley Smith, *Formerly Headmaster Bede Hall, Billingham.* **Congregationalism**

Maurice Assad, *Assistant General Secretary, Department of Education, Middle East Council of Churches.* **Middle East: Christian Education in the**

David Atkinson, *Anglican Chaplain, University of Hull.* **Diocesan Advisers: Church of England; Diocesan Syllabuses: Church of England**

David Attfield, *Team vicar, St John's, Drypool, Hull.* **Concepts; Nurture; Proselytism**

Jean-Pierre Bagot, *Professeur de Pedagic, l'Institut Catholique, Paris.* **France**

Edward Bailey, *Rector of Winterbourne, Bristol.* **Civil Religion; Common Religion; Folk Religion**

John Bailey, *County Chief Inspector, Bedfordshire County Council.* **Music**

John R. Baker, *Senior Lecturer in Education (Physics), University of Leicester.* **Science and Religion**

Mordechai Bar-Lev, *Deputy Head, School of Education, Bar Ilan University.* **Israel**

Vida Barnett, *Principal Lecturer, City of Liverpool College of Higher Education.* **Artefacts, Use of; Comparative Religion; Ritual; Standing Conference on Inter-Faith Dialogue in Education**

Patrick Barry OSB, *Formerly Headmaster, Ampleforth College.* **Religious Communities in Education**

Ulrich Becker, *Professor for Theology and Religious Education, University of Hanover.* **Ecumenical Education; World Council of Churches**

Ian H. Birnie, *Adviser for Religious Education, Lancashire.* **Biography; Heroes; Social Issues; Social Morality Council**

Reimund Blühm, *Lecturer, Naumburg High Seminary, Federal Republic of Germany,* **Eastern Europe**

John Bradford, *Course Tutor in Urban Education, Open University.* **Social Studies; Spiritual Rights**

Desmond F. Brennan, *Director, West London Institute of Higher Education.* **Media: Use of in RE; Resource Centres**

Colin Brock, *Chairman, International Education Unit, Institute of Education, University of Hull.* **World Studies**

Elizabeth Browett, *Head of RE, King's High School, Warwick.* **Allegory**

Alan Brown, *Schools Officer (RE), General Synod Board of Education.* **The Fourth R; Meaning, Quest for; Neo-confessional**

David Brown, *Formerly Bishop of Guildford.* **Dialogue**

Douglas A. Brown, *General Secretary, Methodist Division of Education and Youth.* **Free Church Federal Council; Joint Education Policy Committee; Methodist Church**

K. E. Bugge, *Professor of Religious Education, The Royal Danish School of Educational Studies, Copenhagen.* **Denmark**

Joseph P. Bysh, *Religious Education Adviser, Humberside.* **Grouping of Pupils**

W. S. Campbell, *Head of Religious and Theological Studies, Westhill College, Selly Oak.* **Journals; Tolerance**

Douglas S. Charing, *Rabbi, Director, Jewish Education Bureau.* **Bar/Bat Mitzvah**

Geoffrey Chorley, *Head of Religious and Moral Education, Homelands Comprehensive School, Derby.* **Cowper-Temple Clause; Management of RE in the Secondary School; Newsom Report; Plowden Report**

Rodney Cocks, *Adviser for Religious, Moral and Personal Education, Dorset.* **Provision for RE**

W. Owen Cole, *Senior Lecturer, West Sussex Institute of Higher Education.* **Founders of Religions; Multi-Racial Society; Shap Working Party on World Religions in Education**

David Cook, *Director, Church Educational System (CJCLDS) in the British Isles and Africa.* **The Church of Jesus Christ of Latter-day Saints ('Mormons')**

Benjamín Cortés, *Pastor.* **Latin/Central America**

Edwin Cox, *Emeritus Reader in Education, University of London.* **Agreed Syllabuses; Bible: Use of in RE; Moral Education**

Joan H. Craig, *CEM Secretary for Scotland.* **Scottish Joint Committee on Religious Education**

Bernard Crick, *Professor of Politics, Birkbeck College, University of London.* **Political Education and RE**

Sue Cross, *Director, Northampton Youth Dance Theatre.* **Dance and Drama**

Vince Cross, *Musical Director, Northampton Youth Dance Theatre.* **Dance and Drama**

John C. Dancy, *Professor, School of Education, University of Exeter,* **Independent Schools**

N. Daniel, *Secretary, All India Sunday School Association,* **India**

Jill Davies, *Advisory Teacher in Personal Relationships, ILEA.* **Personal Relationships: Teaching about in RE; Pastoral Care**

Rupert Davies, *Warden, John Wesley's Chapel, Bristol.* **John Wesley: Educational Work of**

Dorothy A. Dixon, *Formerly Assistant Professor of Education, University of Missouri-St Louis.* **Spiritual Area of Experience; Spiritual Development**

Peter Donovan, *Senior Lecturer in Religious Studies, Massey University, New Zealand.* **Religious Language and Use of Language in RE**

Althea Draper, *Head of RE, Seaford School, East Sussex.* **Yoga**

Frank Earle, *Adviser for Religious Education, Cheshire LEA.* **Sixth-Form**

W. J. H. Earl, *Formerly Staff Inspector for RE, DES.* **Acts of Parliament; Conscience Clauses; Inspection of RE**

David L. Edwards, *Senior Lecturer in Religious Studies, Edgehill College of Higher Education.* **Inter-Schools Conferences**

F. Elkin, *Professor of Sociology, York University, Toronto.* **Socialization**

Susan Elliott, *Education Officer, Programme Support and Development, IBA.* **Broadcasts: Independent Television and Independent Local Radio**

Trond Enger, *Senior Lecturer in Theology and RE, Halden College of Education, Norway.* **Norway**

Kenneth D. Exley, *Formerly Head of Andenshaw Grammar School.* **Head Teacher: Role of in RE; Sheffield Report; Spens Report**

Ian C. M. Fairweather, *Formerly Lecturer in Religious Education, Jordanhill College of Education, Glasgow.* **Emotional Development; Skills**

M. C. Felderhof, *Senior Lecturer in Modern Theology, Westhill College, Selly Oak.* **Tolerance**

Michael Fortounatto, *Priest, Russian Orthodox Church, London.* **Icon; Orthodox Church**

Leslie Francis, *Research Officer, Culham College Institute for Church-Related Education.* **Prayer: Children's Concepts of; Use of in School; Young Men's Christian Association; Young Women's Christian Association**

Carol Fry, *Lecturer in Religious Education, Dundee College of Education.* **Cognitive Education in RE; Miracle**

Erika Fuchs, *Vicar, Reformed Parish, Vienna.* **Austria**

F. W. Garforth, *Senior Lecturer, Department of Educational Studies, University of Hull.* **Classics and RE**

Brian E. Gates, *Head of Religious Studies and Social Ethics, St Martin's College, Lancaster.* **God**

John Gay, *Director, Culham College Institute for Church-Related Education.* **Colleges of Education: Church Colleges in the United Kingdom**

Peter Gee, *Publications and Press Officer, Overseas Development Institute.* **Student Christian Movement**

William Gilbert, *Director of Programme, Anglican Diocese of Ottawa.* **Canada**

Peter Gilliat, *Humanities Adviser, Avon.* **Humanities and RE**

John Gray, *Senior Lecturer in Ethics and Practical Theology, University of Edinburgh.* **Christianity: Theology and Education; Secularism**

James Green, *Chairman, Division of Religion and Theology, Sunderland Polytechnic.* **Peace Studies; Values Education**

William Greenwood, *Senior Lecturer in Religious Studies, West London Institute of Higher Education.* **Assessment of Students**

John E. Greer, *Lecturer in Education, The New University of Ulster*. **Attitudes; Clergy/Ministers: Role of in** RE **and Right of Entry in Northern Ireland; Ireland: Northern**

Michael Grimmitt, *Lecturer in Religious Education, University of Birmingham*. **Christianity: Place of in** RE **in Britain; Curriculum Development; International Seminar on Religious Education and Values; Worship**

Norman Habel, *Principal, Kodaikanal School, Tamil Nadu, India*. **Magic in Religion**

Christopher Halliday, *Formerly CEM Regional Secretary North West*. **Textbooks**

Paula Halliday, *Head Teacher, Lancasterian School, Manchester*. **Special Education, Special Schools**

Anthony Hanson, *Professor, Department of Theology, University of Hull*. **Hermeneutics; Qumran Scrolls**

Joan Hazelden Walker, *Leverhulme Emeritus Fellow and formerly Research and Publications Secretary, Institute of Religion and Theology*. **Higher Education**

Reijo Heinonen, *Lecturer in Didactics of Religion, University of Tukuru*. **Finland**

James Hemming, *Consultant Psychologist*. **British Humanist Association; Humanism**

Christopher Herbert, *Vicar, St Thomas-on-the Bourne, Farnham*. **Death: Pastoral Aspects of** RE; **Death: Teaching about in** RE

Ian L. Higgins, *Chaplain, Methodist Ladies College, Melbourne*. **Phenomenological Approach in** RE

Donald Hilton, *Minister, United Reformed Church, Norwich*. **Church Education; National Christian Education Council; Partners in Learning**

Michael Hinton, *Headmaster, Broadoak School, Weston-super-Mare*. **Ethos; Hidden Curriculum**

Paul H. Hirst, *Professor of Education, University of Cambridge*. **Philosophy of Education**

Sheila M. Hobden, *Head Teacher, The Margaret Glen Bott Comprehensive School, Nottingham*. **Assembly; Empathy**

Jack W. G. Hogbin, *Head of Religious Studies, Didsbury School of Education, Manchester Polytechnic*. **Examinations; History**

Raymond Holley, *Lately Senior Lecturer in Religious Studies and Chairman, Subject Area of Religion, West London Institute of Higher Education*. **Revelation; Ultimate Questions**

Jean Holm, *Principal Lecturer in Religious Studies, Homerton College, Cambridge*. **Jesus: 4. Teaching about in** RE; **Methods in** RE: **A Survey; New Zealand; Religion**

Roger Homan, *Senior Lecturer in Education, Brighton Polytechnic; Director, Centre for the Study of Religion and Society, University of Kent*. **Culture; Institutions; Sociology of Religion**

Morna D. Hooker, *Lady Margaret's Professor of Divinity, University of Cambridge*. **Jesus: 1. Evidence for Life of; 2. Significance for Christians**

Sue Howard, *ISCF Secretary*. **Inter-School Christian Fellowship**

Kenneth G. Howkins, *Senior Lecturer in Religious Studies, Hertfordshire College of Higher Education.* **Evangelical Attitudes**

Herbert Hughes, *Senior Lecturer in Religious Education, University of Wales.* **Wales**

John M. Hull, *Senior Lecturer in Religious Education, University of Birmingham.* **Indoctrination; RE: Nature of; Theology: 2. Theology and RE**

Edward Hulmes, *Professor, Department of Theology, University of Durham.* **Farmington Institute for Christian Studies; Neutrality; Qur'an, al-**

Keith Hurt, *Secretary, Higher and Further Education Affairs, Methodist Church Division of Education and Youth.* **Further Education**

Andrew Hutchinson, *Secondary Education Adviser, Christian Aid.* **Development Education and RE**

John Huxtable, *Formerly Executive Officer of the Churches' Unity Commission.* **Ecumenical Movement in Britain**

Muhammad Iqbal, *Adviser to Overseas Students and Senior Lecturer, Huddersfield Polytechnic.* **Islam, Islamic RE**

Robert Jackson, *Senior Lecturer in Arts Education, University of Warwick.* **Unions**

G. C. Jain, *Head of Department of Prakrit and Jainagama, S. Sanskrit University, Varanasi.* **Jainism**

Tony Jasper, *Broadcaster, author, journalist.* **'Pop' Music**

David E. Jenkins, *Professor of Theology, University of Leeds.* **Theology: 1. Definitions of**

Arthur Jennings, *Senior Lecturer in Education, University of London, Institute of Education.* **Baptist Church**

Margaret E. Jervis, *Formerly Senior Lecturer in Education, University of Bristol.* **Greek, New Testament**

Alistair Kee, *Reader in Religious Studies, University of Glasgow.* **Marx, Marxism**

David Keep, *Senior Lecturer in Religious Studies, Rolle College, Exmouth.* **John Calvin; Pilgrimage; Quiet Rooms in Schools**

Trevor Kerry, *Head of Department of Applied Social Studies, Doncaster Metropolitan Institute of Higher Education.* **Evaluation**

Cecil King, *Lecturer in Religious Education, Kwamw Nkrumah Secondary Teacher's College, Kabwe, Zambia.* **Africa: Eastern**

D. Paul King, *Adviser for Religious Education, Devon.* **Advisers; Local Education Authorities; Plural Society; RE Room**

Ursula King, *Senior Lecturer in Theology and Religious Studies, University of Leeds.* **Mysticism**

André Knockaert, *Directeur du Centre international d'Etudes de la Formation religieuse, Brussells.* **Belgium**

David Konstant, *Roman Catholic Bishop in Central London.* **Catechetics; Roman Catholic Church**

F. H. Kuiper, *Senior Lecturer in Religious Education, Vrije University, Amsterdam.* **Netherlands**

J. J. Laidlaw, *Adviser in Religious Education, Tayside.* **Association of Teachers of Religious Education in Scotland; Millar Report**

Stephen Lambden, *Research student, University of Newcastle upon Tyne.* **Baha'i**

John Lawson, *Reader in the History of Education, University of Hull.* **Cathedral Schools; Monasticism; School Boards**

Clive A. Lawton, *Headmaster, The King Davids High School, Liverpool.* **Judaism**

Brenda Lealman, *RE Adviser, Secondary Schools, CEM.* **Affectivity; Aims of RE in LEA schools; Art; Mystery; World Religions**

Philip Lee-Woolf, *Minister of United Reformed Church; formerly General Secretary CEM.* **Christian Education and RE; Conscientization; Ministry: Informal/Auxiliary Courses**

Anza A. Lema, *Associate General Secretary, Lutheran World Federation.* **Lutheran Church: Involvement in Education**

James E. Loder, *Mary D. Synnott Professor of Philosophy of Christian Education, Princeton Theological Seminary.* **Creativity**

Roy Long, *Head of Religious Studies, Lodge Park Comprehensive School, Corby; Secretary for Christian Education, Lutheran Church in Great Britain – United Synod.* **Luther: Educational Work of**

Alan Loosemore, *Staff Inspector for Religious Education, DES.* **Department of Education and Science (DES)**

J. R. B. McDonald, *Head of Religious Studies, Stanmillis College, Belfast.* **Ireland: Eire**

Sallie McFague, *Professor of Theology, Divinity School, Vanderbilt University.* **Parables**

Donald M. McFarlan, *Formerly Head of Religious Education, Jordanhill College of Education, Glasgow.* **Clergy/Ministers: Role of in RE and Right of Entry in Scotland; Scotland**

Henry McKeating, *Senior Lecturer in Theology, University of Nottingham.* **Bible: Biblical Models of RE**

R. J. McKelvey, *Principal, The Northern College, Manchester.* **Theological Colleges**

Duncan M. MacPherson, *Senior Lecturer in Religious Studies, St Mary's College of Higher Education, Strawberry Hill, Twickenham.* **Christian Theological Critiques and RE; Hinduism; Schools Council**

Timothy J. Mark, *Principal Lecturer, Department of Applied Social Sciences, Doncaster Metropolitan Institute of Higher Education.* **Adolescence**

Howard Marratt, *Assistant Principal, West London Institute of Higher Education; Chairman, Religious Education Council of England and Wales.* **British and Foreign School Society; Colleges of Education and RE; Commitment; Religious Education Council of England and Wales; Teachers**

Robert Martineau, *Formerly Bishop of Blackburn.* **Church of England: Policy in Education**

John Marvell, *Senior Lecturer in charge, RE Centre Essex.* **Home, Role of; Social Education**

J. Kenneth Meir, *Formerly Secretary, Methodist Youth Department*. **Sunday School Movement**

Barbara Menzies, *Senior Lecturer in Education, Edge Hill College of Higher Education*. **Religious Development in Childhood; Infant School, RE in**

Graham B. Miles, *Senior Lecturer in Religious Studies, Homerton College, Cambridge*. **Interdisciplinary Approaches to Education; Transcendence**

Robin Minney, *Lecturer in Religious Education, University of Durham*. **Festivals; Knowledge**

David Minton, *Head of RE and Co-ordinator of Personal Development, Benjamin Britten High School, Lowestoft*. **Jesus: 3. Place of in World Faiths**

Basil Moore, *Lecturer in Religious Studies, South Australian College of Advanced Education*. **Typology of Religion**

Heather Moore, *Teacher, Norbury First and Middle School, Harrow*. **Middle School: RE in**

Gabriel Moran, *Associate Professor of Religious Education, New York University*. **United States of America**

Alasdair Morton, *General Secretary, Church of Scotland Department of Education*. **Presbyterian Churches, Church of Scotland**

Basil Moss, *Provost of Birmingham Cathedral*. **Baptism**

R. P. Moss, *Professor of Geography, University of Salford*. **Environmental Studies**

John Mott, *Director, Bloxham Project*. **The Bloxham Project; Chaplains: Role of in Schools**

Kenneth Mullis, *Senior Lecturer in Religious and Theological Studies, Westhill College, Birmingham*. **Jean-Jacques Rousseau**

Carol Mumford, *Formerly Senior Lecturer in Religious Education, Margaret McMillan College, Bradford*. **Nursery Schools: RE in**

David Naylor, *Adviser for RE, Hampshire*. **Implementation of Agreed Syllabuses**

Graham Neville, *Director of Education, Diocese of Lincoln*. **Clergy/Ministers: Role of in RE in England and Wales; Doctrine, Teaching of**

Timothy Newell Price, *Director of Religious Studies, Leighton Park School*. **Community Service; Work Camps.**

K. E. Nipkow, *Professor of Religious and General Education, University of Tübingen*. **West Germany**

Robin Norbury, *Formerly Principal Lecturer in Environmental Studies, Bretton Hall College, Wakefield*. **Environment; Environmental Education**

D. Nwosu, *Lecturer, Faculty of Education, University of Ilorin*, **Africa: West**

Carl-Eber Olivestam, *Professor of Theology, University of Umå*. **Sweden**

Judith Ollington, *Formerly Senior Lecturer in Religious Studies, Whitelands College, Roehampton Institute of Higher Education*. **Imagination; Openness in RE; Personal Relationships: Development of Teaching about in RE**

Krister Ottosson, *City Centre Chaplain, Newcastle upon Tyne*. **Pentecostal Churches**

Michael Paffard, *Formerly Senior Lecturer in Education, University of Keele*. **Sensitivity**

David A. Pailin, *Senior Lecturer in Philosophy of Religion, University of Manchester.* **Philosophy of Religion**

Gwen Palmer, *Senior Lecturer in Religious Studies, Hertfordshire College of Higher Education.* **Child-Centred RE; Junior School: RE in; Myth; Symbolism**

Martin Palmer, *Formerly Director, Sacred Trinity Centre for the Study of Religion and Education, Salford,* **Inner City, RE in the**

Robin T. Pearce, *Head of Humanities, Castle School, Taunton.* **Sacred Places**

John H. Peatling, *President, Values Research Services Ltd.* **Theories of Development**

Chantal van der Plancke, *Professor, l'Institut Lumen Vitae, Brussells.* **Belgium**

Colin Price, *Head of RE, Bradford Girls' Grammar School.* **Computer Assisted Learning in RE**

Jack Priestley, *Lecturer in Education, University of Exeter.* **Health Education and RE; Story; Themes**

Richard Pring, *Professor of Education, University of Exeter.* **Conscience**

Patrick Purnell SJ, *National Adviser for Religious Education to the Bishops of England and Wales (Catholic).* **Diocesan Advisers: Roman Catholic; Diocesan Syllabuses: Roman Catholic**

Elizabeth Ramsey, *Primary RE Development Officer, St Martin's College, Lancaster.* **Primary School: RE in**

Garth T. Read, *Director, Regional RE Centre (Midlands), Westhill College, Selly Oak.* **Australia**

John Reardon, *Secretary, Church and Society Department, United Reformed Church.* **United Reformed Church**

Jean Richardson, *Regional Youth Officer, Methodist Church.* **Handicapped, Mentally: Religious Education of**

James Robertson, *Formerly Secretary, United Society for the Propagation of the Gospel.* **Mission Schools**

Edward Robinson, *Director, Religious Experience Research Unit, Manchester College, Oxford.* **Religious Experience; Religious Experience Research Unit**

Mary S. Robinson, *Lecturer in English, University of Constantine, Algeria.* **Africa: North-West**

Ralph Rolls, *Producer Religious Programmes and formerly Senior Producer Religious Programmes in Schools, BBC Television.* **Broadcasts: BBC**

Arthur Rowe, *Senior Lecturer in Religious Studies, Avery Hill College.* **Association for Religious Education; Community Relations, Contribution of RE to; Evangelism and Education**

P. S. Sambi, *Chairman, The Sikh Information Centre, Leeds.* **Sikhism**

G. E. W. Scobie, *Lecturer in Psychology, Glasgow University.* **Psychology of Religion**

Alan P. F. Sell, *Theological Secretary, World Alliance of Reformed Churches, Geneva.* **Rationality**

David Sellick, *Senior Lecturer in Education, College of Ripon and York St John.* **Secondary Schools: RE in**

Robin H. Shepherd, *General Adviser in Religious Education, Bedfordshire.* **Career Value of RE; Confessionalism**

Noël Barrett Shuell, *Assistant Professor of Religious Education, Memorial University, Newfoundland.* **Canada: Newfoundland and Labrador**

David Sibrey, *Director, Jehovah's Witnesses Information Office.* **Jehovah's Witnesses**

Ninian Smart, *Professor of Religious Studies, University of Lancaster; Professor of Religious Studies, University of California, Santa Barbara.* **Explicit Religion; Implicit Religion; Phenomenology of Religion**

Michael B. Smith, *British Field Representative, ACE; Principal, Emmanuel Christian School.* **Christian Schools**

David Stacey, *Principal, Wesley College, Bristol.* **Bible: Trends in Modern Biblical Scholarship**

E. M. Stamper, *Senior Lecturer in Religious Studies, Huddersfield Polytechnic.* **Vacation Term for Biblical Study**

Dennis Starkings, *Lecturer in Arts Education, University of Warwick.* **Professionalism: Its Meaning and Growth in RE**

Alan M. G. Stephenson, *Rector of Steventon with Milton.* **Lambeth Diploma**

H. Stopes-Roe, *Senior Lecturer, Department of Extra-Mural Studies, University of Birmingham,* **Life Stance**

Doreen Storr, *RE/Voluntary Children's Work Adviser, Diocese of Lincoln.* **Infancy**

Peter Street, *Senior Inspector in RE and Humanities, Essex.* **Standing Advisory Councils for Religious Education**

Vincent Strudwick, *Director of Education and Training, Diocese of Oxford.* **Adult**

D. Sullivan, *Senior Teacher, St Katherine's County Primary School, Snodland.* **Crowther Report, 1959; Gifted Children**

Kenneth Surin, *Lecturer in Theology, College of St Paul and St Mary, Cheltenham.* **Experiential: Definition of; Experiential Approach to RE**

John M. Sutcliffe, *General Secretary, CEM.* **British Council of Churches; Christian Education and RE; Holy Communion and Children; Professional Council for Religious Education; World Church**

Lyndon Taylor, *Lieutenant-Colonel, Salvation Army, Territorial Commander, Ghana.* **Salvation Army**

D. G. Temple, *Formerly General Secretary, Christians Abroad.* **Christians Abroad**

Ronwyn Goodsir Thomas, *Director, Nether Hallam Conference and Retreat Centre; Secretary of the Institute of Religion and Theology of Great Britain and Ireland.* **Meditation: Use of in RE**

June B. Tillman, *Teacher, Pimlico School, Furzedean Primary School and ILEA Centre for Young Musicians.* **Music**

D. Tomasetto, *Secretary, Italian Sunday School Council.* **Italy**

Roger Tomes, *Lecturer in Old Testament, Northern College, Manchester.* **Dissenting Academies**

John Trillo, *Bishop of Chelmsford.* **Christian Education Movement**

Paul Turton, *Director, National Society* RE *Centre, London.* **The Christian Year; Life Cycle; National Society of Religious Education**

Harry Undy, *Deputy Director, Council for Education in World Citizenship.* **Christianity: Teaching as a World Religion**

Owen van den Berg, *Professor of Didactics, University of the Western Cape.* **Africa: South**

Robert Waddington, *Dean of Manchester.* **Confirmation; Reserved Teachers; Voluntary Schools**

Rex Walford, *Lecturer in Education, University of Cambridge.* **Games**

Maurice O'Connell Walshe, *Deputy Director, Institute of Germanic Studies, University of London.* **Buddhism**

David Warwick, *Director of Curriculum, Farnham College, Surrey.* **Correlation in** RE**; Integration of Curriculum and** RE

Peter R. Watkins, *Principal, Price's Sixth Form College, Fareham, Hampshire.* **General Studies and** RE **in Sixth Forms**

Derek Webster, *Lecturer in Educational Studies, University of Hull.* **Poetry and** RE**; Research in** RE

John White, *Head of English, Dunraven School, London.* **Prejudice**

Donald C. G. Whittle, *Head of Religious Studies, Bath College of Higher Education.* **In-Service Education of Teachers of** RE**; Personal Belief of Pupils**

Richard Wilkins, *General Secretary, Association of Christian Teachers.* **Association of Christian Teachers**

John Wilson, *Lecturer in Educational Studies, University of Oxford.* **Autonomy**

Derek G. Winter, *Area Secretary, Church Missionary Society, Dioceses of Hereford, Gloucester and Bristol.* **Missionary Societies**

Peter Woodward, *General Inspector of Schools, City of Birmingham.* **Multi-Faith Schools; Sacred Books; Traditional or Tribal Religions**

Ian Wragg, *HMI and formerly County Adviser for* RE*, Derbyshire.* **Slow Learners**

Philip Wragge, *General Secretary, Quaker Social Responsibility and Education Department, Society of Friends.* **Religious Society of Friends (Quakers)**

D. S. Wright, *Professor of Education, University of Leicester.* **Moral Development**

Alain Wyler, *Pastor, Faculté de Theologie charge de Recherches Catechetiques.* **Switzerland**

Frances Young, *Lecturer in Theology, University of Birmingham.* **Early Fathers**

Richard Zipfel, *Secretary, Community Relations Committee for Roman Catholic Bishops' Conference of England and Wales.* **Rastafarianism**

ABBREVIATIONS

ACT	Association of Christian Teachers
AG	*Adi Granth*
ARE	Association for Religious Education
BCC	British Council of Churches
BFSS	British and Foreign School Society
CEM	Christian Education Movement
CNAA	Council of National Academic Awards
CSE	Certificate of Secondary Education
DES	Department of Education and Science
HMI	Her Majesty's Inspector (/ate)
ICE	Institute of Christian Education
ILEA	Inner London Education Authority
LEA	Local Education Authority
ME	Moral Education
NEB	*New English Bible*
NT	New Testament
OT	Old Testament
RC	Roman Catholic
RE	Religious Education
RERU	Religious Experience Research Unit
RI	Religious Instruction
RS	Religious Studies
SACRE	Standing Advisory Councils for Religious Education
SCM	Student Christian Movement
UK	United Kingdom
UNO	United Nations Organization
UNESCO	United Nations Educational, Scientific and Cultural Organization
USA	United States of America
WCC	World Council of Churches

* An asterisk denotes a reference to another article in the *Dictionary*

Acts of Parliament

The statutory framework for religious education in the schools of England and Wales is that laid down by the Education Act, 1944. All previous legislation was either superseded by or incorporated in this Act and subsequent developments in the practice of religious education have been brought about through changes in the interpretation of the basic Act and not through legislative change. The only direct references to religious education in later Acts up to 1982 are in Section 7 of the 1946 Act, which defines where collective worship is to take place, and Section 12 of the 1981 Act, which re-enacts Section 33 of the 1944 Act relating to Special Schools.

The Acts of 1967, 1968 and 1975 affected the administration of aided schools and the Act of 1980 has altered the system of government of all schools, but none of these Acts has modified the religious education provisions of the 1944 Act, although it should be noted that the Education (School Information) Regulations 1981 (Statutory Instrument 1981 No. 630), made under the 1980 Act, require all schools to publish information on their religious affiliations, if any, and on the religious education provided as well as on the arrangements for parents to exercise their rights under the conscience clauses*.

The provisions of the 1944 Act are best understood in the light of the attempts made during the previous century to solve the 'religious difficulty', which arose then, as it inevitably arises in any state which provides education and practises religious toleration, since the educational policy of the state must reconcile its concern for its own unity with the fact that its citizens may hold widely differing views on the nature of ultimate reality and are likely to wish their children to be educated in accordance with these views. The two most common solutions in the West are the secular one, excluding religious instruction altogether from state schools (as in France and the USA), or some variety of the confessional one, giving representatives of religious bodies opportunity to instruct their members in school (as in Germany). The solution worked out in England and Wales follows neither of these courses and is, it would appear, unique.

The 'difficulty' raised its head, in Parliament and outside, as soon as the state made its first intervention in education, in 1833, even though at that time it did no more than make a modest grant for building schools to two existing denominational societies, the National Society* and the British and Foreign School Society*. The building of schools was further facilitated in 1836 by the School Sites Act, the first of the Education Acts. Three years later the government provoked a storm when it not only set up, by order in Council, the 'Committee of the Privy Council on Education' to administer the grants but proposed to appoint inspectors to supervise their use and even to establish an interdenominational 'normal school' for the training of teachers. The government got their inspectors (the first two HMIs) only at the cost of giving a veto on appointments to the churches and they had to give up the proposed normal school.

Kay-Shuttleworth, the influential secretary of the Committee, commented later that the aims of the government in 1839 were to 'assert the claim of the civil power to the control of the education of the country' and to 'lay the foundations of a system of combined education in which the young might be brought up in charity with each other rather than in hostile camps for future strife'. Succeeding governments have had similar aims.

The real and lasting decisions were taken when the 1870 Act introduced the first state-provided, and not merely grant-aided, system of education. W. E. Forster, its architect, was only too well aware of the danger that his bill might be wrecked, as others had been, by denominational strife. The solution embodied in the Act was to offer the new School Boards three options: 1. no religious instruction; 2.

Bible reading with no comment; and 3. Bible teaching without denominational instruction. The London Board, chaired by T. H. Huxley, chose the third option and was followed, in due course, by most of the others. This choice, linked with the Cowper-Temple clause* and the conscience clause*, established the distinctive principles of the Anglo-Welsh system of religious education: in state-provided schools, religious education is the responsibility of the members of the teaching staff, and the teaching must not be denominational; in other words, the teacher must not use his position to influence his pupils in favour of any one denomination. All subsequent legislation is founded on these principles.

The Act of 1902 established the Board of Education, the LEAS and the Dual System; in matters of religious education it merely confirmed the 1870 settlement, adding a further conscience clause to give some protection to teachers. The most important feature of the next forty years was the development of prototype 'agreed syllabuses'* by the West Riding (1923) and Cambridgeshire (1924) and the rapid spread of the idea to other authorities. By 1944 almost all local authorities had adopted such a syllabus and both religious instruction and a daily act of worship were normal features of school life, but neither worship nor instruction was compulsory.

The Butler Act of 1944 reflected a mood of national unity and it was, of course, an all-party measure. In making compulsory and codifying more precisely what was already normal practice, it relied on the well-tried device of the agreed syllabus, combined with the Cowper-Temple clause and the conscience clauses, to consolidate the success achieved by the principles of 1870 in fostering agreement between confessional rivals.

The basic clauses on religious education occur in Section 25. It should be noted that the Act uses 'religious education' to cover both worship and teaching, and 'religious instruction' when it refers to classroom teaching. This article follows the same usage.

To begin with religious instruction, Section 25 (2) says: 'religious instruction shall be given in every county school and in every voluntary school'. The wording is surprisingly imprecise in some respects, but it has usually been assumed that it is meant to apply to every pupil in an establishment conducted under the Schools Regulations and that the 'instruction' should be given every week. There is no mention of the number of periods, but a possible implication of the withdrawal clauses is that the framers of the Act had at least two periods in mind.

Section 26 is much more explicit on the nature of what is to be taught. In county schools and, with certain exceptions, in controlled schools, the teaching is to be in accordance with an agreed syllabus and it must not be distinctive of any particular denomination. The agreed syllabus must be drawn up by a conference constituted according to the Fifth Schedule of the Act. The conference is to be convened by the LEA and must consist of committees to represent (a) 'such religious denominations as, in the opinion of the authority, ought, having regard to the circumstances of the area, to be represented'; (b) the Church of England (except in Wales): (c) teachers' organizations, (d) the authority. Recommendations must be unanimous and the committees have one vote each, which gives each a power of veto. There are provisions for an appeal to the Secretary of State if the conference and the authority fail to agree over the adoption of a recommended syllabus.

The position of voluntary schools* is slightly more complex. The Act superseded the previous Dual System by setting up two major classes of voluntary school. Controlled schools are wholly maintained by the local authority, which has a majority on the governing body, but in aided schools the outer fabric is maintained by the trustees and they have a majority on the governing body and receive a grant, now set at eighty-five per cent, direct from central government. The Act also established a small class of special agreement schools whose administration approximates to that of aided schools and which come in the same category as aided schools in respect of religious education.

In Section 28 it is laid down that religious instruction in an aided (or special agreement) school shall be under the control of the governors and in accordance with the trust deeds (or normal practice) of the school, but that if any parents ask for agreed syllabus instruction it must, under certain conditions, be provided. Conversely, under Section 27, religious instruction in a controlled school must be in accordance with an agreed syllabus, but if parents ask for instruction in accordance with the trust deed of the school, then 'reserved teachers' (who must not include the head teacher) must be appointed to provide it.

In all schools, whether county or voluntary, including boarding schools and special schools, parents and teachers have the right to invoke the conscience clauses.

Since 1944 the operation of the agreed syllabus procedures has developed, within the existing law, to meet changing conceptions and changing circumstances. It may be said, indeed, that the wisdom behind these clauses has been shown by their flexibility. One aspect of this flexibility is seen in the changing form of the typical syllabus. The early syllabuses were all sizeable documents covering each year's work in considerable detail and, as changes could only be made by the rather cumbersome procedure of convening a full Fifth Schedule conference, it was all too easy for them to become outdated. Several authorities then discovered the usefulness of Section 29 which authorized them to set up a standing advisory council on religious education to advise on methods of teaching and similar matters. The constitution of such a council is left to the discretion of the LEA and it is therefore easier to convene than a full conference. The usefulness of this became apparent when some authorities, such as Hampshire, began, in effect, to modify their syllabuses by supplementary papers from the advisory council and even more evident when others (led by the now-defunct Bath authority) decided to issue a new syllabus in the form of a short basic document, supplemented by material from an advisory council, which could easily be modified, or by approved material from elsewhere. The first major authority to issue a syllabus in this form was Birmingham, which in 1975 adopted a syllabus of only four pages, with a supplementary handbook of over 400 pages. Legal discussions over the issue of this syllabus appear to have established that, provided the basic document is sufficiently explicit and structured to be recognized as a syllabus and not merely a generalized statement of intent, this is an acceptable arrangement within the framework of the Act, and most syllabuses issued since 1975 have followed some variation of this pattern. It is common for the LEA to adopt the obviously convenient procedure

of treating the statutory conference as its advisory council for the purpose of drawing up the supplementary material.

The second major development has been the widespread inclusion in syllabuses of material about non-Christian religions and, in several areas, the inclusion of representatives of these religions in the Fifth Schedule conference. The Act does not say that religious instruction must be confined to Christianity, presumably because the drafters were conscious of the well-established rights of Jewish schools and Jewish parents, and what is to be taught is left to the statutory conference. As adherents of other religions settled in Britain, it became clear that they must have the same rights as other parents, including not only the right of withdrawal but also the right of participating in the agreed syllabus system if they so wished. The West Riding syllabus of 1966 and the London syllabus of 1968 both contained sections on non-Christian religions and London took the further step of including Jewish and Muslim representatives in committee (a) of the conference which produced its syllabus. This precedent has been followed by Birmingham and other authorities and it now seems to have become general practice to include representatives of other religions among those of the 'denominations' in committee (a) where local numbers warrant it.

A more controversial point has turned out to be the position of non-religious philosophies and their representatives. Again, the West Riding and London syllabuses set the precedent of referring to such belief systems, but the position was closely debated when the Birmingham syllabus was in preparation. The legal opinion then expressed was that it was reasonable to include the study of non-religious philosophies in order to 'clarify the distinctive features of religious faith'. This debate seems to be largely a matter of definitions, on which philosophers and lawyers may disagree.

Another development not foreseen in 1944 was the inclusion of religious instruction in schemes of integrated studies. There appears to be nothing illegal about this and several agreed syllabuses encourage it, but it does raise problems over the conscience clauses and, in aided schools, the scope of inspection*. A sound guiding principle, more than once given official backing, is that the element of religious instruction in such schemes should be sufficiently identifiable to permit the exercise of the conscience clauses.

Morning worship, the other aspect of religious education covered by the Act, can be dealt with more briefly. (Incidentally, the Act never uses the term 'assembly'*.) Section 25 (1) says that 'the school day in every county school and in every voluntary school shall begin with collective worship on the part of all pupils in attendance', subject, as is later made clear, to the conscience clauses. The arrangements must provide for a single act of worship unless the premises 'are such as to make it impracticable'. The Act of 1946 adds that the act of worship must always take place on the school premises, with the sole exception that an aided school may on special occasions conduct it elsewhere, provided that parents are given sufficient notice to enable them to exercise their right of withdrawal. It has been held that, with a similar proviso, the wording of the Act would permit a controlled or county school to do the same, so long as the pupils have attended morning worship at school first.

The only element of flexibility in the wording of this section of the Act would appear to be the phrase relating to the premises, which explicitly leaves the determination of what is 'impracticable' to the LEA, or, in the case of a voluntary school, the governors. It is significant that the 1982 Report of the Commons Select Committee on Education singled out this clause as the one area in which legislation might be called for, in the interest of the flexibility which they commended.

In contrast, the Act is remarkably flexible when it comes to the form of the act of worship. Section 26 states merely that it 'shall not, in any county school, be distinctive of any particular denomination'. Nothing is said about the form of worship in voluntary schools, whether aided or controlled.

Section 33, re-enacted by Section 12 of the 1981 Act, provides that 'so far as practicable' every pupil attending a special school shall attend or be withdrawn from religious worship and religious instruction in accordance with the wishes of his parents.

The sections of the Act relating to independent schools make no reference to religious instruction or religious worship, and the sections relating to county and voluntary schools do not apply to such schools.

See also **Conscience Clauses, Cowper-Temple Clause, Inspection of RE.**

———

G. Taylor and J. B. Saunders, *The Law of Education,* Butterworth [8]1976.

W. J. H. EARL

Adolescence

The concept of *adolescence* within the life-span of an individual is rooted in three general premises. 1. It represents a socially defined stage in the course of a person's life and refers to the years of development which occur between childhood and adulthood. 2. The social reality of adolescence varies from one social setting to another and this fact limits the possibility of making broad generalizations regarding the nature of adolescence. 3. Since human development is a life-long process, investigations into adolescent development must be interpreted with reference both to development in the years of childhood and to the post-adolescent years of adulthood.

The notion of *religious development* in adolescence is concerned with changes which are observed amongst adolescents in their attitudes, beliefs, behaviour and thinking with regard to religion. Some scholars such as Goldman have suggested that this development is partly of a clearly defined series of stages and others, including Murphy have questioned the adequacy of stage theory to provide a sufficiently rigorous conceptual framework into which to fit the evidence. Several techniques are used by researchers to describe and analyse religious development. A favourite method is to administer group tests and questionnaires to large samples of children and to analyse the responses by statistical procedures. Such 'concurrent' cross-sectional measurements involve the collection of data from children at different age-levels and produce 'mean values of description' which provide evidence of general trends, but the results often obscure the personal individual differences which are found within any particular group of children from which a 'mean' or 'average' value has been obtained. The results of such investigations need to be compared with the findings of 'longitudinal' measurements, in which the same experiment is repeated at intervals, ideally with the same group of people perhaps over a period of years, and also with the findings derived from other techniques such as individual oral interviews, attitude scales, essays and projective pictures. Most recent investigations into religious development are cross-sectional concurrent studies and as such they do not provide direct evidence of developmental changes in the same children, although they do provide evidence which is suggestive regarding the course of development.

In evaluating research reports, attention must be given not only to the design of the investigation and to the reliability of the test instruments but also to the definition of religion which is employed. Most investigators use definitions of religion which emerge from an institutionally orientated understanding of Christianity, but some recent British studies have employed functional definitions in which religion is defined as response to chaos and fundamental concerns.

Attitude to religion and religious behaviour
The differences in attitudes to religion of adolescents, their involvement in religious practices and their ability to think about religious concepts have been documented by several researchers. Differences due to the effects of age and sex are clearly discernible. Attitudes to Christianity and involvement in the activities of the church become less positive as children get older. Where involvement in the church is maintained attitudes to religion remain positive. Girls consistently show more positive attitudes than boys and greater involvement, but a linear decline in attitude to religion and in religious involvement is associated with increase in age.

Hyde made a broad enquiry into the problems of religious education by assessing the religious behaviour, attitudes and attainment of 1,997 children in four secondary schools. His results indicated that the children's attitude scores were related to their professed religious behaviour and also that their attitudes appeared to influence their conceptual development. Children with higher attitude scores, indicating stronger religious involvement and interest, showed greater conceptual insight than children with lower attitude scores. An illuminating insight derived from Hyde's work was the result that

the age at which a marked deterioration of attitude is observed coincides with the period of mental development when abstract thinking emerges.

Francis reported the design and use of an instrument to measure the attitudes towards religion of children aged eight to sixteen years. The items on the scale were deliberately restricted to six concepts which would be familiar to primary school children: God, Jesus, the Bible, prayer, church services, and religion in school. Nine hundred children in two secondary and two primary schools were tested during 1974. His results gave substantial support to the earlier findings of Hyde, but with one importance difference: the reported deterioration in attitude to religion among secondary school children was found to begin during the primary school years and to extend into the secondary school years in a linear fashion. In a 1978 replication study the same linear trend is reported with an accelerated decline beginning in the fourth year of the secondary school. Greer administered the Francis religious attitude scale to a sample of 2,149 Roman Catholic and Protestant boys and girls in Belfast schools, aged eight to sixteen years. His data was collected in 1979 and the results confirmed the earlier findings of Francis of a significant decline in positive attitudes to religion associated with the first four years of secondary schooling.

In an unpublished dissertation, Timothy J. Mark investigated the attitudes* to religion, religious behaviour and religious thinking of 2,096 adolescents aged eleven to sixteen years in two comprehensive schools. Hyde's attitude to religion scales were used to obtain a measure of attitudes to traditional Christian religion and new scales were developed to measure attitude to non-institutional religion in which religion was functionally defined as response to chaos and the search for ultimate meaning. Measurements of religious behaviour (frequency of church attendance, attendance at Sunday School, habits of prayer and Bible reading), general intelligence and religious thinking were also obtained. Four main results were obtained from this investigation: (i) the earlier finding of Francis was confirmed, showing a linear decline in attitude to traditional Christian religion associated with increasing age; (ii) attitude to non-institutional religion, that is, attitude to others and to fundamental concerns, also showed a linear decline associated with increasing age; (iii) girls consistently obtained higher scores than boys on attitudes to religion and religious behaviour measures, and girls generally obtained higher scores than boys for attitude to others, for religious thinking and for general intelligence; (iv) within the adolescents' thought world their attitudes to institutionalized religion, their attitudes to non-institutionalized religion and their ability to understand and use religious concepts operate along three separate and distinct continua.

Religious cognition

A developmental process associated with age is also observed in children's ability to think about religious concepts. Many adolescents move through a Piagetian concrete operational mode of thought to the mastery of formal operations. Older children are consistently more successful at understanding religious concepts and ideas than younger children. A strong correlation exists between religious thinking and general intelligence. The evidence regarding the connection between religious attitude and religious thinking is equivocal. Children with higher attitude scores indicating strong religious involvement can show greater conceptual insight than children with lower attitude scores. On the other hand, the child with negative attitudes to Christianity and with no contact with church or Sunday School can show a marked success at understanding the complexities and significance of religious language. Goldman analysed children's responses to three projective pictures. A categorization of the responses into stages of religious thinking was then made and it was demonstrated that from a mental age of thirteen plus children are capable of formal operational thought applied to religious concepts. Goldman suggested that there is a gap between a child's theological view of the world and his logico-scientific view which widens during adolescence and which is often accompanied by a regression in the ability to think about religious concepts. General support for Goldman's conclusions has been demonstrated by later studies but the adequacy of stage development theory to provide an appropriate description of the development of religious thinking continues to be debated. Mark compared the scores

obtained on a religious thinking test with scores derived from attitude scales and from a general intelligence test. Religious thinking scores were found to be generally independent of attitude scores but strongly and significantly correlated with general intelligence. Greer, using the attitude to religion scale developed by Francis and the thinking about the Bible scale developed by John H. Peatling, concluded that there was a significant but not a close relationship between religious thinking and religious attitudes. William K. Kay found that older and more able pupils scored more highly on Peatling's thinking about the Bible scale and therefore tended to interpret the Bible more metaphorically and abstractly. Significant differences in test scores were also found between Church of England, Ulster Protestant and Ulster Roman Catholic schools. According to Kay, religious cognition is clearly influenced in different ways by the type of school which the pupil attends.

Conclusion

It is clear from the evidence reviewed here that sex and age differences are the key to understanding the religious development of adolescents. Generally speaking, girls show greater interest and involvement in religion than boys and are also more successful at thinking about religion. Also, generally speaking, adolescents, both boys and girls, show less positive attitudes towards Christianity, less involvement in church activities, but more success in mastering religious concepts as they grow older. There are exceptions to these general trends, however, and some adolescent children maintain with increasing age positive attitudes and involvement in the church. Although many adolescents appear to reject the institutionalized forms of Christianity represented in the church and Sunday School, and although there is widespread agnosticism, there is also evidence that most adolescents are immensely interested in religious questions more generally defined as a search for values and meaning. There is certainly no evidence of any widespread atheism. Although from the point of view of research methodology it is useful to investigate the affective and cognitive elements of religious development as distinct and separate domains, it is necessary to recognize that in the adolescent's experience of religion they are inter-related: his attitudes, his membership of religious groups, his religious practices of prayer, worship and Bible reading, his understanding of conventional religion and his search for values and meaning must be seen as parts of a complex network of inter-related influences. Research reports must be interpreted within the context of this inter-dependence.

Glen, H. Elder Jr, 'Adolescence in the Life Cycle: An introduction', *Adolescence in the Life Cycle: Psychological Change and Social Context*, ed. Sigmund E. Dragastin and Glen H. Elder Jr, John Wiley and Sons 1975; D. Elkind, 'The development of religious understanding in children and adolescents', *Research on Religious Development*, ed. M. P. Strommen, Hawthorn 1971; Ronald J. Goldman, *Religious Thinking from Childhood to Adolescence*, Routledge & Kegan Paul 1964; John E. Greer, 'Stages in the development of religious thinking', *British Journal of Religious Education*, 3, 1, 1980 and 'Religious attitudes and thinking in Belfast pupils', *Educational Research*, 23, 3, 1981; Kenneth E. Hyde, *Religious Learning in Adolescence*, Oliver & Boyd 1965; Timothy J. Mark, 'A study of religious attitudes, religious behaviour, and religious cognition', *Educational Studies*, 8, 3, 1982 and 'Compassionate attitudes in two comprehensive schools', *Journal of Moral Education*, 11, 2, 1982; Roger J. Murphy, 'A new approach to the study of the development of religious thinking in children', *Educational Studies*, 4, 1, 1978.

TIMOTHY MARK

Adult

In the major world religions, adult religious development takes place either within a community of faith based on childhood schooling and matured through the pedagogic role of liturgy or as a personal quest for enlightenment through spiritual disciplines. Both approaches are often present.

In the Christian West, it has been nurtured in a theological framework of hermeneutics, dogmatics and liturgical worship. Spiritual direction and guidance on personal and social behaviour has been based on this framework and the didactic transmission of the deposit of this knowledge have been seen as the main work of adult religious education.

From time to time there have been those who have encouraged a significantly different approach, placing spiritual experience before cerebral knowledge. 'I would rather feel compunction than know its definition' wrote Thomas à Kempis in his *Imitation of Christ*. Spirituality is seen to begin in the perception of the created world and in self-awareness, rather than in a deposit of knowledge. During the second half of the twentieth century, this tradition appears to be in the process of asserting itself anew.

Three main influences are at work. The first is that of social change which has forced members of the church to question the theological framework and to examine the inhibitions which this places on individual understanding and corporate action. Earlier this century, ventures such as the Catholic Social Guild and the 'Life and Work' Group of the Ecumenical Movement found themselves posing questions about the gap between apostolic and contemporary experience. Half a century later Paulo Freire placed this questioning in a new framework. He said that an educational system will either liberate or domesticate; it can never be neutral. Domestication is the process of conditioning in which a person is led to accept the situation in which he finds himself and to believe that he can do nothing about it. Liberation, however, makes people believe in themselves and take responsibility for their own lives so that they might contribute to changing society.

The second influence has been a renewed understanding of the person and work of the Holy Spirit. If the Holy Spirit is active in the world, then it should be possible for ordinary men and women to discern what he is doing and learn how to co-operate with him in doing it. Religious development, therefore, can and should happen in the world as the choice place of God's love. The force of this theology has helped some Christians to venture out from their communities of faith into the world, even though they are regarded there as eccentric to some degree.

The third influence is that of the liberal humanist tradition of education, itself shaped early in the century by Christian leaders like Mansbridge and Temple who challenged the view that systematic education had to be completed by a specific age by which time the person was then equipped with the educational luggage necessary for the journey of life, apart from casual additions. They insisted on the concept of lifelong education and in the years following the 1939–45 war the churches forged a partnership with secular adult education provision and initiated new projects of adult learning, some of them associated with the radio. Although in the late 1950s and 1960s the churches withdrew from adult education and concentrated anew on congregation building, the publication of the Russell Report (1973), combined with the other influences already mentioned, has helped to renew interest in the concept of continuing education.

Church programmes of adult religious education in Britain reflect differences in framework. A good deal of local education is concerned with congregation building by enhancing their membership's understanding of the Christian faith and its implications through Bible study, prayer circles and house groups led by the clergy. There is, however, a growing and complementary approach that seeks to begin with present experience formulated by laypeople and clergypeople together and based on their perception of the everyday world. They can be divided into three categories.

1. Those concerned with the major issues of our planet, including the distribution of resources and survival against the possibility of nuclear holocaust, social and racial disintegration and ecological disaster. Conscientization is a word that has been invented to describe how we become aware of the ways in which we are oppressed by the structures of society and what needs to be done in order to change things and give us the self-confidence to act. The churches are forced to ask, 'Who are the poor and oppressed and how can they be enabled to take responsibility for their own programmes?'

2. Programmes concerned with family and community life at neighbourhood level. Community development projects, job creation programmes and programmes concerned with exploring social attitudes are being widely offered.

3. Sensitivity training, personal growth and a study of the ways in which a group has power over its individual members which can control, alter or influence their behaviour as learners. These insights have been most influential in changing the style of learning in all adult education work. The personal growth movement has yet to work out fully its relationship with a more traditional exploration of contemplative prayer and programmes of retreat and renewal.

All the major British churches have national officers and most of them have networks to enable adult education to take place, and in 1978 a Christian Association of Adult and Continuing Education was formed. The movement towards consciousness and conscientization has begun to draw some Christians away from the traditional structures of the church into communities of quest through prayer and service. While diverse in origin and inspiration, there is nevertheless a unity in their questioning spirituality which often gives rise to a critical attitude towards the prevailing framework of ecclesiastical and social order and encourages the growth of projects for social change. Whether or not these learning communities are ephemeral, they are an impressive expression of one generation's conviction that if the soul within us dies so will the world we build around us.

Paulo Freire, *Pedagogy of the Oppressed,* Sheed & Ward 1972; F. W. Jessup, *Lifelong Learning,* Pergamon Press 1969; Margaret Kane, *Theology in an Industrial Society,* SCM Press 1975; George Lovell, *The Church and Community Development,* Grayle Publications 1972; John Taylor, *A Church Re-shaped,* CMS 1975.

VINCENT STRUDWICK

Advisers

The appointment of RE advisers originated from two sources. Before 1944, inspectors appointed by Church of England dioceses inspected religious knowledge in 'council' as well as in church schools (Carlisle Commission report, *Partners in Education,* 1971). At the same time, from the early years of this century, London and other larger local authorities established their own inspectorate as distinct from Her Majesty's Inspectors (HMI), who are nationally appointed within the DES. The first LEA subject appointments, often termed 'organizers', were in curriculum areas which could involve physical danger for pupils or in which many teachers lacked initial training. Only in the 1960s, the emphasis then changing from inspection to advice, did a few LEAS appoint advisers specifically for religious education, the first being in the West Riding of Yorkshire, Inner London, Norfolk, Hampshire and Devon. By 1971, the British Council of Churches' report, *The Recruitment, Employment and Training of Teachers concerned with RE*, noted that 'only 13 out of 164 local authorities have so far appointed such advisers'. Two years later there were over thirty.

Since local government re-organization in 1974, new authorities have planned more co-ordinated services to provide advice on all aspects of education, although this may involve one person covering several subjects or also having a general role in primary or secondary schools. Most LEAS have designated one officer as responsible for RE, but the amount of specialist work often depends upon the range of other commitments. In addition, some have also appointed advisory teachers for the subject. Under the 1944 Education Act, RE in church-aided schools remains the responsibility of the churches rather than of the LEA whose duties, however, cover controlled as well as county schools.

The RE adviser has four main tasks: advice to schools and colleges, in-service education*, reports to LEA committees and officers, and public relations. Most time is spent in schools and usually in classrooms so previous teaching experience is essential, but effectiveness depends as much upon personal relationships as upon subject knowledge and professional skill. Every school is different and needs to be known in some detail if advice is to be welcomed or applicable. Requests for support come mainly from secondary schools and colleges with specialist staff, but needs are often greater among primary teachers.

The overall task in schools is to nourish the highest expectations for RE among head teachers, governors, staff and pupils. The appointment of competent teachers trained in the subject is a first priority: only since about 1960 have most secondary schools designated specialist RE posts and the last twenty years have seen a considerable increase in such appointments. The adviser is then concerned with support during the period of probation and with promotion of heads of department.

Further concerns are the curriculum and physical provision for the subject. Advisers are normally involved in the design and furnishing of new school buildings but more frequently in improving facilities and equipment in RE rooms*. Delicate negotiations with senior staff may be necessary to ensure adequate teaching time for the subject (at least five per cent) and that RE teachers are not taking so many classes that they know few pupils well. Agreed syllabuses* generally allow flexibility in the detail of RE schemes and teachers value the opportunity to discuss the development of their work with an adviser acquainted with other local syllabuses, curriculum projects and integrated courses. The purchase of new books and materials, coupled with financial support from both within and outside the school, are further topics for discussion, as is the development of external examination courses in religious studies.

In-service education* for teachers involves universities, initial training institutions, HMI and local teachers' centres, as well as courses organized directly by the adviser. The latter, however, co-ordinates these activities within an LEA and considers secondments for RE staff undertaking further professional training. Many advisers organize short residential courses or lead school-based programmes which are especially valuable for RE in primary schools. Teachers' centres are the venue for one day, half-day or evening meetings.

The central role of the adviser is to interpret the needs of the subject to LEA committees and officers. Initially this related mainly to the agreed syllabus conference and standing advisory committee, but recently it has also involved responses to DES circulars on such topics as information to parents and curriculum policy statements. The RE adviser can also be concerned with discretionary grants to students undertaking religious or ministerial training and with LEA surveys on particular aspects of education.

Public relations for RE have become increasingly significant with the emergence of local radio and television as well as press interest. An LEA's agreed syllabus is a public document and religion is sometimes equated with controversy. Positive attitudes among parents and within local religious communities are important assets in sustaining the morale of the subject among teachers and pupils.

D. PAUL KING

Aesthetic Aspects of RE

see **Art; Dance and Drama; Media; Music**

Affectivity

There is a tendency to create a dichotomy between affect (feeling) and cognition (thinking) in RE. Cognitive development is recognized as being more amenable to objective analysis and measurement and the study of it has the advantage of providing factual material for academic courses. Recently there has been some reaction against this one-sided stress on the explicitly conceptual, and the primacy of the affective in religion has been stressed by e.g. Westerhoff, Durka, Harris, Lealman and Robinson. At the same time, this view emphasizes the importance of interpreting all ways of knowing, affective, intuitive and intellectual.

Research indicates that there are two ways of knowing, two modes of thinking and of consciousness (e.g. the work of R. Ornstein). One is rational, intellectual, processes information in a linear, logical way and is largely verbal in its expression; the other is intuitive, affective, often passive and generally non-verbal. Psychological studies may suggest the existence of distinct mechanisms for the processing of cognitive and affective stimuli, but the interaction of the two is a matter of everyday experience. No religion has long survived that does not appeal to all sides of human nature.

It is recognized that an important part of RE is the development of attitudes* such as tolerance* and appreciation of religions and cultures different from one's own; sensitivity to social problems and human needs; awareness of human values. Such education of attitudes represents some movement into the affective domain.

More fundamentally, perhaps, affective growth makes possible an apprehension of the non-rational heart of religion. Religious awareness begins in the intuitive mode of consciousness, and its growth depends greatly on the sharpening of the senses. It is through the use of imagery, metaphor and symbol that this growth is possible and a sensitivity to different levels of reality can be expressed and communicated.

See also **Cognitive Education.**

B. Lealman and E. Robinson, *Exploration into Experience*, CEM 1980; B. Lealman, 'The Ignorant Eye', *British Journal of Religious Education*, 4, 2, 1982.

BRENDA LEALMAN

Africa: Eastern

1. *History*. When the countries of Eastern Africa were under colonial rule, RE in schools was controlled by Christian missions and churches. It was denominational church education aimed at producing committed church members. In the few government schools, pupils were usually divided by denomination for religion classes and outside teachers from the churches would come in to take these classes. The religion of the schools was Christianity. Indigenous traditional religious values were transmitted through the family and the village; Islam was taught at the mosque; Hindu religious values were passed on in Hindu homes.

After all these countries except Zimbabwe achieved independence in the 1960s, the rapid increase in the number of government schools, the handing over to governments of many church schools and the vast increases in the number of pupils in school meant that individual churches could no longer provide religious instruction for all pupils in schools. Also the new governments desired to promote national unity and could not allow denominational or religious division of classes in schools. Therefore, in most countries of Eastern Africa the major churches working in schools produced Joint Syllabuses for RE. In the 1970s most of the governments, except in Ethiopia and Mozambique where Christian RE was associated with church support for previous oppressive regimes, were implementing in schools and training teachers to teach Christian RE syllabuses, while the churches did most of the curriculum development and production of materials for these syllabuses.

2. *Aims*. In all Eastern African countries there are different opinions about whether or not RE should be part of the government controlled school curriculum and about the

nature and purpose of RE in schools. Most churches believe that the aim of RE in schools should be to create, foster and develop Christian commitment. Governments do not see it as part of their task as governments to teach the Christian faith and wish to draw a distinction between church education and RE. But because of the past and, in some countries, present importance of the churches in education and national affairs, Christian RE syllabuses have been accepted by governments for all schools provided they are joint inter-denominational syllabuses. The public pressure on governments to include RE in the school curriculum reflects the strong desire for moral education of young people at a time when rapid social change and urbanization have broken the hold of traditional moral values, but most RE syllabuses are not designed to give moral education as such. As governments make more efforts to introduce locally relevant curricula in schools, RE has to justify its inclusion in the curriculum on educational rather than traditional, confessional or political grounds. RE must become locally appropriate because government resources are scarce and so governments are unwilling to include in school curricula subjects which make no contribution to national development. The pressure to change RE syllabuses is illustrated by the Zimbabwe government's demand for a new RE syllabus that reflects the ideals of the new Zimbabwe (1981) and the Zambian government's decision to change the name of the subject to Spiritual and Moral Education (1979). The trend is for RE to cease to be exclusively Christian and to reflect more African traditional values and modern indigenous philosophies and to draw material from Islam and Hinduism in countries where these religions are significant. The trend is also for RE to be more concerned with helping pupils to clarify values, to make moral decisions and to understand religious ways of thinking, in order to equip them better for adult life in their societies, where religion is an important factor socially, politically and culturally.

    3. *Syllabuses.* Primary schools in Eastern Africa are permitted to have RE periods on the official school timetable whether the school is government or church controlled, except in Ethiopia, where RE is taught only in church-managed schools, and Mozambique. The RE lessons may be taught by teachers on the regular school staff, except in those two countries and in Tanzania, where the local headteacher decides on the arrangements for RE teaching in the school. In most of the countries, there is a Christian RE syllabus for primary schools agreed by the churches and accepted by the government. Sudan, Kenya and Tanzania have Islamic RE syllabuses as well as Christian. Uganda and Tanzania have separate Catholic and Protestant RE syllabuses for some or all primary school grades. In several countries the Joint Syllabuses are either confined to Bible knowledge or have been prepared to include only the religious teaching on which all the churches agree. But syllabus revision is going on in most of the countries in order to develop pupil-centred, life-based RE syllabuses for primary schools. The Eastern Africa Inter-church Consultation on Primary School RE, which has been meeting annually since 1981, includes both government and church personnel working on primary school RE and has stimulated a more professional approach to the development of RE curricula and the study of the moral, educational and developmental aims of primary school RE.

    The Pastoral Institute of the Roman Catholic dioceses of Eastern and Central Africa (AMECEA) at Eldoret in Kenya has produced Christian RE syllabuses for secondary schools and initiated international and interdenominational co-operation in RE since the 1960s. The Institute's 'Developing in Christ' syllabus for junior secondary schools and 'Christian Living Today' syllabus for senior secondary schools have been used or adapted for use by most Eastern African countries. These syllabuses integrate African values and Christian teaching and use a life-based approach. Some Eastern African countries have Bible Knowledge syllabuses for the senior secondary School Certificate examinations, but increasing use is being made of the 'Christian Living Today' syllabus which explores such values as justice, work and the family in contemporary African society, traditional African society, the Bible and African church history.

Curriculum Development Centre, Lusaka, *Grade 8 RE Pupils' Book*, Mission Press, Zambia 1983; John Henze, *RE Thinking*,

Mufulira Teachers' College Resource Centre, Zambia 1981; Pastoral Institute of Eastern Africa, *Teacher's Handbook for Developing in Christ,* Chapman 1981; Pastoral Institute of Eastern Africa, '*Christian Living Today' Teacher's Handbook,* Chapman 1981.

CECIL KING

Africa: North-West

Nearly all North Africans are Muslim and Islam* is the state religion of the three countries of the Maghrib – Morocco, Algeria and Tunisia. Yet not one of the three states has an Islamic government and this is made quite clear in their titles: the Kingdom of Morocco, the Democratic and Popular Republic of Algeria, the Republic of Tunisia. All three countries have become independent nation-states within the last twenty-six years and are determined to develop modern, technological societies. Therefore, it is essential that they have modern, scientific systems of education; and in each country it is the government which sets the standards and controls all education, including religious education. Religious instruction is given in the primary schools, and Islamic history is taught in both the primary and the secondary schools. Yet in the public schools there are no teachers who have been specially trained to give religious instruction and in all three countries a large part of the population feels that their children acquire a very inadequate knowledge of Islam through the public school system.

Consequently, the public school is not the primary means of religious education. Just as during the period when North Africa was under French colonial domination, it is the family which provides the basic religious education so necessary in a Muslim land. For Islam is more than a religion; it is a whole way of life, an environment. From the time when a grandmother or an aunt whispers 'In the name of God' into the ear of the new-born baby, the Muslim child acquires a Muslim reflex. All actions, from the most insignificant to the most important, are undertaken with a spoken or unspoken reference to God and the whole rhythm of life is based on the recurring cycle of Muslim holy days and months.

More and more North African families are turning to another traditional means of religious education – the Quranic school – in order to ensure that their children are brought up in the true faith. Independent Morocco has given more official recognition to traditional religious education than have the other two Maghribi countries. Moroccan children have to receive some instruction in a Quranic school before being admitted to primary school. Nevertheless, Moroccans have felt a need to improve the education given in the Quranic schools and in 1979 the Ministry of Islamic Affairs supervised 21 pilot Quranic schools with 31 teachers and 1385 pupils. Algeria and Tunisia, in their zeal to promote scientific education controlled by the state, discouraged the continuation of traditional Quranic schools and in both countries such schools became rare and were not recognized officially. However, during the 1970s Algeria experienced a rapid growth of 'free' mosques where *imams* dispense Quranic instruction and commentary to children, young people, and adults. Also large numbers of young Algerians are attending private groups of religious instruction, many of them organized by Muslim Brothers and Muslim Sisters. In 1980 the Algerian government decided to create special schools for Quranic study because children were not learning enough about the Qur'an* in the public schools. Unofficial religious instruction has also increased in Tunisian mosques, and an unusual private development in the field of religious education is the Association for the Protection of the Qur'an. Officially approved by the Tunisian government, this association has branches in most Tunisian towns, encourages the memorizing of the Qur'an, publishes a magazine and appeals for a return to traditional Islamic values. In what might be interpreted as an admission that traditional religious personnel should be given more control over religious education, the Tunisian government in 1980 transferred responsibility for Quranic schools from the Ministry of Education to the Office of Religious Affairs.

The governments of these countries are also finding that more attention must be given to higher Islamic education, to the founding of theological schools and to the training of mosque personnel, particularly *imams,* who are responsible for leading prayers, giving Quranic instruction in the mosques and preaching the special Friday sermon. Only in Morocco is there still a Muslim university, the famous Qarawiyine University founded in Fez in the thirteenth century; and there are Islamic Institutes in other Moroccan cities. In Tunisia the 1300-year-old Zaytuna University has been reduced to a faculty of Islamic law and theology attached to the University of Tunis. Algeria, however, has no Muslim faculty of theology or chair of Islamics in any of its numerous universities. The Islamic Institutes (secondary level), built in all Algerian cities and large towns soon after independence, were transformed into ordinary secondary schools under the Ministry of Education in May, 1976. The University of Islamic Law, under construction in Constantine for many years, has yet to be finished. Nevertheless, since 1979 the Algerian government has reversed some of its earlier decisions concerning Islamic education and now takes every opportunity to recognize publicly the importance of such education. Islamic Institutes have been reopened in several towns. Islamic sections, on an equal footing with the scientific, literary and technological sections, are to be created in secondary schools. After receiving the baccalaureat, students from these Islamic sections will continue their studies in the Higher Institute of Islamic Sciences soon to be opened in Constantine.

Without a doubt the movement of Islamic renewal, which has been gathering momentum in North-West Africa since 1976, has played a major role in changing the attitude of the state towards RE. In the past the state seemed to use Islam to reinforce its own influence and to promote national unity. Nowadays the governments of the three North-West African countries realize that they must deal with Islam on its own terms; for, as the president of Algeria has said, Islam is one of the fundamental components of the Maghrebi personality. An era of debate and, for the most part, creative tension has begun in North-West Africa, where workers, intellectuals, government officials and religious leaders are seeking to define true religion and its relevance to modern life.

See also **Islam**; *Qur'ān, al-*.

Christiane Souriau (ed.), *Le Maghreb Musulman en 1979*, Editions du Centre National de la Recherche Scientifique, Paris 1981.

MARY S. ROBINSON

Africa: South

Religion, and Christianity in particular, has had an enormous impact on education in South Africa. In the schools established by the Dutch in the seventeenth and eighteenth centuries, Calvinist Christianity constituted virtually the whole curriculum, a situation reinforced in society by the pious religiosity of the settlers.

As elsewhere in the colonial world, the lifestyles and belief systems of the indigenous peoples were denigrated by the European settlers. As a result, the early colonial schools aimed at inculcating a Christian life and worldview in the consciousness of all the inhabitants, while schools for the indigenous population also aimed at socialization into a European culturo-economic paradigm, coupled with equipping these people for an appropriately obedient and subserviant role in the labour market. By the middle of the nineteenth century most of what is now South Africa had been brought under the subjugation of the European population, a process enhanced by the acquisition of the Cape by the British and by an influx of British settlers.

The basic assumptions of the European population and of the missionaries who flocked to South Africa during and after the evangelical revival consolidated the religiosity of the school and the desires to destroy the alternative belief systems followed by the indigenous population. In an increasingly racially segmented society, the twin aims of Christianization and labour stratification were pursued consistently, a situation neatly summed up as follows by Cape Governor Grey in an address to the Colonial Parliament in 1855: '. . . we should try to make them [the indigenous people] part of ourselves, with a common faith and common interest, useful servants, consumers of our goods, contributors to our revenue: in short, a source of strength and wealth for this colony, such as Providence designed them to be'.

The rising tide of Afrikaner identity from the 1860s, in reaction to British Imperialism, and the growth of capitalism via the discovery of diamonds and gold soon afterwards, further consolidated both racial and class consciousness among the 'whites' and accelerated the proletarianization of the numerically superior 'non-white' groups. These trends eventually fused into a racial and class ideology that found its educational expression in the policy of Christian National Education. This policy of CNE was adopted by the National Party at its victory in the 1948 election and has remained the dominating factor in all South African education since.

The basis of Afrikaner Nationalist ideology – and therefore of CNE – is that the diversity of races or peoples is God-given and supported by scripture and that it is therefore a Christian responsibility for the individual to cherish and develop his own cultural-national adherance and to submerge himself into his nation. South Africa's people are not viewed as one but as several nations, which have to live and be educated separately. The Afrikaans-speaking 'whites', however, are to be viewed as the trustees of all the other nations in the South African geopolitical entity, with a divine 'calling and task' to Christianize and determine the future of all the other nations. In addition, there is to be no levelling: an education of others is not to be at the expense of the 'whites', inequality is expressly acknowledged as a pillar of Christian-National ideology. It must be noted, however, that the most enduring and consistent opposition to Afrikaner Nationalist ideology has come from the Christian churches (other than the 'white' Afrikaner churches).

The immediate effects of this policy for all education in South Africa are (a) segregated schooling, first on the basis of language (Afrikaans-speaking 'whites' are schooled separately from English-speaking 'whites') and secondly on the basis of racial classification; (b) unequal educational provision in the sub-systems for those not classified 'white'; (c) the suffusion of all the educational sub-systems by the particular ideology of the Afrikaner power elite; and (d) the argument that such policies are to be understood as 'Christian'. That education has to be 'Christian' and 'National' is written into the major educational legislation. It is in this context that RE in South African has to be understood.

Since the Second World War, RI in South Africa has remained with the pattern established in the United Kingdom at that time; while the situation in the UK has altered significantly since the 1960s, the South African school syllabuses have remained virtually unchanged for thirty-five years. They follow the 'agreed syllabus' format, though the views of the Afrikaner 'white' churches are those which have been determinative. The subject is compulsory in all schools, although parents and teachers have the right to withdraw from participation. The syllabuses are essentially confessional, evangelical, Bible-based (with a smattering of church history), repetitive, historically rather than contemporaneously oriented, and focussed on a personal piety rather than on issues such as social justice, secularization and the like. The underlying assumption is that it is the responsibility of the school to expose children to substantial sections of biblical material to increase the likelihood of their becoming Christian; school inspectors expect those teaching the subject to be evangelical Christians.

The religious pluralism of South African society is not acknowledged by the syllabuses, which do not even offer sections dealing with what is traditionally known as apologetics: the assumption is simply that a uniformly Christian society exists. In those few schools with a significant Jewish enrolment, alternative Jewish religious instruction is usually permitted, but in schools with a substantial Muslim clientele the subject has all but disappeared rather than adapt to the challenge of religious pluralism.

While the current strategy towards RE is generally accepted by the population at large and does not generate any significant public debate, criticism of existing practice and assumptions coupled with reflection on possible alternatives has begun to occur. Those changes that have begun to be implemented are occurring mainly in private church schools, where innovation is more easily achieved. The subject undoubtedly has an extremely low status in the great majority of schools: this is exacerbated by the extreme importance attributed to examinations in South African schools, for 'Scripture' or 'Religious Instruction' is a non-examination subject.

At the tertiary level, biblical studies (also an examinable, but not very popular, school subject) is taught in most cases in the same evangelical way – in fact, considerable but subtle pressure is placed on all prospective teachers to include at least some such study in their training – but in a very few English-language institutions courses akin to British Religious Studies courses are offered.

Census figures reveal that a substantial proportion of the South African population still calls itself Christian and church attendance is still far more widespread than in Western Europe. Sunday Schools therefore reach a sizeable number of children, drawing most of their teaching materials from similar movements in the UK, the USA and Australia.

RE in South Africa, certainly as far as the schools are concerned, is in an atrophied state. It is only in a few, more enterprising classrooms that the subject is deemed to be relevant by the pupils of the schools.

                              OWEN VAN DEN BERG

Africa: West

This article is concerned mainly with a descriptive survey of religious education in Anglophone West Africa (Nigeria, Ghana, Liberia, Sierra Leone and Gambia), although much of its content would also be applicable to the Francophone countries of the sub-region (e.g. Benin Republic, Togo, Ivory Coast and Senegal). RE in West Africa relates mainly to Africa's three major religions: African Traditional Religion, Islam and Christianity.

Among the Anglophone countries already mentioned, Nigeria is by far the biggest – in land mass and population. For instance, the country has a land area of about 1,000,000 sq.km., while its closest rival, Ghana, has an area of 238,537 sq.km. Nigeria is populated by about 77,000,000 and Ghana by about 10,310,000 people. In many aspects of life, Nigeria is fairly representative of West Africa, remaining for long the melting pot of the sub-region.

The label 'Religious Education' is not generally used in West African schools. More usual are: Bible Knowledge/Christian Religious Knowledge, Islamic Religious Knowledge, and very rarely, African Traditional Religion. This educational nomenclature tells its own story – the absence of proper religious education in West Africa.

Curriculum
1. *African Traditional Religion (ATR)*

Character training featured prominently in traditional or indigenous African education – an education characterized by a significant religious content. Discussing his study of the

Yoruba of South-Western Nigeria as an example, Majasan asserts that 'Religion is so important in Yoruba society that it has been made the main objective of Education and most of the other objectives are pursued through it – philosophy . . . art . . . and morality. . . . It also includes understanding nature and the Universe through religious explanations and establishing rules of conduct through religious authority.' Besides, among the adherents of the Abvoi cult in Southern Zaria, Northern Nigeria, education of the child is never devoid of references to Abvoi, who is believed to 'swallow' stubborn and ill-behaved people; while among the Akwapims of Ghana, the Akonodi Shrine or cult plays an important role in education by seeking to stamp out vices like incest, stealing and adultery.

In the light of all this, one of the most conspicuous features of RE in West Africa is that ATR does not feature in the syllabus and timetables of primary and secondary schools. The reason for the development of this situation is that modern education was introduced to West Africa by Christian missionaries who, statistically and effectively, dominated education in the sub-region even as recently as 1970, ten years after most African countries had attained sovereignty. Since the missionaries generally saw their schools as effective instruments of evangelism, and since the practice in their home countries in Europe or America was to teach Bible Knowledge or Christian Religious Instruction, they paid no attention to the inclusion of ATR in the curriculum. Many of them condemned ATR as being fetish, idolatrous or devilish. Even with government assumption of control of education in most countries, and monopoly of education in some, the situation has remained unchanged because products of mission schools, and the government schools that adopted the missionary pattern, preponderate in West African bureaucracies. Those who are not Christians are generally Muslims who do not care about ATR either. In addition, political authority in the sub-region rests solidly with Muslims and Christians.

At the tertiary level, however, beginning from the Higher School Certificate (HSC) Advanced Level ('A' Level) class, ATR becomes an academic subject. Even here, the subject is not studied in its own right, but simply as an appendage to Christian Religious Studies (CRS) and Islamic Religious Studies (IRS). The West African Examinations Council which is the main Ordinary Level/ School Certificate and HSC/'A' Level examination board in Nigeria, Ghana, Liberia, Sierra Leone and Gambia, offers 'West African Traditional Religion' as an alternative to 'History of Christianity in West Africa' and 'Islam in West Africa' in its HSC/'A' Level CRS Paper III and IRS Paper III. Consequently only a fraction of the CRS and IRS students study ATR. In colleges of education and universities, the situation is not radically different as departments of ATR are hard to come by. Generally, again, ATR is either appended to the CRS or the IRS programme.

2. Islam

Historically, Islam was the second of Africa's three religions to appear on the West African scene. Islam's possession of a Holy Book, the Qur'an*, and its association with the nineteenth century Fulani jihad (holy war) resulting in the entrenchment of Islamic governments in various parts of West Africa and the British Colonial authorities' respect for such Islamic regimes and Islam itself all ensured that, unlike scriptureless and politically unsponsored ATR, Islam remains today part and parcel of the West African curriculum, from primary to university level. In Ghana, however, Islamic teaching did not enter and take root in the educational system until the 1960s when the Ahamadiya Mission started its educational efforts, and the 1970s, when IRK became part of the curriculum in state schools respectively.

At primary and junior secondary levels, the various national, or in some cases regional/ state, governments allow their agents or schools to prescribe the IRS syllabuses for the two levels. Often such syllabuses are set on a fraction of the IRS syllabus prescribed by the West African Examinations Council (WAEC). In Kaduna State (Nigeria), for example, the IRS syllabus for junior secondary school students is based on some parts of the 'O' level syllabus. At 'O' level or school Certificate stage, the programme of study, as in all other subjects, is the one established by WAEC for the entire sub-region. The course title given to the study of Islam at this stage is Islamic Religious Knowledge (IRK). It would

seem that West Africans do not want their IRK/IRS and BK/CRS 'adulterated' with any other form of religious study, for the WAEC expressly states that IRK/IRS 'may not be taken with Bible Knowledge' (CRS) and vice versa; nor is either to be taken with ATR. For those who proceed to higher education, the study of Islam becomes Islamic Religious Studies.

3. Christianity

Christianity, making its debut in West Africa, nominally in the sixteenth century, but effectively in the nineteenth century, has made a greater impact on West African education and society. Since Christianity constituted the medium by which modern education spread to and within West Africa, it is only to be expected that the study of the religion should be 'a popular and important subject in the curriculum' of the sub-region.

As with Islam, determining the programme for the study of Christianity in the primary and junior secondary school is more or less a matter for the national or local political authority or its agents.

RE and Pedagogy

At the primary level, children get about two periods of BK or IRK a week, each period lasting 25–35 minutes depending on the school. In secondary schools, the number of periods is about two or three, and the duration 35–40 minutes. In the teacher training colleges that produce primary school teachers, part of this time, from form III on, is spent on methodology. From the HSC/'A' level on, the CRS/IRS or Religious Studies (RS) course entails four to six periods of 50–60 minutes each per week. For trainee teachers at the tertiary level, part of the syllabus also centres on methodology. The criticisms made by some of the products of the West African system however show that too often only a general 'Methods' is taught and the students are not exposed to a thorough strategy specific to RE or to particular subjects.

Methodology. Here we start off with objectives since, logically, objectives should influence not only what is taught but also how it is taught. The BK/CRK, CRS, IRK and IRS class in West Africa is generally seen by teachers and the public as a forum for academic work and religious nurture. Hence the 'aims and objectives' of Bible Knowledge, for example, have been described as preparing 'a student to pass his examination by helping him acquire solid knowledge of the facts in a given area of instruction. More important, Bible knowledge aims at making a student a God-fearing, Christ-centred and responsible citizen.' Some authorities have also advised that Christianity and Islam should be 'effectively taught and learnt, not only as an academic subject, but as an instrument for correct and acceptable personal and social behaviour', especially as 'everybody is interested in well ordered Society'.

On the professional side, however, it has been argued that the objective of a CRK Methodology Course has to do with problems of CRK in schools and, naturally, the aims of teaching the subject. With regard to the latter, the following have been identified: personal, national, social and knowledge aims, as well as moral, religious and spiritual objectives.

One of the basic assumptions of the teacher of Christianity or Islam in a West African school is that his pupils or students are already members of the faith. Consequently, the teacher does not aim at conversion. Another basic assumption is that there is need to deepen the learner's faith in the religion and the teaching method is tailored to that end. Naturally, either religion is presented as the only true and perfect religion, a situation which dictates that other religions be ignored except for references indicating their defects.

Most of the time, from the primary to the university level, the story-telling/lecture (or scripture reading/explanation) technique is predominantly used in imparting knowledge of the religion in question. However, it is now felt that these methods need urgent and drastic innovations.

On the Islamic side some trained Muslim religious educationists make even stronger criticisms of what goes on in the Islam class. One of the observations that have been made of Ghana for example is that the IRK in many schools is simply an exercise in memorization and rote learning. Many people in Sierra Leone, Gambia and Nigeria would easily corroborate this view. The case of ATR is even worse. In the few West African higher institutions where ATR is studied, the student relies exclusively on his lectures and text books. Sometimes there are provisions for expression work or class activity. In primary

schools this could take the form of modelling, drawing and answering of questions. Social work as a follow-up to the religious knowledge class is rarely heard of in West Africa. At the higher cadres, written assignments predominate. But in teacher training institutions of secondary or tertiary status, student activity occasionally includes the making of relevant teaching aids. Nonetheless, construction and use of teaching aids are yet to receive adequate attention in West African education in general and in RE in particular. There is such a dearth of visual aids as to suggest that the sub-region does not bother much about them. Sometimes, very rarely, film strips and films are used to illustrate the Christian or Islam lesson/lecture.

Examinations. An aspect of pedagogy has to do with assessment and examinations which mirror, to some extent, the effectiveness of the teaching/learning process. In this regard, the religious knowledge examination in primary schools is under the control of national, regional or state authorities. In the junior secondary school, it is generally the responsibility of individual schools, except in Nigeria where the new National Policy on Education warrants a state/central control of the form III examinations as from June 1984. This is because for many, if not most, of the students these are the final examinations they will take. The School Certificate and 'O' level, as well as the HSC and 'A' Level, exams are run by the West African Examinations Council for the people of Nigeria, Ghana, Liberia, Sierra Leone and Gambia. The mode of examination is nearly always a combination of context and essay-type questions based exclusively on the specific courses. Continuous assessment is not used in WAEC's religious knowledge or religious studies examinations, but Nigeria plans to make continuous assessment constitute half of the 'O' level examination. In many tertiary institutions, however, continuous assessment is now part of the examination in religious studies.

Religious Education outside public institutions
Since ATR is not 'a religion of the book', it has not yet assembled a literary corpus, nor has it yet developed any outstanding, modern formal organization. One does not therefore talk of ATR schools, seminaries or theological

colleges, for they just do not exist. The religion is learnt and practised informally and its priesthood is trained informally, without books and through a master and apprentice type of procedure, since most of the adherents are illiterate. However, an exception has to be made for the Akonodi cult of Ghana whose leader, a woman called Nana Operebea, is literate, and some of whose functionaries are also well read. Nana's secretary, for example, is said to be a university graduate. The cult is partly run along the lines of modern organizations, with paid, literate staff, and facilities like guest houses. The Ijo Ibile Ti Enia Dudu (Orunmila Religious Group) among the Nigerian Yorubas is also undergoing formalization and 'modernization'. The sect has now made a definition of its creed and its formalization is seen in the fact that 'the mode of worship of this faith seems tailored to that of the church'.

As for Islam, religious education for the adherents outside the public school is carried out mainly in the Quranic schools. Various studies and writings in West Africa show that fees are not paid and that learning is loosely organized in these schools. There is usually no established timetable or syllabus, the house of the mallam (teacher) constitutes the school, while 'a cane and rote learning process' constitutes the methodology. There are also provisions for more advanced Islamic studies; some, where 'such things as rules and prescriptions concerning Islam, inheritance, marriage . . . (and) fasting . . .' are learnt; and a third phase or 'post-secondary level' of study which includes Islamic Law and jurisprudence as well as religious and mystical studies – for those who hoped to set up as independent mallams. Naturally, the students in Quranic schools are generally children, while those at 'post-secondary level' are usually adults, often elderly people. A small group of the latter is occasionally seen in Muslim areas squatting on mats with its mallam, in front of the mallam's house, all peering into some fat Islamic books.

On the Christian side, things are much more formalized, organized and perhaps sophisticated. Catholic and Protestant churches in West Africa offer various types of religious education in their churches, some formal, some informal. There is also, on both sides, the age-long Sunday School in almost every church. A recent study of the Sunday School in Protestant churches voices certain reservations about the practice and calls for some reform. The general enthusiasm of the children for Sunday Schools was capitalized upon by the diversity of programmes within Sunday School activities in West Africa. Organization and operation were mainly in the hands of missionary-trained teachers closely supervised by a pastor. However, the operation of Sunday Schools is now being eroded as rapidly changing organizational priorities within the church mean that church hierarchies attach less importance to the work of Sunday Schools. This is even more the case following the institutional take-over by the government in the wake of the secularization of education in Nigeria.

There is a need for investigation into the lack of expression work for pupils, lack of visual aids and a serious lack of trained Sunday School teachers and other personnel.

More formally, the Protestant and Roman Catholic churches have their own Bible colleges, catechist institutes, pastoral institutes, seminaries and theological colleges scattered across West Africa. Some are only for the training of priests but others admit both laymen and priests as students. In some cases the theological colleges and major seminaries are affiliated to local or foreign universities, and most major Catholic seminaries award their degrees in religious studies through such affiliations.

See also **Islam**; *Qur'ān, al-*; **Traditional or Tribal Religions.**

E. A. Ayandale, *Missionary Impact on Modern Nigeria,* Longmans 1966; W. J. Kalu, *West African Religion,* vol. XIX, 1/2, University of Nigeria 1980; E. Luke (ed.), *Christianity in Independent Africa,* Rex Collins 1978; D. Nwosu, *An Introduction to the History of Christianity in West Africa,* n.d.

D. NWOSU

Agreed Syllabuses

Like many other legal documents, the Agreed Syllabuses of Religious Education prescribed by the 1944 Education Act were intended to provide a practical solution to an historical problem. In the late nineteenth and early twentieth centuries, suspicion between the Christian denominations had reached a point of acrimony that threatened to make impossible any teaching about religion in the increasing number of local authority schools. A modicum of denominational agreement on the content of that teaching was needed.

The growing realization of this need was shown between the two world wars by the making by some local authorities of voluntary agreed syllabuses, the West Riding of Yorkshire doing this as early as 1923. The purpose of these syllabuses was to define an area of agreement between the Christian denominations and to state what content teachers might use in their lessons without giving offence to any Christian body and without being in danger of being accused of indoctrinating in a way that was unacceptable to some.

The 1944 Act extended agreed syllabuses to the whole country and made them statutory. Since then, every local authority has been required to make its own syllabus of RE, or to adopt one made by another authority. Consequent upon the Act, there was a period of active syllabus making and certain syllabuses, such as those of Surrey (1947) and Cambridge (1949), were used widely throughout the country.

In order to construct a syllabus, an English local authority has to convene a Syllabus Conference consisting of four panels; one representing the Church of England; one representing 'other religious denominations' (which, in effect, meant originally 'other Protestant denominations', since the Roman Catholics did not co-operate and no other religion was envisaged); one representing the local authority; and one representing teachers' organizations. Nothing may be included in a syllabus to which any of the panels take exception and so each has a right of veto.

In the years immediately following the 1944 Act, the churches took keen interest in Syllabus Conferences and the two religious panels tended to include a high proportion of leading ecclesiastics and theologians, whose interests and concerns greatly colour the early syllabuses. The tacit assumption of the older syllabuses is that RE in schools is intended to impart the Christian faith to the young of a Christian country and their preambles state their aims in such phrases as giving pupils 'knowledge of the common Christian faith held by their fathers for 2,000 years' (Surrey)

and leading them to 'a life of worship and service in the Christian community' (Sunderland). Furthermore, because Christian denominations found it easier to agree on the inspiration and efficacy of the Bible than on doctrine or liturgical practices, the syllabuses were mainly schemes of Bible study.

Events subsequent to 1944 have made these strongly ecclesiastical and biblical syllabuses seem less appropriate to the classroom situation and recent syllabuses have mostly had a different form and function. Britain has become a less homogeneous Christian society; immigration has brought practising believers of other major world faiths, as well as less orthodox forms of Christianity, such as Rastafarianism* and the Jesus cults: agnosticism, humanism* and materialism are more openly espoused; the 'New Theology' has made doctrines which previously seemed unquestionable the subject of debate; and psychological research into the development of children's religious thinking has cast doubts on the wisdom of an unvaried diet of Bible-study and has brought new theories of how religion is learned and understood.

Reflection on the educational implications of these influences has brought a widening of the borders of RE, which has, in its turn, modified the syllabuses. Five changes are to be noted. 1. The accent has moved from 'agreed' to 'syllabus'. Syllabus Conferences are now more concerned with what children have to be taught to understand religions than with what churches agree can be taught. This was shown first by the West Riding of Yorkshire Syllabus (1966) which did not call itself primarily an agreed syllabus, but was entitled 'Suggestions for Religious Education'. 2. The warnings of Goldman and others about the difficulty that young children have in understanding religion has influenced what is prescribed for primary schools. This is often an investigation into the children's surroundings and relationships, with little explicit religious teaching, and it is not always clear in what way this teaching counts as RE. 3. Teachers have had a larger part in syllabus construction and the religious panels of Conferences have been less predominant. In certain cases the majority of the work has been done by teacher working parties whose recommendations were ratified by the full Conference. 4. Representatives of non-

Christian religions have participated. They were admitted to the Birmingham Syllabus Conference under the category 'other religious denominations' and the resultant syllabus of 1975 established that religions other than Christianity may legally be included in the syllabus. 5. Recognizing the need for teachers to select material appropriate to their pupils and local conditions, the syllabuses prescribe less detailed content. Some, such as Avon and Hampshire, have been content to specify suitable aims and objectives for broadly defined age groups. This, however, gives less help to the inexperienced or hard-pressed teacher and authorities often issue handbooks or supplementary material to complement the official syllabus.

The temper of the majority of syllabuses produced since the middle 1970s is shown by these quotations:

It is no part of the responsibility of a county school to promote any particular religious standpoint (Hampshire, 1978).

Religious Education . . . is most appropriately seen as an introduction to an individual's religious quest and some of its contemporary expressions in belief and practice (Northamptonshire, 1980).

See also **Acts of Parliament; Implementation of Agreed Syllabuses.**

M. Cruickshank, *Church and State in English Education,* Macmillan 1963; J. Hull, 'Agreed Syllabuses, Past, Present and Future', *New Movements in Religious Education,* Temple Smith 1975; H. Loukes, *New Ground in Christian Education,* SCM Press 1965, ch. 4; *What Future for the Agreed Syllabus–Now?,* Religious Education Council 1977; *Learning for Living,* series of articles on agreed syllabuses in Vol. 11 No. 1 (Sept. 1971) and a symposium on the Birmingham Syllabus in Vol. 15 No. 4. (Summer 1976).

EDWIN COX

Aided Schools   *see* **Voluntary Schools**

Aims of RE in LEA Schools

The process of clarifying aims in RE is itself important. It focusses attention on what is meant by 'religious' and what is meant by 'education'. Understanding kinds and functions of aims, and the criteria of overall aims, precedes choice of content in RE.

Four kinds of aim have been distinguished: general, phase or stage, scheme, lesson (cf. Raymond Holley, *Religious Education and Religious Understanding,* and Humberside Education Authority, *Agreed Syllabus 1981*).

The function of overall aims is to indicate the general direction rather than the targets of RE and the kind of approaches and attitudes which are required. They help to give cohesion to activities in RE across different schools and within any particular school.

General aims are sub-divided into a series of objectives. Phase or stage aims or objectives cut across schools and depend upon the pupils' stages of intellectual, emotional and social development. They are influenced by relevant psychological studies. Scheme and lesson aims take shape within the context of a particular school and vary from school to school. Scheme aims give precise direction to particular units of work and give coherence to various activities and methods. They reflect selection of material by particular schools in the light of general and stage aims, the abilities and ages of pupils, the school environment, the knowledge, skills, enthusiasm of the teachers. Lesson aims indicate content to be handled during a particular period of time and reflect provision made for RE in terms of timetable organization, room space, resources.

Holley suggests dimensional (religious), educational and social criteria which overall aims should satisfy.

The early LEA syllabuses reflect the overall aim, as the goal of certain procedures, of helping children to grow up within the Christian faith: 'To teach Christianity to our children is to inspire them with the vision of the glory of God in the face of Jesus Christ, and to send them into the world willing to follow him' (*Cambridgeshire Agreed Syllabus*, 1949). The procedure was to inculcate the values associated with Christianity by teaching Christianity mainly through the use of biblical material.

In the 1960s, Harold Loukes pointed to the relevance of young people's own experiences and the religious and moral questions these throw up. Greater awareness of the child's experience in the learning process, confidence in the development model of Piaget and the application of his concepts to the study of religious thinking and general religious awareness (cf. R. Goldman, *Religious Thinking from Childhood to Adolescence*) led to emphasis on life themes.

Discussion of personal and social problems often formed a large part of the secondary school syllabus. Pupils' experience and contemporary situations provided ways into Bible texts. The aim of helping children to grow up in the Christian faith and the acceptance of RE as the main vehicle for the transmission of traditional values still underlay work of this period.

Aims widely accepted during the 1970s were conceptually rooted in Ninian Smart's multi-dimensional, phenomenological analysis of religion, and were discussed within the context of educational theory and practice. RE came to be seen as the study of religion; content depended on a descriptive definition of religion. The overall aim, in summary: to help pupils to understand religion without themselves necessarily accepting its claims.

A document of major influence was the Schools Council Working Paper 36, *Religious Education in Secondary Schools* (1971). This made use of the terms confessional/phenomenological, implicit*/explicit*; the concepts behind these terms have played a part in the shaping of recent statements of overall aims.

Two Schools Council publications of the 1970s contributed to the defining of aims. *Discovering An Approach* (1977) pointed to four processes at work in RE: the exploration of religion; the exploration of experience; the development of capacities (e.g. meaning conveyed through symbols/empathetic understanding); the development of attitudes* (e.g. respect for those holding a different view). *Groundplan* (Schools Council 1977) put the emphasis on the identification of skills*, concepts* and attitudes to be developed rather than on knowledge to be imparted, and made understanding and evaluation* the key aims: 'Whatever else religious studies might aim at, they must be centrally concerned with (a) pupils coming to understand as far as possible the claims of at least some religions and the significance of those claims for both adherents and non-adherents, and (b) the progressive development of the pupils' capacities to make responsible personal judgments or evaluations on the many matters with which these religions are concerned.'

One of the RE feasibility studies in connection with 'N and F examination proposals' (Schools Council 1977) suggests these aims: to know enough about religion to be able to understand and evaluate its claims and insights, and to be able to apply those insights as appropriate.

Curriculum 11–16 (DES 1977) says the intention of RE is to 'help pupils to value emotional and spiritual capacities no less than intellectual ability or physical skills; to understand the nature of religious questions and affirmations; and to develop a personal and intellectual integrity in dealing with the profoundest aspects of their own experience'.

Starting with the Avon syllabus (1976), LEA syllabuses have concentrated their attention on aims rather than on content. Two of them suggest the following overall aims: 'The principal aim of RE in schools within the public sector is to enable pupils to understand the nature of religious beliefs and practices and the importance and influence of these in the lives of believers' (*Agreed Syllabus for Religious Education*, Hampshire Education Authority 1978). Religious Education 'helps children to understand religion' (*Humberside Agreed Syllabus* 1981).

Understanding is currently thought to be a worthwhile overall aim in RE. But, what is meant by understanding? Is there sufficient awareness of the complexities and of the broad range of the kinds and ways of understanding? Holley refers to the 'penetrative insight' of understanding 'whereby the agent sees and grasps the inner character and hidden nature of things.' He provides an overall aim based on a conceptual analysis of ideas about the spiritual: 'The provocation of intellectual understanding of the spirituality of personality', or elsewhere expressed as 'the provocation of spiritual insight'.

It is questionable that there exists, yet, a definition of religion which can provide adequate criteria for educational practice and which allows aims to be shaped through consideration of pupils' needs within an appreciation of religion as it is recognized and experienced. Perhaps aims need to reflect more clearly the processes involved in coming to understanding as a creative, synthesizing and liberating experience, but, at the same time, should point to the limits of understanding in RE.

R. Goldman, *Religious Thinking From Child-*

hood to Adolescence, Routledge & Kegan Paul 1964; Raymond Holley, *Religious Education and Religious Understanding,* Routledge & Kegan Paul 1978; Harold Loukes, *Teenage Religion,* SCM Press 1961.

BRENDA LEALMAN

Albania *see* Eastern Europe

Allegory

Allegories come into Western religious education mainly from Graeco-Latin and Judaeo-Christian sources; they are found in literature and art as well as specifically religious material.

To allegorize is by definition: *allos* 'other' and *agoreuein* 'to speak from', used by rhetoreticians who, in a series of metaphors, spoke of one thing in terms of another. A sustained one-to-one relationship, e.g. 'I am the vine, you are the branches', characterizes an allegory. It is a mode of expression, useful for clothing thought in words wherever figurative thinking is found.

Literary evidence shows that allegory is generally found when people become self-conscious and aware of the need to think about right and wrong, to make judgments and also when they need to go on finding meaning in, and to preserve, threatened concepts.

This happened in Greece when the Stoics preserved the ancient gods as abstracted attributes of the *One*. Their thinking may have influenced Jewish teachers. The figure of Wisdom is a personification of the Law which is of the mind of God. It is significant that in Jeremiah's new covenant (Jer. 31.33) the Law is to be written in men's hearts.

As schools and synagogues developed, wisdom teaching was sometimes put in euphemistic allegories to make it suitable for religious instruction. The history of exile and oppression was taught in allegories of attacks by 'the beasts that perish'; hope of deliverance by God was put in familiar biblical metaphors of the chariot and cloud.

In the inter-testamental period, Philo, a liberal Alexandrian Jew, used allegory to commend his religion to educated pagans. This device was continued by early Christian scholars, such as Clement and Origen, when looking for significance in plain statement or to get over difficulties such as contradictions or unacceptable customs.

After AD 70 the Christian church increasingly lost touch with Jewish antecedents. The spread of the gospel among pagans brought in different ways of thinking and vocabulary. All this made religious education more difficult. Allegorizing became fanciful, as in the interpretation of the Good Samaritan attributed to Ambrose of Milan in which the wounded traveller is sinful man rescued by Christ and healed in the church.

Augustine of Hippo, AD 354–430, formidable allegorist himself when he was a pagan rhetoretician, struggled more critically as a Christian bishop with the problems of limited understanding and diversity of opinion. His dictum, 'Let Truth herself bring forth concord', shows the need for a general balance of interpretation. This need may lie behind the practice of using four heads of interpretation: 1. the literal: what happened; 2. the allegorical: what should be believed; 3. the moral: how we should behave; 4. the anagogic: where we are tending.

The turmoil of world history and the passing of time led to general ignorance of actual historic events; these circumstances made the first head of interpretation difficult and the others often unacceptable by the criteria of modern scholarship.

There are many important allegories now generally classed as literature but which are part of Western Christian heritage and of religious education, e.g. Langland's *Piers Plowman*; the mediaeval morality plays and parts of Chaucer's *Canterbury Tales*. From the Latin tradition via France comes the civilizing effect of the concept of courtly love and the *Romance of the Rose*. This tradition produced Spencer's *Faerie Queene*, a socio-religious allegory of epic standard.

There is a long tradition of works more specifically about life, death and judgment. Dante is the great allegorist in this field; his deep understanding of love within himself is projected as the figure of Amor: light/love. Modern Jungian psychologists hold that the 'dark' side of man is shown in such figures as dragons and Apollyon.

In Renaissance and Reformation times, the rediscovery of Greek, Luther's interest in the biblical text, and the power of the Swiss reformers re-directed religious education; Pilgrim in his Progress travels the Pauline-Calvinist road of Salvation.

Literary allegory has now moved into the novel and at present has a more socio-political concern for 'the chief end of man'. Kafka's *The Castle* and Orwell's *Animal Farm* are good allegories in that they stand on their own feet regardless of inner meaning; this excellence may raise questions about the rightness of unconscious influence and 'double-think'.

Religious educationalists have now a new opportunity to consider allegories in the light of modern study through:

1. The progress of Jungian research on symbols and allegory.

2. Better relations with Jewish scholars and understanding of the literal and metaphorical elements in the OT. More knowledge of interpretation in the NT text.

3. Work in educational psychology on child development in understanding.

ELIZABETH BROWETT

Anglican Church
see **Church of England: Policy in Education**

Art

RE encourages the exploration of meaning and mystery. This exploration must take place in the light of personal experience and insight. It is not the task of RE to provide or to create what might be called religious experience*. It should, however, take seriously the experience of young people and do all it can to help them to explore that experience in whatever form it may come, whether it is recognizably and explicitly religious or not. Visual imagery can play a key role in RE in the achieving of such aims.

To the question 'What is the function of visual art in RE?' there are a number of possible answers.

1. Works of art make a demand; teachers and pupils are required to give them attention – a way of waiting is needed to respond to them, to relate them to experience. The artist himself intends this. 'A work of art, restricted to what the artist has put in it, is only part of itself; it only attains full stature with what people and time make it' (Naum Gabo). Works of art trigger off the creative imagination and creative processes.

2. A work of art does not only reflect the artist's skill; it also reflects his vision of the world and his whole response to life. By learning to give attention to his work, perceptions can be heightened and so lead to awareness of new possibilities, of hitherto unsuspected levels of reality.

3. A work of art can suggest to those who look at it, ways of expressing their own experience and thus of sharing it with others. To enable pupils to recognize the depth and mysteriousness of their experience, to find means of articulating it, and to have confidence in its authority for them, is an important function of RE.

4. The function of art is not to give information but to provoke fresh insight. It communicates its meaning indirectly and this method of communication is at the root of RE, i.e. the method of appropriation and assimilation which thrusts into deeper self reflection and appropriation of truth on an existential level. It should not require the impersonal acceptance of truth as objective. This is in line with Socratic method and that advocated by Kierkegaard who wrote about education as a process of awakening. This way of communication is in metaphoric mode and avoids giving too precise a definition to reality.

There is a place in RE for visual art which is religious in quality, not necessarily in content. Religious art may broadly be defined as that which has a concern with man's experience of the transcendent; it should not be confined to that art which the artist intends to be religious.

Works of art may be regarded as visual aids, i.e. as illustrating an idea which has already been presented in some other form, but they should not be regarded primarily as having this function.

There is also an important place in RE for the study of the art of the major religions as it reflects the experience and beliefs of those traditions, e.g. the patterns and the arabesques of Islamic art which suggest an infinite field of vision; the rich representationalism of Hindu art and the architecture and structure of its temples which reflect the Hindu idea of the structure of the cosmos and of the human personality.

G. Heyer, *Signs of Our Times*, Handsel Press 1980; *In the Image of Man: the Indian Perception of the Universe through 2000 years of*

Painting and Sculpture, Weidenfeld & Nicolson 1982; Hans Küng, *Art and the Question of Meaning*, SCM Press 1981; B. Lealman and E. Robinson, *The Image of Life*, CEM 1980; James E. Loder, 'Creativity in and beyond Human Development', *Aesthetic Dimensions of Religious Education*, ed. Gloria Durka and Joanmarie Smith, Paulist Press 1979; M. Tickner and D. H. Webster, *Aspects of Education: Religious Education and Imagination*, 28, University of Hull 1982.

BRENDA LEALMAN

Artefacts, Use of

Learning *about* another person's faith seems irrelevant to many students and the narrow dissemination of factual information sometimes increases prejudice and does not lead to understanding and involvement. Learning *from* another's faith, however, enriches each student's own personal quest for meaning in life. Ideally students need to meet believers, share their thoughts and in some measure participate in their worship at home and in community. Such encounters can be deepened, or where necessary replaced, in the classroom by the use of artefacts.

Artefacts give life to the spoken and written word. The careful way in which they are handled mirrors the depth and importance of the phenomenon of personal faith. Artefacts, however, are not ends in themselves. They are the starting point or the focal point for an explanation of the meaning and relevance of faith.

A small Sefer Torah scroll, reverently handled, may first be examined for its symbolism with reference to history, to biblical narratives and to religious concepts. Reference can then be made to the writing of synagogue scrolls, their use on Shabbat and during festivals, their 'disposal' when replaced, emphasizing the implications of the practices for personal belief. Slides, concentrating on the facial expressions of people involved, will help create the atmosphere for discussion. Literary references to the grief caused to worshippers by the misuse of scrolls – e.g. in Leon Uris, *Mila 18* – will raise questions. How reasonable is it to suffer persecution for a symbol? The possibilities of exploring universal questions are legion if the artefact 'opens a door' and is not merely a static point of information.

The difference between the symbolic and the superstitious use of artefacts must be stressed. The dropped icon* may distress the worshipper but he should not fear 'divine retribution' for misuse or lack of use. That to which the symbol bears witness is not affected by accident or forgetfulness. An accompanying slide of an unconcerned caretaker carefully replacing the burnt out electric light bulb in the synagogue's *ner tamid* (eternal light) points to the depth, not the superstitious nature, of the artefact – to what is universally important and not what is immediate and peripheral.

A single expensive artefact, e.g. a large Hindu shrine figure or a beautiful Christian chalice, illustrates the importance of faith to individual and community. The simple and inexpensive, bought or made, can be equally effective. Paschal and havdalah candles provide opportunities to explore the concept of light, deepening understanding, bringing sudden perception of victory over evil, of continuing relationships. A Muslim prayer mat achieves its fullest symbolic impact when placed beside a clean handkerchief and illustrated by a slide of a desert bedouin drawing a rectangular outline in the sand. Intention supercedes the actual physical object or action and gives them life. Muslim prayer beads are a reminder of many beliefs concerning God's relationship with man. The implications of their acceptance by the individual are part of the universal quest and universal response. 'What difference would it make to our life if. . .?' Thus the artefact becomes a means by which each student explores his own questions and responds to the mystery of life, whatever his beliefs and uncertainties.

VIDA BARNETT

Asia

A vast region with a population of 2.8 billion. In the field of education there is a variety of methodology, approaches, philosophy and levels of development. It is difficult to talk about North-East Asia (including Japan with one hundred per cent literacy and high school enrolment of ninety-four per cent) together with the Indian subcontinent where the literacy rate is between twenty and thirty per cent (actual readership rates are a fifth of the above percentage). Likewise, in the field of RE, there are differences between the countries with Buddhist, Confucian, Hindu or Muslim backgrounds. RE in the Philippines, where Christianity is a predominant religion, cannot be discussed together with Thailand, where Christianity is a weak minority. Almost all churches in Asian countries borrowed the philosophy and style of their RE from Western churches, especially from American churches. Now they are in the process of indigenization of curricula, methods and teaching materials as well as their programmes for self-support.

There are restrictions on Christian education in some Asian countries. However, Asian people and governments in general take a favourable attitude towards Christian education. There is no open persecution against Christians or Christian education in Asia. The YMCA* has now reopened its programmes, although Christian schools will not revive in China.

Censorship of books and publications is common in most Asian countries, but it does not affect RE much except in Taiwan. In Burma there is a problem of the rationing of paper. Printing machines and, in some countries, audio-visual media also need licences.

Governments in Asia take RE more seriously than those in so-called developed countries. The Thai Government requires Buddhist ethics in all Thai schools, and Muslim countries are requiring more Islamic studies. In these countries, Christian education in Christian schools is permitted in either regular or extra-curricular classes. In Indonesia, Bangladesh and Sri Lanka, the government permits Christian education in state-supported schools for the children of Christians, along with religious education for children of other faiths. In Hong Kong and Singapore, the governments include the Bible as one of the subjects for secondary school examinations.

The education ministry of Asian churches is extended to the people outside the churches. Asian churches are financially sponsoring aids to educational programmes in Vietnam, Laos and Cambodia. Here only Sunday Schools, Christian schools and other Christian education agencies, such as Boys Brigades, YMCA, YWCA*, can be discussed. In some Asian countries Sunday Schools are called 'church schools' and in other countries Christian schools are called 'church schools'. Christian schools in Asia are not only institutions for RE they are also agencies of community outreach.

In many Sunday Schools, there are more children from non-Christian homes than from Christian families. In North-East Asia, Christians usually relate to churches individually. Non-Christian parents are willing to send their children to Sunday Schools or to Christian kindergarten and nurseries. In most Asian countries, Sunday Schools are patterned on American or British styles and philosophy. In some parts of Indonesia, children's worship follows Dutch or German traditions. In the past most curricula in Asian Sunday Schools were translated from American models, but now national councils of churches and major denominations in Asia have their own curricula. However, the churches under foreign missionaries or para-church groups still use Western materials and methods. The Presbyterian Church in Taiwan produced its own curriculum in 1980. The National Council of Churches in Pakistan is considering building its own curriculum. Nepal is probably the only country in Asia where there is no native Sunday School curriculum.

Where Christians are a minority, it is very difficult to produce materials for RE for financial reasons. For example, the Church of Christ in Thailand has an Office of Education capable of producing quality books, but when there are only 200 Sunday Schools it is difficult to print good books. Where the churches are divided it becomes more difficult. The curriculum and materials of the United Church in Japan are adopted by many churches. The Hong Kong Christian Literature Council produces a Chinese curriculum for the Sunday Schools of overseas Chinese. The Lutheran Churches in Hong Kong, Taiwan, Malaysia and Singapore share common curricula both in English and Chinese. The Christian Conference of Asia has been supplying Asian-made RE materials to Asian churches through offices of the national councils of churches and major denominations.

The churches in Asia are adopting traditional teaching methods and teaching aids as well as inventing new media. Indonesian churches adopted *wayang* (shadow play) in RE. *Kamishibai* (paper play) from Japan is used in other Asian countries, especially in the areas where there is no electricity. Christian kindergarten in Japan are using video cassettes.

When most children in Sunday Schools come from non-Christian families, the goal and contents of the curriculum are different from those of 'Christendom'. Where Christians are a minority and placed under strict government control, the Sunday School curriculum includes very little social application of the gospel. The Burman Council of Churches is exceptional, and its adult education encourages Christians to be controversial and to overcome fears of being socially involved. Curricula in Japanese churches and Christian schools include peace education or environmental conservation, but it is difficult to deal with 'peace' in most Asian countries.

In southern Asia, where the literacy rate is low, Western approaches to education through printed media are not so effective. However, literacy rates among Christians are not noticeably higher than others. Missionaries built schools side-by-side with church buildings in Asia. The Jesuits and other Catholic missionaries in the sixteenth century built colleges and seminaries. Protestant missionaries also built schools. Today there are nearly 20,000 Christian schools in Asia. One third of them are in India. There are fifty Christian universities and colleges and eighty theological seminaries in Japan. But there is only one theological seminary in Bangladesh.

Christian schools used to be known as 'mission schools', but many of them were built and funded by the native Christians. Also the 'mission' spirit was lost among many of the Christian schools. Nevertheless, moral and personal education is still a very strong sales point of Christian schools. Some Christian schools were primarily built for literacy education, as well as Christian education, in lieu of public elementary education. These schools are found in India, Indonesia, Pakistan and Bangladesh. It is very significant that literacy rates are very high in Southern and North-Eastern India where the Christian population is also high.

Many of these schools were nationalized in China, Pakistan, Sri Lanka, Burma and Bangladesh. In Bangladesh, Baptist churches had to give away their schools for financial reasons. However, English media schools were spared by the government. In the age of missionary moratorium and self-support,

English media schools are mushrooming in India and Pakistan to the detriment of native language media schools. These English language schools are enrolling rich people's children.

English-language education was a strong sales point of Christian schools in Asia. In southern Asia, institutions of higher education heavily depend on English textbooks and, English being an international language, Christian schools are popular among non-Christians.

International education is another feature. Christian schools in Japan are not only self-supporting but also hire native English teachers, and 'missionary associates' who teach English are in high demand. Nevertheless, these self-supporting Christian schools are more and more dependent on government, big business and rich parents. This trend is not without ideological sacrifices. The Japanese government and local governments subsidize both Christian schools and their students. In Singapore, all schools, including Christian schools, can be aided by the government up to one hundred per cent. The government has the right to appoint their principals.

In Hong Kong fifty-one per cent of secondary schools are Christian schools where British colonial policy took advantage of Christian missionaries from the West. In order to cover the shortage of secondary schools the Korean Government assigns students to mission schools by drawing lots.

In Indonesia, the Council of Churches insists on giving opportunities for Muslim children to study Islam at Christian schools because they function almost as public schools. However, the Council of Christian Education in Indonesia considers that Christian schools were founded to give Christian education to all their students.

In order to improve curricula and develop better teaching methods or recruit and train good teachers, there are Christian school unions in many Asian countries. In India, there is close co-operation between Catholic and Protestant school unions. They are united at the level of higher education. The Association of Christian Universities and Colleges in Asia consists of Catholic and Protestant universities but does not include all Christian universities and colleges.

One of the Christian contributions to Asian

societies is educating minorities and op-pressed people. Christian education for women in Asia is highly valued by non-Christians. Many leaders of women's libera-tion movements are graduates of women's Christian colleges, although many more grad-uates are found in middle class or upper class homes. Missionaries and local Christian leaders founded girls' schools when the status of women in Asia was low. In lieu of the government sponsored schools, the churches and missions built schools for the blind, for the deaf and dumb, for orphans, and homes and schools for mentally-retarded and other handicapped children. Today the emphasis of Christian education in Asian churches is not so much *for* the handicapped people but together *with* them and *with* the oppressed people.

Camping is not well developed in the chur-ches' educational programmes in Asia but there are many conference centres and retreat houses. There are academies and lay-training centres for Christian social concerns, but at present their number is small. YMCAS and YWCAS are found in most Asian cities. However, in Singapore and Taiwan, student YMCAS and the Student Christian Movement* are considered as 'pro-communist' organiza-tions. Some churches use Boy Scouts or Girl Scouts either for Christian education or for churches' community service programmes. In some countries, the churches organize Boys' Brigades and/or Girls' Brigades. There is a favourable mood among the governments in Asia toward 'uniformed' education.

Tosh Arai and Rob Evans (eds), *Church and Education in Asia*, Christian Conference of Asia 1980; Tosh Arai (ed.), *Children in Asia*, Christian Conference of Asia 1979; Barbara Stephens (ed.), *Christian Education News-letter*, Christian Conference of Asia.

TOSH ARAI

Assembly

When the Education Act (1944) prescribed that 'the school day in every county school . . . shall begin with collective worship on the part of all pupils in attendance at the school . . .' and that the collective worship should not be distinctive of any particular religious denomination, it was speaking to a specific generation. The books produced to help head-teachers to carry out the Act had a clearly defined view of worship – 'nothing less than the rendering unto Almighty God of the honour, the veneration and – most perfect of all worship – the adoration which is due to Him as Creator and Redeemer and the love which is due to Him as Himself Eternal Love'. From this base, assembly books of the 1940s and 1950s contained traditional prayers and hymns, as well as biblical and a limited number of extra-biblical readings. Their emphasis is somewhat introverted – prayers for animals, armed forces and Armistice Day and with concentration on the Christian virtues. They show a cosy, orderly view of life with little about the great issues of the world in which young people were growing up and of which subsequent generations were to become more acutely aware (economic injus-tice, victims of oppression, disasters, etc.). It must, however, be said that the nation was at that time far less pluralistic and that religious perceptions and assumptions about religious allegiances went largely unchallenged.

In the 1960s assemblies began to change. To the secularized society which was being identified and which had came about through the rise of Communism, materialism, scien-tific thinking and developments in mass com-munication, the attitudes and assumptions which had characterized assemblies in earlier decades were no longer acceptable.

The societal changes were matched in the world of schools. The creation of large comprehensive schools in the new social climate opened up the possibility, indeed the necessity, of a re-examination of the place of assembly in schools. The fresh look began to explore changes both in the methodology which produced assemblies (including greater involvement by pupils in the preparation and production of them) and a greater relevance of content to the secular, pluralist world in which these pupils were living.

The third area which had its influence on a rethinking of assemblies was that of theology. The lively and public theological debates of the sixties meant that as worship came under scrutiny in the churches, resulting in new forms and expressions of spirituality, its effect was necessarily felt in schools.

Thus, not only were newer forms being considered, but a whole debate was being opened concerning the nature and purpose of assemblies.

In the BCC report, *Religion and the Secondary School*, Colin Alves wrote that assembly should be thought of as 'an educative instrument, a means to insight, an evocation of vision'. Material began to be produced in the 1970s more from this viewpoint. By 1975 the thrust of that thinking was impelled to the logical conclusion that an understanding of school assembly as worship should be abandoned and the assembly left free to relate in new ways to the curriculum. The most articulate suggestion of the way forward for school assembly came from John Hull: 'The objectives of school assembly will be to provide ceremonies, celebrations and other events, which while not assuming the truth of any one controversial statement will present the issues to the pupils in such a way so as 1. To widen the pupil's repertoire of appropriate emotional response . . . 2. To encourage a reflective approach to living, a way which transcends the immediacy of experience . . . 3. To demonstrate the values which are not controversial and upon which democratic society depends (freedom of speech, equality before the law etc) . . . 4. To provide some experience and understand of what worship is so that the way of worship, along with other life styles will remain an option for anyone who wishes to follow it and so that all will have some insight into what it is like to live a religious life. But this provision will not require anyone to worship and will certainly not commit the school to corporate acts of worship.'

It is, he argued, the task of these assemblies to select from the various aspects of the tradition of worship those which are compatible with educational goals. These issues can be treated in an open way and contribute to the moral, aesthetic and religious development of the pupil in a rational, freedom-enhancing way.

This viewing of assembly as a focal point of the curriculum and the whole enterprise of the school means that assembly planners of the 1980s face new demands. No longer are books of 'Assembly Services' either needed or produced. Material which has been most widely used in recent years centres more on material for experimental and local approaches of the 'Assembly Workshop' type.

Flexible organization and imaginative approaches are called for. Assemblies, less the responsibility of the head, are more arranged by a working party or committee so that themes from a variety of areas can be explored. If the working party is drawn from a wide team of staff having a good overview of the school, they are able to draw out connections and common themes. Assemblies prepared in this way, focussing for example on courses run in the school and their aims in terms of preparation for life beyond school, are not 'an irrelevant interlude before the educational work of the school begins but the centre for the illumination and integration of the whole curriculum'. The school and its relationship to the community are brought more into focus by using music*, drama, poetry*, slides, films and inviting speakers from all aspects of the community, not only its religious life. Rather than the exposition of religious truth, the starting point of assembly today is much more that of what pupils are concerned about – families, friends and relationships, success, failure, the future, concerns about society and awareness of the world wide community. The aim is to encourage them to consider seriously such concerns, to move from the trivial to the significant, from the immediate to that which is lasting – the ultimate concerns of life.

School assembly, seen as a time of sharing of ideals and visions, offers a wide range of subjects and attitudes to be explored. Its function is not to secure commitment nor to profess faith but to deepen understanding and facilitate choice.

C. Alves, *Religion and the Secondary School*, SCM Press 1968; C. L. Berry, *The Teacher's Handbook* to *A Book of Morning Worship*, Dent 1946; John Hull, *School Worship: An Obituary*, SCM Press 1975.

SHEILA M. HOBDEN

Assessment of Students

All teachers make assessments of their pupils' progress, using a wide range of techniques which take account of a variety of skills, aptitudes and qualities in an attempt to provide, over a period of time, a total picture of individual performance and achievement. In this respect the teacher of RE is no different from any other teacher; yet there are significant emphases which relate specifically to the approach to RE adopted by the individual teacher.

Pupil activity in most first and middle schools is unlikely to be subject-specific (except in a denominational context). In so far as the total profile of a pupil at this stage will be concerned not only with cognitive skills but will also take account of such abilities as perseverance, the development of self-reliance, of social skills and of a sense of responsibility, the teacher will be able to 'feed in' the RE component. In particular, participation in co-ordinated activities in which RE plays a part, such as school assembly or community service, will be noted and commented on. In addition, the affective domain is especially significant in discovering an approach to RE during the first and middle years of schooling and, where a teacher believes in implicit* rather than explicit* RE, assessment will be based on the degree of sensitivity and response evoked by such a method of teaching.

Likewise, secondary school RE teachers will adopt an approach to assessment which accords with their philosophical stance. Those who emphasize the affective dimension of religion may well argue that its assessment is inappropriate and unexaminable in any formal sense. Others will stress that assessment of the pupil is an inherent part of any monitoring process and will take into account every dimension, the affective, the conative and the cognitive. If the mark of a religiously educated person is the possession of a 'disposition to assign a positive value to and to attain an ultimate confidence in life' as well as 'the ability to integrate his experience in itself with that of others in a total value system' (as argued by M. C. Brown in *New Movements in Religious Education*), some attempt must be made to identify the acquisition of such characteristics. Such an aim may not be susceptible to traditional forms of assessment, such as examinations*, but, nevertheless, many RE teachers believe it important to assess pupils' achievements and argue that the status of the subject needs to be bolstered by its being treated in the same way as any other 'academic' area of the curriculum. It is recognized that the curriculum in RE is influenced (as is the case with many other subjects) by public examina-

tion syllabuses, hence the importance of nationally agreed criteria and especially of clearly stated aims and objectives. Such aims and objectives for an examination in religious studies must be seen to cohere and be compatible with those for RE *sui generis*. It would seem that some examination boards have not made this distinction in the past: it is difficult to see how the aim 'to bring children into a encounter with Jesus Christ' is translatable into an assessment objective. A fundamental question which needs to be posed is whether there are skills and abilities which are unique to RE and how far they are identical or similar to those used in other subjects (e.g. history) but applied to religious studies.

Assessment of pupils who have completed a course in religious studies as part of their religious education should be based on clearly defined objectives. Such may well include the following abilities: (i) to give a clear account of key religious beliefs and practices based on the acquisition and assimilation of essential information; (ii) to demonstrate a knowledge of religious language, vocabulary and terminology; (iii) to show understanding of the application of this knowledge to differing contexts of past and present; (iv) to interpret the beliefs and practices of religions, from the point of view of the adherent and the non-adherent; (v) to show evidence of having thought clearly and rationally about their own and other people's beliefs and values.

Modes and methods of assessment in RE are mixed. Most teachers use a combination of continuous assessment and terminal examination, if they assess formally at all, and many prefer a similar mixed pattern for public examination purposes. It is especially important that pupils be encouraged to develop skills* of insight, understanding, empathy and personal judgment. Many teachers find the activity usually subsumed under the generic title 'project' a very valuable means of developing and exhibiting those skills. It is often in this context that breadth of viewpoint and qualities of perseverence and originality can be developed. However, there are obvious drawbacks: danger of plagiarism, over-dependence on secondary sources, unthinking regurgitation, as well as difficulties in standardization and marking. Strict criteria need to be applied to all forms of assessment, for only by such means will public credibility be maintained. The fact that Religious Studies, as an examination subject, is not an easy option is now generally recognized but certification of pupils must command public confidence. It needs to be recognized that the teacher and/or examiner is not 'assessing' belief in the sense of grading pupils on a sliding scale according to their degree of commitment to any one particular viewpoint. On the other hand, an open-ended approach should not result in indecisive or vacuous responses from pupils. A further and crucial point to be considered is that in assessing the pupil the teacher assesses the quality of the work which is being done and is thereby evaluating the worth of the subject. Assessment assesses the assessor and by this means RE is subjected to a process of continuous self-appraisal.

See also **Evaluation**.

WILLIAM GREENWOOD

Association of Christian Teachers

Formed in 1971 by a co-operation of three previously existing bodies. The Teachers' Prayer Fellowship and the Christian Education Fellowship were merged in the new Association. The teachers' professional activities of the Inter-School Christian Fellowship were absorbed, although ISCF's work amongst pupils remained separate. ACT's full doctrinal statement is firmly in the tradition of inter-denominational evangelicalism. Membership is open to all who can sign a much briefer basis of belief.

ACT is active in RE and produces a termly review of resources, holds regular RE conferences and courses, and publishes occasional booklets. Nevertheless, its aims of asserting Christian principles and values in education, promoting Christian participation in public discussion about education, and stimulating prayer, study, witness and fellowship among Christian teachers, result in a membership which is wider than RE alone.

RICHARD WILKINS

Association for Religious Education (1969-83)

ARE was concerned solely with the professional aspects of RE. Professional involvement in the subject was the one link between members drawn from all levels of education. ARE affirmed that RE was an essential part of the school curriculum. Its activities included: the publication of a termly bulletin *Area* and occasional papers; the encouragement of research and support for teachers in the classroom; the organization of conferences and the exchange of information and ideas; and the representation of the professional interests of RE teachers to politicians, publishers, industry, commerce, the media and other bodies. On 1 January 1984 the Association united with the Christian Education Movement's Professional Committee for Religious Education to form the Professional Council for Religious Education*.

_____

P. Lefroy-Owen, *A Professional Approach to Religious Education*, ARE Working Paper 3, 1972.

ARTHUR ROWE

Association for Teachers of Religious Knowledge
see **Christian Education Movement**

Association of Teachers of Religious Education in Scotland

Formed in 1962 it acts as a professional subject association promoting the subject and teachers' interests in Scotland. Secondary teachers form a large majority of the membership and secondary education concerns predominate but primary teachers can be associated.

The Association makes representations to the Scottish Education Department and other bodies with influence in Scottish Education. It submitted evidence to the Millar Committee whose report, published in 1972, mentioned in favourable terms the ATRES views on the aims of RE. Since the Millar Report*, ATRES has taken the opportunity to offer comments on numerous statements on education promoting the concern of the subject.

The Association publishes a termly bulletin, *The Scottish Journal of Religious Education*. Six branches provide local meeting points. A national conference is held annually (usually in May).

J. J. LAIDLAW

Attitudes

The concept of attitude has an important place in the social sciences and there is a substantial body of literature about it. Attitudes cannot be directly observed, but they are hypothesized on the basis of consistent responses and 'latent predispositions' (Elms) shown by human beings to features of the world about them. Attitudes have been defined in a number of different ways and there is no one correct definition. It is commonly argued that attitudes have three components or aspects, cognitive (belief), affective (evaluative) and conative (behavioural) (Stevens), but some psychologists prefer to define attitude as relating only to the evaluative dimension and to consider belief separately. Attitudes are said to be relatively enduring and are learned and not instinctive or inherited. They dispose a person to act in a certain way and are said to have certain psychological functions.

What then is meant by 'attitude to religion'? Some writers (e.g. Wilson) speak of 'the religious attitude', by which they mean givenness to certain experiences or types of commitment which are held to be characteristic of religion. Ambiguity can be avoided by taking 'attitude to religion' to mean the psychological construct of attitude applied to the religious dimension of human life. 'The religious attitude' may then be used, if desired, to characterize a particular type of appreciation or apprehension of religion.

Workers in the tradition of social science research have operationalized the concept of attitude to religion in such a way that it is open to empirical investigation. Accounts of research into attitudes to religion may be found in the published journals or unpublished doctoral theses. The debate about whether attitude should be defined as cognitive, affective and conative or only as affective is reflected in the studies which have been carried out into attitude to religion. It is, however, difficult to see how a person's attitude to particular religious concepts, persons or objects, can be separated from his beliefs about these referents.

In discussions of curriculum planning, it is commonly argued that teachers' objectives must include the changing of attitudes. This has been discussed in relation to RE by Naylor. But examination of the relevant literature supports Lee's claim that relatively little work has been carried out on the way in which attitudes to religion are formed or influenced by RE. Among the few studies which have been carried out, reference may be made to

that by Hyde which concluded that the development of religious thinking, as measured by ability to select the orthodox definition out of four possible definitions of a number of theological terms, was dependent on positive religious attitudes and behaviour. Miles (1971) reported that a planned course of instruction in RE delayed the decline in favourable attitudes towards religion among 'O' and 'A' level pupils. Francis found that there was no significant difference in attitude between English pupils educated in state schools employing the traditional form of agreed syllabus and pupils in state schools employing the modern form of agreed syllabus, and he concluded that the latter form had not achieved an improvement in pupil attitudes. Finally, Kay found that the content of the RE syllabus appeared to have effect on attitude to religion as measured by the Francis scale. For example in state schools in Northern Ireland and in English Roman Catholic schools teaching world religions appeared to damage attitudes to Christianity. In contrast, teaching about the Bible in Church of England schools promoted positive attitudes to Christianity.

Up to the present, relatively little research has been carried out into the development of attitudes to religion by the formal process of RE in schools. There is clearly a great deal of investigation to be carried out, which should be helped by two factors. In the first place, while questions of the definition of attitude have not been resolved there is now much greater clarity about the concept of attitude to religion. In the second place, the production of valid and reliable instruments has made it possible for attitude to religion to be measured and this must facilitate empirical enquiry.

A. C. Elms, *Attitudes*, Open University 1976; L. J. Francis, 'Paths of Holiness? Attitudes Towards Religion among 9–11 year-old children in England', *Character Potential*, IX, 3, 1980; J. E. Greer, 'Attitude to Religion Reconsidered', *British Journal of Educational Studies*, 31, 1, 1983; K. E. Hyde, *Religious Learning in Adolescence*, Oliver and Boyd 1965; W. Kay, 'Syllabuses and Attitudes to Christianity', *The Irish Catechist*, 5, 2, 1981; J. M. Lee, *The Flow of Religious Instruction*, Religious Education Press, Mishawaka 1973;

D. Naylor, 'Curriculum development', in N. Smart and D. Horder (eds), *New Movements in Religious Education*, Temple Smith 1975; Schools Council Religious Education Committee, *A Groundplan for the Study of Religion*, Schools Council 1977; R. Stevens, *Attitudes and Beliefs*, Open University Press 1975; J. Wilson, *Education in Religion and the Emotions*, Heinemann 1971.

JOHN E. GREER

Australia

Education in Australia is a state responsibility, therefore variations in administrative procedures and curriculum provisions exist between the different states. It is also important to note that each state has a dual system of Government and Independent schools. The Roman Catholic Church maintains an extensive system of primary and secondary schools, and several other churches and groups have significant numbers of schools, mainly secondary, in each state. This survey concentrates on provisions for RE in state schools.

By the middle of the twentieth century, most state legislation reflected a two-tiered approach to the teaching of religion in Government schools.

1. Some form of general religious teaching by classroom teachers was allowed or required. Examples from the New South Wales and Queensland legislation will suffice to illustrate this kind of provision. The quite specific reference to particular content in the Queensland Act makes an interesting comparison between these two examples.

'In all schools under this Act the teaching shall be strictly non-sectarian but the words "secular instruction" shall be held to include general religious teaching as distinguished from dogmatical or polemical theology and lessons in the history of England and in the history of Australia shall form part of the course of secular instruction' (N.S.W. – Public Instruction Act of 1880 (43 Vic. No. 23.) Section 7).

'Instruction in accordance with regulations in that behalf shall be given in State primary and special schools during school hours in selected Bible lessons. A separate reading book shall be provided for such purpose. Such instruction shall not include any teaching in the distinctive tenets or doctrines of any religious denomination, society or sect' (Queensland – Education Act 1964–1970 Pt III State Schools, Division 1. General 20 (2)).

2. Religious groups were afforded the privilege and legal right to send authorized representatives into schools, usually during school hours, to present to the children of their adherents their own particular beliefs and doctrines. Clauses from the Victoria Education Act illustrate this 'right-of-entry' provision: 'when religious instruction is given in any State school during the hours set apart for the instruction of the pupils: '(*a*) such religious instruction shall be given by persons who are accredited representatives of religious bodies and who are approved by the Minister for the purpose; (*b*) such religious instruction shall be given on the basis of the normal class organization of the school except in any school where the Minister, having regard to the particular circumstances of such schools, authorizes some other basis to be observed; (*c*) attendance at any class for such religious instruction shall not be compulsory for any pupil whose parents desire that he be excused from attending' (Victoria Education Act 1958, Section 23(2)).

In every state, provision was made within the legislation to allow parents the right to withdraw their children from any and all religious teaching and activity in the school. A similar right to 'opt out' was available to teachers in most states.

During the 1960s, increasing numbers of people were asking serious and probing questions about the appropriateness of these legislative provisions and about the effectiveness of actual school practice in relation to them. Several attempts at reform were made, especially in Tasmania. However, all came to a head in 1969 when several major Christian denominations in South Australia indicated that they would cease to exercise their right of entry to Government schools to give special or denominational religious instruction. This action, along with requests from several churches to the Government for reform, resulted in the establishment of a Committee of Enquiry to investigate the whole matter of RE in the state schools of South Australia.

From this point, and throughout the 1970s, debate about RE in Australian state schools was focussed in a succession of Government enquiries. In most cases, lengthy and detailed reports issued from these investigations and are listed here, using their popular titles rather than their lengthy more formal titles.

The *Gutekunst Report*, Queensland 1972 (not publicly available)

The *Steinle Report*, South Australia 1973

The *Russell Report*, Victoria 1974

The *Nott Report*, Western Australia 1977

The *Rawlinson Report*, New South Wales 1980

Reference to RE also appeared in general reports on state educational provisions in Tasmania (*The Tend Report*) and in the Australian Capital Territory (*The Campbell Report*, 1972).

While considerable variations exist in the degree of acceptance afforded the reports and their recommendations by state authorities, each re-affirms the belief that there is an appropriate and important place for the study of religion in schools and that the ability and will to maintain such courses, is, or can be made available to state schools throughout Australia. The major concerns reflected in each report are practical ones and are expressed either as a desire to find alternative structures or to provide more effective means for supporting the established two-tiered structure.

The New South Wales report actually recommends the retention of the two-tiered approach. In Queensland, Victoria and Tasmania, political decisions and educational practice subsequent to the issuing of their respective reports, and, maybe in direct opposition to the recommendations contained in them, have clearly indicated a continuing commitment to the two-tiered structure. In South Australia and Western Australia, decisions were taken to strengthen school-based responsibility for the study of religion rather than the externally controlled activity operating through 'right-of-entry' provisions. In the Australian Capital Territory, all curriculum decisions, including those relating to RE are matters for individual school boards and therefore may vary considerably between individual schools in the Territory.

Interesting variations are also found in the ways in which some state educational authorities have sought to support the subject either through traditional or newly established structures. Queensland set up a curriculum project team within its State Education Department to produce teaching materials for use by religious groups exercising their right of entry to schools and to provide extensive in-service and resources provision for these people. In 1982 multiple copies of a new version of the Bible were supplied to state primary and special schools and a teacher was seconded to prepare reading schemes to help class-teachers respond to the needs of the second tier of the system, namely the school-based Bible reading required by state legislation. South Australia also established a very strong curriculum team which produced a wide range of teacher and pupil material to promote the development of the school-based subject. Extensive in-service and piloting provisions were also developed by this team in an impressive investment by the state in the development of a fully recognized school subject. On the other hand, Western Australia adopted a school-based curriculum development model, linked with a centrally administered in-service and advisory service. A Development Officer was appointed within the State Education Department to encourage and help individual schools develop their own religious studies programmes.

Differing curriculum emphases are also found, especially between the three states where state educational authorities have taken deliberate steps to influence the content and procedural styles of classroom programmes. In the South Australia materials, religion is viewed in the widest possible sense to include most of the major religious traditions represented in Australian and indeed world society. In Western Australia the breadth of content to be covered is a matter for negotiation within schools. Because of factors such as a particular core subject structure, previous bad experiences with RE as an optional subject, variations in teacher knowledge and attitudes, the thrust has been towards integrating religious material into core subjects in secondary schools and into general thematic work in primary schools. In Queensland, apart from the Bible reading provisions, curriculum decisions in RE remain with religious groups exercising their 'right-of-entry' to schools. The materials produced by the state curriculum project team are freely available to and may be used by these groups. These materials use important human experiences and concerns and relate them to religious beliefs and practices drawn almost entirely from the Christian tradition.

While there is not a strong tradition in Australia of offering RE as an examination option in secondary schools, interesting developments in this regard have run parallel with the movements surveyed above and with the expansion of Religious Studies departments in institutions of higher education. Space does not permit a detailed survey of these developments and of the variations in procedures and curriculum emphases which are emerging in the different states in relation to examination work in RE.

RE remains a problematic area of the curriculum for many educational systems around the world. The activities described here represent particular Australian responses to these problems at a time when the nation is becoming increasingly conscious of its own religious pluralism and of the complex pluralism which exists in the 'global city' in which many Australians wish to receive full suburban status and in which they seek to play formative and participating roles.

GARTH T. READ

Austria

The Austrian Constitution professes the basis principle of religious freedom. It includes, however, the concept of state-recognized churches and religious communities which receive protection and aid from the state. It is in the context of this state aid that RE in Austrian schools must be seen.

On the one hand, religious instruction is given within the school system as a regular, compulsory subject (although with the possibility of opting out), which can also be selected as part of the final examinations. Religious school books, like all other school books, are supplied by the state; teachers are paid from public funds (by the Federation in the case of general and technical schools and by the local authorities for primary schools). On the other hand, the determining of teaching agendas, the choice of teaching aids, the employment of teachers and their training, as well as technical control of instruction, are all exclusively the business of the churches. The training of teachers for primary schools is undertaken through a system of courses, while for secondary schools the training takes place in the theological faculty of universities (these again are state-aided in order to fulfil the requirements of church teachers and pastors).

Basically, only confessional religious instruction is foreseen, but inter-confessional working groups, exchange of experience between Catholic and Protestant teachers of religion, etc., are becoming more frequent. Within the context of the recent Reformed-Roman Catholic dialogue, the intention was even expressed of submitting schoolbooks to one another for mutual approval and review. Further, there is now a tendency (although often difficult to realize) towards subject-overlapping education. For teachers of religion, this offers a special opportunity to have their subject fully integrated into the whole educational process. And it would seem also to be an appropriate method of keeping down the amount of non-attendance at classes. While in primary schools absences are few, their number increases among the older pupils. The reasons vary: overloaded timetables, religious instruction at unfavourable hours, etc., are certainly at least as indicative as basic lack of interest or simply refusal to attend. The tendency to absenteeism is greater in schools where technical subjects are taught, perhaps because the method of passing on knowledge here is rather inappropriate to the teaching of religion – however, nor can you generalize here.

The number of hours of religious instruction suggested per week is two for groups of ten or more pupils. Groups of between five and nine pupils will be given only one hour per week. If there are less than five in a class, then pupils from several classes and even from different schools must come together for instruction. All this means that, within a basically similar legal situation, there often arises a completely different case for Catholic and Protestant RE. While everywhere Catholic instruction can take place for two hours a week within the regular school timetable, in the main, Protestant pupils will receive instruction for one hour only and then often together with pupils from other classes, from other age levels and sometimes even other schools – factors which obviously impair the efficiency of instruction. The situation is also disadvantageous for Protestant teachers. Because of the small numbers of pupils, they must often teach in more than one school and rush from one to another without really belonging anywhere. (This is also true, of course, for the smaller churches or religious communities, e.g. Old Catholics and Orthodox.)

The connection of RE with the life of the local parish is made more difficult because of the scattered nature of the Protestant Church in Austria. The administration and control of RE, however, falls within the jurisdiction of the parish pastor. This principle is valid also for Vienna, although here the local parishes have joined together and elected inspectors. It is difficult everywhere to fulfil the intended inter-action of RE and life in the community; it is most likely to be valid among Catholic primary school children. Elsewhere the boundaries of the school domain and the church domain simply do not coincide and certainly do not in the case of secondary schools.

Concerning the teaching curricula, it should be noted that the curricula for Roman Catholic RE are set thematically and that teachers are supplied with precise, authoritative study materials. The teaching programmes for Protestant RE on the other hand, are conceived according to the principle of 'evangelical training' and are biblically-orientated. However, they simply map out the framework in which the instruction has to take place so that many possibilities are left open to the teacher to deal with questions which arise directly or indirectly from the experience of the pupils. This, of course, obliges the teacher to be always well informed and to be constantly aware of appropriate teaching materials. A revision of the teaching programme is at present under discussion which proposes a new assessment of the elements of church history.

Although RE in schools is problematic in some cases, in general, Austrian churches view it positively, since it offers them an opportunity to win over also those children and adolescents who at home are given no introduction to any teaching about the church.

ERIKA FUCHS

Autonomy

The concept marked by 'autonomy' is by no means a clear one; but it is at least clear that two things are ruled out by it. 1. A person's belief and actions are not supposed to be dictated by any sort of unquestioned authority. Authorities may be accepted, but only if there is good reason to accept them. 2. A person's beliefs and actions are not to be governed by internal impulse or desire: 'autonomous' is not to be equivalent to 'autistic'. There must be reasons why his belief is thought to be true or his action right.

What rules out both of these is the necessity of following reason, in a broad sense of that phrase. In that (broad) sense, the necessity is undeniable: briefly, because the words that stand for all that we think valuable are connected with reason. If we think our beliefs and actions 'true', 'wise', 'sane', 'perceptive', 'worth having', 'proper', 'justified', 'right' or almost anything else, then we are saying that they are *well grounded:* that they rest not on blind obedience or impulse, but on some kind of *evidence* or *reasons*. Further, it is part of what we mean by 'reasons' ('evidence', etc.) that I cannot pick and choose what is to be a good reason or a weighty piece of evidence. It is not a matter of my choosing, but of it being or not being so, not just for me but for anyone else.

Religious believers who face these facts and respect autonomy can thus only educate pupils in any serious sense if they are clear about what, in the case of religious belief, counts as a good reason. (As in other subjects: if we did not know this in the case of science or mathematics or history, we could not teach them, because we would not know how to do the subjects.) Education *in* religion (not just *about* religion or particular religions, which is no more than a guided tour or a kind of window-shopping) rests on this question.

An objective analysis suggests that the central and *sui generis* element in religious belief is the assertion that some object is worthy of worship, that a certain mental or emotional attitude is appropriate to it. Religious education is thus centrally a matter of educating the emotions, which in turn is centrally a matter of uncovering and inspecting the pupil's beliefs – both conscious and unconscious – so that he can understand and control them. It is for the pupil to answer the question, 'What, if anything, or whom, ought to be worshipped (revered, admired, etc.)?' It is for the teacher to help the pupil to answer this *reasonably* – that is, with understanding and insight. In this way, a proper religous education both respects the pupil's autonomy by not demanding adherence to a particular preordained answer and enhances it by giving him more control over his unconscious feelings and compulsions.

JOHN WILSON

Awe *see* **Childhood, Religious Development in**

Bahā'ī

The religion founded by Mirza Husayn 'Alī, 1817–92 (Bahā'u'llāh). The Bahā'ī faith, is pre-eminently a religion of the Book. Bahā'ī doctrines, laws and spiritual teachings are set out or rooted in the voluminous Bahā'ī scripture, i.e. the Persian and Arabic treatises and letters of Bahā'u'llāh and secondarily the interpretations of those writings by Bahā'u'llāh's eldest son and successor, 'Abdu'l-Bahā (1844–1921), and his great-grandson, the late Guardian of the Faith Shoghi Effendi (1897–1957). A good many passages are contained in this Bahā'ī sacred literature, more especially in the writings of 'Abdu'l-Bahā, that in one way or another relate to educational theory. It is the case, however, as Shoghi Effendi pointed out in 1939, that the teachings of Bahā'u'llāh and 'Abdu'l-Bahā, 'do not present a definite and detailed educational system'. They simply offer, 'certain basic principles and set forth a number of teaching ideals that should guide future Bahā'ī educationalists'.

To date, no detailed Bahā'ī educational philosophy has been worked out. Bahā'īs in different parts of the world derive educational guidance from the Bahā'ī writings available to them and from the various institutions within the Bahā'ī administrative order which operate on local, national and international levels.

The majority of Bahā'u'llāh's more direct references to education are to be found in the writings of the 'Akkā period of his ministry (1868–92) or, more explicitly, after he had completed his book of laws or *Kitāb-i-Aqdas* in 1873. The *Kitāb-i-Aqdas* (Most Holy Book) itself contains one or two passages relevant to education. In it every father is exhorted to instruct or have his children instructed, 'in the art of reading and writing and in all that hath been laid down in the Holy Tablet'.

If, however, he is too poor to provide this instruction, the responsibility falls upon the 'House of Justice' or Bahā'ī administrative institutions. In his *Tablet of the World (Lawḥ-i-Dunyā* and *Splendours (Ishrāqāt)*, Bahā'u'llāh reiterates these and similar themes and it may be said that 'Abdu'l-Bahā subsequently, on the basis of these texts, advocated compulsory education. In his *Kitāb-i-Aqdas*, Bahā'u'llāh also recommends that world leaders consult together and choose what should become the international auxiliary language and script and in other writings, notably his *Glad Tidings (Bishārāt)*, states that when adopted they should be taught to children worldwide. This, he further comments, would be instrumental in promoting the oneness or unity of mankind.

In his *Lawḥ-i-Maqṣūd* and elsewhere, Bahā'u'llāh indicates that the great Messengers of God who appear from age to age to found new religions or communicate divine guidance are the ultimate sources of human education. Faith in these Messengers of God and knowledge of their teachings is seen by Bahā'īs as the basis of human education. Throughout his ministry Bahā'u'llāh called upon men to acquire spiritual perfections, giving knowledge an exalted position among them, and came to underline the importance of the 'fear of God' in human spirituality and education. A balanced education, one may gather from many passages in Bahā'u'llāh's writings, should be both practical and spiritual or religious and scientific. Though Bahā'u'llāh in his *Words of Paradise (Kalimāt-i-Firdawsīyih)* taught that schools should first educate children in the principles of religion, he made it clear that this should be done in such a way as not to lead to ignorant fanaticism or bigotry.

In connection with the practical aspect of education, Bahā'u'llāh gave great importance to the various arts, crafts and sciences. Music and philosophy were highly regarded by him, though he frequently counselled men not to waste their time studying fruitless sciences or occult and metaphysical abstractions. Thus in his last major work, his *Epistle to the Son of the Wolf (Lawḥ-i-Ibn-i-Dhi'b,* c.1890), Bahā'u'llāh wrote, 'Such sciences and arts . . . as are productive of good results . . . and are conducive to the well-being and tranquillity of men have been, and will remain, acceptable before God.' In his *Lawḥ-i-Maqṣūd* he characterized man as a 'mine rich in gems of inestimable value' and stated that education alone can 'lay bare the treasures of mankind'.

'Abdu'l-Bahá in his *The Secret of Divine Civilisation (Risála-yi-Madaníyih)* which was written as early as 1875 and which, inspired in large measure by Bahá'u'lláh's 'Tablets to the Kings', sets down a programme for the reformation and modernization of Iranian society, lays great stress on the importance of both scientific and religious education and the eradication of ignorance and fanaticism. He is clearly aware of the importance of education: 'The primary, the most urgent requirement is the promotion of education. It is inconceivable that any nation should achieve prosperity and success unless this paramount, this fundamental concern is carried forward.' Though 'Abdu'l-Bahá took up similar themes in his *Treatise on Politics (Síyásíyih, c.*1893) which was primarily addressed to the Bahá'ís of Iran, the vast majority of his pronouncements relating to education are to be found in his innumerable letters and recorded speeches. The following few paragraphs summarize some of the major themes that bear upon Bahá'í educational philosophy in these sources.

'Abdu'l-Bahá often spoke of man as possessing 'two natures': a higher spiritual nature and a lower or selfish nature. While all human beings are born pure or sinless, each individual has a distinct intellectual capacity and manifests from infancy a natural inclination towards selfishness. Education should enable man to overcome his selfish inclinations and to realize the full his intellectual and spiritual capacities. Human progress is without end since man cannot, either in this world or the worlds that the immortal human soul enters after death, attain absolute intellectual or spiritual perfection.

In a talk delivered at 'Akká in about 1905 'Abdu'l-Bahá maintained that individual human characters have an essentially threefold make-up: 1. an *innate character* (the God-given perfections of the human soul); 2. an *inherited character* (genetically determined human traits); 3. an *acquired character* (socially conditioned human behaviour patterns). Education, he taught, has a tremendous effect upon man's acquired character. He similarly divided education into three categories: 1. *material education* (physical education,

health, hygiene, etc.); 2. *human education* (arts, crafts, sciences, technology, etc.) and 3. *spiritual education* (moral or religious education). Having made this categorization, 'Abdu'l-Bahá argued that man ever stands in need of a divine authority or Messenger of God who will communicate guidance in each of these three spheres of education. It is important to note that the Bahá'í writings make no rigid distinction between matters secular and religious. Science, art and philosophy for example, are regarded as ultimately deriving from the 'Holy Spirit' as actualized by creative human endeavours.

Great importance was given by 'Abdu'l-Bahá to the education of children which he referred to as 'the foundation of the Law of God and the bedrock of the edifice of His faith'. He regarded mothers as the 'first educators' and stressed the importance of an early moral education mediated by loving and spiritual parents. Since mothers are the first educators, the education of girls, neglected in the East, is equally if not more important than that of boys. 'Abdu'l-Bahá emphasized that the education of girls and the consequent emancipation of women would contribute to progress and peace in all spheres of human endeavour.

Frequent reference was made by 'Abdu'l-Bahá to the difficulty of character reformation after puberty. Spiritual education must therefore be given from infancy as indicated by the fact that he wrote a good many prayers to be recited for and by children as well as a prayer to be read by the pregnant mother for the future spirituality and success of her child. This emphasis on the education of children should not be taken to imply any kind of dogmatic or Bahá'í indoctrination. Bahá'í parents are encouraged to exhort their children to investigate truth for themselves and to educate them in religions other than the Bahá'í religion as well as the Bahá'í religion. Though Bahá'í youth are brought up as Bahá'ís, it remains their decision as to whether or not they choose to follow some other religious or secular ideology.

'Abdu'l-Bahá suggested that a universal curriculum would contribute to world unity. Among the subjects he recommended be taught to children are included (apart from distinctly religious subjects): reading, writing, music, languages, mathematics and the sciences, arts, crafts, technology, history, physical education, kindness to animals and 'the expansion of consciousness'. Children should receive a disciplined though liberal and universal education and be prepared for a socially worthwhile career. Both Bahā'u'llāh and 'Abdu'l-Bahā condemned idleness, begging and asceticism, exhorted Bahā'īs to acquire a trade or profession and regarded work performed in the spirit of service to mankind as the worship of God. During his tour of Europe and the United States and Canada (1911–13), 'Abdu'l-Bahā often counted universal compulsory education as one of the 'twelve cardinal principles' of the religion founded by his father.

The first Bahā'ī schools were opened in the Middle East around the turn of the last century with the encouragement of 'Abdu'l-Bahā and in the light of the limited opportunities for formal education. As early as 1897, a boys' school was being operated by Bahā'īs at Ishqabad in Russian Turkestan (a girls' school was opened there ten years later) and in 1904 the Tarbiyat school for boys in Tehran, Iran, was officially recognized (the Bahā'ī school for girls was opened in Tehran in 1912). Such early Bahā'ī operated schools provided education for fairly large numbers of both Bahā'ī and non-Bahā'ī pupils and were, in certain cases, aided financially and administratively by Western Bahā'ī communities. A few of them attained considerable prestige.

By 1963 about twenty-seven Bahā'ī schools or teaching institutes were operating in (among other countries) Bolivia, Ecuador, Gilbert and Ellice Islands, Guatemala, India, Mentawei Islands, New Hebrides, Swaziland, Uganda and Vietnam. To date, the number of pre-primary, primary, secondary and 'tutorial schools' (simple schools in which a Bahā'ī teacher conducts classes for children in reading, writing and elementary subjects) opened by Bahā'īs in some forty countries adds up to ast least seventy-five and plans are being made to open many more. In addition to these schools, hundreds of less formal classes are held by Bahā'īs in countries where state school systems meet the general need for education. Bahā'ī children's classes are being held regularly in at least fifty such countries.

Bahā'ī institutes, popularly known as 'summer' and 'winter' schools and often running for one or more weeks, were first operated in the United States and have since spread to many other countries. They were primarily designed to provide facilities for the study of Bahā'ī doctrine and history and its relationship to other faiths and ideologies. The three original 'summer schools' held in the United States at Green Acre, Eliot Maine (from 1929), Geyersville, California (from 1927) and near Davidson, Michigan (the 'Louhelen Bahā'ī school' from 1931) were referred to by Shoghi Effendi in 1944 as 'embryonic Bahā'ī educational institutions'. He hoped that such 'summer schools' or 'Bahā'ī Institutes' would evolve into the Bahā'ī universities of the future, though no such development has yet taken place: there are no officially recognized and sponsored Bahā'ī universities.

In his *Kitāb-i-Aqdas*, Bahā'u'llāh speaks of the need to erect Bahā'ī 'Houses of Worship' (*Mashriq Al-Adhkār*, literally the dawning-place of the praise (of God)) in every city and village. 'Abdu'l-Bahā subsequently mentioned a number of dependencies that could cluster around the central House of Worship including schools and colleges or universities. The central House of Worship where Bahā'ī and other sacred scriptures should be chanted or sung, and its auxiliary institutions, should become the focal point of spiritual, humanitarian, administrative and educational Bahā'ī activities. Though five Bahā'ī Houses of Worship exist in the world today, formal educational institutions have not as yet been built alongside them.

Shoghi Effendi, on a number of occasions, mentioned the great need for a profound and co-ordinated Bahā'ī scholarship. During his Guardianship (1921–57), he lamented the lack of profoundly knowledgable Bahā'īs but predicted the eventual emergence of Bahā'ī scholars who would be of great benefit to the Bahā'ī world. A new generation of Bahā'ī scholars may indeed be said to have emerged in the West (particularly in Western Europe, the United States and Canada) since the late 1960s and bid fair to raise the level of Bahā'ī intellectual life to greater heights of academic integrity. An increasing interest is being shown in Bahā'ī studies by non-Bahā'ī academics and the basics of Bahā'ī belief are being taught in many secondary schools alongside those of the great world religions. In recent years the Bahá'í Universal House of Justice (Bahá'í world authority) has reiterated Shoghi Effendi's statements about the importance of Bahá'í studies and steps have been taken in both East and West to ensure its continuation and growth.

Bahá'í Education, Bahá'í Publishing Trust (UK) 1976; *Bahá'í Quotations on Education,* National Spiritual Assembly of the Bahá'ís of the Hawaiian Islands 1971; H.T.D. Rost, *The Brilliant Stars, The Bahá'í Faith and the Education of Children,* George Ronald 1980; H.T.D. Rost, *The Possible Nature and Establishment of Bahá'í Universities and Colleges Based Upon a Study of Bahá'í Writings,* University Microfilms Inc 1970.

STEPHEN LAMBDEN

Baptism

The traditional initiation rite of the Christian church. In the early church, adult baptism was the norm, but a household would be baptized with its head (Acts 16.15 and 33; I Cor. 1.16), including children.

During the centuries of persecution, an extreme separation between the church and the rest of society controlled the understanding of baptism. Although the expectation of an imminent Second Coming of Jesus faded, there was fear of relapse, and in the fourth century the risk of post-baptismal sin caused many to delay baptism until the point of death.

But, in the Christianized society that followed, infant baptism became universal. In the Orthodox East, the baby is baptized by a priest as if it were an adult and after immersion and anointing it is given Holy Communion (wine on a spoon). In the West, successive Popes insisted that the anointing and/or laying on of hands, and reception into the church, should continue to be reserved to the bishop. Since in Northern Europe bishops were few and travel was bad, baptized children had to wait, often for many years, for the 'confirmation'. With this development came a shift in Western theology. Baptism effects the washing away of a baby's *original* sin and guilt; 'confirmation'* by the bishop becomes an additional sacrament of strengthening and equipping the (older) child for adult life. Admission to communion faded in importance as lay reception declined. Only since

1910 has Roman Catholic practice been (i) infant baptism, (ii) first communion at 7 years, (iii) episcopal confirmation *after* first communion.

The churches of the Reformation which kept infant baptism gave a pedagogic purpose to confirmation. The baby, brought to baptism by others, must later receive instruction, learn a catechism, so that 'at the age of discretion' he may *confirm for himself* his baptismal vows: baptismal grace is then *confirmed to him* by the laying on of hands with prayer for the gifts of the Spirit. In the Reformed tradition, the baptism of infants is justified, not as a 'magical' sacramental act, but as a recognition that the child of Christian parents is within the covenant of grace: he is to be admitted to the church in hope and faith that the nurturing of the child in a Christian home and a worshipping, practising congregation will bring him forward to take his own responsibility to follow Christ in the church. A very different attitude to Christian initiation is represented by the Baptist tradition. Baptism is appropriate only for converted adults who have committed themselves in faith to Jesus Christ. The dedication of infants is widely practised, but young children as such are in a state of innocence and immaturity: they cannot strictly speaking be nurtured as Christians.

The secularization of Western society and the erosion of traditional Christian belief and practice has caused renewed attention to Christian initiation among those 'mainstream' churches which practise infant baptism. There is a strong movement towards limiting it to the children of committed and practising Christians, or towards making adult baptism once more the norm.

The church as a minority society of believers must continually seek to admit a new and younger generation to its faith and community life in a way that guarantees the continuance of that faith and life. It is perceived more clearly that religious education (involving suspension of belief or unbelief) is different from 'nurture' or 'formation' (which pursues growth in understanding in the context of active faith, commitment, prayer and response). Those churches which retain infant baptism increasingly stress that the child has to be helped to 'become what it is'.

BASIL MOSS

Baptist Church

Any understanding of the policies of Baptists towards education must be based on an appreciation of the Baptist view of the church. Indeed complex historical strands help explain the origins of the different branches of Baptist witness today. In England, Ireland, Scotland and Wales, there are groupings of Baptist churches which are called 'unions'. The major grouping of Baptists in the United Kingdom is the Baptist Union of Great Britain and Ireland. Other Baptist churches include the strict Baptists and a significant number of independent Baptist churches that tend not to join any affiliation of churches.

The Baptist tradition lays particular stress on the authority of the Bible, the autonomy of the local church and the principle of individual religious freedom. The Word of God is the supreme authority for Baptist doctrine and the practice of the church. The church is the local gathered community of believers, and entry to membership is usually preceded by confession of faith in Jesus Christ as Lord and Saviour, followed by baptism of the believer. The autonomy of the local church derives from the position of the church meeting which, informed by scripture and guided by the Holy Spirit, has the authority to determine policy and action.

In practice, many Baptist churches seek to support and encourage one another by voluntary groupings. County or regional associations provide for mutual support of churches which are affiliated to the Baptist Union. Thus leadership and co-ordination of activities of local churches may be exercised at association and denominational level. Therefore, in describing policies with regard to education, it is possible to identify guidelines developed and approved by the Baptist Union Council, but it is important to recognize that these policies cannot be enforced in the constituent churches, though they may well receive substantial consent and adoption. Equally, local churches in good standing with the Union may develop distinctive educational policies and practices and many small churches, lacking ministerial leadership, may have little educational awareness.

1. *Policy towards education.* It has not been Baptist policy to maintain denominational schools. Along with other non-conformists, Baptists accepted the religious provisions of the 1944 Education Act and this remains the recognized position. Therefore, the Baptist Union is concerned about the quality of education provided by the county schools and supports the continuation of RE within the agreed syllabus arrangements. From time to time, Baptist viewpoints on specific education issues are forwarded to the DES though this is usually done in concert with other non-conformists through the agency of the Free Church Federal Council*.

Baptist monitoring of and involvement in the education system may be perceived at three levels. At denominational level, within the Mission Department, a member of staff and the education committee keep abreast of developments within schools and liaise with other church groups on educational matters through the Free Church Federal Council and the British Council of Churches*. At county and regional level, some associations have education committees that take an interest in local school policies and Baptists are numbered amongst Free Church representative members of county education authorities. At local church level, many ministers and church members, especially parents of school-age children, have an involvement in school governing bodies and in parent-teacher associations. At all levels, the desirability of a Christian presence within county schools is recognized. Some responsibility is felt for encouraging Christians to share in the teaching of RE, but the importance of the Christian witness of teachers of other curriculum subjects is equally appreciated.

While many Baptists spend their careers in education and some ministers and parents become intimately involved in schools, it is probably a fair judgment to say that the Baptist Union has a sympathetic and interested orientation towards state education but that education rarely becomes a major issue in the life of either the denomination or of the local church. Recently, however, a small number of independent evangelical Baptist churches have decided to establish their own schools primarily for the children of church members, in order to provide an education which is soundly biblical and in distinct contrast to the secularism of modern society. At present the number of these schools does not reach double figures.

2. *Church membership preparation.* Classes for potential church members are usually called enquirers' classes and are arranged whenever an individual or group of people have expressed an interest in joining the church. Normally conducted by the minister, the series of classes extends over several weeks and focusses upon Baptist principles and the significance of baptism, the Lord's Supper, the importance of personal devotions and the responsibilities and duties of church members. In some churches, enquirers will be expected to back up the classes with personal reading and Bible study.

Church membership is restricted to those who have made a conscious, responsible decision to follow Christ and to join his church. Consequently, in most churches, enquirers' classes are for those who have at least achieved their teenage years when, it is considered, a responsible decision to the call of Christ can be made, though there are Baptist churches which will receive younger persons into membership.

If, at the end of the series of classes, an enquirer expresses a desire to join the church, then visitors are appointed, usually two in number, who meet with the candidate to talk about his/her experience of Christ and commitment to follow him. The discussion also explores the candidate's understanding of the church and willingness to share in the life of the church fellowship. The church meeting receives the report of the visitors and comes to its decision about admission to membership. For many converts, the sacrament of believers' baptism by immersion provides an occasion for public witness to new life in Christ. Often the first communion follows and it is at this communion service that the minister, in a simple ceremony, formally receives the new member into membership of the church and extends the right hand of fellowship. In some churches the new member is invited to sign the church roll and may be given a membership card and a copy of the church rules. Some Baptist churches have a closed membership system, so that only adults baptized as believers may be admitted into full membership in the manner that has been described. Today, however, many churches have an open membership in which believers' baptism is not essential and in these churches Christians in good standing with other denom-

inations may be received into membership by transfer. Church visitors may visit these persons before the church meeting agrees to membership, but local practice is variable. In closed membership churches, Christians from other backgrounds may be accorded an associate membership status.

3. *Church education courses and policy.* Baptists hold strongly to the priesthood of all believers. Consistent with this philosophy, the Baptist Union launched a Christian training programme in the early 1970s. The purpose of this scheme is to equip Christians with a better knowledge of the scriptures to enable them to interpret that understanding in the contemporary world and, through selected courses, to sharpen skills for leadership. The three principal areas covered by the training manuals are (i) biblical and doctrinal (ii) historical and contemporary and (iii) Christian leadership. This third theme provides for the specialist needs of different groups including Sunday School teachers, church administrators and Christians in industry and commerce.

The manuals have been designed for the widest possible range of educational abilities. All assessment is through assignments and students can proceed at their own pace. Assistance and encouragement is provided by a local tutor. An introductory programme of units leads to the Baptist Union Certificate and successful completion of a requisite range of courses earns the Baptist Union Diploma. Nevertheless a student may study just a single unit and in some churches a unit may be selected for the basis of a house study group.

Since its inception, the scheme has grown steadily both in the number of students and in the breadth and diversity of course manuals available. Indicative of the growth and continuous updating of the materials is the revision of ten manuals during 1981 and preparation of three additional manuals on Christianity and politics, the reformation, philosophy and religion. About 3,000 students have been enrolled and about 600 local tutors guide their studies. The Christian training programme has attracted considerable interest overseas and manuals have been supplied to many countries including Zaire, Poland, Kuwait and to many places in the United States and Western Europe.

A selection of units of the Christian training

programme forms the basis of the studies for a probationary lay preacher. Upon completion of the course of study and after meeting requirements in terms of conduct of worship and preaching, a lay preacher may be formally recognized by the Union as an accredited lay preacher. The Union has also introduced a comparable scheme to recognize those who work with children and young people. Practical experience, together with approved study courses, forms the basis for recognition and the Equipped to Teach units of the Christian training programme may be offered as part of this training.

Whilst there is at present no formal recognition scheme, it is also the policy of the Baptist Union for youth workers to receive appropriate training. Youth leadership programmes are arranged through the agencies of both the Union and the associations. Also, the manuals of the Christian training programme are regularly complemented by numerous, practically-orientated, denominational publications geared to assist ministers and leaders in local churches in specific aspects of their local witness.

While children are not, in the literal sense, members of the local Baptist church, Baptists have traditionally invested substantial resources on the nurture and training of children and young people. Sunday classes for instruction in the faith are normally supported by a mid-week programme of youth activities, frequently graded for age and, in larger churches at least, include uniformed and non-uniformed activities.

In common with other free churches, Sunday Schools meeting in the afternoon separately from the worshipping church have now given way in most churches to a morning programme in which the children share a time of worship with the whole church but also receive teaching in graded departments. Whilst this pattern of 'family worship' and junior church may be regarded as the norm, there are many other patterns. In a minority of churches, a form of all-age Christian education has been developed on Sunday mornings. There are also churches that have replaced Sunday School with a mid-week Bible School and still other churches hold a sequence of morning service and Sunday School sessions in order to accommodate all those who attend. Further diversity is found in the lesson materials used with children in Baptist churches. The Baptist Union does not publish lesson guides, but was a partner in the British Lessons Council and many churches use *Partners in Learning** materials, and Scripture Union and Scripture Press along with lesson guides from other sources are now in common use. Some churches prepare their own lesson materials and some of these attempt to use a common theme for the address to the adults and for the graded lessons for junior church, but this is only practicable where there is a good preparation session involving minister and teaching staff and this situation does not hold in all churches.

Despite the diversity of patterns of junior church and the variety of lesson guides used, there is common ground first in seeking to nurture the growing child within the family of the church. This is consistent with the pledge of the church when parents bring their baby for the dedication service. On this occasion, parents and church promise to bring up the child in the knowledge of the Lord Jesus Christ. Secondly, the challenge of the gospel will be presented to the young people so that a considered decision may be made concerning the claims of Christ.

Baptist Union, *The Child and the Church*, Carey Kingsgate Press 1966; D. F. Tennant, *Children in the Church – A Baptist View*, Baptist Publications 1978; A. C. Underwood, *A History of the English Baptists*, Kingsgate Press 1947.

ARTHUR JENNINGS

Bar/Bat Mitzvah

A Bar Mitzvah is not something you do, it is something you become, whether or not you do anything about it. It is in no sense a sacramental rite. It confers nothing, imparts nothing, creates nothing; it merely celebrates and thus it is wrong to attempt a comparison with Christian Confirmation. Every Jewish boy who attains the age of thirteen years and one day (a girl reaches her majority at twelve years and one day) is automatically a Bar Mitzvah and remains one for the rest of his life.

The term 'bar mitzvah' means son of the commandment or duty. In post-biblical Jewish literature, it was stated that 'thirteen [is the age] for [the fulfilment of] the commandments', and that 'a man is responsible for his son until the age of thirteen; thereafter the father should recite the blessing "Blessed be He Who freed me from responsibility for this child" '. Although it appears that it is a fairly old Jewish tradition to set thirteen apart as a religious milestone, specific ways of observing it have been developed only in the last few hundred years. The first written record of a special ceremony comes from the thirteenth century.

Bar Mitzvah refers to the person and the event. A Bar Mitzvah acquires three new privileges. He can be included in the *minyan* (quorum of ten males needed for public worship); he can be called to the reading of the Torah; if he is an Orthodox Jew, he now puts on his *tefillin* (phylacteries) daily. This is what is meant by being an adult in the Jewish sense. A bar mitzvah can take place on any day the Torah is read, namely a Sabbath, Monday, Thursday, New Moon or Festivals. The favourite day is the Sabbath. Some Reform congregations in America opt for Friday nights. Strictly Orthodox Jews prefer Monday or Thursday so that distant relatives and friends can travel, which is forbidden on Sabbaths. In British Orthodox synagogues, the average boy will read (this means chant) the *maftir* which is the last paragraph of the *sidra* (weekly Torah portion). He will also usually read the *haftara* (reading from the Prophets), although the London United Synagogue does not allow this as a right, but only after the boy has reached the prescribed standard of Jewish knowledge. In Progressive (Reform or Liberal) synagogues, the boy will usually read (not chant) a portion from the Scroll, in both Hebrew and English, and *haftara*, which is normally read only in English, and in some congregations he will also be expected to conduct the whole service. Some synagogues (both Orthodox and Progressive) also include a prayer recited by the boy. At every bar mitzvah, the rabbi or minister will address the boy and present him with a Bible or prayerbook. In Israel, many bar mitzvah ceremonies take place at the Western Wall in Jerusalem.

A ceremony for girls is very recent and was one of the Reform innovations of Germany and the United States, before it was extended in other countries. A growing number of Orthodox congregations allow such cere-

monies. A girl is usually referred to as a Bat Mitzvah (daughter of the commandment) or Eshet Chayil (woman of valour). In most Progressive synagogues, the ceremony is identical to that of the Bar Mitzvah, but, in Orthodox synagogues, it is usually held on Sunday afternoons in a group ceremony, each girl reading a few verses from the Bible or prayerbook. A number of Reform congregations abolished bar mitzvah and replaced it with a ceremony for both sexes at around the age of sixteen, since they felt that children in Western society were not mature enough to be considered adult at the age of thirteen. They called the ceremony 'Confirmation' and it usually takes place on Shavuot (Pentecost), the festival which celebrates the birthday of the Jewish religion by the giving of the Torah. It often takes the form of group participation. Due to social pressures, many of these synagogues also now include bar and bat mitzvah. Many also dislike the name of this later ceremony and prefer to call it *kabbalat mitzvah* (acceptance of the commandment) or Ben (or Bat) Torah, son (or daughter) of the Torah.

The status of a Jew is not affected in any way should he have no Bar Mitzvah ceremony. Ideally, being Bar Mitzvah should be the beginning of serious Jewish religious education, not the end.

B. Efron and A. Rubin, *Coming of Age*, Union of American Hebrew Congregations 1977; H. Levy, *Becoming and Remaining Barmitzvah*, United Synagogue, 1971; A. Marcus, *Bar and Bat Mitzvah*, A. R. E. Denver 1977; M. Patterson (ed.), *The Bar Mitzvah Book*, W. H. Allen 1975.

DOUGLAS S. CHARING

Belgium

1. *General situation.* Belgium is divided into four linguistic regions constitutionally established since 1971; in Flanders, the language most generally used is Dutch; in Wallonie, French; in the Eastern cantons, German; Brussels is bilingual. The Episcopal Conference holds separate assemblies for the two principal linguistic groups.

The officially recognized religions in Belgium are: Catholic, Protestant, Jewish and Muslim. They benefit from government grants for their ministers and professors.

2. *The Catholic system.* (*a*) Institutional

Organization. Since the Schools Agreement (1958), *all* schools *must* include two hours a week religious or non-confessional moral education in their timetables. It is up to parents to enrol their child/ren for religious or moral instruction. Catholic schools offer instruction in the Catholic religion only, while taking into account the number, often considerable, of non-Catholics. The proportion of specialists in RE being insufficient, RE is often in a state of penury.

(*b*) Religious programmes and catechetical options. The two interdiocesan commissions authorized by the Belgian hierarchy relating to RE in primary and secondary education, each opted, at a national level, for 'existential catechetics'. This decision having been taken, the sub-committees have worked, through linguistic regions and levels of teaching, at elaborating a common programme for schools in all the regions.

(*c*) The Catechetical 'Movement'. Progress in educational methods, but above all the impetus given by Vatican II and the changes in Christian society and pluralist society, at first accentuated the tendency towards biblically-based catechetics. It is against this background that the present trend towards 'existential catechetics' has established itself. This latter evolves from several approaches: analysis and interpretation of actual experience (individual and collective); confrontation of this experience with analogous situations, lived through faith, reported in scripture and in church history; the relating of this existing situation with the life of Christ and of witnesses to the faith, from early times to the present day.

Among the principal creators of programmes in the Dutch language are the Rev. J. Bulckens, Fr Lefevre and Fr M. van Caster, SJ; in French for primary schools, Fr P. Ranwez, SJ, and for secondary schools, the Rev. R. Waelkens.

This inductive system at catechetics calls for more theological competence than was called for by the traditional doctrinal system. It is not necessarily a question of 'starting from life' in order to reach the gospel (which would not be life . . .) but of facing daily life and gospel life in order to promote an actual relationship with Christ. The evolution of recent official documents is characterized by a double emphasis, pedagogical and doctrinal.

The emphasis on the scholastic character of RE tends to promote a more systematic and rigorous teaching in regard both to the pedagogical and religious aims, and the dialogue between Christian thinking and the humanities. The doctrinal emphasis aims to help young people to relate better their Christian identity with church tradition and its theological dimension.

(*d*) Institutions for Catechetical Formation. Belgium has an important network of colleges for the training of teachers of RE. The Catholic 'écoles normales' train teachers for all subjects (including religious education) at different levels. The Institutes of Higher Education (RE) train specialists and professors (whose diploma relates to RE only) and professors of all disciplines (for which they are qualified elsewhere) who seek an additional formation for RE.

3. *Family and parish catechetics.* Family catechetics are informal. Their principal dynamism comes from the family and the presence of parents engaged in parochial or scholastic catachetics. It is usually during their second primary year that children are prepared for first communion, jointly in the family, school and parish, each of these networks having its specification and specific catechetical role.

Besides the church preparation for first communion, the highly structured parochial catechetics revolve round two axes: (i) the preparation for the profession of faith and confirmation, which takes place between ten and eighteen years – but generally at the age of eleven, during the last primary year. ('Post-catechetics', are more informal and occur for a year or two after the sacrament of confirmation.) Preparation for confirmation is composed of two years of weekly parochial catechetics over and above the RE given in school. (ii) The liturgy of the word for children in the framework of the Sunday eucharistic liturgy which gathers together all ages (but there are still Masses for the young).

4. *The permanent formation of adults and catechumens.* More and more Christians attend centres or participate in groups and sessions relating to permanent formation of faith. Certain parishes also prepare lay people for specialist ministries (to the sick, engaged couples, married couples and the stimulation of communities which are without a priest).

Adult catechetics is developing. It relates

both to adults seeking entry into the Christian community and to the baptized who, for various reasons, have never been catechized or have not been able to integrate their faith into their daily lives.

ANDRÉ KNOCKAERT/
CHANTAL VAN DER PLANCKE

Belief   *see* **Personal Belief of Pupils**

Bible: Biblical Models of RE

All societies must ensure that the young learn their traditions and customs and the values enshrined in them, and the people of God in biblical times were no exception. We may look for our biblical models of education, therefore, in any setting in which the people of God offered its members an introduction to its own 'way': its story, its laws and standards of behaviour, its wisdom.

One of these settings was undoubtedly the sanctuary and its cult, governed by the priesthood. Though it is often assumed that the priest in biblical times was primarily concerned with sacrifice, originally this was not so. Primarily the priest was 'the handler of the *torah*', i.e. 'teaching'. Priests would give decisions on specific questions put to them and on points of dispute, but there were at least occasions in some periods of history when more general instruction was offered. Nehemiah 8 describes such an occasion (see especially v.8), but this was evidently not unique. II Chronicles 35.3 describes the Levites (the priestly tribe) as 'the Levites *who taught all Israel*'.

But the liturgy itself must have been, at all periods, one of the most potent educational influences. The celebrations of the great festivals inevitably included the recital of the particular story of salvation being celebrated. Passover/Unleavened Bread celebrated the deliverance from Egypt; the Feast of Tabernacles, the wanderings in the wilderness; and, by NT times, the Feast of Weeks (Pentecost) had become firmly associated with the lawgiving on Mount Sinai.

Not only is all this implictly education, it was sometimes explictly so. In the Passover liturgy there is a specific place, and a very large place, for the exposition of the significance of the feast (Ex. 13.14f; Deut. 6.20ff.).

The biblical tradition draws no sharp distinction between education and worship. Worship inevitably has an educational dimension and, conversely, all learning, if done in the right spirit, leads to the praise of God.

All of this involves *instruction*, i.e. an authoritative statement of what the tradition *is* and what the events are which are being celebrated, but it also involves invitation or appeal. The worshipper is being invited to join, or to remain within, the community which is defined by these traditions; to regard himself as a member of the people to whom these things happened; to accept the story as *his* story; to say '*we*' and '*our* fathers'. The exercise is an authoritarian one in that it states unambiguously what the tradition is that is being offered; but the events it celebrates are themselves acts of grace, to which God's people are being invited to respond with faith and commitment.

It may be significant that our evidence for explicit instruction in the meaning of the cult is associated with Passover. Passover was originally a domestic festival and became so again after the destruction of the temple in AD 70. It is in the domestic setting that education most readily and naturally takes place.

Doubtless this happened for the most part informally, but Deuteronomy seems to be advocating a quite formal and systematic domestic education in the law and traditions of Israel. 'And you shall teach them diligently to your children, and shall talk of them when you sit in your house, and when you walk by the way, and when you lie down, and when you rise' (Deut. 6.6–9).

Much of the material in the wisdom writings may also reflect a system of instruction and guidance given within the family. The advice is at any rate often addressed to 'sons'. This evidence is not unambiguous, however, for in the biblical period such words were often used by teachers addressing pupils (see e.g., John 21.5).

Even though some of the wisdom material may have its roots in the family, much of it certainly reflects use in the *school*. The 'wise' in Israel evidently did gather students around them (and no doubt casual enquirers too) and attempt to impart the life skills that they thought young men would need. (The wisdom writers address themselves exclusively to young *men*. Education as the Bible witnesses to it is heavily male-centred.) In the OT period, such schools seem to have concerned themselves largely with what we should think of as the more secular aspects of education, but in the inter-testamental and NT periods the 'wise' came to see themselves principally as teachers of the religious law.

By NT times there was a considerable body of recognized teachers, many of them of the pharisaic persuasion, who gave more or less intensive instruction to bodies of disciples and who were evidently available also for questioning and discussion with casual enquirers. The story of the boy Jesus in the temple (Luke 2.41–51) implies the existence of a sort of 'open forum' where a young man up from the country could bring his sharp questions and observations to the experts.

There is no compulsion involved in such schools. The wise simply make themselves available (and, within the biblical period, accepted no fees for their services). In the wisdom literature, the figure of Wisdom herself is an evangelical one. She *invites*; and her invitation is to all who will listen (Prov. 8.1f.; 9.1–6). Those who respond to her invitation are already displaying wisdom by valuing what she has to offer. And they will gain more wisdom. Those who despise her riches are fools, and will remain fools, for foolishness shuts itself out from wisdom's house and wisdom's feast, and sets no value on the pearl of great price which is in her gift.

This 'take it or leave it' quality of wisdom is evident in Jesus own approach. No call could be more authoritative and imperative than that of Jesus. Yet by some it is refused and Jesus accepts the inevitability that some will refuse it. He recognizes that there will be those who 'hear these words of mine and do them', and those who will not (Matt. 7.24–27 and parallels). He issues his invitation and when it is refused does not plead, or offer it a second time (Mark 10.17–22 and parallels). There will be others who will accept (Luke 14.16–24 and parallels).

In the apostolic church, *proclamation* is what is appropriate when addressing those outside the church, *teaching* is normally addressed to those who are already inside. The epistles might suggest that the content of the teaching largely concerned Christian behaviour, but if the gospels themselves were written for the instruction of Christians they redress the balance by showing that the traditions about the ministry and the death and

resurrection of Jesus were also part of the content.

To conclude: there are without doubt strongly authoritarian elements in the Bible's understanding of education and learning, and also strongly evangelical ones. To those within the community of the people of God, the tradition or way is presented as a birthright which they are *entitled* to appropriate. But it is also a yoke which is laid upon them and the summons to make that way their own is an imperative one, which it is their *duty* to accept. At the same time it is an invitation to respond gratefully to what God has already done for his people, is prepared to do now, and able to do in the future. The traditions themselves contain both the record of those acts of salvation and grace and the summons to obedience which they entail.

HENRY MCKEATING

Bible: Trends in Modern Biblical Scholarship

The most important consequence of applying the form-critical method to both OT and NT has been the realization that few biblical books, other than certain of the epistles, can be regarded as documents written by a single author as a single undertaking. OT books especially must be seen as the product of a long process of transmission and modification. Some scholars have put forward bold theories to the effect that most of the transmission was in oral form until the exile, but they have not won general support. Nevertheless, the emphasis is now thrown on the contexts in which the forms developed. Here the over-riding importance of the cult has been widely recognized. It has always been clear that some types of literature, such as psalms and ceremonial laws, were developed in a cultic setting, but recent research tends to show that the influence of the cult was wider than previous generations recognized, that the antipathy between prophets and the cult had been much exaggerated, and that most of the literature of the OT owed its preservation and therefore its colouring, at least in part, to the various functionaries and institutions of the cult.

It follows that the distinction between 'authentic' and 'inauthentic' material is hardly valid. On one hand, it has to be recognized that the precise words of the original speaker or writer cannot, save in a few rare cases, be determined with any confidence. On the other, it must be acknowledged that the process itself contributes to authenticity of a different kind. A psalm that has been in use for generations is authentic because it is an expression of Hebrew faith rather than because it might have been written by David.

There has been much discussion over whether the cult, now recognized to be of so much importance, was a unique phenomenon of the ancient world or whether Israel borrowed heavily in form and in substance from her neighbours. The debate about myth and ritual patterns and the discussion of whether Israel's autumn festival was in any sense an enthronement festival are concerned with this point. As a generalization, it might be said that scholars with a background in anthropology are inclined to see extensive links between Israel and her neighbours, whereas those with a background in theology are more likely to regard Israel's cult as unique.

Large advances have been made in the field of archaeology, both in actual discoveries and in the refinement of techniques for interpreting what is found. This has greatly affected the study of Hebrew life and religion. Study of the text of the Hebrew Bible has profited from the finds at Qumran and elsewhere.

For some decades OT theology has been established as a distinct discipline, not to be confused with a study of Israel's religion. A large number of OT theologies have now appeared, but there is nothing approaching unanimity among scholars regarding the presuppositions and method of OT theology, nor regarding the relationship of the OT to the NT.

The course of NT studies has not been altogether dissimilar. The most important factor has been the recognition that the NT was not the work of individuals anxious to chronicle the past, but the product of vigorous and fast-developing Christian communities facing up to their problems. The gospels were written because believing, worshipping and often persecuted Christians needed them in their own particular circumstances. It follows that the NT provides answers to questions about the church's belief, rather than about the actual facts of the ministry of Jesus, and interest has moved away from the original

words and the actual happenings to the theological work of the evangelists in the various practical situations in which the final versions of the gospels were set down. This stress upon theological factors means that, at one significant point, the divergence between the synoptics and the fourth gospel has decreased. The notion that the synoptics reproduce the evidence of eye witnesses whereas John is a theological reflection on the ministry of Jesus, is now thoroughly out-dated.

Though the redaction critic's question, 'Why did the evangelist mould the tradition in the way that he did?' is of great importance, he depends on the results of source critical studies and the 'assured results' of source criticism are increasingly questioned. Even the assumption of the priority of Mark and the existence of the source Q (at least as a single document) are under attack, and L and M are now regarded as no more than convenient labels. Much attention is being given to christology and much illuminating work has been done on the use of the OT by the NT writers. Different Christian communities had to affirm their faith in Christ in ways that made sense to them. So the different gospels are seen as affirmations about Christ made in different contexts rather than different records of a series of events. In these circumstances, the attempt to write the definitive life of Jesus has largely been abandoned. Nevertheless historical questions cannot be avoided. What precise happenings gave rise to the life of the early church? On this matter there is no sign of agreement. Some argue that whereas we have plenty of evidence for NT faith, the historical causes of that faith are now beyond recovery; others that only if the record is substantially accurate can NT faith be explained at all.

The debate about the Jewish and Hellenistic background of the NT has entered a new and more complex phase. There is a general recognition that Judaism itself had been influenced by Hellenism 'higher up the stream' so that the thought forms inherited by the NT writers were already coloured by contemporary Hellenistic culture. Here, as in many other ways, the evidence of the Dead Sea Scrolls has been invaluable. Paul's relationship to Judaism has been scrutinized again and, perhaps because the modern understanding of first-century Judaism is more sympathetic than it was, the result is a more subtle and complicated explanation of both Paul's dependence on Judaism and his quarrel with it.

The writing of NT theology is also now more problematic than it was, for whereas the unity of the NT around the figure of Jesus is as clear as ever, the diversity of forms of expression make a unified and systematic treatment of the material impossible. It is now more common to speak of the various theologies represented in the NT than of NT theology pure and simple.

――――――

G. W. Anderson (ed.), *Tradition and Interpretation: Essays by Members of the Society for Old Testament Study,* Oxford University Press 1979; R. E. Clements, *A Century of Old Testament Study,* Lutterworth Press 1976; Patrick Henry, *New Directions in New Testament Study,* SCM Press 1980; I. Howard Marshall (ed.), *New Testament Interpretation,* Paternoster 1977; C. F. D. Moule, *The Birth of the New Testament,* A. & C. Black 1981.

DAVID STACEY

Bible: Use of in RE

Study of the Bible has provided the major syllabus content in RE, especially in Britain, with the exception of Roman Catholic schools. The reasons are practical and historical. For many years a copy of the Authorized Version of the Bible was the only religious text available for study in schools and the Bible was the area which Christian bodies agreed could be taught without infringing denominational interests. With the Cowper-Temple clause* forbidding the inclusion in RE of any formulary distinctive of any denomination, Bible study, often 'without note or comment' was the most obvious method of procedure.

The teaching was largely uncritical and the findings of biblical scholarship were often ignored. It was generally assumed that pupils would approach the study with Christian assumptions and that acquaintance with the Bible text would lead to Christian faith, practice and morals.

Since 1960, there has been less Bible study, though it still has a strong presence in some syllabuses and some schools. The reasons for this change were multiple. Researches in the early 1960s (such as those of Goldman, Hyde and Loukes) raised questions as to whether young children understood the Bible in a way that did it justice, or whether they acquired a distorted and over-literalist view. The arrival of immigrants with other faiths drew attention to the fact that there are other sacred books* that might be studied. The change of RE from Christian initiation to a search for meaning in life and to a phenomenological study which aimed to give acquaintance with all dimensions of religion meant that Bible reading became less central. Furthermore, recognition of the complex nature of biblical literature evoked the realization that it needs more subtle treatment than can be accorded it in the average classroom. Nevertheless, the Bible plays such a significant part in Christianity, and has contributed so much to existing culture, that it remains an important ingredient in the RE of a pluralistic world.

Unless the teacher adopts a thoroughgoing fundamentalist position, there are four problems in teaching about the Bible in a multi-cultural environment. 1. It is a literature that comes from long ago and from distant countries. Its understanding requires a considerable knowledge of the culture from which it comes and a well-developed historical imagination. Young children may not have either of these and are inclined to understand the stories from the perspective of the culture in which they have been reared, so misunderstanding what the literature is saying. 2. The language and the assumptions of the scriptural writers differ from those current today. They were less tied to empiricism and expressed their ideas in more figurative and allegorical ways than does the twentieth century. This often leads to the mistaking of the imaginative and the metaphorical for the historical and scientific, which can produce misunderstanding and consequent rejection of what is being studied. 3. Because of their use in liturgical worship and in private devotions, the writings of the Bible acquire, for Jews and Christians, a significance and a set of associated meanings which go beyond the intrinsic meaning of the words. The context in which they have been used enriches them with overtones and nuances, so that believers understand them differently and react to them differently from unbelievers. This can cause problems in mixed classrooms, with pupils responding in diverse ways to the study. 4. There is the problem of dealing with the belief in inspiration and revelation. Those who accept the Bible as sacred do so because they believe it is inspired and brings certain knowledge of God and of reality which human beings could not acquire otherwise. This involves an initial act of faith in the nature of the literature, which not all pupils have made. If the teacher is a believer there may be a tendency to ignore this, to assume that all accept Bible inspiration and to present the revealed knowledge, not as depending on an act of faith, but as objective fact, universally unquestioned. It is such insensitivity that frequently brings upon RE the charge of being indoctrinatory.

In view of these difficulties, the teacher has to consider how to use the Bible in lessons in an educationally approved way. This may vary according to the context. In a faith situation, where teacher and all pupils recognize the Bible as inspired and use it at other times liturgically and devotionally, the teacher may feel justified in presenting it as God's truth and the arbiter of sure beliefs and sound morals. In a multi-cultural situation caution may be necessary. In that context, the following activities can be attempted without infringing pupils' intellectual freedom:

(*a*) Teaching that there are those who hold that the Bible is sacred and brings them information which they believe to be true.

(*b*) Imparting information about what is claimed by such persons to be revealed in the Bible.

(*c*) Showing how Jews use the OT and Christians the whole Bible in worship and meditation and explaining how this affects their beliefs and conduct.

(*d*) Discussing with more mature pupils how far the claimed revelations are borne out in conduct and thereby verified. Occasionally it may be possible to go further and discuss the phenomenon of inspiration and what leads men and women to feel they have intuited truth directly from God.

The essence of this approach is that RE is concerned to teach how Christians and Jews understand and use their scriptures, rather than to insist that all students, whatever their beliefs or doubts, ought to understand and use them in a similar way.

P. Cousins and M. Eastman (eds), *The Bible and the Open Approach to Religion Educ-* *ation*, Tyndale Press 1968; E. Cox, 'The Bible in Religious Education', Smart and Horder, *New Movements in Religious Education*, Temple Smith 1975; A. Dale, *The Bible in the Classroom*, Oxford University Press 1972; Robert Davidson, *The Bible in Religious Education*, Handsel Press 1979; Paul D. Fueter, 'Teaching the Bible in School', *British Journal of Religous Education*, Vol. 2 No. 1, Autumn 1979; John Gray, *What about the Children?* SCM Press 1970; D. S. Hubery, *Christian Education and the Bible*, Religious Education Press 1966; C. M. Jones, *Teaching the Bible Today*, SCM Press 1962; H. Loukes, *New Ground in Christian Education*, SCM Press 1965.

EDWIN COX

Biography

The study of the life of a person has traditionally played a significant part in the RE programme of schools and religious communities. That this should be so tells us something about approaches to questions concerning the nature of people and how we have understood the process of education.

The use of the word *education* in association with religion is striking. In our schools we have not normally used the terms English education, history education, science education, mathematics education, but we have become accustomed to speaking about physical education, social and moral education, education in personal relationships, health education, *et al*. There is some significance in attaching the word education to these curriculum areas for it could be said that in such territories an attempt is made to influence the development of the pupil in some way. The word *education* derives from the Latin verb *educare*, meaning to lead out or fulfil. A useful analogy here is that of the leading of an army out of a barracks in order that it should fulfil its destiny as a fighting force. Truly an army does not fulfil its purpose by being confined to barracks. The view of education as being a process through which and by which persons are nurtured toward self-fulfilment has been widely accepted in Western society, notwithstanding the controversial nature of ideas concerning human fulfilment.

At the heart of this view of education there is an assumption about human nature, and that is that the future, or development of a person, is not predetermined biologically but is, on the contrary, an open-ended historic process. Teachers are particularly aware of the impact of the social, political and technological revolutions of our world on the pupils with whom they work. In such a world, events explode in the everyday life of people, deeply influencing their attitudes, values and beliefs. Feelings of helplessness in the face of change and of meaninglessness at the centre of life are not only intellectually known but emotionally grasped. We are reminded of some words from the Crowther Report* published by the Central Advisory Council for Education in 1959. 'The teenagers with whom we are concerned need, perhaps above all else, to find a faith to live by. They will not find precisely the same faith and some will not find any. Education can and should play some part in the search.' Education, so regarded is about equipping people for discovering what it means to be human and how to live hopefully and humanly in a world which is largely denying human values and human distinctiveness.

Precisely because education has seen itself exploring the capacities of a human being and through so doing raises, in many different ways, the question of what each of us might become, religious education is able to locate a distinctive contribution in the process. The subject has the task of introducing the religious experience of mankind to persons who are becoming increasingly sensitive to ultimate questions arising on the boundaries of their experience.

The study of the history of persons, biography, is in this sense an essential element of a mature programme of RE seeking as it does to develop in pupils sensitivity to questions of meaning and purpose in life. Whether the pupils be in schools or voluntary groups intent on nurture within the faith, that which presents itself evidentially in life through the experience of men and women cannot be avoided. Neither can claims of what is true for persons be evaded. On the contrary, the very controversiality of human experience ensures that programmes of RE excite interest when they introduce pupils 'to what men have found'. Truth claims encountered in and through a study of the biography of persons may all be wrong, and given the variety of claims they clearly cannot be all right! The pupil will need to understand this if he is to begin to grasp what it means to take up a faith position in life.

See also **Heroes**.

IAN H. BIRNIE

Bloxham Project, The

An educational charity set up to enquire into the way boarding schools, many of which are Christian foundations, communicate ideas and values. It works with schools to consider the distinctive role of Christian schools in modern society by evaluating approaches to authority, communication, change and personal relationships in schools, and by exchanging knowledge and experience of developments in school worship, religious education and confirmation preparation. A survey was published in 1971 (Richardson and Chapman) and the Project has held national conferences and residential consultations for heads, chaplains, housestaffs and RE teachers. The Director visits individual schools and organizes area meetings and study groups. A termly newsletter is available and a report called *Heirs and Rebels: Principles and Practicalities in Christian Education* was published by the Project in 1982.

R. Richardson and J. Chapman, *Images of Life: Problems of Religious Belief and Human Relations in School*, SCM Press 1971.

JOHN MOTT

British and Foreign School Society

The title given, in 1814, to the Lancastrian Institute for Promoting the Education of the Labouring and Manufacturing Classes of Society of every Religious Persuasion (originally founded in 1798 by Joseph Lancaster). It rapidly established 'British' schools throughout Britain where the poor were taught to read the Bible, attracted the support of George III and such leaders as Wilberforce and Mill, and soon extended its work to Europe, Africa, India, America and the West Indies. The 'monitorial' system also created teacher training institutions – first at Borough Road (1798, which moved to Isleworth in 1890) and afterwards at Stockwell (1861), Darlington (1872) and Saffron Walden (1884). The contraction of teacher training in the 1970s, however, resulted in the closure of all these colleges, except Borough Road, which amalgamated in 1976 with two neighbouring institutions to form a new voluntary college called the West London Institute of Higher Education (where the BFSS Archives are now available for consultation). Since the 1870 Education Act in which the Cowper-Temple clause* enshrined the Society's principles of religious toleration, it has gradually withdrawn its support for schools and concentrated on three activities in line with its Royal Charter: a prominent share in the West London Institute (whose constitution also requires the provision of training for RE); the provision of grants for needy students and for certain voluntary organizations; and the development of research into, and of provision for, the needs of the deprived, of the handicapped and of multi-cultural education. The Society's patron is the Sovereign, and the Vice-Presidents include the leaders of the major Christian denominations in the United Kingdom.

HOWARD MARRATT

British Council of Churches

Formed in 1942, an Education Department was established early in its life. This brought together representatives of the churches, all levels of education, the teacher unions and government, with the services of a full-time secretary. The Department became closely linked with the CEM, two of whose staff were members of its executive committee and another served as Education Consultant to the Council. The Department sponsored two major enquiries into RE in schools. The published reports were *Religious Education and the Secondary School*, by Colin Alves (SCM Press 1968) and *The Recruitment, Employment and Training of Teachers concerned with Religious Education in Schools in England and Wales* by Howard Marratt (BCC 1971). An open and reflective approach to RE teaching was adopted by the Department which encouraged its discussion and support in local Councils of Churches.

Following the reorganization of the Council in 1974, five divisions were created to cover the scope of the Council's work, and education became part of the brief of one of these – the Division of Community Affairs. An Education Working Party contributed to the Conference (1977) and report *Britain Today and Tomorrow* (Collins 1978).

See also **Dialogue**.

JOHN M. SUTCLIFFE

British Humanist Association

There are three national Humanist organizations in Britain, of which the British Humanist Association (BHA) is the largest and has the widest field of activities. The other organizations are the National Secular Society and the Rationalist Press Association. In addition, the South Place Ethical Society has close links with the Humanist movement. The BHA is a membership organization as well as including fifty local groups many of which are affiliated to the Head Office in London. The BHA publishes a monthly newsletter, pamphlets and information leaflets; it also holds an Annual Conference. Social work includes a vigorous Housing Association, which provides flats for the elderly, a counselling service and the Independent Adoption Society. Members of BHA are frequently asked to officiate at funerals, when a non-religious ceremony is requested. The BHA is affiliated to the International Humanist and Ethical Union to which forty-three organizations belong. IHEU, with its headquarters in Utrecht, has consultative status with UNESCO and the United Nations. The BHA in its present form – its roots go back to the last century – was founded in 1963.

JAMES HEMMING

Broadcasts: BBC

The School Broadcasting Department of the BBC has been in existence for over fifty years and religious broadcasts to schools have been part of that output for almost as long. Since the early beginnings in the 1940s, radio broadcasts for school worship (and later for school assemblies) and for classroom education increased to as many as eight separate series by the mid-70s, spanning an age range of eight to eighteen. In 1979, 'Something to Think About', a long awaited series for infant school assemblies aged five to seven, was added to widen further the resources available to the RE teacher,

Titles of past series tell their own story of style, content and attitude towards RE. The series for sixth forms began as 'The Christian Religion and its Philosophy' then became 'Religion and Philosophy' before developing into 'Religion in its Contemporary Context' and eventually 'Religion and Life' in 1972. In 1980 the series was discontinued, the emphasis shifting to the needs of younger listeners and to areas of RE with fewer resources.

The very popular service designed for school worship began in 1940 as a service for eleven-year-olds and above. In 1961 it divided into a junior and senior series: 'A Religious Service for Primary Schools' (eight to eleven) and 'An Act of Worship' (eleven to sixteen). In 1974 the junior series was broadened in outlook and re-named 'A Service for Schools'. It remained, however, a Christian celebration, though by the end of the 1970s a Christian standpoint on the part of the listener was no longer assumed, in recognition of a changing multi-racial society. At the beginning of the 1980s, the audience for this series had risen to a record one and a quarter million children each week. In 1977 'Contact' was added as an additional resource for assemblies of eight to twelve year olds. It reflected a broader view of school assemblies in a multi-cultural context, as did its senior counterpart which replaced 'An Act of Worship' with 'Material for Secondary Assemblies'.

Religious broadcasts to schools have always taken a lead in educational innovation through the content of the programmes and in the guidance given in accompanying teachers' notes. In style, the broadcasts have drawn extensively from the resources of radio-commissioned drama, poetry, music, actuality, interviews – reflecting the vigour of contemporary debate and the intellectual provocation of ideas.

The early radio dramatizations of biblical scenes were the backbone of education for many years. Then in the late 1960s the medium of Radiovision (a 35mm colour filmstrip accompanied by programme sound, recorded by schools for use thereafter with the pictures) made a significant contribution to the study of world religions in an 'Encounter' series – Hinduism, Buddhism, Judaism, Islam, Christianity. In subsequent years, programmes about religions other than Christianity have been regularly broadcast as have been programmes directly involving the main immigrant religions.

In 1979 the first BBC television programme in support of RE was provided, though there had been occasional elements within other series which looked at matters of faith and morals. The series was offered as resource units for eleven to thirteen-year-olds studying religious and moral education.

All BBC broadcasts to schools are approved by the Programme Committees of the School Broadcasting Council, supported by advice and guidance from the council's education officers and research staff. It was established in 1929 and re-organized in 1947: its purpose is to guide the BBC in its educational provision and to represent the educational world and its needs to the BBC.

RALPH ROLLS

Broadcasts: Independent Television and Independent Local Radio

Since the 1944 Act enshrined religion, the approach to religion as a school subject has changed. Generally now 'Religious Education' has displaced 'Religious Instruction'. Independent Broadcasting's contribution to this matter reflects that change. While the religious output on television included series for young people that were recognizably 'RI' – such as Yorkshire TV's networked 'God's Story' based on the *Ladybird Bible*, and Grampian's 'Sunday School' and 'Look and See' – in the output for schools the concept of 'RE' provided a thread through the maze of a multi-faith society.

There has been a tendency to emphasize the moral, rather than doctrinal, aspects of religion since this is what many teachers request. Examples of such programmes were Granada's 'The Messengers', Associated Television's 'Starting Out' and Scottish Television's 'Play Fair'. Specific education about religions was provided in ATV's 'Believe It or Not' launched in the Spring Term of 1973. Intended for eleven to fifteen-year-olds, the series was taken in its first year by under four per cent of secondary schools, in 1981 by twenty-three per cent. The aims of the series in 1982 were: 1. To give a clear exposition of custom and ritual in five of the world's main faiths. 2. To provide a sympathetic insight into what is distinctive and characteristic about each religion's practices and ethos. 3. To avoid caricature, or such preoccupation with the bizarre that the adherents of a religion may seem uniformly 'peculiar'. 4. To pose through various situations the basic ques-

tions that religions raise; and to suggest a number of 'answers' meriting consideration.
5. To approach difficult questions about the 'truth' of religions, and about the truths in various religions.

There is uncertainty about what contribution TV can make to primary RE. Many of the social and moral issues with which religions are occupied in day-to-day practice are introduced into infant, junior and middle school programmes, in a variety of contexts. A series for the younger age-group (eight to nine years) was produced by Grampian TV, reflecting 'A Curricular Approach to Religious Education' as recommended by the Scottish Central Committee on Religious Education (see **Scotland**). This series has subsequently been shown to schools on a network basis. When Independent Local Radio was established in 1973, the Independent Broadcasting Authority decided not to require ILR stations to provide formal educational broadcasting aimed at schools and educational institutions. ILR educational programming aims chiefly at the listener at home. The number of stations and the diversity of programming is such that a conspectus of what informal 'religious education' is provided by ILR is not possible in a brief account: but what is done can fairly be characterized as moral and social rather than specifically 'religious' in the sense of 'doctrinal'. In addition, there are regular 'religious' broadcasts on ILR as on ITV, which provide RE incidentally.

SUSAN ELLIOTT

Buddha   *see* **Buddhism**

Buddhism

There is no formulated Buddhist philosophy of education. The teaching as a whole is a course of spiritual education, one of the Buddha's titles being *satthā devamanussānam'*, 'Teacher of gods and men'. Gotama the Buddha (*c*.566–486 BC) was one of a numerous class of wandering teachers in the Gangetic plain who disputed in complete freedom among themselves and with orthodox Brahmins. Rejecting 'signs and wonders', he approved only the 'miracle of education', summarized as: 'Reason in this way, do not reason in that way. Consider thus, and not thus. Get rid of this disposition, train yourself, and remain, in that.' The whole content of

the Pali Canon is a systematic exposition of the course of training whereby monks and lay followers may break free from the cycle of rebirths and gain the ultimate release of *Nirvāṇa*. The teaching is summarized in the Four Noble Truths: 1. the truth of *dukkha* (inadequately rendered 'suffering' – all that is unsatisfactory, painful and frustrating in life); 2. the origin of *dukkha* which is *taṇhā* (lit. 'thirst', i.e. craving and self-oriented desire); 3. the cessation of *dukkha* (equalling *Nirvāṇa*); and 4. the way leading to that cessation, the Noble Eightfold Path, whose eight steps are subsumed under the three heads of Wisdom, Morality and Meditation (or, better, 'mind-training'). The immediate goal is called 'entering the stream' (*sotāpatti*), whereby one is irrevocably set on the right path. The decisive factor is the practice of mindfulness (*sati*) leading to increasing self-knowledge (and, finally, to the realization that what we call 'self' is unreal). The Buddha's non-authoritarian attitude is noteworthy: on his deathbed he refused to name a successor, and in a famous sermon to the Kālāmas he told them not to depend on any teacher's word – even his own! – but to find out for themselves those things that were profitable and keep to them. Buddhism has never sought to set up its teachings as divine commandments backed by legal sanctions.

All is set forth as a process of self-training: 'You yourselves must make the effort – the Tathāgatas (Buddhas) are pointers of the way'. The foundation for such training is morality: the 'five disciplines', to refrain from 1. taking life, 2. theft, 3. sexual misconduct, 4. wrong speech and 5. use of intoxicants and sloth-inducing drugs. For monks, there are 227 rules of conduct. Instruction took the form of discourses, often highly compressed and meant to be learnt by heart. There was much repetition and lists of items or factors played a large part. Sometimes, especially when dealing with lay enquirers, the Buddha adopted 'Socratic' methods. Interlocutors were made to clarify their premises and then led on to admit the truth of the Buddha's position. In most cases, this process is represented as being successful, with the questioner (whether originally hostile or genuinely enquiring) expressing wonderment and delight, and requesting acceptance, either as a member of the Order, or as a lay-follower 'as long as life shall last'. Many such opponents are either arrogant Brahmins or members of other sects.

The Buddha varied his methods according to the pupil, expounding the same ideas in many different ways. He illustrated his teaching with stories and analogies from daily life or in vivid images. In one sermon, he likened a greedy and conceited monk to a beetle gorged with dung; one with uncontrolled impulses is compared to a man who has tethered six animals together – a snake, a crocodile, a bird, a dog, a jackal and a monkey. Each pulls in a different direction and finally they go the way of the strongest. In the *Kūṭadanta Sutta*, he pictures an elaborate Brahmin sacrifice which is bloodless, since all its elements are treated symbolically. At the end of it, his Brahmin interlocutor grants life to the hundreds of bulls, goats and other animals he had planned to offer up and becomes a disciple, gaining the first stage on the path (*sotāpatti*) through the realization: 'Whatever has a beginning contains the seeds of dissolution.' An early example of 'visual aids' is found in the story of how Maudga-lyāyana (Moggallāna, a leading disciple) illustrated the twelve-linked formula of Dependent Origination (*paṭicca-samuppāda,* i.e., 'the predispositions are conditioned by ignorance', etc.) by a picture of a twelve-spoked wheel, which the Buddha caused to be displayed over a monastery gateway – the origin of the Tibetan 'wheel of life' and similar representations. Basic teachings were sometimes put into pithy stanzas and a collection of such verses formed the *Dhammapada*, one of the most famous and beautiful of Buddhist scriptures. The *Sigālovāda Sutta* sets out the ideal relationship between teacher and pupil. The teacher should show affection to his pupil, train him in virtue and manners, carefully instruct him in wisdom, speak well of him and guard him from danger. The pupil should minister to the teacher, rise in his presence, listen attentively to his words, attend to his needs and follow his instructions. Elsewhere, three kinds of teacher are mentioned. One who teaches a doctrine of disenchantment with decay-and-death, of dispassion leading to its cessation, is called one who teaches Dhamma. If he has trained himself accordingly, he is called one trained in conformity with Dhamma. If through such training he is liberated from grasping, he is called one who has attained Nirvāṇa.

The monastic life, austere as it may seem, is seen as the middle way between the extremes of self-indulgence and the self-torture often practised, then as now, in India. It is a life not of penance but of withdrawal from the world's enticements. Meditation, as the way to the goal, is possible in the 'house-hold life' but easier in the monastic context. Developing a calm state of mind by concentration (*samādhi*) is needful, but the 'heart of Buddhist meditation' is the practice of mindfulness (*satipaṭṭhāna*), described as 'the only way to the attainment of purity . . . to the end of pain and grief . . . to the realization of Nirvāṇa'. It involves the close objective 'monitoring' of one's body, feelings, mental states and mind-objects. When these are seen 'as they really are', dispassion arises leading to enlightenment. Though such meditation should be incumbent on all monks, today this is far from being the case in practice. However, in recent years a powerful impulse in this direction has come from Burma, whence it has spread to Thailand, Sri Lanka and latterly also to the West. It should be added that much that passes for meditation in the West today has little in common with the true Buddhist tradition. The Buddhist contribution to psychology, based on meditative experience, has not yet received the recognition it deserves. The *Abhidhamma* (the abstruse third section of the Pali Canon) includes matter of varying date and unequal value, but some portions contain perhaps the most penetrating analysis of the nature of consciousness to be found anywhere.

Traditionally, in Buddhist countries, education was centred on the monasteries. Tambiah, writing of pre-1767 Thailand, refers to 'the sending of young boys (and, less frequently, girls) to the monasteries to learn elementary Dhamma and reading, writing and arithmetic', adding that this is reported from other Asian countries as well. He cites a Dutch report of 1636: 'Till their fifth or sixth year the children are allowed to run about the house; then they are sent to the priests to learn to write and read and to acquire other useful arts. When they can read and write properly they are sent to learn a trade . . . frequently, however, the cleverest of them are allowed to pursue their studies . . . instruction, secular as well as religious, is given solely by the priests, till they are qualified to fill public positions and offices. They then discard their yellow robes, but many intelligent and talented pupils remain in the monasteries, in order to become Heads of temples and schools, or Priests.' Until the nineteenth century, the way to secular advancement lay almost only through such monastic training. The custom of young Thai men spending up to three months in the robe is still widespread. Many stay on for several years before entering public life, even though normal opportunities of secular higher education have long been available. Despite the mixed motives of some, this custom still does much to uphold Buddhist influence in an increasingly secularized society.

At another level, Rama III in 1835 sought to make Wat Pho (the famous temple of the Reclining Buddha) into a 'popular university' by adorning its walls with educational paintings and inscriptions for the edification of young and old – a kind of forerunner of the two Buddhist universities established in Bangkok in the 1940s on foundations laid some fifty years earlier. The system of study for monks is organized round a series of scriptural examinations (*pariyan*) up to a very high standard and the main entry is for monks with a good *pariyan*, though there are also 'extension' courses for women and for foreigners. At Mahamakut University 'instruction is given by four departments – social sciences (sociology, education), philosophy (Buddhism, comparative religion), languages (Thai, Pali, French, German, Chinese), psychology (including biology and the physical sciences). English is compulsory.' All this is very much in keeping with the 'purification' of Buddhist teaching inaugurated by King Mongkut (1851–68), who held that true Buddhism when purged of 'popular' accretions was fully in keeping with a modern scientific outlook.

Buddhism is probably seldom or never taught as an independent subject in British schools. Some suggestions may usefully be made for its treatment in any general course on world religions. One stumbling-block for many is the fact that it is non-theistic – leading to doubts as to whether it is really a religion at all. Conversely, the idea that the Mahāyāna (northern) schools *are* theistic (as opposed

to the Theravāda school discussed here) is incorrect: Buddhas and Bodhisattvas are not 'deities' and any so-called 'gods' occupy a subordinate position. What, then, of ultimate reality? A significant passage declares: 'There is, monks, an Unborn, Unbecome, Uncreated, Uncompounded, and if there were not this Unborn . . . there would be no deliverance here apparent from what is born, become, created, compounded. But since, monks, there is this Unborn . . . therefore there is here apparent a deliverance from what is born, become, created, compounded.' Christians and other theistic believers can accept this statement as true in itself, with whatever qualifications or additons they would wish to make. It therefore serves as something of a bridge between the faiths. Indeed, the statement quoted might be taken as *the* fundamental proposition of all genuine religion. If so, it would provide an effective criterion for distinguishing 'religion' from such surrogates as Marxism* or Humanism*.

The importance of morality is no less strongly stressed in Buddhism than in theistic faiths, though the motivation differs in that, for Buddhists, good and bad deeds bring their own karmic reward or retribution without divine intervention. While Buddhists may fairly rebut the occasional charge that Buddhism is 'selfish' by pointing out that the very idea of self is considered illusory, this merely deepens the mystery for some, particularly in relation to the doctrine of rebirth through many lives. The short answer is that if 'I' am an illusion in this life, that same illusion can persist into other states. Be that as it may, acceptance of the bare possibility of a series of lives on either the Buddhist or the Hindu model can, in present conditions, produce a social bonus by defusing current debates on the importance of 'heredity' versus 'environment': once it is admitted that mental traits and abilities could even conceivably be 'inherited' by the individual from past lives, these two seemingly exclusive alternatives lose something of their relevance.

S. Dutt, 'Buddhist Education', *2500 Years of Buddhism*, Government of India 1956; H. von Glasenapp, *Buddhism, A Non-Theistic Religion*, Allen & Unwin 1970; A. W. P. Guruge, 'Buddha as a Teacher', *The Young Buddhist*, Singapore 1979; D. Nanyakkara,

'Education, Concept-Input, Mind', *Buddhist Quarterly*, XII, 1980; Ven. Nyānaponika, *The Heart of Buddhist Meditation,* Rider 1962 and *Abhidhamma Studies: Researches into Buddhist Psychology,* BPS 1965; S. J. Tambiah, *World Conqueror and World Renouncer,* Cambridge University Press 1976; B. J. Terwiel, *Monks and Magic,* Curzon Press 1975; E. J. Thomas, *History of Buddhist Thought*, Routledge 1933.

MAURICE O'CONNELL WALSHE

Bulgaria   *see* **Eastern Europe**

Calvin, John

John Calvin (1509–64) studied for the church at the Collèges de la Marche and de Montaigu in Paris and then Civil Law at Orleans and Bourges. Suspected of Lutheranism, he fled to Basle in 1535. From 1536–38 he was lecturer, then pastor, in the independent republic of Geneva. After exile in Strasbourg he was invited to return in 1541. His ministry made the city the model for reformed theology and practice. Calvin's *Ecclesiastical Ordinances* for church government were accepted by the General Council of the City on 20 November 1541.

Calvin extended the apostolic threefold ministry by adding doctors (teachers) to the pastors (bishops), elders (presbyters) chosen from the councillors, and deacons. Their function was to train the young in languages and theology to fit them for the two lay orders, or for the chief offices of pastors and magistrates. He also planned a school for children. Initially this scheme proved impracticable. A school had been established in Geneva before 1400, but it had closed in 1531. A new college was formed in the former convent of Rive in 1535, but it was difficult to find staff. Sebastian Castellio (1515–63) followed Calvin from Strasbourg but was expelled in 1544 after disputes over scripture and administration. Education was still largely the frequent expository preaching, which was the application of mediaeval method to the original scriptures.

In 1558 Calvin was able to complete his plans. Public subscription paid for the Collège de Genève which opened on 5 June 1559. Failing to attract Mercier from Paris, Calvin appointed Theodore Beza (1519–1605) as Rector. He was joined by the faculty from Lausanne. Calvin taught the Old Testament.

Within five years the college had expanded to a 1200 student secondary school (*schola privata*) and a 300 student academy (*schola publica*). This was granted a Charter by the Emperor Maximilian II in 1566. The grammar school had seven classes. The first three years learned writing, Latin and French. In the fourth, students read Cicero and Ovid and began Greek. In the second class they added Luke in Greek and Logic, and in the first class, Paul's letters and rhetoric. This was the reformed humanist structure based on Johannes Sturm (1507–89) at Strasbourg. It equipped its students to communicate throughout Europe and to go on to study theology, the Queen of the Sciences. Each lecture began with prayer and pupils heard three sermons each week.

There were five professors in the academy, two theologians and one each for Greek, Hebrew and the Arts. There were twenty-seven lectures each week, a theological seminar and a monthly disputation. Discussion was free within the very strict limits of acceptance of the Bible, the confessions of the four General Councils and the theology of Calvin's *Institutes* (1536–59). This thorough system of indoctrination produced highly trained Pastors and Elders and may be compared with the Jesuit system of Ignatius Loyola (1491–1556), who followed Calvin at Montaigu. It was not intended to foster liberal thought or science, though Geneva became a refuge for political and intellectual refugees.

―――――

Calvin: Theological Treatises, Library of Christian Classics Vol XXII, trans. J. K. S. Reid, SCM Press 1954; James Mackinnon, *Calvin and the Reformation,* Longman 1936; T. H. L. Parker, *John Calvin,* Lion 1975.

DAVID KEEP

Canada

Canada is by background and by the nominal affiliation of her people a Christian country. A substantial proportion of the population, perhaps twenty to thirty per cent, can be described as active Christians. The largest church is the Roman Catholic Church with forty-five per cent of the people and its largest concentration in the Province of Quebec. The various Protestant churches and the Anglican Church hold another forty per cent of the people. The remaining fifteen per cent are divided between the Orthodox churches, small sects and cults, Jews, adherents of other religions, agnostics and atheists.

Public education in Canada is a provincial responsibility. In the past, in provinces where religious instruction was permitted in the public schools, it was along the lines of Christian nurture. Nowadays, outside Newfoundland and Quebec, the public school systems are largely secularized and there is no formal religious education of any kind. Attempts to bring in programmes which seek to introduce students to the religious heritage of mankind have not met with much success. Moral and values education is a current fashion, however. Nevertheless, there is a growing minority of Christians who are so disenchanted with the public schools that they are starting private schools. The Dutch Reformed community has been prominent in this regard.

In most Canadian universities there are now departments of Religious Studies. These offer courses leading to undergraduate and graduate degrees in Arts. The major traditional churches have seminaries located on university campuses. In Vancouver, Toronto, Montreal and Halifax these resources are combined in ecumenical consortiums where students registered in one college take many of their courses in colleges of other traditions.

Adherents of non-Christian religions are a small but growing segment of the Canadian population. Buddhist temples and Moslem mosques are beginning to appear in large cities. The Hindu and Sikh religions are represented amongst new Canadians from India. The Jewish community is much more in evidence. All of these groups, and others, nurture their adherents in the beliefs and practices of their faith traditions. Interfaith associations such as The Canadian Council of Christians and Jews and the World Conference on Religion and Peace promote mutual understanding and common action.

For the different denominations, religious education is an important part of church life.

1. *Roman Catholic Church.* The parochial day school is still the main agent of Christian formation in the Roman Catholic community. Generally across the country in the 1970s, the traditional question and answer catechism was replaced by a contemporary Canadian Catechism, produced in both English and French versions under the auspices of the hierarchy by Canadian scholars and educators. The Canadian Catechism is a graded programme, similar to a Protestant curriculum. It is under constant revision and has been adapted for use in parish Sunday Schools with children who do not attend Catholic day schools. It has been used enthusiastically by some Anglican parishes.

The Roman Catholic Church has not been immune to the influences of secularism affecting all religious communities. The educational programme of the average parish does not differ markedly from its counterpart in the other churches. The hierarchy is amongst the most progressive in the context of worldwide Catholicism. There is a strong social conscience and a willingness to co-operate with other Christians in educational and outreach programmes such as Ten Days for World Development.

2. *Anglican and Protestant Churches.* For many Protestant and Anglican Canadians, Christian education is synonymous with Sunday School. Parents bring their children to church on Sunday morning. In one widely accepted pattern, they attend the service together until the time of the sermon when the children depart for their classes in the education centre.

Since the mid-1960s, there has been a massive decline in the number of children attending Sunday School. The United Church reports losses as high as 100,000 students. The Anglican and Presbyterian declines are proportionately as large. In part, this decline is due to a falling off in the birth rate, but it is also symptomatic of the general secularization of the North American culture.

Despite this loss in numbers, local congregations are arguably stronger centres of faith and witness. Christian parents continue to demand a Sunday School as the major community effort in education outside the home. The local congregation is much more active now in the selection of curriculum materials. This reflects a trend away from denominational uniformity. The United and Presbyterian Churches have co-operated with American churches in the production of ecumenical resources. Booklets have been produced by denominations, which offer guidance in the evaluation and choice of materials. American religious educators such as John Westerhoff have conducted workshops in various parts of the country. National and regional judicatories employ religious education consultants to advise local congregations. Nevertheless, there is a lack of distinctly Canadian resource materials.

Adult education has become important. Universities offer courses in religion, Christian councils sponsor lay schools of theology and churches offer practical training programmes in specific forms of lay ministry, such as hospital visiting. The introduction of contemporary forms of worship has involved much explanation and teaching. Many congregations are introducing classes of instruction for parents prior to the baptism of their children and are offering them ongoing help for Christian education in the home.

The alarming increase in marital breakdown partly explains the proliferation of programmes such as marriage preparation, marriage encounter and marriage enrichment. Often these are held at Christian conference centres in residential, weekend, community building settings. There is a large market for religious books and a wealth of quality materials available. However, the majority of Protestant and Anglican churchgoing adults in Canada are still likely to be influenced most for good or ill in an educational way by their experience of Sunday morning worship and sermon.

3. *Evangelical and Pentecostal churches*. The Evangelical and Pentecostal churches continue to emphasize biblical literalism and authoritarian teaching. These characteristics are evident in Christian education materials for use with both children and adults. The materials are produced in very attractive formats with detailed instructions for teachers in simple form. They are popular with some teachers in traditional churches although frowned upon by experts.

From this part of the Christian community has come the television evangelist, several of whom have developed large audiences and staggering incomes. This approach is resisted by the major denominations, who have experimented to some extent with ecumenically produced programmes. For the most part, however, the churches have not been able as yet to tap the tremendous educational potential of radio and television. This is true in terms both of the public airwaves and of private cassette production made possible

now by the availability of reasonably priced video equipment.

4. *Recent Trends*. The charismatic movement has had an impact on all the churches and, while it may not have directly influenced everyone, it has encouraged general spiritual renewal. The Cursillo Movement, an intense three-day experience of immersion in Christian teaching and community life, is spreading beyond its origins in a Roman Catholic context. Bible study and prayer groups are growing and Christian healing is promoted by associations such as the Order of St Luke.

There is increasing interest in congregational renewal. From evangelical Protestantism has come the Church Growth Movement. Many congregations are seeking to apply its principles and methods. Annual stewardship programmes which culminate in a home visit seeking the commitment of time, talent and money, are also common. Such programmes have worthwhile educational components. Denominations have launched mission study and fund raising programmes to extend work in the Canadian north and overseas.

WILLIAM GILBERT

Canada: Newfoundland and Labrador

Arrangements for RE are the result of the history and structure of the provincial schools. All primary and secondary schools are church schools, each being related to one of three Denominational Education Committees (DEC) – Pentecostal, Roman Catholic and Integrated – which are responsible for school construction and operation. The province's Department of Education finances the schools fully through grants to each DEC in proportion to the number of students. All post-secondary education is non-denominational. This article is mainly concerned with RE in denominational schools.

Every school's programme includes RE and worship. Each DEC develops the RE curriculum for its schools, but local school districts determine the format of worship. Individual students may withdraw from RE or worship if their parents so request. Religious, moral, social and denominational development are specified aims for all schools; but each DEC pursues them differently depending on its understanding of the relation between school and church. All three RE programmes aim to achieve 1. critical understanding of religion, 2. appreciation of the individual and social importance of religion, and 3. personal enlightenment through consideration of religion's major issues. Single-denomination schools also aim at religious commitment, belief and observance.

Pentecostal schools have 6,000 students in one province-wide school district. RE includes formal study of the Bible, emphasizing familiarity in primary school, and critical and apologetical skills in secondary where one year is allotted for the study of non-Christian religions. Parental involvement is especially sought in lower primary. The entire programme underwent revision in 1982, with North American influences dominating through the network of Pentecostal Assemblies.

Roman Catholic schools, with 55,000 students in twelve school districts, include study of many aspects of the heritage, with emphasis on liturgy and theology. Life experiences such as celebration, growth and community are emphasized for fives to fourteens and parental participation is actively sought. Formal study of scripture, ethics, church history, theology and world religions is done by the fifteen to seventeen age group. While aiming to nurture RC commitment, RE is ecumenically oriented and allots two years for studying non-Christian religions. Courses for sixes to sevens and fifteens to seventeens are being revised and the church is developing RE programmes for the deaf. RE planning is guided by the Canadian Conference of Catholic Bishops and RE specialists often seek graduate degrees in Ontario and the USA.

Integrated schools, teaching 83,000 students in twenty-one districts, resulted from the 1969 consolidation of former Anglican, United Church of Canada, Salvation Army, Presbyterian and Moravian schools. Formal Bible study is done in the last two years of both primary and secondary schools, but in other courses students learn about themselves and their world, ancient and modern non-Christian religions (three to four years), church history and current social, ethical and religious issues. Special parental involvement is not expected and denominational development is left to individual churches in Sunday Schools. RE for the eight to eleven age-group

is presently being revised. Curriculum development* has been influenced mainly from England through Edwin Cox's work in the province, contacts with John Hull and the Christian Education Movement*, and graduate study by RE specialists.

In primary schools all three programmes use activity-centred learning and evaluate by observing student behaviour and project work. Secondary students learn through lecture, discussion and project methods and are evaluated by written work and classroom exams; in their final year, they may also write a provincial exam prepared by the DEC.

Teacher education at the university includes elective courses in religious studies and RE, summer institutes, and teaching practice in local schools or in Essex (England) county schools at the residential campus in Harlow. In-service training is conducted by the RE programme coordinator for each school district and by the interdenominational Religious Education Special Interest Council (RESIC) through workshops, annual conferences and newsletters.

The development of RE teachers and the creation of criteria and methods for evaluating RE programmes are two major tasks for the future.

Colloquium on the Future of Religious Education in the Province of Newfoundland and Labrador, Memorial University Extension Service, St Johns, Canada 1971; *Colloquium on Religious Education and the Student: Implications for the 80s*, Integrated Education Committee, St John's, Canada 1980; Frederick W. Rowe, *Education and Culture in Newfoundland*, McGraw-Hill Ryerson 1976.

NOËL BARRETT SHUELL

Career Value of RE

The nationally recognized public examination boards in England and Wales examine religious education, usually as Religious Studies (RS), under the same terms as those for all other school subjects. (In Scotland and Ireland too, despite historic differences, the subject has become examinable.) Standards are set and moderated; the religious background of candidates even from Roman Catholic and Jewish schools is not a factor. Graded certificates are awarded normally at 16+ (GCE 'O' level or CSE) and 18+ (GCE 'A' level).

Universities, institutions of higher education, professional bodies and employers usually require applicants to have a minimum number of 'A' level and/or 16+ passes ('O' level grades, A, B and C and CSE 1 being acceptable). As these minimum entry qualifications are generally not subject specific, RS is not excluded.

Some courses and occupations ask for particular subjects, particularly English language, mathematics, the sciences and a modern language. However, RS is never obligatory for university entrance, even for a degree in religious studies, though an interest at school is a consideration. For any career, the subject is *per se* neither a requirement nor an obstacle, but in practice the imperatives in some fields for specific subjects leave students little alternative but to omit RS from their optional courses. At 18+ especially, when normally only three subjects fulfil the demands in the scientific, technological and medical spheres, religious studies and the humanities curriculum suffers.

Formal recruitment and selection policies discriminate in favour of other subjects, but not against religious studies. However, decisions are often made by individual professors or managers, some of whom may believe that RS does not stand with 'academic' subjects such as history and English which have general and universal meanings open to everyone. Rather, they perceive RS as dependent on particular abilities which may be God-given rather than attained and not equally accessible to all students; music and art may be other examples. An understanding of the rigour of the academic demands on students and teachers in RS will dispel this misconception.

As the image of the subject changes, religious education is being valued positively for the study skills* of assimilating and recapitulating information, weighing evidence, forming judgments and expressing them in clear, usually written, form. Students are given an understanding of people, knowledge of ethical issues and standards, insights into culture, historic and multi-faith, and an appreciation of human values. RS is a useful background subject for a wide range of careers – medical and social work, teaching, distributive and service industries, personnel and sales departments. In providing insights for

personal and social development it lays a foundation for a successful 'career' whether in paid employment or in the creative work of living life to the full.

See also **Further Education; Higher Education**.

ROBIN H. SHEPHERD

Catechetics

The word used (particularly within the Roman Catholic Church) to describe the process of the education in faith of the Christian; the process is known as catechesis. This is broadly defined as 'a dialogue between believers'. A more complete description of catechesis is: 'Throwing light on the whole of human existence as God's salvific action by witnessing to the mystery of Christ through the word, for the purpose of awakening and fostering the faith and prompting men to live truly in accord with the faith' (Higher Catechetical Institute of Nijmegen, *Making All Things New*, Divine Word Publications, Illinois 1966). The literal meaning of catechesis is 'echo'. It occurs in the NT only in its verbal form where it is used in a derived sense to mean oral teaching. Later it came to be applied to the teaching given to catechumens preparing for baptism (baptismal catechesis) and to neophytes recently admitted into membership of the church (mystagogical catechesis). There is a rich body of catechetical homilies dating from the third and fourth centuries. As the practice of infant baptism became more common the catechumenate, intended primarily for adults seeking initiation into the church, gradually disappeared, and at the same time the term catechesis also fell out of use.

Those to be instructed were now more usually young children, baptized in infancy. The instruction was codified in books known as catechisms, many of which were published at the time of the Reformation, e.g. Luther's *Kleiner Catechismus* (1529), the *Heidelberg Catechism* (1563), Bellarmine's *Catechism* (1598), the Catechism of the Council of Trent (intended mainly for priests) (1566). These catechisms were scriptural and christocentric. Later catechisms moved towards a strictly doctrinal content – creed, commandments, sacraments and prayers – with the emphasis on memorization. During the early part of this century, a movement was growing for the development of a form of catechesis for children which would take greater account of their immediate needs; latterly the importance of continued catechesis throughout adult life has been stressed.

There are four principal sources of catechesis or languages of faith, which together determine the content: scripture, doctrine, liturgy and experience. Scripture is the Word of God; it is normative, permanent and central, and is a unique source for grasping and penetrating ultimate mystery. Doctrine is the expression of the substance of faith which can be grasped by the mind; it is the main rational element in catechesis and is essential for the promotion of dialogue. Liturgy is the way the community of believers expresses its faith in worship; it allows for a non-cognitive articulation of faith and it deepens faith precisely through its celebration. Experience, both overt religious experience and the day by day experiences of life, forms the context within which faith becomes relevant; it can lead to an explicit religious understanding of life and consequently to a more deeply Christian way of life.

The current direction in catechetics is towards the development of forms of education in faith appropriate to particular stages in an individual's life (e.g. at marriage) and to particular groups within the RC church (e.g. the handicapped).

See also **Roman Catholic Church.**

J. Hofinger, The ABC of Modern Catechetics, William Sadlier 1961; Pope John Paul II, Catechesis in Our Time, Catholic Truth Society 1979; J. A. Jungmann, Handing on the Faith, Herder 1959; K. Nichols, Cornerstone, St Paul Publications 1978; R. M. Rummery, Catechesis and Religious Education in a Pluralist Society, E. J. Dwyer (Australia) Pty Ltd 1975; M. Van Caster, The Structure of Catechetics, Herder & Herder 1965; E. Yarnold, The Awe Inspiring Rites of Initiation, St Paul Publications 1971.

DAVID KONSTANT

Cathedral Schools

From the church's infancy, each bishop had necessarily to provide for the education of his clergy in areas without schools. Accordingly, he received into his household boys and young men whom he taught himself or through a priest who was both secretary and schoolmaster (scholasticus). Certain bishops' schools became important centres of Christian and classical education during and after the Carolingian age; the eighth-century school at York, with its library and wide-ranging curricula is well documented in the writings of its former pupil and master, Alcuin.

As the bishop's household became detached from his cathedral, control of the school passed to the cathedral clergy. This happened in England after the Norman Conquest when nine cathedrals were reorganized as secular foundations each governed by a dean and chapter. Here the school became the responsibility of the chapter's scholasticus (later chancellor), who appointed a schoolmaster as his deputy. In the eight cathedrals served by monks, there being no chapter, the school remained the bishop's responsibility and became the city school, the convent having schools of its own. In England as in France, during the twelfth century certain secular cathedral schools flourished as centres of higher education; that at Paris developed after 1170 into one of the first universities. With the rise of these in the next century, the cathedral schools took second place as grammar schools and the provision of one of these by every cathedral to teach the clerks of the church and other poor scholars become a canon-law obligation.

Every pre-Reformation secular cathedral was staffed by a hierarchy of clerks below the canons, all with functions that required some proficiency in Latin. The grammar school was thus an indispensable if subordinate part of the establishment. Its pupils covered a wide age range from boy choristers to junior vicars and other 'inferior ministers' of the cathedral staff, as well as city boys and local parish clergy. The master was usually required to be an MA and might have regular choir duties to perform, but he was never a prebendary. Hardly less important for the cathedral's daily routine was the song school which the precentor controlled. His deputy, the song master, trained the choristers and younger vicars in plainsong and polyphony and sometimes also was the organist. Less permanent and institutionalized was the chancellor's theology school in which he or a substitute lectured. As chancellors tended to become non-resident, these lectures lapsed, with only occasional periods of revival.

The Reformation left these cathedrals and their schools undisturbed. At the dissolution the monastic cathedrals and six abbey churches were re-established by Henry VIII as secular cathedrals, each obliged (Winchester, Norwich and Oxford excepted) to maintain a grammar school; several of these were refoundations of older schools, some were later known as King's Schools. All became indistinguishable from other grammar schools of the time, providing for boys an education based on the classics and Anglicanism. Most continue, now largely independent of cathedral control. Some are public schools, others LEA controlled. Choir schools, some of them also preparatory schools, are maintained by cathedrals of both modern and ancient foundation.

J. F. Burnet (ed.), *Public and Preparatory Schools Year Book*, A. & C. Black 1981; Nicholas Carlisle, *Endowed Grammar Schools*, 2 vols, 1818; Kathleen Edwards, *The English Secular Cathedrals in the Middle Ages*, Manchester University Press 1967; Nicholas Orme, *English Schools in the Middle Ages*, Methuen 1973.

JOHN LAWSON

Chaplains: Role of in Schools

Many independent boarding schools have an ordained chaplain on the staff, as do some independent day schools. The role of the chaplain ranges from being close to that of a parish priest to being a fully committed teacher with additional sacramental and pastoral duties, and there is often a tension between these two aspects. The key element in his role is that he symbolizes and provides a focus for the Christian presence in the school, of which the celebration of the sacrament is the single most apparent feature. He comes into his own most clearly when the school community faces ultimate issues of life and death. So it is that he ministers to those in distress and has an important official function on occasions of public celebration in the school year. He is also responsible, directly or by delegation, for all acts of Christian worship in the school, of which there may be a considerable number and at which attendance may be compulsory. This involves him in having to adapt and present liturgical services for adolescent congregations of which perhaps the majority of the members are not committed in any way.

Most chaplains place great emphasis upon their pastoral ministry and work alongside housestaffs and tutors, providing help and advice upon all manner of problems. This ministry also includes the staff, both academic and ancillary, and their families and, at times, the chaplain may well be drawn into the family problems of pupils. The exercise of this ministry requires considerable time and flexibility on the chaplain's part. His most important relationship is with the head, to whom he may be a personal chaplain, able to listen in confidence and providing support in time of stress. He ought to be able to speak freely to the head, particularly since he is not a career teacher. This may enable him to bring an almost prophetic role to his ministry which can be exercised at all levels of the school and can constitute a considerable force for good in the community, often bringing about lasting change and development.

All chaplains do some teaching and most teach as much as house staff. This can be the mainstay of the chaplain's ministry, particularly if he has an academic subject other than RE, but not all chaplains have teaching qualifications and a distinction must be made between the confessional role of the chaplain as a preacher – who inducts pupils into Christianity (through confirmation classes in Anglican schools) – and the impartial educational role of the teacher in the classroom. In view of this it is surprising that so many chaplains are also expected to undertake the additional role of head of RE, particularly since running a good educational department may well impose an extra burden upon a busy chaplain.

The chaplain's work can be very demanding and challenging and he will find support from The Chaplain's Conference (formerly the Association of School Chaplains and School Masters in Holy Orders).

JOHN MOTT

Central America
see **Latin/Central America**

Child-Centred RE

The notion of a child-centred approach to education is often contrasted with that of a teacher-centred or knowledge-based approach. The latter is said to focus on the transmission of knowledge and the former on the development of self-awareness and the enrichment of individual experience. Child-centred education implies 'beginning from where the children are' rather than from the subject matter. No doubt such polarization is over-crude and open to a great deal of criticism. In practical terms, the two approaches are seldom so clearly separated. Nevertheless, theories supporting either one or the other have long been part of the educational debate.

The Plowden Report* (1967) traces the child-centred movement back to Rousseau*, Pestalozzi, Froebel, Montessori and others. Plowden itself, like the Hadow Report some thirty years before, stressed the importance of individual experience and of the child being 'the agent in his own learning'. The compilers of the report argued: 'We certainly would not wish to undervalue knowledge and facts, but facts are best retained when they are used and understood, when right attitudes to learning are created, when children learn to learn. Instruction in many primary schools continues to bewilder children because it outruns their experience.' Plowden saw the child as central to and actively promoting his or her own educational process.

Psychological theories have also been influential in the movement towards child-centred education. Following the work of Piaget in particular, educational practice increasingly has attempted to take into account children's intellectual development. More recent studies, for example those of Bruner and of Gagné, have indicated the importance of active involvement and of guided discovery in facilitating learning. Such theories do not exclude the need for careful structuring of the material and of the skills* to be learned, but they do imply that central to educational planning should be a consideration of the learning processes of the child.

It is within the primary school, and especially in the early years, that child-centred approaches have had their greatest influence upon the curriculum. Primary schools, particularly since the widespread abolition of examinations at 11+, have been relatively free to experiment with a wide variety of ways of organizing learning. In structural terms, this freedom has led, for example, to vertical or family grouping, to the integrated day and to individualized learning. It has also led in some instances to an apparently undifferentiated curriculum. The organization of learning by means of topics, themes and projects is closely associated with child-centred approaches. In theory, it would seem that where child-centred approaches are dominant the traditional subject areas are less likely to be offered to the child as discrete areas of learning. Within the secondary sector, however, child-centred approaches appear to have had little impact upon structure or across the curriculum, despite attempts to integrate humanities or other subject areas.

An examination of the development of RE in both primary and secondary schools shows the subject-centred tradition on which it was founded. The Parliamentary Returns of 1879 and 1906 demonstrated not only that religious instruction was Bible-based, but also that, within the school it was separated from secular instruction. Syllabuses published before and following the 1944 Education Act concentrated upon subject-matter and were largely Bible-centred. It was not until the research of Dr Ronald Goldman in the early 1960s related the findings of developmental psychologists to RE that agreed syllabuses became in any real sense 'child-centred', although it must be said that the aims of many of the earlier syllabuses often related the choice of subject matter to the faith-development of pupils.

Yet the shift from Bible-centred approaches to RE, particularly in secondary schools, began even prior to the work of Goldman. Harold Loukes (1961) advocated the use of the problem-centred approach in RE in secondary schools. Christian teaching, he argued, would only be relevant to the adolescent if it shed light upon his or her personal experience and the problems arising from that experience. By 1965, Loukes recorded that although the main aims of RE teachers in secondary schools still related to the transmission of biblical knowledge, aims concerned with the development of personal and moral insights ran a close second. The problem-centred approach, centred on discussion of problems arising from individual experience, encouraged self-awareness as well as understanding of Christian teaching, and involved the secondary pupil as agent of his own learning.

Goldman's influence was perhaps most marked in the primary sector of state education. His conclusion that the Bible was taught too much and too soon provoked considerable controversy and confusion. The more positive aspect of his work was his emphasis upon relating RE to the needs and experience of children (1965). The influence of contemporary child-centred approaches upon what Goldman called 'developmental religious education' can easily be seen. He advocated religious education by means of 'themes, based upon the real life experiences of the children' and called this 'teaching by life-themes'. There is an emphasis upon natural interests, upon first-hand knowledge and experience, and upon personal exploration. Life-themes can therefore be argued to be child-centred. The major problem posed by them was that the 'religious bit' (i.e. the Bible story) was often tacked on at the end of the theme in a way that separated it from the child's experience, or attempted to integrate the biblical material in such a way as to demand from the child the ability to apply a different level of thought from that required by the rest of the material presented within the theme.

By 1970, child-centred approaches to RE were provided with a common justification rooted in the nature of man. The contention of the Durham Report on Religious Education (*The Fourth R**, 1970) was that: 'Man is a creature who finds himself perplexed with the mystery of his existence . . . The great religions of the world find their frame of reference within these ultimate questions which man has asked and continues to ask . . . Young people share in the human condition. They should have some opportunity to learn that religion is a feature of this condition.'

Enabling children to reflect upon their experience, to explore questions of meaning for themselves, to develop an awareness of the human condition as exemplified in themselves and in others was recognized as a justifiable concern of RE as much as, or even more than, of other areas of the curriculum.

Schools Council Working Paper 36 (1971) asserted that, at the time of writing, RE was understood in one of three ways. The 'confessional' and 'phenomenological' approaches owed little to child-centred movements in education; whereas the third way, the 'personal quest for meaning', promoted the notion of the child as agent of his own learn-

ing, and of the subject matter (whether 'confessional' or 'phenomenological') as one focus of his enquiry. It was argued in *Working Paper 36* that RE 'should be both a dialogue with experience and a dialogue with living religions, so that the one can interpret and reinforce the other'. 'Confessional' and 'phenomenological' subject-matter was subsumed within a child-centred, enquiry-based, theory of education.

During the 1970s, a variety of approaches to RE emerged which were less obviously child-centred and aimed more at bridging the gap between the experience of the child and the major world religions*. Michael Grimmitt (1973) rejected the child-centred life-theme approach as confessional in aim and lacking an educationally acceptable basis. He offered a framework for RE based on existential theology, the phenomenological* study of religion, a context of social pluralism, and a view of education as to do with the total development of persons. The framework was held by him to be child-centred in that it was underpinned throughout by developmental psychology. Within Grimmitt's scheme, encounter with the dimensions of religion occurs concurrently with the pupil's exploration of depth themes (aimed at developing the individual's skill of reflecting at depth on his or her own experience) and of situation themes (concerned with the ability to see how a person's beliefs and values affect his behaviour and his way of life). Grimmitt argued that the dimensional and existential approaches must be related in practice in order to enable pupils to build conceptual bridges between their own experience and the central concepts of religions.

Jean Holm (1975) also saw religious education as contributing to the development of children as persons. The 'personal quest' approach adumbrated by *The Fourth R* is followed through here. Children may learn what it means to be fully human by reflecting upon their experience and by considering ultimate questions*, questions concerned with the meaning of life. The religions of the world offer interpretations of human existence and are thus also concerned with ultimate questions. Human experience themes are sequenced by Holm alongside explicit study of aspects of religion, and the use of the imagination* as well as the intellect is advocated as a tool for developing understanding.

The importance of equipping children to act as agents in their learning has been stressed in addition to the need to use their immediate and structured experiences. The role of the emotions and of the imagination have been emphasized as necessary adjuncts to the use of reason and of the intellect if understanding and empathy are to develop within RE. Bridging the gap between the developing child and the religious experience of mankind is now recognized to be a highly complex endeavour. The polarization of child-centred and subject-centred approaches is an inadequate description to deal with the stage in RE reached by the end of the 1970s. Raymond Holley (1978) took the child-centred approach further than most in arguing the task of the religious educator to be the provocation of spiritual insight into personal life, with the phenomena of religion as aids and guides only to the development of spirituality. It could be said that Holley has brought the child back to the centre in a somewhat different way from that of his contemporaries, most of whom attempted to relate the development and the experience of the child to religion, often by means of experiential themes.

The personal quest, as part of child-related rather than child-centred education, continues to appear in the majority of recent new or revised agreed syllabuses. The logic of starting from the child's experience and relating it to religion is integrated with developmentally sequenced objectives. In the syllabuses of, for example, Avon (1976), Hampshire (1978) and Hertfordshire (1981), we read sentences such as 'Religious Education fosters the personal search for meaning and purpose to life in the wider context of the religious traditions of mankind.'

Yet child-related, as child-centred, approaches are not without their critics and their problems. One problem that has been identified is that the role of RE in enabling the child to reflect upon his experience and discover meaning in it is often over-stressed. This is surely the task of the whole curriculum, as the latter is understood within the liberal tradition of education. Enabling the child to build bridges between his own experience and the religious experience of man is also fraught with difficulties. Questions arise as to the kind and quality of experiences which are apparently being set one against another, and the validity of the connections and even of the expectation of connections being made. John Hull (1980) has drawn attention also to the inadequacy of the view of religions as merely presenting answers to the ultimate questions arising from human experience. He argues that an 'enquiring model of religion' should be constructed and used with an 'enquiring mode of education' to provide a coherent rationale for RE. Exponents of child-related RE still have far to go in devising satisfactory structures on which practical classroom work may be based.

Child-related approaches to RE have grown out of child-centred approaches but have preserved those things which are important. Respect for children as persons in their own right, acknowledgment of the importance of their felt experience and of their attitudes, continue to form part of the context of development. The danger of limiting learning to existing interests or of ignoring the role of the teachers in facilitating learning is, it is hoped, past. Child-centred and subject-centred approaches are seen to be complementary, rather than in opposition, and the problems and possibilities of relating child to subject continue to be explored, both in RE and in the curriculum as a whole.

Ronald Goldman, *Religious Thinking from Childhood to Adolescence,* Routledge & Kegan Paul 1964 and *Readiness for Religion,* Routledge & Kegan Paul 1965; Michael Grimmitt, *What Can I do in RE?,* Mayhew-McCrimmon 1973; Raymond Holley, *Religious Education and Religious Understanding,* Routledge & Kegan Paul 1978; Jean Holm, *Teaching Religion in Schools,* Oxford University Press 1975; John Hull, 'Editorial', *British Journal of Religious Education,* Winter 1980; A. V. Kelly (ed.), *Curriculum Context,* Harper & Row 1980; Eric Lord and Charles Bailey (eds) *A Reader in Religious and Moral Education,* SCM Press 1973; Harold Loukes, *Teenage Religion,* SCM Press 1961 and *New Ground in Christian Education,* SCM Press 1965; Carol Mumford, *Young Children and Religion,* Edward Arnold 1982; Schools Council, *Working Paper 36: Religious Education in Secondary Schools,* Methuen Educational 1971.

GWEN PALMER

Childhood, Religious Development in

Not only have children had fewer life experiences than adults, but the research of psychologists such as Piaget and Bruner suggests that they have a more limited ability to form the concepts necessary for a meaningful interpretation of these experiences.

Piaget has suggested that there are clearly marked stages in the development of conceptual thought through which all children will pass, although not necessarily at the same rate. Goldman related his study of children's notions about religion or, more strictly speaking, of children's interpretation of the religious ideas contained within particular Bible stories, to the work of Piaget.

On starting school at the age of four or five years, the child is at what Piaget describes as the 'intuitive' stage. He sees the world piecemeal and depends entirely upon perceptual judgments: he may deduce that someone is older because he is taller. He makes relationships between things and events which are not valid: if a thunderstorm follows his misbehaviour he may think that he has caused it. His thinking is not reversible: he may know that children will grow into adults, but not that adults were once children. He is not always able to separate his feelings about a situation from the facts which surround it.

Goldman described this stage as that of 'pre-religious thought'. Ideas which can be interpreted in physical and human terms are viewed in this way and those which cannot are classed as 'magic'. A problem here is the child's inability to make a clear distinction between reality and fantasy. The appropriate criteria for distinguishing between the animate and the inanimate are also hazy.

New knowledge can only be assimilated as it relates satisfactorily with existing knowledge and the verbal explanation of an adult is often not sufficient to enable the child to build a conceptual 'bridge' between one idea and another. We can easily be misled by a young child's ability to make an appropriate verbal response. Religious ideas can only be explained by the child in the context of the relevant developmental stage in his thinking and further questioning will often reveal gross misunderstanding.

The young child will feel things long before he is able to understand them and through his feelings can undoubtably 'know' the joy of celebrating a religious festival, can sense the awe surrounding experiences of life and death and will wonder at the magnificence and the mystery of natural and man-made phenomena. The child can be helped to reflect upon his feelings and it will be appropriate to enrich and extend these through stories, which often provide a useful stimulus for sensitizing his imagination.

At about the age of seven or eight years, the child will begin to transfer to what Piaget has described as the stage of 'concrete operations'. By this stage the child can use both inductive and deductive reasoning successfully, but only in relation to concrete situations. He can now deal with more than one relationship at the same time. Gradually he begins to acquire concepts of conversation and, in grasping the concepts of time, speed and distance, stories and information relating to other times and places can now be better understood. He is increasing in awareness of his feelings and emotions, has the verbal facility to discuss them and is able to exert a greater control over them.

When the child at this stage relates the language which he hears with the situations or ideas which are described or explained, a lack of sophistication in differentiating between language uses will often cause confusion. The child will question the language of religion because he is interpreting imagery and metaphor in a literal way. Concrete thought restricts his moving beyond an anthropomorphic view of God*, and he will often see a conflict between religious ideas and the world of reality (as in 'God is everywhere'). Goldman describes this stage as that of 'sub-religious thought'.

Facts are gathered avidly by children of this age, who are continually excited by the discoveries which they are making about the world in which they live. They are constantly experimenting and testing their knowledge, but the tests most appropriate to the stage of concrete operational thinking are those of the empirical kind. Disillusionment occurs when these tests are applied inappropriately to check a religious interpretation of experience.

Children's interest can now be aroused in the buildings, customs and practices of religion in the community, and in hearing about the actions of people motivated by their faith. As the child is beginning to move away from a wholly egocentric standpoint, he is better able to enter into the thoughts and feelings of others and may be becoming aware of beliefs and value systems which are different from those held in his own home.

The stage at which Piaget suggested that a facility for thinking in symbolic and abstract terms becomes possible probably occurs at about the time when we might consider that a child passes from childhood to early adolescence (eleven to twelve years), although Goldman thought that, with religious concepts in mind, the concrete operational stage continued until about the age of thirteen to fourteen years. However, he accepted that the stage from eleven to thirteen years is a period of transition, when many children will be moving towards an ability to think in the abstract. An example of thinking about God at this stage would be 'A piece of sky or something, maybe a cloud with a face on it. God is the sky' (Grimmitt).

It has been acknowledged that the transition from concrete to abstract thinking is a crucial stage for religious education. This is not to underestimate the importance of religious development in childhood: 'If a child is to understand religion he must first reflect upon the nature of human existence – what it is to be a person, relationship with others and with the natural world' (*Discovering an Approach in Practice*). This would seem to be an eminently suitable exercise to be pursued throughout the years of childhood.

See also **Development, Theories of; Emotional Development**.

Ruth M. Beard, *An Outline of Piaget's Developmental Psychology,* Routledge & Kegan Paul 1969; Mollie Brearley *et al., Fundamentals in the First School,* Basil Blackwell 1969; Ronald Goldman, *Religious Thinking from Childhood to Adolescence,* Routledge & Kegan Paul 1964; Michael Grimmitt, *What Can I Do in RE?*, Mayhew-McCrimmon 1973; Schools Council Religious Education in Primary Schools, *Discovering an Approach in Practice: Conveying Meaning,* Macmillan 1977.

BARBARA MENZIES

China   *see* **Asia**

Christian Education and RE

Christian education needs, but includes more than, religious education. Christian doctrines/theologies of human nature traditionally emphasize human fallibility or sinfulness and conversely its potential for personal and corporate wholeness or redemption. Views of Christian education based on traditional theology affirm that education contributes to growth into wholeness. To this end a Christian education properly understood does not confine itself to the Christian religion. Religious education in a general sense is needed by and included within Christian education. Learning about religion and about faiths other than Christianity will be seen as part of the whole Christian process, as a contribution to understanding between people, to love of neighbour, and as making for critical openness. Similarly, educational disciplines other than RE fit into the Christian scheme of education as not different in kind or less 'religious'; for instance language contributing to communication and understanding between people, science making possible stewardship of the creation, crafts encouraging creativity, and other disciplines similarly, are all naturally part of a Christian education.

RE in general is concerned with the immensely important role of 'religion' in human affairs; it has to do both with the proper meaning of 'religion', itself a matter of fundamental debate, and with the teachings and practices of the various 'religions', including Christianity itself. A Christian education, on the other hand, includes 'religious education' as well as other disciplines affecting human life in society, seen *'sub specie aeternitatis'*, and in particular in the perspective of Christian faith in God. In practice most of Christian education may look little different from other education: but its roots, inner meaning, self-understanding and eschatology are its own. It grows out of and points to the Christian understanding of God as active creatively and redemptively in human history. It thus has rich content both spiritually and intellectually: the content is provided by the created order understood as *created* and by human activity. In a broad sense, it has political, social, even commercial reference, for instance geography may arouse concern for the disparate provision of resources; history may raise questions about the justice practised in human communities; and so on.

It follows that the Christian teacher is not confined to education in Christian faith or to religious education. As historian, or geographer, or teacher of literature, he has a responsibility for the 'truth' in his subject, making for as much comprehensive understanding as possible, and enabling learners to be as understanding as is possible. As in all relations of persons, the Christian teacher is in a pastoral relation to the learner. If the Christian teacher's subject is RE, the criteria indicated elsewhere fully apply.

Christian education may be expected from a school which is a church foundation, or which reflects a society's Christian tradition. Such a school's purpose is different from that of the church: and in the sense indicated here, most churches do not have, in any full way, programmes of Christian education. They do involve children and adults in a critical experiential process of what it means to be part of the Christian community, to practise Christianity and to express Christian belief in human affairs. In that a church does not teach across a wide, inclusive curriculum, it has a narrower function than a school. In its demands on persons and involvement in social, charitable and political activity, a church can be expected to be much more committed and involved than a school.

JOHN M. SUTCLIFFE/
PHILIP LEE-WOOLF

Christian Education Movement

In 1892 a group of Cambridge undergraduates arranged a holiday camp for sixty-seven schoolboys. This led two years later to the founding of the Universities Camps for Public Schools. Similar camps for girls followed and in 1898 the Federation of University Camps for Schoolgirls was launched after the Annual Conference for college students organized by the Student Christian Movement* of Great Britain and Ireland.

A Schools Department, incorporating the Universities Camps for Public Schools, was established in the Student Christian Movement (SCM) in 1923 in order to promote voluntary activity in schools, primarily through holiday parties, voluntary groups and Sunday meetings.

In 1931 former members and staff of the

SCM ran a conference for teachers which set up a Christian Education Group to see if teachers of Religious Knowledge would welcome an institute to help them in their work. Dr William Temple (later Archbishop of Canterbury) became the active and enthusiastic Chairman of this Group. About the same time, two other groups were formed with similar aims: the Association for Teachers of Religious Knowledge and the Committee for Co-operation between Educationalists at Home and Abroad. Four years later these three bodies combined to form the Institute of Christian Education (ICE). Dr Temple became the first President and the Institute rapidly became influential.

The Institute of Christian Education was a professional body with a large membership, including heads and teachers from every kind of school, HMIS, lecturers in universities and teacher training colleges, and clergymen and ministers concerned with education.

The next breakthrough, in 1943, was inspired by William Greer, General Secretary of the SCM, later Bishop of Manchester. Anticipating the passing of the Education Act of 1944, the Student Christian Movement in Schools (SCMS) was established as an independent organization, yet preserving strong links with the parent body. The SCMS took off and prospered under the vigorous leadership of the Anglican, Fred Welbourn, and the Baptist, Robert Walton. Heads were widely concerned to implement the opportunities offered by the new Act in the statutory obligations to conduct a daily assembly* and to promote religious education throughout their schools according to the new agreed syllabuses*. At this time, the Movement worked mainly in the rapidly expanding sixth-forms of grammar and public schools, offering a lively and intelligent account of the Christian faith and ethic, through day conferences in groups of schools, through residential conferences, through publications and a great network of school groups, which were serviced by members of school staff and the growing number of peripatetic regional secretaries of the SCMS.

In 1954 the University Women's Camps for Schoolgirls combined with SCMS to make a single instrument of Christian witness and service in schools and in 1955 a highly successful move was made, guided by the Rev.

Eric Lord, later a senior HMI, into the realm of younger school leavers, that is those who were leaving school at fifteen rather than entering the sixth form. The field of work widened dramatically and many secondary modern schools became associated with the Movement.

In 1946 the ICE created the Overseas Appointments Bureau (now part of Christians Abroad*), which has recruited thousands of teachers of many subjects to serve in schools and colleges abroad, mainly in Africa and the West Indies.

The ICE and the SCMS were merged in 1965 into the Christian Education Movement (CEM) at a ceremony in the Jerusalem Chamber of Westminster Abbey under the Presidency of Robert Stopford, Bishop of London, and with the backing of the British Council of Churches*.

At the same time, with the help of the Conference of British Missionary Societies and, later, Christian Aid, the CEM appointed an International Secretary and created an International Department, which has promoted informed concern about the Christian world mission, race relations, world religions, international affairs and teaching Christianity as a world religion. The department has sponsored many conferences and school visits. It has contributed to CEM's publications programme and advisory service to teachers.

The CEM like its predecessors, was run largely by, and for the sake of, its teacher members. During the 1960s, however, there was an increasing emphasis on 'professionalism' in the practice of RE and in 1967 the Teachers' Committee was created in the CEM. The potential for the growth of the work was seen to be immense and a Primary Department was established which soon affiliated thousands of primary and junior schools.

During the 1970s and 80s, the general work of CEM as described grew, serving teachers and pupils, and the very active professional association for RE teachers, the National Teachers Committee for Religous Education, was consolidated and took over the running of an Easter Vacation Course for teachers. In 1981 this committee was re-named the Professional Committee for Religious Education and in January 1984 it amalgamated with the Association for Religious Education* to form the Professional Council for Religious Educa-

tion*. A wide range of booklets, pictures and papers for teachers, parents and pupils was published.

Outstanding among the publications was the journal, *Religion in Education*, first published in 1934. In 1961 this became *Learning for Living* and then, in 1978, *The British Journal of Religious Education*. This journal has throughout provided a forum for the subtle changes and developments in the teaching of RE down the years.

The ICE's Research Committee sponsored research or development projects; see for instance H. Loukes, *Teenage Religion*. This tradition has been continued by CEM, through its Research Committee. Most recently there have been published reports on 'Religious and Moral Education in Inner City Schools' and 'Religious Education in Special Schools'.

In 1980, in co-operation with the Diocese of Manchester, the Centre for the Study of Religion and Education in the Inner City was established in the Church of the Sacred Trinity, Salford. This resource centre open for children, teachers and university and college students also provides a base for the CEM's projects in Greater Manchester, and houses the notable Student Christian Movement Library. In 1981 the British and Foreign School Society* established a link with CEM; plans were made to continue some of the work of the BFSS through CEM. In 1983 CEM Video was established.

In 1983 over 2,500 Secondary Schools, over 3,500 Primary Schools and all colleges of Education, Polytechnic and University Departments concerned with RE received the CEM's termly mailing. The work of the CEM that year was carried on by twelve full-time and forty part-time members of staff.

JOHN TRILLO

Christian Schools

What has become known as 'The Christian School Movement' originated in the USA, as a reaction to the 'secularizing' of the public schools in that country, which happened because, 'the influence of the church and religion gradually diminished and the civic authorities assumed support and control . . . religion was no longer the centre of the curriculum; in fact it was eliminated altogether or reduced to a minor place in the course . . . with the aims and the curriculum predominantly nonreligious'. For many committed Christians, this position was unacceptable and as early as the turn of the century independent schools* were beginning to be established.

A new, specifically Christian philosophy of education has been formulated in contradistinction to that now generally held stressing the importance of Christian revelation as the very foundation of education; so that whatever is part of the school's curriculum, whether history, science, literature, or anything else, it must be presented within the context of that revelation. Berkhof has succinctly put it like this: 'Education . . . may not be merely physical and intellectual with a smaller ingredient of surface morality added to it. It should be very decidedly religious and the religion should be . . . the religion that is taught in and required by the Word of God.'

In Great Britain during the past ten years or so, a similar disenchantment with state education has produced the same results. Christian teachers and parents, feeling that LEA schools are too humanistic and many of the voluntary aided schools arguably little better, have become vocal and active to provide a suitable, profoundly Christian alternative. So, independently of each other, various groups have set about establishing their own Christian schools. There are, broadly speaking, three classifications. 1. Private schools have been established, either by one person, or by a board of trustees. These would appear to be in the minority. 2. There is quite a powerful move at present to establish schools as an integral part of local churches. This movement is very well organized, predominately in the United States, but increasingly in the whole of the free world. The philosophy behind this type of programme envisages the education of children within the Christian world as parallel to that of the Hebrew system, and as a part of the church's supportive ministry to the home, providing adequate spiritual, moral, academic, and skill instruction for its children. 3. There is a considerable body of opinion that believes that as the scriptures lay the responsibility for education squarely at the parents' door, it is necessary for Christian parents themselves to work towards establishing their own educational programme. Thus what could be termed 'co-operatives' are being set up in in various parts of the country, in which parents from one or several churches form governing bodies and establish their own private schools.

From the increasing interest that is being shown in Christian education, it is apparent that the Christian School Movement could be a major sociological factor during the next decade or so, and, far from being a very small minority, the evidence suggests it could well have repercussions throughout the educational world.

L. Berkhof, *The Christian School, The First Line Trench*, National Union of Christian Schools, Chicago 1938; Donald E. Boles, *The Bible Religion and the Public Schools*, Iowa State University Press 1961.

MICHAEL B. SMITH

Christian Theological Critiques and RE

The word 'theology' can mean 'The science treating of God, his nature and attributes and his relations to man and the universe' (*Pocket Oxford Dictionary*). It can also refer to a specific school or system of theology. Thus a theological critique might easily be seen as an application of this 'science' or one of its schools or systems to the evaluation of the theory and practice of RE in schools. This would probably represent the usual understanding of the title of this article. However it is not the sole approach, nor is it necessarily the most useful. Many modern theologians set out to transcend the gap between theory and practice, between reflection and action. If this line of thinking is followed, the professional educator involved in producing or modifying syllabuses will be seen as *doing* theology just as certainly as the professional theologian who evaluates and criticizes his work. It follows, therefore, that any such critical evaluation is not to be regarded as the judgment of theology upon the non-theological enterprise of the religious educator. Instead it should be seen as the evaluation of one theological perspective from the standpoint of another.

There are two possible objections to this approach. One is that the professional theologian writes from outside the school situation and needs to take into account only the criteria of divine revelation whereas the producer of syllabuses has to consider various educational, social, administrative and even economic factors. The seond objection is that although producers and teachers of RE syllabuses are often Christians they are not all required to be. Thus if Christian religious educators are doing theology what is it their non-Christian colleagues are doing?

To the first objection it can be countered that the professional theologian too is limited by the relativities of time and place. He has a particular class outlook and personal psychology. To the second objection it can be maintained that many human activities can be undertaken either with a theological understanding or without one. Dialogue between those engaged in such activities can only be dubbed *theological* when the parties to the dialogue have a shared belief in God* which informs their discussion. Obviously believers in God include Hindus, Jews, Muslims and others and it may be possible to elaborate an inter-faith theology of RE. Such a venture will be methodologically extremely difficult however and it is probably easier to divide the enterprise between Christian theological dialogue on the one hand and educational or philosophical dialogue on the other.

Church school RE. The theology of church school RE usually stresses the links between catechesis and sacrament. Although virtually all pupils in church schools in Britain have been baptized in infancy, first Holy Communion, Confirmation and (in Catholic schools) First Confession are important milestones in RE which, together with regular participation in the life of the church help to structure the syllabus for church school RE. The church school is seen as at once the extension of the Christian family and of the Christian liturgical community seeking to deepen the faith that is assumed to exist in the home and making better appreciated and understood the faith which is celebrated in the church.

A negative evaluation of such a theology usually, though not always, turns into an attack upon separate church schools. It is argued that Christian denominational schools exhibit a defensive perspective which proceeds from an inadequate theology of mission. Valuable resources, both financial and human, are diverted to maintaining the influence of the church over its members rather than upon service to the world. The fact that large numbers of the pupils do not come from genuinely Christian homes illus-

trates still more strongly the weakness of the traditional position.

Many defenders of church schools would respond to these criticisms by an attempt to reform the content of RE in the church schools, seeing such schools as extensions of the Christian family which prepares members of a diaspora church for an active apostolic involvement in the world. However, some of those who have attempted this ambitious and exciting work have come instead to advocate a concentration upon voluntary *adult* Christian RE.

County school RE. In the non-denominational state schools RE has passed through two distinct phases. The first phase began with the 1944 Education Act which produced local authority 'agreed syllabuses' concentrating upon Scripture Knowledge as the content of county school RE. The second phase, which began in the sixties, shifted the emphasis to thematic teaching and problem-centred discussion lessons. Under the influence of the *Schools Council** this emphasis was gradually broadened to take in the teaching of World Religions* as part of the subjective study of religion as a global phenomenon. More recently there has been an emphasis upon the dimensions of religious experience* and pupils have been encouraged to identify in their imagination with adherents of the different faiths. In other quarters there has also been a conservative movement to re-instate 'Christian' teaching (presumably the old 'Scripture Knowledge' approach).

It can be argued that each of these phases and movements in RE can be examined for its theological rationale and criticized from the point of view of other theological positions. The post 1944 Scripture Knowledge style of agreed syllabuses had an underlying theology which saw Christianity as essential for 'good citizenship' and moral development, and the Bible as a non-controversial positive influence. Doctrinal and other disputed questions were invariably avoided in favour of consensus Protestant Christianity. Theological critiques of this position drew attention to the way in which it reduced the gospel to a national ideology. As the ecumenical movement matured, theologians also questioned whether doctrinal differences should not be openly and fairly discussed in the RE lesson rather than simply ignored. Churchmen of all kinds also objected to the way in which the Bible was studied in isolation from the community of believers – an objection which gained strength from the increasing evidence that many children without church affiliation were becoming completely alienated from the study of the Bible and were proving unable to remember even the most basic information.

The shift to thematic teaching in the late sixties involved the theological perception that the outsider could only be asked to examine the claims of Christianity in the context of an exploration of values, meanings, and problems in life – that the gospel dimension could be introduced as one possible perspective which many people held and found centrally important for living.

The sociological fact of enlarged immigrant communities led to a widening of this approach to take in the perspective of other faiths. The *theological* justification for such a development could have been provided by the new and positive developments in the Christian theology of world religions. Some Christian critics have attributed the development to either pan-religious indifferentism or to post-Christian agnosticism. However the 'phenomenological approach'*, with its claim to treat religions impartially as objects of academic study, blocks out such accusations and leaves them unproved. Religions are studied *because they are there* and because people believe in them. Applied consistently the phenomenological approach is non-theological; compatible with all theological approaches and none. It has been attacked by many of those who favour direct Christian instruction and has been diluted by its original proponents in favour of an orientation towards religious experiences.

Those who support the movement back to Christian RE often have a strongly traditional theological model of catechesis. Very often this model can tend to be authoritarian, politically conservative, have an inadequate theology of world religions and sometimes fail to assimilate any of the new theological insights on the rights of individual consciences or of religious freedom.

The other current trends towards the experimental dimension could be seen as based on any of a number of theologies of religious experience*. These theologies begin to overcome the problem of treating religion as though it could be understood at a purely cerebral level but they often conceal an uncriticized and unspecified assumption about the unity of all religious belief and experience. Too frequently questions of relative truth claims are subordinated to an idealist conception of the needs of community relations and international understanding. The RE teacher easily falls into the role of an evangelist for some 'religious dimension' and those Christians who sympathize with secular theology or religionless Christianity will clearly baulk at such a role.

A balanced *Christian* theology of world religions will have to do justice both to the centrality of Christ and to the reality of God's self-disclosure in other faiths. However a practical theology of RE will also need to take on board new theological insights about (for example) childhood*, commitment*, sexuality, secularism*, atheism and personal and political freedom. Only in this way can syllabuses and text-books begin to address themselves to 'the nature of God', his attributes and his relations to men and the universe.

R. Jackson, *Approaching World Religions*, John Murray 1982; Joseph Andreas Jungman, *Handing on the Faith*, Burns & Oates 1955; Gabriel Moran, *Theology of Revelation* and *God Still Speaks*, Burns & Oates 1967; Kevin Nichols, *Orientating: Six Essays in Theology and Education*, St Paul, Slough 1977; D. J. O'Leary and T. Sallnow, *Love and Meaning in Religious Education (An Incarnational Approach to Teaching Christianity)*, Oxford University Press 1982.

DUNCAN M. MACPHERSON

Christian Year, The

As part of the experience of all children in the West, understanding of the Christian year's structure is an educational necessity. Ways in which Christian festivals* interpret basic human experience may be examined, e.g. the return of light and hope (Christmas), suffering and new life (Easter), the need for help and power (Whitsun). Study of the total pattern of the Christian year gives an overall view of the content of the Christian religion and underlines the human need for a basic pattern of recurring events to celebrate.

Educational difficulties arise from the fact

that both Christmas and Easter fall in school holidays so that school activities will take place in the penitential preparation period. The significance of events such as the Ascension and the celebration of saints days will need special attention in school if they are to be covered since they are not widely observed in all churches. In using the Christian year for teaching, full use should be made of the various associated symbols, e.g. the colour of robes and hangings, the crib, the Easter garden and regional customs such as Whit walks in the north-west of England.

Ways in which other religions reflect the underlying human needs expressed in the Christian year constitute an important linked area of study.

R. Brandling, *Christmas in the Primary School,* Ward Lock Educational 1970; J. Harrowven, *Origins of Festivals and Feasts,* Kaye and Ward 1980; F. Nesham and H. Kilminster, *The Christian Year Cookbook,* Mowbray 1980; *Together for Festivals – a resource anthology,* CIO 1975.

PAUL TURTON

Christianity: Place of RE in Britain

An educational rationale for the study of religion in county schools cannot be based on the theological presuppositions of any one of the faiths to be studied because these presuppositions constitute part of the content that is studied. The educational principles underlying the teaching of Christianity must, therefore, be the same as those underlying the teaching of any other religion. As in relation to other faiths, the teacher's concern in teaching Christianity is to introduce pupils to the variety of forms in which central Christian beliefs receive expression in the world today – through liturgy and worship, through art*, literature*, music* and architecture, through personal, family and community life – and then to explore with them the authority which Christians find for their beliefs in their scriptures and in the continuing experience of the Christian church.

This emphasis on exploring contemporary expressions of the Christian faith prior to any detailed or systematic study of its origins and scriptures represents a new departure for many RE teachers who, like the agreed syllabuses* of the past, have tended to equate the study of the Bible with studying Christianity. But the Bible's significance and authority as the word of God arises from the experience of the Christian community, where the study and use of the Bible is inexorably linked with worshipping and preaching, participating in the sacraments, witnessing to and caring for others, etc. Any study which removes the Bible from this context and seeks to treat it in isolation either divests it of its religious and faith-promoting significance by treating it as literature or history, or treats pupils as Christian catachumens cut off from the faith-sustaining, corporate life and witness of the church.

In terms of timetable time and curriculum content, there are cultural, historical and educational reasons why the study of Christianity should be treated generously: 1. Despite the complexities of a multi-cultural, pluralist and increasingly secular (though not secularist) society, there are clear indications that Christian presuppositions and values continue to exert a dominant influence on the British way of life. An understanding of the relationship and interaction of Christianity and Western culture is, therefore, an essential part of a young person's education at a time when cultural diversity presents an increasingly important and challenging opportunity. 2. Allowing for regional differences, it is still more likely for a young person in Britain to come into direct contact with forms of Christian expression, albeit architecture and literature, than of any other religion. It is appropriate that the close proximity and familiarity of Christian traditions should be fully used in RE as a mean of encouraging a deeper understanding of at least one religion. 3. Because liberal educational ideals have arisen from the complex interaction of Christianity and Western culture, there is a marked compatibility between the critical and rational spirit of Christianity and that encouraged by a contemporary view of education. The scholarly study of Christian theology and philosophy can thus be of considerable intellectual and personal value to older pupils, irrespective of their own religious stance. 4. Although RE neither seeks to promote faith nor deter it, cultural factors make the likelihood of conversion to a faith outside the immediate cultural history of a pupil's family very remote indeed. But given that more pupils in British schools come from homes which at some time have had links with the Christian faith, it is appropriate that such pupils should be presented, if indirectly, with an option of faith which is realistic. For most, that option is Christianity.

J. Frost, 'Learning about Christianity', *New Movements in Religious Education,* ed. N. Smart and D. Horder, Temple Smith 1975; M. H. Grimmitt and G. T. Read, 'Teaching Christianity in RE', *World Religions: A Handbook for Teachers,* ed. W. Owen Cole, CRE 1976; N. Smart, *The Phenomenon of Christianity,* Collins 1979.

MICHAEL GRIMMITT

Christianity: Teaching as a World Religion

If Christianity is presented only in the cultural form familiar to the teacher, its integrity as a major world religion is denied. It is not necessary to adopt unusual syllabus elements in order to achieve the wider dimension; it would normally be sufficient to extend references and resources by consciously determining not to imply that 'our' direct limited experience of Christianity is the norm. The point may conveniently be made by considering four common syllabus elements.

1. *The Spread of Christianity.* Although the New Testament refers to a Southern development through the Ethiopian eunuch (Acts 8.26ff.) and the family of Simon of Cyrene (Mark 15.21; Rom. 16.13), its Euro-centric nature may result in an emphasis on only the Western expansion of early Christianity. There is no biblical reference to Mark's links with Alexandria (AD 42–68), which are so important in the self-awareness of many African church leaders, or to the early appearance of the Coptic and Ethiopian Orthodox Church.

Legends related to the Eastward journeys of Thomas introduce the growth of the Syrian Orthodox (Nestorian) churches within a generation of the resurrection. Christian presence in the area of modern Pakistan (evidenced by the Taxila Cross from Sarkap, pre AD 100) and in Sri Lanka by AD 560 makes an interesting comparison with the journeys of Columba to Iona. The meeting of the Syrian Orthodox mission and Duke Fang Xuanling (representing Emperor Tai Zong) at Changan in AD 630–635 is recorded on the Xi'an Monument. Christianity reached European Russia via Armenia and the Crimea by AD 988. For the 'missionary age' (about mid-eighteenth to early twentieth centuries), the cultural conditioning of missionaries should be noted in considering their achievements. If 'mission' is to be brought up to date, contributions of Asian and African Christians to a theology of mission may be interesting for some classes, but the present activities of missionaries from all six continents to all six continents is likely to be a more popular resource, as well as indicating the scope of mission today.

2. *The Bible.* In looking for the meaning to the writer and to the Christian reader, illustrations culled from beyond Europe can do more than just match the rural environment of the text. They can help the discovery that Christian criteria challenge any culture more than they legitimate it. While the 'Western' church may mythologize Jesus' references to 'the poor' and 'justice/judgment' as spiritual metaphors, many Christians elsewhere read these passages as declaring God to be on the side of the poor and oppressed.

Experiences of the church working among the poor (in relief and in prevention/correction) become key resources in a study of, for example, the prophets. The righteous anger of Amos against those who evicted widows from their homes and peasants from their land, and the cost to Hosea of reconciliation, can be paralleled in many modern situations.

In these and many other parts of the Bible, the vision of the wider church enables the pupil to experience the Bible as a source of religious authority for everyday life.

3. *Life Issues.* Within a World Religions syllabus, Jewish or Muslim, etc., attitudes to many issues can clearly be seen as different from the mores of society. The same should be true of Christian judgments and priorities, though this is difficult if it has been suggested that pupils live in a 'Christian country'. The introduction of other avowedly Christian views makes for a more robust classroom discussion and a greater understanding of religious feeling.

Bonhoeffer's changing attitude to violence can be compared with the varied policies adopted by Christians in societies where the prime violence is state oppression and the tensions between reconciliation and liberation and where counter violence is a consciously adopted policy of action. The assumption that Christian marriage 'is the union for life of one man and one woman to the exclusion of all others' is illuminated when pupils know that in some cultures Christians try to establish a true marriage before they have a wedding. The relationships and responsibilities on which Christian marriage depends might be clarified by discussing the baptism of a polygamist if that means he must divorce one or more wives in a society where a divorced wife is an outcast.

Attitudes to stewardship, economy and sharing can be illustrated by reference to material relevant to Development Education*. This might include discussion of a Doctrine of Man through a comparison of the attitudes of Jesus with some images used in fund raising.

4. *Church Structure and Activity*. A typical Western view of the church would be dominated by familiar denominations. Description of patterns of participation and of seats of power should guard against giving inappropriate predominance to the northern nations and churches. Globally, although the confessional families should be noted, the number and variety of United Churches throughout the nations is significant, especially when the reasons for union are considered.

Common Western assumptions about the structure and order of congregations are not universally applicable. Despite important differences between countries, the strength of Christian Base Communities (cbcs) shows that they are not a passing phenomenon but a major factor in the development of 'church'.

Arising in many ways from the cbcs, there is a growing challenge to the assumption that theology is what is read, studied and taught by those who attain certain intellectual status. The 'informal theologies' to which pupils could relate include Theologies of Liberation (Latin America), Minjung Theology (Korea), and Black Theologies (Africa and usa).

The worship, hymnody and witness of Christians is also important and some hymnbooks in English include translations of hymns (to original or Western tunes). This makes the material more accessible than the more traditional creeds.

HARRY UNDY

Christianity: Theology and Education

Whereas in the past attempts have been made to produce a Christian theology of education, particularly in the work of Nels F. H. Ferré and Paul Tillich, the concern here is with the special contribution of theology to Christian education and religious education.

A primary theological insight is that education in the Christian sense involves a particular content. Christianity claims to be a historical religion with a revelation divinely given. This revelation is closely bound up with the scriptures, which provide a content to be known and understood. This basic content is extended historically to include creeds and catechism as summaries and guides to scriptural and doctrinal understanding. In the past (and perhaps reviving), the acquiring of such a content was associated with rote-learning and the hidden assumption that the more 'content' acquired, the more 'Christian' the learner would become. With the decline of rote-learning as a method and other pressures, this intellectual emphasis on necessary knowledge to be acquired tended to weaken and almost to disappear. Yet Catholic and Protestant theologians alike still emphasize the need for something to be learned. So Gabriel Moran speaks of the need for 'detailed knowledge', and T. F. Torrance argues that 'only with Christian information can a child learn to think in a Christian way, and to learn Christian truth'. For such theologians, the dominical word 'go teach' must still be heard by the Christian educator.

Christian theology, however, has more to offer than insistence on the necessity for knowledge. Horace Bushnell speaks of 'the Lord's way of education, having aims appropriate to him'. Such an aim must be 'mature manhood, measured by nothing less than the full stature of Christ' (Eph. 4.13 NEB). This requires what Montessori calls 'supernatural growth' and such growth comes about only through 'nurture' or 'formation', the preferred theological words for 'education'. Two theologians have made special contributions here. Horace Bushnell claims the baptized child is a full member in Christ's family, receiving all the benefits of Christ for his spiritual nourishment and growth in grace through his Christian family. Aquinas, with development also in view, looks upon the crisis situations of life as challenge or threat to growth and the church sacraments as affording the special supply needed for effective growth. Basically, the role of the Christian community as the divinely appointed agency and context is stressed as absolutely essential for Christian education. Such insight is specially valuable in the present time in relation to such questions as the best age for confirmation, the admission of baptized children to communion, which have theological and educational reference, as well as the larger question of what constitutes a Christian community for the purpose of nurture. The whole approach emphasizes that 'learning about Christ' must happen in~a human situation where he is present. For such an incarnational approach is 'God's pedagogy'.

But Christian theology offers a further contribution. Kierkegaard has noted how even those who have shared in these educational advantages can remain detached, 'admirers' rather than 'followers' of Christ. Christian theology recognizes that there is a life to be lived as well as a lesson to be learned or a status to be enjoyed. This especially Christian quality of life cannot come about without identifying with Christ and becoming a 'disciple' in the full sense of personal attachment and following which is implied in the way that word is used in the New Testament. Liberation theology has reinforced this teaching and given it a new urgency. What has not yet emerged is the kind of educational practice which would help to deepen discipleship by affording opportunities to experience a Christian style of life and training in ethical decision making. The revived interest of theology in Christian ethics demands an equal educational response. The early church attempted this with its converts and apparently achieved a measure of success in relating confession to conduct, and some modern attempts at Bible study and action groups are developing techniques for training in discipleship.

A further service which theology can render to Christian education is to show the limitations which must apply to all its schemes and practices. There cannot be an infallible scheme of Christian education which will inevitably increase the faith of the faithful and produce no renegades to unbelief and selfishness. Wesley*, curiously enough, recognized this in his own way by declaring that baptismal grace was so worsted by original sin that evangelism and not education had to take the strain. Most theologians would not, however, be so pessimistic as Wesley but wish to make the point that only God himself, as he begins the educational process in revelation, can complete it. So Augustine can speak of 'the interior teacher', Christ himself, and Kraemer really makes the same point when he describes success in teaching as a miracle, something which cannot be achieved without divine help. Yet theologians have never sought to set divine illumination over against human efforts at nurture and formation, and Calvin*, for one, stresses the human element as necessary. The theologian, then, is reminding the teacher that he labours with God, who alone can bring his works to good effect – a lesson well grasped by Augustine, theologian and teacher, speaking of one apt to learn; 'we should rather say much on his behalf to God, than say much to him about God'. Such thinking keeps alive a dimension often forgotten by the Christian educator.

These are some of the insights which theologians can provide for the task of Christian education as a church activity. How these insights apply to the school will, at least in part, depend upon how Christian theologians regard the school. For most theologians in the Catholic tradition, the school would ideally be an extension and agency of the church with a Christian religious education content and worship and sacramental observances such as childrens' masses entirely appropriate. Reformed theologians, historically, tended to make the state responsible for education but expected the godly magistrate to make the school a school of faith, and some still stand in this ambivalent position. But although both Emil Brunner and Paul Tillich have sought to grapple with this problem and highlight the difficulties, Christian theology on the whole has not yet come to grips with what religious education should, or can be, in the community schools of a mixed and growingly secular society.

J. A. Jungmann, *The Good News Yesterday and Today*, W. H. Sadlier 1962; P. Tillich, *Theology of Culture*, Oxford University Press 1969; T. F. Torrance, *Handing on the Faith*,

James Clarke 1959; R. Ulich, *A History of Religious Education,* University of London Press 1968.

JOHN GRAY

Christians Abroad

Its present form was established in January 1973 in order to 'encourage and assist Christians to respond to needs and opportunities to advance the Christian religion through work and witness abroad . . . and to recruit Christians for work which satisfies such needs or affords such opportunities and to prepare them for their lives and work abroad'.

Supported by a large number of mission bodies connected with the British Council of Churches*, Christian Aid and the Catholic Fund for Overseas Development, it provides an extensive information service about opportunities for work, particularly of a skilled kind, outside Britain, and makes teaching appointments as requested in a number of countries particularly in the less industrialized world.

It is built upon the pioneering operations of the Overseas Appointments Bureau, originally a department of the Institute of Christian Education, which, from beginnings soon after the Second World War, recruited teachers for schools, mostly in Africa and mostly having original connections with churches and missionary societies. Later this work was conducted parallel with Catholic Overseas Appointments, to be merged eventually into the creation of Christians Abroad. In recent years, it has also arranged introductions to overseas churches and help in preparation for Christians going abroad through industry and other secular channels. Christians Abroad is a notable instrument of lay service for British Christians interested in working outside Britain.

See also **Christian Education Movement**.

D. G. TEMPLE

Church Education

Early this century, Sunday School attendance was high but buildings, quality of teaching and equipment rarely matched the opportunity. George Hamilton Archibald observed that they were more a mission to the poorer children than a nurturing medium in which children were led to become members of the church family. He advocated a child-centred* approach, division into age-groups, effective training of leaders and systematic courses.

In the early 1940s, identifying a gap between Sunday School and church, H. A. Hamilton inspired Congregational churches to see that as children grow naturally in the home, so they have a natural place in the household of faith. Many Congregational churches, and others, moved their children's work to Sunday morning and began with a period of family worship, though this was sometimes only a change of method rather than of attitude.

The churches were greatly affected by the ferment of thought in the 1960s. The *Honest to God* debate affected the content of religious education, as did the educational research of Ronald Goldman. Christian educators found themselves obliged to take the emotional and psychological development of children more seriously, and to recognize that by presenting adult concepts to children much of their work had been counter-productive. Harold Loukes, who had tested the effectiveness of RE in schools and argued for a problem-based syllabus derived from the young people's own experience, was paralleled by Douglas Hubery, who, in the 'experiential approach'*, urged church educators to begin with the experience of children. Both endorsed M. V. C. Jeffrey's contention that religious truth is normal experience understood at full depth. The British Council of Churches report 'The Child in the Church' (1976) drew out the contrast between the OT where children are 'the Israel to be', and the NT conviction that 'the reign of God is already exercised among children and the childlike'.

Others have helped churches to see the nature of their life as a community. A consultation at Glion, Switzerland (1973), recognized that 'the church was seen to be an adult organization by its members and that it tolerated children rather than gave them rightful place within the church family'. John Sutcliffe, commentator on the consultation, has re-affirmed that Christian education involves asking crucial questions about the very nature of the community of faith, and has gone on to widen the task of the Christian educator to that of creating a new future for persons and society.

Although the work of individuals is formative in church education, the influence of weekly educational programmes cannot be over-estimated. *Christian Education Handbooks* pioneered by H. A. Hamilton, material produced by Westhill College, Birmingham, *Partners in Learning* and *Alive in God's World*, have all played important parts in the radical changes this century has seen.

The Child in the Church, British Council of Churches 1976; H. A. Hamilton, *The Family Church*, REP 1941; John M. Sutcliffe, *Learning Community*, Denholm House Press 1974 and *Learning and Teaching Together*, Chester House Press 1980.

DONALD HILTON

Church of England: Policy in Education

1. *Schools and Colleges*. Since before the Norman Conquest, the church in England has been engaged in the field of education and until the seventeenth century almost all schools in England were run by the church. The control may have become less direct, but the connection no less strong, by the formation of the SPCK in 1698, of the (Free Church) British and Foreign School Society* in 1808 and of the National Society* in 1811. Limited partnership with the state began in 1833 with the first government grant to aided schools.

The 1870 Education Act established local school boards with board schools sufficient for all children to receive elementary education. All church schools received grant aid, and thus direct partnership between church and state in this field began and provided the foundation of the dual system which came into being with the 1902 Education Act. County schools and voluntary (or non-provided) schools became part of one educational system, maintained by the newly-formed Local Education Authorities*.

Special provision was made by the Cowper-Temple Clause* in the 1870 Act, which has been reaffirmed in subsequent education acts, that in voluntary schools* RE could be given according to the principles of the providing body (Church of England, Roman Catholic, Jewish, etc.), but that in other schools there should be religious instruction of a kind which is 'not distinctive of any particular denomination'.

The dual system applied at first only to the elementary sector, but the 1936 Education Act extended the partnership to the secondary sector and enabled LEAS to contribute towards the provision of voluntary senior schools. The 1944 Education Act took this provision a large step forward by requiring secondary education for all children. The church (and the providing bodies) could not afford to adapt or enlarge all its senior schools to meet the new needs and an arrangement came into being which strengthened the partnership between church and state in this field. Two categories of voluntary schools* were defined – voluntary aided schools, grant-aid being given by the central government, and voluntary controlled schools which were entirely paid for by the LEA but in which the original providing body retained a number of rights. In aided schools, religious instruction could be given according to the principles of the providing body; in controlled schools it was to be given according to an agreed syllabus*, but with special provision for parents to ask for denominational instruction. Equally, parents of children in county schools were given the right to withdraw their children from religious instruction and from the act of worship which begins each school day.

From the first, the ultimate purpose of the church's involvement in schools was an expression of its concern for society. Without losing this aim, the domestic concern, that of training church children in church schools staffed by church teachers, became more prominent. The National Society includes this in its foundation document and in 1812 founded a central training school for teachers. Some dioceses founded their own diocesan training schools shortly after. Many of the present church colleges of education* were founded as teacher training colleges in the 1840s.

Since the 1870 Education Act and the subsequent establishment of the dual system, the role of the church in its schools has changed back to that of taking its share in educating the youth of this country in a Christian context. The role of the colleges changed similarly to equip teachers with a Christian understanding of education for the schools of the country as a whole. In the mid 1970s, when there was reorganization of all colleges of education (as they had become), there was an understanding between the church and the Department of Education and Science* that as approximately one sixth of all teachers were being trained at that time in church colleges of education, that proportion should continue to apply as some colleges closed or merged with others. At the same time, there was a change of role in all colleges through the introduction of diversification. Most colleges now offer degree courses, and not only leading to a BEd; and most, if not all, cater for in-service training* in RE for teachers who qualified in some other subject. In this way, the church is taking its share in higher education as a whole. In addition, the religious needs of children and the ways of meeting those needs form part of the basic professional course in all colleges.

2. *Confirmation Training*. The *Book of Common Prayer* presumes that every child baptized will, in due course, be presented to the bishop for confirmation, having first learnt the basic fundamentals of the Christian faith as expressed in the Catechism. The proportion of baptized persons who are not subsequently confirmed has increased greatly in the last century. One of the reasons is that today the initiative is expected to come from the child or his parents; in 1662 the initiative was expected to come from the incumbent of the much more static parish.

Confirmation* today has two main aspects. There is the acceptance by the child of his baptized status and preparation for admission to Holy Communion; there is also an act of commitment to the Christian way of life. There is no single Church of England policy in this. Clergy who emphasize the first aspect tend to favour candidates of a younger age and the instruction is weighted on the side of the privilege of church membership and understanding of the sacraments. Clergy who emphasize the act of commitment tend to favour confirmation at a later age and the training is more general and weighted on the side of the responsibility of Christian discipleship.

The Ely Commission set up by the Church Assembly recommended that admission to communion should not depend on confirmation, but that there should be two events to express the two sides of what is now one composite act. They recommended formal admission to communion at a younger age (about nine years old) and a commitment to discipleship with confirmation in late teenage or early adulthood. The General Synod was divided on this issue and the recommendation was defeated by a small majority in February 1974.

However, a number of changes in practice in recent years indicate the way the church is moving in this matter. Confirmation services are held more frequently in most dioceses; small parochial confirmations are normal and services for large groups of parishes are scarce. In many dioceses there are some confirmation services for adult candidates only, where the distinction between mature professions of faith and a growing-up ceremony is further stressed. Parochial services are often held in the setting of a parish communion, making the event less individual and more corporate. The candidate's incorporation into the communicant fellowship of the church is made more real and the impact of the confirmation of some on the fellowship of the rest is made more clear.

In a small but growing number of parishes, lay people (Bible class or club leaders) are involved in the training of the candidates; also in a growing number of parishes meetings (rather than classes) are held with the parents. The practice of having confirmation sponsors obtains occasionally. In all these ways the corporate rather than the individual nature of confirmation is brought out.

The revised forms of the confirmation service do not speak of renewing baptismal vows but of giving one's whole self to Christ, penitence for the sinful past and turning to Christ and renouncing evil for the present and future. These promises are the same as the revised baptismal promises but the link is nowhere stated – the whole emphasis is that of asking for the strength of the Holy Spirit to live the Christian life in the fellowship of the church.

In consequence, training before confirmation is far wider than an exposition of the Catechism, and booklets for candidates cover a much wider field than most communion manuals. With no deliberately stated policy, the Church of England is developing a practice which is half-way between the Roman Catholic system of early confirmation with admission to first communion before that and the Free Church profession of faith leading to full adult membership of the congregation.

3. *In-Church Education*. Since the founding

of the Sunday School Movement* in 1780 by Robert Raikes in Gloucester, Sunday Schools for children have been a normal part of English parish life. A recent survey revealed that eighty-five per cent of all parishes in England have a Sunday School and that about half a million children are involved. More than half of all Sunday Schools meet at the same time as a church service and in many cases the children and teachers come into church for parts of the service. There is, therefore, a definite trend towards the integration of the Sunday School with adult church life and worship, away from the previous custom of the Sunday School being almost a separate institution. There is no common pattern in the syllabus or lesson courses used in Sunday Schools; about one third uses courses produced by the Board of Education, one third uses courses produced by societies such as the Scripture Union and others, and one third makes up its own courses. In the majority of parishes there is a 'family service' at least once a month, often combined with a parade of Scouts and Guides, etc.

In contrast with the widespread existence of Sunday Schools, there is a clear dropping off at secondary level and the Young People's Bible Class is almost a thing of the past. This is partly explained by the trend towards earlier confirmation in parishes where the main, or only, Sunday morning service is a Parish Communion. The proportion of those confirmed who are regular communicants even three years later is small. Thus, though instruction in a separate grouping has given way to nurture within the church fellowship, there is still a long way to go. There is a growing concern to involve parents and friends in the task of the Christian nurture of the children. In parts of the Episcopal Church in the USA, a parent wanting his child to attend Sunday School (Church School) is expected to take his turn at teaching or helping from time to time.

Training for Sunday School teachers is an established practice, but often takes the form of a preparation class to explain next week's lesson rather than training the teacher to teach. Since the publication of *The Child in the Church* (1976) there has been a growing concern, not least among Diocesan Advisers* for Voluntary Religious Education, for parent education. Changes in the pattern of family

life, the increase in family mobility, the desire of young people for active adventure rather than passive instruction, are gradually being taken into account.

Since the publication of Dr Goldman's work, there has been a growing readiness in voluntary religious education to adopt a child-centred, rather than a content-centred, approach. This is evident in material such as 'Alive in God's World', produced by the Wadderton Group. This Group came into being in 1965 under the auspices of the (then) Children's Council, but now has an independent existence and seeks to produce material for adults as well as children. The Group is concerned to help adults with methods of teaching and to understand the way a child learns, and the teaching material is produced accordingly.

Adult Education in the church has developed similarly over the same period. Until the mid 1960s, there were occasional evening-classes, diocesan lecture courses and various parochial study-groups. Since then, group methods, with a strong dependence on the Parish Life Conference approach as used in the Episcopal Church in the USA, have been made available through the Board of Education and in a different way through Clinical Theology Groups. In-service training for clergy has become almost a standard part of diocesan life, and the courses held at St George's House, Windsor, for senior clergy set a pattern which is being reflected at diocesan level. In all these, the understanding of the role of the Christian in contemporary society takes precedence over a detailed knowledge of the facts of the Christian faith.

ROBERT MARTINEAU

Church of Jesus Christ of Latter-day Saints, The ('Mormons')

Since its foundation in 1830, The Church of Jesus Christ of Latter-day Saints has developed and promoted both secular and religious education in those places where the church is established. Joseph Smith, the prophet and founder of the church, stated in 1843 that 'Whatever principle of intelligence we attain unto in this life, it will rise with us in the resurrection' (*Doctrine and Covenants*). The education or development of an individual to his/her full potential is an important aspect of religious life for all 'Mormons' and the church therefore seeks to promote this.

In practice, this has led to the development of the Brigham Young University, Utah, which provides a wide range of academic and non-academic subjects for both members and non-members. There are numerous other schools and colleges, particularly in South America where a literacy programme also has been established.

Religious education is supported by the church in that it helps broaden the minds of children to different aspects of life, particularly where the parents might fail to teach their own children, and ideally it should be more than a simple discussion of ethics, or moral standards. The church has developed its own religious education courses to cater for areas where 'Mormon' religious education is not available in schools and these are now available to members worldwide.

The church has also a course developed specially for enquirers to inform them about the church and to prepare them for membership. Taught by trained missionaries, the course comprises approximately eight one-hour sessions, given privately within the home, which cover the basic doctrines, history and background of the church. Presentations may also be given to non-member groups such as school classes, clubs etc. All of these presentations are without charge and available through a local mission.

Within the church, there is an extensive programme for all members in which they may learn a variety of skills and subjects:

1. *Sunday School.* Like most churches, the Church of Jesus Christ of Latter-day Saints provides a Sunday School in a local meeting house. From the age of twelve, all members of the church are enrolled in a Sunday School class to learn about doctrinal topics. The classes are systematic, i.e. they follow an annual prescribed course which is followed by the church worldwide from January to December. Such a course may be a book of scripture, church history, or lives of prophets and apostles, all adapted to the particular age group. In addition to this, there is a class for 'investigators' or new members not yet fully conversant with church teachings; this is specifically designed to more fully acquaint them with the 'Mormon' church.

2. *Relief Society.* Also presented weekly within the meeting house is a course of lessons designed for the women of the church over the age of eighteen. As with Sunday School, there is a prescribed course in which four different subjects are covered each month, i.e. a doctrinal lesson ('Spiritual Living'), a guide to helping mothers teach children ('Mother Education'), a guide to helping with social problems ('Social Relations'), and finally an art and cultural lesson ('Cultural Refinement'). Also, once monthly, a midweek practical lesson is also given ('Homemaking').

3. *Young Women.* Girls aged from twelve to eighteen attend a series of lessons designed to help them socially, and to enable them to see how their religion relates to them.

4. *Priesthood Classes.* Since the church has no paid clergy, all male members aged twelve and over, of good standing within the church, are ordained and play a part in the ministry. A study guide is provided each year for personal gospel study, supplemented by a weekly priesthood lesson, at which instruction, counsel and advice on the performance of various church ordinances is given.

5. *Primary.* Children from three to eleven attend a weekly two-hour combined singing and learning session with specifically designed church-related courses.

All the above mentioned are regular Sunday activities, taught and organized by lay teachers, who are supervised and have the opportunity for once-monthly training to assist them.

The course of study which was developed by the church for those of school or college age to help balance the lack of religious education, is also available in the UK with the aim of balancing school education with Latter-day Saints' teachings. It may be divided into two sections: 'Seminary', for fourteen to eighteen year olds, and 'institute', for students aged eighteen to twenty-six. Seminary and institute are organized on a home-study basis, with weekly attendance at a class, except in some areas where classes are taught on a daily basis. Locally these classes may be taught also by lay teachers, but the programme is supervised by professional teachers, since this is essentially a course at school or college level. Both courses are involved with an in-depth study of scripture, and how the prophets and their teachings relate to individuals today. Each course lasts one year and approximately coincides with the academic year. Unlike other courses within the church, specific goals are made for achievement and attendance which may result in 'graduation'.

As a summary, it may be said that the church provides its involved educational programme on all levels to assist each individual member of the church to be better equipped for a more balanced and fulfilling life.

Doctrine and Covenants, The Church of Jesus Christ of Latter-day Saints, Salt Lake City, Utah.

DAVID COOK

Church Schools   _see_ **Voluntary Schools**

Church of Scotland   _see_ **Presbyterian Church, Church of Scotland**.

Civil Religion

Civil religion (or, sometimes, civic religion, but the two could usefully be distinguished) is an old concept, as well as an ancient reality. But it has enjoyed a new prominence, especially in the United States*, since 1967, when R. N. Bellah borrowed the term from Rousseau*. Bellah's description of what he meant is worthy of consideration because of its proven utility for thought about society. This includes its possibilities for the study of religion and its potential, albeit hardly exploited as yet, for religious education.

Bellah said that 'this religion – or perhaps better, this religious dimension – has its own seriousness and integrity and requires the same care in understanding that any other religion does'. This 'national faith' was neither Christianity, on the one hand, nor merely 'the American Way of Life', on the other. Indeed, it was 'rather clearly differentiated from the churches'. But if they were somewhat hostile to it, this was partly because of the influence it had upon them (cf., in the UK, folk religion*).

According to Bellah, civil religion is seen in such solemn public occasions as presidential inaugurations, when it is expressed in the inaugural address. Analysis of these and other expressions showed that its God was majestic and unitarian, moral and universal, to the extent of being not only benevolent but also active. It was specifically national, in seeing the winning of Independence as its Exodus, Washington as its Moses, and Lincoln its saving martyr, etc. But 'precisely because of this specificity, the civil religion was saved from empty formalism and served as a genuine vehicle of natural religious self-understanding'.

The concept of civil religion is an application, in Bellah's case to the national, societal level, of Weber's comment that every group has its own religion. But it cannot be assumed in advance that this is always mere nationalism, or some other form of self-idolization. Bellah has shown that historically, for instance in the USA, it has contained a strong sense of vocation, and hence an eschatological sense of judgment, including the possibility of an apocalyptic condemnation. British readers can detect parallels in their recent history, to which it is difficult to do justice, except in this way.

The study can be seen, then, as a way of 'discerning the spirits', and 'naming the gods'. It could be applied, for instance, to the different political parties and, on the larger scale, to international agencies such as the UNO or UNESCO. The recent awareness of a 'hidden curriculum'* in educational institutions shows a similar concern, but the low-key analogy discourages a full phenomenological exploration of the moral fervour or ontological assumptions that may be implicit in it.

Edward Bailey 'The Implicit Religion of Contemporary Society: an orientation and plea for its study', _Religion: Journal of Religion and Religions_, XIII, 69–83, Academic Press 1983; R. N. Bellah, _The Broken Covenant: American Civil Religion in Time of Trial_, Seabury Press 1975 and 'Civil Religion in America', _Daedalus,_ Journal of the American Academy of Arts and Sciences, XCVI (1), Winter 1967; R. N. Bellah & P. E. Hammond (eds.), _Varieties of Civil Religion,_ Harper & Row 1980; Philip E. Hammond, 'The Sociology of American Civil Religion: a bibliographical essay', _Sociological Analysis_ 1965, 37, 2.

EDWARD BAILEY

Classics and RE

Though the roots of Christianity are mainly Hebraic, it was born and grew within the context of Graeco-Roman civilization and its political structures. The early church drew on the concepts and imagery of contemporary classical culture to explain its faith: the language of the NT, including the gospels as we have them, is Greek; Latin became for centuries the medium of the Christian scriptures in Western Europe. A knowledge of classical civilization and its languages must surely therefore enlarge our understanding of Christianity.

The religious experience of Greece and Rome, drawing on different ethnic and cultural sources, covers an enormous and complex spectrum. It includes the anthropomorphic antics of the Olympian pantheon, the formal rituals and festivals of the state cults (including that of the Roman emperor, with which many Christians found themselves in painful conflict), the 'mysteries' of Eleusis, Orpheus, Dionysus and Mithras, the revelries of Bacchanalia and Saturnalia, as well as the spiritualized and mystical conceptions of Plato, Aristotle, the Stoics, Epicureans and later philosophers. Like us, the Greeks and Romans sought meaning and consolation in a perplexing and hostile world and their problems are ours: suffering, injustice, mortality, the nature of divinity and our relations with him (or her). Though rooted in different traditions, many of their concepts and practices are familiar to us: the soul and its salvation, sin, repentance, sacrifice, incarnation, resurrection, revelation, prophecy, prayer, conversion.

The study of this manifold experience illuminates understanding by similarity and contrast. It emphasizes the universality of religion as a human phenomenon arising within a common human predicament and sharing with Christianity and other religions a common range of concepts, expressions and ethical ideals. Yet there are differences – and correctives: the classical religions have no basis in the Hebrew scriptures; many are closer to nature and to primitive human emotions than we are, and less inhibited by moral prudery; in some their deity is dominantly or exclusively female. They disturb complacency and pose

questions, of which not the least is, 'What is different about Jesus?'

J. Ferguson, *The Religions of the Roman Empire*, Thames and Hudson 1970; W. K. C. Guthrie, *The Greeks and their Gods*, Methuen 1950; R. M. Ogilvie, *The Romans and their Gods in the Age of Augustus*, Chatto and Windus 1969; H. J. Rose, *Ancient Greek Religion*, Hutchinson 1946 and *Ancient Roman Religion*, Hutchinson 1948.

F. W. GARFORTH

Clergy/Ministers: Role of in RE in England and Wales

So long as most educated men belonged to the clergy and most education was in some sense religious there could hardly be a specific clerical role in RE. From the fourteenth century, with the establishment of English as a written language, an educated laity broke the clerical monopoly; but it was not until the efflorescence of secular academic disciplines in the eighteenth century that RE began to be contrasted with education in general. The clergy responded by insisting that religion provided the only adequate basis for general education. That was an assumption common to the Charity School movement in the seventeenth century, the Sunday School Movement* in the eighteenth, the promotion of voluntary schools* in the Victorian era, and the expansion of the so-called public schools since the time of Dr Thomas Arnold (1795–1842). The same was true of the Welsh circulating-school movement inspired by the evangelical Rector of Llanddowror, the Rev. Griffith Jones (1683–1761). But the secularization of European thought which has dethroned theology, the 'queen of the sciences', has also promoted the rise of religious studies as a non-confessional discipline. The clergy, being professionally committed to induction into the faith and practice of the church, have faced a choice, or chosen to alternate, between the phenomenological approach* to RE and some form of neo-confessional* teaching. The rationale of the latter has been more fully explored by clergy in the USA, where RE is forbidden in the public schools.

Except in the case of church related voluntary schools, the clergy has no right of entry into schools and no automatic relationship with schools. Many serve as school governors;

a few develop a pastoral ministry to a particular school's staff and pupils. Many ministers and clergy have developed a specialist interest in RE and contribute to its teaching in development in Higher Education and through the LEA Advisory Service and Her Majesty's Inspectorate.

John Macleish, *Evangelical Religion and Popular Education,* Methuen 1969; David Newsome, *Godliness and Good Learning,* Murray 1961; Anthony Russell, *The Clerical Profession,* SPCK 1980; John Westerhof, *Will Our Children Have Faith?,* Seabury 1978.

GRAHAM NEVILLE

Clergy/Ministers: Role of in RE and Right of Entry in Northern Ireland

The present place of RE in schools in Northern Ireland was laid down by the Education Act (Northern Ireland) 1947, the provisions of which were continued in the Education and Libraries (Northern Ireland) Order 1972. This legislation allows clergy 'reasonable access at convenient times' to schools, for two different purposes; to give religious teaching to children of their own denomination which may be distinctive of that denomination, and also to inspect the religious teaching given by the teachers. Since clergy are not professionally qualified to inspect specialist RE teachers on probation and Department of Education inspectors are prohibited from inspecting this subject, such teachers are assessed by the principal of the school.

In practice, today relatively few clergy of the Church of Ireland, Methodist Church and Presbyterian Church make use of the right of entry to give denominational teaching in controlled schools. Until recently the inspection of RE was carried out by groups of local Protestant clergy who visited a school on the same day. This form of inspection has in places lapsed or been replaced by more informal visits by clergy over a period of time. Despite some changes, clerical inspection has come under criticism and an alternative policy has been suggested (Greer and Brown 1981). Each diocese of the Roman Catholic Church has appointed one or more priests as specialist inspectors who have total responsibility for the inspection of RE in church schools. Since 1975, these clergy have been renamed Diocesan Advisers, reflecting their changing role in the schools.

A number of clergy in Northern Ireland have come to occupy other influential roles by virtue of their professional involvement in RE. Protestant clergy have lectured in Stranmillis College and the New University of Ulster and have been appointed as Area Board Advisers in Religious Education. Roman Catholic clergy have lectured in St Mary's and St Joseph's Colleges of Education and in the New University. A number of clergy have become full-time specialist teachers of RE in secondary schools.

J. E. Greer and W. Brown, 'The Inspection of Religious Education in Northern Ireland Schools', *The Northern Teacher*, 13, 4, 1981.

JOHN E. GREER

Clergy/Ministers: Role of in RE and Right of Entry in Scotland

The schools of Scotland fall into two general categories: the former voluntary and church schools which transferred to state control in 1872, subsequently known as 'public schools', and the denominational, almost entirely Roman Catholic schools, which transferred under the Education (Scotland) Act of 1918 but retained church rights of appointment and religious instruction.

A minister has no statutory right to enter a public school. He is there only by invitation of the head teacher and the formal approval of the education authority. As chaplain he is welcome to meet staff and pupils, to conduct regular worship, to attend school occasions, to be kept informed of personal or particular needs where he may supply pastoral aid at the request of the head teacher.

In practice, the chaplain or team of chaplains conducts regular school assembly and occasional church services in the local church particularly to celebrate a festival of the Christian year, such as Easter and Christmas or to mark the beginning or end of term. In the primary school the usual practice is worship in the classroom. In all cases the minister's task is devotional rather than instructional, though in some cases he may undertake classes in RE in the upper school at the request of the head teacher. In Roman Catholic schools the appointment of the chaplain is made directly by the church and he is regularly in the school to participate in assemblies and to conduct classroom Mass.

DONALD M. MCFARLAN

Cognitive Education in RE

The 'cognitive' is one of the three domains of learning classically described by Bloom in his taxonomy of educational objectives; the other domains being the affective and the psycho-motor. It includes 'those objectives which deal with the recall or recognition of knowledge, and the development of intellectual abilities and skills'. As well as knowledge, this domain therefore includes such skills as comprehension, translation, interpretation, extrapolation, application and evaluation.

The type of knowledge involved will be dependent upon the aims of the subject. For example, at the time when RE was largely 'confessional' in aim, it followed that the knowledge involved was mainly that of the life of Christ and of the doctrines of Christianity. When that aim was current, the affective domain was dominant because of the change in attitude involved in coming to a particular form of commitment. With contemporary understandings of RE, the scope of the cognitive domain is necessarily wide-ranging. In general terms, the knowledge and skills involved may be seen as those which enable the learner to become 'religiate' (Gates). The phenomenological approach* is frequently employed as a means of identifying the areas of knowledge concerned. This is based on Smart's analysis of the six dimensions of religion: the ritual (the activities of a religion, and the artefacts and symbols associated with them), the mythological (the traditional stories told within a religion), the doctrinal (beliefs and their formulations), the social, the ethical, and the experiential (the believer's own religious experience or sense of the 'other'). Whilst the use of the phenomenological approach is not without its difficulties, it is a method which is relatively free of presuppositions made within any particular community of faith.

The cognitive is not confined to the acquisition of factual knowledge of religion and religions: it includes a range of skills* necessary for the understanding and evaluation of this knowledge. Among these are the recognition of symbols and symbolic forms, as well as of the variety of types of language and modes of expression employed in religion. The ability to identify religious issues as religious is another skill which the pupil may be expected to demonstrate. Ultimately, the understanding involves 'understanding (as from the point of view of an adherent) of the concepts, feelings and actions of the tradition(s) being studied, and their integration within the characteristic life-style of an adherent' (*Groundplan*). Evaluation of the truth claims, value-systems and internal coherence of a religion also comes within the cognitive domain. This evaluation will be both from the pupil's own point of view and from the point of view of established disciplines of investigation. Evaluation from the latter stance will necessarily involve a further element of knowledge, knowledge of the discipline concerned.

B. S. Bloom, *Taxonomy of Educational Objectives*, Vol. 1, Longmans Green 1956; Brian Gates, 'Religious Education: a proper humanism', *London Educational Review*, II(3), 1973; R. Holley, *Religious Education and Religious Understanding*, Routledge & Kegan Paul, 1978; Schools Council, *A Groundplan for the Study of Religion*, 1977; Scottish Central Committee on Religious Education, *Curricular Guidelines for Religious Education*, CCC 1981; N. Smart, *The Religious Experience of Mankind*, Fontana 1971.

CAROL FRY

Colleges of Education and RE

The title 'Colleges of Education' marked the transformation, in the 1960s, of teacher training colleges, which were mostly founded by Christian bodies to staff, first voluntary and then also county schools, until LEAS also undertook teacher training (especially after 1945). The intended development of an all-graduate teaching profession, combined with the imminent fall in the school population, led in the 1970s to three further major changes: the closure of many institutions or their amalgamation with other colleges (or polytechnics); a reduction in colleges providing 'monotechnic' training (to avoid the continued isolation of teacher education); and the replacement of the Certificate in Education by BEd courses, validated by the local university or the Council for National Academic Awards. In these re-organized and diversified colleges, Religious Studies, where it continues to be provided, may comprise two aspects – the study of religion and the pedagogy of Religious Education. In some BEd courses the two aspects are inter-related; in others (especially in colleges which provide for both BEd and BA courses) the study of religion may be undertaken in the same classes by students following different degree courses, whereas the methodology of RE is taken separately by BEd students. Other BEd courses may replace the traditional study of at least one subject (e.g. English or RS) for its own sake at the student's level, by more general syllabuses reflecting the needs of the school curriculum. Because colleges of education have provided training particularly for the first and/or middle years of schooling, they should also offer non-specialist training in the statutory provision of RE, but such curriculum courses vary in depth, in breadth and in the obligation to attend, especially at colleges not providing teachers for denominational schools. Some colleges also provide postgraduate courses in RE for primary and/or secondary schooling, and occasionally the opportunity to specialize in RE at either main or subsidiary level.

See also **Teachers**.

HOWARD MARRATT

Colleges of Education: Church Colleges in the United Kingdom

The first English colleges were foundations of the 1840s and by 1847 all but one of the twenty colleges were Anglican. State institutions only emerged after the Cross Commission's Report of 1890 and there were then forty-three colleges, all of them voluntary institutions and the great majority still Anglican. In addition were several Roman Catholic colleges, one Methodist, one Congregational and a few others run by non-religious bodies.

Between 1890 and 1945 both the Anglicans and the Catholics gradually expanded the numbers in their colleges and it was only after 1945 that the churches' substantial responsibility for teacher training was seriously challenged when the development of new colleges was restricted to the LEA sector. However, during the expansionist 1960s church institutions were able to grow again and between 1963 and 1970 the Anglican teacher training places doubled to 18,000 and the Catholic

went up from 4,500 to 11,000, which, with the addition of one Free Church and two Methodist colleges, gave the churches a twenty-eight per cent involvement in the total teacher training system.

Despite recent contractions, both the Catholics and the Anglicans retain enough diversified colleges of higher education to give them a formal stake in England's future educational system. Despite their three small colleges, the Free Churches have always favoured a strong involvement with LEA colleges, particularly within their RE departments.

In Wales, one of the two Anglican colleges survived the recent cuts, while in Scotland the two Roman Catholic colleges have now been merged into one. In both provinces the Free Church influence is strong in the state training institutions. In Northern Ireland, a denominational system of schooling led to a segregated training pattern with two explicitly Roman Catholic colleges and one implicit Protestant college.

The relationship between the teaching of religion and the church colleges has been crucial. The state college model of 1890 explictly excluded RI from the curriculum and there were unsuccessful attempts in 1908 to turn RI in church colleges into a voluntary option. By making RI mandatory, the 1944 Act gave the church colleges a major boost, as strong departments of divinity had always been one of their distinctive features.

The secularization processes of the 1960s, followed by reorganization, contraction and diversification pressures in the 1970s combined to leave question-marks over the colleges' religious rationales. Increasingly they pointed to their RE work as being distinctive and so they were anxious to develop good academic and professional RE courses. Many of them also run RE centres and major in-service training courses and curriculum development schemes. Recently, resources from the closed church colleges have been used to help RE.

Historically the church colleges were the main source both of teachers and of ideas in RE. The post-war development of neo-confessional approaches has undoubtedly reduced the prominence of the church colleges and even raised suspicions about their real intentions. Nevertheless at the national level and in the popular mind the link between RE and the churches remains close and so the church colleges will continue to play a significant role in the subject's future development.

H. C. Dent, *The Training of Teachers in England and Wales 1800–1975*, Hodder and Stoughton 1977; J. D. Gay, *The Christian Campus? The Role of the English Churches in Higher Education,* Culham College Institute, Abingdon 1979; P. S. Gedge, 'The Church of England Colleges of Education since 1944', *Journal of Educational Administration and History*, 1981; J. Lynch, *The Reform of Teacher Education in the United Kingdom,* Society for Research into Higher Education 1979.

JOHN GAY

Commitment

The relationship between the teacher's own commitment and his professional task is particularly acute in the field of RE. Except in church schools where, at the choice of parents, the teacher may be involved in transmitting to their children the whole ethos of the Christian faith, the task of RE no longer reflects the conditioning once associated with Divinity or Religious Instruction. Whilst indoctrination* in its best sense may be a part of all education, the teacher who is concerned to practise respect for others, as well as to encourage true wholeness – and not merely to transmit truths and facts – will be sensitive to the fact that teaching becomes conditioning rather than education when the teacher 'intends' his pupils to be committed to certain beliefs, regardless of the evidence or of the development of rationality or autonomy. Such intention is more effective than even the selection of biased contents or methods.

RE teachers in county primary and secondary schools must, like all teachers, be committed to the importance of their subject, but in the classroom must ensure that their commitment to a particular faith avoids any evangelism. Whilst some educationalists identify procedural with personal neutrality* in the classroom, research shows that the teachers most effective as educators and most respected by pupils are those whose commitment is neither concealed nor obtrusive but who treat with respect a variety of religious

beliefs and standpoints. The nature of a teacher's commitment (whether religious, ideological or political) is usually affected by the object of that commitment and its procedural ethos (e.g. some absolutist religions deny the possibility of open educational dialogue on even second-order matters). Moreover there may be certain matters (e.g. the morality of murder or lying) on which any educator cannot be neutral, and other aspects of religion in which the non-adherent cannot fully appreciate the faith or practice of another religion, and which cannot be brought empirically into the classroom of a state school. Nevertheless, through empathy and the use of the affective domain and through visitors or visits, it is possible to meet the requirements of truth and to provide a sensitive and understanding education, and so to maintain one's own commitments and show pupils the importance of commitment.

The Fourth R, SPCK 1970; I. A. Snook, *Concepts of Indoctrination,* Routledge & Kegan Paul 1972.

HOWARD MARRATT

Common Religion

One of a cluster of expressions used to refer to similar realities and which began to gain wider use in the 1970s, it is unusual in having been defined with some care. According to its main progenitor, Robert Towler, it is composed of 'those beliefs and practices of an overtly religious nature which are not under the domination of a prevailing religious institution'. Its parts are the remaining elements of a folk religion*, which has been driven underground by the official adoption of a universal religion, and survives as an unofficial religion among the common people. However, it 'need not necessarily be' 'found in contradistinction to official religion'. In India, for instance, it is to be found in popular Hinduism. In sixteenth- and seventeenth-century Europe, it appeared in the 'remarkable outbreak of accusations of witchcraft'.

So, although official religion itself is often hostile to common religion, the two are not usually seen as incompatible. Indeed, each 'system' can supply something lacking in the other and individuals may operate publicly in both traditions. So, to 'provide an adequate gauge of total religiousness' in any society, each of them requires attention.

Towler says his 'common religion' stands midway between official religion and the 'natural religion' which Luckmann described when he spoke of 'the anthropological condition of religion'. This was seen in the intersubjective process of establishing symbols and so was an inevitable part of being human. In contemporary societies it took the form, not of ecclesiastical religion, but of an 'invisible religion'.

Towler said his 'common religion' shared with this, the natural religion of contemporary societies, a highly thematic character. But, in contrast to Luckmann's 'modern religious themes', such as 'individual "autonomy"', self-expression, self-realization, the mobility ethos, sexuality and familism', 'common religion' attempts to meet life's perennial insecurities, such as health, marriage, procreation and death. It does so by concentrating on predictions and charms.

The concept of common religion is, therefore, similar to that of folk religion, which was used in ecclesiastical circles in the 1970s. On the other hand, it differs from civil religion* in being social rather than corporate in character; of the common people rather than common to the whole people. It has a similar potential for the study of religion, and not least for RE, to that of 'folk religion' and 'civil religion'.

Edward Bailey, 'The Implicit Religion of Contemporary Society: an orientation and plea for its study', *Religion: Journal of Religion and Religions*, XIII, 69–83, Academic Press 1983; Thomas Luckmann, *The Invisible Religion: the problem of religion in modern society*, Collier-Macmillan 1967; Robert Towler, *Homo Religiosus: Sociological Problems in the Study of Religion*, Constable 1974.

EDWARD BAILEY

Community Relations, Contribution of RE to

Community Relations is a shorthand expression for the way different groups of people within a given locality deal with each other. The centripetal forces which bring such groups into existence include the arts, sport, race and religion. If 'religious education has two main aspects: the development of the pupils' own religious interpretation of life; and the growth of their understanding of other people's religious life and throught' (*Journeys into Religion*), this suggests two contributions RE can make to the development of good community relations. 1. It can help the pupil to understand himself, his own identity and significance in relation to his family, his peers, his ethnic group and society, whether or not he comes from a religious family. It is here that the arguments of Edward Hulmes, against the teacher pretending to a neutral role and instead that he should subject his own commitment to critical scrutiny, are so important. Pupils can be helped to handle their own convictions about contentious issues with those who differ from themselves, by seeing how the teacher handles his own views. 2. RE can promote understanding of those central ideas and values of the different groups which make up the community. Not that mutual understanding and respect flow automatically from the raising of religious issues. The teacher needs sensitivity to avoid 'treading on other men's dreams' and care in dealing with pupils' attitudes. A direct approach intended to change prejudice, for example, can be counter productive. Attitudes are influenced indirectly by the way the teachers and the school function together and interact with the local community. At the same time, prejudice often stems from ignorance and RE provides information which can help to reduce popular misconceptions and encourage the acceptance of religious differences as normal, while also indicating those values which different religions have in common. A third contribution of RE can be helping all pupils to understand the roots of a culture and society within which the community is allowed to be plural in the fundamental beliefs of its members.

W. Owen Cole (ed.), *Religion in the Multi-Faith School*, Hulton 1983; Brian Gates (ed.), *Afro-Caribbean Religions*, Ward Lock Education 1980; Edward Hulmes, *Commitment and Neutrality in Religious Education*, Geoffrey Chapman 1979; Robert Jeffcoate, *Positive Image*, Chameleon Books 1979; Schools Council, *Journeys into Religion,* Teacher's Handbook A, Granada Publishing 1977.

ARTHUR ROWE

Communities in Education, Religious

Religious communities in general are christocentric; they are dedicated primarily to the following and imitation of Christ. From this springs necessarily a desire to share in the teaching mission of Christ. Expressed first of all in the training of their own novices it gradually tended to include others. In monasteries from the earliest times the teaching of *oblati*, who were offered by their parents to be trained as monks, figures in the work of the community and this work is referred to by St Benedict in his Rule. During the Middle Ages it became common for monasteries to accept also lay candidates (*the externi*) for similar training. Apart from teaching in literacy and the humanities religious teaching was integral to their curriculum.

It was not until the sixteenth century that an extensive development of this enterprise took place. The Jesuits were the leaders with their Colleges, and as time went on they were imitated by other religious orders for both men and women and this movement also inspired the extension and development of monastic schools for the laity. The aim was to train the young in the humanities (and later in science also), while at the same time providing a religious education which was seen as central to the whole undertaking. This religious education took its inspiration from the dedication and rule of life of the religious communities themselves. The religious were often, as in the case of the Brothers of Christian schools (founded in the early eighteenth century) and many other congregations of men and women religious, committed to the Christian education of the poor. The work they undertook was pioneering work in uncharted regions but, as other secular initiatives in education developed during the nineteenth and twentieth centuries, they learnt quickly to integrate their efforts with secular demands. The fundamental religious aims remained unchanged and took their inspiration from the communities' life of dedication to the following of Christ. There was some tension between the two aims. The spirituality of a religious community could not be applied without some mutation to lay life. There was some recognition of the difficulty and the spirituality of, for instance, St Francis de Sales exercised a helpful influence. For many, however, who passed through these schools the ideal of Christian lay spirituality was still thought of as being that modelled on that of religious communities of men and women.

In all this Vatican II proved to be a watershed. It did not so much initiate change as recognize the significance of changes which had already taken place. The Council's clear recognition that lay spirituality and understanding of Christianity had a validity of its own in parallel and not subordination to the spirituality of dedicated religious was crucial. In some minds the question arose whether religious communities as such had much to contribute to the complex tasks of education for Christians in the contemporary world. Might not even explicitly religious education be better committed to believing lay men and women? Certainly the limited number of religious communities could no longer hold the central position which they still held in the nineteenth and early twentieth centuries. It became common for men and women religious to go out from their communities to work in schools which were no longer under the control or direct influence of religious orders. Where religious communities still ran schools their increasing reliance on lay teachers diluted the communities' influence.

On the other hand the development of retreat centres and catechetical centres opened new ways in which monastic and other communities could influence and contribute to the religious education of both young and adults. It is in such centres, as much as in those schools which still remain in the control of religious communities, that the relationship between lay spirituality and that of dedicated religious is being worked out.

The influence and contribution of religious communities is still significant but often in quite new ways. In an age of aggressive secularism the dedicated religious community preserves an archetype of the following of Christ which, though not the only one, retains its traditional significance. It provides an inspiration and a point of reference for Christian laity trying to work out a commitment and spirituality appropriate to lay life. The significance of this is the greater as the idea of community in the following of Christ receives even greater emphasis in developments of parish life and the whole theology of the church. It is arguable that this sort of influence will in the future prove to be more effective in adult life. However, where it has been preserved and developed in tune with the times, it still has a very significant influence in schools. The ethos of a school run by a religious community is distinctive. Where good understanding and co-operation with lay teachers has been established such schools have a great deal to offer in the development of religious education. Their aim is to present the sort of understanding of Christianity and practice of spirituality which is appropriate to lay life. This calls for the highest standards in religious studies and an understanding and flexible approach which has moved a long way from the older pattern in which the pupils were given only a modified version of the spirituality and practice of the community itself. Whether in schools or in the various enterprises of adult religious education the source of a religious community's contribution remains fundamentally the same, namely their own dedication in community to the following of Christ.

PATRICK BARRY OSB

Community Service

Service by pupils to individuals and groups within the school's local community has been a major development from the 1960s onwards. From the youngest child in the first school to sixth-formers, there is a well-documented literature on the theory and, particularly, the practice of every variety of community service by young people, each according to his or her age and skill. Food parcels for the needy at Christmas; concerts for senior citizens' lunches; outings for the handicapped; home-helping; tree-planting; wheel-chair surveys; fetching and carrying to local shops and the public library: these are typical evidences of community service.

Community service is full of transaction skills and maturing challenges. The 'Learning for Life' tradition of education has made good use of it and it has blossomed best where there has been a close link with the in-school curriculum skills such as those of the engineering and general workshop, music-making and social history.

Historically, the motivation has been largely Christian and, in the main, connection has been with RE in one guise or other. Much of the underlying theory, however, has been 'educational' rather than 'religious', though it is implicitly highly theological. The educational concerns have been with the need for greater social awareness among children, not only in co-tutoring and working with each other (seniors helping juniors with reading, for instance), but in taking them outside to gather first-hand evidence from the environment and generally increase their range of perceptions of people and environments. The experience has often been highly therapeutic (for the teacher, as well). It has proved its worth for pupils of widely differing backgrounds and temperaments. Often the withdrawn, the aggressive and the reluctant return to school with a determination to communicate as never before – in conversation and on paper.

Many an RE teacher makes a simple and direct connection between the challenge of community service and Christian social witness. To some of them (Christian) religious education is community service. Not too many young people, particularly the more emancipated, would see it that way, though they might accept the example of Christ, the servant, the man for others, a humanist good-worker rather than a redemptive Christ.

The theological dimensions are various, though not necessarily much to do with the local church. Indeed there is often a strong element of 'anti-Church' and anti-adult in general about community service, in that most young people hope to triumph where they feel grown-ups in the churches, the voluntary organizations and usually, more particularly, the statutory services ('the government') have failed. On the other hand, alert and forward-looking local churches have been quick to help promote community service as part of their concern to redeem the social idealism of the young.

The promptings 'to serve' may be of compassion or of indignation – sometimes a moral injunction. The tasks often seem too demanding, particularly in terms of emotional challenge. Winning through is the reward: so are new insights into human deprivation and suffering. The acceptance of gratitude and affection from the person being served may be a new experience and so are the many ways in which the young person discovers new dimensions and qualities in himself.

This learning is perceived as experiential rather than didactic. It is 'more real' and 'more challenging' than normal school. It is based on active involvement rather than passive learning. Horizons of a better and more just and caring society emerge, suggesting the most exacting and, potentially, beneficial outcomes of a process that education can initiate.

Western education, both in the West and where it has been imported, has been based on a derivative and emasculated intellectualism. Learning is by delimited subjects fed through an examination system up to the age of twenty-one at least, for the academically bright. Community service has only reached the timetable for the less bright. The academic high-flier has to find time in areas of the school timetable away from main examination subjects or in 'free' time.

The world cannot wait for the young intellectual to volunteer at his leisure and the most exciting developments in the community service principle are in the Third and Fourth Worlds. Education there is becoming community based, providing survival and development skills necessary to build a future for the rural area and the rural poor, in particular. Education is for the whole community to re-invigorate its culture and political life and to help to develop appropriate technologies for survival and a bit more, at least. Service for the community becomes service by the community: an enriching self-help. This is the model for most education in the future.

TIMOTHY NEWELL PRICE

Comparative Religion

The title 'Comparative Religion' was coined in about 1860. Increasingly anthropological and sociological research and the debate concerning evolution raised the question, 'How should we study religion?' Geneva established a chair in Religious Studies (1873); Harnack opposed a similar department in Berlin (1901), believing religious scholarship required a context of linguistic and cultural knowledge – an opinion to be heeded if not always accepted. In Britain, Manchester established a chair in Comparative Religion (1904).

After the setting up of a chair in religious studies at Lancaster in 1967, the term 'compa-

rative' was soon questioned. Too often it was used to imply superiority and inferiority. Ritual and doctrinal 'facts' were 'compared' without reference to the worshipper and *his* understanding of his faith. Comparison invited a slick 'supermarket' approach. An emphasis on primal religions and on living religions within the village setting often contributed to superficial generalizations.

In Britain, the main impetus to the study of comparative religions across the whole educational curriculum came from the publication of Parrinder's *Comparative Religion* and from the work of scholars and teachers brought together by the Shap Working Party on World Religions in Education (1969)*. Many recognized the need for a less controversial title, e.g. the (scientific) study of religion, world faiths in education. Intentionality and methodology were the most crucial issues in the debate. Simplistic comparison and description were rejected. Religions should be studied within the context of their own unique claims of truth and practice. The meaning of the experience for the worshipper was very important. Vague syncretism and generalizations were debilitating, though the study of religion was enriched by appreciation of common insights and recognition of occasional perceptive borrowing. Ninian Smart called not for an historical study but for an interweave of doctrine, myth*, ethic, experience, ritual* and institution.

Today there is a flowering of resources and increased opportunities for study at every level as the search for creative aims and methods continues.

J. R. Hinnels (ed.), *Comparative Religion in Education,* Oriel Press 1970; G. Parrinder, *Comparative Religion,* Allen & Unwin 1962.

VIDA BARNETT

Computer Assisted Learning in RE

There are five jobs a computer can do: 1. solve mathematical problems; 2. offer computer control to devices such as slide projectors; 3. store, organize and select information on a large scale; 4. display stories interactively; 5. build models and run strategies and simulations. Except for (1), all the functions can be used to enhance religious awareness.

The storage facility means that much information can be brought into schools in compact form such as floppy discs or through computer networks. This database would include text, pictures, graphic displays and diagrams from all the world religions. Interactive display means that the computer-user can become part of each unfolding story, be it from the Bible, *Pilgrim's Progress, Lord of the Rings* or the *Jakatas*. With colour and sound, these can open up the student in a unique way to an appreciation of transcendental reality glimpsed through ritual, saga, myth and symbol.

The computer can be used for programmed or machine learning in which, Pavlovian fashion, with stimulus and response, learning is advanced through encouragement and reinforcement without the direct use of a teacher.

Simulation models enable the student to alter variables and judge their effect. A Third-World development model might examine how aid is to be distributed, so that, on utilitarian principles, the greatest good might be achieved for the greatest number. Similarly, models can be constructed from simple encounter and conflict situations, in which the various outcomes of moral, social and psychological pressures and their personal consequences can be determined by user-selected options. Family stress, courtship, marriage, moral and social situations can thus be role-played; the user learns of, and is sensitized to, situations which as a young adult he or she has yet to experience directly.

Colin Price, *Religion and the Computer*, CEM 1984.

COLIN PRICE

Concepts

The bricks out of which the house of thought is built. In any subject concepts are important because the understanding of a discipline demands a grasp of its key notions. Hence to teach anything requires promoting acquisition of its central, distinctive and characteristic concepts. In modern education, great attention has been given to the concepts children need to have in order to reach a real comprehension of mathematics and science, etc., so as to avoid the childish verbalism which has been only too often produced in the past, particularly among the younger and less able children.

If the goal of RE is understanding and critical choice on the part of pupils among world-faiths, it is vital to realize that both belief and unbelief, agnostic positions and intelligent exploration, equally presuppose a grasp of and competence in using religious language* rationally and correctly. Concepts are central to God-talk, to the articulation of religion, to faith, worship and devotion, as of every other human activity and experience. Setting aside pre-linguistic concepts and those animals may possess, a good definition is: 'Concepts are . . . specific mental abilities exercised in acts of judgment, and expressed in the intelligent use of words (though not exclusively in such use)' (Geach). RE then involves teaching competence in religious language in which concepts are manifested.

Therefore RE requires theologians and philosophers of religion to analyse the crucial concepts of a faith (e.g. God, sin, prayer, Brahman, Nirvana) in either its orthodox or other contemporary forms and those concepts of other disciplines, such as history or morality, and of common sense, that theology makes use of in expressing its claims. Further distinctions among concepts are important for RE. If its aim is to produce religiously educated people who can be simple believers, if they choose, then among the crucial concepts we need to distinguish the categorial from the religiously essential notions; more than that would be too burdensome for the normal pupil! The categorial concepts are those, such as God, which underlie the spiritual dimension as a whole and which conceptualize the distinctive object of numinous and mystical experience, without which theistic propositions could neither be true nor false. Yet another kind of concept is that essential to the articulation of the simple belief of the saint or the unbelief of the ordinary sceptic.

RE need not present the further concepts inessential to simple faith but required in the more advanced pursuit of the spiritual life, like those of affective prayer or of meditation*, since producing a developed understanding of a faith is too ambitious an intention for the normal child. Nor is RE concerned to introduce children to the technical concepts of theology, for instance the *filioque*. Training clergy or even equipping 'A' Level students is not our purpose. But it should also be noticed that those concepts a faith borrows from other disciplines are indispensable for a religiously educated person and the acquisition of such notions comes through a good general education. Here the RE specialist relies on his colleagues to attend to the concepts proper to their several fields.

Further study will reveal the conditions logically necessary to the acquisition of religious concepts and any logical order in which they have, at least initially, to be gained so that teachers can plan deliberate programmes of presenting the requisite conceptual structures. Factors, too, in childhood, in life and in the social climate, that help or hinder this presentation, can also be deduced *a priori* from the character of a faith and its articulation in language.

In logic it is at this point and not before that conceptual research needs to take account of cognitive developmental psychology. Empirical investigation of how and when concepts are acquired by children and what promotes or prevents this is essential. In the twentieth century, the epoch-making work of Piaget has placed educators in his debt and shown the gradual way children gain concepts over the years in terms of general logical stages and particular kinds of operation. Using this framework and methodology, in the 1960s the work of Goldman and his followers in exploring children's understanding of the Bible was seminal and has exercised a profound influence on primary education in particular.

Although the conceptual research so far done by psychologists in the service of RE has proved to be of great value, the philosophical issues discussed above have been largely ignored and the results of empirical investigation are not always clearly of use to the open-ended, multi-faith approach most teachers desire today, as opposed to the amalgam of child-centredness and the New Theology in vogue in the 1960s as the neo-confessional* approach. The philosophical, theological and educational presuppositions of Goldman and others would not command universal assent in RE today.

Thus, before empirical investigations into children's conceptual growth can be profitable, there must be prior agreement on the aims* and objectives of RE in respect of the

Christian and of other faiths, so the concepts to be presented can be mapped and their inter-relations displayed. Then applied cognitive psychology may be employed to disclose how the notions we want to teach are currently being gained or not being gained and why, and better programmes of teaching tested. In the light of such research, which would have to be a joint endeavour of theologians, philosophers, psychologists and experienced teachers, more realistic and effective syllabuses and schemes of work for pupils at all ages and stages might be devised.

Conceptual research also aids evaluation. For example, the question how far and in what aspects has the pupil grasped the categorical concept of God* can only be answered when the logic of this crucial notion is delineated. Then the teacher is equipped to ask the right questions about what the child knows. From the puzzles of the infant class to the debates of the sixth-form, growth of religious understanding can only be effectively promoted by the educator who is clear about the terms he wants to convey and is sophisticatedly self-conscious about the concepts such as God which they express.

David Attfield, 'A Fresh Look at Goldman: the Research Needed Today', *Learning for Living*, November 1974, 'Conceptual Research in Religious Education', *Learning for Living,* Spring 1976, and 'A Taxonomy of Religious Concepts', *Learning for Living,* Winter 1976; J. H. Flavell, *The Developmental Psychology of Jean Piaget*, Van Nostrand 1963; Peter Geach, *Mental Acts*, Routledge & Kegan Paul 1957; Ronald Goldman, *Religious Thinking from Childhood to Adolescence*, Routledge & Kegan Paul 1964; Schools Council, *A Groundplan for the Study of Religion*, Schools Council RE Committee Bulletin 1977.

DAVID ATTFIELD

Confessionalism

Together with the associated terms, confessional, confessionalist and neo-confessionalism, this probably derives from the phrase 'confession of faith' – a formal declaration of doctrine or religious principles usually formulated as a public testimony by a religious group, e.g. the Confession of Augsburg, the Westminster Confession. It is not related to the sacrament of confession or to confessing sins in prayer. The curious use of these words in the 1970s in Britain alongside or instead of apparent synonyms such as 'indoctrinatory', 'dogmatic', 'doctrinal' or 'evangelistic' may owe something to contact with Northern European religious educators, especially the Swede, Sten Rodhe.

These terms appear in print in relation to RE for the first time in *Religious Education in Secondary Schools* (1971). The Schools Council team based at the University of Lancaster attributed a confessional approach in RE to religious leaders and compilers of agreed syllabuses*. Even syllabuses based on openness to children's needs and interests were dubbed neo-confessional in that the ultimate importance of the Christian faith *for the pupils* was not an open question.

For some of those who accepted the Working Paper arguments against confessionalism and for the phenomenological approach*, the terms became weapons with which to derrogate others. Frequently, confessional was used as an antonym for 'professional'*. On the other hand, teachers who had taught the Bible and church history academically, and who did not see themselves promoting any denominational confession, objected to the implication that they were unprofessional. It was asserted that religious bodies, even those, such as the Christian Education Movement*, devoted to promoting educational approaches in RE were *per se*, confessional.

Used to connote instruction in particular beliefs to the exclusion of all others, the confessionalism group of words had validity, but amidst the acerbity of the 1970s RE debate the terms became debased and gradually lost currency. Newbiggin's attack on the assumed undogmatic stance of the Birmingham agreed syllabus justified commitment, of one kind or another, as an essential prerequisite for education in or about religion. No longer could confessional be used as an unqualified 'boo' word.

See also **Professionalism**.

Schools Council, *Religious Education in Secondary Schools* Working Paper 36, Evans/ Methuen 1971; *Learning for Living*, 17.2, CEM.

ROBIN H. SHEPHERD

Confirmation

Part of the rite of initiation used in Eastern, Western Catholic and some Reformed churches. Historically it has included laying-on of hands by a bishop, anointing with oil (chrism) together with the imposition of the sign of the cross (usually on the forehead).

Though the laying-on of hands is referred to in the New Testament (see for example Acts 8. 14–17 and 19. 1–7), no distinct link between this action and the developed rite of confirmation has been conclusively established. By the third century the rise of Christian initiation conducted by a bishop included the blessing of a font, baptism by water, the actions described above that form confirmation, and the Eucharistic rite. With the rapid spread of Christianity, bishops delegated to priests some of the acts in the rite of initiation but retained the laying-on of hands, chrism and the imposition of the sign of the cross. So confirmation became a separated rite. Only the Eastern churches have retained a unified rite of initiation (in infancy) which includes confirmation by anointing, the oil for which has been blessed by the bishop and distributed to his clergy.

The Western Catholic and some Reformed traditions have continued the practice of a separate rite of confirmation. In the Roman Catholic Church, for example, this is conducted by a Bishop with chrism, the imposition of the sign of the cross and hands extended in blessing, when children are about seven years old. The Church of England retained the laying-on of hands but the use of oil ceased in 1549 and the imposition of sign of the cross in 1552. The rite is generally administered at about twelve or thirteen years of age, sometimes in the mid-teens.

Christian initiation has always been preceded by a period of preparation. In the early church it was called the Catechumenate and would consist of instruction with questions and scrutinies. The intentions and preparedness of candidates were summed up within the rite itself in the form of baptismal vows, taken for life. From an early date designated teachers were in charge of the Catechumens: some places even boasted Catechetical schools. (The writings of St Cyril of Jerusalem provide an early example of Catechesis.) The process of education involved knowledge of the doctrines of the church, involvement in the Eucharistic fellowship and the growth of a commitment that would allow a sincere acceptance of lifelong vows. This nurture in the faith changed radically as the practice of infant baptism grew and confirmation developed as a separate rite. Adult sponsors or Godparents were now required at baptism to speak on behalf of the child and to make the vows. Confirmation at seven or in the early teens extended the period of nurture. Two practices emerged: separate general instruction in groups or classes over a period of years, unconnected with confirmation and sometimes with only tenuous relations with the worshipping fellowship; and a fixed period of preparation immediately prior to confirmation. This latter tradition emerges clearly in the 1662 Book of Common Prayer where confirmation is described as for those who have 'come to years of discretion'. The book provides a Catechism which requires recitation by the child of the Creed, Lord's Prayer and the ten commandments. Present practice has been influenced by the liturgical movements in some churches and by contemporary educational theory and practice. These influences confirm the wisdom of the early church in combining within the preparation for initiation instruction, worship, fellowship and the fostering of commitment.

In many churches interest at present is centred, with a variety of emphases, on the following: (a) the possibility of re-introducing a unified rite of initiation in infancy after which nurture in the faith will be a life-long process; (b) postponing confirmation until adulthood and viewing it as a commissioning to lay ministry; (c) the admission of children to Communion before confirmation on an experimental basis: (d) the use of a 'catechumenate' for adult candidates closely linked with a worshipping community; (e) the introduction of children's nurture which relates congregation, instruction and the family; (f) the development of a theory of 'faith development' which combines theology and psychology.

There is continued uncertainty about the theology of confirmation as well as a somewhat bewildering variety of practice.

ROBERT WADDINGTON

Congregationalism

Congregationalists share the Reformed Churches' enthusiasm for education. Every church member must be able to read and understand the Bible, and, in a Congregational church, be prepared to take full part in every aspect of church activity. Congregationalist emphasis upon the total depravity of unredeemed human nature had, for educational purposes, to be allied to a belief in the validity of human powers of reasoning. The 'end of learning', wrote Milton, is 'to repair the ruins of our first parents'.

Congregationalists were therefore strong supporters of the eighteenth-century charity schools movement. Perhaps the most influential defence of those schools against their detractors was a pamphlet by Isaac Watts. Watts was by no means the first to realize the special needs of children in the realm of hymns, but his *Divine Songs attempted in Easy Language for the use of Children* (including 'How doth the little busy bee') became the principal children's hymnbook for all Protestants for more than a century.

Elementary education remained a central interest of Congregationalists. It appears that the majority of ministers, in small rural churches at least, were expected to enhance their meagre stipends by teaching the village children.

A more determined attempt to meet the educational needs of the whole population waited till the early years of the nineteenth century. Schools were now organized in connection with churches of all denominations. Congregationalists took a large part in the beginning, in 1808, of the interdenominational, non-Anglican British and Foreign School Society*.

The separation of church and state is a central tenet of Congregationalism. The beginning of government grants to schools in 1833 thus created a dilemma for those who regarded education as the province of the church. In fact, nonconformists had received for nearly a century a small annual gift from the royal purse, for the relief of their ministers' widows. This *regium donum* later caused unease and was discontinued in 1851. Meanwhile, however, it provided a precedent for acceptance of state aid. Nevertheless many Congregationalists came to see state grants to their schools as incompatible with their principles. Some, but not all, refused the grant.

The Congregational Union, meeting in Leeds in 1843, established the 'Congregational Board of Education to promote the advancement of popular education, upon strictly religious principles, free from all magisterial authority'. 1845 saw the foundation of Homerton College, to train teachers for the numerous Congregational schools springing into existence.

This stand against state interference could succeed only if there were a possibility that voluntary effort might succeed in providing universal education. There was no hope of this. The Rev. R. W. Dale of Birmingham became, therefore, a leader of the National Education League, demanding in 1867 a state system of entirely secular education. This was not, however, what came out of the 1870 Education Act. It set up school boards to provide schools where provision by the churches was insufficient (which meant nearly everywhere) and left each board to decide whether or not to include religious instruction. As drafted, this permitted a board to specify denominational instruction. Provision was made for conscientious withdrawal by parents. The bill was made a little more acceptable to congregationalists by the addition of the Cowper-Temple clause*, forbidding, in board schools, instruction distinctive of any denomination. Dissatisfied though they were, Congregationalists nevertheless in general worked with the 1870 Act and in most cases handed over their schools to the boards or discontinued them. This attitude was not universal: at the end of the century, a new nonconformist voluntary school was founded in Bournemouth.

The 1902 Education Act transferred to local authorities and their rates the maintenance of board and church schools alike. Churches had merely to maintain the premises. A considerable movement of 'passive resisters' included many Congregationalists, whose refusal to pay rates led to distraint sales of their possessions. This movement failed to achieve any improvement to the Act and was brought to an end by the upheavals of the 1914–18 war. Congregationalists now learned to accept a system quite incompatible with their principles. Indeed, in the discussions leading up to the 1944 Education Act, with its substantial further financial concessions to church schools and its imposition of mandatory religious instruction and worship on all schools, Congregationalists were often found siding, perhaps unenthusiastically, with those who called upon the state to provide religious teaching. Congregationalists might have emphasized, but often did not do so, their belief that the 'Gentiles' do possess a moral law and that that – and not an appeal to a Christian faith which many pupils and parents reject – must be the basis for moral education in schools.

If, however, in 1870 and 1902 the concept of undenominational religion in school had seemed practicable, the emergence of a multicultural society in post-1950 Britain confused the issue. What is to be done in a school with a sizeable proportion of pupils from homes of non-Christian faiths? A pioneering attempt to show how this question might be answered, the Schools Council's Secondary RE Project, was led by a Congregationalist, the Rev. Donald Horder.

Another stream of popular education, which diverged increasingly from the day school, was that of the Sunday School. During the nineteenth century all churches had their Sunday Schools. These did not, even in the most successful cases, bring every one of their pupils into church membership. Children did gain from the friendship and care of the teachers; and from the inculcation of moral standards. Congregationalists could not be satisfied with this. Mistrustful of rules, not only as a spurious aid to salvation but also as restrictions upon the free response of the redeemed Christian to the leading of the Holy Spirit, Congregationalists were much involved in attempts to improve the quality of the teaching. These included the National Sunday School Union and Westhill College. By the early years of the twentieth century, it was becoming clear that the Sunday School, however much it might be benefiting its members, was bringing few of them to any commitment to Christ and his church. In 1924, Ealing Green Congregational Church (Rev. Wilton E. Rix) began 'Little Church'; children attended morning worship, sitting with their parents or with other adults who each undertook to be 'friend' to one or two children. After the second hymn the children moved in procession to their own chapel, where they used a liturgy which involved participation by those of various ages, and listened to an address. In 1939, the Rev. H. A. Hamilton of the Congregational Union Young People's Department produced *Family Church* with its accompanying graded lesson schemes, including plans for occasional major festivals when all the children remained with the adult congregation and made contributions to the worship. Similar ideas subsequently came to be the norm in children's work in all denominations.

In all this, secondary education had not been overlooked. Amongst the earlier attempts to extend the upper level of ordinary schooling was Titus Salt's School at Saltaire, founded in the mid-nineteenth-century to serve the model village he built for his employees. Meanwhile, the needs of ministers to be free to move without interrupting their children's schooling had led to the foundation of several boarding schools, including Mill Hill, Caterham, Silcoates and (for girls) Milton Mount, early in the century.

In Wales, the activities of Congregationalists not only paralleled those in England, but also included an additional component – the language. Throughout the later years of the nineteenth century and until after the 1914–18 war, official policy discouraged the Welsh language, on the grounds that its speakers were disadvantaged in an English-speaking island and an increasingly English-speaking world. Welsh opposition to this policy was spearheaded by the Welsh-speaking Congregationalists, the Union of Welsh Independents. The only denomination using no language but Welsh, they led the provision of educational activities of various kinds and at all levels, to encourage and stimulate the use of the language and the preservation and enhancement of the culture.

The nonconformist academies began as clandestine one-man attempts to provide a substitute for Oxbridge, for those excluded by the anti-nonconformist measures of the 1660s. Oxford was closed to non-Anglicans; Cambridge was technically not closed, but compulsory chapel attendance and the requirement to subscribe the Anglican articles before graduation were severe disincentives. Some fifty tutors, mainly Congregationalists or Presbyterians, tried to fill the gap.

The surprising feature of these early academies is the extent to which the tutors did not confine themselves to the provision of an accurate copy of the Oxbridge in which they themselves had been educated. Instead, they ventured on a variety of innovations. In some cases, these innovations e.g. scientific experiments, politics and logic, were suggested by experiences in other countries; in others, they seem to have been inventions of the tutor from his own mind, accustomed to respond to the leading of the Spirit.

Congregationalism's refusal to envisage any priesthood except that of all church members implies that the minister's special role is in teaching. Theological colleges are thus indispensable. The special needs of missionary training were recognized with the foundation, jointly with Baptists and Presbyterians, of Carey Hall, Birmingham in 1912.

A Congregational church calls to its pastorate the man or woman whom it believes God to have raised up for that office. Where that minister has not been to theological college, he will usually take advantage of arrangements provided by the denomination (the Congregational Federation) for training by short residential courses and correspondence. Similar courses are provided for lay preachers. Congregational principles imply that the ordinary church member must equally seek ways to enhance his understanding of his faith. This need is met, in many churches, by regular weeknight meetings. Denominational provision of materials for the ordinary church member has met with a somewhat disappointing response and it has been commented that too many members of Congregational churches are content to ignore the duty, laid upon them by their church membership, of taking seriously their need of continual education.

Acceptance into membership is preceded by suitable sessions for instruction and discussion. The content of these varies considerably from church to church; a number of handbooks, with varying emphases, have been issued from time to time. It is of the essence of Congregationalism that Christ's church ideally includes local churches which respond to diverse leading by the Spirit, finding their unity not in agreeing on details of their structures, activities or theologies, but only in their allegiance to Christ as Lord and Saviour. Thus any uniform system of education, at any level, would deny their churchmanship.

See also **United Reformed Church**.

Joe W. Ashley Smith, *Birth of Modern Education: the Dissenting Academies,* Independent Press 1955; R. Tudur Jones, *Congregationalism in England 1662–1962,* Independent Press 1963.

J. W. ASHLEY SMITH

Conscience

Often referred to as an 'inner voice' that tells you what is right or wrong. Of course, this is only a metaphor. But it is a convenient one for describing the kind of knowledge which is concerned with what one *ought* to do. On the other hand, it can be misleading in a way that has considerable moral and religious significance (see below).

There are different kinds of knowledge – scientific, philosophical, mathematical, etc. We do, however, ask questions not only about matters of fact, of religion, or of arithmetic, but also about our duties both in general and in particular cases. In so far as there are reasonable and often convincing answers to these questions, one can talk about moral knowledge, too. I believe, as an example of general knowledge, that one ought not to hurt people simply for the fun of it. I know, more particularly, that I personally ought to visit Mr Smith in hospital. The *internalization* of those general principles forms my conscience and it is reflected in my sense of duty on particular occasions. It must be remembered, however, that like any inner or outer voices, this conscience, or internalization of principles of action, is a process of reasoning or pondering or conversing. In other words, the conscience is the product of reflection and reasonings about one's duties or principles and manifests itself in particular convictions about what one ought to do.

Such convictions are reflected in one's feelings. I have a *feeling* of duty to act in certain ways, and I *feel* guilt or remorse when I do not act in the way that I know I should. The sense of duty and the feelings of guilt and remorse embody the practical moral knowledge that we identify with 'having a conscience'. And they also explain why conscience is often seen as 'an inner voice'. Very often, external distractions and temptations or the reasonings of others fail to extinguish that inner conviction which is reflected in the feelings of duty, guilt and remorse.

Two aspects of the 'inner voice' metaphor need to be noted, since different emphases lead to quite different, especially religious, understandings of conscience.

1. The stress upon 'voice' points to the importance of reasoning about your duties, of seeing your duty (and thus the convictions of your own conscience) as something that you can justify to and question with others. That is, you are keen to internalize, and to act according to, *right* reason. What is good or bad is not just a personal matter. There are objective criteria for deciding between right and wrong. A properly formed conscience, therefore, would be one that has internalized those principles which are in some objective sense the correct ones. And part of the moral education of children, therefore, would consist in teaching them what the correct principles are. At the risk of being crudely simplistic, one could say that the Catholic moral tradition has stressed the objectivity of morals and of the need to form the conscience of children according to the traditions embodied in the Catholic Christian community.

2. However, more stress is sometimes given to the 'inner' aspect of the voice of conscience. It is essentially a *personal* conviction, where right and wrong are not a matter of publicly agreed knowledge in the way that mathematics and science are. There is a stress upon individual responsibility and, within the more Protestant tradition of Christianity, upon the formation of that inner conviction of God, unmediated by the church as a moral authority.

This is of course a rather crude oversimplification and essentially a question of emphasis. But, in different ages, different emphases are given to these two aspects of conscience. The Catholic Church still, of course, plays an active part through its teaching in forming the conscience of its members, but is at pains to stress that ultimately a person must make up his or her own mind in the light of the church's teaching. General principles need to be applied. They can never anticipate the many different situations of our complex lives in which they are to be applied. Therefore, each person will need to respond as he or she thinks fit on particular occasions in the light of the general principles. Acting according to one's conscience reflects the unavoidability of personal responsibility for what one does.

There are three important aspects of the formation of moral conscience that need to be remembered. 1. Conscience requires the capacity to see things from a moral point of view and for making judgments according to general principles of justice or fairness. We know from developmental psychologists that such a capacity only gradually develops in children and under certain conditions. 2. The actual judgments of conscience that one makes will depend upon the sort of moral concepts one has and therefore upon the particular moral traditions one is exposed to. 3. The formation of conscience can so easily be stunted in the early stages of child development, so that he or she might be left with strong feelings of guilt totally disconnected from the reflective reasoning that is characteristic of the mature adult.

RICHARD PRING

Conscience Clauses

The basic conscience clause, the right of withdrawal, has been embodied in every Act relating to RE since 1870; in fact it had become a compulsory feature of the trust deeds of all schools receiving grant even before that. The 1944 Act therefore did little more than re-enact the existing law.

Under Section 25 (4) the parent of any pupil in a county or voluntary school has the right to ask that he or she be excused from attendance at either religious worship or religious instruction, and his request must be granted – a right which, of course, applies to no other subject.

Furthermore, the pupil may then be withdrawn from the school, though only at the beginning or end of a day, to attend religious instruction in accordance with the parents' wishes. In a county secondary school, though not in a primary school, this may, under Section 26, be given on the school premises, so long as no costs fall on the LEA, and the LEA does not find the proposed arrangements unreasonable.

A less well-known clause, Section 25 (3), which also has a history going back beyond 1870, provides that a pupil's attendance at a county or voluntary school may not be made dependent on his attendance or non-attendance at a Sunday School or place of worship.

Section 25 (7) gives parents of pupils at maintained boarding schools the right to demand facilities for religious instruction and Sunday worship in accordance with their beliefs – so long as no costs fall on the LEA.

The rights of teachers are safeguarded under Section 30. No teacher may be disqualified from appointment to any school because of his or her religious opinions, no teacher may be required to give religious instruction, and no teacher may suffer in promotion or emoluments because of his religious opinions, but teachers in aided schools and reserved teachers* in controlled schools are specifically excluded from the first two of these provisions since, under Sections 28 and 27 respectively, they may be required to give religious instruction.

The conscience clauses make no mention of independent schools*, since attendance at such schools is purely a matter of parental choice.

See also **Acts of Parliament**.

W. J. H. EARL

Conscientization

An approach to education which became widely known in the 1960s and is associated especially with the Brazilian, Paulo Freire. According to this approach, real education is aimed at freeing people from all forms of oppression, both those deriving from social circumstance (class, poverty, being taught, etc.) and those based on inner condition, e.g. ignorance. By conscientization a person's consciousness is awakened so that he recognizes his own true place in nature and society while becoming growingly aware of his dignity and moving to take part in action to change that place and advance that dignity.

Education as 'conscientization' is contrasted with 'banking education', a process in which the attempt is made to transfer knowledge from the teacher who knows to the learner who does not, as capital is moved into the bank account of the recipient. In 'conscientization', it is held that no man can give liberation, the aim of the process, to another. The subject must experience his own world in a process of teaching-learning-action arising from the participant's own life and experience.

The concept has produced a rich growth of theory and development, indicated in *Learning for Living* Vol. 13, No. 3, 'Is School Dead'. The definitive accounts are in the works of Paulo Freire (e.g. *Pedagogy of the Oppressed*) and Ivan Illich (e.g. *Deschooling Society*).

See also **Latin/Central America**.

PHILIP LEE-WOOLF

Correlation in RE

The 1944 Act had the effect of encapsulating RE within a weekly 'statutory period' and emphasizing its separateness through daily morning assemblies. Moves to counteract these tendencies and to bring it once more into a constructive relationship with other subjects in the 1960s often resulted in the evaporation of the discipline within schemes of integrated studies, or a further narrowing of its purview.

This erosion of the spiritual element within the curriculum was noted by the DES and Her Majesty's Inspectorate in a series of documents arising from the 'Great Educational Debate'. Here it was seen as a major area of experience at secondary level, as Goldman and Ross had shown it to be within the primary and middle schools respectively. In 1980, LEAS were instructed that RE should be part of any core curriculum whilst the Inspectorate, who three years earlier had explained *how* this might be done, stressed the importance of its role.

Given overall aims accepted by all who work in a school, the teacher in the primary classrooms should be able to demonstrate the religious aspects of all that is done. Here insights into cognitive development supplied by Piaget, Goldman and Kohlberg are important. At secondary level emphasis has moved over the last decade away from Tooke's attempts to indicate ways in which each subject could be used to teach RE and towards an understanding of how almost every discipline includes a religious dimension – literature*, art*, history*, music* and drama* being especially important in this respect. The teacher responsible for RE must now ensure the existence of the spiritual element *across* as well as *within* the curriculum. This puts the teacher in a strong position to influence not only what is taught and the nature of that teaching, but also how the school is run. Theo-logy might have lost its former predominant position as 'Queen of the Sciences', but if it works in this way, with and not against the currents in society at large, it will have discovered just as effective a voice for the transmission of its message. What is more, that voice will be an appropriate one for the 'open' and cosmopolitan world it must now serve.

See also **Integration of Curriculum and RE**.

DES *Curriculum 11–16*, HMSO 1981; DES, *A Framework for the School Curriculum*, HMSO 1980; DES, *The School Curriculum*, HMSO 1981; DES, *A View of the Curriculum*, HMSO 1980; R. J. Goldman, *Religious Thinking from Childhood to Adolescence*, Routledge & Kegan Paul 1964 and *Readiness for Religion*, Routledge & Kegan Paul 1965; M. Holt, *The Common Curriculum*, Routledge & Kegan Paul 1978; A. M. Ross *et al.*, *Curriculum in the Middle Years*, Methuen/Evans 1976; Schools Council, *The Practical Curriculum*, Methuen 1981; D. Warwick, 'Teaching Methods and Strategies', *Religious Education in Integrated Studies*, ed. I. H. Birnie, SCM Press 1972.

DAVID WARWICK

Cowper-Temple Clause

An amendment in the 1870 Elementary Education Act initiated by the Liberal W. E. Forster. William Francis Cowper-Temple (1811–1888), Liberal MP for South Hampshire, introduced the amendment after objections to the original bill from Free Churchmen threatened its successful passage. The issue at stake was that of the provision of new schools (which presumably would teach the Christianity of a particular denomination) from the *local* rates as distinct from central government grants to existing denominational schools, which Free Churchmen had generally come to accept.

The Clause (section 14 sub-section (2) of the Act) read as follows: 'No religious catechism or religious formulary which is distinctive of any particular denomination shall be taught in the school.' It applied in England and Wales and only to the newly-established Board Schools as a condition of financial aid.

The Clause is an educational landmark in two ways. 1. The Act, finally passed by a coalition of Liberals and Conservatives, was

essential for securing a national, and later compulsory, system of elementary education.
2. The Clause established by legislation the neutrality of the state in regard to competing Christian denominations. It also implied that religion was only one element of the curriculum, rather than providing the basis for it.

The idea of the Clause was by no means peculiar to the England of 1870. Undenominational Christianity had been part of the programme of the British and Foreign School Society* from the first quarter of the century. There were tensions in both Western Europe and the United States over whether education should be religious or secular and whether it should be controlled by church or state.

Like the already legally-established Conscience Clause*, permitting dissenters to withdraw from Anglican religious instruction, the Cowper-Temple Clause can be seen as a defence of the rights of the family to bring up children in their own faith and not to be usurped by corporate bodies such as church or state.

The Clause represents the solution whereby some schools provide a 'generalized Christianity', the common ground of the Christian churches, which in practice very often came to mean the teaching of the Bible. It precluded teaching on the sacraments, whereas the Apostles' Creed was apparently envisaged as possible, although often omitted.

Despite attempts to repeal the Clause, particularly at the time of the 1902 Act, it has remained in force, being incorporated in Acts of 1921 and 1944. It has been valued by the Free Churches especially. However, the underlying principle of the Clause was limited in 1902 by legislation permitting *rate* aid to voluntary schools and in 1936 by allowing the churches to build new senior schools. This has been counterbalanced by the decision of the 1944 Act to apply the clause to LEA secondary schools and partially to church schools which chose the option of controlled status.

The development of LEA agreed syllabuses* of RE was an outgrowth of Cowper-Templeism, because they represented what could be taught in schools in accordance with the Clause as agreed amongst the churches.

To some extent the Clause is now a period piece. The issues it reflected are no longer so urgent. The blurring of denominational differences and the trend of professional religious education to reject initiation into a specific faith as an aim of contemporary RE have removed the need to avoid certain items of content. Recent agreed syllabuses no longer reflect the Cowper-Temple Clause. However, in today's multi-faith society, the Clause could be re-interpreted as a historical symbol of the need for the neutrality of the state towards RE.

GEOFFREY CHORLEY

Creativity

In a Christian context, its ultimate significance comes from the biblical notion of divine creation. In bringing the created order into being out of nothing (*creatio ex nihilo*), God provides the definitive creative act with respect to which all human creativity is contingent and relative. However, as a free act, human creativity has the potential of being directed either towards God, reflecting and glorifying him through his creation, or towards self-glorification and manifold forms of idolatry.

Whether human creativity is directed towards God's purposes or works against them, it follows a basic pattern upon which there are many variations. This consists of four phases: preparation, incubation, illumination, and verification.

1. In preparation, a range of personal resources, prototypes, information and cognitive competence are brought to bear upon some complication, puzzle or conflict within a given context. Out of the interplay among these resources will come a series of new approaches to the original complication.

2. Between the preparation and the final illumination falls the period of incubation, which may range in time from seconds to years. It is a period of unconscious psychological activity in which the elements of the precipitating dilemma, together with learned or inherited prototypes, are scanned, sorted and integrated. Alpha rhythm activity and the contributions of the right hemisphere work under the surface of awareness towards some resolution of the original dilemma.

3. Illumination comes to consciousness with spontaneity and surprise, and conveys an insight that is felt with intuitive force. The dilemma may be resolved all at once, or a series of illuminations may combine to

compose the resolution. At this phase of the process, the resolution is held with subjectively convincing force and it resides in the personality as an image, feeling and/or vision. Thus, a final phase, verification, is called for as essential to the integrity of the creative act.

4. Verification, a predominantly left-hemisphere function, is the act of matching the substance of the illumination with elements of the dilemma to see if it can be publicly demonstrated that an adequate resolution has indeed been given to the illumination.

A classic illustration of the process is the account of Archimedes' discovery in hydrostatics. After being commissioned by the tyrant, King Hiero of Syracuse, to determine the relative purity of the King's gold crown, but without melting it down, Archimedes fell into a severe dilemma. Baffled at first, he put it out of consciousness and went to the public baths. There as he immersed himself, he watched the water rise against the smudges on the wall, and then illumination struck him. In an intuitive realization, he 'saw' that by immersing the irregular shape of the crown in water he could measure the displacement of water to find the volume of the crown. With knowledge of the specific gravity of gold he could then determine whether the crown was pure gold or not. As legend has it, he was so ecstatic that he ran naked through the streets of Syracuse shouting 'Eureka!'. Fortunately, he was able later to verify his discovery and set down the first principles of hydrostatics.

Although this process is often ascribed only to genius, all persons are by nature creative and can at some time recognize in their own experience instances when this process has worked for them. It may even be argued that simply to develop as a person is to undergo a process of creation and that to know anything is to invent it. Since creativity as a process of invention and transformation pervades human nature, it is used educationally to alter patterns of conformity, stereotyping and prejudice. Creativity combines spontaneity with sustained continuity of intention, so it should also be distinquished as a process from mere play and the generation of novelty, the bizzare or the outlandish. Although frequently fragmented, creativity as a process drives towards completion of all four steps, even when one has entered the process in the middle by having illuminating answers before one knows what the question is.

Educationally, creativity is generally fostered by placing a positive value upon stress and conflict, by affirming that the inner life of fantasy and feeling may be a source of truth, by working in a context where there is no absolute human authority, by emphasizing complexity rather than simplicity except when simplicity genuinely masters a wide range of complexity ($E = MC^2$), and finally by recognizing and accepting personal differences.

The unique value of creativity for Christian education lies in its inherent potential for reflecting in human terms the nature and purpose of the on-going creative work of Christ's Spirit (*Spiritus Creator*).

JAMES E. LODER

Crowther Report, 1959

Issued in two volumes: Volume I was the lengthy report itself and Volume II the surveys which provided much of the background to Volume I.

The report was wide-ranging in its vision. It addressed itself particularly in Part 3 to 'Secondary Education for All'. This included strong arguments for the raising of the school leaving age to sixteen, both for the benefit of the individual and in the national interest. Recognizing the potentially large increase in the number of sixth-formers, the report attempted to define the sixth-form in terms of the sixth-formers themselves, the staff, the structure and, above all, the curriculum.

The report defined 'Technical Challenge and Educational Response' as neglected educational territory. In surveying the whole area of further education (part-time and full-time) the report consistently stressed the need for expansion. It called for much better integration between schools and further education, less reliance on evening classes for under-eighteens and, above all, a long-term aim of developing vocational training into a 'coherent national system of practical education'.

In Part 7, 'Institutions and Teachers', we find some strong opinions on the nature of comprehensive schools. It is valuable to re-read these in the light of Michael Rutter's *15,000 Hours*. Commenting on the qualities of a good teacher, Crowther commends boldly: 'an integrity and a humility in their work which clearly puts their pupils' interests before their own'.

Finally, Volume II (the surveys) provides a remarkable insight into the life and background of young people in the late 50s – particularly school leavers, those just having taken up National Service and those involved in technical courses.

D. SULLIVAN

Culture

The concept of culture in the social sciences owes something, if not a great deal, to the meaning it conveys in the natural sciences: for example, Hutchinson's biological definition 'the class of all the behaviour exhibited by the group is called the culture of the group' usefully stresses the qualities of sharing and uniformity among members of the community, by which characteristics they are distinguished from outsiders.

The inadequacy of such a definition for the social scientist, however, lies in its emphasis upon observable performance rather than upon latent tendencies such as values, knowledge, belief, law and ideology, which are not necessarily manifested in behaviour. The definition of Kluckhohn and Kelly is therefore more typical of sociological formulations: a culture is a historically derived system of explicit and implicit designs for living, which tends to be shared by all or specially designated members of a group.

These explicit* and implicit* 'designs for living' are of particular interest to the sociologist and it is this prescriptive dimension that is often signified in references to 'cultural revolution'.

Of special interest, too, is the category of 'subculture' which has dominated a number of important studies in the last two decades. A subculture prevails within a section of a given community such as a generational or status group: often there are visible or audible symbols of differentiation such as dress, hairstyle, music and language and the subculture maintains insularity by means of postures of rejection or aggression towards other sections. A classic examination of a generational subculture is provided by T. R. Fyvel's work on the Teddy Boys: this has been periodically succeeded – as have his subjects – and some later subcultures, such as hippies, have lent their relatively explicit ideologies to

appreciative study. In an important recent work, Bernice Martin has surveyed the complexity and diversity of youth culture in the post-war period and has presented it as a critical factor of contemporary cultural change.

The badges of affiliation are borne into the Western classroom – jewelled nostrils and metallic green hair in London, Arab headscarfs in Hamburg. The young are rallied around conscientious causes by, among others, the Anti-Nazi League in England and the Green People in West Germany. Youth subcultures are both conspicuous and influential and the designs for living which belong to them command serious attention in religious education: so, too, does the critique of traditional designs implied in the normative posture of rejection.

Both in national cultures and in the cultural life of minority communities, religions play an important role in validating dominant ideologies and in organizing and integrating communities. In complex multi-cultural societies such as Great Britain and the United States, the study of religion necessarily addresses problems of community relations and the conditions and criteria of cultural differentiation.

T. R. Fyvel, *The Insecure Offenders: Rebellious Youth in the Welfare State,* Chatto 1961; G. E. Hutchinson, 'Marginalia', *American Scientist,* 38, 1950; C. Kluckhohn and W. H. Kelly, 'The Concept of Culture', R. Linton. *The Science of Man in the World Crisis,* Columbia U. P. 1945; Bernice Martin, *A Sociology of Contemporary Cultural Change,* Blackwell 1981.

ROGER HOMAN

Curriculum Development

The content of the RE curriculum in county schools in England and Wales is prescribed, by law, through the agreed syllabuses* of the local education authorities*. These official documents therefore provide a clear indication of the developments that have occurred in the theory and, possibly, the practice of RE during the present century, especially the effects these have had on curriculum content. Although most agreed syllabuses make some provision for the study of any distinctive religious features of the region for which the syllabus is intended, until the 1960s the syllabuses conformed to a similar pattern, based upon the assumption that RE consisted of a study of the Bible* as history with special attention being given to the foundation documents of the Christian church. They were also similar in purpose, namely to provide an understanding of the Christian tradition and to foster Christian faith.

Several new considerations emerged in the 1960s, which called in question both the assumptions underlying the existing agreed syllabuses and the content they prescribed. For example, religious educators found that they could no longer ignore the changes that were taking place in other subjects in the school curriculum as a result of their accommodating new insights from developmental psychology, child-centred theories of education and from the philosophy of education. Initially these changes were seen as necessary for the promotion of more effective ways of learning. The application of Piagetian insights into concept formation and the use of experience-based methods of learning and teaching would, it was believed, enable traditional subject matter to be understood and learned more easily. But the effects of such accommodation on RE were more far reaching; they led to the educational value of the traditional content being questioned and challenged religious educators to re-formulate their understanding of RE itself. The same consequences emerged from the application to RE of conceptual analysis techniques taken from the philosophy of education. Instructing pupils in the Bible with a Christianizing intention could not be said to constitute an acceptable educational activity. Historical precedent was an insufficient ground to guarantee RE's place in an overcrowded curriculum.

Although the traditional disciplines of education played a decisive role in establishing the boundaries within which development of the curriculum should take place, it was a new discipline, Curriculum Theory, which set itself the task of providing the actual theories and techniques of curriculum analysis, construction and change. In the 1960s, a number of curriculum development models were devised, the earliest being the so-called process models, in which the identification of aims and objectives and their classification as knowledge*, skills* and attitudes* was seen

as being logically prior to selection of content. Recognition of the inter-dependence of content and method led to the concept of devising learning experiences able to promote the sort of learning stated in the objectives and to incorporating into the process an opportunity for the learning experiences to be evaluated, again in terms of the objectives. In order to increase the efficiency of the process, it was recommended that objectives should be stated in behavioural terms. Although the model had an obvious relevance to science teaching, it was regarded as being applicable to the development of the curriculum in all subjects and able to be applied to both cognitive and affective domains.

RE in the UK has never totally embraced this form of curriculum model, but its influence on curriculum development in RE during the 1970s is apparent in various publications, syllabuses and curriculum projects. For example, both the Avon Agreed Syllabus of 1976 and the Hampshire Agreed Syllabus of 1978 chose to abandon the practice of prescribing content and to offer teachers sets of educational objectives for each age-range, which left them free to decide on content and learning experiences which might most appropriately, in their own teaching context, lead to their achievement. It is, perhaps, the built-in flexibility which allows teachers to be actively involved in curriculum decision-making that has made the Hampshire syllabus a popular choice for adoption by many local authorities, but at the time of its publication there were signs that a more content-centred approach to curriculum development would persist. This was a consequence of the search for the educational justification for RE being directed towards establishing the subject as a descriptive and critical study of the world's religions. Curriculum development in RE thus appeared to proceed on the basis that the more comprehensive the content of RE became, the stronger became its case for educational legitimation. This view was reflected in the Schools Council* publication, *A Groundplan for the Study of Religion*, and in the decision to include the study of non-religious stances for living in the Birmingham Agreed Syllabus of 1975, although existing legislation prohibited this study from taking place on equal terms with the study of religions. It is noteworthy that this renewed interest in content was hardly influenced by the insights from developmental psychology so apparent in the 1960s, even when considering whether the curriculum should be organized by means of themes* or typologies* or each religion treated separately.

The existence of the legislative machinery for creating agreed syllabuses may have been responsible for encouraging the view that it is both possible and desirable for a grand, comprehensive theory of RE to be developed which can be implemented in schools by means of a curriculum that is true to the inner logic of religion and which takes full cognizance of the learning characteristics and the needs of pupils. A similar view may have lain behind the setting up of the two Schools Council curriculum development projects in RE in the early 1970s, although the Primary RE Project challenged this view and departed from it. But in recent years, despite the introduction by the DES of the concept of a common curriculum, curriculum theorists have largely eschewed the notion of an all-embracing theory of curriculum and come to recognize that effective curriculum development is best conceived on a small scale with the focus upon what actually happens in the classrooms and upon how innovation can and does take place. Here responsibility for curriculum development devolves upon the individual teacher working in the highly specific context of a particular school. Such a teacher may then find that curriculum development is as much concerned with the development of political and management strategies (such as how to influence the school's curriculum decision-making policies, especially in such matters as which subjects, if any, are to be integrated, offered as options, examined etc., and how to negotiate for more teaching time, resources and staff) as with developing teaching strategies and making decisions about content. Without this grass-roots involvement in curriculum development (variously referred to as school-based curriculum development, school-based in-service education and training, action research, etc.,) on the part of the classroom practitioner, the most carefully and imaginatively conceived agreed syllabuses of the local authorities are rarely implemented as they were intended.

M. H. Grimmitt, *What Can I do in RE?*,

Mayhew-McCrimmon 1973; B. Lealman (ed.), *The Total Curriculum in Relation to RE*, CEM 1980; D. Naylor, 'Curriculum Development', *New Movements in Religious Education*, ed. N. Smart and D. Horder, Temple Smith 1975; Schools Council, *Religious Education in Secondary Schools*, Working Paper 36, Evans/Methuen 1971; Schools Council, *A Groundplan for the Study of Religion*, Schools Council RE Committee Bulletin 1977; P. H. Taylor and C. M. Richards, *An Introduction to Curriculum Studies*, Humanities Press 1979.

MICHAEL GRIMMITT

Dance and Drama

In attempting to find a satisfactory third way in RE between the morally unfashionable vigour of a 'confessional' approach, in which the object is to somehow persuade the pupil of the validity of a particular religious stance, and the morally impeccable drabness of a 'descriptive' method, in which the world religions* are merely compared and contrasted in a neutral observer mode, dance and drama may be very valuable.

The conscious taking of the role of another, in life or in the context of drama, entails the development of a greater or lesser degree of empathy with the person or object studied and a consequent widening of our own experience and understanding, even our capacity for love or religious awe. According to Scheff, vicarious experience may have a cathartic effect and add to our lives an element of ritual that is often missing, to our detriment. Dance and drama are exciting and motivating methods of teaching when exercised in an appropriate environment by a competent and imaginative teacher at home with the demand these disciplines make on his or her flexibility and class-control.

The powerful mixture of myth* and history* to be found in the world's religions is a rich source of plot and character, often permitting a setting in period or a relocation in contemporary life. The ethical codes of religion abound with possibilities for the moral dilemmas which are the stuff of drama. Where ethnic groups mingle, an appreciation of their differing traditions in drama and dance may be a key to wider understanding and sympathy. Worship itself, at its best, is an activity with affinities both to dance and drama, and there seems to be a growing awareness in Western Christianity, of the potential of these skills for enhancing church life. The individual teacher will no doubt be able to judge which particular topics are right for dramatic treatment in his or her situation, though a number of the works listed in the bibliography will give guidance and encouragement to experiment.

However, the written word is of scant help to an RE teacher wishing to widen his or her teaching repertoire in these respects. The literature specific to RE and dance/drama is very sparse, though dance and drama in themselves are well-covered subjects. In any case, expertise in these area, whether as teacher or performer, is best acquired by doing, preferably by attending courses if these are available.

The wise teacher will exercise sensitivity with respect to pupils' (and pupils' parents') attitudes to the human body. Some pupils may object to dance on moral or religious grounds: many more will be straightforwardly shy, particularly boys during or after puberty.

Religion, too, often attracts more female participants in Western cultures during adult life. Is this because our sexual stereotyping demands that boys channel their physical energies into the limited emotional repertoire of sport rather than the wider possibilities of dance and drama?

Drama and dance can greatly enrich school assemblies. It is for each teacher and class to decide whether a piece of work is for themselves alone or for an audience. There are those who feel that performance may detract from the immediate value of an experience by over-stressing rehearsal and 'correctness'. Others would argue that the understanding of people and issues intrinsic to dramatic work is only fully realized when communication with an audience is attempted, and certainly performance very often generates a peculiar intensity of experience for the performer, which is not quickly forgotten.

V. R. Bruce and J. D. Tooke, *Lord of the Dance – an approach to RE*, Pergamon Press 1966; R. Burbridge and M. Watts, *Time to Act,* Hodder & Stoughton 1979; M. Evening, *Approaches to RE,* Hodder & Stoughton 1972; V. Green, *Drama in RE,* Blandford 1979; A. Long, *Praise Him in the Dance,*

Hodder & Stoughton 1976; T. J. Scheff, *Catharsis in Healing, Ritual and Drama,* University of California Press 1979; J. K. Thornecroft, *RE Through Experience and Expression,* Edward Arnold 1978.

VINCE AND SUE CROSS

Death: Pastoral Aspects of RE

Everyone knows what it is to suffer loss – whether that loss be relatively trivial or very profound. It is common ground upon which all human beings stand – common to both teacher and child. Dealing with bereavement therefore requires sensitivity and understanding. Whilst it is true that loss is common to all, the ways of responding to that loss are infinite. In broad terms, it is possible to talk of 'stages' of grief, but to suggest a definite chronology is to over-simplify.

In RE the pastoral care* of a child will depend not so much upon the subject matter as upon the relationship between teacher and child. Even though 'counselling' and 'care' have a fairly high status in some schools, it is worth asking whether or not children ought to be expected to look to their teachers for help. They may or may not. Often the teacher is the last person with whom they want to talk. The child's own integrity must be respected and acknowledged. They will choose who they want to ask for help – and if it is not the teacher, then so be it. The pastoral care will impinge directly upon RE (though not necessarily more than in, say, English literature), when questions of meaning are being explored. Then the teacher needs to be aware of the individual circumstances of the child, and lead that exploration with care and skill.

A number of agencies concerned with pastoral care, for example, Marriage Guidance Councils and Social Services Departments, are very willing to share insights they have about bereavement. The same is equally true of clergy*, who are in constant contact with bereaved people, and of hospice staff.

N. Autton, *Pastoral Care of the Bereaved,* SPCK 1967; H. Gollintzer (ed.), *Dying we live,* Fontana 1974; Elizabeth Kübler-Ross, *On Death and Dying,* Macmillan 1970; *To live until we say goodbye,* Spectrum 1979; S. Stephens, *Death Comes Home,* Mowbrays 1972.

CHRISTOPHER HERBERT

Death: Teaching about in RE

'Death' is the one subject in the RE curriculum where all are agreed that the cognitive and affective domains meet, where implicit* and explicit* beliefs converge. If nothing else, this should indicate the sensitivity and skill required in handling the subject. This too is an area where the beliefs, uncertainties, fears, hopes and anxieties of the teacher are exposed and vulnerable. The same may be said with equal force about the child. Existentially, it is the dying teaching the dying about death.

The choice of how to tackle the subject has to be left to the individual teacher, who takes account of local factors. At the cognitive level, it is clear that each major religion has beliefs about the process of dying, death itself and the afterlife which are worth studying. But this must be done with an awareness of the integrity of the whole value-system of each religion. A morbid and macabre trip around the more exotic manifestations of belief-systems is not called for. The study should include: (a) the beliefs about the destiny of the person after death, e.g. heaven, hell, reincarnation, etc; (b) the origin and development of those beliefs; (c) the architectural and artistic expression of those beliefs; (d) the social and personal expression of those beliefs; (e) the religious expression of those beliefs in language, symbolism and behaviour.

If the teacher chooses to work initially in the 'affective' area, then the concern is to help the child come to terms with death for himself; to help him express his own feelings and beliefs, and to deepen his own understanding and grasp of religious approaches to death. This is likely to involve poetry*, drama, dance*, photography, music and painting. This approach needs very careful handling for obviously the teacher will be in touch with the deepest levels of the child's personality.

CHRISTOPHER HERBERT

Denmark

1. *Historical background.* With the Lutheran reformation (1536), catechetical instruction became a vital concern of the church. This endeavour was powerfully undergirded in 1814 through the introduction of compulsory education for all – including RE. When the constitution of 1849 spoke of the state's duty to support the Lutheran church, it was generally agreed that the teaching of RE in schools was one of the ways in which the state could honour this obligation. Early twentieth-century regulations demonstrate the close alignment between church and school. The aim of RE was to develop sympathetic understanding of the basic tenets of Lutheranism. The main curriculum content was Bible-teaching, hymns and catechism. The schools of a diocese were all supervised by the bishop and at local level by the pastors.

In 1933, supervision of schools was transferred to secular authorities. At the same time, theologians of liberal inclination advocated a non-confessional teaching of RE. These developments called forth a vociferous public protest. A new education act passed in 1937 terminated the debate through compromise. School supervision remained secular, but it was codified by law that RE should be taught in accordance with the Lutheran confession. When the next education act was passed in 1958, the clause concerning the confessional character of RE was re-enacted without much debate.

2. *Challenges and responses.* The 1960s witnessed a growing dissatisfaction with the confessional aim of RE. A series of new challenges nourished a general feeling of uncertainty. A 'Humanist Society' appeared in 1960. In theology, the provoking de-mythologization ideas of Bultmann were widely discussed. Affluence contributed to the dissolution of traditional ethics. The student generation was influenced by the anti-conventional ideas of hippie-subculture, Eastern religion and neo-marxism.

The challenge was met through various initiatives at different levels. A law concerning teacher training (1966) considerably improved the academic standard of RE teachers. At the highest level of school education, i.e. the three pre-university classes (10.–12.), RE had, since 1903, been taught on a non-confessional basis, with the inclusion of non-Christian religions, but without examination. At the same level, a new, concentrated, two-year course was established in 1966, with RE as an obligatory examination subject. The government appointed inspectors for the teaching of RE at all levels including teacher training colleges. Also the teaching of RE in primary and secondary schools was revitalized. In 1958, the Association of RE Teachers altered its confessional statement of purpose into a purely educational formulation. Already in 1954 the association had established a resource-centre, the activities of which were much expanded in the 1960s. An increasing number of teachers attended in-service training courses. At the Royal Danish School of Educational Studies (Danmarks Laererhoejskole), an Institute of Religious Education was established in 1962. The Institute offers in-service training and degree courses and conducts research in RE. In the field of teaching-aids, comprehensive series of books appeared covering the total range from beginners to school-leavers and dealing both with Christianity and other world faiths.

The Ministry of Education appointed a commission (1967–1974) to explore the whole area of RE. The commission published a short report (1970) concerning RE at pre-university level and a longer one (1971) covering primary and secondary education. The commission advocated a non-confessional aim for RE and offered detailed suggestions for curriculum improvement.

3. *Recent development.* The confessional aim of RE was cancelled in the Education Act of 1975. The dogmatical clause has been superseded by an educational directive stating that the central area of information is to be the Lutheran Christianity of the Danish church. The act passed by the home rule legislative assembly in the Faroe Islands (1979) retains the confessional formulation of previous Danish legislation. A striking innovation of the present act is the distinction between Christianity and 'religion', i.e. non-Christian religions. For the *subject* 'Christian knowledge', government regulations prescribe a minimum number of lessons per week. At several stages the number of lessons prescribed for the subject is only one, which creates a difficult educational situation. 'Religion', together with non-religious stances, is classified as a *theme*, for which the number of lessons is decided by local authorities. Finally, the present law introduced new provisions for exemption from RE. Previously the condition for exemption was membership of a non-Christian religious community (or none). The act of 1975 requires only the written demand of the parents. A survey conducted in 1980/81

(excluding the Faroe Islands and Greenland) reveals that one or two per cent of the pupils in the classes 1.–9. are exempted from RE. Provisions for exemption similar to the present Danish law are found in the education act (1979) passed by the home rule legislative assembly in Greenland.

In the wake of the present law, the Ministry of Education has issued extensive guidelines both for the teaching of the subject Christian knowledge and of the themes religion and non-religious stances. But all is not well. The economic recession of the 1970s has limited the publication of teaching-aids and is narrowing the field of in-service training. The falling birth-rate raises premonitions of unemployment among teachers. In cities, the settlement of Muslim immigrants creates tensions hitherto unknown. Together with the increasing unco-operativeness of pupils, these problems have led many RE teachers to a sense of frustration. Other teachers react by returning to authoritarian orthodox ideas of former times. Still others seek to meet the harsh realities of the day as a challenge calling for inventiveness.

Although the situation is in many ways difficult, there are nevertheless signs of new development. A renewed interest in what goes on in other countries is noticeable. Danish RE has traditionally sought inspiration from Germany. The late sixties and early seventies have witnessed a considerable interest in British RE (Goldman, Smart, Grimmitt) and in the concept of religious language. Most recently, narrative theology has developed ideas which seem to be useful, especially because for more than a century Denmark has had a strong tradition for basing RE on stories. The ethical confusion in school and society has evoked inquiries into Moral Education*, a neglected area in Danish RE. Another promising new field of investigation is RE for handicapped children. Finally the emerging pluralistic pattern of society has led to courses and studies dealing with cultural encounter.

P. E. Andersen and S. Johannessen, *Haandbog for religionslaerere*, 1977; K. E. Bugge, *Vi har rel'gion*, 1979, and *Dansk krist-endomsundervisning 1900–1975*, 1979; A. Nellemann, *Schools and Education in Denmark*, 1964.

K. E. BUGGE

Department of Education and Science (DES)

Created in Britain in 1964 when the Ministry of Education and the Office of the Minister of Science were combined. It is responsible to the Secretary of State for Education and Science, who is a member of the Cabinet and is assisted by a Minister of State who has special responsibilities for the arts and three Parliamentary Under Secretaries of State. The 1944 Education Act requires the Secretary of State, 'to promote the education of the people of England and Wales and the progressive development of institutions devoted to that purpose and to secure the effective execution by local authorities under his control and direction, of the national policy for providing a varied and comprehensive educational service in every area.'

The principal concern of the Department is to formulate national policies which are administered through various branches dealing with schools, further and higher education, buildings, finance and legal matters. Schools III Branch, for example, is concerned with school curriculum, school examinations and educational technology. This branch is also responsible for liaison with the Schools Council* and contains the Assessment of Performance Unit (APU). This Unit's task is to develop methods of assessing and monitoring the performance of pupils throughout the school system.

DES has few executive functions: it does not provide or administer schools or colleges and it does not prescribe their detailed curricula. Schools are provided and administered by the local education authorities*, although their expenditure is financed largely by central government. The education service is therefore aptly described as a 'national system locally administered'. It is essentially a partnership between DES, LEAS and the teaching profession.

This distinctive feature of the education service in England and Wales is well illustrated in the provisions for RE. The subject is required by law as laid down in the 1944 Education Act, but each local authority has the responsibility of preparing an agreed syllabus* as the basis for religious teaching in county and controlled schools. The notion of partnership in education is stressed in the DES

publication *The School Curriculum* (1981), which offers guidance to LEAS in England and Wales on the curriculum covering the whole period of compulsory education. 'The place of religious education in the curriculum and its unique statutory position accord with a widely shared view that the subject has a distinctive contribution to make to a pupil's school education. It provides an introduction to the religious and spiritual areas of experience and particularly to the Christian tradition which has profoundly affected our culture. It forms part of the curriculum's concern with personal and social values, and can help pupils to understand the religious and cultural diversity of contemporary society. The Secretaries of State consider that local education authorities should keep under review the provision made for religious education, bearing in mind the requirements of the Education Act 1944 as regards collective acts of worship and religious instruction; and that they should also reconsider from time to time the appropriateness of the Agreed Syllabus for their area in the light of the needs of particular groups of pupils and changes in the society in which the pupils are growing up' (*para.* 27).

DES is particularly concerned with educational standards, and in exercising this responsibility it is assisted by members of Her Majesty's Inspectorate, whose primary role is to report on trends and standards throughout the education service on the basis of inspection and to provide the Secretary of State and DES with professional advice. HM also offers advice to LEAS, schools and colleges, conduct short courses for teachers and prepares publications of various kinds. These publications include two national surveys – *Primary Education in England* (1978) and *Aspects of Secondary Education in England* (1979). A small number of Inspectors have as a major part of their assignment a responsibility for RE under the leadership of a national specialist, the Staff Inspector for RE who also serves as an Inspectorate link with such bodies as the Religious Education Council*, the Christian Education Movement* and the Association for Religious Education* (amalgamated 1984). The HMI subject committee contributed the supplementary paper on religious education to *Curriculum 11–16 Working Papers by HM Inspectorate: A Contribution to Current Debate* (1977).

This HMI statement deals with the scope of religious education, the RE programme at the secondary stage, the context of the subject in society and schools and, finally, expectations and assessment in RE. The role of RE in the curriculum is described in the following terms: 'Religious Education shares with other subjects the task of helping children to acquire the skills, knowledge and social competence necessary for their personal development and life in society. Consequently it shares with other subjects a concern for basic skills such as attention to evidence, careful reasoning, the communication of ideas through the written and spoken word, as well as providing opportunities for pupils to work independently and display initiative. . . . However, Religious Education also makes a distinctive contribution to the curriculum in directing attention to the religious understanding of human life and to the central values (many of them derived from religion) which society seeks to uphold and to transmit. In this consideration of religion and values, the intention is to help pupils to understand the nature of religious questions and religious affirmations, and to develop a personal and intellectual integrity in dealing with the profoundest aspects of their own experience now and in adult life.'

ALAN LOOSEMORE

Development Education and RE

The origins of the term date from the 1960s when there was a growing recognition by aid agencies and educators of a fundamental division in the world. Economic wealth and political power were increasingly concentrated in a minority of rich industrialized countries in the North, whilst the majority of the world's population remained powerless and exploited at very low income levels in the countries of the South. Development education attempts to describe and to explain this global division and to stimulate thought and action on how to remedy the injustice of the situation. Broader acceptance that the processes of underdevelopment create poverty both within nations and between nations has resulted in development education being concerned with issues of human welfare, human rights, social justice and the moral and ethical dilemmas that these issues

pose, in both 'developing' and 'developed' countries.

The objective of development education is to enable people to comprehend and participate in the development of themselves, their local communities, their country and the world. It requires an educational approach which provides an understanding of the power structures, interdependencies and processes which influence patterns of development at the local, national and global level. A key element in the process of development education is participation, based on the principle that everyone has the potential to contribute to the creation of a world of greater justice.

Any study of moral and ethical dilemmas requires a consideration of the contextual values and value systems of societies. The contribution RE can make to development education lies in this area of values and morality. In a world where an increasing population is in competition for the finite resources of the planet, RE can help pupils develop moral judgments about the allocation of these resources and the solution of conflicts arising from the struggle for global justice, drawing on the insights and values of the world's great religions, the teachings of religious leaders and the example set by some of their adherents.

John J. Shepherd, *Religion and World Development*, Extramural Division, School of Oriental and African Studies, University of London 1982.

ANDREW HUTCHINSON

Development, Theories of

Human development is far from a settled matter for religious education. Some religious educators tend to deny it, while others tend to regard it as irrelevant. While that is unfortunate, it is a fact that only the psalmist's fool could ignore. Even so, development or its functional equivalent (ordered change across time) seems inescapable. Across any twelve to eighteen month period most humans change or develop: it is almost impossible for them to be the same at the end as they were at the beginning.

During the twentieth century there have been a number of important contributions to a theory of development. The most general and persistent such contribution is the legacy of Charles Darwin. Evolution is a theory of development on a truly vast scale. In these final decades of the twentieth century the theory of evolution is more than a hundred years old, remarkably alive, and surprisingly difficult to either prove or falsify. However, for many the battles over evolution are now as dead as those ecclesiastics who are remembered only in the footnotes to histories of science.

Many but not all Christians found ways to accommodate the evolutionary thesis early in the twentieth century. Thus, for many committed persons the resurgence of an anti-evolutionary creationism in the 1980s was a sign of severe cultural lag. Still, for some religious educators, the denial of development on a vast scale probably seemed like a more worthy enterprise than it will at the start of the twenty-first century.

In the early years of the twentieth century three persons made significant contributions to the theory of development: Alfred Binet (France), John Dewey (USA), and Maria Montessori (Italy). Binet was a psychologist, Dewey was an educator, Montessori was a physician. Their contributions can best be understood as the expression of their basic disciplines. Yet each of them was concerned with education. In addition, both Dewey and Montessori were also concerned with religious education. In the middle half of the century, Dewey lost that interest but Montessori retained it until her death in 1952.

During the middle years of the twentieth century five persons made significant contributions to the theory of development: Alfred Adler (Austria), Charlotte Buhler (Germany), Erik H. Erikson (USA), Robert J. Havinghurst (USA), and Jean Piaget (Switzerland). Adler and Erikson were both psychoanalysts. Buhler and Havinghurst were both psychologists. Although often considered the developmentalist, Piaget considered himself to be a genetic epistemologist. Each of them contributed ideas important to education, although many of those ideas have now become part of a folk wisdom that is enshrined in popular secondary and tertiary interpretations or applications.

As the last quarter of the twentieth century began, the ideas of Jean Piaget seemed to be most influential. The work of Ronald J. Goldman (Australia), Lawrence Kohlberg (USA) and James Fowler (USA) are all variations on a theme by the Swiss genetic epistemologist. Each of these has affected RE although only Fowler has persistently been interested in religion. Goldman moved on to other problems when he emigrated from Britain to Australia. Kohlberg has rarely shown any real interest in RE. Thus, religious educators have a very real need to go behind Goldman, Kohlberg and Fowler to Piaget himself. In addition, there is much to be rediscovered in Adler, Binet, Buhler, Dewey, Erikson, Havinghurst and Montessori.

Any developmental theory supports belief that humans are very complex creatures. Most developmentalists also recognize that humans have an often overpowering desire for simplicity, especially when faced with genuine complexities. The simplifying endemic to popularizing is developmentally understandable, even if it often involves over-simplification of the complex educational realities religious educators continually encounter. While the occamist's razor is quite useful, too often mere models of complicated developmental sequences are popularly presumed to be full, detailed and accurate descriptions.

After careful developmental analyses of over 12,000 instances of a standard set of Piagetian tasks involving difficult biblical material, and more than 3,000 responses to a Piegetian puzzle concerned with authority, Peatling reached three conclusions about human development. 1. The empirical evidence does witness to a direction, the presence of pattern, and the reality of differences. 2. The rate at which persons in various religious groups move in a developmental direction is noticeably different. 3. The range of differences within religious groups is such that some persons from groups with very different rates exhibit precisely the same developmental level. Thus, simple characterizations of religious groupings are often inaccurate and usually inadequate to the complex reality of most such groupings. Rules of thumb are never more than that and, often, quite disfunctional educationally.

In these last decades of the twentieth century, theories of development perform one invaluable service for RE: they keep religious educators from becoming no more than biological teaching machines. The realities of direction, pattern and difference mean that religious educators must both attend closely to their students and continue to be ingenious in adapting materials, goals and curricula to their true interlocutors, their students. Less is an effective denial of developmental fact, theory and research: something very like culpable ignorance.

John Dewey, *Democracy and Education,* The Free Press 1961/1966; Martin S. Dworkin (ed.), *Dewey on Education,* Teachers College Press 1959; Erik H. Erikson, *Childhood and Society,* W. W. Norton ²1963; Erik H. Erikson and Joan M. Erikson, 'On Generativity and Identity', *Harvard Education Review,* 2 May 1981, pp. 249–69; James Fowler, *Stages of Faith: The Psychology of Human Development and the Quest for Meaning,* Harper & Row 1981; Ronald J. Goldman, *Readiness for Religion,* Routledge & Kegan Paul 1965; Robert J. Havinghurst, *Human Development and Education,* Longmans Green 1963; Lawrence Kohlberg, *The Philosophy of Moral Development: Essays in Moral Development,* Vol. 1, Harper & Row 1981; Maria Montessori, *The Absorbent Mind,* Holt, Rinehart & Winston 1967; John H. Peatling, *Religious Education in a Psychological Key,* Religious Education Press 1981; Jean Piaget, *Science of Education and the Psychology of the Child,* Grossman Publishers 1970; Jean Piaget and Barbel Inhelder, *The Psychology of the Child,* Basic Books 1969.

JOHN H. PEATLING

Dharma *see* **Hinduism**

Dialogue

May occur whenever people of different religions meet within a common social environment. In most situations it happens spontaneously and haphazardly: since religious beliefs and practices are the framework of reference to many questions about holidays and festivals*, family life, birth, marriage and burial customs, dietary laws and rules of hygiene, religious dialogue is often only implicit, and it is closely linked with culture and race.

Paul's activity in Hellenistic Ephesus was described as 'dialogue' (*dialégesthai*, 'to argue, discuss', is used in Acts 19.8–9). His speech on the Areopagus (Acts 17.22ff.), containing references to Stoic and Epicurean philosophies, shows the style which the author of Acts thought appropriate to such an audience. A living and appreciative dialogue with current philosophies continued within the church, particularly at Alexandria, alongside hostility towards them. Ambivalence has continued to mark the attitudes of Christians towards other religions all through the centuries.

In recent years, several factors have compelled churches and educational institutions to pay greater attention to inter-religious dialogue: the growth of the churches in Asia and Africa, renewal of other major religions in reaction to Western imperialism (political, economic and cultural), easier and quicker transport, development of the media through radio, television and satellite, labour mobility and the development of world community. Few societies, except in isolated areas, remain homogeneous.

Following Vatican II, the Vatican Secretariat for Non-Christians was established in 1964. In 1970 the World Council of Churches* set up a Department for Dialogue with People of Living Faiths and Ideologies. Handbooks and discussion material have been published and many conferences and consultations held, often with participants from other religions. The British reference point is the British Council of Churches'* Committee for Relations with People of Other Faiths. The institutions of other religions have begun to develop similar initiatives.

In the educational field there has long been a tradition of academic dialogue in universities and the departments of religious education in colleges of further and higher education. The Department of Education and Science* has drawn attention to the need for a pluralist religious education to meet the needs of contemporary society (*Education in Schools,* 1977), and appropriate provisions are now embodied in some agreed syllabuses*, following the pioneering activities of the Birmingham Education Authority. Valuable contributions have been made by the Shap Working Party on World Religions in Education*, and the Standing Conference on Inter-Faith Dialogue in Education*. A succinct account of the principles involved is given in a BCC pamphlet *Education Principles in RE*. The representatives of other religions play an increasing part in the construction of syllabuses appropriate to the needs of a pluralist society. The Centre for the Study of Islam and Christian-Muslim Relations at the Selly Oak Colleges, Birmingham, is doing much to help Muslim groups relate to the unfamiliar situation in Britain.

Dialogue takes place in the classroom in RE lessons, but also at many points in the curriculum and in the social relationships between groups in class or in school. Certain guidelines must be observed if dialogue is to be beneficial and not divisive.

1. Dialogue is between people: every individual represents the beliefs and practices of a particular community and expresses them in a personal and distinctive way.

2. Truth must be told about different religions even-handedly, if possible in terms acceptable to each particular religion. There can be no dialogue unless there is mutual understanding and mutual trust. To tell the truth is to allow each person to speak without fear or embarrassment.

3. Dialogue can only be conducted helpfully if every participant accepts a common loyalty to the well-being of the whole society and recognizes the rights of those who are different to share in it.

These guidelines are essential not only for planned inter-faith discussions in the classroom but also for the many other encounters which occur in other contexts. The attitudes learnt in class are important to guide people belonging to different religions and cultural groups in their relations with one another. In this way, schools prepare children for citizenship in a pluralist society and a world commonwealth.

Many people fear that dialogue leads to a loss of confidence in particular religious truths and traditions, and diminishes commitment to them. On the contrary, dialogue enables people to understand their own beliefs more clearly, but in a way which reflects the wider context of other people's beliefs and practices. 'We commend the way of dialogue as one in which Jesus Christ can be confessed in the world today; . . . we assure our partners in dialogue that we come not as manipulators but as genuine fellow-pilgrims, to speak with them of what we believe God to have done in Jesus Christ who has gone before us, but whom we seek to meet anew in dialogue.'

David Brown, *All Their Splendour*, Fount

1982; Kenneth Cracknell, *Considering Dialogue*, BCC 1981; John Hick, *God and the Universe of Faiths*, Fount 1977; M. Y. McDermott and M. M. Ahsan, *The Muslim Guide*, Islamic Foundation 1980; S. J. Samartha, *Courage for Dialogue*, WCC 1981.

See also **World Religions**.

DAVID BROWN

Diocesan Advisers: Church of England

Almost all dioceses have implemented the recommendation of the Carlisle Report that a diocesan education team should include an RE adviser. Some follow the pattern of that report and have one officer responsible for work with children in both church schools and also in the voluntary context. Others have split the responsibility between two officers, on the lines of the distinction between RE and Christian nurture*, set out in *The Child in the Church* (1976).

The task in relation to church schools is to provide a consultancy and advisory service. While advisers have no direct access to county schools, they normally work closely with colleagues in the LEA service and contribute a good deal to the support and development of RE in general.

In addition to offering a service analogous to that of LEA advisory staff, they help clergy to relate effectively to their schools. They may have some responsibility for the training and support of foundation governors and for the provision of church school inspectors (often referred to as 'visitors'). They have an important interpretative role between church and school, bringing together the insights of both educational and theological disciplines.

The task in relation to the voluntary context is similar. While there is often still a considerable emphasis on training voluntary staff for Sunday Schools and providing them with resources, there is an increasing concern to enable local churches to work out the implications for their life of the presence of children within the Christian community. This will often be focussed around the provision of ideas and resources for family worship. Advisers may also have responsibility for the development of confirmation preparation programmes.

They may provide opportunities for

children to take part in diocesan activities, e.g. holiday courses, festivals or projects based on the cathedral.

The main thrust of their work is, however, directed towards advice, support, training and pastoral care for those adults who are responsible for the religious education and the Christian nurture of children in church schools and parish churches.

The Child in the Church, British Council of Churches 1976; Report of the Carlisle Commission, *Partners in Education: The Role of the Diocese,* National Society/SPCK 1971.

DAVID ATKINSON

Diocesan Advisers: Roman Catholic

Appointed by the bishop to implement the religious education policy of the diocese, the adviser may be a priest, a religious or a layperson and will have a supervisory and facilitating role over the whole field of RE from preschool children to the elderly or will specialize in one particular area. The adviser works as a field officer visiting parishes and schools and setting up courses both centrally and in a particular area. An adviser whose particular brief is parishes will be responsible for helping them to develop up-to-date eucharistic and confirmation programmes for both candidates and their parents, in co-operation with the local clergy. One whose brief is schools will not only be concerned with classroom programmes but will also promote teacher training courses, for example, the Catholic Teachers' Certificate. An adviser engaged in adult work will be involved in looking at every possible way in which to find opportunities for adult religious education, for example, the encouragement of parish group learning, talks on theology, scripture, etc., the use of local radio, newspapers, etc. There are, therefore, RE advisers working for primary and secondary school children and their parents, for the deaf, for the physically and mentally handicapped, for travelling people, for young people and for adults. An adviser needs to have had practical experience in working in his/her chosen field, to have the necessary knowledge and the ability to communicate, and the willingness to work with others, generally as part of a diocesan team.

PATRICK PURNELL SJ

Diocesan Syllabuses: Church of England

According to the 1944 Education Act, controlled schools are required to teach RE according to the agreed syllabus* of their local authority, but can provide denominational teaching to supplement it. Aided schools can, however, use their own (denominational) syllabus. Diocesan syllabuses have been developed to assist aided schools in this provision. At present there are twenty-four dioceses (out of forty-three in England) that have adopted a syllabus and another seven are considering doing so. There appear to be sixteen different syllabuses in use. All of these have been published between 1970 and 1981.

The assumption underlying most such diocesan syllabuses is that 'the purpose of religious education in an aided school must be as it was defined for the county school . . . that is, to explore the place and significance of religion in human life and so to make a distinctive contribution to each pupil's search for a faith by which to live. Where it will differ from religious education in the county and controlled schools is in its freedom to achieve this purpose through involvement in one particular religious tradition' (Ramsey). They tend, therefore, to be similar in their educational approach to the agreed syllabuses, while differing in content.

They tend, as might be expected, to be more confessional, (although Blackburn, for instance, has a World Faiths Supplement), and to see more readily that 'the local faith community is a prime resource in the teaching of RE in schools'.

The syllabuses are mostly concerned with primary and middle schools, reflecting the paucity of aided secondary schools. They are not mandatory, and quite clearly (as some of them recognize) not always appropriate for aided schools in multi-faith areas, or for those which act as neighbourhood schools. They will often need to be used alongside agreed syllabuses and their claims to be guidelines rather than schemes of work need to be taken seriously.

Brian E. Gates (ed.) *Religious Education Directory for England and Wales*, Religious Education Council of England and Wales 1982; I. T. Ramsey (ed.) *The Fourth R,*

Durham Report on Religious Education, National Society/SPCK 1970.

DAVID ATKINSON

Diocesan Syllabuses: Roman Catholic

In the years immediately after Vatican II (1963–1965) there was a very considerable renewal in school RE programmes. This renewal was world-wide, and a number of RE programmes from elsewhere were introduced into Britain, for example the work of Maria de la Cruz. Among the earliest programmes produced in this country was the 'Over To You' series from Digby Stuart (Roehampton) College of Education, but it was the Christian Education Centre of the Archdiocese of Liverpool under Fr A. Bullen which quickly became well known for its syllabus for primary schools. Later the diocese of Westminster issued the Konstant Syllabus, first for the primary and then for the secondary school. Next came the Liverpool syllabus for secondary schools. Over the years, the work done in Liverpool has developed and the Liverpool secondary religious education programme has become one of the standard texts for the whole country. Its Primary Syllabus has been recently published by Fr G. O'Mahony, SJ. The diocese of Shrewsbury has also produced a syllabus for the primary school. However, in recent years the Irish Catechetical Programme has achieved a very notable success and has been adopted by very many of the dioceses in England and Wales as their official programme for primary schools: this has come to be known as the Veritas Programme. It is important to note that whereas once the syllabus carried with it the weight of officialdom, in the sense of 'this had to be taught', today it is presented as a teaching tool to help teachers share their faith with the children they teach.

PATRICK PURNELL SJ

Dissenting Academies

The Act of Uniformity (1662) excluded from the Church of England all those clergy who could not accept either the *Book of Common Prayer* or episcopal ordination. The statutes of Oxford and Cambridge forbade them to admit any who were not members of the Church of England. Dissenters therefore had to make other arrangements for the training of their ministers and the higher education of their sons.

In the latter part of the seventeenth century, individual ministers who had themselves been educated at Oxford or Cambridge tried to give pupils the kind of education they had enjoyed. The theology they taught was generally an orthodox Calvinism. Otherwise the curriculum depended on the interests and abilities of the tutor, and pupils frequently migrated from one to another. At Newington Green, under Charles Morton, Daniel Defoe learned five languages and studied mathematics, science, logic, geography, history and politics as well as theology. Morton was exceptional in teaching in English instead of Latin.

Early in the eighteenth century, Queen Anne and the Tories attempted to close the academies. The Schism Act (1714) prohibited anyone from keeping a school without declaring assent to the Prayer Book and obtaining the bishop's licence. Some academies did close. However, the Hanoverians and the Whigs were more tolerant towards Dissenters and during the century the academies became more stable institutions, with more than one tutor and support from denominational funds. One of the best documented is the academy Philip Doddridge maintained at Northampton (1729–1751). He made his pupils consider both sides of controversial questions, so much so that they were accused of having no convictions of their own.

The academy which did most to provide general education was the one at Warrington (1757–1783). It was founded to train 'ministers free to follow the dictates of their own judgments in the inquiries after truth' and to give 'some knowledge to those who were engaged in commercial life as well as in the learned professions'. The leading tutors were John Aikin and Joseph Priestley.

In strong contrast were the academies founded towards the end of the eighteenth century under the influence of the Evangelical Revival. Here, training to preach to the unconverted was all important and other studies were unnecessary, if not corrupting. Academies such as Trevecca and Hoxton contributed most to the growth of the nonconformist denominations in the early nineteenth century. Eventually the traditions of learning and evangelism were combined, as at Homerton under John Pye Smith.

It would be a mistake to exaggerate the achievements of the dissenting academies. They were not all progressive and those which did teach modern subjects were following rather than pioneering change. Nevertheless, at their best they maintained the Puritan ideal of a conscientious and learned ministry and provided an efficient substitute for university education. Their role in training for the ministry is continued by Free Church theological colleges today, but their contribution to general education diminished when the secular universities were founded from 1828 onwards.

Nicholas Hans, *New Trends in Education in the 18th Century*, Routledge & Kegan Paul 1951; H. McLachlan, *English Education under the Test Acts*, Manchester University Press 1931; Geoffrey F. Nuttall, *The Significance of Trevecca College 1768–91*, Epworth 1969; Irene Parker, *Dissenting Academies in England*, Cambridge University Press 1914; J. W. Ashley Smith, *The Birth of Modern Education: the Dissenting Academies*, Independent Press 1955.

ROGER TOMES

Doctrine, Teaching of

Educational attitudes to the teaching of doctrine in RE are largely determined by two factors: (*a*) the degree of religious pluralism in the relevant society; (*b*) the extent to which the dominant religions emphasize the need for doctrinal orthodoxy.

In a pluralistic society with competing orthodoxies (e.g. the USA), all religious intruction may be relegated to the private sphere. In England and Wales, the combination of a broad Christian consensus with sharp denominational differences produced the present dual system of county and voluntary schools. Church schools are free to develop their own syllabuses of doctrinal teaching, but in county schools RE, according to agreed syllabuses*, has until recently avoided contentious doctrinal issues and confined itself largely to biblical studies.

Since the Second World War the situation has changed radically. There is no longer a broad consensus in religion and morality, either among parents or teachers. The teaching of doctrine has been criticized as indoctrination* (in spite of its ineffectiv-

eness), and has been forced to adopt a phenomenological guise. Moreover, the wide acceptance of Piaget's account of children's development has led many teachers to declare that doctrinal teaching is impossible, even if desirable, before the secondary stage of schooling. Most recently, however, a new emphasis has been put on the religious experience of young children and although this is unlikely to lead to the rehabilitation of doctrinal teaching, it focusses attention on the nature of religious doctrine as the crystallization of experience and identifies experience as a pre-requisite for the understanding of doctrine.

Ronald Goldman, *Religious Thinking from Childhood to Adolescence*, Routledge & Kegan Paul 1964; I. T. Ramsey (ed.), *The Fourth R*, SPCK 1970; Schools Council, *Religious Education in Secondary Schools*, Methuen/Evans 1971; Ninian Smart, *The Teacher and Christian Belief*, James Clark 1966.

GRAHAM NEVILLE

Drama   *see* **Dance and Drama**

Dual System   *see* **Acts of Parliament**

Durham Report   *see* **Fourth R, The**

Early Fathers

Education in the ancient world was largely based upon the study of literary texts and aimed at producing public speakers skilled in debate and elaborate stylistic embellishment. Christian attitudes ranged from outright condemnation on the grounds that the literature was full of pagan myths and immoralities (e.g. *Apostolic Tradition, Didascalia Apostolorum*, Tertullian, Epiphanius), to almost whole-hearted acceptance in an integrated programme with a theological summit (Origen and the Alexandrian school). By the fourth and fifth centuries, Christianity now being the official religion of the Empire, church leaders were socially prominent and drawn from the educated and cultured classes. Recognizing the need for skilled debaters, exegetes and preachers, for upholding the church's position in society, they advised parents and young people to allow the usual educational curriculum to train the mind while discriminating between the morally useful and the harmful and avoiding the temptations of worldly success and 'vainglory' (e.g. Basil the Great, *Address to young men on how they might profit from pagan literature;* John Chrysostom, *On Vainglory and the education of children*). Yet committed Christians would abandon the rhetorical profession (e.g. Basil and his brother, Gregory of Nyssa), and a frequent charge against heretics was that they depended upon dialectical skill rather than commitment to truth. The inherent ambiguities in these attitudes are illuminated by the reign of Julian who, on coming to the throne, revealed his apostasy from Christianity and, amongst other anti-Christian moves, promulgated an edict banning Christians from the schools and the teaching profession (A D 362): a teacher, he argued, should honour the gods honoured in the literature he taught. The reaction was dismay: that the edict was intended to undermine the effectiveness of the church was never doubted. Some, by writing alternative epics, tragedies and comedies using biblical stories and putting the Gospels into the form of Platonic dialogues, attempted to provide an alternative syllabus (the Apollinarii, father and son); others attacked the claim that mathematics, music, poetry, etc. belonged to paganism, arguing that these subjects were a universal legacy deriving from many races and religions (e.g. Gregory of Nazianzus). The crisis quickly passed; so the ambiguities were never resolved. The classics remained the basis of education in a nominally Christian society. Christian education proper remained within the home and the church and did not affect the educational system as such. Some parents sent their sons to monastic schools, but Chrysostom (op. cit.) did not recommend this for the majority; rather he concentrated on the moral and spiritual environment desirable in the Christian home. The duty of Christian parents to bring up their children in the Christian way was based upon the New Testament (Eph. 6.1–4) and it was expected that the home background would counterweigh the influence of the pagan schools. Most of those who became influential bishops were brought up in this way.

Meanwhile, the church had developed its own system of Christian catechesis* for converts and adults seeking baptism. The local bishop was responsible for a very considerable educational enterprise, unique in its universality: all classes, illiterate as well as highly cultured, were bound to participate before baptism in a course of lectures during Lent, learning by rote the creed and the Lord's Prayer and sometimes substantial portions of the scriptures, and listening to expositions outlining the principal doctrines of the faith. Reading the extant series of lectures (those of Cyril of Jerusalem, John Chrysostom and Theodore of Mopsuestia), one is struck by the seriousness with which the task of imparting doctrinal theology was taken. Intellectual difficulties were tackled and a paramount task was the arming of converts not merely against immorality but also against paganism and heresy: polytheism, Judaism, dualism and other plausible but false doctrines were countered. The lectures were the culmination of several years 'probation', during which study suitable to the educational level of the convert was supervised by the catechist. The *Great Catechism* of Gregory of Nyssa and Augustine's *De Catechizandis Rudibus* are illuminating instructions to catechists, each in their own way concerned to adapt Christian education to the needs of individual enquirers.

In some respects, the church took on the role of the philosophical school teaching the true philosophy. The sermon or homily corresponded to the philosophical lecture, being at first a moral exhortation, later an exposition of scripture. In both forms it owed a great deal in style and technique to the educational practices of rhetors and philosophers, with the Bible substituted for classical texts.

M. L. Clarke, *Higher Education in the Ancient World,* Routledge & Kegan Paul 1971; Edwin Hatch, *The Influence of Greek Ideas on Christianity,* 1888, Harper & Brothers 1957; M. L. W. Laistner, *Christianity and Pagan Culture,* Cornell University Press 1951.

FRANCES YOUNG

East Germany   *see* **Eastern Europe**

Eastern Europe

In the Soviet Union, Bulgaria and Albania, no religious education of those under eighteen is allowed by law. In Poland, R E is prohibited at school, but constitutionally is allowed in the church, including the institution of catechist centres. The legal and actual situation is similar in Yugoslavia. In the Czechoslovakian Republic and Hungary, the teaching of RE in schools using a school syllabus is legal, but it is not obligatory and so rarely happens. Here, and in the German Democratic Republic, RE is the responsibility of churches and congregations in different ways and dimensions.

With the exception of establishments for the education of clergy, RE has been eliminated from schools throughout Eastern Europe since the end of the Second World War. In all these countries, a comprehensive school system has been established, more or less based on the ideology of Marxism-Leninism. The claim to represent the most progressive order of society includes the conception of pushing back the influence of any religion on education. At school, religion is treated as a historical phenomenon. Where RE exists, it is organized as a responsibility of the church or takes place within the family. Religiously inspired works of cultural tradition can be considered as incidental factors of RE. Occasionally, information about religion is obtained through the promulgation of atheism. In most countries of Eastern Europe, there are no direct links from RE to teaching institutions or research. The conditions for RE in Eastern Europe differ according to its historical importance, or the present strength of religion, or earlier conflicts, depend on political ideology, and vary from toleration to under-privilege or repression. RE in Eastern Europe is related to tradition and mission.

Information about RE in the Soviet Union is very sparse. It is impossible to be precise about this subject. In the Russian Orthodox Church, Christian education is based on the divine service with its holy liturgy, paintings and customs and on family prayers. In the Orthodox divine service, it is possible to move and participate in an individual way; here there is contact with another environment, another language, metaphorical expressions and symbolical activities and objects. Such experiences can affect the motivation of the worshipper who is beginning to learn the Christian tradition and adopting Christian attitudes and patterns of life. This is especially true of the spirituality which is characteristic of the Orthodox faith. The transmission of Christian norms and thinking from one generation to another in the Orthodox Church is founded in liturgy. RE is considered more as

the way to attain the vocation of participating in the spiritual life than teaching on an intellectual level. So baptism, for example, becomes important for RE. It is difficult to estimate to what extent such education is able to assist people to look critically at the social and rational conditions and challenges of a secular environment. In the Soviet Union conditions for RE in the Protestant tradition, which is much more related to verbal teaching and communication, are also complicated. RE is conducted in small groups as it is difficult, especially for the Roman Catholic Church, to invite children to larger meetings (masses for children are not allowed). Methods of religious education in the several churches and congregations correspond to their different traditions.

In Poland, all churches have an extensive system of religious education, including Sunday Schools and camps, and there is a Catholic university at Lublin. The Polish Roman Catholic Church, feeling itself both as part of the Roman universal church and as an integral part of Polish history and identity, has based RE on the priesthood. This instruction, given by priests and catechists, is mainly directed to observing ritual norms and to learning Catholic doctrines. Each child is called to share in a ministry of telling other children about preaching and religious instruction, praying, divine service and consolation.

In Hungary, instruction is given in the first classes of schools for a small number of children. However, the intruction given in the churches themselves has greater importance. In the Protestant churches, RE is almost always Bible-centred. In the Orthodox Church of Romania, RE is considered as part of the pastoral service of the priest visiting parishioners with ritual acts and prayers. Meetings in groups are not allowed. The situation in Bulgaria is similar. In the Protestant churches in Romania – churches of ethnic minorities – there are Sunday Schools, e.g. in preparation for confirmation.

In the German Democratic Republic, the only socialist country with a history considerably shaped by the Lutheran Reformation, the Protestant churches have formed a new structure for RE (now named Christian Education) as a result both of historical developments and of such theological reflection as developed in the fascist period. RE has been integrated into the other activities of the church and takes place as instruction, free working with children, Sunday School, family divine services, weekend courses, and regional children's days or camps. Usually there are small groups of mixed ages. In many church districts there is a shortage of catechists, therefore the church has tried to get lay co-workers. In 1980 the Federation of Protestant Churches in the GDR rearranged the education of 'parish-teachers'. In 1976, after a period of more doctrinal and Bible-centred instruction, the Federation of Protestant Churches in the GDR established a curriculum project intending to deal with the extensive changes in family, society and church, in theology and doctrine. Christian education is recognized as being a complex process. The general aim is to qualify people for witness and service in a socialist society. Christian education aims to give children assistance and information to equip them for their life. The confessional character of RE does not dominate real education. Catholic RE in the GDR is directed more towards commitment than is the Protestant. A monthly journal for RE, 'Die Christenlehre', is published in Berlin.

The hardest burden in RE in Eastern Europe is isolation in a social system within the different groups on which individuals depend and the inner conflict of the divided loyalties felt by everyone who wants to combine faith with loyalty to his own country. The general approach that RE should be related to context is demanding in practice: individuals and communities must face processes of adjustment, completion or correction. The answer depends on context and theological persuasion. One opportunity for RE in Eastern Europe is to raise issues and experiences which are neglected in the environment. Everywhere it is important for Christian religious educators to make possible, on the one hand, appreciation of the tradition of faith, and, on the other, the finding of meaningful answers to the issues of context (Jer. 29.7). In Eastern Europe, RE is faced with the problem of coming to terms with the education system of real socialism, based on a view of historical determinism. In this sense, it is deeply involved in the history and presence of this complex and dynamic area. This implies difficulty, but also hope.

G. Barberini, M. Stöhr, E. Weingäter (eds.), *Kirchen im Sozialismus, Kirche und Staat in den osteuropäischen sozialistischen Republiken*, Frankfurt/Main 1977; Trevor Beeson, *Discretion and Valour*, Collins 1974.

REIMUND BLÜHM

Ecumenical Education

The task of ecumenical education has always been considered a fundamental one where Christians, acting in congregations, churches and ecumenical bodies, work towards visible Christian unity and a common Christian witness. Inasmuch as ecumenical education is one dimension of the ecumenical movement, it has always formed part of and been related to such activities as encounters, meetings, conferences, joint services, statements, publications, etc., carried out in this context. Thus, it has been an integral part of all ecumenical activities, but, in addition, it has always found its own distinctive form of expression.

In defining ecumenical education more precisely, three motives which determine the understanding of 'ecumenical' have to be taken into consideration:

1. The ecclesiological motive, which gives rise to the question of how Christians of different churches, confessions and denominations can contrive to move towards more visible unity.

2. The missionary motive, which requires a global awareness and a new understanding of the inter-relatedness of the proclamation of the gospel and social commitment, of evangelism and humanization.

3. The social-ethical motive, which, by linking the unity of all Christians and the unity of all human beings, stresses the commitment to the cause of peace and justice in a world seen as a single dwelling-place for all human beings.

The word 'ecumenical' binds these three motives together. Therefore they are also constitutive for ecumenical education. In a particular learning project, one of the motives may prevail. No one of the three, however, can be completely lacking.

Thus ecumenical education can be described as fostering 'understanding of, commitment to, and informed participation in the vision of the one, missionary church in process of renewal. When grasped it leads then to ecumenical commitment, i.e. to participation in the process of letting the churches be more truly the church' (World Council of Churches, 1957).

Therefore, ecumenical education can no longer be limited to the communication of the facts, history, background, structures and functions of the ecumenical movement as part of a curriculum in theological, religious or Christian education. Rather, it is the comprehensive task of equipping Christians to live as one liberating and reconciling community in a divided world. It is, therefore, a dimension rather than a segment of the whole educational task of the churches, although it appears also in particular learning projects or programmes such as development education* or education for mission.

Its pedagogical dimension and all the factors which must be considered if such ecumenical learning is to take place need further discussion. As early as the 1950s came the call for new methods of ecumenical education, and first steps towards a 'learning theory for ecumenical education' were envisaged. Finally, Ernst Lange pleaded for ecumenical didactics, a theory and method 'for producing an atmosphere, a situation of tension, in church and society, in which individuals, groups, communities and church officials are really set free for a learning process which carries them beyond their previous level of information and awareness'.

There are already some cornerstones for building an ecumenical learning theory. But further work is necessary to find a clear answer as to 'how Christians can grow so as to contrive to be adequate for the world in which they are called to believe, to love and to hope' (E. Lange). To work on this means finally to bring new aims, new contents and new methods to the churches' total teaching.

Christian Education and Ecumenical Commitment, Youth Department of the WCC and World Council of Christian Education, *Risk*, II, 1, Geneva 1966; Paul A. Crow, 'Unity, Mission, Truth: Education for Ecumenism in the 1980s', *Mid-Stream*, XIX, 1980; Ernst Lange, *And Yet it Moves*, WCC, Geneva 1979; Werner Simpfendörfer, 'Ecumenical and Ecological Learning: "Becoming at home in the wider household of the inhabited earth" ', *The Ecumenical Review*, 34, 1982

ULRICH BECKER

Ecumenical Movement in Britain

When in 1971 the World Council of Christian Education was integrated with the World Council of Churches*, a seal was set on the increasingly ecumenical fashion in which discussions of Christian education had been conducted in the present century. In that development, bodies like the YMCA, the YWCA, the Institute of Christian Education, the Student Christian Movement* and the World Student Christian Federation had each played a significant part.

The Education Act of 1944 is a symbol of that increased mutual understanding. It was a landmark in English church history because the provision of RE in schools would not have been possible apart from an agreement between Christian bodies, which was in marked contrast to the sharp controversies which had been a feature of their differences earlier in the century. This change was the fruit of growing mutual respect and understanding which the growing ecumenical movement encouraged, largely in this country under the leadership of such men as William Temple and John Scott Lidgett.

One of the consequences of this Act for RE was the production of agreed syllabuses* which were prepared by experts from several Christian traditions. Among the best known of the early syllabuses are those of Cambridgeshire, Surrey and Sunderland, and in the 1960s, the West Riding. These syllabuses showed that RE may include, at appropriate levels, material other than scriptural material, such as the history of the church, its expansion in recent centuries, and Christian responsibility in international affairs. It is now widely recognized that it is not as easy to separate scriptural material from theological and ecclesiastical interpretation as was once supposed.

The ecumenical context of discussion has been of great benefit in two other areas of educational concern.

Since 1944, questions have been raised about the very nature of RE and about what can and should be taught at this or that stage of a child's development, and whether in fact it is educationally 'right' to teach scripture to young children. The BCC* and the Free Church Federal Council* (often in discussion with the Roman Catholic Church) have sponsored discussion of these themes, as has also the Christian Education Movement*, itself another evidence of ecumenical activity.

In more recent years, another serious issue has occupied the thinking of Christian and other religious leaders: how to relate RE (understood as Christian) to those whose countries of family origin are closely related to a different religion. While no general agreement has been reached on this question, it seems that some churches (cf. *Religious Education in County Schools*, Free Church Federal Council) would urge that education in the Christian religion should be given to all children living in England, if only on the ground that a person cannot be at home in a country if he does not understand its religious tradition. On the other hand, teaching should also be given in the religions largely represented in the country, so that mutual understanding and respect be promoted. The fact that the Ecumenical Movement is, in the end, concerned with the unity of all mankind, and not just close co-operation and unity between churches, may well make it possible for Christians together to work at this important issue.

See also **Young Men's Christian Association; Young Women's Christian Association.**

JOHN HUXTABLE

Egypt *see* **Middle East, Christian Education in the**

Emotional Development

While it is unwise to justify RE simply on the ground of its contribution to emotional development, it is legitimate to ask how RE does contribute to it.

1. What is emotional development?
Emotional development is among the least explored of all aspects of a child's growth, but we know sufficient to realize how important a factor it is in personal development. 'Learning (in the widest sense of the word) and emotion, the cognitive and the affective aspects of development, intellect and feelings are so closely interwoven and from so early an age as to be almost indivisible' (Pringle). 'Among the most significant emotional experiences for children are those which have to do with personal-social relationships' (Munro). These experiences are significant both in the learning process and in the emotional well-being of children. Through others, children learn and

become successful – or the reverse. Through others, they see themselves as valued and worthy of acceptance and respect – or the reverse.

But what is the goal of such development? While there is considerable agreement among psychologists as to children's basic emotional needs, it is arguable whether our choice of goal for emotional development is a purely psychological question. The goal we set for it seems to be determined by our value judgments which describe the kind of adults we desire children to grow into – e.g. 'the mentally healthy adult', 'the well-adjusted personality', or 'the free and responsible person'.

It is here assumed that in education we are aiming at the development of the person to maturity, however that is to be characterized. All education is aimed at changing pupils, whether it is to have the correct concept of a cow, a triangle or responsibility. Similarly, we help pupils to grow and develop as persons. We must be aware of the paradox of the person. We only become persons as we relate to others: but we never fully become persons because we never relate completely to others. (Christians call this 'sin'.)

Emotional development is here taken broadly to be:

(*a*) One aspect of personal development whereby the child becomes or does not become a fully responsible adult capable of forming social relationships.

(*b*) A process of encouragement, direction, control and refinement (but not elimination) of emotions, so that the pupil's emotional responses to experience become more specific and differentiated and are associated with particular and appropriate people, events and states of affairs, which are evaluated in a certain light: e.g. we are angry with the other driver, not because we don't like his face, his clothes or his car, but because we see him as thoughtless and a danger on the road. Further, this process results in all the varied emotions experienced by children being combined to build fundamental attitudes to others and the world, such as trust/acceptance/confidence/love or distrust/rejection/fear/hatred.

(*c*) A process which may be influenced by various environmental factors, including the family, the school-community, the curriculum, other children, but especially by adults such as parents and teachers with warm, accepting attitudes.

2. What is the connection between RE and emotional development?

Pupils' basic emotional needs and their emotional response to experience vary as a result of these needs being satisfied or unsatisfied. The connection between RE and emotional development can be fully understood when we realize that these needs, together with experience, provoke existential/religious questions. The RE teacher will encourage pupils to raise these questions and will teach the main answers given by world religions.

The relationship of RE to emotional development can be seen in the following examples:

(a) The need for love and security, that is for acceptance for what pupils are in themselves and not for achievement or good behaviour, produces a response (especially to people and events and objects associated with them) which may involve love/hate; courage, acceptance/fear, unease, jealousy; trust/distrust; joy/sadness; anger, a sense of guilt or shame. The existential/religious questions related to such a response are: who am I in relation to others? how should I treat other people? what is the best way of living together? am I related to a transcendent being who is loving and gracious?

(b) The need for new experiences will provoke responses of wonder at or about, or apathy; a desire to explore, surprise, interest, appreciation and enjoyment of the world, or disinterest. The related questions are: why am I here? where am I going? is death the end? have I (and others) any significance in this vast universe? why this universe and not another? why is there anything and not just nothing?

(c) The need for praise and recognition including the awareness of having value in oneself produces various responses – a sense of being accepted or rejected, of being important or unimportant in the eyes of others and even in one's own eyes, self-confidence or diffidence, a sense of defeat or hope after failure. The related questions are: do I matter? am I important? where do I get my self-value? why are there physical pain, mental agony and suffering? are suffering and failure a denial of personal value?

(d) The need for responsibility, freedom and a growing independence from adults will arouse a sense of being trusted or alternatively distrusted and frustrated, of being responsible and accountable or alternatively a 'couldn't care less' attitude, a sense of self-praise or blame and of being a person in one's own right. The related questions are: am I free but limited? how shall I act responsibly? what considerations should guide my choices? what is it to be a person and how do I become one? am I always in the presence of God who relates himself to me and calls for my response?

These examples do not analyse human experience but indicate some ways in which RE and emotional development are connected. Many connections can be made between each example. The need for love and security (a) may be strongly related to a need for praise and recognition (c). It follows that there will be a similar link between the emotional responses made and the questions asked.

3. How does RE contribute to emotional development?

A contribution to the personal development of pupils is made by the whole life of the school, rather than by the learning of particular subjects, though success at learning *something* (whatever it may be) generally contributes to self-confidence and self-esteem.

Yet RE teachers have far greater opportunities to make such a contribution than teachers of some subjects. (a) RE has an interest in the exploration both of the pupils' experience and of human experience generally, and such exploration will help younger children to make specific, differentiated and appropriate emotional responses to situations.

(b) RE teachers and those concerned with the emotional development of the child and young person share an interest in helping pupils evaluate situations. As religions are interpretations of life and experience, RE teachers aim to make pupils aware of the difference to behaviour such value-judgments may make: e.g. whether we see a stone as a weapon to be thrown or as a work of art to be carved into the likeness of an elephant, or whether we see people as enemies or as fellow human beings. Emotional maturity is being advanced when a child's judgments based purely on emotional 'likes' and 'dislikes' are replaced with value-judgments based on appropriate reasons of a non-prudential kind: here the goal of the process is taken to be when people are seen as persons with a value in their own right, and not simply as rich aunts, luscious blondes or VIPS.

(c) RE contributes to emotional development when its curriculum is informed by an understanding of the correlations between pupils' emotional needs, their emotional responses to experience and the existential/religious questions outlined above. For example, the existential question 'From where do I derive my importance?' was in the past answered by pupils when they acquired employment on leaving school: they achieved in this way a sense of value. If, however, a high level of unemployment is to be a permanent feature of our society, it will be educationally appropriate for the RE teacher at least to point pupils to Christianity which sees worth in every person – a worth not dependent on the attainment of any standards of achievement or goodness.

Margaret Munro, *The Psychology and Education of the Young*, Heinemann 1969; Mia Kellmer Pringle, *The Needs of Children*, Hutchinson 1980.

                                    IAN C. M. FAIRWEATHER

Empathy

1. In its sense of 'the power of projecting one's own personality into (and so fully comprehending) the object of contemplation', it can be said that without empathy an artistic emotion is purely intellectual and associative. By means of empathy a great painting becomes a mirror of the self. 2. More commonly, empathy is understood as 'the power of entering another's personality and imaginatively experiencing his experiences'. Thus the goal of all reading is empathy with the content and spirit of the material read. This intellectual identification with or vicarious experiencing of the feelings, thoughts or attitudes of another shows empathy to be more enduring and valuable than romantic love. In empathy we permit our feelings for others to become involved.

In RE the importance of both senses is apparent.

                                    SHEILA M. HOBDEN

Environment

In order to give the term rather more meaning than just another word for surroundings, we need to look at what constitutes an environment, and, more importantly, what makes things environmental.

The interaction of people or other organisms with their environment is a direct activity. The environment is exploited by us to a greater or lesser degree whatever the location. Study of the environment requires close observation, clear analysis, use of a whole range of support resources and data, and it implies decisions to be made about the nature of that environment and its future management. Since any environment, particularly in our urban society, implies human work, habitation and cultural life, the decision-making process for the environmentalist is a similar one to that of a person engaged in religious study; the judgments made being ethical and moral.

Rural settlements in Britain and elsewhere have changed so radically in the last fifty years. Church and squire as centres of life have given place to distance commuting and the countryside is now seen as a public amenity. The role of churches and chapels, of priests and parishioners is a fluid one. Villages, however, present people with a community unit of manageable and understandable size for study, and the focus of human needs within a community of any kind introduces us all in a practical manner to the part that religion plays in society.

When we turn to urban life, the historical role of the church as protector, provider, vehicle for culture, stimulus for change in the pre-modern city, and the architectural part it plays in townscape, can be set alongside the newer concepts of religious buildings as non-liturgical institutions. Modern town planning is an extension of the concerns of the Victorian evangelists, and the considerable needs of contemporary social problems ought to be seen as a priority cause for concern of all religious bodies. Indeed, the multi-cultural society, the inner city*, the tower block and life in the spreading suburban housing estate all pose issues which are at the heart of religious education.

Pollution and conservation ask us to consider very basic human values and rights, from the unprotected miner working a dangerous substance like asbestos in an African state, and the culling of seals in the North Atlantic, to the demolition of a listed building in our local town.

Almost any study issue in human ecology is as much a study of the environment as it is of religion in society.

ROBIN NORBURY

Environmental Education

There are strong parallels between the study of religious education and environmental education. The principal motivation for both is first-hand experience. In simplest terms, one could be said to be the study of 'Who am I?' and the other to be of 'What am I doing?' In this sense they are closely related to working methods. What both need is an extended awareness, sensitivity and exploration of significance.

As studies are made of the role of an individual in a rural community or small industrial village, the basic human needs approach is most suitable. In subsistence economies and in their developed equivalents, the relationships between material and spiritual needs is evident. This is frequently formalized, and use of church and other records constantly reveal the realities of parish life. In urban study, the structure of urban society and its relationship with church government is clearly evident, whilst the impact of the religious reformers such as Angela Burdett Coutts and her East London working-class housing, and that of George Cadbury and Bournville, are vital landmarks in the process of improvement in nineteenth- and twentieth-century urban form and conditions.

When dealing with human ecology, the relationship is evident but sometimes subtler. To understand the problems of population, pollution and conservation, study of religious and other cultural life is vital. Probably the most valuable product of this study for the student is the accumulation of tolerance, understanding, concern and commitment to change the nature of society and its exploitation of resources. The humanitarian concern which is implied in decisions on low or intermediate technology, the value judgments which cannot be purely scientific or economic when considering nuclear power or war and peace, are evidence of a close link between RE and environmental study.

ROBIN NORBURY

Environmental Studies

The religious and moral dimension of environmental studies is fundamental for three principal reasons. 1. All religions, including humanism and scientific rationalism, imply a view of the relation of man to nature, the content of which affects the way in which the environment is treated. 2. Policy decisions themselves involve evaluations of nature and the environment which may properly be considered moral. 3. Environmental problems of pollution, the conservation of resources, the preservation of nature itself, the growth of population globally and locally, and of migration and aggregation into burgeoning urban complexes, cannot be set apart from social and economic questions which have an undisputed moral dimension. Furthermore, the multi-ethnic character of modern society, together with the complex intellectual and religious history of Christendom, has produced a plethora of more or less conflicting viewpoints. It is clearly the task of RE to attempt to unravel some of these interlocking threads.

There has been much debate concerning the Judaeo-Christian view. Some have seen it as essentially exploitative; others have argued strongly that this is a misconstruction of the true picture, which emphasizes the notion of stewardship, of man responsible to God for the conservative management of the natural world. Evolutionary humanists have tried to develop an environmental ethic from the notion of survival value, or of reverence for the process of evolution itself; but some have turned to Eastern religions for an explicit or implicit pantheism to provide a moral underpinning for an ethic. It has been argued that Islam sees man's responsibility in the light of the 'khalifate' of man over nature under God. Less sophisticated societies live and work within a very different framework, often not without some real concept of a single omnipotent creator or god who is, however, too remote for direct relationship and responsibility. The significance of man's relationship to his environment as an element of his worldview is therefore virtually universal and exercises considerable ideological influence on his behaviour.

E. Ashby, *Reconciling Man with the Environment*, OUP 1978; J. N. Black, *The Dominion of Man*, Edinburgh University Press 1970; C. Derrick, *The Delicate Creation*, Stacey 1972; R. P. Moss, *The Earth in Our Hands*, Inter-Varsity Press 1982; M. Nicholson, *The Environmental Revolution*, Hodder & Stoughton 1970; J. Passmore, *Man's Responsibility for Nature*, Duckworth 1974.

R. P. MOSS

Ethos

The ethos of a school is its characteristic spirit, its prevailing tone. In part, it is the product of explicit intentions; in part, it reflects the attitudes which the members of the school community bring to their activities and relationships. Intentions and attitudes often differ, even within the same individual; a teacher may try to inculcate courtesy by being peremptory and aggressive. A coherent ethos is most likely to emerge from a careful and corporate consideration of aims, and from a stress upon a characteristic way of doing things – a school style – which is appropriate to those aims. Even then, the consensus is likely to be only approximate and the ethos consequently weakened or modified.

The English tradition of school ethos is ambivalent. On one hand, more emphasis has been laid upon the affective, the moral and the spiritual than is common in other countries; on the other, the actual practice of schools has often been much more functional than their pronouncements on principle and has been directed almost exclusively towards the acquisition of skills* and of paper qualifications. RE won its place in schools because of one aspect of the tradition; the effect of the other has sometimes been to vitiate it. In a functionally orientated school, RE commands little resources or respect except in so far as it wins itself a place among publicly examined subjects. Even in a school with a broader ethos, the subject is still under threat. The religious education which served past generations is now so far from most children's experience that it can easily be seen as irrelevant and sterile by the pupils even if taken seriously by the staff. Hence the need for the approaches adopted in most recent agreed syllabuses*; hence too new thinking about

morning assembly* and the part religious considerations should play in school life as a whole. In a school with a balanced ethos, religious education is most likely to play its proper part if it can both claim academic respectability and be shown to relate to children's experience and personal needs.

See also **Hidden Curriculum.**

P. E. Daunt, *Comprehensive Values*, Heinemann 1975.

MICHAEL HINTON

Evaluation

Much time, energy and expense are consumed by teachers in teaching and learners in learning. Assessment of the effectiveness of this effort is known as evaluation. Evaluation can be carried out at the level of the individual lesson, for a course, or upon such longer-term issues as the effectiveness of an agreed syllabus* or the value of a child's total educational experience in a given subject. It can scrutinize the content of teaching, its processes, and the efficiency and quality of the learning. It may be carried out by the teacher or by an outside researcher.

In many classrooms, evaluation has traditionally been confused with examinations* or testing. At the end of a course, teachers have used norm-referenced tests to assess pupils' attainment. Educationists now accept that there is more to learning than is measured with these relatively blunt instruments.

Evaluation cannot be carried out in a vacuum. Even in the individual lesson, the teacher begins from a set of intentions, aims or objectives. These condition the choice of subject-matter and the selection of appropriate teaching methods and strategies. After the lesson, the learners should have progressed some way towards meeting the original intentions. By articulating clearly the intentions of a lesson and devising learning experiences designed to achieve them, a teacher is evolving the criteria against which appropriate measures of learning success can be devised and an evaluation of lesson effectiveness be made. The same basic comments apply to working through a scheme or syllabus or even a whole curriculum.

It is not possible to evaluate RE until one decides what constitutes 'religious education'.

We take the view that RE consists of knowledge about religion, moral competence and a spiritual response. Since most RE is taught in secular schools it is doubtful whether any measure should be made of the third element.

The work of Loukes in the 1960s served to show that RE had come to be conveyed as knowledge alone, a set of historical and geographical facts. The facts were taught to pupils, through the medium of biblical stories and history, many times in a school career. Retention of the information, however, was poor.

Application of the work of Jean Piaget convinced many that this biblical narrative teaching was also positively harmful because it was given before children's religious and moral thinking had developed to the stage where it could cope with, for example, the dilemma of the God of love who drowns the Egyptian forces in the Red Sea.

Piagetian theory encouraged Goldman, Kohlberg and others to suggest a developmental view of children's religious and moral thinking. In Kohlberg's theory the first four stages correspond to Piaget's model. This kind of stage theory has implications for the content, sequence and structure of agreed syllabuses* and schemes of work, and also for the evaluative criteria appropriate in judging pupils' growth and development in RE. Suppose a pupil has been studying the Joseph story. The 'knowledge about' component might be judged by the pupils' ability to: 1. Say what a 'saga' is compared with a book of history; 2. know some historical facts about Egypt at about the time when 'Joseph' took place; 3. argue (at an appropriate level) the pros and cons of Joseph as a real person in a set of real events; 4. say why the story came to be written in its present form in the light of the Jewish view of history; 5. describe the place of the story as part of the wider development of the idea of 'the one true God', even at a crude level (God the true interpreter of dreams); 6. show some appreciation of the style of the story and to say how it might be written today; 7. recognize some literary allusions to the story and say what they mean; 8. know the basic factual outline of the story.

On the other hand, moral competence (the ability to make judgments and, potentially, to act on them) might be shown by the pupil if he could cope with the skills listed by Taba:

1. sensitivity to the feelings and attitudes of others; 2. understanding of, and the ability to predict the consequences of, behaviour; 3. identification with the feelings and attitudes of people in different circumstances from himself; 4. explanation of other people's behaviour and appreciation of the place of past experiences in determining it; 5. insights and ability 'to read between the lines', 6. objectivity in discussing his own behaviour; 7. the bringing of emotional response into the field of intellectual and rational control.

What has been said so far has considered evaluation as a means of exploring whether curriculum objectives have been met. The word is also used to describe studies of the effectiveness of teaching process, the management of learning, the effect of innovation or the usefulness of specific curriculum materials.

Evaluation of teaching processes is usually done by trained observers using either systematic observations or a case-study approach. Many teachers of a given subject are observed and the components of effectiveness are teased out by the researcher. Increasingly, teachers are being asked to use sound or videotape or to keep written records in order to scrutinize their own behaviour and performance: self-evaluation.

Some professional evaluators have major interests in how decisions at LEA, school, or classroom levels affect pupils' learning.

Evaluation studies in innovation (e.g. what happens when an LEA goes through the processes of adopting a new agreed syllabus) tell us about the more effective management of change.

Nowadays, before reputable authors and educational institutions market curriculum materials, these will have been put to the test in trial schools, their content, format and language checked in the field, and the users asked to respond to detailed questions about their strengths and weaknesses. This kind of formative evaluation will lead to a more polished product, which may itself be subject to further evaluative study.

See also **Assessment of Students.**

Ronald J. Goldman, *Religious Thinking from Childhood to Adolescence,* Routledge & Kegan Paul 1964; Lawrence Kohlberg, 'Continuities in Childhood and Adult Moral Development Re-visited', *Lifespan Developmental Psychology*, (eds) P. B. Bates and L. R. Goulet, Academic Press 1973; Harold Loukes, *New Ground in Christian Education*, SCM Press 1965; Jean Piaget, *The Moral Judgment of the Child*, Routledge & Kegan Paul 1932; Hilda Taba, 'Nine Collected Works', *Mirrors for Behaviour*, Vol. 5, (eds) A. Simon and E. Boyer, Research for Better Schools Inc. 1967.

TREVOR KERRY

Evangelical Attitudes

Evangelicals hold firmly to the historic Christian faith and while they are open to, and use, the methods of modern scholarship in biblical and religious studies, they are not able or willing to accept all the presuppositions of some scholars.

They consider that RE should be both religious and education. Education is not the same as evangelism, for education aims at spreading understanding of the faith, while evangelism aims at spreading acceptance of it.

Religion entails commitment of the deepest sort. Evangelicals hold that for the teacher, such commitment, far from being a liability, is a great asset, in that it gives him the insight and understanding to be able to communicate such insight and understanding to his pupils. Teaching RE involves showing that religion requires choice and commitment, but it does not involve pressing for commitment; such pressure must be rejected on theological, professional, moral and psychological grounds.

Attempts to teach RE phenomenologically or objectively were a reaction to actual or imagined use of pressure, but they fail in the most central issue of showing what religion really is. Evangelicals consider that being objective is a bogus ideal for anyone; but being fair is vital as a matter of integrity.

The good evangelical RE teacher will be fair to his own understanding of his faith and fair to other people's different understandings. He will be fair also to other religions and fair to his pupils, of whatever age. While he will not parade his own faith, neither will he attempt to conceal it, but he will not attempt to impose it.

KENNETH G. HOWKINS

Evangelism and Education

Evangelism is the presentation of good news with a view to the conversion of the hearers to the evangelist's faith. Education has in view understanding religion. Evangelism includes teaching because the good news and the reasons for conversion need to be understood. For this reason, within a religion which evangelizes such as Christianity, education has always had an important role. In American church schools, 'Evangelism and education come together within the overall purpose of Christian Education.' In Britain, on the other hand, evangelism has been regarded as the responsibility of the churches and in county schools at least education does not include the same Christian purpose. This distinction was clearly expressed in the Durham Report: 'To press for acceptance of a particular faith or belief system is the duty and privilege of the Churches and other similar religious bodies. It is certainly not the task of a teacher in a county school. If the teacher is to press for any conversion, it is conversion from a shallow and unreflective attitude to life. If he is to press for commitment, it is to the religious quest, to that search for meaning, purpose and value which is open to all men.'

Both evangelism and education involve advocacy. The teacher implies he is introducing something worth knowing but the evangelist goes further: this is worth your commitment and your life. The teacher stimulates critical consideration and questions, the evangelist proclaims and persuades. In teaching, the expectation is that understanding will be within the student's existing mental framework but in evangelism the objective is a radical change in the whole way of thinking. Essential to both must be respect for the personalities of those addressed. Indoctrination* should be avoided but the challenging nature of the subject should also be respected and allowed to make its impact.

The Durham Report on Religious Education, *The Fourth R*, National Society and SPCK 1970; Michael Green, *Evangelism in the Early Church*, Hodder 1970; Randolph Crump Miller, *The Theory of Christian Education Practice*, Religious Education Press 1980; Angela Tilby, *Teaching God*, Fount 1979.

ARTHUR ROWE

Examinations

Well established in the field of RE and have been conducted under a variety of titles – Scripture, Religious Knowledge, Religious Studies. The titles reflect trends in thinking about the subject over the last forty years. Current usage is Religious Studies, although critics of this title express the anxieties of those who fear that examinations in religion stress the cognitive aspects of the subject at the expense of the affective.

Most public examinations have, over the years, included Religion, whether the old School Certificate and Higher Schools Certificate, its replacement the General Certificate of Education (at Ordinary, Advanced and AO levels) and the more recent Certificate of Secondary Education. A new opportunity is the provision for the subject in the International Baccalaureat examination.

At present in Britain there are thirteen CSE boards and eight GCE boards, offering a wide variety of syllabus choice and several modes of examination, mostly board based or school based. This structure is currently under review in the context of developing a new common examination for pupils aged 16+. Major attempts have taken place over the last twenty years to reform public examinations but these have so far failed to secure the necessary public support. The future of 16+ proposals remains to be seen. Efforts have been made to restructure 18+ examinations (GCE 'A' level) with the general aim of broadening the sixth-form curriculum. As a 'minority subject', Religious Studies has stood to benefit from such changes since entry to specialist higher education in the subject has never depended heavily on candidates achieving a GCE 'A' level pass in Religious Studies. A very interesting modular syllabus design was developed in the context of these proposals, but work lapsed in 1980 when the Secretary of State decided to retain the existing 'A' level structure. Logically, 18+ reform will eventually follow any 16+ reform.

The largest number of entrants for public examinations in the subject undoubtedly relate to GCE 'O' level and CSE. In 1978, the numbers entering for GCE 'O' level were over 50,000 and for CSE over 60,000. No doubt falling numbers in secondary schools in the rest of this decade will result in smaller numbers of entrants.

Attempts to replace this dual system by a common examination have been taking place for over ten years, but the pace has accelerated since 1981 when the Secretary of State for Education and Science requested the production of national criteria for each subject. Widespread national consultations have taken place and draft criteria circulated.

Some major issues have emerged. Should there be a common core study of Christianity? Should study of more than one religion be compulsory? Should there be compulsory project or course work? The trend seems to be towards permissiveness on these issues rather than compulsion. The dominant public discussion of content ought not to hide the importance of relating methods of assessment to the skills and processes of learning appropriate to the subject. Religious Studies should become a more practical subject in the future and this should be reflected in forms of assessments that demonstrate what pupils can do as a result of studying this area.

See also **Assessment of Students; Evaluation**.

JACK W. G. HOGBIN

Experiential: Definition of

In the theory of knowledge*, the term characterizes knowledge that is gained by observation. Such knowledge, derived from sense-experience, is usually contrasted with knowledge that is acquired through the use of the principles of reason. In the context of RE, however, the term tends to have a more general reference and its connection with sense-experience may be less direct and less specific. Thus, it is often used to refer to anything connected with the realm of 'lived' experience or human existence, as opposed to the process of merely analysing or reflecting theoretically upon such experience or existence.

KENNETH SURIN

Experiential Approach to RE

Sometimes referred to as the existential approach, it is based on the principle that *all* experience is essentially religious. As such, this approach is often contrasted with the phenomenological approach*, which maintains that since religion is a *sui generis* experience, it cannot therefore be reduced to any other form of experience.

In the classroom, the application of this approach will take as its starting-point the ordinary, everyday, experiences of pupils and teachers, and the encounters between teachers, teachers and pupils, and the pupils themselves. How, and on the basis of what principles, pupils and teachers respond to these experiences and encounters, constitutes the subject-matter of RE (according to the experiential approach). The idea here is that religious concepts grow out of man's experiences of awe and wonder, guilt and anxiety, joy and sadness, etc. The objectives of the experiential approach, therefore, are to get the pupils to reflect on these fundamental experiences, to recognize the cognitive and affective significance of these experiences in their lives and to make reasoned judgments (including value-judgments) about them.

Teaching methods are devised in accordance with these objectives. Pupils will be encouraged to acquire a 'feel' for religious phenomena before they proceed to examine such phenomena at an intellectual level. Pupils acquire this 'feel' from their ordinary experiences and the experiential approach thus requires these experiences to be related, at an intellectual level, to those experiences which are characteristically regarded as religious. The child's ordinary experience is thus regarded as a sort of hermeneutical 'bridge' which is used to interpret (intellectually) concepts and symbols found in holy books, forms of worship, doctrinal tracts and so on.

Michael Grimmitt, *What Can I Do in RE?*, Mayhew McCrimmon 1973; Harold Loukes, *Teenage Religion*, SCM Press 1961; Schools Council, *Humanities for the Young School-leaver, An Approach Through RE*, Methuen/Evans 1969.

KENNETH SURIN

Explicit Religion

A contrast between the ways in which RE explores explicit and implicit* religion has figured in discussions of the field since the early seventies. Explicit religion refers to the way religions manifest and express themselves, for example, in their history, in their doctrines, architecture, feelings and so on. If, therefore, RE concerns itself primarily with

what is 'explicit', it is then chiefly exercised in conveying the facts and meanings of recognized religious and perhaps 'quasi-religious' traditions and movements. The latter category of human belief-systems, such as Marxism* and Humanism*, is sometimes included under the definition of religion. The educational reasons for this are at least twofold. First, in fact in the wider world the secular ideologies often compete with and combine with traditional religions (consider Kampuchea, Latin American liberation theology, Islamic nationalism, etc.). Second, non-religious stances for living are explicit possibilities for the young person who is experiencing religious education. The case is further reinforced by the fact that 'implicit religion' relates to secular and thus non-explicitly religious experience.

The distinction between explicit and implicit religion was first made systematically in *Schools Council Working Paper 36* (1971) and was developed in various ways by Donald Horder during his work as Deputy Director of the Schools Council Project on Religious Education in Secondary Schools (1969–1973) at Lancaster University. The notion of explicit religion was presented then in terms of the six-dimensional analysis of religion, which is a kind of checklist of aspects of religion which need to be attended to if a realistic and balanced account of a religion is to be explored in a curriculum. The dimensions are: the doctrinal, the mythic (or mythological), the ethical, the ritual, the experiential and the social (or institutional). Thus an account of (say) the Roman Catholic tradition should include reference to its distinctive and central doctrines, its sacred narrative (concerning Christ, the foundation and development of the church, the Virgin Mary), its ethics (attitudes to marriage, for instance), its ritual (notably the nature of the Mass and other sacraments, its iconography and so on), its experiential emphases (devotion, the mystical tradition, etc.) and its relationship to society and the shape of its institutions (the Papacy, the priesthood, the role of the laity, etc.). Thus a rounded view of explicit religion is one that takes account of feelings and the standpoint of the believer and is not just informational in an external sense – for the experiential dimension of religion lies at the heart of the analysis. Other ways of providing checklists are not excluded, of course: it is just that the notion of 'explicit' RE was initially worked out in relation to Smart's six-dimensional account.

Ninian Smart and Donald Horder (eds), *New Movements in Religious Education,* Temple Smith 1975; Ninian Smart, *The Religious Experience of Mankind,* Collins 1971; *Schools Council Working Paper 36,* Methuen Educational/Evans 1971.

NINIAN SMART

Farmington Institute for Christian Studies

An independent research centre in Oxford which began its work in RE in 1974. The staff consists of a Director and six research associates. Although the primary interest is in Christian Education, the Institute is concerned with Christian approaches to other faiths and with a consideration of contemporary critiques of Christianity to be found in other religions and ideologies. It is held that these wider issues are of importance in *Christian* studies.

Farmington continues to be involved in the following work: 1. In organizing consultations (in Oxford and elsewhere) for those with a special interest in RE. 2. In providing a centre where people can meet informally to discuss aspects of RE and to deepen their understanding of the claims of religious faith. 3. In exploring the nature of Christian commitment, and in encouraging a greater sensitivity to the religious affirmations of adherents of other faiths.

EDWARD HULMES

Federation of University Woman's Camps for Schoolgirls
see **Christian Education Movement**

Festivals

The social occasions which a community celebrates. Festivals may serve as public calendar, or may publicly mark steps in the life passage of an individual or family. Alternatively a festival may arise spontaneously to celebrate a victory, a rich harvest or other special occasion, and this may or may not be remembered thereafter by a regular re-enactment. Some festivals are tied to a particular place, but the celebration of sacred (or special) time is more common. There are also festivals which,

though seasonal, recall or centre on a particular place (e.g. Bethlehem, Mecca). If religion is very broadly defined then all festivals can be seen as religious. It is more usual today, however, to recognize that many festivals are marginal to religion (Mardi Gras) or not religious at all (music and beer festivals).

Celebrations provide a good starting point for religious education in the school or home setting. They are usually joyful occasions which give scope for creative, expressive and altruistic activity together, and the few which are solemn or penitential should be left until later. Celebrations in children's own lives provide a lead in, such as birthdays, confirmations, family weddings, all of which are social occasions. Festivals in education help children to develop a sense of occasion and to share with each other at an affective level, as well as learning information. In multi-cultural settings festivals promote understanding and help to lower barriers. Festivals also provide a link between classwork and assemblies where this is required.

1. Ancient Religions
Ancient festivals like the Olympic Games brought large numbers of people together for entertainment as much as for worship, and they caught a sense of a power beyond that of individuals. No travellers' accounts, however, not even sacred texts give an adequate understanding of what took place. Attempts were made by the 'Myth and Ritual' school to reconstruct the New Year festival of ancient Israel, but remain unconvincing. Participation in a living festival is the only reliable guide.

2. Hinduism*
'Hinduism' includes primal religions, fertility cults, poly- and mono-theisms, deep spirituality and mysticism. Astrology impinges on all. Thus hundreds of festivals reflect enormous variety. Some are closely linked to theism, but others hardly involve gods except as they too inhabit the universe. The following are widely kept.

Divali is a four day festival of lights (October-November). People devoted to Vishnu celebrate the triumph of Rama (a Vishnu incarnation) over evil. In Western India, Divali is also New Year, especially for traders: houses are cleaned and new account books opened. Honour is paid to Lakshmi, goddess of wealth. People give sweets, put on new clothes and exchange greetings.

Dussera (Durga Puja, Navarati) is a ten day festival (September-October) in honour of the great goddess. In Bengal she is Durga, the destroyer with bloody teeth, for some Kali the terrible, or Sakti lusting for the corpse of Shiva. But she is the kindly mother too, or the virgin Kumari, and other manifestations in other parts of India. Maharajas celebrated Dussera by staging grand military parades.

Holi is the Spring full-moon (February-March). There is noise, colour and a boisterous atmosphere when proprieties are broken. Though probably older than current gods, some link Holi with Rama or Krishna (both Vishnu incarnations), others to Kama, god of love.

Shivarati is sacred to Shiva and includes a night of fasting and austerity followed by bathing and fairs (February-March).

Gokul Ashtami, or *Janmashtami*, is Krishna's birthday (monsoon time, July-August) and kept wherever he is worshipped. There are many joyful customs. However long or complex the festivities, the moment of birth is precisely kept, midnight on the 8th Shravan (the Hindu calendar has lunar months with intercalary days added to level up).

3. Buddhism*
Buddhists recognize gods as existing but irrelevant to salvation (nirvana) according to Theravada tradition. Festivals draw on local customs, with or without Buddhist associations. Specifically Buddhist is the full moon of Wesak which marks Gotama Buddha's birth, enlightenment and death (pari-nirvana). Relics of the Buddhas and their shrines are centres for pilgrimage and some have famous annual festivals, e.g. the Tooth at Kandy in Sri Lanka. Mahayana Buddhists have elaborate festivals in honour of their bodhissattvas, or other local spirits. The influence of astrology and pre-Buddhist practices is often marked.

4. Judaism*
Selfconscious monotheism demands that all celebrations centre on God and his people. Jewish festivals are joyful, except for *Yom Kippur*, and also serious and instructive. The year of twelve months (lunar with intercalations) begins with *Rosh-ha-Shanah*, New Year, in September-October. It is followed by *Yom Kippur* on the tenth, then *Succoth* (ancient Tabernacles). At winter solstice is *Chanukah*, festival of light, *Purim* in March, *Pesech* (Passover) linked to the Spring moon, and *Shevuoth* (Pentecost).

5. Christianity*
The biggest feast centres on the suffering, death and resurrection of Jesus Christ. As a spring festival, Easter has attracted folk customs linked to new life, as well as the preceding fast of Lent leading to crucifixion day (Good Friday). Christmas marks the birth of Christ, and family members come together to feast and exchange gifts and play games. Linked to Christmas Day (25 December) is Epiphany (6 January) which celebrates the showing of Christ to the gentiles. In the West, Christmas Day is the focus, but in the East it is Epiphany, the baptism of Jesus being also recalled then. Between these, New Year's Day is a big festival for some but Christian links are slight. Other feasts include Ascension and Whitsun, Harvest Thanksgiving (autumn, date fixed locally), and the patronal festival of a particular parish church. This can be rich in local customs and celebrations.

6. Islam*
Islam has two major festivals, both called *Id* (or *Eidh*). *Id-ul-Adha* evokes the *Haj* (pilgrimage to Mecca) and the sacrifice of an animal at Mina with feasting which concludes pilgrimage on the 10th of the month of *Haj*. *Id-ul-Fitr* ends the month long fast of Ramadan kept by Muslims wherever they are. Mosques are lit throughout the month, and for *Id* people put on new clothes, exchange greetings and sweetmeats. The Muslim calendar has twelve strictly lunar months without intercalations and thus the Islamic year is noticeably shorter than everyone else's. Shi'i Muslims have an additional festival in Muharram (the first month) to bewail the martyrdom of Hasan and Husayn. The climax is *taziah*, a kind of passion play on the 10th, preceded by days of austerity. This is most dramatic at Kerbela in Iraq, the place of Husayn's death. This festival is ignored by Sunni Muslims (the majority). Other celebrations include New Year of Hijra, the Prophet's birthday and local saints' days.

7. Non-religious Festivals

There have probably always been celebrations to mark special events, or feelings of release after a time of scarcity, whether cold winter or parched summer. Modern festivals too abound: music festivals, jubilee, May Day (whether parades or dancing), and carnivals, of which those in Rio and Trinidad are best known.

Teaching about Festivals

For children, who are learning the ethos of family and society, festivals build feelings of excitement and togetherness. Basically the teacher needs three things: knowledge of the pupils; *rapport* with the community whose festival it is; and some idea of the significance of the festival chosen. Because celebrations confirm a group's identity, festivals should be kept in their right time and place. To study an unfamiliar tradition without the help of a living community, is more difficult and requires even greater sensitivity and humility on the part of teacher and pupils. Because of their love for dressing up and imaginative play children can easily share in the joy of festival whatever the tradition it arises from. Appropriate stories from the important writings of different religious groups can be read, dramatized and mimed. The importance of meals in many religions at festival time can be used effectively. In discovering about the various traditions through such participation, children also learn the value of preparing and working together, but above all develop for themselves the consciousness and feeling of celebration.

ROBIN MINNEY

Finland

1. *Christian religious education before the public school system.* Christian public education was established in Finland by the Roman Catholic Church between the thirteenth and fifteenth centuries. The Swedish/Finnish Lutheran Church administration of 1571 established the oldest complete school system which was even then considering compulsory education. The founding father of RE in Finland is considered to be Juhana Gezelius Sr (1615–90), who, in a circular letter in 1666, prescribed the establishment of ambulatory schools in every parish. The ambulatory school system remained predominant in preparatory education until the early 1900s.

The chief aim of this system was to teach the student to read, recite his catechism from memory, and to prepare for confirmation school – the only required public school until compulsory education came into operation in 1921. Religious instruction at home, with catechetical supervision (*kinkerit*) from the clergy, had great significance in religious instruction at preparatory level. Literacy became prevalent in the 1700s mainly as a result of the confirmation schools.

2. *Religious pedagogics in the public education system.* A commune-directed public elementary school which paralleled the church-directed instruction came into being in the 1860s. In 1869 the responsibility for this new form of public education transferred to the Department of Public Education. In the first decades of the public elementary school system RE continued to hold its central position with an average of six lessons per week. However, the establishment of an independent Finnish government in 1917 led to fundamental changes in the relationship between church and state two years later. For centuries Finland had been dominated by Sweden; from 1809 it was bound to Russia as an autonomic grand duchy. Throughout this period the state was closely committed to the Lutheran confession but the new constitution began with the elimination of confession and the introduction of the idea of impartiality in religious issues. Marxist-socialist and cultural-liberal circles contested the position of RE in schools demanding its abolition and offering to substitute religious history and instruction in non-religious morality. This controversy was legally resolved in 1923 by the legislation of the public school system which preserved elementary RE and its confessional nature. The Social Democratic Party withdrew its demand for the abolition of RE. One obvious reason for the preservation of RE as confessional is the mandate given to the Evangelical Lutheran Church (ELC). In 1920, 98% of the community were ELC members while only 1.6% were members of the Orthodox Church. In 1980 the corresponding figures were 91% cent and 1.2%.

3. *Secondary schools.* Finland's secondary school system can trace its roots to the Catholic Church's maintenance of monastic and cathedral schools. In 1649, during the period of Lutheran orthodoxy, the school system recognized three kinds of secondary school.

These were mainly concerned with the education of priests and secondary education in general was in the care of the church until the establishment of the Department of Public Education in 1869. In order to develop the preparation for scientific education, in 1872 school regulations provided for an eight-year lyceum and a five-year high school as a basis for further vocational studies. From these two basic forms the intermediate school and senior high school developed during the 1910s. Together with the primary school this formed the basic educational unit until the reformation of the comprehensive and senior high school system during the 1970s. Religion has traditionally had a place in the secondary school curriculum.

4. *Comprehensive school reformation.* On the basis of the school ordinance of 1968 RE was recognized as a compulsory subject for every church member throughout the nine years of education in a comprehensive school. Following the deliberations of the Educational Planning Committee in 1970 RE was established as one of the main objectives within the comprehensive school, and currently (1982) work is being done to reform the content of RE at comprehensive school level. A considerable reduction in the number of RE lessons has caused many problems.

5. *Senior high school reform.* The senior high school reformation began with the decision made by the State Council in 1974 that vocational training institutions and the senior high school system should be integrated to the comprehensive school system on the one hand and on the other to university studies. Following the demands made in the 1960s for non-confessional religious studies, the Senior High School Educational Planning Board decided in 1977 to drastically reduce the teaching of RE. However, in 1980 the State Council issued a statute which reaffirmed the position of RE in the senior high schools; accordingly there should be five courses for the three school years of RE for all students registered with the church. Part of the background of the decision was a parliamentary church-state committee's statement of 1977: because of the religious-political situation prevalent no change was needed.

The most fundamental reform concerning methods and organization of RE in senior high school was the changeover to periodical study.

After a trial period in 1981 this amended curriculum was introduced in 1982. The subjects contained in it were: biblical knowledge, knowledge of the church or church history, Christian doctrine and ethics and also knowledge of the Church of Finland. Orthodox students have their own courses with an emphasis on the liturgy. When compared with the previous approved curriculum of 1967 the following changes are clear: the proportion of church history is reduced; biblical knowledge has been taken as a senior high school subject; ecumenical instruction is reinforced; religious themes linking art and religion have been expanded.

The nature of religious confessional instruction in schools has been defined by the parliamentary church/state committee as 'pedagogically confessional'. Thus, study courses contain mostly subjects relating to the doctrine and functions of the two churches. The central point of RE is the Christian confessional form within which children are raised. From this it proceeds to world religions and different world views. According to the general aims of the school the method of instruction emphasizes an objective and critical understanding of the subject.

6. *Educational activities of the Evangelical Lutheran Church.* Confirmation school comprises the most significant part of the church's educational activity directed towards the young and during the 1970s the attendance of those in the fourteen to fifteen age group was as high as 90%. The complete educational activities of the ELC which took place during the 1970s included reform of the confirmation school based on Harold Louke's concepts of 'life questions'. The episcopal conference of 1980 approved the confirmation school scheme for the whole country. Confirmation school and religious instruction in schools are mutually supportive even though each has a different degree of religious commitment. The view of RE taken by the Orthodox is close to that of the church in the shared idea that the aim of RE is to guide the individual towards becoming a confirmed parish member.

7. *Traditions of religious pedagogy.* From the end of the 1800s the Herbart-Zillerite influence began to take a central position in Finnish pedagogues. The Herbartian view which approved a historical study of the Bible had previously been disapproved of but these

views, which were internationally appraised, were strongly represented in Finland between the 1890s and 1940s. The most significant representative of these views was Mikael Soiminen (1860–1924). He believed that treatment of the subject matter was to be determined by the so-called 'home locality principle'. Instruction should be based on familiar community church affairs. Through guidance the teacher should bring the pupil from the perceptual to the conceptual level and from that to practical application.

In contrast to this view, the progressive pedagogy began to point out that broader attention should be given to the child's own situation and to issues of developmental psychology. The most significant representative of this new trend in RE was Martti H. Haavio (1897–1966).

Three main instructional plans have guided the teaching of RE in secondary schools this century. These are: the curriculum design of 1916; an amended version of this design made in 1941; and the 1967 curriculum scheme which attempted to assimilate all criticism which had been directed at RE since the Second World War. The central objective of the curriculum plan of 1916 was to transfer the emphasis from teaching dogmatics to historical contents. This echoed the prevailing trend of the 'young church movement' to closely connect church doctrine and culture. The church historians' work was to demonstrate Christian principles as the basis of morality and civilization. When later during the Second World War the reforms did not bring substantial change, the breadth of the subject of church history came under strong criticism which went on throughout the 1950s. The President of the Association of the Teachers of Religious Instruction in Finland, Päiviö Virkkunen (1905–1980) emphasized that the curriculum had to meet the psychological and spiritual needs of the student. Although objectives aiming for a personal conviction were emphasized less than in the discussion of the 1950s, the curriculum plan of 1967 included this statement: 'The purpose of religious instruction is to familiarize students with the Bible, Christian traditions and way of life . . . as well as – if possible – to lead to a personal acceptance of Christian belief.' While in West Germany* there was a transfer from a hermeneutic instruction to a problem orientated one, in Finnish religious pedagogics there were features of the German post-war religious pedagogical discussion (*evangelische Unterweisung*).

The comprehensive school reform which was initiated a few years later brought with it powerful shifts towards problem orientated teaching and these were soon reflected in course materials. This change was influenced both by the external criticism of RE and the shift of religious pedagogics towards empiric research. Before this Haavio and Virkkunen were already demanding greater attention to the real life needs of the students. Support for the implementation of these requirements was obtained in 1974 when Kalevi Tamminen (1928–) started a broadly based research project which illuminated the structure and content of religious thinking in children and young people.

A change in RE from the Bible and church history-centred instruction to life problem orientated instruction took place on two levels – in the comprehensive school curriculum of 1970 and the reformation of the confirmation school in 1973.

REIJO HEINONEN

Folk Religion

An expression which began to be used, especially by British ministers of religion in the 1970s, to refer to those aspects of life which seemed to be religious in some way, but were not part of orthodox Christianity as that was understood, mainly in the light of biblical and existentialist theology. Described in this way, the concept might appear somewhat judgmental, even patronizing. But the term has also been used by some who wish to urge upon the stricter kind of churchman a sympathetic attitude towards contemporary expressions of perennial religiosity.

The first extended, sociological study to use this term is by David Clark (1982). However, Bruce Reed, 1978, gave a number of examples of what he meant by the term. They included the desire of non-churchgoing mothers to have their children baptized, and popular outcries against proposals to demolish church buildings. But they also included practices shared with churchgoers, such as hanging medals of St Christopher in cars, wearing a cross for protection, or opening the Bible at random to find guidance.

So far, then, 'folk religion' is not so much a distinct system as an interpretation of various items. Indeed, Reed defines it as being inevitably conservative, because nourished by the unconscious. It is 'the outward expression of deep emotions which are kept unexamined through ritualization'. Thus it tends to bolster the *status quo*, and flourishes in totalitarian regimes of the left or right, with or without official encouragement.

The concept may be seen as an eccelesiastical (and especially Anglican) parallel to the common religion* of the sociologists, or what tends to be called, in continental Europe especially, 'popular religion'. Each of these terms attempts to highlight, in a sympathetic way, the middle ground and/or the overlap between the canonical religion (Christianity, in this case) and the merely secular. It tries to focus upon that part of human life that appears to be religious, either because of its inner meaning or because of its outer method, and yet which is overlooked by an exclusive concern with explicit religious systems or non-religious sciences.

A comparable trend, in some ways, was seen among religious educationists in the 1970s, in their use of the expression 'implicit religion'*, to refer to spontaneous experiences of transcendence. They may be seen as an individual, introspective, subjective form of a similar reality. The other side of that latter coin is the civil religion* which received so much attention from all three groups (ecclesiastical, psychological and educational) in the United States during these years. They may be seen as the characteristically contemporary expression in the individual and social spheres, of what, when looked at in historical perspective, is called folk or common religion.

Little empirical work on folk religion in industrial societies has yet been attempted. Indeed, the term, and the concept, hardly appear in the standard works on religion. It is, however, clearly related to the 'little traditions' and 'practical religion' of anthropologists, to the 'natural religion' of theologians, to the 'folk lore' of historians and to the 'primitive' or 'primal' religion of phenomenologists. The door is thus open for research by schools, provided agreement can be reached on its meaning and title. On the other hand, as these must be non-evaluative, at least initially, an alternative term may be preferred.

Edward Bailey, 'The Implicit Religion of Contemporary Society: an orientation and plea for its study', *Religion: Journal of Religion and Religions*, XIII, 69–83, Academic Press 1983; David Clark, *Between Pulpit and Pew*, Cambridge University Press 1982; Bruce Reed, *The Dynamics of Religion*, Darton, Longman & Todd 1978.

EDWARD BAILEY

Folk Song   *see* Music

Founders of Religions

Before beginning to teach about any founder of a religion, the teacher needs to answer two questions: to what extent was that person the founder of the religion and how is he viewed within the particular tradition being studied? Can Jesus, for example, be described as the founder of any expression of Christianity which exists today? Christians would, however, describe Jesus as the founder of Christianity, meaning that he is the rock upon which it is built, but Muslims would not regard Muhammad in the same way – God alone is the founder of Islam. Muhammad is the last prophet, but no more – hence their distate for the name 'Muhammadan'. Not only must the teacher have decided how these issues are to be resolved, but also there is a need to consider when and how they are to be brought to the attention of pupils, for to neglect them is potentially to reduce teaching about founders (perhaps 'messengers of God' is a preferable phrase – but what of the Buddha?) to story-telling. These people are famous and revered for what they said and did, and for the place which they hold in their respective religions, and that is why stories about them are still told.

The first task of the teacher is to transmit the tradition, to convey the portrait of Jesus, Muhammad, or the Buddha which Christians, Muslims or Buddhists treasure. This might be regarded as solving by evasion the problem of distinguishing between the Jesus or Guru Nanak of history and the Jesus or Guru Nanak of faith. However, a religious studies approach to religious education would suggest that the starting point should be the received tradition. Sketchy or patchy beginnings can take place in the early years of schooling. Between the ages of ten and twelve, pupils should find a topic 'Who was Jesus (Muhhamad), and what kind of person was he?' helpful in bringing together the pieces of knowledge accumulated over the years.

When they have some acquaintance with the messenger as a real person of flesh and blood, the next step is that of presenting his message and the way in which he conveyed it. In the Christianity syllabus, this might result in the parables of Jesus being presented more intelligibly and intelligently if they are seen to be the provocative observations of a perhaps typical Jewish teacher. The emphasis in the miracles might then fall in the right place: not upon the deeds but upon the signs contained within them.

The final task, that of explaining the significance of the founder within his respective tradition, will have been implicit in much that has gone before. However, there is a need to be explicit too.

There are two other issues. 1. The overriding question of revelation, a study of how human kind believes that God reveals himself. 2. The task of helping pupils to recognize how religions regard the messengers of other faiths. Within Islam, Jesus is highly respected as a prophet and as messiah, but he is not divine and Muslims do not believe that he was crucified. There is little point in arguing which document is right, the Bible or the Qur'an*, but an attempt to understand how and why Jew, Christian and Muslim differ in their evaluation of Jesus can be both positive and profitable.

W. OWEN COLE

Fourth R, The

A report of a commission on RE established by the Church of England Board of Education and the National Society was published in 1970 under the title *The Fourth R*. The commission, chaired by Ian Ramsey, Bishop of Durham, surveyed the condition of religious education in England and Wales and considered its underlying principles.

The major themes of the report are: the origins and development of RE in England; theology and education; RE and moral education*; RE in schools, particularly county schools; RE in independent and direct grant schools; RE in other Western societies; and the church within both the Church of England and other educational institutions.

There are sections on contentious issues, such as the relationship of moral education to RE and an influential appendix on 'Indoctrination' by Basil Mitchell.

ALAN BROWN

France

Originally RE was synonomous with catechetics* and until the French Revolution practically all schools were run by members of religious orders. These were supressed during the Revolution of 1789 but reappeared after the Concordat of 1801. During the nineteenth century there was an upsurge of such schools, which are now known as 'écoles libres' and in which RE is taught. With the separation of church and state at the beginning of the twentieth century, the teaching of religion in state schools and universities was forbidden, though religion was and is recognized as 'a fact of civilization'. Today some twenty per cent of French schools are 'écoles libres', of which ninety-five to ninety-eight per cent are Catholic, and there are Instituts Catholiques (for higher education) in Paris, Angers and other cities.

There are several catechetical systems – Catholic, Protestant, Orthodox. This last centres on the liturgy and iconology. Catholic and Protestant catechetics differ in origin, which for the former is doctrine and for the latter the Bible. The teaching of both was aimed at an intellectual acquisition of knowledge. The evolution in teaching methods, linked to new needs, has transformed a denominational, apologetical approach and favoured ecumenism.

Before Vatican II, the aim of catechetics was to prepare children for their 'profession of faith' at the age of twelve. This involved four years of doctrinal teaching (dogma, morality, liturgy) in the condensed form of the catechism, which was a book of questions, the answers to which had to be learnt by heart. There were parochial catechism classes to supplement the learning done at home.

Cultural changes resulted in this form of teaching being less and less related to actual Christian experience, and this provoked research into the content of teaching, the ways in which children learn, and the consequent appropriate methods of teaching. This attempt at renewal ended in a setback, the condemnation by Rome in 1957 of 'progressive catechetics'. From that time on, however, catechetics for adolescents, less bound to the official system, developed a new orientation.

Vatican II gave permission for renewed research. Priority was given to rediscovering, in new ways, the links between doctrine and the life of the child. Catechetics began to take place more and more in the framework of small groups, often on the initiative of parents, and based on an 'obligatory foundation', i.e. a collection of doctrinal texts to be used in various forms and taking account of sociological and religious factors. New psychological understanding led to catechetics for adolescents developing from being deductive in form (progressing from doctrine to actual experience) to being inductive (passing from known experience to the Christian gospel).

This research was upheld by the *Directory of Pastoral Catechetics* published by the Episcopate in 1964 and by the Sacred Congregation of the Clergy's, *General Directory of Catechetics* (1971). The Synod on Catechetics (1977) resulted in John Paul II's apostolic exhortation 'catechesi tradendae' (1979).

The cultural crisis of May 1968 accelerated the breakdown of the old ways of thought and teaching. This led to a new danger: the socializing of catechetics, which risked being little more than the imposing of Christian views on an already coherent humanism. It was difficult to see how to introduce the Christian message.

Catholic catechetics now took a new direction. It sought to put children and young people in touch with the whole Christian community and to initiate interaction with the great Christian witnesses of the past and present, the Bible, the liturgy and the history of the church. Children and young people were encouraged to express their faith intelligently in the light of their own developing experience and in union with the whole church. It is therefore no longer a matter of deduction from given facts, nor inference of belief from an experience which tends to eliminate all external revelation, but rather a rediscovering and reaffirming of beliefs through a constant dialogue with tradition.

Numerous documents were published about the teaching of religion. In 1980 the Episcopal Conference promulgated 'a text of reference for the use of authors of catechetical publications and those responsible for the pastorate' and 'a collection of authorized documents' as a point of reference for the various catechetical systems. This was intended to enlarge experience which is too easily limited by the local and the temporal, by opening it to the dynamism of revelation.

Some of the first schools run by Protestants in France were opened in the nineteenth century. Before 1968 catechetics for Protestant children was essentially Bible-based. It aimed to initiate children into salvation history through knowledge of the Old and New Testaments. Adolescents added to this the study of contemporary Christian belief. The rigidity and bookishness of this teaching became evident during the cultural crisis of 1968. Sunday School leaders were constrained to think out new programmes which took into account changes in society, pedagogical renewal and the findings of modern sociology and psychology. While remaining Bible-based, instruction lost its encyclopaedic character. No longer was there a seeking to teach the whole of salvation history, but rather to explore themes related to the needs of the children and to the life of the community.

As well as using a selection of biblical lections, group teaching is based on a theme or a person and on constant interplay between biblical texts and daily life. This aims to relate the teaching more pertinently to the life of young people. Relationship with Jesus Christ thus loses its too theoretical character and becomes a living experience.

JEAN-PIERRE BAGOT

Free Church Federal Council

Formed in 1940, it unites the National Free Church Council established in 1892 and the Federal Council of Evangelical Free Churches established in 1919. It provides for joint action and representation of its member churches. Apart from the Hospital Chaplaincy Board, the Education Committee is the main specialist committee. This Committee is concerned to support and promote religious education in its widest sense as an integral part of the whole curriculum for the whole person in all schools. It takes into its purview therefore the whole range of concerns with regard to county as well as voluntary schools*. From time to time it publishes reports and discussion documents on RE, on its place in the curriculum, and on the supply and training of teachers of RE.

The committee is concerned also in higher* and further* education, promoting, or co-ordinating, for example, the appointment of a free church chaplain in certain institutions.

It receives and comments on consultative and other documents from the Department of Education and Science* and other agencies. It promotes active involvement in local education authority committees and in Standing Advisory Committees for Religious Education (SACRE)* by members of the free churches. It appoints the free church members of the Joint Education Policy Committee* and establishes liaison with other bodies such as the Religious Education Council*.

Free Church Federal Council, Working Party Reports: *Religious Education in County Schools*, 1976; *Education in the 1980s*, 1981.

DOUGLAS A. BROWN

Friends   *see* **Religious Society of Friends**

Further Education

While the term 'further education' is variously used, it may conveniently be taken to refer to the whole area of post-compulsory education outside the school sixth-form and the so-called 'higher' education* sector of university, polytechnic and colleges of education*. It also includes adult education and the increasingly popular evening classes. It is generally assumed that most students in further education are in the sixteen to nineteen age group, following programmes of study related to their daily work, but more students are over twenty-five than under nineteen and an increasing number of people are taking up some kind of formal education in adult years.

In colleges of further education generally there is little place for RE in a formal or explicit sense, that is, if RE is understood as meaning courses with traditional theological, biblical or world religions content. Some colleges do teach General Certificate of Education courses in RE to 'O' and 'A' level, but demand for these is limited. The religious provisions of the 1944 Education Act do not apply to the post-compulsory sector so that any religious teaching in British institutions, in contrast to that in some countries such as Germany, normally has no pedagogical content. On the other hand, there is an increasing demand among interested adults for classes in the general area of religion and philosophy, including not only a study of the Bible and Christian theology, but also a wide-ranging consideration of morality, ethics and especially world faiths. Contemporary pluralist society evinces a growing interest in matters of a multi-faith and inter-faith nature and this is increasingly reflected in both the content of courses and the identity of students.

At the same time, a great deal of the work in colleges of further education could be described as 'religious education' in an implicit sense. The 'religious dimension' is a valid part of human experience to be considered alongside, for example, the mental, physical, moral and aesthetic dimensions. Education, including further education, is about people and is concerned with a total process of personal development. The approach to education therefore depends upon the view taken of human beings.

Some teachers deliberately seek to involve themselves from the specific stance of a particular religious commitment, including Christianity, as they recognize the place of moral and spiritual development in further education and its involvement with each person's individual search for meaning. Teaching in further education, like all teaching, inevitably involves the transmission of values. There is a growing willingness to examine these critically and to be concerned with the nature and quality of relationships both between individuals and institutions. In recent years the Christian churches have become especially concerned with these questions and have established a body committed to their promotion. This is the National Ecumenical Agency in Further Education (NEAFE) whose membership includes all the main Christian churches in England and the professional associations concerned with further education.

NEAFE has also highlighted another area in further education which might also be seen as a matter of religious education, that is, the pastoral care* of staff and students. Chaplaincy provision within the area of further education is a specialist concern, complicated by the part-time and home-based nature of most students. There are, however, signs that both further education institutions and religious bodies are becoming more aware of its importance and possibilities.

KEITH HURT

Games

The development of games and simulations as a technique for learning has been a significant development in many branches of education since 1950. The essence of the activity is in the creation of a model of reality (simplified in structure and usually compressed in space and time) and the involvement of students as participants in that activity. Where the involvement demands the conscious adoption of a particular role, the technique is usually known as 'role-play'; where there are rules constraining decisions, rounds of activity and intended progression, the term 'game' is usually applied. Other forms of simulation include 'in-basket' and 'action-maze' situations (often designated for individual use) and mathematical and hardware simulations.

Following a long history in military training (war-gaming), the idea of using games and simulations has spread via management education to a wide general use in schools and in adult education. Voluntary agencies and charities have been extensive users of the technique since one of its well-documented characteristics is the quick creation of high motivation and interest. Its major claims, however, centre on its superiority over formal techniques in developing empathy for the predicament of others and in showing interactions and processes at work. In RE it is probably most used to highlight the many-sidedness of some social and ethical problems (e.g. in a classic game such as *Starpower* (Christian Aid) – a simulation about privileged and under-privileged groups). However, there are also examples of biblical situations simulated effectively (e.g. the problems facing Solomon, Pilate, the early apostles), of metaphysical dilemmas (e.g. Ken Jones' *Is God There?*), and of church life (e.g. Brian Wren's *Giving and Receiving*, Christian Aid).

Much of the expertise about simulation and gaming is gathered in the membership of SAGSET (Society for the Advancement of Games and Simulations in Education and Training).

P. Baker and M. R. Marshall, *Using Simulation Games*, Joint Board of Christian Educa-

tion for Australia and New Zealand 1974; A. Davison and P. Gordon, *Simulation Games in Action*, Woburn Press 1978; D. E. Miller, G. F. Snyder and R. W. Neff, *Using Biblical Simulations*, Judson Press 1973; J. L. Taylor and R. Walford, *Learning and the Simulation Game*, Open University Press 1978.

REX WALFORD

General Studies and RE in Sixth-Forms

The term General Studies entered the vocabulary of curriculum discussion in the late 1950s, in the context of concern about the high degree of specialization which characterized the English sixth-form*. The Crowther Report* (1959), whilst fully endorsing specialization in a group of two or three, usually related, subjects, coined the phrase 'minority time' to describe the remainder of the pupil's timetable. Some of this would be spent by arts and science students together and would include as well as art, music and physical education, 'religious education and all that goes to the formation of moral standards'.

The idea of General Studies gained coherence through the formation of the General Studies Association (1962), the spread of the General Studies 'A' level examination, introduced by the Joint Matriculation Board in 1957, and the creation of a General Studies subject panel by the newly formed Schools Council in 1964. The idea was one thing, the identification of aims and objectives, curriculum content and skills, however, was another, whilst the Crowther Report recognized the further problem that minority time did not represent a major commitment for either pupils or staff. These problems have remained. Recent work on the curriculum has identified 'forms of understanding' (P. H. Hirst) or 'realms of meaning' (P. H. Phoenix) which should form part of every pupils education. Amongst these, RE should contribute to the ethical and spiritual areas.

In any institution run under Schools Regulations – including both schools with sixth-forms and sixth-form colleges – 'religious instruction' is compulsory, whilst, paradoxically, in any institution run under Further Education Regulations – including tertiary and technical colleges – compulsory religious instruction is forbidden. In most sixth-forms and sixth-form colleges in the maintained sector, however, RE forms part of the General Studies programme. In very few, is it a compulsory component for all students throughout their course, partly because a single period each week is hard to defend educationally and also because one compulsory element in a curriculum open to choice in other aspects is resented by pupils. Many schools and colleges offer optional courses, recognizing that they will be taken up by a minority. Some, however, require students to select one or more courses under the general heading 'Beliefs and Values'. Some recently-produced agreed syllabuses* offer guidance in planning appropriate programmes. The Northamptonshire syllabus (1980) specifies that 'the option or rotation system must enable all students to participate in at least one RE course in each year of their sixth-form studies'. The selection offered in the syllabus includes religious belief and language*, theology and ecology, meditation* and yoga*. The Hampshire handbook to RE, *Paths to Understanding* (1980), includes a description of the 'Beliefs and Values' programme at one of the county's twelve sixth-form colleges, where 'students are expected to complete three of these courses during their first five terms in the college'. The approach of some courses is through religious traditions, whilst others use human experience as a vehicle for a consideration of beliefs and values. Courses include Indian Religion, the Bible, Archaeology and Modern Problems, Christianity Today, the Business of Being Human and the Artist's View of Life, as well as an opportunity for a Youth Leadership course and a residential conference on 'Community Today'.

PETER R. WATKINS

German Democratic Republic *see* Eastern Europe

Germany, Federal Republic of
see West Germany

Gifted Children

Identifying gifted children and helping them to reach their full potential is an issue which has concerned educationalists for many years. There is still considerable discussion as to whether such children should be truly identified as 'gifted' or 'exceptionally able'.

What is beyond question, however, is that gifted children have special needs. They can so often exhibit confusion and frustration in their lives. They can easily become isolated from their peers because they are at times prematurely aware of problems before they have developed an emotional security to deal with them. If they are underachieving, they can be a disruptive influence in school.

Belle Wallace, Advisory Teacher for Gifted Children in Essex, has said that the major needs of gifted children are: 1. recognition; 2. understanding of their emotional, social and intellectual needs. Is there no room for the spiritual? Frequently, gifted children reflect on how they seek the meaning of life and how they delve into the world's great philosophies and major world faiths.

Here is an opportunity for RE to contribute to the development of a particular group of children. Gifted children have an ability to absorb information, to perceive ideas and attitudes sharply, to understand consequences and outcomes. The aims* and objectives of RE can be adapted to these special abilities. Such children may very quickly reach the heart of what religion is about and they may have a fascination with and firm grasp of historical details and facts. An exciting, open religious education can take them further by recognizing their high intelligence and creativity. It can help them relate their talents to man's search for meaning. Above all, it can help sharpen their sense of belonging by encouraging them to recognize their uniqueness and its worth and value to the future of the community.

D. SULLIVAN

God

Whether within the context of a church-, gurdwara-, or synagogue-going family, or alternatively a county school, the process by which a boy or girl comes to any understanding of God is complex and varied. It cannot be exhaustively described because at both poles there are qualities of infinity. This is true by definition of references to God, but arguably also with reference to the richness of individual childhood experience.

At one level, few children even in a secular Western democracy grow up without any understanding whatever of religious vocabulary in general and the word 'God' in particular. It is part of their socio-cultural inheritance, bequeathed to them by the environment of stories, jokes, oaths, festivals*, adverts, etc., within which they learn. In this respect, the degree of association with a local religious community through home or school does affect the attitude and content of their religious learning, but some minimal familiarity remains fairly universal even without explicit religious belonging.

The status of children's conceptions of God is, of course, open to dispute. There are social historians who would suggest that they are little more than the terminal moraine of yesterday's beliefs, to be acknowledged in the way that myths and legends are, but, like acne, to be outgrown by a normal healthy adolescent. There are behaviourist psychologists who are inclined to believe that God concepts are no more than miscues to stimuli that have been wrongly interpreted to mean more than they actually do: like pigeons, children are reinforced in their superstitious ideas in expectation of promised reward or punishment (Skinner). Neither of these views allows much independent validity to religious belief, but both acknowledge its occurrence.

The psychoanalytic tradition presents different glosses on this same claim. According to one view, children's conceptions of God are genetically prompted, individual recapitulations of the stages of religious belief that humankind has gone through – polytheism – monotheism – atheism. Freud, too, rooted religion in the childhood of the human race, but stressed as well the individual infancy of any child's dependent relation on parents as a source for the 'religious illusion'. Faced with the harshness of the real world (war, starvation, inequality), what is a child to do but fall back on the security of a power even more protective and benevolent than the immediate parents, although ideally patterned on them. Empirical studies to check the correlation between emotions and concepts associated with parents and those associated with God indicate some interdependence, but less exclusively tied to the father than Freud suggests. In any case, the centrality or otherwise of parental motifs varies from one religious tradition to another, as also for the atheist.

It is an important characteristic of psychoanalysis that it calls attention to the unconscious depths of human personality. The adult's emotional life is largely determined by childhood experiences (from earliest pre-natal ones to adolescence). Jung shared in this, but where Freud relates the unconscious life and religion to biological and physical drives, Jung makes spiritual needs and energies central. Childhood is still of major importance for emotional and religious development, but Jung sees this positively: the potential deriving from the childhood inheritances provides the path for personal integrity in middle age and beyond, when due attention can be given to more than the basic priorities of becoming materially independent in life. In a sense, for Freud the sooner a child's religious concepts can be outgrown the better, while for Jung their promise is explored only many years after leaving school.

So far it has been claimed that concepts of God are derived from social context and emotional needs. According to developmental psychology, however, the concepts derive also from the cognitive reasoning processes. Questions about the beginning and end of the universe, as also about the whys and wherefores of life in it, are asked by young children and 'God-laden' responses are often found in this connection, whether derived from adult's comments or emerging from conversation with their peers. Piaget identified such references as typical of a myth-making stage in the development of children's thinking. Applying his general account of cognitive development directly to religious thinking, others (notably Goldman in England, Godin in Belgium, Elkind and Peatling in the USA) claim to have demonstrated that it follows the same sequence of development as do for instance mathematical, historical and moral reasoning. The earliest stage is labelled pre-operational and even pre-religious; reasoning here is restricted in that arbitrary connections are made following intuition and fancy. Father Christmas, fairies and God belong in the same sphere. This gives way in middle years, 7/8 to 11/12, to concrete thinking where reasoning is content specific and dependent on hard evidence for its validity. God is believed in because Jesus was seen to be alive again after crucifixion, or not believed in because spacemen failing to find the divine location. Only during adolescent years do boys and girls show themselves capable of fully operational thinking, taking into account the importance of intentions, hypothetical possibilities and the total context. God is believed in now as final source of meaning in life, or rejected as incompatible with human freedom or the facts of suffering in the world.

There is a strong implication from some cognitive developmentalists that children's God-concepts are 'sub-religious' until this last stage is reached. Such a verdict ignores the significance of the thought-forms found in earlier childhood whose apprehension of God is just differently expressed.

From these accounts it is apparent that children's conceptions of God can be approached from several different angles, some more mutually exclusive than others. They all deserve to be reckoned with when considering how to introduce children and young people to religious language. Do the child's emotions and attitudes make him/her more, or less, receptive to the content to be shared and how might receptivity be increased? If RE also goes on in middle age and beyond, what can most usefully be done earlier to peg out foundations that will not subsequently need to be changed? Do certain modes of thinking predominate at certain ages and, if so, what forms of communication will then be the most effective? What associations has the individual child already made for God from those who surround him? Above all, what point has he reached in his appreciation of God? These are all questions that a parent or teacher may well want to ask in preparation for any formal use of religious language with a child.

However, it would be a mistake to attend to only one side of the educational equation. Children need to be understood as a preliminary to any understanding of their concepts of God. But, in turn, concepts of God can affect both what is looked for, and found, in and for the children. To be sure, concepts of God are often institutionally labelled as such, deriving from specific and direct use of religious vocabulary: this is true, irrespective of the religious tradition in question. It needs to be recognized that overt familiarity with such words as God, Almighty, Lord, Allah, Vishnu, etc., is no guarantee of any particular degree of understanding. Each points to a reality which is believed to be far greater than any words could signify and each community of faith which uses any such word has generated a rich store of language to express itself

and assist communication. It is vital therefore for the teacher or parent concerned for religious development to be familiar with the range of available language which can be used, i.e. not just prophet, priest and king, but father, friend or companion: artist, judge or clown: volcano, river or sun: fortress, bridge or hospital: all-loving, all-demanding, all-wise. Depending on the tradition, the words may be more, or less, personal, and with, or without, historical reference. Categories of height, or of depth, will be used, with perhaps more emphasis on the former in a tradition that streses the 'otherness' of God, or the latter in one that stresses 'within-ness'. Greatness may also be expressed in terms of the dimension of time – at the beginning and end of time, or a sense of timelessness even in the present now.

Picture language abounds throughout the religious experience of mankind and can be drawn on as a resource for apprehension of how others see God. The taboo against images, as found in Islam*, Judaism* and strands of Christianity, in this context may best be regarded as a warning against the misplaced concreteness of identifying one verbal or visual image with God. With this proviso, so as not to become frozen and fixed, imaging in words or pictures can be employed with even the youngest child (and surely will be by them).

Because the language which is used of God and the experiences which are referred to are so diverse, it is inevitably the case that the bounds of institutional religious labelling are exceeded. In the same way that verbal and visual images, such as those selected above, drew on a wide range of human experience, so too children may cross the religious threshold in their own experience without realizing it. They may have sensed wonder and awe in some big city-centre, on a forest pathway, or just looking up at the stars: they may have been moved to cry out at the sight of pointless cruelty on the roadside or on TV, and to follow it with an expression of fellow-feeling; or they may have been overjoyed, thrilled and delighted with a pleasure that has come to them personally for being who they are – in for example a birthday or festival celebration. Any of these can give glimmerings of the experiences that for the religious believer may be associated with a God concept and the child who has 'been there' already may be better able to make a connection or see new meaning in formal religious language. Similarly, Violet Madge used to speak of the sense of being lost and found as a model for the warmth and security of a God who seeks to be the lover of humankind. Again, a child may know inwardness from moments of quiet, solitariness, or gentle reflection in front of a fire: the isolation and desertion, the burning and transience, as well as the gentleness and warmth that may be known with feeling, can disturb and deepen, and so lead beyond the realm of surface meaning.

In many ways children introduce themselves to God concepts, but there is always the task in RE to explore much further into God-ward territory, and to help with the identification of false idols by leaving the shallows behind. This is the least that any self-respecting atheist could demand of RE. At the same time, it may also be that the initiative for conceiving God will come to a child from without his immediate world. Were that not the case, the concept of God would itself have become but a tamed superstition for children to recognize as such.

Fynn, *Mister God, This is Anna*, Collins 1974; R. Goldman, *Religious Thinking from Childhood to Adolescence*, Routledge & Kegan Paul 1964; R. S. Lee, *Your Growing Child and Religion*, Penguin 1965; E. Lewis, *Children and Their Religion*, Sheed & Ward n.d.; V. Madge, *Children in Search of Meaning*, SCM Press 1965; *A Kind of Believing: Report to General Synod of Church of England*, CIO 1980.

BRIAN E. GATES

Greek, New Testament

In the past, New Testament Greek was almost always studied in universities or theological colleges by students who already had considerable knowledge of one or more of the classical Greek dialects. More recently, as the opportunities for studying classical Greek in schools have become fewer, the New Testament dialect is often taught to pupils with no other knowledge of Greek and perhaps very little of any other foreign language. Courses offered to such pupils in the senior forms of schools have proved to be well worth the trouble taken to provide them.

There are indeed a number of advantages in beginning Greek in this way; the subject matter of the New Testament is generally familiar to the pupils, the amount of vocabulary needing to be learnt is relatively small and the sentence structure in the majority of the books is simpler than in many classical Greek authors. It is, moreover, a particularly rewarding study for young people and, with the development of modern methods of language teaching emphasizing comprehension and appreciation of written passages rather than disembodied grammatical knowledge, it has been possible to devise courses which appeal to and meet the needs of those with a general interest in religion as well as of potential scholars and critics. From a very early stage pupils can begin to feel that they are coming into direct contact with the New Testament authors and beginning to understand the dilemmas of the translators. Discussion of a passage of the Greek text is also often the most appropriate and helpful way of beginning to consider a biblical theme or theological question.

Ernest C. Colwell and Ernest W. Tune, *A Beginner's Reader-Grammar for New Testament Greek*, Harper & Row 1965; D. F. Hudson, *New Testament Greek,* English Universities' Press 1960 and Hodder & Stoughton 1980; Dora Pym, *Outlines for Teaching Greek Reading*, John Murray ²1961.

MARGARET E. JERVIS

Grouping of Pupils

Teaching groups are formed according to several criteria. Most school groups include children of the same age although vertical grouping for educational or economic reasons does exist, especially in small schools. Age ranges are wider in those countries where pupils are promoted on achieving a standard. Intellectual ability has been a major grouping factor. This has resulted in rigid streaming which is now giving way to broader banding or setting. In a setting arrangement where a pupil is in a teaching group according to his ability in that subject, RE sets are often the same as those for other humanities subjects. Mixed ability teaching has become more common with pupil groups being formed in a random way, often based on pastoral groups formed alphabetically by pupils' surnames or geographically by where pupils live. Other administrative devices can determine the composition of a teaching group; sometimes RE is taught to one sex while the other sex is timetabled for games or music. If children are withdrawn from lessons on religious grounds, this will result in new groupings.

In larger schools where block timetabling is operating, the RE teacher may have the opportunity to regroup several classes, or even subgroup one class. This could be done on the basis of Thelen's 'preference grouping', where teachers assemble a group of pupils they enjoy teaching, or by Moreno's 'sociometry', allowing for pupils' professed friendship groups, or by Eysenck's 'personality of pupils', or by the pupil's particular learning style. Such arrangements can avoid personality clashes but careful reviewing is necessary as friendship patterns can change rapidly.

A teaching group can vary in size from one pupil to several hundred. Individual learning is practised for advanced studies, interest projects, homework, written work or silent reading. Pairs of pupils could be engaged in instant discussion after a talk, or on some research or community service. Small groups of three to five pupils might be working on a role play or a display. Groups of six to ten pupils (i.e. an average sized class divided into four groups) are the ideal size for discussion and such groups also can be used for tasks rotating round the class.

Half-class size groups are used for remedial purposes or where some are withdrawn for counselling, and were encouraged by the Humanities Curriculum Project to facilitate discussion. Class sizes of up to thirty or so pupils are commonplace and are most used to foster group identity, to set tasks or hear reporting back, or for straight informational instruction.

While acknowledging that every group of pupils is unique and has a distinct group personality, a major determinant of how any group reacts is the teacher. Each teacher has his own philosophy, practice, preference and personality. Teachers need to understand group dynamics and communication, especially when their subject is not merely cognitive, but includes substantial elements of attitude formation. Teachers work best with a group system in which they believe.

The accommodation provided for any group is also important. Many RE specialists have found themselves without a permanent base or isolated in a mobile classroom. Others are successful in acquiring a large carpeted room, with easy chairs and facilities for projection, drama and music. The ideal group arrangement depends on the task to be tackled.

See also **RE Room.**

R. Berenda, *The Influence of the Group on the Judgments of Children*, Columbia University 1950; J. L. Moreno, *Who Shall Survive?*, Nervous and Mental Disease Pub. Co. 1934; R. W. Napier and M. K. Gershenfield, *Groups: Theory and Experience*, Houghton Mifflin, Boston 1973; O. A. Oeser, *Teacher, Pupil and Task*, Tavistock Institute 1960; P. B. Smith, (ed.), *Group Processes*, Penguin 1970; H. A. Thelen, *Dynamics of Groups at Work*, University of Chicago Press 1954; E. C. Wragg, *Teaching Mixed Ability Groups*, David and Charles Ltd 1976.

JOSEPH BYSH

Handicapped, Mentally: Religious Education of

It is only during the past few years that serious attempts have been made to develop the subject of RE in Special Schools. Prior to that, most research had been undertaken by the Roman Catholic Church in Europe by Professor Henri Bissonnier, and more recently Professor Paulhus, and David Wilson in England. In 1978, CEM set up a project to explore the place of RE in the curriculum of Special Schools. Recommendations from that project included the adoption of an implicit* approach to the subject, with only occasional explicit* teaching, which requires of the teacher a sympathy with or commitment to the religious dimension of human experience. (This is especially the case in schools for the severely handicapped.) The project reported that it was possible both to guard against the risk of indoctrination and at the same time to prepare schemes of work based on an implicit* approach to RE which all teachers would be able to use. It was possible to select from teaching programmes those areas of work having a religious potential, with a view to considering ways in which this potential could be developed further. The report suggested ways of putting these recommendations into practice. Many schools have used the report as a guide to introduce the subject into the curriculum. Teachers participating in a Curriculum Development Project came to the conclusion that rel*g*ous education should receive its focus in the school assembly* and be related to a theme, e.g. fire, water, food, particular festivals*. The approach and content should be adapted to the mental development of the children in the school. In schools for the severely handicapped the theme should be explored in such a way as to heighten awareness of the religious dimension to life. In schools for the moderately handicapped, the theme should become the starting point to a more explicit* approach to the subject. Research and experiments continue as more Special Schools recognize the importance of including RE in the curriculum.

See also **Special Education, Special Schools.**

Henri Bissionnier, *Catechetical Pedagogy of the Mentally Deficient Children,* Lumen Vitae Press 1967; R. Gower, *The Formby Project,* Sefton LEA; Jean Richardson, *Religious Education in Special Schools,* CEM 1978; David G. Wilson, *I am with You,* St Paul Publications 1975.

JEAN RICHARDSON

Head Teacher: Role of in RE

At both the primary and secondary stages of schooling, the role of the head teacher in religious education is specially significant. Since under the 1944 Act the subject is mandatory in all state schools in England and Wales, no head teacher can, in law, ignore it. At the same time, the head's personal view of the aim and purpose of the education the school provides will be critical in determining the place occupied by RE, both in the curriculum and in the general life of the school. It is not just a question of classroom priorities and the allocation of resources, important as these are. The most important single factor in determining the quality of the education provided in a school is the leadership exercised by the head teacher (*Ten Good Schools*, HMSO 1977).

Religious education suffers because its boundaries tend to become ill-defined and also because its function as perceived by many people becomes subsumed at the secondary level under other headings such as Personal*

and Moral Education*. The lack of adequately trained specialist teachers in secondary schools and the low priority sometimes given to the subject in the training of primary teachers too often means that the teaching of the subject is unenlightened, uninspired and woefully mechanical, if it is seriously attempted at all. At a time when resources are scarce and there are considerable pressures on schools to include a whole range of new subjects in the curriculum it is too easy to relegate RE to the lower end of the head teacher's priorities. Consequently the head has a peculiar and heavy responsibility in relation to the provision of RE in his or her school. If, at the primary level, the school has a coherent philosophy based on the worth of the individual child and at the same time seeks to implement the best current practice in primary education, then many of the implicit aims of RE will be achieved in what is done. However, difficulties will arise in the area of explicit* religious education and it is here that the positive leadership of the headteacher is vitally necessary. The head needs to subscribe to the view that 'no boy or girl can be counted as properly educated unless he or she has been made aware of the fact of the existence of a religious interpretation of life' (*The Spens Report*, HMSO 1938), and that the best place to begin this is in the primary school. The head teacher must provide opportunities and encouragement for the staff concerned to prepare themselves through in-service and other courses, and must make sure that the teachers are aware of the wide range of excellent material now available to help them. At the very least, RE must be placed on the same footing as any other timetable activity and must have adequate resources.

In the secondary school the task is made harder by the changing view in society of the proper function of a school, the widespread neglect of the spiritual dimension of life, the uncertainty of belief which inhibits many teachers and the confusion which surrounds the purpose of RE in a multi-faith society. It is the head's responsibility to make clear the view that religious education matters and that the school is concerned with the development of the whole person. Therefore the spiritual elements of personal development cannot and must not be neglected. How this message is conveyed is crucial to its success and will depend essentially upon the head teacher/staff relationship. It will only be achieved by the exercise of positive leadership from a head who is aware of the problems facing the teacher and who is sensitive to the unspoken needs of his or her students. Further, it is the headteacher's duty to give as much moral and practical support as possible to the teachers and to provide for them whatever practical assistance may be available.

KENNETH D. EXLEY

Health Education and RE

The connection between health education and religious education is two-fold; historical and conceptual.

Historically, as can be clearly seen from early agreed syllabuses*, health education appeared within the RE lesson. Nor was the separation accidental. In the early 1960s, quite explicit attempts were made to isolate what were regarded as the facts about health from the moral and metaphysical systems in which they were encapsulated.

However, a decade later, Schools' Council Working Paper 57 asserted that, 'Health Education depends for its success on the formation and development of attitudes,' commenting also that, 'little is known about methods for affecting attitude change.' In an appendix of the same document, Backenbury goes so far as to say that health education is concerned with helping children to evolve a considered basis for morality, and even talks of personal and sexual relationships as sometimes having sacramental significance. The main report discusses the need to raise such questions as, 'Who am I?', 'What is my worth?', 'Where am I going?'

This rediscovery of a dimension which is the legitimate concern of religion is not to be wondered at. Conceptually, health and religion are very close. Health education is essentially the whole life of humankind considered from the viewpoint of health which, in turn, is that to which we aspire. The General Confession calls Christians to repent because 'there is no health in us'. Health has to do with well-being and wholesomeness and the *Oxford English Dictionary* defines it as 'spiritual, moral and mental soundness'.

Health is also culturally relative. It derives from social, philosophical and metaphysical values. To reject the religious is necessarily to substitute some other basis. There is, therefore, a choice to be made between secular health education and religious health education. What is the distinction? In simplistic terms it is seen in a question such as, 'Was Father Damien a healthy person in working among lepers?'

J. G. Priestley and Nicholas DeSausmarez, 'The Existentialist Theologian and the Battery Hen: some thoughts on the relationship beween RE and Health Education', in B. Lealman (ed.), *The Total Curriculum in Relation to RE*, CEM 1980; Schools' Council Working Paper No. 57, *Health Education in Secondary Schools,* Evans-Methuen 1976; Kenneth Slack, *Is Sacrifice Outmoded?,* SCM Press 1966.

JACK PRIESTLEY

Hebrew: Study of in RE

The study of Hebrew has been practised among Jews from OT times, and at first Western Christian scholars were entirely dependent upon the work of Jewish teachers. It was the Reformation which injected a new impetus into the study of Hebrew among Christians because Protestants sought to base their polemics upon the Bible and, as an alternative to the Latin Vulgate, translated the scriptures into the vernacular from the original languages. Logically, the doctrine of verbal infallibility of the Bible demanded a knowledge of Hebrew and Greek* if it was not to be based on a selected translation. The aim of both Reformation and Renaissance was therefore to extend the knowledge held by scholars from their common language, Latin, to include these other languages as well. Erasmus refers to this in his ideal of *trilinguis homo*, 'trilingual man'.

Study of Hebrew as an academic subject has continued to the present and in 1975 it was being taught in twenty-three British universities to about four hundred and fifty undergraduates. More recently, however, it has become less and less a compulsory element of a degree course in either theology or biblical studies, let alone religious studies.

The main argument against its inclusion in such courses is the amount of time which must be devoted to acquiring the rudiments of the language in the context of pressures from economic forces to shorten degree courses.

The real question at issue is how that time should be used and whether it could be more profitably spent by the prospective teacher in studying less strictly biblical subjects such as sociology*, Marxism* and the psychology of religion*. In contrast, the arguments for its continued study within training courses for clergy and RE teachers, even when Hebrew is unlikely to be a subject which they will actually teach, is that their integrity in handling the OT and the authenticity of their interpretation will be enhanced by their ability to handle material at source in the original language.

J. Barr, *The Bible in the Modern World*, SCM Press 1973; E. R. Bevan and C. Singer, *The Legacy of Israel*, Clarendon Press 1927; E. V. N. Goetchius, W. Harrelson and G. M. Landes, 'Teaching the Biblical Languages', *Theological Education*, III, 1967, pp. 435–507; N. Smart, *Secular Education and the Logic of Religion*, Faber 1968; J. Weingreen, *A Practical Grammar for Classical Hebrew*, Oxford University Press ²1959.

D. R. AP-THOMAS

Hermeneutics

The discipline which teaches how to study a given text. It is something which has always exercised the minds of Christian scholars, but it has been given a new orientation by the rise of biblical criticism. Pre-critical writers were always in danger of understanding the text quite out of its context and also of reading into it their own presuppositions. These dangers have not always been avoided by critical scholars either.

Since the last war, a whole hermeneutical school has arisen, particularly in Germany. They maintain that the student who wishes to interpret a text rightly must face two distinct questions: 1. What did the original writer mean? 2. How do we today make sense of what he meant? But some (e.g. W. Pannenberg) distinguish a 'double gap' as far as concerns the sayings recorded of Jesus: we must ask 1. What did Jesus originally mean? 2. What did the early church make of his meaning? Similarly, when we are seeking to interpret the OT we must be prepared for a similar double question: 1. How do the NT writers interpret this text? 2. What are we to make of their interpretation?

It was on the basis of this approach to hermeneutics that Rudolf Bultmann elaborated his famous programme of 'demythologizing'. He held that much of the language of the NT was basically mythological and needed to be transposed into terms intelligible to modern man (or indeed abandoned altogether). Since Bultmann's day, students of linguistics and meaning theory have entered this field, sometimes with confusing results.

For RE, the most important significance of hermeneutics is that it warns us against a naive, anachronistic, or dogmatically tendentious interpretation of the Bible* and points to the pitfalls which lie on the path of the unlearned student. The technique can, of course, be applied to the sacred texts of other religions also.

H. W. Bartsch (ed.), *Kerygma and Myth*, SPCK 1953–62; C. E. Braaten, *History and Hermeneutics*, Lutterworth 1968; R. Bultmann, *Jesus Christ and Mythology*, SCM Press 1960; J. Macquarrie, *The Scope of Demythologising*, SCM Press 1950; S. M. Ogden, *Christ without Myth*, Collins 1962; A. Thisleton, *The Two Horizons*, Paternoster 1980.

ANTHONY HANSON

Heroes

Examination of the curriculum recommendations contained in agreed syllabuses* of RE reveals a suggested major commitment to the study of famous lives. Until quite recent years, these lives have been largely those of Christian heroes associated with the development and expansion of the religion in Britain immediately following the collapse of the Roman Empire, the witness of men and women during the turbulent fifteenth, sixteenth and seventeenth centuries and the missionary exploits of those who followed the military expansion of Europe into Africa, Asia and the South Pacific. The many publications produced to support such teaching erred in a number of respects. The approach tended to be heavily historical, tracing the life of the person simply in terms of key events, with little or no exploration of personal search for meaning and purpose in life. Such heroes all too easily lost their real earthy humanity and for many pupils had little or no relevance as they took their natural place in Victorian stained glass. The view of *mission* represented in those nineteenth century lives of men and women who addressed themselves to the heathen dark continents would not now be shared by the major missionary societies of the Christian church. The mass of heroic examples were the witness of the dead.

More recent trends in RE have seen the importance of introducing pupils to the faith response of contemporary figures from not only Christian but all backgrounds. Pupils discover the living history of persons in their own community and the wider world who, like them, have lived with the vexing questions which are characteristic of life: What can we really know about ourselves and the world? Why is there a world supporting human life? Where do human beings come from and to where they go? Why is the world as it is? What meaning can be discovered at the heart of reality? What ought we to do? Why do we act as we do? Why and to whom are we finally responsible? What deserves our forthright contempt? What deserves our love? What is the meaning of suffering? What is the point of loyalty, friendship? What really matters for people? What can we hope for? Why are we here? What is life all about? How can I face death? What is there left for a person after death? Does the fact of death render all talk of meaning and purpose meaningless? What will give us courage for life? What will give us courage for death?

These questions are vital in the process of developing self understanding, and heroism illustrated through the content of RE is the courage with which people have faced such questions and the personal cost they have borne as a result of a faith position adopted.

While stressing the importance of the contemporary experience of mankind it can be of great interest for pupils to discover that just such issues have been issues for all men down the centuries and are likely to remain so in the centuries which lie ahead. Each pupil is in the process of finding a route through life and in this he or she is in solidarity with all mankind. Schools are disposed to talk of developing maturity in the young and this can be understood in terms of how a person copes with his existence in what for many children now is a terrifying universe.

To the extent that teachers are successful in bringing heroes down from the stained glass windows into a conjunction with the real experience of the pupils, it may be that this aspect of RE will in a lively way be a significant resource for the pupil in his or her search.

See also **Biography.**

IAN H. BIRNIE

Hidden Curriculum

The curriculum is the sum total of the teaching and learning within a school. It has two aspects. The public curriculum is the formal content of departmental syllabuses. The hidden curriculum is the learning which takes place because of values which are taken for granted and because of the ways the members of the school live their lives within it. The hidden curriculum can support or endanger the public one. It probably has more effect, because it works at the level where feelings are engaged and attitudes formed. Certainly the ethos* of a school depends more upon the hidden than upon the public curriculum.

The phrase 'hidden curriculum' has fallen out of favour recently because, with an increasing awareness of the phenomena to which it refers, has come an increased determination to take them consciously into account. In addition, it has been government policy to press schools to define their aims. This task, if undertaken with sensitivity, must involve a consideration of elements in the hidden curriculum – for example, the expectations of staff, parents and pupils; the influence of assessment* procedures on school life; the extent and nature of voluntary activities; and the affective consequences of classroom teaching methods. In general, the less hidden the hidden curriculum, the greater the likelihood that it will be purposive and fruitful.

Classroom religious education is as susceptible to the influence of the hidden curriculum as other subjects are, but the outcomes may well be different. Pupils often approach the subject with a predisposition against it, believing it to be boring and irrelevant. They are more inclined than in any other subject to claim that they are being taught opinion as fact and that they are being compulsorily indoctrinated. In a school where teachers are usually regarded as experts beyond question the RE teacher is likely to be seen as an exception, and to have a difficult task. In a school where open-mindedness and awareness of uncertainty are common classroom attitudes, a predisposition against RE is more easily dealt with. Similarly, a tradition of rigid, impersonal classroom discipline is likely to make the effective teaching of RE more difficult than a tradition of firm and sensitive friendliness.

The hidden curriculum is of even greater importance in its effects on religious education in the wider sense – as an effect of the messages carried by school life as a whole. A church school may strive to ensure that its life reflects at every point the Christian attitudes which prompted its foundation, while allowing at the same time for the fact that its intake may in large part be from non-Christian homes. A maintained school may strive for an atmosphere of sensitive caring congenial to spiritual growth, without either forcing consciences or alienating goodwill. In either case, the endeavour is to encourage, or at worst leave room for, a spiritual dimension in school life. If that endeavour is lacking, the effect may well be that the hidden curriculum is one of unremitting secularism; as indeed it sometimes is.

P. E. Daunt, *Comprehensive Values,* Heinemann 1975; M. Hare Duke and E. Whitton, *A Kind of Believing*, General Synod Board of Education 1977; Michael Hinton, *Comprehensive Schools: A Christian's View,* SCM Press 1979; *A View of the Curriculum*, HMSO 1980.

MICHAEL HINTON

Higher Education

Since 1945 the study of religion in institutions of higher education has seen more changes than any other discipline. The new variety of learning programmes reflects the increase in interest of the young in questions about meaning, and also more general and widespread interest in the phenomenon of religion itself. Degree patterns going far beyond traditional Christian studies, often where Christianity takes its place as one of the several faiths which may be selected and studied within the complexities of their cultural heritage, are now commonplace. The permeation of the modular degree into European higher education is widespread, and in Britain the inclusion of religious studies within this structure was the innovation of the 1970s. Two specific events contributed to the increase in the study of religion within modular or unit degrees: 1. the formation in 1970 of a Theological and Religious Studies Board by the Council for National Academic Awards; 2. in 1971 The Open University introduced 25,000 students to its first courses and prepared the ground for the inclusion of religious studies as a discipline within the Faculty of Arts.

1. *The study of religion at university.* The choice of courses leading to degrees in theology or RS on offer in the university sector is excellent. Alongside degrees in theology, some faculties or departments offer BAs in specialized areas, in combined and in general studies structures. Degree courses in religious studies are all of fairly recent origin, and all include a range of options in the study of the major world faiths. Some include a substantial component of social and cultural anthropology, psychology* and sociology of religion*. The more traditional-type degrees in theology for those who wish to concentrate on Christianity* reveal the growing emphasis on contemporary socio-religious studies. Postgraduate taught courses are equally wideranging from architecture and liturgy to ecumenical and pastoral or practical theology. The Open Univerity, which adopted a unit degree structure allowing students to build up credits from different disciplinary areas, has seen an expanding market in the study of religion.

2. *The study of religion in the non-university sector.* One of the very positive factors to emerge from the re-organization of the former colleges of education has been the expansion of religious studies in LEA insitutions, including polytechnics. Colleges having a religious foundation, although not necessarily credited with the monopoly of academic excellence in the study of religion, had nevertheless enjoyed better staffing ratios and resources for the teaching of religion. This is no longer true.

(*a*) *Polytechnics.* Many provide courses in religion leading to Dip.HE, BEd or the BA degree within the faculty of humanities and are staffed and resourced accordingly. Where there is no specific department or division of RS, often courses are offered which have distinctive religious content, whether historical, philosophical or sociological, within the total humanities programmes. The contribution to the academic study of religion within the polytechnics is now considerable. All degrees and diplomas are CNAA validated.

(*b*) *Institutes and Colleges of Higher Education.* The former colleges of education contributed greatly to twentieth-century developments in RS. Faced in the immediate post-war years with the demands for RE specialists in schools, several colleges ran 'One-year Supplementary Courses in Divinity'. No sooner was this task virtually completed when they were required to embrace the new approach to religious education and so equip students not only with some understanding of the contemporary religious thought, belief and practice but also with some degree of expertise to meet the changing face of English society, particularly that of the inner-city* schools. A working knowledge of all world religions* appeared essential. Colleges expanded and RS departments grew into mini-faculties with appropriate specialist lecturers. In the late sixties, religion became a popular main study area in the new four-year BEd. At this time colleges were constituent members of the appropriate school, faculty, institute or department of education and were therefore validated by the parent university. Hence BEd patterns tended to conform to local usage although there was considerable freedom within teacher's certificate courses. Since the reorganization, many institutes and colleges have sought CNAA validation for both BEd and new BA single, combined honours or humanities degrees. Others have found closer ties with the university sector and some have been absorbed within a university education school. The overall picture within this sector of higher education is a healthy one which has seen tremendous activity and enthusiasm of staff, whether in the production of new degrees and diplomas or in closer working ties with parent universities.

3. *Theological Colleges.* Seminaries and theological colleges reflect current trends in the study of religion. The impending demise of the London external BD has had startling repercussions in this area of vocational training and was the reason for the establishment of the Theology and Religious Studies Board of CNAA in 1970. The freedom that a CNAA degree has given to those institutions which have sought its validation has been well exploited. The broadening of the traditional theological courses has been welcomed by staff and students alike. Many theological colleges of differing denominations are closely affili-ated to their local universities and the students read for degrees and diplomas provided by the university. Other denominational institutions, formerly almost solely concerned with the training of ordinands, are integral parts of the university, many from their original foundation. Most theological colleges have long since opened their doors to students of both sexes and to those not necessarily bent upon ministerial training.

4. *Current Research.* One of the first tasks undertaken by the Institute of Religion and Theology was to set up a register of current research in religion and allied disciplines. This register entitled *Current Research*, although still far from complete as a survey of all relevant research undertaken in the UK and Ireland, has highlighted the considerable interest in the area. With its new computerized records and search service its facilities have become internationally known and used.

See also **Colleges of Education.**

JOAN HAZELDEN WALKER

Hinduism

The term 'Hindu' was originally coined by the Persians and the Arabs to refer to the people of the Indus Valley. As a religious system 'Hinduism' lacks a historical founder, a creed, or a set of universally accepted dogmas. Hinduism is not therefore easily susceptible to generalizations. Indeed there is a serious problem of defining what Hinduism is, and this problem directly affects both the philosophy and the practice of Hindu religious education. It also creates problems for the treatment of Hinduism as a world religion in British RE syllabuses and textbooks.

Hinduism is often used as a shorthand term for the complex of religious beliefs and practices of those Indians, Nepalese and Balinese who cannot be identified as members of any other religious community. Despite the tremendous variety of Hindu beliefs and practices however, historical, geographical and cultural factors have produced a remarkable degree of coherence in general beliefs and outlook and this coherence includes the broad outline of a Hindu philosophy of education.

Hindu philosophy of education. Traditional Hinduism recognizes four legitimate goals of life: moral and social duty (*dharma*); pleasure (*kama*); power (*artha*); and spiritual release or escape from the cycle of rebirth (*mokśa*).

In proper harmony with each other the first three go to make up a balanced society and balanced life, but none of them offers the ultimate fulfilment which is seen as the goal of the ascetic's quest. This attempt at harmonizing apparently divergent goals is mirrored in the four stages of life (*āśramas*). In this ideal systematization the individual passes through the childhood to the student stage (*brahma-cārin*) then to that of householder (*grhasha*), forest dweller and renouncer (*vānaprastha*) and finally total renouncer, (*sannyāsin*).

The student stage (*brahmacārya*) centres on the relationship between teacher (*guru*) and disciple and is characterized by celibacy, austerity and a single-minded devotion to spiritual learning; a idealized picture which has captured the imagination of many modern Hindu educationalists.

In classical Hindu spiritual teaching the pursuit of spiritual release is often seen as achievable through the realization of the fundamental unity between the individual soul (*Ātman*) and the pervasive ultimate reality (*Brahman*) and modern Hindu thinkers such as Rabindranath Tagore and Swami Vivekenanda have used the teaching as the basis for an idealist philosophy of education. According to this philosophy the mission of education is to help in the realization of the principle of the unity of all knowledge and to harmonize the various elements of man's mind and spiritual being.

The universalistic character of this vision often leaves little room for direct and specifically religious teaching and many modern Hindu references have excluded it. Tagore regarded it as divisive and Gandhi limited it to the teaching of the Hindu epic literature. For them and other thinkers the all important spiritual truth was 'caught rather than taught' through the personal influence of the teacher.

The neo-Hindu *Ārya Samaj* sect also placed a strong emphasis upon the disciple-guru model, revived the institution of *brahmacarya* making it the basis of its Gurukula movement which promoted a very Indian type of education and laid specific emphasis upon direct Hindu religious education based upon the study of the most ancient Hindu scripture, the Vedas. Other less nationalistic neo-Hindu movements have promoted syncretistic approach to the teaching of religion. The Ramakrishna movement for example advocates the teaching of the 'true eternal principles' found in all religion.

Religious Education within Hinduism. The concern of modern Indian thinkers has tended to produce a model of Hindu religious instruction and religious formation to compete alongside the religious schooling of Muslims and Christians. This tendency has led to some attempts at doctrinal self-definition by Hindus along lines similar to the semitic religions. However, in the traditional life of the village, where four-fifths of the Indian population still live, religion permeates every social experience and activity and religious education is assimilated in informal ways. Simple human activities such as morning ablutions in the preparation and eating of a meal are regarded as important religious rituals. The rites of passage* (*samskāras*) which mark the progress of the individual from conception to final dissolution give a religious character to the cycle of a human life in the same way as the numerous festivals* of the Hindu year punctuate the seasons of the year with religious meaning.

Social relationships are governed by fundamentally religious and Hindu understanding of ritual purity and pollution evidenced particularly by the institution of caste which physically separates different hereditary social groups, excluding all inter-marriage and even, in the case of untouchables (*harijans*), of physical contact.

The village abounds in shrines to tree-gods, spirits and village deities as well as to regional and India-wide gods. Large numbers of Hindus also visit temples and undertake pilgrimages to holy places sometimes hundreds of miles from their own villages.

The rich and varied mythology of Hinduism is contained in the epic literature and in the collections known as the Purāṇas, but at a popular level the mythology is constantly being reworked and retold. A Hindu village child will normally learn numerous versions of the same myths from grandparents, temple priests and story-tellers, dramatic performers and others. His counterpart in the town will also have the opportunity to see the myths at the cinema and to read them in 'comic-strip' versions.

The chaotic richness of Hindu popular religion excludes easy generalizations on the content of Hindu RE, but the average Hindu will grow up with a predictable range of assumptions and attitudes. These will usually include: belief in Bhagvan 'the Lord' (a supreme embodiment of Godhead whose unity is quite consistent with the myriad personifications of the deities of Hinduism); the caste system; respect for parents, the four goals and the four stages of life, the doctrine of reincarnation and the law of karma (action) which determines future rebirth.

In India the school system will often reinforce this knowledge. In Britain as elsewhere in the Hindu diaspora the main source of religious education is the home and the community. Many Hindu families in Britain still observe the main traditional festivals and domestic shrines are a feature of most Hindu homes. Hindu mythology and ideas will often be passed on by parents, and more importantly by older relatives. Temples are also assuming greater importance as centres for the maintenance of community identity. Apart from the daily rituals, these temples also become centres for the singing of devotional hymns and for sermons by visiting religious teachers from India. Some temples have also set up 'evening' or 'Sunday' schools which educate the children in their traditional language and often provide some element of formal religious intruction.

Those Hindus who become most assimilated to British society can expect some difficulty in defining what precisely constitutes their 'Hinduism'. In this respect the Hindu 'sects' with defined rules and doctrines can be expected to have greater appeal.

The teaching of Hinduism in British schools. The problem of definition also reappears when considering the treatment of Hinduism in RE in British schools. Together with the other major world faiths, Hinduism now features in a number of agreed syllabuses* and school textbooks, receiving attention both in its own right and in the development of thematic topics. Several CSE examination boards offer Hindusim as a part of their examination syllabus and a few GCE boards include an option in Hinduism at Ordinary and Advanced level.

The gradual emergence of Hinduism in British RE is partly a result of the new orientations provided by the Schools Council* and partly by a desire to utilize the educational opportunities provided by the presence of the Hindu community in Britain. The complexity and confusion attached to Hinduism may have put off some teachers from including it in their teaching, but these teachers can be encouraged to make a selective use of Hindu beliefs and symbols in their thematic teaching.

Moreover the problem of general ignorance and confusion about Hinduism should become less with the improvement in the availability and quality of school resources in Hinduism. Also as the Hindu community becomes more established in this country we can expect it to become more vocal on its own behalf and to attract more interest and recognition.

See also **Yoga.**

William Cenker, *The Hindu Personality in Education: Tagore; Gandhi; Auribindo*, Manohar, Delhi, 1976; S. S. Dikshit, *Nationalism and Indian Education,* Sterling Publishers, Delhi 1966; H. Kanitkar and R. Jackson, *Hindus in Britain,* London School of Oriental and African Studies 1982; S. Weightman, 'Hinduism and Religious Education', *Perspectives on World Religions*, ed. R. Jackson, London School of Oriental and African Studies 1978.

DUNCAN M. MACPHERSON

History

Religious Studies is a multi-disciplinary field and among the disciplines involved history may lay claim to be a major contributor. But history is not antiquarianism, or merely chronology, or simply a collection of facts about the past. History is about people, evidence and values. The facts of history can only be appreciated by imaginative experience – the imaginative reconstruction of the past disciplined by the evidence. The motives of past people cannot be known directly but only by inference and intuition. History and religion share a common task in enabling pupils to develop empathy. Pupils must be put into a position to enter into the minds and feelings of those involved in an event, so as to appreciate their differing attitudes without necessarily approving of their beliefs, attitudes or values. By enquiry pupils will seek to understand why, given the particular situation, people acted in the way they did. Pupils need to perceive their involvement in the past:

this means relating the pupil to his/her own past, including a religious past (if any), and exploring the immediate physical environment. It involves questions like 'Why was Grandad a Quaker?' or 'Why are there so many synagogues in this part of town?' or 'Why does Walid fast during Ramadan?' The challenge of values in history may be equally direct: 'Why do so many Asians live in the poor part of town?' or 'Why are all the people who go to church posh?' The use of urban trails that relate local history to the challenge of beliefs, attitudes and values, and that consolidate personal identity with critical openness are a recent venture in RE that is deserving of wider use by teachers of the subject.

The syllabus in RE, including its historical contents, can affect attitudes and assumptions about racial groups, nations, cultures and religious communities. Properly handled, the historical dimension of religious traditions can lead to a more critical frame of mind which will enable pupils to challenge easy generalizations. In this respect, of course, the teacher of RE will be aware of the tensions that may arise between religious truth claims and the analytical and critical skills fostered by the development of historical study. Advocates of the study of world religions* have sometimes recommended a 'willing suspension of disbelief' in the study of the religious beliefs and traditions of others. In part, such detachment is necessary, but it remains but part of the process. Any teacher knows that pupils are constantly involved in expressing opinions and making judgments – it is an essential part of growing up in a lively classroom at whatever age. Comparisons and contrasts, similarities and differences, need to be discussed openly. The use of the historical dimension in RE is not a means of avoiding personal judgments in some seemingly neutral or objective study. Pupils will respond and make judgments about people, about beliefs and about evidence: it is the teacher's job in RE utilizing the tools of history and other disciplines, to enable pupils to make informed and responsible judgments. Such judgments will in due course influence the decisions and the life style of every pupil.

See also **Biography; Heroes.**

JACK W. G. HOGBIN

History of RE in England

Although religious teaching had been part of English schooling from the very beginning, its place became firmly established only when the 1870 Education Act incorporated it into the new 'national' system of education, though its nature was confined by the Cowper-Temple clause*. The vague 'Bible theism' which this restriction produced began to be developed and enriched once the idea of an 'agreed syllabus'* had been mooted. The Cambridgeshire Syllabus of 1924 was the first breakthrough in this area and this concept of an agreed syllabus soon became so widely accepted that it was able to be used as a central plank of the 1944 Education Act.

The settlement of 1944 gave statutory force to two practices which were already widespread in schools, the giving of religious intruction according to an agreed syllabus and the holding of school prayers. Together, these two practices were described as 'religious education', and it was as if the classroom lessons were an exposition of (or background to) the Bible passages being read at the morning assembly*. Both the appropriateness and the effectiveness of such an approach were fairly soon called in question and a number of enquiries were set up by bodies such as the Institute of Christian Education (who published two surveys, in 1953 and 1961). The later survey was conducted by Harold Loukes and written up by him under the title *Teenage Religion*. It pointed the way to a new approach, sometimes labelled 'pupil-centred', sometimes 'problem-centred', derived in part from the approach to theology then associated with the name of Paul Tillich, and in part from the old educational adage, 'Start where the pupils are'. A similar approach with young children was advocated by Violet Madge, whose first book was significantly entitled *Children in Search of Meaning* (1965). Also in 1965, Ronald Goldman, in *Readiness for Religion* tried to answer the question, 'Where exactly is the point at which our pupils find themselves at various stages in their lives, so that we may more clearly know from where to start in our pupil-centred approach?' The labels 'experiential'* and 'implicit'* were often applied to the style of RE advocated by both Loukes and Goldman, either because it drew heavily on the child's experience (and/or sought to enhance that experience) or on the grounds that man's religious experience was implicit in his 'ordinary' experience.

Goldman's ideas helped to shape a whole new generation of agreed syllabuses, of which the West Riding's *Suggestions for RE* (1966) was both the first and the most widely used. But more fundamental questions were already being asked, not just about where to start from, but about where the whole process of RE was supposed to be leading. Most of the earlier agreed syllabuses, even though they were intended for county schools and not for church schools, had implied (and some had actually stated) that the purpose of RE was to encourage commitment to Jesus Christ through membership of a Christian church. This view was now coming under serious challenge. Edwin Cox's *Changing Aims in RE* (1966) was a sign of the times, but the most weighty endorsement of the new thinking came in *The Fourth R** (1970), the report of a Church of England commission chaired by the Bishop of Durham: 'To press for acceptance of a particular faith or belief system is the duty and privilege of the Churches and other similar religious bodies. It is certainly not the task of a teacher in a county school.'

Throughout the 1970s aims were to be expressed in terms of knowledge* and understanding: commitment was out; openness, neutrality and objectivity were in. The content of many new syllabuses included much material on religions other than Christianity (notably the Birmingham Agreed Syllabus of 1975) reflecting the work of Ninian Smart at Lancaster University. But his move to widen the content of RE was parallelled by a growing concern for clear identification (in positive terms) of the aims and objectives of the subject. The pioneer here was the Avon Agreed Syllabus (1976), but the most widely used of the syllabuses adopting this new approach was the one from Hampshire (1978). Meanwhile the Schools Council* had published *A Groundplan for the Study of Religion* (1977), which led in its turn to the attempt (in the studies for the projected N and F level examinations) to construct an examination syllabus purely on the basis of stated objectives*.

This growing unwillingness to specify a universally applicable content, linked with the repudiation of religious commitment as a legitimate educational aim, caused alarm in some conservative circles and attempts were made to prevent the spread of 'Hampshire-style' syllabuses. Similarly, the motive of the British Humanist Association* in taking up membership of the RE Council* was questioned by some. Despite the uncertainties implied by these developments, the Commons Select Committee on Education in its second report (1982) reaffirmed its support for the religious clauses in the 1944 Act, while at the same time signalling its approval of the changes achieved since 1960 by welcoming the substitution of RE for RI as the proper title of the subject.

This symbolic change of title acknowledges a clear educational role for the subject, concerned with the development of understanding as opposed to its earlier concern with the instilling of values drawn from one particular (though broadly interpreted) tradition. But, in establishing this new role, the subject may at times have been in danger of stressing too much its analytic function and forgetting that (in the terminology used by Phoenix) religion has a synoptic role. Just as in art education the development of true artistic insight comes from something more than the exercise of analytic skills on information acquired, so in RE the development of true understanding does impinge inescapably on the realm of values. To realize this in practice, without compromising the principles hammered out over the past two decades, is the task facing RE in the next decades.

See also **Acts of Parliament.**

Edwin Cox, *Changing Aims in RE*, Routledge & Kegan Paul 1966; Ronald Goldman, *Readiness for Religion*, Routledge & Kegan Paul 1965; Harold Loukes, *Teenage Religion*, SCM Press 1961; Violet Madge, *Children in Search of Meaning*, SCM Press 1965; Schools Council, *A Groundplan for the Study of Religion*, 1977.

COLIN ALVES

Holy Communion and Children

Debate about the participation of children in the sacrament of Holy Communion has arisen mainly in Protestant churches, in many parts of the world. It reflects experience in congregations with a developed sense of community.

Where churches take seriously the experience of individuals and their place in the corporate whole, questions tend to be raised about children, their place in it, their contribution to it, and their need of ministry from it. The participation of children, in practice, has raised both explicit and implicit questions about the nature of the intitution of the church and of the liturgy. This is turn has led to the development in some places of new forms of community life and to the creation of new liturgies. In response to grass-roots experiences, some churches, e.g. the Presbyterian Church in the USA, have now changed their church rules. This debate is not new.

The Orthodox* churches have maintained the practice of baptized infants participating in Holy Communion from the time of their baptism. Cyprian and later Augustine bear witness to the participation of infants in the eucharist. Both argue that baptism and eucharist are necessary for membership of the church, together with continued participation in the eucharist. In the mediaeval church, a similar argument was followed by St Thomas. At the Reformation, reference back was made to Augustine, Cyprian, Bernard and Chrysostom. The practice of communicating infants was restored by the Hussites in Bohemia and was an element in the controversy between John Whitgift and Thomas Cartwright in England. The practice was adopted by the nineteenth-century Catholic Apostolic Church.

The argument against the participation of children is usually based on the children's need to understand both the nature of their own sin and of God's judgment, pardon and grace offered through the death and resurrection of Christ. Children, it is said, must be instructed first. This view raises questions about what is meant by understanding, the communicative power of a community and its symbols, and the meaning of baptism. Those in favour of the participation of children argue that the exclusion of children obscures the meaning of the gospel of grace. The covenant love of God is offered in baptism and the Lord's Supper unconditionally; it does not depend on the good works, merit or worth of the communicant. Since baptism is the normal mode of entry into the church, those who are baptized as infants (or as adults) should be helped to feel that they belong to Christ and

his community. Within an accepting community, children are able to make commitments appropriate to their age. Further, informal research shows that children are able to perceive meanings and to respond imaginatively and sensitively to the eucharist to the extent of having insights to contribute to the church's adults. The practice of communicating children is usually safeguarded by requiring that only children accompanied by adults may participate.

A major strand in the discussion concerns the nature of the child's belonging to the church. The sacraments of baptism and Holy Communion can be closely related only where either baptism is of adults, or confirmation (or church membership) is separated from admission to Holy Communion. It has been suggested that the true biblical order is: belonging to Christ by birth and baptism; believing that we belong through experience in the community of Christ and participation in Holy Communion; and understanding and professing belonging. This latter would include confirmation, but would to a great extent be a life-long process and be part of the interaction of life and faith.

(Throughout this article eucharist, Holy Communion, Lord's Supper are used as synonyms.)

Children and Holy Communion, ed. G. Grundy, Joint Board of Christian Education, Australia 1978; . . . *and do not hinder them*, ed. G. Müller-Farenholz, World Council of Churches 1982; *Austin Seminary Bulletin*, April 1976 and October 1979; *Reformatio* 11/12, 1979.

JOHN M. SUTCLIFFE

Home, Role of

Individual human life gains its meaning from social roots. Home and school both have important roles to play in the socialization of young people. This is critically so in the matter of fundamental beliefs concerning the underlying realities of life.

The home is both chronologically and in terms of fundamental influence the primary socializing influence in any person's life. The parent transmits, through shared family experience, ways of perceiving and understanding life and the world around. As the child assimilates the culture of his family he gains a world view. This is particularly encapsulated in the language which he is acquiring. By this means, the child will inherit the traditional world view of the family and of the society to which it belongs.

This process can also be observed in modern secularized societies. In this situation, however, the world view transmitted by the family may well be a considerably modified version of that traditional within the society of family origin. In addition, the child will develop a sense of autonomy as he grows up which will lead him to question traditional views about religion and morality which form the basis of his society's value system and even to abandon them.

In a traditional society, the school's task is seen as giving the pupil a personal understanding of the community's faith and an understanding of the adult moral and social responsibilities he will have in that society. It will be supplementing what is already being undertaken in the home.

In a modern secularized society, the school's task is much more complex. In such a society, adults have great freedom with regard to personal faith and religion. There is also considerable flexibility in public and private mores. Accordingly, the individual is faced with complex decisions and choices which do not exist in traditional societies. RE has to impart to the rising generation the skills*, knowledge*, abilities and understanding to make informed and rational moral and religious commitments. The task of socialization within the school will be widely based but RE will have a key role in seeing that the ultimate questions in life are dealt with, the place of religious commitment in life is understood and an open attitude to the ways and beliefs of others is encouraged.

In a modern complex democratic society, the school must promote understanding and open, tolerant attitudes in pupils, but only the home and community can give experience of belonging to a community of faith. Bernstein has suggested that the change to an 'open society' has been accompanied by a change to 'open schools'. One aspect of this is a much greater communication between home and school. This needs special development in the area of RE if the separate but joint tasks of home and school are to be undertaken with mutual understanding and without friction.

P. L. Berger, *The Social Reality of Religion*, Faber & Faber 1969; B. Bernstein, 'Open schools, open society?', *School and Society*, ed. B. R. Cosin *et al.*, Routledge & Kegan Paul 1971; T. Luckman, *The Invisible Religion*, Macmillan 1967; J. Marvell, 'The formation of religious belief in a multi-racial community', *Learning for Living*, Autumn 1975.

JOHN MARVELL

Humanism

An approach to life which goes back to ancient Greece and has since been modified by the impact of the Renaissance and the Enlightenment. The major factor, however, in the re-emergence of the naturalistic spirit of Greece has been the scientific revolution of the past 200 years.

Modern Humanism is a view of reality built on these insights and is motivated by the continuing search into the nature of human existence and the universe of energy, matter and life of which it is a part. Humanism does not look to supernatural explanations for the natural order but relies for insight upon the study of the natural order itself, including the higher manifestations of human consciousness. Creativity – the potentiality for fruitful change – is regarded as inherent in the nature of things. This conception excludes the need for ideas of particular creation and design. The fundamental energy and potential in the natural order, combined with the dynamic generated by interaction between the products of that energy, is considered to be an adequate explanation for what exists. In the later stages of evolution, intelligence, reason, feeling and imagination, themselves outcomes of the creative process, are seen as becoming involved in understanding and influencing the process. Hence, humanity is held to be increasingly responsible for the future of life on this planet.

Moral values. Humanists regard moral values, not as edicts from some supernatural source, but as the principles, discovered during evolution, upon which good human relationships and coherent individual life depend. Such values include love, respect for truth, honesty, integrity, a sense of justice, caring, co-operation, sacrifice for the common good, if necessary, and the acceptance of responsibility for one's own behaviour and the well-being of others. Humanists believe that these human values lie at the heart of societies and civilization, however much they may be ignored in practice. To be healthy, a society must honour such values and succeed in transmitting them from generation to generation, as well as refining them to meet the complexities of social and technological change. Respect for these values is held to be a pre-condition for civilization itself because such principles of relationship are fundamental to the emergence of society. It follows that these values must have existed, and been respected among men and women, long before the era of the great religions, the leaders of which reinforced and elucidated these values, but did not originate them. The Golden Rule – do unto others as you would they should do unto you – epitomizes Humanist moral values as well as being the central human value which is common to all religions.

Humanists regard religions not as of divine origin but as outcomes of the human struggle for understanding, support, involvement and significance. The *values* religions teach may be acceptable to Humanists in general, but the *beliefs* most religions also insist upon are not found to be credible. Humanists reject the idea that moral values cannot exist without the underpinning of divine sanctions. They prefer to build up and inspire the natural human potentialities for love, understanding and responsiveness to ideals.

Humanists set great store on enhancing the quality of life at all levels of experience, therefore on the maximization of freedom to develop and attain self-actualization, limited only by the rights of others to do the same. They are not, however, hedonists in the narrow sense since they see happiness as residing not in transitory pleasure but in the fulfilment of every individual's creative potential. They also believe that such fulfilment is intrinsically social in character: people become themselves *with* others, not at the expense of others, or in isolation from them. Humanists deplore the inequitable distribution among the nations of the world of all that makes for a full and happy life.

The social perspective of humanists. Humanists believe in the Open Democratic Society as the right social/political basis for human life and growth. This because people need the dignity and satisfaction of informed involvement in the affairs with which they are concerned. It is held to be obvious that corruption and secrecy are associated. Accordingly, a healthy society is seen as one in which, although privacy and confidentiality are protected, 'the cards are on the table' to the fullest possible extent, so that decisions can be made in the light of the facts and the likely consequences. As a corollary to this, Humanists are among those who prefer small to large institutions and self-government to bureaucratic control. The concept of the Open Society implies the search among people for shared goals and values in a climate of tolerance, and of respect for one another's points of view.

Since Humanists regard human beings as responsible for the future evolution of life on this planet, they find themselves in association with those working to remove poverty and inequality, and those concerned to conserve and enhance life and to sustain the ecological system and natural habitats upon which life depends. Humanists actively support the World Disarmament Campaign. They also cooperate with those concerned for the full equality of women and for the responsible enjoyment of sex; they regard these as essential elements of personal freedom.

Spectrum of viewpoints. Humanism does not set out to present a monolithic system of ideas, since it regards knowledge, feeling, understanding and perspective as evolving. Humanism as a formal entity seeks to avoid dogmas but, rather, represents an association of people who share a common outlook on the universe and on human responsibility. It includes within its ranks atheists and agnostics, strict rationalists, and religious Humanists, who are especially interested in ultimate relationships and the human search for self-transcendence. The core of Humanism is the rejection of the supernatural as either the origin of what is, or as a force intervening in the affairs of the planet or mankind. Humanists do not, however, reject the concept of mystery. A universe in which consciousness is gradually extending its range, as knowledge and perception expand, cannot but be mysterious, since penetration into the known perpetually opens up new vistas of the unknown. To Humanists, mystery is a stimulus in the struggle to push back the frontiers of ignorance, faulty perception and insufficient sensitivity.

Humanism in education. Humanists believe that young people, during their school years, need an opportunity to acquire the perspective, moral insight and set of principles on which they can build a stance for living that makes sense to them and gives structure and guidance to their lives. Such a life stance includes ways of looking at and understanding the ultimates of existence: What am I? Why are we here? What is existence? What is behind it all? Where is it going? What is the meaning of life? – questions which all young people are interested in. It follows, Humanists believe, that the Humanist life stance should be taught in RE along with religious life stances since they represent different approaches to the ultimates of existence.

Humanists see the modern situation as presenting new challenges to religious education and to the socialization of the young. The characteristic approach of the past to the problem of providing the young with a stance for living was the inculcation of a particular set of beliefs and explanations and, indeed, this is still the approach of authoritarian régimes. Such an approach is, however, not feasible in the context of modern democracy, not only because indoctrination is undemocratic, but also because the young are today distrustful of authoritarian dictates. Furthermore, it is no longer possible to make claims for absolute certainty in religion or anywhere else. The acquisition of a viable philosophy of life for the young has, then, become a two-way process, in which the ideas of the young people themselves interact with the various points of view that exist in a modern society, with the teacher as mediator to help clarify and consolidate their ideas.

In this situation, religious education assumes two roles in particular: to inform young people about the range of life stances, religious or other, and to help each individual to arrive at a position which provides him/her with insight, understanding, support and, if possible, inspiration. Humanists believe that these roles cannot be fulfilled adequately by isolated periods of RE, but require an approach to education which pervades the whole school, supported by allocation of time for the special study of the issues involved.

All subjects are seen as having a part to play in developing those values and attitudes with which both Humanism and religions are concerned. History, geography and social studies bring teacher and taught into situations involving moral choices. English literature is about character and relationships, right and wrong behaviour and their consequences. Mathematics and the sciences epitomize the value of integrity, respect for truth, and the acceptance of responsibility for the use of knowledge. The arts nourish feeling, sensitivity, imagination and depths of insight.

Humanists support the view that the quality of the school community also has a powerful influence upon the moral development and human perspective of young people. They believe that the values and attitudes manifest in the life and relationships of the school profoundly influence all those subjected to them: a caring school will tend to produce caring people. The school's relationship with the wider community is also held to be significant; for example, the opportunities that exist for social service, and the value that the LEA and the managers of any particular school put upon it.

Thus, religions and Humanism are, in essence, both concerned with promoting human values in society, even though they differ in the explanation of the origin of those values. For the religious person, abiding by human values represents doing the will of God; for the Humanist, living by such values represents true human fulfilment through the acceptance of human responsibility. There is, therefore, a large area of common purpose, even though Humanists reject the supernatural, authoritarian and punitive aspects of religious teaching.

Since there is a good deal of overlap in what both religious people and Humanists respect, in pragmatic terms, it is, Humanists believe, all the more educationally desirable that religious and naturalistic systems of values and beliefs should be treated together in helping young people come to terms with themselves and life, rather than by seeking to impose any particular outlook on the young. They believe that co-operation, between people of a religious orientation and Humanists, is not only possible but necessary if human values are to be cultivated in schools.

The Humanist attitude to RE. The Humanists' difficulties with RE arise only if 'religious' is interpreted narrowly, a position which, they feel, is encouraged by the present legal requirement for compulsory Religious Education (originally Religious Instruction). They believe that compulsory RE is not only undemocratic but unfortunate in its consequences. Whereas a well-developed sector embracing social, moral and religious education is a proper part of a well-designed contemporary curriculum, any legal obligation to include RE as an isolated subject can only have the effect of, on the one hand, separating it from the main curriculum and, on the other, precluding a proper development of the sector as a whole.

Humanists also reject the legal obligation upon schools to start the day with an act of religious worship. They recognize the value of assemblies which confirm a sense of social unity, promote common purpose, and can be used as a source of inspiration by celebrating all that is challenging, exalting and enobling in human experience and achievement. Treated as acts of worship, however, they feel that assemblies present as certainties ideas which are, in fact, hypothetical.

Finally, Humanists believe that there is no place, within the state system of education, for denominational schools. They believe these to be dangerously divisive, especially at a time when it is vital to achieve a sense of social unity – though not conformity – among the many cultural traditions that, in the modern world, are to be found in all countries. Humanists believe that mankind must strive for a consensus of social/moral values to guide the affairs of our inter-dependent world. They believe that our schools should be concerned to promote insight about these universal human values rather than becoming caught up in sectarian differences.

JAMES HEMMING

Humanities and RE

There are many interpretations of the term humanities. In the Western academic tradition, it has tended to refer to the classics, and the term has often been used in contrast to religion: secular learning as opposed to divinity. Today the frontiers of humanities vary from one academic institution to another, but they are likely to include art*, history*, literature*, music*, philosophy and religion; the social sciences are also sometimes included,

i.e. anthropology, economics, geography, politics, psychology and sociology. In the English educational system humanities embraces such subjects, at an appropriate level, as history, geography, RE, economics, sociology and social studies*.

In the early years of the primary school, humanities subjects are usually introduced through a topic framework, whereby children draw on material from different subject disciplines. This integrated approach may well continue with children above the ages of eight or nine, but in the upper part of the primary school separate subjects become more distinctive. At secondary level, some schools during the late 1960s and early 1970s replaced history, geography and RE courses with inter-disciplinary programmes of work in the lower part of the school. This never became a universal practice and in many schools inter-disciplinary courses have not developed beyond year one. In the upper part of the secondary school, examination courses in the social science subjects have become increasingly popular, although there have been very few successful inter-disciplinary examination courses in the humanities. In the non-examination general studies area of the curriculum there has been a growth of personal*, moral* and social education* courses, often related to RE.

In general terms, humanities subjects can help pupils to understand the world in which they live and to explore values which give some meaning to their personal lives. A study of religion has a very important contribution to make but teachers have sometimes found it difficult to establish the RE element within humanities work; either it disappears into a 'religion is in everything we do' approach or it stands apart defending an 'essential content'. RE within humanities needs to be clear about its distinctive skills*, especially those related to communication and imagination, and about its key ideas; where this happens, RE can make a very effective contribution to a humanities curriculum.

Ian H. Birnie (ed.), *Religious Education in Integrated Studies*, SCM Press 1972; The Schools Council/Nuffield Foundation, *The Humanities Project: An Introduction*, Heinemann Educational 1970; Schools Council,

Exploration Man: An Introduction to Integrated Studies, Oxford University Press 1972.

PETER GILLIAT

Hungary *see* **Eastern Europe**

Hymns *see* **Music**

Icon

1. *The incarnation has revealed perfection.* 'Be ye perfect, even as your Father which is in heaven is perfect' (Matt. 5.48). Among those born on earth from the dawn of time, the incarnate Son of God, the 'first-born from the dead' (Col. 1.18), alone must be recognized as truly perfect; every other man, woman and child ontologically falls short of perfection in having become sinful and mortal; and one cannot represent and venerate that which is disfigured. Through Christian baptism, however, grafting as it does the baptized person into Christ, the possibility of perfection is restored to man, and in Christ holiness becomes depictable. The Orthodox* understanding of *Iconoclasm*, including the ban on images imposed by Moses in the OT rests on the recognition that man is essentially imperfect before and outside Christ. The incarnation is the corner-stone of iconography, and iconoclasm is logically a pre-Christian phenomenon. Thus, the first and foremost icon of the church is that of the incarnate Son of God, himself the 'image of invisible God' (Col. 1.15).

2. *Persons are represented.* Every icon painted in the tradition of the church, bears the name(s) of the saint(s) represented on it. This universal practice stems from the patristic affirmation that both God and man are seen as persons: God in the Trinity, and man, the image of God, in the church. It would be wrong to divide the person, to single out a part or an isolated virtue and paint it (e.g. the virginal purity of the Mother of God, the heart of Jesus, the might of God in the sacred calf). This fragmentation of the person leads to the risk of losing sight of the whole person, to caricature, to blaspheming, to idolatry. Paganism, being nurtured through an overwhelming vision of nature, ascribes worship to created things, with no adequate reference to the true Creator. The Christian icon, in representing individual saints, carries the inscription 'saint' next to the name, indicating

by this word that the person depicted is a saint in virtue of God's holiness. Man's created spirit should not be confused with the divine person of the Holy Ghost, whose grace it is, dwelling in man, that makes man a saint. The halo is a symbol of this.

3. *Icons are venerated.* God's perfect purpose in creating all things was to make them good: 'and God saw that it was good' (Gen. 1.4ff.). The created world, being good, is also representable. Thus the visible matter of this world becomes, in Christian liturgical art, a vehicle for the image of the person of the Son of God and of his saints. This image, or rather the holy persons represented on the icon, the 'prototype', sanctifies the physical icon and, through the colours, the lines, the name of the saint, calls the beholder to veneration. God is worshipped (*latreia*) while icons are venerated (*proskynesis*). This occurs in the Christian home and in the liturgy, particularly at a vigil of a feast day when the priest solemnly censes the icon of the day and the members of the congregation bow before it and kiss it.

4. *The icon in education.* From the earliest time the icon, with the word of God, fulfils the important didactic function of guiding the believer into the knowledge of God and of his saving acts. Children of all ages are particularly responsive to this medium. The figurative art of the icon includes murals, mosaics, sculpted icons, as well as the better known panel icons. They depict holy persons and events of the OT and NT particularly the Lord himself, and vrious events of the gospel story to cover those essential facts of our sacred history which form the basis of our Christian faith. In every Orthodox home and classroom an icon hangs in a prominent corner and prayers are said in front of it at appropriate times. On every major feast day, the icon of the sacred event powerfully tells its story, leaving the beholder, particularly the learning child, with the immediate impression of a thing seen transcending time and space. Through an icon one believes oneself to be taking part in the event.

MICHAEL FORTOUNATTO

Imagination

The development and use of imagination are of central importance in RE. Its significance is often stressed in three rather different contexts: in the religious education theme where the concern is to explore experience in depth; in the recognition of the symbolic, metaphoric and narrative form of most religious expression; and in the multi-faith approach to the subject where religious education necessarily involves imaginative insight into another's vision of life. What links these superficially disparate uses of the term is the fact that imagination is that human power which enables us to go beyond the immediate situation, whether by linking one image with others as in poetry*, or in shaping experience in symbolic forms, or by passing beyond the confines of one particular view of the world. In this context imagination needs to be distinguished from fantasy. Fantasy takes us beyond the world in order to create a realm divorced from reality, unconsciously as in madness or consciously as in play. Imagination on the other hand takes us beyond the immediate in order that we may grasp what is really possible, gain vision to extend frontiers and recognize that there is more in life than the mundane. It is because of this power of transcendence that imagination is closely linked with religion.

There are three contexts in which imagination is necessary in religious education:

1. It is imagination which gives depth to the life experience themes suggested in many approaches to religious education. The kind of subjects chosen for such work, seasons, birth and death, light and darkness, indicate their imaginative importance. It is through imagination that these are linked together with other experiences. The object of such work is to enable the child to gain a sense of wholeness or meaning of life. This poetic sense of the world provides a vital basis for religious education in the future. Much of the best teaching in this area may well be done indirectly, through the use of evocative pictures, poems, or music*, and the sensitivity which allows space for listening and reflection.

2. When considering the explicit* teaching of religion it is important to recognize that the material being handled is often in imaginative form. Through story*, gesture and ritual, music and drama, dress and food, people find expression for their faith and all forms are combined in the great festivals*. In such ways religions suggest the transformation of the every day and give symbolic meaning to time

and place. When introducing children to this realm it is necessary to be aware of the difficulties they experience with the metaphoric language of others, and yet recognize how responsive they are to symbolic form. Young children are intensely imaginative and the images formed in the early years may have a profound effect on later attitudes.

3. Imagination plays a crucial role in any religious education which is concerned with giving pupils an understanding of differing views of life. If it is not possible to enter into another's experience and yet return to one's own, the whole enterprise is either a form of indoctrination*, or involves a rather meaningless acquisition of strange facts and customs. The work of great novelists and of some anthropologists bears witness to the fact that such understanding is possible. It is however the achievement of a mature mind and much work with school-age pupils will be laying foundations which make such insights possible in later years. Through the careful use of biographics, role play and drama, film and video, and by providing the opportunity for meetings with men and women of many different visions, much can be done to develop imaginative insight.

***

Gloria Durka and Joanmarie Smith (eds), *Aesthetic Dimensions of Religious Education,* Paulist Press 1979; John Prickett, *The Place of Imagination in Religious Education,* BCC 1978; Edward Robinson, *The Original Vision,* Religious Experience Research Unit 1977; Mary Warnock, *Imagination,* Faber 1976.

                                    JUDITH OLLINGTON

Implementation of Agreed Syllabuses

Since 1944 the agreed syllabus* has been a powerful agency in curriculum development*. Surveys have shown that schools, in their actual schemes of work, have largely followed the agreed syllabus currently applicable within their LEA. Despite practical constraints, and the reservations (even opposition) of some teachers, agreed syllabuses continue to exert much influence.

The 1944 Education Act made each LEA responsible for adopting an 'Agreed Syllabus of Religious Instruction' for use in its schools, on the recommendation of a duly constituted Statutory Conference. The Fifth Schedule

(Section 29) of the Act specified the composition of such a Conference, namely. representatives of: (a) Such religious denominations as, in the opinion of the authority, ought, having regard to the circumstances of the area, to be represented. (b) Except in the case of an area in Wales or Monmouthshire (at that time an English county), the Church of England. (c) Such associations representing teachers, as in the opinion of the authority, ought, having regard to the circumstances of the area, to be represented. (d) The LEA (i.e. elected members of the Education Committee).

To the professional educator such a constitution looks distinctly unpromising for the task of implementing fresh approaches to the subject. However, careful reading of the provisions and subsequent experience of working the system reveal scope for the formation of Statutory Conferences appropriate to the changing nature of British society (e.g. representatives of non-Christian religions have sometimes been included in (a)). Furthermore, it has been common practice to delegate tasks to working parties of teachers. Some religious educators nevertheless wish to unshackle curriculum development from such statutory constraints, arguing that these, coupled with the unwelcome connotations of compulsion, have stultified growth in the subject. Others argue that community involvement in curriculum development is healthy and that the machinery has given scope for RE to articulate its contribution and to fit into a hierarchy of decision-making which involves: 1. National expression of a desire to have RE in the curriculum of schools. 2. Local authority guidelines. 3. School application of the syllabus and guidelines in a scheme of work. 4. Individual teachers applying their distinctive professional skills to achieve the desired objectives. Syllabuses produced in the late seventies and early eighties have provided frameworks for RE without putting teachers into straitjackets.

The provisions of the 1944 Education Act also empower (but do not require) a local authority to constitute a Standing Advisory Council for Religious Education (SACRE)*, a body which, being less tightly controlled in constitution, is often composed predominantly of professional teachers. The SACRE can offer potentially valuable support for the subject, especially in the crucial and continuing task of implementing the agreed syllabus.

The adoption of a new syllabus is often the climax of a lengthy process of investigation, discussion and composition; it is also the starting-point of a process of implementation which may take several years if the objectives of the syllabus are to be achieved. For any truly innovatory syllabus (e.g. Hampshire 1978 since adopted by several other LEAs) is likely to demand two considerable changes of the sort which do not happen overnight or by chance: 1. a change in understanding the nature and scope of religion, and therefore of RE; and 2. a change in teaching practice, with the teacher's role becoming less that of a transmitter of a body of knowledge, more that of a questioner or interpreter concerned to develop appropriate skills for both the understanding of religion and religious understanding.

For implementation to be effective, LEAS on the one hand and individual schools on the other must create the optimum conditions.

1. LEAS should provide for and co-ordinate: (a) *Curriculum Development* and consultation in order to put 'flesh' on the 'bones' of the syllabus and to share good practice between schools. Hence the publication by some LEAS of handbooks which offer guidance, suggestions and information about resources. (b) *In-Service Education**. Good in-service provision creates cells of activity, overcomes the isolation of individual teachers, and makes possible the sharing of good ideas. Some authorities have increased the impact and value of a newly adopted syllabus by 'launching' it within the context of discussion and debate, e.g. in short conferences, initially for all head teachers and followed by a range of in-service opportunities at all levels: i.e. (i) Secondment for post-graduate work. (ii) Secondment for shorter courses (1 term or 1 day a week). (iii) Residential Conferences (2–3 days). (iv) One-day Conferences. (v) Use of 'occasional days' for school based in-service work. (vi) Evening courses in Teachers' Centres. (c) *Resource Provision* to service (a) and (b). Resource Centres* set up within a co-ordinated programme of curriculum development and in-service education can be really effective and escape becoming museum pieces. Resources can usefully be classified

and stored in a manner closely related to the various sections of a syllabus.

2. School provision should include: (*a*) *Support from the head teacher*, who needs to be well enough informed to recognize that a curriculum which fails to make the key concepts and methods of religious studies accessible to pupils would be seriously defective. (*b*) *Adequate Time*. In secondary schools, the minimum should be five per cent of curriculum time (i.e. 2 periods per week in a 40-period week). In primary schools, only careful checking can ensure that RE receives sufficient attention, surfacing in the curriculum in a planned way. (*c*) *Adequate Staffing*, with appropriate specialist qualifications and proper opportunities for further in-service education. (*d*) *Fair Resourcing*, calculated on the basis of the number of pupils being taught. Secondary schools should provide specialist accommodation, with facilities for a wide range of learning experiences (including audio-visual methods of communication), and a rational, easily manageable system of storage and retrieval for resources. Facilities and finance should be available for educational visits and for receiving visitors.

The establishment of these optimum conditions requires a partnership between the local authority and the schools. The role of the County Adviser with special responsibility for RE is crucial in developing and maintaining such a partnership: an agreed syllabus needs a capable, mobile and available adviser, not burdened with an impossible job specification.

At the highest level, national organizations are needed to monitor and stimulate both thinking and practice in RE, to maintain dialogue with interested bodies (e.g. the British Humanist Association*), and perhaps to exert pressure on such powers as Teachers' Unions*, LEAS and DES. Working towards these ends are, among others, the Christian Education Movement*, the Religious Education Council* and the Schools Council*.

DAVID NAYLOR

Implicit Religion

The terminology of 'implicit' and 'explicit'* in relation to religious education goes back to the *Schools Council Working Paper 36* (1971) setting forth various approaches to RE and stemming from the work of the Lancaster Project on Religious Education in Secondary Schools. But the idea of implicit religion is found earlier in the thinking of Harold Loukes and others in their concern to stress pupils' own experience and life questions. Briefly: implicit religion refers to the range of experiences and questions which are concerned with the meaning of life and which arise in this context independently on the explicit teachings and practices of recognized religious traditions and movements. The notion thus relates to Tillich's idea of ultimate concern – religion being what concerns man ultimately (and this independently of whether it takes the form of explicit religious belief). The educational importance of the implicit religion approach is that it ties RE to the immediate experience and world of pupils.

Loukes' worry was that biblically and traditionally based instruction was too remote from pupils' lives and did not meet them where they were. His own and Goldman's work had, in the early sixties, shown the problems in a particular form of explicitly religious education. Implicit religion should not only explore the pupils' experience and the questions of meaning and purpose they raise, but should in an open way help them to make their own choices of worldview and morality. This approach makes it essentially difficult to disentangle religious and moral education* (perhaps this is no bad thing), for the autonomy of morals and thus of ME is a doctrine about the relationship of moral judgments and religious beliefs (and thus of 'explicit' religion).

There is a fair amount of consensus that it is important to combine both the explicit and implicit approaches. The former without the latter fails to meet some of the real questions of pupils. The latter without the former fails to inform pupils about some of the formative ideas and passions which have helped to shape their own civilizational past and that of other societies.

To complicate matters 'implicit religion' is a phrase arrived at independently by Edward Bailey, who has organized a number of consultations on the theme from 1978 onwards, and discussed in his paper to the XIVth Congress of the International Association for the History of Religion in Winnipeg, 1980. It means roughly the religious dimension of ordinary life, and relates to R. Bellah's notion of 'civil religion'*, though the latter deals with the religion implicit in state ceremonial and the like and has a more official and corporate connotation (e.g. the religion implied in US inaugurations). It has relationships too to the kind of symbolic analysis which arises both from modern anthropology (Victor Turner and Mary Douglas) and from cross-cultural history of religion (Eliade). Thus 'implicit religion' is sometimes used as shorthand for the symbolic value system of ordinary folk – e.g., the 'regulars' of a pub or the ethos of a game.

The two senses of 'implicit religion' are not in conflict, but they tend to cover a different range. They meet educationally in the notion that part of RE is making pupils capable of clarifying and analysing their own and others' values and meaningful activities.

See also **Meaning, Quest for.**

Harold Loukes, *New Ground in Christian Education*, SCM Press 1965; *Schools Council Working Paper* 36, Evans/Methuen Educational 1971.

NINIAN SMART

Independent Schools

The independent schools of the UK, whether boarding or day, are all fee-paying schools and therefore the clientèle are inevitably with few exceptions well-to-do and/or middle-class. Such homes are now chiefly secular and some may even contain no Bible; yet many non-religious parents are willing, even keen, for their children to have some exposure to religion.

Most of the better known schools have an explicitly religious foundation, usually Church of England, though there are also Roman Catholic, Methodist, and United Reformed Church public schools. In some of them religion has become something of a formality and there are few now where the majority of the staff are active Christians. But officially the schools remain Christian. Among secondary schools, most boarding and many day have a chapel and a chaplain*. More important, a high proportion of headmasters and headmistresses take their religion and its responsibilities seriously, and so probably do most of those key boarding-school figures, housemasters and housemistresses.

Traditionally 'school chapel' took place every day. Recently however obligatory attendance has been heavily curtailed: on weekdays worship is often voluntary, on Sundays it may be optional, with a secular educational alternative. Where this has happened, a 'community' event such as an assembly* has sometimes been introduced – ironically, just at a time when assemblies are declining in maintained schools. These changes have brought both gain and loss. But one clear result is that variations of commitment are now as visible at school as in adult society. There are those who 'go to chapel' regularly – not in any way regarded as peculiar. There are those who conscientiously abstain. And, to judge by the number confirmed at fourteen or fifteen, the majority probably still practice 'high day and holiday' Christianity – but chosen by themselves, not under pressure from school or parents.

Classroom RE differs in two main respects from that in maintained schools. 1. It exists – normally right up the school into the sixth-form, and for two periods a week. 2. It is largely taught by amateurs (often co-ordinated by a professional RE teacher), a system which again has its strengths and its weaknesses.

The larger independent secondary schools have often a recognized churchmanship and theology. Apart from RE and Free Church schools, there is within the Anglican group a range from the relatively 'high' churchmanship of the Woodard Schools to the evangelical tradition of the Allied Schools. But most fall somewhere in the middle and indeed may have features of both: the 'parish communion' is now the most common form of Sunday worship, but it usually coexists with prayer and Bible-study groups. Only the charismatic movement is absent.

The theological picture is less clear cut. The demythologized social gospel of the sixties now seems somewhat *vieux jeu*. In its place one can perhaps refer to no more than an eclectic pluralism.

Running through all the activities and concerns of the majority of British independent schools remains a firm thread of sincere Christian faith and practice. To say this is to say no more than can be said of any adult British community. What distinguishes 'public school religion' is its social setting. At its worst this breeds pharisaism. At its best however it is a focus for a prophetic radicalism which challenges the materialistic values of society at large and of many of the homes from which the pupils come.

JOHN C. DANCY

India

Christian education programmes in India began as a result of the initiative and planning of the missionary bodies working in different parts of the country in the last part of the nineteenth or the beginning of the twentieth century. An important factor in this planning was the linking of Christian education in Sunday Schools with the day school set-up of the missions. In many parts of the country teachers in the village mission primary schools were entrusted with the task of running Sunday Schools. This arrangement worked fairly well for some time till the primary schools in villages were taken over by the government. In urban areas day school teachers played such an important role in Sunday Schools that it gave rise to a strong feeling in the churches that Sunday School work was the sole responsibility of day school teachers. This association of Sunday School work with the day schools may give the impression that it was the outcome of a comprehensive approach to Christian education. This was not true. The missionary bodies only looked at it as a workable arrangement. Perhaps it was this type of planning which was responsible for the lack of interest on the part of many churches in Christian education.

During the past three or four decades the churches have shown special interest in Sunday School work and have adopted a comprehensive approach to Christian education. This is evident from a variety of new structures that came into being: 1. The Church of North India has a committee for Religious Education and Lay Training. 2. The Calcutta Diocese of the Church of North India has a Committee for Lay Training and Mission. 3. Some of the Dioceses of the Church of South India plan Christian education as part of lay Training programmes. 4. The Tamil Inter-Church Committee for Religious Education (TICCRE) is the result of a common concern of the churches in one language region to plan Christian education and moral education programmes in day schools and Sunday Schools. 5. The Convention of the Baptist Churches in Northern Circars has a Board of Christian Training which covers theological education, lay training, youth work and Sunday School work. 6. At the national level the National Council of Churches in India constituted a Christian Education Council of India (CECI) which is aimed at serving the cause of Christian nurture of children, youth and adults. These are only a few examples of many new structures that have come into existence in the recent past. They are indicative of the growing trend among churches in India to look at Christian education with a broader perspective.

An outcome of this trend was the concern for preparing moral education and Christian education curricula for use in day schools. After 1947, when India attained independence, great emphasis began to be laid on secularism in political and educational fields. Although RE as such was not banned, many restrictions were imposed on schools which wanted to teach religious education. Education is a state responsibility in India; different states adopted different policies which in varying degrees affected the RE programmes of Christian schools. But a few years later there was a new development. In response to a growing demand in educational circles the Government of India appointed a committee headed by Sri Prakasa to make a detailed study of the entire question of religious and moral instruction in the educational institutions in the country. The report of this committee, which came to be known as the 'Sri Prakasa Report', was published in 1959. It is a landmark in the development of religious and moral education programmes in India. It is significant that this report avoided the traditional terms 'religious and moral education' but pleaded for education in moral and spiritual values. The report was based on the premise that moral and ethical life can only be the result of education linked and based upon the life of the spirit. The Day School Curriculum Project sponsored by the India Sunday School Union by and large followed the guidelines suggested by the Sri Prakasa Report. The result of this project are published in the 'My Life at its Best' series of books (Orient Longmans). The lessons in the 'My Life at its Best' courses follow experiential and exploratory approaches. When the Day School Curriculum Project was taken up, there was already in existence a set of books on moral sciences which followed a strong didactic approach.

The Day School Curriculum Project also resulted in an outlined scheme of Christian education entitled *Believing is Living*. It contained lesson courses for all the classes in the day school. The lessons in this scheme follow the experiential approach. Another scheme of Christian education, known as the 'Charter house Scheme', was in use even prior to the Day School Curriculum Project. This scheme, prepared by E. L. King of Leonard Theological College in Jabalpur, and mostly used in Methodist schools, consisted of teaching materials for thirteen years and aimed at building up Christian character among pupils. It has a strong moral emphasis.

The planning and preparation of Christian education schemes and curricula for use in Sunday Schools in India has a long history. The India Sunday School Union published Graded Study Notes for the use of Sunday School teachers until the early fifties. Representatives of all the major churches in India participated in two curriculum conferences in 1955 and 1957. Two sets of curricula, 'Light of the Bible Series' were published: 1. Group graded series for use in urban Sunday Schools. 2. Broadly graded series for use in rural Sunday Schools. This was a thematic curriculum which was widely used for nearly three decades. In the late sixties the Evangelical Fellowship of India introduced another curriculum which is popularly known as CEEFI (Christian Education of the Evangelical Fellowship of India). It has a strong evangelical emphasis and is claimed to be a Bible-centred curriculum. This is now being widely used in India. The Christian Education Council of India, an agency of the National Council of Churches in India, prepared a curriculum known as the 'Growing Together' series which is used in many Sunday Schools. In addition to these all-India curricula there are others which may be termed denominational schemes.

Scripture examinations are quite popular in certain regions. They are held every year on a prescribed syllabus for both pupils and teachers. The questions set for younger children are mainly factual requiring knowledge of the text: those set for older children seek their opinion as well as knowledge of prescribed passages. Questions set for teachers cover lesson preparation and other topics in teacher training.

The Methodist Church (Episcopal) in India has emphasized the importance of Christian education in the day schools. For instance the Church has a Council of Christian Education which publishes a periodical entitled *Christian Education* which is aimed at serving the cause of Christian schools in India. Christian education programmes of the Roman Catholic Church to a large extent follow a catechetical approach. It is rendering a great service to the cause of education through the programmes of the All India Association of Christian Higher Education, which publishes a journal entitled *New Frontiers in Education*.

See also **Hinduism.**

N. DANIEL

Indoctrination

Content, social environment, intention and method must all be borne in mind when seeking to understand the nature of indoctrination. The content most characteristic of indoctrination will consist of political and religious doctrines, and we may thus distinguish indoctrination from other forms of persuasion, such as the attempt to induce an unswerving, emotional attachment to a certain advertised product, which possess other features of the indoctrinary process, but lack a doctrinal content. A doctrine is a proposition which forms part of an ideology or a theology. It is a cognitive element of a world view.

There are many world views and this plurality is an essential aspect of indoctrination. Plurality leads to comparison and controversy. Indoctrination attempts to give its content an authority and a normative value to which in fact the doctrines have no rightful social or intellectual claim. The indoctrinator thus attempts to conceal from his hearers the controversial status of his doctrines. Indoctrination has to do with the social status of beliefs. If a doctrine did in fact possess unquestioned social authority in a given society, it is hard to see how it could be a content for indoctrination, since this element of deception about its status could not arise.

Considerations of content and social context enable us to distinguish indoctrination from socialization, the latter seeking to create conformity with accepted social mores and attitudes, whereas indoctrination is concerned with cognitive conformity. Moreover, socialization does not presuppose a plurality of world views.

Indoctrination is best regarded as an intentional activity. It is sometimes argued that indoctrination is inevitable because we cannot avoid influencing others, but this argument seems unconvincing. We can become aware of the sort of influence we are having and we ought not to seek to have the particular kind of influence which is properly described as indoctrination. Although it is important thus to emphasize intentionality in order to distinguish indoctrination from mere influence, it remains the case that indoctrinators may differ in their shrewdness or their naivity. We may best think of a naive indoctrinator (one who does not fully intend to indoctrinate) as being an agent of the indoctrination process rather than being an indoctrinator to the full sense. The intention of the indoctrinator is to cause his subjects to accept his controversial doctrines as if they were uncontroversial assertions, and to adhere to them with an unquestioning emotional and intellectual loyalty. The indoctrinated person holds certain beliefs in a certain way.

The method of indoctrination is calculated to induce such acceptance, and characteristically includes repetition, reinforcement by associated rewards and punishments, isolation from other points of view, and the use of a wide variety of techniques intended to heighten susceptibility and to minimize individual judgment. Indoctrination attempts to bypass the reason. It is an assault upon the values and dignity of the person.

Religious, moral* and political education* can and should be sharply distinguished from indoctrination. Indoctrination and education are mutually exclusive. They spring from quite different beliefs about the nature of human beings. It must also be understood that there are teaching/learning processes other than education and indoctrination which occupy some ground between these two sharply opposed forms of communication. It is an oversimplification to claim that all forms of religious communication which are not educational must be indoctrinatory. The public dissemination of political and religious views by advocates of those views (evangelists or party political broadcasters) is not an educa-

tional activity, but it need not be an attempt at indoctrination either. Another example of an intermediate process would be the means whereby a religious community attempted to deepen the faith and commitment of its members (religious nurture*). It may be difficult for religious communities in pluralist societies to perform this task without falling into indoctrinatory methods, since the temptation to exaggerate the intellectual and social status of the religious tradition is so severe, and the desire to protect the members of the religion from becoming attracted to alternatives tends to be overwhelming. In spite of this, religious nurture need not be indoctrinatory. The practices and intentions of each religious community must be examined one by one. Some will indeed be found to exhibit the features of indoctrination, but others will display an awareness of plurality and an open, critical rationality which, combined with the distinctive features of the religious tradition in question, will be sufficient to establish that form of religious nurture as being neither religious education (in the general educational sense) nor religious indoctrination.

In considering whether British religious education is a history of religious indoctrination, great care must be exercised. The deliberate suppression and exclusion of religious doctrines during the period 1870 to the mid-1920s and the concentration upon historical and geographical material does not suggest an indoctrinatory intention. Religious education in Britain certainly became much more doctrinal from the mid-1920s. The use of the Cowper-Temple clause* to exclude controversial material and so to create an authoritative core of normative belief may certainly be regarded as an attempt at Christian nurture through religious instruction, but even here care must be taken not to assess the practices of previous decades in the light of distinctions with which they were not familiar. During this 'doctrinal' period in British religious education there never ceased to be an emphasis upon the freedom and dignity of the pupil, and one must also remember that British society was neither as secular nor as pluralist as it is today.

It is more difficult to defend school worship, which, with its assumption of unanimity and its authoritarianism, does appear to present features of an indoctrinatory process, although this is in most cases conventional rather than intentional.

————

J. Elliott, 'Problems of RE Syllabus Construction in a Democracy', in J. M. Hull (ed.), *New Directions in Religious Education*, Falmer Press 1982.

JOHN M. HULL

Indonesia *see* Asia

Infancy

The religious development of the child in infancy is largely dependent upon the quality of the child's formative experiences within the family. From birth the child learns by living in and experiencing the world, a world which is bounded in the first instance by the cot, the pram and mother's arms. The feelings of warmth and cold, of hunger and satisfaction, of comfort and fear will teach the child about the world into which he or she has come.

As the child grows, the range of learning situations becomes wider and in a secure family setting the child is given confidence and encouragement to explore the world beyond. At this stage religious development is diffuse and cannot be isolated from the rest of the experiences of the world around the child.

The acquisition of concepts as a necessary prerequisite for later religious understanding are conditioned by the calibre of the relationships the child encounters. These will determine the extent to which the child's own self-image is formed and will in turn govern the child's ability to form loving relationships with other people including peers. The child's self-image is reflected from people who are close and important to him or her. The reflections reveal whether the child is valued or not valued, liked or disliked, loved or not loved. The child who is not loved will have difficulty in giving love.

The level to which the child's sensitivity to the world is awakened will be determined by the sensitivity being fostered and encouraged. An awareness of colour, beauty, shape, pattern and texture will arouse feelings of awe, wonder and mystery. The nurture of the child's natural delight in the resplendence of the world, in the mastery of bodily skills, is enhanced by the child's associates being able

to enter upon and share some of the same feelings of delight.

Some children will have contact with formal religious practices and customs. Patterns may be established within the home about saying grace and prayers and attending worship. The child may be aware of a reverence and awe which adults, who are important to him or her, have for a certain church or artefacts. The young child is likely to be influenced by this and by the atmosphere and ethos which is felt by contact with a loving, open, worshipping community so building up positive feelings towards religion.

Religious language and the idea of deity hold little meaning for the pre-school child. Prayers can be said by the child in a repetitive way and usually go alongside the repetition of nursery rhymes and favourite stories.

The stage of development of the pre-school child, known in Piagetian terms as the intuitive stage, lasts for about six years and spills over into the first years of formal schooling. During the pre-school years the child should have had opportunities of building up concepts of his or her own self-image, of having begun to establish loving relationships with others and having been made aware of the world in which he or she lives. It is upon these foundation experiences that religious understanding at a later stage can be built.

————

Joan Cass, *Literature and the Young Child*, Longmans 1967; R. Lee, *Your Growing Child and Religion*, Penguin 1965; Carol Mumford, *Young Children and Religion*, Edward Arnold 1982; J. Piaget, *Play, Dreams and Imitation in Childhood*, Norton 1962.

DOREEN STORR

Infant School, RE in

Constraints are imposed upon the work which can be attempted in the infant school both by the limited capacity for concept formation of the age-group and also by the brevity of its life experience (see **Childhood, Religious Development in**).

This is not the stage at which children might be expected even to begin to understand the various doctrines on which religious traditions depend. A great deal of education at this early stage is affective, not intellectual, and children may be helped to sense the religious dimension in human experience long before they are able to understand it.

At an early age a child is curious and is usually highly motivated to explore the natural and man-made world and to find his place in it. The main task of the teacher will be to help him to extend his experiences so that the world of which he is aware is enlarged, and to reflect upon and ask relevant questions of his experiences so that meaning can be found in them. Teachers will give children time and encouragement to look, touch, listen, wonder, talk about and develop sensitivity towards their discoveries.

Although the boundaries of the traditional subject areas of the school curriculum are not clearly defined at this stage, the teacher will be aware that questions of many different kinds should be raised, for example: mathematical, scientific, aesthetic, moral, religious. Significant in differentiating between these questions is the particular language use appropriate in dealing with them. The child's initiation into more subtle and complex uses of language will necessarily be accompanied by the relevant practical experiences.

Teachers who are themselves aware of the 'life' questions with which religions are concerned may be able to lead children towards the time when they will raise these questions for themselves. Even young children will be confronted with situations in which questions may arise about birth and death*, pleasure and pain, beauty and ugliness, feeling safe and feeling afraid. In helping children to face this kind of question at their own level in daily experience, teachers are contributing in a fundamental way to their education into an appreciation of the religious dimension in man's make-up.

Care should be taken in dealing with children's questions at this stage, in order to leave the way open to later questioning when thinking abilities, wider experience and greater maturity make fuller answers comprehensible. It may be unwise to give children oversimplified versions of complex thought forms which will need to be 'unlearned' later. There is a danger that the simplified form will never be discarded and will become a barrier to understanding in later years, 'difficulties which can turn the secondary school into a vast repair shop' (Copley).

The child's own experiences will become the starting point for a developmental approach to his religious education. Situations in which this work can be pursued will be both spontaneous and contrived. Infant schools abound with appropriate stimuli: natural and man-made objects, people and pets, pictures and stories, poetry and music. Often something experienced will lead to a heightening awareness from which there may arise feelings of wonder, awe, delight, sadness, anger, compassion, fear and frustration. These basic feelings are at the root of many questions which could be identified as having religious significance. In helping a child to reflect upon these feelings, then, a teacher would be making an appropriate contribution to his religious education.

Stories are an excellent medium within which a child can identify with the thoughts, feelings and motives of others. It would seem that this is more likely to be profitable when the characters and situations portrayed are not too remote from those of his own personal experiences. As the concept of time is extremely hazy at this stage, a story which relies upon its historical context is unlikely to be fully appreciated. It is also unlikely that the child is able to conceive of an adult as ever having been a child. Teachers should ask themselves whether the conceptual difficulties encountered by the child at this stage in interpreting religious myth* are a sufficient reason for excluding certain stories to be found in religious literature.

It has been suggested that it is through the imagination that we appreciate the imagery of a story* (Priestley). This thought will raise two further questions for those who teach this age-group: how can we help children to develop an imaginative response to literature*, and how soon will they be able to explore profitably, through their imagination, the imagery in stories such as those to be found in the Bible?

Many children of this age have not the necessary language with which to handle their feelings, and infant schools will have freely available opportunities for expression and exploration through the visual arts, through sound and movement, and through imitative, constructional and imaginative play.

The experiences which some children bring to school will include those more directly concerned with religious practices such as prayer* and worship*. These experiences can be discussed with the same spirit of enquiry and exploration as might be afforded to any other personal experience which it would be appropriate to discuss with individuals or with groups.

Opportunities may also be sought to extend the experience of children who have little or no contact outside the school with religious people or religious practices. It is of value for children of this age to share in the enjoyment of the celebration of religious festivals*. They can begin to understand that certain occasions have particular significance for particular groups of people, although they will be unlikely to understand why this is so until a later stage.

At this stage, the attitudes and values which are promoted will be as important as the skills and knowledge that are acquired. A condition of successful religious education in the infant school would be a welcoming and challenging environment, where children are encouraged to observe, explore, question and evaluate. And the starting point in religious education, as in other aspects of the curriculum, will be the children's own thoughts and feelings evoked by their own personal encounters with the small but steadily enlarging world of which they are becoming increasingly aware.

Mollie Brearley *et al., Fundamentals in the First School*, Blackwell 1969; Terence and Gill Copley, *First School RE*, SCM Press 1978; Michael Grimmitt, *What Can I Do in RE?*, Mayhew-McCrimmon 1973; Carol Mumford, *Young Children and Religion,* Edward Arnold 1982; Jack Priestley, 'Religious story and the literary imagination', *British Journal of Religious Education*, Autumn 1981; Schools Council Religious Education in Primary Schools, *Discovering an Approach,* Macmillan 1977; Joan Tough, *Focus on Meaning,* Unwin Education 1973.

BARBARA MENZIES

Inner City, RE in the

Recent research, the experience of teachers and the perceptive insights afforded by working-class autobiographies constantly stress that despite (or even because of) the poverty, the inner city is for many children their own

territory to be explored, experienced and interpreted. It affords opportunities such as close proximity to city centres, strong family and community links, as well as problems such as poverty and unemployment. Children of the inner city will be less familiar with institutional Christianity than their suburban counterparts, though they will often know more about other religions. They will have a very wide experience of issues which legitimately hinge on RE. Their language will often reflect the norms and assumptions of mass media, but there are many fruitful areas within that for the sensitive teacher to explore and expand the children's insights.

Recent research has shown the influence of teacher expectation. Predominantly middle-class teachers may bring to work in the inner city disgust, fear and apprehension of the physical environment of the inner city which severely affects their expectations of the children. If the children often base their language on models found in the mass media, it is no less true that teachers operate on popular stereotypes of what inner city life is like. This profoundly limits the teacher's ability to affirm the children's own lifestyle and experiences, from which so many rich areas of exploration may arise for RE.

Political and economic forces have meant that inner city schools are often in a poor condition. Old buildings, scant space and lack of easily available parental financial support means that resources are particularly limited. Thus in many inner city schools RE is hampered by a shortage of books and audio visual equipment. Yet the very environment, so frequently derided, is a resource of considerable value. There are old churches, museums, art galleries, industrial chaplaincies and so on. Furthermore, many areas now have mosques in old terraced houses, Sikh gurdwaras, Hindu temples, Islamic centres, sari shops, Buddhist grocers, Jewish craftsman living around the corner. The schools themselves often reflect this wider religious pluralism.

John Nicholson, *Religious and Moral Education in Inner City Schools*, CEM 1983; Michael Rutter, *Fifteen Thousand Hours: Secondary Schools and Their Effects on Children*, Open Books 1979.

MARTIN PALMER

In-service Education of Teachers of RE

In-service education is particularly relevant in religious education since 1. many teachers receive little initial training in RE; 2. the nature of the subject is changing; and 3. the introduction of new agreed syllabuses* makes it important for teachers to keep abreast of such changes. Some courses are designed primarily to provide the opportunity for teachers to re-examine their own assumptions and attitudes about religion and to consider the aims* and objectives* appropriate for the subject. Other courses are intended to help teachers to become better equipped in terms both of content and in classroom skills. Many of these courses would be introductory in scope, providing the enthusiastic teacher with a chance to explore, say, festivals* in Judaism, Islam and Christianity; sacred literature; the use of literature* in RE; RE and movement; working out RE in relation to the general thematic or topic work undertaken in primary education; or 'O' and 'A' level examination syllabuses.

The length and style of courses vary considerably. Courses often occupy that 'twilight zone' after school, when the level of concentration and quality of participation cannot be high. If teachers can be released for a day, or half-day, through a term, then a more valuable and profitable use of time is likely. Longer residential courses are also available and these provide additional opportunities for teachers to discuss more informally their personal and professional concerns.

Most of these courses are held away from the school, and often with only one member of the staff from each school attending. A totally different style of course is one designed for a whole school staff, held on their premises, and linked with curriculum development* in that school, often related to the introduction of a new agreed syllabus.

In-service provision is usually mounted by the LEA advisory team, but increasingly in England, the institutions of higher education have been taking a lively interest in this work and are often able to provide useful centres for curriculum development.

DONALD C. G. WHITTLE

Inspection of RE

Section 77 (5) of the 1944 Act states clearly that in any county or voluntary school religious instruction given in accordance with an agreed syllabus* may be inspected only by one of Her Majesty's Inspectors, an inspector temporarily employed by the DES, or an officer of the LEA. Religious instruction given in a voluntary school* otherwise than in accordance with an agreed syllabus may be inspected under arrangements made by the governing body. In other words, agreed syllabus religious education is to be treated like any other subject and it may only be inspected by authorized officers of central or local government, a provision which has the effect of protecting religious education from denominational or other pressure groups by ensuring that it is inspected only by persons professionally engaged in education. The converse of this is that both central and local inspectorates have consistently tried to give educational considerations priority when dealing with the subject in school, even though, in this subject alone, legal provisions must also be given due weight.

The fact that the subject is open to inspection has also meant that both central and local inspectorates have built up a body of specialists who are available for short courses or short forms of in-service training.

RE in aided schools (or other voluntary schools) which is not given in accordance with an agreed syllabus is exempt from inspection by HM or LEA inspector and the usual arrangement has been for the governors to pass on their responsiblity to the appropriate church authorities. Practice has varied widely and many churches and dioceses have found it difficult to maintain a consistent policy. The (Anglican) Carlisle Report, *Partners in Education* (1971), made certain recommendations on diocesan inspection, (saying, for instance, that it should be 'advisory' rather than 'inquisitorial') and firmly endorsed the recommendation of the Durham Report, *The Fourth R* (1970)*, that RE in aided schools should be open to inspection by HMI. It has since become not unusual for HMI to be invited to look at such religious education and for HMI to do so, though always with the understanding that this is by invitation only. A further consideration may well be that in some schools integration has made it all but impossible to avoid looking at religious education while inspecting some other subject.

In independent schools* it is long-established practice for H MI to ask whether the head wishes R E to be inspected.

In Scotland* all religious education has until recently been exempt from inspection by H MI or L E A inspector, and it is of interest that in 1972 the Miller Report* suggested that the subject had been the loser by this arrangement. The Education (Scotland) Bill 1981 contains a provision for R E in all schools, including denominational schools, to be inspected by H MI.

W. J. H. EARL

Institute of Christian Education
see **Christian Education Movement**

Institutions

In sociology the term 'institution' is normally applied to a recognized and established pattern of behaviour, usually authoritatively enforced. An adequate definition would refer to the standardization of behaviour and to the existence, where appropriate, of a supportive structure. Examples of religious institutions would include established roles and status levels within a sacred hierarchy, ceremonies such as those expressing sacraments and sacrifices, rituals of initiation, and times, days or seasons appointed for significant religious purposes. Religious institutions are standardized practices by which believers enact in symbolic form their relationship to the supernatural.

There is, however, a broader meaning to the term 'institution', which stresses the organizational dimension. Such a usage prevails in everyday speech and in the language of behavioural science, and the sociologist Joan Brothers has produced a book on *Religious Institutions* which is in fact about religious communities such as churches and denominational schools.

However understood, the concept of institutions is a powerful enabler of the study of beliefs and practice as objects or phenomena. It allows for emphasis not upon the symbolic function of religious behaviour but upon the social arrangements for its negotiation and validation. Further, the concept provides for a kind of levelling of forms of religious behaviour: primitive rites and the Christian sacrament of confirmation are comparable as institutions and called by the same name of initiation or *rites de passage*. In a similarly inadequate way, the focus upon religious organizations is likely to have regard for formal and public features such as size and inter-denominational relations and to blur the spiritual and emotional commitments of the individual believer.

During the 1970s, books for school use and new syllabuses reflected an increasing interest in the institutional features of the world's religions. Factors favouring this trend include the desirability of a detached observation of alternatives in culturally pluralist societies and the attractiveness of religious institutions to the illustrator, photographer and television producer.

The effect is to demythologize religious behaviour. In the age of phenomenology and the zoom lens, the domain of the sacred is readily penetrated and the faithful at prayer are in the name of education made objects of legitimate observation.

Joan Brothers, *Religious Institutions*, Longman 1971.

ROGER HOMAN

Integration of Curriculum and RE

Every subject on the timetable should take its direction from and exemplify the central aims of the curriculum as a whole: 'the public expression of [a school's] educational thinking'. Curriculum planning involves the balancing of each of its internal divisions, be they pastoral or academic, so that each complements the other and they all interrelate in the furtherance of such goals. It also includes the monitoring of this whole process on a regular and centralized basis. Hence phrases such as 'integrated studies' are tautologous – an unintegrated curriculum would be a contradiction in terms.

Subject integration should therefore rely more upon a skilful division of the 'seamless cloak of knowledge' than a mere stitching together of its separate parts. If the latter does for any reason become necessary, then it is essential for the R E teacher to be fully conversant with the curricular fabric he has in his hands – its key concepts, essential ideas, central knowledge*, the basic skills* required, etc. If these can be accommodated within such a scheme, then the school's work may well be strengthened by the amalgamation of various subject areas.

Various factors will determine the precise nature of the integration: How explicitly are the individual subjects to feature within the scheme? How tightly is it to be structured? What precisely will be the role adopted by the teacher and by the learner? What is the age and the ability of the pupils? How experienced are the staff? What materials and facilities are available? A wide spectrum of possibilities will be delineated by the answers to such questions. At one extreme will be a series of wide, open-ended, child-centred enquiries. A more directive approach ensures inter-connection between such theme-teaching within some larger and more structured framework, whilst the formal integration of specific areas of the curriculum appears on the timetable once faculties are created. Finally, and at its most formal, integration can also be said to have been achieved when autonomous subjects continue as separate entities but steps are taken to ensure that their inter-relationship is made clear to all (Related Studies).

The vigilance of the RE specialist is required in any form of theme-teaching, otherwise the essence of his discipline may be lost. Its integrity is guaranteed in Related Studies, but the appearance of faculties presents a particular difficulty. Each of these accentuates a different aspect of religion – within the Humanities the historical element will emerge, in Expressive Arts it will be the experiential, in Communication Studies the literary aspect will prevail, in Social Studies* contemporary moral issues, and so on. RE cannot generally find a satisfactory home within all of these areas. Some forms of team-teaching ensure its appearance in cyclic fashion, others on a modular basis. The subject then becomes a servicing agency for each area. Some teachers object strongly to this, others feel that it is precisely how RE should operate. But, whatever the answer to this and the other questions raised, it is certain that the RE teacher has to know more and not less about the precise nature of his subject with the advent of Integrated Studies than he would under a conventional timetable.

See also **Correlation in RE.**

I. H. Birnie (ed.), *Religious Education in Integrated Studies,* SCM Press 1972; M. Holt, *Schools and Curriculum Change,* McGraw Hill 1980; M. Marland and S. Hill, *Departmental Management,* Heinemann Educational 1981; Schools Council, 'Journeys into Religion' Series, Hart-Davis Educational 1977–82; D. Warwick, *Integrated Studies in the Secondary School,* Univ. of London Press 1973 and *Team Teaching,* Univ. of London Press 1971.

DAVID WARWICK

Interdisciplinary Approaches to Education

A school subject, like biology or geography, must be distinguished from a discipline or form of knowledge. A discipline, or form of knowledge, like science, mathematics or religion, has its own distinctive concepts (salvation, Torah, Nirvana, in religion), its own logical structure, truth criteria and techniques of study.

From this it follows that integration in the physical sciences involves the use of one discipline or set of methods of analysis, but that some school subjects, like geography and religious education, are already 'areas of study' which use many disciplines, and are themselves forms of interdisciplinary enquiry.

'Integrated studies'* is an ambiguous term. It may refer to interdisciplinary enquiry, in which case it is a proper method of educational study in which questions are answered in their appropriate discipline. Sometimes 'integrated studies' refers to a study in which knowledge is undifferentiated, e.g. a treatment of a theme* like Easter in which no distinction is made between religious, empirical or other questions and their appropriate discipline, or in which no distinction is made between fact and value. Such an approach may create more confusion than understanding.

Interdisciplinary enquiry may be necessary: 1. to explore a number of subject areas which contribute to a topic like 'the Vikings' or 'the Reformation'; 2. to investigate a topic like 'Easter', in which questions are related to their appropriate disciplines; 3. to study a question of practical living, often controversial, which is not the preserve of one subject, like 'relations between the sexes', or 'living in a multi-racial community'; 4. for a pupil to explore his chosen area of interest, like medical ethics, which will involve answering questions in the appropriate disciplines.

Materials, such as those of the Schools Council* Humanities and Integrated Studies Projects, if used with interdisciplinary methods, often help to make areas of study more relevant and meaningful to pupils.

I. H. Birnie (ed.), *Religious Education in Integrated Studies*, SCM 1972; M. Brown, 'Religious Education in Integrated Studies' in N. Smart and D. Horder (eds), *New Movements in Religious Education*, Temple Smith 1975; J. Holm, *Teaching Religion in School*, OUP 1975; A. V. Kelly, *The Curriculum*, Harper 1977; R. Pring, *Knowledge and Schooling*, Open Books 1976; Schools Council, *Working Paper No. 36. Religious Education in Secondary Schools*, Evans/Methuen 1971; J. P. White, *Towards a Compulsory Curriculum*, Routledge & Kegan Paul 1973.

GRAHAM B. MILES

International Seminar on Religious Education and Values

This is an informal association of RE scholars. Its aims are to promote research in the area of its concern and understanding between religious educators from many countries, and so to influence the development of RE in the various countries represented. The seminar is concerned both with RE as a subject taught within national and public education systems, and also with religious education as found in a variety of religious communities*. The seminar includes an interest in moral education*, values, character formation and human development in so far as this may be related to RE. The founding session of ISREV took place in the University of Birmingham, in 1978, and subsequent biennial sessions have been held in the United States and Holland. ISREV has no formal membership. Participants are invited to join the seminar and to share in its ongoing work.

MICHAEL GRIMMITT

Inter-School Christian Fellowship

The Inter-School Christian Fellowship is a part of the schools ministry of Scripture Union and exists to support, encourage and train voluntary Christian groups in schools to live as Christians in their own situation and to reach out to others in demonstrating the love of Christ. Some of the groups (perhaps called a Christian Union or Christian Fellowship) are staff led; others are led by senior pupils. ISCF offers help to individuals and groups who need advice, materials, training and inspiration. This service is available to primary and secondary schools. It organizes a number of different kinds of residential activities for young people including 'A' level courses, summer holidays and Broads cruises. ISCF also runs holiday activities for the nine to twelves.

ISCF has a team of full-time staff who work in co-operation with local teachers and pupils. Some of the staff visit schools over a whole region, others are locally based.

SUE HOWARD

Inter-Schools Conferences

Inter-schools day and residential conference programmes have been a part of the British religious education scene for many years.

In principle such enterprises should: 1. relate to the education of the whole person and the importance of values; 2. commend pupils to practise their own roles as participating agents helping to transform their environment; 3. advance support for school initiatives which maximize the spiritual and religious dimensions of its corporate life; 4. oppose forces within education which tend towards materialist and reductionist views of human beings; 5. encourage 'happenings' which help young people to share, widen and deepen their experiences.

In practice schools conference programmes: 1. provide a creative force in the senior forms' General Studies/Religious Education curriculum either within a course or to draw together thoughts on a course which has been completed; 2. stimulate ideas and through subsequent contributions inform young people's thinking; 3. bring together youngsters from different schools and backgrounds to explore a topic which interests them, thus facilitating an exchange of ideas and clarification of views; 4. confront youngsters with expert speakers and leaders who might otherwise be unavailable to schools thus enabling developments not as easily reached in the classroom; 5. encourage students to think about modern religious and social issues and to make proposals concerning them.

Selection and investigation of a particular situation or context which does not have to be overtly religious but which allows for theological elaboration and statement are the primary strengths of such inter-schools enterprises. These programmes have been a regular feature of the work of the Christian Education Movement* and of the Student Christian Movement* before it. Part of CEM's work is directly with young people at school for one of the Movement's aims is to encourage open, reflective and socially responsible education.

DAVID L. EDWARDS

Ireland: Eire

General background. The system of education inherited by the first Irish government in 1922 has been described as a 'voluntary or managerial system of privately owned, privately staffed, state-aided (as regards building and staff-remuneration), state-supervised schools, theoretically neutral but denominational in practice' (King). The constitution adopted in 1923 laid it down that all citizens had a right to a free elementary education and in Article 8 placed all recognized forms of religion on an equal basis. In contrast the new constitution adopted in 1937 declared that 'the State recognizes the special position of the Holy Catholic Apostolic and Roman Church as the guardian of the faith professed by the great majority of the citizens'. It went on to add that 'the State also recognises the Church of Ireland, the Presbyterian Church in Ireland, the Methodist Church in Ireland, the Religious Society of Friends in Ireland, as well as the Jewish Congregations and the other religious denominations existing in Ireland at the date of the coming into operation of this Constitution'. These two parts of Article 44 were deleted by referendum in 1972 leaving only the acknowledgment that the homage of public worship is due to Almighty God. Here is indicated the religious, though not necessarily Christian, dimension of citizenship.

Articles of the constitution accord with Roman Catholic social teaching on the rights of parents, churches, the state and the child in the matter of education: thus Article 42.1 'The State acknowledges that the primary and natural educator of the child is the Family and guarantees to respect the inalienable right and duty of parents to provide, according to their means, for the religious and moral, intellectual, physical and social education of their children.' In giving aid there is to be no discrimination between schools under the management of different religious denominations and there is a right of withdrawal from attending religious instruction.

The official *Rules for National Schools* emphasize the place and significance of religious instruction within school life: 'Of all parts of a school curriculum Religious Instruction is by far the most important, as its subject matter, God's honour and service, includes the proper use of all man's faculties, and affords the most powerful inducements to their proper use. Religious Instruction is, therefore, a fundamental part of the school course, and a religious spirit should inform and vivify the whole work of the school.' Periods of formal religious instruction have to be indicated on the timetable and teachers in the national schools traditionally have taught classes in religion and have taken part in the preparation of children for 'first communion', 'confirmation' etc. In recent years some teachers have called for the right to refuse to do this without this refusal affecting their employment or promotion.

In the *Programme of Primary Instruction* it is stated 'that the prescribing of the subject matter of Religious Instruction, the examination of it, and the supervision of its teaching are outside the competence of the Department of Education'.

At the secondary level, as the vast majority of the schools have been owned and run by various religious institutes, the teaching of religion would normally have been the responsibility of teachers in religious orders, or, in the much smaller number of schools in which Protestant pupils were educated, by those teachers willing to undertake this helped by local clergy. The great expansion of post-primary education which took place in the late sixties and seventies coupled with a decline in religious vocations has meant that lay teachers now outnumber 'religious' by about four to one.

Roman Catholic. In the Roman Catholic Church the traditional view that education is the responsibility of the church and that for the state to take over the provision and control of any aspect of the educational system is dangerous secularization, has been pervasive. From this it follows that the definition of a Catholic school has been in terms of 'authority in and control of the school, the presence of Catholic teachers and pupils, instruction in the truths and practice of the faith, and the visibility of religious symbols' (Brennan). Partly because of the very success achieved in establishing this view, the general upsurge in catechetical activity was slower to develop in Ireland than in America or Europe. Over the past decade the impetus for catechetical renewal at every level has developed strongly and is beginning to be expressed in the struggle to find a different definition of, and philosophy for, a Catholic school. In 1973 the Irish Bishops appointed a team to draw up a catechetical syllabus for primary schools based on the principles of the *General Catechetical Directory* and adapted to the Irish situation. The eight graded programmes of the 'Children of God' series were completed in 1978, and in them 'catechesis or religious education is understood as the communication of the Christian revelation to children in their concrete situation with a view to fostering faith' (Murphy).

At the secondary level more tensions have been experienced between the goals and pedagogical conditions inherent in the general curriculum and those of the Irish Catechetical Programme (begun in 1972 for the 12–15 age-group) and the 'God and Man' series (1977, 15–18 age-group). The general approach of the programmes could be described as 'neo-confessional' and schools are encouraged to relate them to the development of a Christian environment in the school, to involve parents, and to make some co-ordination with church life in the parish. Such goals are proving hard to achieve.

Church of Ireland. In 1972 the Advisory Committee on Religious Education report was presented to the General Synod of the Church of Ireland. The report called for syllabus development at all levels, the development of training for teachers in new methods and approaches, and the appointment of an adviser/priest in each diocese, and it noted that 'on the whole Irish education and church life have not seen it as their aim to prepare people for the bewildering experience of life in a society which is becoming pluralist'. In 1977 *A Curriculum for Religious Education*

in the Primary School was published by the Church of Ireland Board of Education and in 1979 *Guidelines for a Curriculum in Religious Education for Secondary Schools*. A recent survey of religious education in primary schools in the Dublin area, however, has shown that many teachers lack confidence in handling religious education and do not understand the reasons for the great changes that have taken place in method and content. At the same time the approach suggested at the secondary level seems generally to have in mind the needs of more academic streams in urban schools.

Presbyterian and Methodist. The very small number of schools under the control of the Presbyterian Church and the Methodist Church and the fact that pupils attending these schools belong to different denominations means that RE is 'non-denominational' and specific denominational teaching is given through the Sunday School.

Religious Education in the Leaving Certificate. A working party representative of these four churches submitted a curriculum for Religious Education in the Leaving Certificate to a Curriculum Committee set up by the Department of Education and the resultant course became available to schools in 1983. A distinction is being maintained between RE as an examination subject and the continuing pastoral function of catechesis in the school.

The Religious Society of Friends* has a small number of schools in which an emphasis upon the qualities of community living for conveying attitudes and values has attracted pupils of all denominations.

The Jewish congregations in Dublin maintain a primary and secondary school for their children where Jewish/Hebrew Studies are taught as an integral part of the timetable, sometimes by teachers from Israel. Parents of children attending other schools generally make private arrangements for such studies.

Training of Teachers. Since the late sixties the Mater Dei Institute in Dublin and the Mount Oliver Institute for Religious Education in Dundalk have provided recognized specialist courses, one at diploma and graduate level, and the other at post-graduate. Maynooth now offers a degree in theology and arts as well as in theology, and Trinity in biblical and theological studies and a part-time diploma. But whereas teachers in Roman

Catholic schools have had the stimulus of new courses, some linked with extensive curriculum development activity, a serious weakness has been the failure to find way of providing recognized courses through which teachers in Protestant schools could train for, or develop, specialist qualifications in RE. Some help has been given by the 'spare time' course organized by the Church of Ireland Board of Education. Another small but important development has been the Diploma course offered to teachers by the Irish School of Ecumenics.

––––––

Donald Harman Akenson, *A Mirror to Kathleen's Face,* McGill-Queen's University Press 1975; Janet Barcroft, 'Religious Education in the Secondary School: An Approach to the Denominational Issue', *Search*, Winter 1980; Nano Brennan, 'The Catholic School', *The Irish Catechist*, May 1979; Linda Clarke, 'Denominational Teaching – A Defence', *Search,* Winter 1980; John Coolahan, *Irish Education: Its History and Structure,* Institute of Public Administration, Dublin 1981; Charles Hayes, 'The educational ideas of Paul Cardinal Cullen', *Proceedings of the Educational Studies Association of Ireland Conference*, Galway University Press 1979; Timothy F. Kelly, 'Education', *Irish Anglicanism 1869–1969*, ed. Michael Hurley, Allen Figgis 1970; J. D. King. *Religious Education in Ireland*, Fallons 1970; Bill Murphy, 'New Primary Programme', *The Irish Catechist,* Winter 1977.

                                   J. R. B. MCDONALD

Ireland: Northern

Northern Ireland is a deeply divided society in which political and cultural divisions reinforce the religious division between Roman Catholicism and the various strands of Protestantism. Rose termed it 'bi-confessional' because nearly everyone identified himself as either a Protestant or a Roman Catholic. It may be debated whether 'an accentuated practice and orthodoxy' (Martin) is the result of conflicts being thrust into the religious channel, but there is ample evidence of relatively high levels of religious practice and belief.

In such a society, schools inevitably reflect the divisions. It is difficult to find precise figures for the affiliation of pupils at different types of schools, but according to one report,

produced in 1977 (*All Children Together*), 99.5% of Protestant children were at state or Protestant voluntary schools while 98% of Roman Catholic children were in Roman Catholic schools. Religious education in such a society is commonly seen as induction into one particular religious tradition. An account of religious education in Northern Ireland up to 1970 is provided by the Durham Report, *The Fourth R**.

Protestant Religious Education
Before the Northern Ireland state was set up in 1921, nearly all education was provided by the churches. However in 1923 an attempt was made to establish a secular system of education in which religion was not taught by teachers. This attempt failed and following the 1930 Act, Bible instruction became part of the curriculum in county schools, and subsequently most Protestant schools were transferred to the LEAS. The Education Act (Northern Ireland, 1947) extended to the newly created secondary intermediate schools and to grammar schools the provision of 'undenominational religious instruction', that is 'instruction based upon the Holy Scriptures according to some authoritative version or versions thereof, but excluding instruction as to any tenet which is distinctive of any particular denomination'. This provision was continued in The Education and Libraries (Northern Ireland) Order 1972. In 1943, a committee was established with representation from the teacher's organizations and the three main churches (Church of Ireland, Presbyterian Church and Methodist Church). This committee published a programme of 'Graded Courses of Bible Instruction of Day Schools', which continued in use for over twenty years. In 1968, the committee merged with similar groups responsible for secondary (intermediate) and grammar school syllabuses, to form the Religious Education Council, on which were also representatives of the eight local education committees in Northern Ireland. In 1968–71, the Council undertook a major revision of the primary programme of RE based upon the West Riding Agreed Syllabus of 1968. As a result, *Themes in Religious Education* was published by the Council in 1971. However, many teachers were reluctant to change to thematic teaching because they based their religious teaching on

Bible stories and understood imparting Bible knowledge to be an important aim. In 1978, at the request of the Council, a curriculum development project was set up in Stranmillis College to prepare an RE programme for primary schools. *A Programme for Religious Education in the Primary School* was published in 1981 and widely distributed throughout schools in Northern Ireland. It was a substantial piece of work with a clear plan of work for each year from P1–7 and it took seriously the need for children to be actively engaged in learning. However the programme was neo-confessional* in its implicit aims, it was heavily biblical in its selection of content and it paid little attention to the social context in which children lived (Greer 1983).

In 1957 a committee was set up to prepare a syllabus for use in secondary (intermediate) schools. This four-year course was published between 1962–65. The first Grammar School Syllabus was published in 1949 and the most recent syllabus appeared in 1965. This provided a thorough course up to sixth-form level. Both these secondary (intermediate) and grammar school syllabuses were confessional in aim, and largely biblical in content, but tried to make the Christian faith relevant to contemporary life. Since coming into existence in 1966, the Religious Education Council has done little to develop programmes and syllabuses specifically for adolescents. However, in the early 1970s, a group of college lecturers and advisers produced a suggested syllabus for years one to three in the secondary school because previous syllabuses were being used in only a few schools, but this has not really filled the gap which still exists. In 1981, the North Eastern Education and Library Board produced its own *Essential Bible Content Syllabus* for secondary schools as a follow up to its *Essential Bible Content Syllabus* for primary schools (1977).

Protestant religious education in Northern Ireland is neo-confessional, is concerned with biblical teaching which may be related to life in the contemporary world and largely ignores the faith and practice of the Roman Catholic tradition of Christianity. The programmes are somewhat at variance with an important report produced as a discussion document by the Religious Education Council, *Design for Religious Education* (1978), which sought 'to set discussions about religious education in the context of the current general debate in education about the grounds for the establishment of aims and objectives and to articulate an educational rationale for the teaching of the subject in Northern Ireland'. The report also stressed the role of RE in the 'laying of a foundation of tolerance and sympathy towards the religious beliefs and practices of others'.

The progammes tend to have a Protestant tone in that they give relatively little attention to the Christian sacraments. This is probably due to the fact that controlled schools are not related to any one specific church, teachers may consider teaching about sacraments to be divisive and it is not the function of the day school to prepare young people for communicant membership. To nurture children and adolescents in the faith of their own particular denominations and to prepare them for the responsibilities of full church membership, the Protestant churches in Northern Ireland all have systems of Sunday Schools which are attended by large numbers of young people. This system of Christian education is provided by the churches outside day-school time and buildings by voluntary teachers and by clergy.

Roman Catholic Religious Education

In 1923, the Roman Catholic Church was unwilling to accept a secular system of education, and the changes in the 1930 Act and in subsequent legislation did nothing to change this decision. Today, RC schools provide education for nearly all Roman Catholic pupils, and most church primary and secondary (intermediate) schools are in the maintained school category, while church grammar schools are called voluntary schools.

In his survey of catechetics in Ireland, J. D. King has described how in 1964–66 the northern dioceses of the Roman Catholic Church dropped the progamme of religious teaching built around the catechism and adapted the 'On Our Way' series based on the kerygmatic approach to catechetics which had been developed in the USA by Sister Maria de la Cruz. The series had been designed for untrained lay teachers who were teaching children outside the normal school programme. For this reason the lessons were developed in a very detailed way and it became apparent that there was a need for a programme of religious education specifically designed for Irish children. So the Irish Episcopal Commission on Catechetics established a team of catechists to produce a new programme for primary schools. The programme was to cover a period of eight years because transfer to secondary education in the Irish Republic was at twelve years of age, and it was published between 1976 and 1978. This 'Children of God' series provides a national progamme of catechesis for use in RE schools throughout Ireland, from the age of four to twelve. Teachers' books set out a clear rationale of the programme for each year group and of the part to be played by parents, teacher and priest. Cassette recordings of music, excellent posters and photogaphs contribute to an imaginative and stimulating course of study, which included preparation for the sacrament of penance and first communion in P4 and preparation for confirmation in P7. Throughout, the teacher was the catechist, nurturing faith, deepening awareness of God and helping children to respond to him. In comment, it may be said that the programme contains concepts which young children would find hard to understand. It is characterized by 'content-oriented closed-ended catechesis' (Greer 1977) which does not concern itself with helping pupils to understand those who have different beliefs from themselves. The Primary 1–7 syllabus is used in primary schools and the Primary 8 syllabus is used in the first year of secondary education.

In the area of secondary education, the Irish Episcopal Commission on Catechetics established a team of workers to prepare a programme of post-primary catechetics. The junior cycle consisting of three volumes, *Christ With Us, Saved in Christ* and *United in Christ,* was published in 1972–4, providing a pupils' book and a teachers' book for second, third and fourth year secondary classes. From 1978 onwards, the senior cycle of eight titles in the 'God of Man' series began to appear, including *The Mystery of God, Jesus of Nazareth, The Moral Life* and *The Christian Heritage.* The senior cycle completed a comprehensive and impressive progamme of religious education. It is fair to say that the main emphasis of the whole programme is the formation of young people in the Roman Catholic tradition of faith. The secondary syllabus does recognize that most Irish people

who are not Roman Catholics are in fact Protestant, who share many common Christian beliefs. However the religious belief, the practice and the moral teaching of Protestants are not really considered, and the promotion of understanding of those outside the Roman Catholic Church is not an objective of any of the books.

In 1980, the first volume of 'The Christian Way' was published as the first year of a new, experiential presentation of the course for twelve to fifteen year old pupils: *The Risen Lord is present in the Community of Church, in word and in sacrament.* This book goes a long way towards meeting teachers' criticisms that the first version of the Junior Cycle was too academic and difficult for less able pupils. It also goes a long way to promoting understanding of the reformed churches and to encouraging ecumenical contacts and activities.

General Considerations

1. *Conscience clause**. A 'conscience clause' operates in controlled schools which permits teachers to contract out of teaching RE and parents to withdraw their children from RE classes. RC teachers in church schools are required to teach religion if requested by their principal, and the Chilver Committee (1980) was informed by church authorities 'that teachers who are not qualified to teach Religious Education will not be employed in Roman Catholic primary schools and only exceptionally (as specialists) in Roman Catholic secondary schools'.

2. *Public examinations.* While controlled and Protestant voluntary schools provide a confessional type of religious education with a strong emphasis on the Bible and Roman Catholic schools provide a confessional type of RE which is based on the Roman Catholic tradition of faith, in recent years increasing numbers of pupils from both sides of the divide have followed common examination courses provided under the auspices of the Northern Ireland Schools Examination Council. The Certificate of Secondary Education and General Certificate of Education 'Ordinary' level Religious Education were introduced in 1973, and GCE 'Advanced' level in 1975. Large numbers of pupils have entered for these examinations (1982: CSE Mode 1 3475; CSE Mode 3 1790; 'O' level 4257: 'A'

level 4081). This wider study of religion should help pupils to take a more objective and informed view of the subject, though the development of Mode 3 examinations may limit the scope of study to the pupils' own tradition. As in other parts of the country, the debate is taking place in Northern Ireland about the possible introduction of a common examination at sixteen plus to replace the CSE and GCE 'O' level.

3. *Teacher Education.* Teachers are trained for the Roman Catholic schools in St Mary's and St Joseph's colleges of education in Belfast, and for controlled schools in Stranmillis College, a state institution with Protestant Church representation on the Board of Governors. Graduates of Queen's University, the New University of Ulster and the Ulster Polytechnic have also obtained teaching posts in church and controlled schools. One of the most controversial questions in Northern Ireland in 1982 was the British Government's decision to implement the Chilver interim report (1980) which took the view that it was preferable for teacher education to be located in religiously mixed and multi-disciplinary institutions of higher education and recommended the amalgamation of the two church colleges with Stranmillis College on the Stranmillis site. In this Belfast Centre for Teacher Education the voluntary college was promised a distinctive denominational ethos and a separate legal and administrative existence. In the face of considerable opposition to this scheme, the Government decided not to proceed with the amalgamation of the three colleges of education to form the Belfast Centre. However, plans were announced by Roman Catholic Church authorities for the amalgamation of the two church colleges.

4. *Developments across the divide.* Three developments across the religious divide may be mentioned briefly:

(*a*) *Peace Education.* The Irish Council of Churches and the Irish Commission for Justice and Peace have together produced peace education materials called *Free To Be* for use in Primary 5 and 6 classes. These are relevant to and may be made part of a programme of religious education. Other materials have been produced by the two organizations which are suitable for use in secondary RE.

(*b*) *Religion in Ireland.* A curriculum development project called the Project on Religion

in Ireland operated from 1974–77 and 1979–82 in the Education Centre of the New University of Ulster under the direction of Dr John Greer and Fr John McCullagh. Its aim was to develop a rationale and experimental materials for a form of Religious Education which involved secondary pupils learning about and developing sensitivity to religious traditions other than their own.

(*c*) *Lagan College.* In 1981, Lagan College was opened in Belfast as an integrated all-ability college for boys and girls. 'Its aim is to educate the sons and daughters of Catholics and Protestants and of parents having other (or no) religious beliefs, for life in a plural society.' In the curriculum of the school, three periods are devoted to RE each week, one of which is concerned with world religions, one with Christianity and one with the pupil's own religious tradition.

'All Children Together', *News from All Children Together*, 1, 1, 1977; Chilver Interim Report, *The Future Structure of Teacher Education in Northern Ireland*, HMSO 1980; Durham Report, *The Fourth R,* National Society/SPCK 1970; J. E. Greer, 'Attitude to Religion Reconsidered', *British Journal of Educational Studies*, 31, 1, 1983, pp. 18–28; 'The Irish Primary Catechetical Programme', *The Furrow* 28, 11, 1977; 'A New Kind of Teaching: an Exmination of a Programme for Religious Education in the Primary School,' *Compass*, 12, 1, 1983; 'Religion in Northern Ireland' in E. McWhirter and K. Trew (eds), *Northern Ireland: Myth and Reality Social and Political Perspectives*, G. W. and A. Hesketh 1982; 'Religious Education in State Primary Schools in Northern Ireland', *The Northern Teacher*, 13, 2, 1978 and 3, 1979–80; J. D. King, *Religious Education in Ireland*, Fallons 1970; D. Martin, *A General Theory of Secularization*, Blackwell 1978; R. Rose, *Governing Without Consensus*, Faber 1971.

JOHN E. GREER

Islam, Islamic RE

Proclaim! (or Read)
In the Name
Of thy Lord and Cherisher,
Who created –
Created man, out of
A (mere) clot
Of congealed blood:

Proclaim! And thy Lord
Is Most Bountiful, –
He Who taught
(The use of) the Pen, –
Taught man that
Which he knew not.

(Abdullah Yusuf Ali translation of
Al-Qur'an 96:1–5).

This is the very first revelation to the Prophet Muhammad (peace be upon him) which has, over the past fourteen hundred years, inspired the followers of the faith of Islam to acquire knowledge, religious as well as secular. Even in the opinion of the modern educationists, no matter what religious denomination a child may belong to, the most commonly known aims of education, which he has the right to expect, are to fulfil himself, to adapt to a changing world and to become an instrument of social reform.

In Muslim society, one's educational fulfilment means the merging of one's will with the Divine Will. The education provided must, therefore, develop the whole man – both his soul and his body. Religious education becomes imperative for a child who, unaided in this direction, would otherwise accept any kind of food for his moral well-being rather than remain starved. Religious education which is really positive and the very best a society can provide, is, therefore, necessary for the development of a sturdy and a balanced conscience.

Furthermore, Dr Muhammad Iqbal (d. 1938), the philosopher-poet of Islam, has repeatedly advocated in his poems the teaching of Islam to the young and explained the necessity of religious education thus: 'Experience shows that truth revealed through pure reason is incapable of bringing that fire of living conviction which personal revelation alone can bring. That is the reason pure thought has so little influenced man while religion has always elevated individuals and transformed whole societies.'

In the case of a Muslim child he must learn the *Holy Qur'an* and the *Sunnah* (tradition) of the Holy Prophet because the former has the Will of God contained in it and the latter has it explained in it. The *Holy Qur'an* has enumerated the importance of a learned man, i.e. the teacher, several times: 'Allah will exalt those of you who believe and those who are given knowledge to high ranks.' The Holy Prophet has explained it thus: 'The learned are the inheritors of the prophets', 'the ink of the scholars is better than the blood of the martyrs' and 'learning is obligatory upon every Muslim, be he a man or woman'.

As human nature is fundamentally uniform, the teacher, therefore, has the opportunity to make of the child what he wants, according to what he feels in his mind. Ibn Miskawaih, a Muslim educationist of the fourteenth century, shows the child as innocent and his mind a clean slate, on similar lines to J. Locke, who represents the human mind in its first state as an empty chamber which is furnished later by experience. The development of the sentiment of shame in a child, which is the dawn of reasoning, discrimination between good and evil, feelings of humiliation and disgrace, and adjustment to discipline and instruction is, for instance, to Ibn Miskawaih what McDougall defines as 'the sense of respect – the flywheel of character', with all the foregoing characteristics. And this is the time when proper religious education must begin.

Experience has shown that no keen emphasis is laid on religious education, though it is conducted as a matter of routine alongside other arts and sciences. The youths of today especially in the West, some of whom have already made their desires public by travelling to the East in pursuit of transcendental meditation and mental tranquility, need to be equipped with the rudiments of religion, both for spiritual contentment and to reconcile the inner conflict with their material and political values. This illustrates the need for a comprehensive syllabus in religious education for children in all schools, comprising: 1. a résumé of the religious beliefs, 2. religion in practice, and 3. socio-religious issues. The syllabus must essentially be devoid of such issues as may misrepresent religious beliefs and convictions, and should highlight the universal truths, bringing to the forefront the points of difference only when age and time permit. Also the study of Islam at length may involve some of the topics in the above categories with the course and depth left for the individual teacher to decide, taking into account, without fail, the facilities available. This is equally applicable in the case of trainee teachers in colleges of education, with additional readings from recommended books for deeper understanding.

Teaching of the basic liturgical rudiments of Islam are carried out in the mosque-schools. Teachers at these schools are thoroughly briefed on the relevant subjects taught by each one amongst them. They are trained on traditional lines, i.e. reading of the Arabic text of the *Holy Qur'an* from the holy book itself or learning it by heart as well, followed by speaking and writing of Arabic, and have good understanding of Islam. They learn their own mother-tongue, Persian, or Urdu, or Bengali etc., and the vast literature on Islam therein. Above all they are practising Muslims. It has, therefore, been a recognized practice throughout the Muslim world that the *Qur'anic* scriptures are taught to the children as a matter of 'repeat after me'. And a good number of the short chapters of the *Holy Qur'an* are memorized in addition to the text of the daily prayers. There are good many of the *Qur'anic Du'as* (supplications) which have historical meanings and have become a part of the individual worshipper's supplication. The children memorize them. For example, whilst explaining the overall control of God Almighty, the believer must, in the event of an affliction, confess it in all sincerity: 'To Allah we belong, and to Him is our return' (Al-Qur'an 2:156), the Arabic equivalent of which is *Inna lillah-hay Wa Inna Alaih-hay Rajeun* and has become a common and instant utterance at the news or sight of death. Alongside the learning of the *Holy Qur'an* the children are taught in their own mother-tongue the basic belief in the unity of Godhead (*Tauheed*), finality of prophethood of the Prophet Muhammad, other prophets of Islam from Adam to Jesus, the Divine Books, Hell and Heaven, 'pre-destination and free-will', the text and rituals of daily prayers, do's and don'ts of fasting during the lunar calendar month of *Ramadhan*, the benefits of *Zakat* (obligatory charity) and *Khairat* (charity) to the needful and the pros and cons of the *Hajj* (pilgrimage). As children grow older they learn these basic principles of Islam in further details and in the light of the life practices of the Holy Prophet of Islam whose own exhortations as above encourage them to accept education as a life-long process. Stories of the prophets and the tales of the men of Islam are additional readings followed by history of

Islam. At a higher level there are degrees, graduate and post-graduate, available in all aspects of Islam, theological, juridical and philosophical, etc., from universities throughout the world.

In multi-religious Britian, mosque-schools have taken on a vigorous role in the teaching of Islam to Muslim children during the evenings and week-ends as it has not been possible hitherto to undertake the devotional and doctrinal aspects of Islam in the state schools. However, readings from the *Holy Qur'an* have been used in assemblies in ethnically mixed schools and 'O' and 'A' level examinations in Islam have been offered in certain schools. In multi-religious situations, therefore, Islamic education is currently being imparted in a three-pronged attempt, at home, at the mosque and at school.

In the state school system in Britain, the teaching of Islam cannot be entirely satisfactory unless those people to whom the task of preparing the curriculum is assigned are drawn from the Islamic faith, and one cannot be altogether free from apprehension about the solution to such problems as: 1. the child subjected to overwork while learning more about his own religion at his place of worship and home, 2. the teacher needing to determine when to begin the study of one religion and end that of another, and 3. the truth and trustworthiness of one religion against another.

In practical terms, withdrawal classes run with the help of peripatetic teachers are most feasible, even though this kind of arrangement depends on there being an abundance of staff, flexible transportation, and above all, the awareness of parents about the usefulness of such classes and an agreed syllabus for religious learning. The skill and educational attainments required of the teacher teaching Islam during school hours must necessarily be the same as of the RE teacher in normal state schools. Helping the Muslim children occasionally to go to the mosque in the morning or evenings may only mean a withdrawal class is held there, not necessarily periods of worship, because there are always fixed times for saying Muslim prayers. The afternoon prayers that definitely fall within the school day could, perhaps, be a part of the periods allocated for the withdrawal classes.

Finally, from the point of view of the

faithful, the transmission of Islamic tradition is highly desirable regardless of where and how it is conducted in order to avoid any personal dissatisfaction and disillusionment with one's self.

See also Qur'an, al-.

MUHAMMAD IQBAL

Israel

The educational institutions of traditional Jewish society – the 'Cheder' for the elementary school age group and below and the 'Yeshivah' for the secondary school age group and above – were set up in order to impart the elements of Jewish tradition to the younger generation. In these institutions pupils learned mainly Torah and Talmud to the complete exclusion of any form of secular, general or vocational studies. Preparation for practical day-to-day living was left to other agents of socialization – the family, the synagogue, and so on.

During the whole of this long period of the existence of Jewish society as an entirely traditional one, there was only one educational system and there was no need for separate religious education, since the whole of Jewish education was under the sole inspiration and auspices of the world of Jewish values and conduct, which in their substance were also a world of religious values and conduct. All this applied to boys' education while, in most periods and places, girls received no formal education other than socializing influences within their families.

With the weakening of traditional Jewish society as a consequence of the social, political, economic and spiritual changes which took place within it, from about the end of the eighteenth century, dynamic processes of change also affected Jewish educational institutions. During the nineteenth century, there were strenuous efforts by Jewish Maskilim (disciples of Moses Mendelssohn (1729–86) in Germany (and later on in other countries) to challenge the legitimacy of traditional educational institutions, by attempting to create a new form of Jewish education based on modern social foundations, particularly with a wider basis of general and vocational studies. The attempts of the orthodox rabbinical elite to counteract this movement and to prevent this new tendency gaining momentum, were largely unsuc-

cessful. Consequently many Chadarim and Yeshivot in the Diaspora were deprived of the majority of their pupils. It was at this period that institutions of Religious Education gradually began to replace most of the older institutions of Jewish Education.

In Palestine a similar development occurred only towards the end of the nineteenth century – which however did not affect certain minority groups who continued to pursue the old style of Jewish Education – namely the alternative concept of Religious Education, aimed at those parents seeking a solution to the conflict between recognition of the demands of modern society and the need of their sons and daughters for religious identification. A fundamental and lasting solution to this conflict was found after the First World War, following the conscious recognition of its existence by a religious political party, the Mizrachi. It took into account both the new market situation and the likely growth of Jewish settlement in Palestine, which would follow the end of Ottoman rule and the beginning of the British Mandatory Administration, together with the effect of the Balfour Declaration of British sympathy with Zionist aspirations: they also foresaw the economic difficulties of maintaining a private network of religious education for an ever-increasing population. The Mizrachi party conducted lengthy negotiations with the other secular Zionist parties, finally reaching a compromise acceptable to all sides. This granted internal autonomy to religious schools in the field of education, while withholding administrative autonomy. They were thus incorporated into the broad framework of national Zionist education. This compromise agreement was signed at the 1920 Zionist Congress in London and served as a basis for the arrangements which were adopted at the beginning of the establishment of the State of Israel in 1948.

This autonomy led to the formation of a radically different concept of religious education from that of the educational framework in other countries. In the Israeli educational system RE is not concentrated into a few weekly lessons of religious instruction and religious assemblies, but it pervades the whole system – all inspectors, headteachers, form teachers and teachers of every subject, the pupils, the curriculum and the textbooks in every subject, and so on. This all-embracing 'religious education' was also accepted as a blueprint for girls' education, either single-sex or co-educational.

At all events, the acceptance of external autonomy certainly contributed, in the long run, to reducing the social 'distance' between the religious groups and their secular counterparts.

This political agreement enshrined in the 1920 'London Accords' was given legal sanction in 1953, when the Israeli Parliament (Knesset) passed the State Education Act. Its provisions were as follows:

State Education was defined as education provided by the State according to a curriculum with no political, racial or other partisan bias, but drawn up by the State, under the jurisdiction of the Minister or someone appointed by him.

State Religious Education was defined as State Education whose institutions are religious in their way of life, curriculum, teachers and inspectors.

Religious Educational Institution was defined as a recognized educational institution where state religious education was provided.

Supplementary Curriculum was defined as part of the curriculum introduced or authorized by the Minister in accordance with this Law, encompassing not more than twenty-five per cent of the timetable, in a recognized educational institution.

Supplementary Curriculum in a State Religious Institution was defined as a supplementary curriculum which would include teaching of the Written and Oral Law in accordance with the religious way of life exemplified by the institution.

From 1 September 1953 the State Education Law would apply in every recognized educational institution: in any recognized educational institution which in the academic year 1952/53 was affiliated to the Mizrachi or Agudat Yisrael or with the Religious Sector of the Labour movement, State Religious Education would apply.

This formal legislation met with political opposition at various stages, both at local and national levels. However, it led to the development and establishment of a wide-ranging religious educational network, beginning with kindergartens and ending with institutions for the training of teachers, and a religious university – a network which in a period of about thirty years has served between twenty and thirty per cent of the student body in the State of Israel. Within this network there developed an increasing variety of educational streams and options. Today we find in State religious institutions the following types: a Religious School for Seamen; a Religious Military academy for Officers; a religious post-High School Institution for the Training of Opticians and Electronic Engineers; a Religious Institution for Special Education; a Residential High School which combines Yeshivah studies with studies for the State matriculation examinations, all within a framework of intensive involvement in pioneering youth activity, in single-sex establishments called Yeshivot Tichoniot for boys and Ulpanot for girls: a post-High School religious boarding school which combines higher Torah studies at Yeshivah level with a teachers' training course, together with army service in fighting units; a religious post-elementary agricultural school, and so on.

Parallel with this centralized but varied arrangement, there exists in Israel the institutions of independent education (Chinuch Atzmai), which from a legal point of view are 'recognized' institutions which are not 'official'. These institutions cater for six to seven per cent of the school population. They are all single-sex institutions for pupils of the compulsory education age-group (4–15), and include secular studies in their curriculum, although the proportion of time allotted to religious studies is greater than that of state religious schools. These institutions received significant financial support from the government (between 75–90% of the teacher's salaries). State religious schools maintain formal and direct links with various government ministries, but their political links with the National Religious Party (NRP) are completely informal and imperceptible, while Chinuch Atzmai schools maintain formal and direct links with the political party Agudat Yisrael.

Alongside these two trends of religious education in Israel exist 'exempted institutions' (that is, neither 'official' nor 'recognized'): primary schools for boys only, and post-primary and post-secondary Yeshivah-type institutions, again for boys only. These 'exempted' institutions receive no state aid whatsoever, the language of intruction is not

Hebrew, but Yiddish. The most important part of their curriculum is religious studies and most of the teachers have no professional qualifications. The Yeshivah-type institutions, including those mentioned previously, incorporate modern trends (they combine religious studies with general and vocational ones, which are generally found in State Religious Education) and traditional trends which more-or-less maintain the format of Jewish Education in traditional society. Paradoxically, it is in the modern State of Israel that in recent years there has flourished, relatively speaking, the Yeshivah-type of education both at primary level (the Cheder), and at higher level. It should be pointed out that Yeshivah students in Israel are exempted from military service while they are studying (with the exception of students in the Yeshivot Hesder which combine Yeshivah studies with military service).

In conclusion, it should again be stressed that RE in the State of Israel is unique, not only in its scope and comprehensiveness, but also in the wide spectrum of its content and the broad cross-section of the population which it serves, in an age when separation of religion and state is the rule.

See also **Judaism.**

M. Bar-Lev, *Religious Education in Israeli Society*, Centre for the Documentation of Israeli Society, Hebrew University, Jerusalem; Y. Bentwitch, *Education in the State of Israel,* Chachik Publishing House, Tel Aviv 1960; R. Stanner, *Education Laws,* Jerusalem 1966.

MORDECHAI BAR-LEV

Italy

The vast majority of Italians are Roman Catholics and the Constitution of the Italian Republic, issued on 27 December, 1947, decrees in its 7 Article that the relations between state and church are regulated by the Lateran Agreements. This includes a treaty, a concordat, and appendices and lays down the rules for RE in Italy, at least as far as the Catholic population is concerned.

The Concordat of 11 February 1929 (signed by Cardinal Gasparri and Benito Mussolini) states in its 36th Article that 'The Italian state considers the teaching of the Christian doctrine according to the Catholic tradition the basis and finest achievement of state education.'

Therefore it can be said that substantially religious education in state schools is under the jurisdiction of the Catholic Church.

The Italian Protestant churches share a joint religious programme organized by the Federation of Italian Protestant churches founded in Milan in 1967. It's members are the Waldenses (Reformed), Baptists, Methodists, Lutherans, the Salvation Army and Apostolics. The history of Christian education, though, does not begin then as it has its roots in a strong tradition of involvement and spirit of unity.

The Waldensian churches have been present in Italy since AD 1200 and in 1532 (Chanforan Synod) they joined the Reformation becoming a church of the reformed confession. Their presence in Italy was tolerated only in the mountainous regions of western Piedmont where it became a kind of territorial church. The historical situation of a small minority, persecuted and relegated to an alpine ghetto, has coloured Christian education: they have carried out their work in very close contact with the Swiss and French reformed churches, and later with the churches of central Europe. The presence in Italy of the papacy and of a Catholic Church in a dominant position, has forced the Waldenses to assume a polemical position and, as civil and political rights were not granted to them, they have always had a connotation of a popular movement.

The Waldensian churches translated the Bible into French (Olivetan 1535) and donated it to the French-speaking reformed churches, whilst adopting in Italy Calvin's catechism.

The ministers received their theological training in the French-speaking faculties in Europe, while a 'Theological School' was known to have existed in the mountain regions from 1300. As discrimination lasted throughout the centuries, the Waldenses also organized schools for public education in their mountain villages, some of which are still present today. For centuries they were the only non-Catholic church organized in Italy; they resisted persecution and even though exiled, came back to their land of origin. Only on 17 February 1848, with the Edict of Emancipation of King Carlo Alberto, were they recognized as Italian citizens with equal rights.

At that time the historical situation was changing and as Italy became united, a new feeling of freedom favoured the appearance of foreign Protestant missions. Amongst these the two Methodist missions (Episcopalian and Wesleyan) and the two Baptist ones, all supported by the British and American churches, can be noted. This is the period influenced by the Revival and missionary impetus, and the new churches move in this historical perspective and in a vast programme of social work (particularly by opening schools open to everyone to combat illiteracy, orphanages, hospitals). The important thing is that missions present in Italy and the Waldensian churches did not think of building different confessional churches, but rather of working together for a unified Protestant church. This project failed, but it left its mark in the field of Christian education: Baptists, Methodists and Waldenses founded a joint Sunday School Comittee in 1878 and began the publication of the review *La Scuola Domenicale* with a unified syllabus. The magazine used the inter-denominational programme for the study of the Bible and, except for a few interruptions caused by the two world wars, it has been published ever since.

As time went on, through the influence of deepening theological thought and through links with European Protestant churches, the work of Christian education was modified: from a revivalist line it passed to a more deeply Protestant reformed theology. This line has been chosen purposely and maintained in as much as it derives from an analysis of the Italian situation.

It should be remembered above all that in Italy the Reformation was not able to flourish because of the Catholic counter-reformation and inquisition. It must not be forgotten that the Italian situation is unique as it is the seat of the papacy, and that for centuries part of central Italy made up the Papal State, so that the Pope was also a territorial prince.

With the unification of Italy (1870) the Catholic Church lost its territory and only in 1929, with the Lateran Agreements, did it reach a concordat with the Italian state. As far as the cultural and religious situation is concerned, the concordat's clause 'The Italian state considers the teaching of the Christian doctrine, according to the Catholic tradition, the basis and finest achievements of the state education' means that all the teaching in the Italian state schools, except universities, is inspired by Catholic principles. For non-Catholics the exemption from religious instruction is provided on request by the parents. So Catholicism is the state church and all the other confessions are 'free churches', without any financial support from the state. Christian education for the non-Catholic confession is thus a family and church responsibility.

In this historical perspective the work of Protestant churches in Italy consists in educating in a Protestant way its own young people, in building a religious alternative to the Catholic church and in maintaining alive the voice of world Protestantism. The work appears difficult as Protestants in Italy are not more than 100,000 in a population of 55 million Italians, all nominally Catholic.

To respond more effectively to the challenge present in this country, the churches work together in the 'Servizio Istruzione ed Educazione' (SIE), a committee of the Federation of Protestant churches in Italy. The work is done in connection with the other Latin-speaking countries (Portugal, Spain, France, Swizerland and Belgium) with whom there are biennial meetings. Working relations are maintained with the European Conference of Churches (KEK), the European Conference on Christian Education (ECCE) and with the World Council of Churches (WCC)*. These international links help the church not to fall into a national sectarianism, but to keep in touch with the developments in theology and education in the world, particularly in Europe.

Italian student ministers attend the Waldensian Faculty in Rome or, particularly the Baptists, the European Seminary in Rüschlikon/Zürich. All the Protestant churches have a progamme for theological education for lay-persons involved in church work, while special programmes are edited by the women's and young people's federation. The children's sector is taken care of by the SIE which, apart from the magazine *La Scuola Domenicale*, publishes a series of aids for keeping teachers up-to-date.

Apart from the work organized in the churches, there is also the care of isolated families who live in the vast diaspora. During the summer period young people's and teachers' meetings are organized in Protestant summer centres providing a much appreciated opportunity for study.

D. TOMASETTO

Jainism

The term Jainism is an English rendering of *Jaina-dharma* or *Jian-dharma*. It is a religion, a philosophical system, a way of life practised and preached by *Jina* (lit. conqueror of self), the perfect human being. Jainism is a fully developed and well-established religious system. Its philosophy rests on sound foundations and its followers are well-organized as a community. The system is indigenous to India. It retains some extremely primitive conceptions, and happens to be the oldest living representative of the *Sramana* current in ancient Indian culture. It is non-Vedic in origin and probably non-Aryan too. It is neither a revealed religion against Vedic-sacrifices, nor, as held by other scholars, an off-shoot of Brahmanism or Buddhism.

Jaina thinkers or *acaryas* have not written any separate or particular treatise on religious education. But, if we go through the scriptures carefully, we find therein a well-propounded system of education which includes pedagogy and curriculum methods. Thus the Jaina philosophy of education is better understood against its historical and traditional background and its religio-philosophical foundation. Vardhamana Mahavira propounded the religion in 599 BC. Centralization of power and riches in a few hands, gross negligence, and the suffering of the common man in the caste-based society, moved Mahavira as to how to get rid of it. At the age of thirty he left the household and went in for all sorts of austerity and meditation. After twelve years Mahavira became a *Jina*, the twenty-fourth Tirthankara. He began preaching, and continued for thirty years. Before he passed away at the age of seventy-two in 527 BC he organized his followers into two main Samghas: *Sramana-Samgha* for monks and nuns and *Upasaka* or *Sravaka-Samgha* for households. He left behind a strongly organized religious order popularly known today as Jainism.

The teachings of Mahavira were classified into twelve books, called *angas*; as was the practice, these sacred books were transmitted orally through generations.

Later the followers of Mahavira were divided into two groups, which came to be known as *Digambara* or sky clad, and *Svetambara* or white clad. At a later stage *Sthanakavasi* and *Terapanthi* sects came one after the other from *Svetambara*.

Jainism has made substantial contributions to the development of art. Its literature is rich and linguistically varied, preserving forms of language nowhere else preserved. Its followers have developed its doctrinal basis and its effects in religion, philosophy, art, culture and the social order. Jaina philosophy of education is based on the religio-philosophical concepts of Jainism, i.e. reality is uncreated and eternal, the universe is without beginning and without end, consisting of soul, and non-soul, each soul possessing an infinite capacity of knowledge as its intrinsic nature. It is enmeshed in matter and subject to karma: but it can be separated by the efforts of the soul to manifest its true nature. Thus the aim of education in Jainism is to impart knowledge of the fundamental concepts and a way of life for the gradual development of personality, individually and socially up to the highest stage of a *Jina*, or in the religious term to attain *Moksa* or *Nirvana*.

The concept of a Jina is the concept of the best teacher. He is an *apta-purusa*, a fully enlightened person having manifested his true nature. He alone can speak the truth.

The doctrinal basis of Jainism comprises highly developed metaphysics, epistemology and ethics. It is a metaphysical realism, a philosophical non-absolutism, an ethical puritanism and a psychological rationalism. According to Jaina philosophy, the universe is uncreated and eternal. It consists of two fundamental substances or realities, namely, *cetana* and *acetana* or *jiva* and *ajiva* or living and non-living. The living being is described as *atman, jiva* or soul or, in modern terminology, consciousness. Jainism holds that all living beings, from the smallest creature to human beings, have their inherent power of the soul crippled by association with Karmic matter as a result of which they are undergoing births and deaths and various other experiences. The smallest living being can develop itself up to the stage of human being, and reach up to the highest stage of a perfect personality like *Jina*. Thus the progress of a human being is based on the theory of gradual development, psychic and physical, or evolution of personality. The living and non-living (in the form of Karmic matter), by coming into contact with each other, forge certain energies which bring about birth, death and various experiences of life. This process could be stopped and the energies already forged destroyed by a course of discipline. There is no need of an almighty God who creates the world. Such a creator cannot be established logically and, if accepted, the importance of an individual and his efforts to progress are devalued and affected.

Matter or *pudgala* includes everything that is perceptible by the senses. Matter constitutes the physical basis of the universe even as the reality, *jiva* or soul, constitutes the psychical. The elements of nature-earth, water, fire, air, are all gross manifestations of matter. These living and non-living substances keep the world in existence from the beginningless to the endless period. *Jnana* or knowledge is an intrinsic property of the *atma* or soul. Every soul possesses an infinite capacity of knowing. Hence the process of knowing is the process of the manifestation by the soul of its intrinsic nature. This intrinsic nature of a living being is shrouded by matter in which Karma operates. Therefore the process of knowledge differs according to the stages of development. Thus the theory of knowledge is based upon the metaphysical postulate that knowledge is the intrinsic property of the soul. The senses and mind of a living being, up to a certain stage, serve as means or instruments of knowledge. In the case of the soul, it is both the subject and the object of knowledge at the same time. Knowledge therefore, is like a lamp which on account of its luminosity reveals other objects as well as itself. It does not come from outside. It is all the time in the soul itself, waiting to be released or manifested. Knowledge derived from the observation of nature through the senses is the first requirement. Next, step by step, come knowledge of the scriptures or of other people's experiences, of objects remote in time and space, of other minds, and lastly, perfect knowledge of everything. This staged development of knowledge has the following technical terms: *mati, sruta, avadhi, manah-paryaya, kevala*. Of these five types, the first two are possible to any human being, the next two to the sages, and the last to a perfect being only. Human knowledge is always relative. To know is to relate. Therefore our knowledge is essentially relative and limited in many ways. Our thought is relative. The total reality in its completeness cannot be grasped by partial thought. The same is the case with our speech. What we say is also relative and conditioned. No saying can be claimed as absolute. This theory of the relativity of knowledge or non-absolutism is technically called the Theory of *Anekanta*.

Jaina ethical concepts form a very important part of religious education. The ultimate aim of religious education can be achieved only through the practice of these concepts in life. In a single word, the ethical principle of Jaina religious education may be defined as *ahimsa*, and its practice is the *moskamarga* or the path towards the ultimate aim of education. The path is called *ratnatray-amarga*, the three jewels: right faith, right knowledge and right conduct. These three together constitute the path. Jainism does not admit any one of these three in isolation as the path. Of course right faith is the foundation of the latter two, faith without superstitious and wrong belief. Right conduct prescribes the code of conduct for householders as well as for monks and nuns – the religious leaders and preachers. It is technically known as *anuvrates*, small vows for householder, and *mahavratas*, great or full vows for monks and nuns.

The concept of *ahimsa* is based on the philosophical postulates that all living beings are equal, can develop to the highest stage, and deserve to co-exist and progress in society. *Anekanta*, or the concept of non-absolutism, implies intellectual non-violence. It emphasizes a catholic outlook towards all that we see and experience. The concept of *ahimsa* refers to an internal condition whereas its practice is external; both together depict the psychic and physical development of the personality. These religio-philosophical concepts form the philosophy of religious education in Jainism.

The believers in Jainism in present day society have come to form a well-organized community. As already stated above, there are two main sects, namely, *digambara* and *svetambara*, the latter having two sub-sects, *sthanakavasi* and *terapanthi*. These sects and sub-sects have further sub-divisions. These divisions and sub-divisions, though agreeing in philosophical concepts, differ in ethical practices. Regional and cultural influences are also to be observed in the performance of religious activities.

Monks and nuns, as well as professional teachers, give religious education in the manner of their own sect, sub-sect and regional organization. But it is highly important that despite having all such special traits and differences, the followers of Jainism constantly and firmly follow the concepts of their religion, and never compromise if the principle of *ahimsa* is violated in religious practices and performances.

Details of the curriculum prescribed for religious education are well depicted in the scriptures. That curriculum was followed in ancient times: in the present day community it is not. At present the curriculum generally includes: 1. traditional history; 2. the concept of the universe as depicted in the scriptures; 3. the metaphysical and epistemological doctrines; and 4. the code of conduct for monks, nuns and householders, in theory and practice. Besides the original scriptures in the ancient languages, books based on the scriptures written in modern Indian languages form a part of the curriculum. Methods of religious education are defined and depicted in the scriptures. These methods are utilized to explain the nature or the concepts of soul and non-soul etc., as described in the Jaina scriptures. Nowadays, the definitions of most of the methods are taught but not utilized. Efforts are made to keep the candle lit, yet the present day education system has influenced religious education in its all spheres. Consequently today wider means are in use in the Jaina community. For example, 1. the monks and nuns employ the mass media, with or without the use of the book at the time of imparting education as their ancestors did. 2. Regular classes are held in school and major religious institutions, where professional teachers teach the prescribed course of study. 3. For different classes according to their stage, examinations are held, and degrees and diplomas are awarded. 4. Jainism also has been included in university education and forms a part of the curriculum of classical language, linguistics, philosophy, comparative religions, ancient Indian history, culture and education, Indian art, architecture and

epigraphy, besides interdisciplinary resarches in various branches of humanities and social sciences.

The medium of Jaina religious education still continues to be the regional languages for mass education, and education in religious institutions and schools. The medium differs in the universities according to their rules. Thus religious education within the Jaina community forms an important part of the life of the believers.

To sum up, the Jaina philosophy of education embodies in itself the importance of an individual giving equal opportunity to self development, living together and helping each other, knowing one's infinite capacity, and considering one's limitations, psychic and physical, to make for tolerance, so as to develop a perfect human being. Those who sincerely believe in Jainism strive to preach and practise for the welfare of themselves and of the society in which they live.

G. C. JAIN

Japan *see* Asia

Jehovah's Witnesses

1. Education policy

(a) Public education generally. Jehovah's Witnesses view education as a means to become better Christian servants of the Creator, Jehovah God. The Bible is the foundation for their way of life and establishes for them guidelines on education. The version generally used is the *New World Translation of the Holy Scriptures,* published by the Watch Tower Society.

In countries where the need arises, literacy classes are conducted under the care of their congregations. This programme of education is always free and undertaken voluntarily by local Witnesses. *Learn to Read and Write* is the teaching aid specially prepared by the Watch Tower Society for this purpose.

Jehovah's Witnesses work along with education authorities, helping and encouraging their children to make the most of their school years and to study well the subjects of their choice. Parents maintain an active, personal interest in the education of their children. Especially is this so with regard to all aspects of morality. For example, the subject of sex education is not left solely for discussion in school but is incorporated in scriptural discussions at home too.

Jehovah's Witnesses recognize the value of physical education, but accept the scriptural advice that 'bodily training is beneficial for a little' (1 Tim. 4.8) and so do not make it a primary goal. They believe that the scriptures also give sound counsel on some aspects of higher education, warning about the dangers of 'philosophy and empty deception according to the tradition of men' (Col. 2.8). Such 'wisdom of this world is foolishness with God' and for this reason Jehovah's Witnesses are careful to study traditions objectively (I Cor. 3.19; Titus 3.9). In doing this, they know they will safeguard their own spiritual well-being and that of their children (I Tim. 6.20, 21).

(b) *Religious education*. Jehovah's Witnesses look to the Bible as their sole authority in all matters of worship (II Tim. 3.16, 17). Teaching the faith to their children is a responsibility they take very seriously. They bear in mind the charge given to Hebrew parents to inculcate the law of Jehovah in their children. The education of the young boy Samuel and of Jesus himself as a child, provide a guide, just as the teaching of the scriptures to Timothy 'from infancy' by his mother and grandmother later set the pattern for Christian parents (Deut. 6.7; I Sam. 2.18, 19, 26; Luke 2.46–52; II Tim. 1.5; 3.14, 15).

The apostle Paul describes the different offices in the Christian congregation to be filled by mature overseers, also termed elders. These appointed elders exercise great care to ensure that their teachings are accurate and always in harmony with the scriptures (I Tim. 4.16; II Peter 1.20,21). As teachers their purpose is to instruct the members of the Christian congregation (I Tim. 3.1, 2). This arrangement enables all associated with Jehovah's Witnesses to share in making 'disciples of people of all the nations', in turn 'teaching them to observe all the things' Jesus commanded (Matt. 28.19, 20).

2. Church Membership Preparation Course
Although everybody is freely invited to attend meetings at local Kingdom Halls to receive instruction and enjoy Christian fellowship, there are certain steps to be taken before anyone can be officially recognized by the congregation as one of Jehovah's Witnesses. Accordingly, enquirers, who come from all walks of life and backgrounds, religious and otherwise, are given a preparatory study of the fundamentals of the faith (see next section for details). To worship and serve Jehovah God, each individual needs to repent of his former wrongdoings and embrace the Christian way of life, leading to his dedication to Jehovah, through Christ Jesus. This private, prayerful dedication is later publicly symbolized by water baptism (Acts 2.37–42).

Prior to baptism the elders of the congregation will spend many hours with each candidate, talking over basic questions of Christian conduct and doctrine. All are encouraged to express in their own words what their faith means to them, to show that they appreciate fully the significance of the step they are taking. It follows that babies and young children are not baptized by Jehovah's Witnesses.

3. Church Education Course for Enquirers and for Faithful Adults and Children
During 1983, close to 1,800,000 Bible studies were conducted by Jehovah's Witnesses in homes around the world. It is usual for these discussions to be held once a week for an hour or so with family groups or individuals. As a result of this specialized service, freely provided, 161,896 adults were baptized during the course of the year.

The book that has made history as a Bible study aid is *The Truth That Leads to Eternal Life*. For fourteen years it has been a main textbook used for Bible study by Jehovah's Witnesses. The *New World Translation of the Holy Scriptures*, translated by Jehovah's Witnesses directly from the Hebrew and Greek, appears now in eleven languages.

The regular weekly meetings of the congregations are attended by people of all ages. At one of these the Bible is studied with the aid of selected themes featured in *The Watchtower*.

The congregations are taken through a progressive analysis of the Bible books and facts relating to them by means of a school, in which all are invited to enrol. Practical training is also given in public Bible reading and speaking, and in witnessing to others. Children and teenagers have special literature to meet their needs in developing faith in the Bible and to help them build up moral strength. Parents are encouraged to use these Bible aids which are also featured at the meetings.

For all overseers, including those elders who travel and visit the congregations under the direction of the Governing Body of Jehovah's Witnesses, special refresher courses are arranged from time to time.

National (and sometimes international) conventions are held each year as well as bi-annual local assemblies. By means of these counsel from the Bible is imparted. As with all meetings of Jehovah's Witnesses, there is never any charge for admission and no collections are taken.

DAVID SIBREY, JEHOVAH'S
WITNESSES INFORMATION OFFICE

Jerusalem   see Sacred Places

Jesus Christ of Latter-day Saints, Church of   see Church of Jesus Christ of Latter-day Saints, The   ('Mormons')

Jesus

1. Evidence for Life of

The earliest literary evidence for the life of Jesus is found in the letters of Paul. We find references to the birth of Jesus in Gal. 4.4, his Davidic descent in Rom. 1.3, his death and resurrection in I Cor. 15.3ff. (and throughout the epistles), and to the Last Supper in I Cor. 11.23ff. It is characteristic of these references that they are used in the course of theological statements. The same is true, though this is perhaps less immediately obvious, in the case of the canonical Gospels, which are our primary source of evidence. None of these documents is intended to be a biography; they are all presentations of the gospel *about* Jesus. This does not necessarily mean that the traditions about Jesus used by the authors are historically unreliable: it does mean that they have been chosen and used to make particular theological points. Later Christian documents add nothing to our knowledge of Jesus. The material in the apocryphal Gospels is mostly legendary in character.

Evidence from non-Christian authors is almost non-existent. A reference in Josephus (*Antiquities* 18.64) turns out to be a Christian insertion. The Roman historian Tacitus (*Annals* 15.44) refers simply to the execution of 'Christ' by Pontius Pilate and to the 'super-stititon' which derived from him, and his followers are mentioned by Suetonius and Pliny. The Babylonian Talmud (written several centuries later) describes Jesus as a miracle-worker and sorcerer, and says that he was hung on the eve of Passover (Sanh. 43a). The paucity of references outside Christian documents is hardly surprising: there was no reason why non-Christians should have bothered to record his existence, or even been aware of it. The theory that Jesus never existed, which has been put forward from time to time, makes much of this silence but has no other foundation, except the similarity between belief in the resurrection of Jesus and the widespread belief in a dying and rising god found in many cults of the ancient world. It raises enormous problems, since it leaves unexplained why these myths should suddenly have been focussed on a figure called Jesus, who then became the centre of a series of 'historical' statements.

The Gospels devote the greatest space to the passion narrative, and although their accounts clearly reflect theological interpretation, they provide us with more information about the events leading up to the death of Jesus than about anything else: they are agreed that Jesus was put to death by the Romans on an accusation of being a messianic pretender, though the extent to which the Jewish authorities were involved is unclear. There is less agreement between the evangelists about the course of Jesus' ministry, though the Synoptics adopt a common plan. The belief that Mark inherited a summary of the ministry of Jesus, even if it is correct, provides only the most sketchy outline of events. The order in which material is arranged is probably due to the evangelists, and is likely to be thematic rather than chronological. The common notion that the ministry lasted three years is based on John's account, which records three Passovers: since John is clearly using the Jewish festivals to demonstrate the superiority of Christ to Judaism, we cannot assume that his plan reflects knowledge about the length of the ministry. Only Matthew and Luke record the birth of Jesus, and their stories conflict. Both accounts reflect the theological concerns of their authors, and are intended primarily as christological statements which uncover the hidden truths about Jesus, much as the Johannine Prologue supplies a theological exposition of the significance of the incarnation. Similar tensions are found in the Easter stories, again because the evangelists use different traditions about the empty tomb and the appearances of the risen Jesus to express their understanding of the meaning of the resurrection.

The material in the body of the Gospels is also used by the evangelists (as by others before them) for theological purposes. The extent to which stories were 'created' in the tradition, and the degree of historical reminiscence, are matters of debate, and there has been considerable discussion as to whether it is more scholarly to begin with a prior assumption of 'authenticity' or of 'creativity'. It is best to examine each story on its merits, but to remember that the whole is greater than the sum of its parts. Thus one can be far more confident in concluding that Jesus was a healer, than in establishing that he performed any particular miracle of healing, and in maintaining that he spoke and acted 'with authority' than in affirming the authenticity of any particular saying.

G. Bornkamm, *Jesus of Nazareth,* Hodder & Stoughton 1960; H. Conzelmann, *Jesus,* Fortress Press 1973; R. Dunkerley, *Beyond the Gospels,* Penguin 1957; E. Käsemann, 'The Problem of the Historical Jesus', in *Essays on New Testament Themes,* SCM Press 1964; H. K. McArthur, *In Search of the Historical Jesus,* SPCK 1970; A. Schweitzer, *The Quest of the Historical Jesus,* 1911, SCM Press 1981; H. Zahrnt, *The Historical Jesus,* Collins 1963.

MORNA D. HOOKER

2. Significance for Christians

Christian belief was centred on Jesus himself from the very beginning. The feature which distinguished the earliest Christians from their fellow Jews was their conviction that Jesus was God's anointed one or Messiah, who had been proclaimed as such by God himself in raising him from the dead. Since their experience was focussed on Jesus, it was expressed in terms of who Jesus was and what God had done through him.

The evidence of the Synoptics suggests that the teaching of Jesus himself was not centred on his own person, but was concerned primarily with the kingdom of God, and with men's response to God's offers and demands. The all-important shift of perspective took place with the resurrection: Jesus was seen as the one through whom God had been at work, and through whom salvation was offered to God's people. The gospel was now understood as the gospel about Jesus, not simply that proclaimed by him: Christian faith was faith in him, and Christian discipleship meant commitment to Jesus as Lord. This is demonstrated in our earliest documents, the Pauline epistles.

The NT authors express their understanding of the significance of Jesus in a variety of ways. The so-called messianic titles were an obvious way of expressing their belief. 'Jesus is the Messiah' (or Christ) was probably the earliest Christian creed, soon to be followed by 'Jesus is Lord'. These titles, together with others commonly used of Jesus ('Son of God', 'the Son of man'), were probably far less 'ready-made' and fixed in meaning in pre-Christian Judaism than we tend to assume. NT writers also used a variety of images: in particular, OT passages were plundered in order to demonstrate that Jesus was the fulfilment of all man's hopes and all God's promises. The 'I am' sayings in the Fourth Gospel demonstrate one way in which this could be done. These sayings also demonstrate the differences in method between the Synoptics and the Fourth Gospel. In the former, the christological claims of Jesus are implicit rather than explicit: the material is arranged in such a way as to challenge the reader to respond not only in the teaching of Jesus but to Jesus himself. In the latter, the 'claims' of Jesus are spelt out. For all the evangelists, however, the tradition of Jesus' teaching becomes primarily christological material. Jesus is seen as the embodiment of God's kingdom: he is for them not so much the prophet who summons men to repentence as the king who demands their allegiance.

Another way in which the evangelists expressed the significance of Jesus was in telling stories about his activities. The miracle stories were used not simply because they were part of the tradition, but because they present, in dramatic form, the conviction that God was at work in Jesus in a unique way. Stories describing his power to heal and to control demonic forces, to give life and to supply every need, are christological statements about Jesus and his significance for Christian believers.

It is precisely because Jesus was of central importance for Christian faith from the beginning that 'history' and interpretation are inextricably bound together. The attempt to disentangle a 'Jesus of history' from the 'Christ of faith' failed because all the material reflects the beliefs of those for whom Jesus was the Christ.

J. D. G. Dunn, *Christology in the Making,* SCM Press 1980; C. F. D. Moule, *The Origin of Christology,* Cambridge University Press 1977; E. Schweizer, *Jesus,* SCM Press 1971.

MORNA D. HOOKER

3. *Place of in World Faiths*
Interesting insights are gained when a focal figure in any one religious tradition is seen throught the eyes of other traditions. A good example is the case of Jesus Christ. Jesus, like Gotama or Muhammad, can be regarded and presented as a figure belonging to the whole religious experience of mankind and not just as the focus of one particular religion. All the world's other living religions have concepts and language available which provide a bridge across to the central figure of Christianity and in some non-Christian traditions the figure of Jesus is itself present.

Jesus's own religion was Judaism. This was his background and it can be strongly argued that his own religious practices throughout his historical life were determined by Jewish tradition, albeit invested by him with new meaning. In Islam* Jesus holds a position of reverence and significance second only to that of the Prophet Muhammad. He is mentioned many times in the Qur'ān* and it is indicative of his status in Muslim consciousness that a likeness of Jesus is said to have been crucified, and not Jesus himself. Jesus is particularly significant for Sufis, as is shown by al-Ghazali's dictum, 'Take Jesus as your pattern'. The Karmic religions of India and the Far East all have their notions of a periodic incarnation or series of incarnations in whom the ultimate truth or reality is seen as totall present for the purpose of enlightening or saving mankind. Thus, when teaching about Jesus in Judaism*, Islam*, Hinduism*, Buddhism* and traditions related to these, one can take the headings: Jesus as Prophet; Jesus as Avatar; Jesus as Bodhisattva; Jesus as Guru. Such headings

have the double advantage in a Christian context of both explaining the non-Christian concept by applying it to the familiar figure of Jesus and also of providing different cultural terms for expressing the mystery of Christ.

At a more advanced level the different possible ways of relating Jesus to non-Christian faiths can be analysed as follows and illustrated:

1. *Conservative.* This view claims that only the Christian revelation is true and that to describe Christ in terms of other religions can only be misleading.

2. *Neo-Confessional.* This view accepts the uniqueness of the Christian gospel as the *explicit* revelation of Christ, but believes that, if Christ is really universal and if other religions are really sincere, then the latter are bound to find Christ in some sense and to reveal his nature *implicitly*.

3. *Relativistic.* According to this view the different beliefs and focusses of the various religions are historically and culturally conditioned, and when allowance is made for differences of background and context a figure in one tradition can be compared with a figure in another to their mutual enrichment.

4. *Syncretistic.* This view holds that all religions are ultimately and in substance the same and that equivalent figures and concepts are readily transferable from one to another.

J. N. D. Anderson, *Christianity and Comparative Religion,* Tyndale Press 1970; Charles Davis, *Christ and the World Religions,* Hodder & Stoughton 1970; Raymond Pannikar, *The Unknown Christ of Hinduism,* Darton, Longman & Todd 1964; Geoffrey Parrinder, *Avatar and Incarnation,* Faber 1970; and *Jesus in the Qur'an,* Faber 1965; Geza Vermes, *Jesus the Jew,* 1973, SCM Press 1983.

DAVID MINTON

4. *Teaching About in RE*
The life and teaching of Jesus was the most important element in all the agreed syllabuses* which followed the 1944 Education Act. When the biblical element was reduced in the experience-based religious education of the sixties, children in the primary school were likely to encounter the stories about Jesus mainly in the context of themes such as

'Hands' or 'Journeys', although in the early years of the secondary school the Gospel material was often still tackled systematically and CSE and GCE 'O' level syllabuses retained their compulsory section on *The Life and Teaching of Christ*.

Two developments have been responsible for a changed approach to teaching about Jesus:

1. The recognition that nurturing children in the Christian faith is a task for the Christian community and that it is not appropriate for the school to be teaching that Jesus is the Son of God. However, if the school's aim is to help pupils to understand the nature of religion, then part of learning about the Christian religion is coming to understand the significance of Jesus for Christians. This involves learning what he means to Christians today as well as learning about the events recorded in the Gospels.

Any attempt to understand christology obviously belongs in the upper years of the secondary school, but an awareness of the centrality of Jesus in the Christian faith can be gained by younger children through their study of the local church, religious symbols, the ways in which Christians celebrate Christmas and Easter, etc.

When pupils study Islam* they will of course discover the important but very different place which Jesus has in that religion.

2. A realization of the gap between what pupils learn in school and the work of biblical scholars and theologians. Two examples: (a) Pupils' understanding of the Christian scriptures requires a knowledge of the Gospels as faith documents and of the aims of the individual evangelists. Any approach which treats the Gospels as biographies of Jesus, or which presents as the only picture of Jesus one drawn indiscriminately from all the gospels makes such understanding difficult if not impossible. (b) There is a wealth of factual knowledge about the first century and particularly about Judaism* which must not be ignored if pupils are to be given an accurate picture of the religious developments of the period. Through a study of the life of a Jewish child of the time, primary school children can be helped to see Jesus in his Jewish setting. A study of the Pharisees, using Jewish writings of the period, can help their pupils to see not only how close Jesus' teaching was to that of

the Pharisees, but that what eventually caused Christianity to break away from its parent religion was not so much what Jesus taught as what was believed about who he was and the significance of his death and resurrection.

JEAN HOLM

Joint Education Policy Committee

This Committee was formed in 1959 by the Church of England and the Free Church Federal Council* as a forum for resolving questions between denominations arising out of the existence, proposed extension, or proposed closure of voluntary schools. The Minister of Education agreed to recognize it as the approved body to be consulted on these and certain others matters. In 1971 it was extended to include Roman Catholic representation and became known as 'the joint three'. Over the years its function has widened to cover, in a consultative and advisory capacity, any matters of concern to the churches in relation to education in England and Wales.

DOUGLAS A. BROWN

Jordan   see Middle East, Christian Education in the

Journals

1. Professional RE journals: the main journals usually originate from a particular association of people involved in or concerned with RE, and serve also as the organ of that association. Thus the *British Journal of Religious Education* is edited by John Hull and published by the Christian Education Movement.* It is issued termly and contains articles on the theory and practice of RE, resources for teaching, book reviews and correspondence. The CEM also publishes the CEM magazine of religion in education, *RE Today*, three times a year; it is edited by John Sutcliffe and contains articles on RE and the school curriculum, resources and news items.

Religious Education, the official journal (since 1981) of both the Religious Education Association and the Association of Professors and Researchers in RE in the USA, is edited by John H. Westerhoff, and contains articles on all aspects of religious and moral education* from both Jewish and 'main line' Christian educators; it also includes selected papers given at the APRRE annual meeting.

Associated with the above and intended to supplement and complement it in the area of research, is an occasional journal – *Character Potential* – designated as 'an arena for the sharing and publication of research reports in the field of RE'. It is published from Union College Character Project.

The Living Light, the official publication of the Department of Education of the US Catholic Conference, provides a forum for catechists and public educators, designed to present developments and trends, to report on research, and to contribute to decision making in the field of religious education and pastoral action. It is published by W. H. Sadlier.

The Journal of Christian Education, published three times a year by the Australian Teachers Christian Fellowship, shares the pattern of many non-British RE journals which tend not to draw a rigid line of demarcation between RE and Christian Education. This journal is edited by Professor Brian Hill. It includes articles on Religious Education and nurture*, as well as moral education; although it reflects for the most part the Australian scene, it is not limited to it.

The AREA Bulletin, edited by Kenneth Mullis, and published three times a year by the Association for RE until 1983, contains general articles on RE, classroom-related material, resource reviews and correspondence.

The Journal of Beliefs and Values, edited by W. S. Campbell, is the twice-yearly publication of the National Association of Teachers in Further and Higher Education. It contains general articles on RE and RS, reports of conferences and of research projects, as well as book reviews and news items.

Digest is published three times a year by the Association of Christian Teachers*. It contains occasional articles but concentrates mainly on reviewing resources for RE in schools and book reviews. *Spectrum*, a journal for Christians in Education, is also published three times a year by the above association. It contains general articles on all aspects of school, curriculum and community.

An exception to the above pattern is *Lumen Vitae*, an international quarterly review of RE. This journal concentrates on articles on religious education, catechetics and religious development.

Insight, edited by Douglas Charing, Jewish Education Bureau, is published three times a year and deals specifically with aspects of teaching Jewish tradition along with a general interest in resources for religious education.

Shap produces an annual calendar of religious festivals and has a mailing list for the circulation of articles on practical aspects of teaching world religions*, and reviews of resources, etc. This is organized by an editorial panel based at Bishop Otter College.

2. Publications on resources for RE: A number of bulletins and magazines concentrate or resources for religious education. *Resource* published termly by Warwick University Institute of Education contains topical articles on resources and curriculum, book reviews and news items. The RE Centres at Borough Road and Westhill colleges produce termly bulletins on all aspects of resources in RE. Several advisers and teachers centres produce their own bulletins. e.g. *The Avon Bulletin* or the *ILEA News and Views*. *AVA Magazine* reviews films, filmstrips, video and sound cassettes, books and records.

3. Other theological and religious studies journals: Some journals, though they do not normally deal directly with RE, are none the less of interest because they offer material which can be developed for use in the classroom. Occasionally they may offer articles on RE or discuss it in their correspondence. The bi-monthly *Scottish Journal of Theology*, published by the Scottish Academic Press, is a broadly based international and ecumenical journal of theology which also carries articles on biblical and applied theology. The monthly *Expository Times*, published by T. & T. Clark, and the bi-monthly *Theology*, published by SPCK, are similar in this respect. *Religious Studies*, published quarterly by Cambridge University Press may prove helpful on more philosophical issues.

4. Publications on moral education: *The Journal of Moral Education*, published three times a year by the Social Morality Council*, contains articles on all aspects of moral education and moral development. The Social Morality Council Moral Education Information and Resources Centre, St Martin's College, Lancaster, also publishes *Brown Paper* three times a year, with articles on

moral education, classroom approaches, and resources for moral education.

W. S. CAMPBELL

Judaism

1. Jewish Philosophies of Education

The source of the Jewish impetus towards education can be found in the earliest Jewish texts and the roots of Jewish law. In the Bible, Jews are commanded to teach Torah carefully to their children and Moses is commanded to ensure that the Torah is made available to the whole people at public readings.

The tradition was developed by the Pharisees, the expounders and teachers of the Rabbinic tradition at their pinnacle in Roman Judaea. Like the Sophists of fifth-century Athens, they have been severely maligned because the best known representation of them exists in texts inimical to them, but just one of their major contributions to the Judaeo-Christian world that we know was to insist that education was the possession of the people and that it was the responsibility and right of every individual to understand the source of knowledge.

The concept of Torah as embracing every aspect of human life led to the inclusion in the Talmud (the first and major exposition of Torah) of every field of human knowledge: science, medicine, astronomy, history and so on. The further study of this text throughout the Jewish communities of the world ensured that the Jewish community remained literate and bi- (if not tri-) lingual in a world of predominant illiteracy. In addition, since in Judaism there is little dogma, the propensity to argue and discuss has been highly developed over time and no statement stands without challenge and no student is expected simply to sit and accept.

Mainstream Judaism also did not suggest that there was any religious value in removing oneself from the practical day-to-day world and therefore there was always strong encouragement to know about movements in modern education, both for their own sake and the light that they could throw on the interpretation of Torah. Since it is not necessary for the orthodox Jew to be a fundamentalist in his approach to the text, there was a value in understanding new developments in world knowledge and to put them to use in Torah learning. Indeed, fundamentalist approaches

to Torah which reject the significance of the oral tradition of interpretation have been considered heresies of a sort by the mainstream Jewish community.

The age of enlightenment in the eighteenth century and the development of the secular Jew found the Jews already well disposed to knowledge and education. Even when they did not participate in religious education structures, Jews were well tuned to philosophical, legal and medical discussions and developments. Not surprisingly, they took their place in the forefront of many societies in these fields. Many of the crises of religious thought in the face of scientific developments were no problem to the mainstream of Jewish thinking (though there might have been problems for individual Jews) and indeed Jewish scientists were able, if they so desired, to trace back to earliest texts suggestions of some of the most recent discoveries.

Throughout the community today a great premium is still laid upon education, whether it is secular or religious. Much is made in the Talmud of the fact that education is the only portable wealth and that the mind is the only instrument with which one can fully comprehend Torah and help to develop a relationship with God. Therefore any cultivating of the mind has its value.

2. Jewish Religious Education

There are four main contexts in which Jewish religious education is carried out. All are available to both sexes but some will be operated on a single sex basis, particularly as the student grows older and the milieu grows more orthodox. First and most important is the home. It is difficult to divide the religious and social aspects of Judaism and therefore much of home life is influenced by Jewish religious practice – even in circumstances where the family might not call itself 'religious'. These customs and practices are transmitted through the normal process of family life. Values and standards are inculcated in an informal way across the generations, utilizing the extended family structure which is common within the Jewish community.

The second most widespread way is through religion schools (often called Hebrew classes and attached to particular synagogues) which meet on Sunday mornings and, often, weekday evenings as well. In these classes, on a more formal basis, Hebrew and liturgy are taught together with the laws of Judaism, its customs, the history of the Jewish people, the geography of Israel and all other aspects of the multi-faceted nature of Jewish identity.

There is however a strong consciousness that it is almost impossible to devote sufficient time in these part-time classes to all the matters which need to be covered. As a result there is a growing enthusiasm for the Jewish Day School movement, the seeds of which have excited since the arrival of the Jewish community in large numbers in Britain in the mid to late nineteenth century.

Jewish day schools account for a minority of Jewish children (perhaps about 25% in Britain) but are able to integrate Jewish education into the school day and allow the celebration and recognition of community and religious events through the course of the school year. An often overlooked value of a Jewish day school education for the Jewish child is that he is able to grow up feeling 'normal' instead of having to except himself constantly from even the most accommodating non-Jewish school structure.

The fourth means of religious education within the community is that of informal education through youth clubs and youth movements. Be it the celebration of festivals, discussion on matters of Jewish interest, the orientating of art and craft work towards Jewish matters, or the organizing of residential weekends and weeks away in order to enable young people to experience a full Jewish life, the Jewish community finds within its informal youth structure both a vanguard and a safety net for many young Jews who have not found their commitment within the more formal structures offered and have received little support from their homes.

A less widespread but slowly growing area is the development of adult education courses. In very traditional sections of the community adult education is a commonplace since study never stops.

The *yeshiva*, or college of higher Jewish study, is used like a college of further education. There will be evening and lunchtime classes, full-time courses for further study and intensive courses of study for the student who wants to devote his life to such work. A rabbi would normally spend several years in such a college in order to qualify. It is becoming increasingly popular for school-leavers to spend a few months or a year at yeshiva before going onto further secular study or work. Obviously, as with their secular counterparts in Britain, yeshivot reach only a minority of the community and cultivate differing reputations of excellence or style depending on the teachers who make up the faculty.

In the mainstream community there is an increasing consciousness that dislocations such as evacuation during the Second World War, the attempt to outflank antisemitism by a denial of Jewish identity and the rapidly changing mores in the wider society to which Jews are also subject, has led to the growth of a sizeable part of the adult community being too ill-informed to transmit values to their children through the home. All sectors of the community are now cultivating adult education programmes in an attempt to reverse this trend and re-establish the traditional framework where the majority of Jewish consciousness – if not information – could be transmitted from generation to generation within the home.

3. Teaching about Judaism in RE

This is a phenomenon as new as that of world religions* education. Many may think they were doing it before because they studied 'Old Testament' or learnt about the 'Holy Land'. These studies, although often argued as being acceptable to the Jew, were invariably viewing Judaism as the precursor of Christianity and rarely gave Judaism a status of its own in that time, let alone in the present. This is still reflected in the study of Hebrew in Christian circles in an accent wholly unknown in any Jewish community!

However, with the development of the teaching of world religions in schools, Judaism has taken its place in an overview of religious development in the world.

See also **Israel**.

Uriah Z. Engelman, *Jewish Education in Europe 1914–1962*, Institute of Contemporary Jewry, Hebrew University, Jerusalem 1965; Lloyd P. Gartner, *The Jewish Immigrant in England 1870–1914*, Simon Publications 1973; V.D. Lipman (ed.), *Three Centuries of Anglo-Jewish History*, Heffers Publications 1965; Derek Taylor (ed.), *Jewish Education 1981/*

1982, Jewish Education Development Trust 1982; 'Teaching Judaism', *British Journal of Religious Education,* Summer 1981; entry on 'Education', *Encyclopedia Judaica,* Keter Publications, 1975.

CLIVE A. LAWTON

Junior School, RE in

In 1978 a survey carried out by H M Inspectors of Schools in England and Wales noted that the classes of seven, nine and eleven year olds which they visited were provided with 'a religious education based on the Bible and on Christian beliefs and values'. The survey team concluded that 'in many schools the curriculum in religious education was somewhat restricted' and recommended that 'more might be done to make all children aware of other beliefs and to extend their understanding of the multi-cultural nature of contemporary society'.

The problems encountered by the Junior teacher in religious education are many and varied. They range from the levels of development, the mix of ability, and the difference in experience and background of the children, to the demands of the whole curriculum upon each class teacher. Since 1969 the Department of Education and Science* has advocated the provision in primary schools of teachers willing to act in an advisory capacity to their colleagues in this area of the curriculum, but it would appear that the response has been minimal. Recent curricular development has been rapid and demanding and it is hardly surprising therefore, that some teachers have reverted to narrowly based traditional approaches which appear to discount the development of a pluralist society, or that religious education has gone by default.

The statutory position of religious education and the system of agreed syllabuses* does however allow for teachers of all age ranges to receive advice and guidance, as does the network of advisory services provided by LEAS. DES centres and voluntary organizations such as CEM. Similarly the Schools Council* has sponsored a project on religious education in primary schools, with the aim of suggesting 'ways in which teachers can help children to understand religion'.

One of the influences on Junior religious education of recent years has been the formulation of stage-related aims in addition to

general aims for the school continuum. Stage-related aims are based on theories of child development and also on the conviction that continuity and coherence are necessary effectively to progress towards long-term educational goals. The child-centred movement* in RE, particularly in terms of a personal 'quest for meaning'*, has played a part in formulating such aims for pupils as: (*a*) to develop a sense of their own identity and worth; (*b*) to understand some features of human groups and communities; (*c*) to become aware of different forms of verbal communications; (*d*) to appreciate that symbols and artefacts can express human feelings and ideas; (*e*) to explore the natural world and various human responses to it; (*f*) to extend their awareness that people commit themselves to beliefs and causes.

The complexity of religion as well as its diversity is also acknowledged both in the formulation of aims and objectives and in suggestions for schemes of work suitable for implementation in the Junior classroom. Thus alongside 'human experience themes' Jean Holm advocates teaching units on e.g. Creation Myths, Sacred Places*, and specifically biblical themes. The terms 'implicit'* and 'explicit'* religious education are often used to refer to the two inter-connected strands which are said to contribute to the religious education of young children in particular. The danger of claiming too much for the 'implicit' approach was highlighted as long ago as 1971. If 'religion is in everything we do', then how is religious education distinct from education in general?

On the other hand, the nature of religion is such that an overall study of a world religion would seem to be unrealistic in the Junior years. Again, thematic approaches have been advocated and widely used.

Nevertheless, there are pitfalls for the unwary. The danger of syncretism, of playing down the differences between religions, has been pointed out elsewhere. For Junior children there is also the danger of conceptual confusion. The approach depends upon a clear grasp of the elements to be compared. It has been argued elsewhere, 'To build a concept of "church", children need experience of *churches* – not mosques, synagogues and churches.' A thematic approach may cause confusion of categories, if it is not based on sound professional appraisal of the level of understanding, experience and language skills already achieved by the children and on an appropriate selection of material. There is much yet to be done in demonstrating clearly the hierarchical and structural nature of the subject matter in order that the Junior teacher may relate adequately child and content.

A degree of integration between subject areas by means of project or topic-based approaches is often to be found in Junior classrooms. Work on religion may be associated with history topics or topics on other countries, and connections between religious beliefs and moral values are explored in a variety of contexts, including the assembly*. An attempt to identify the contribution of religious education in integrated work was outlined by the Schools Council project on religious education in primary schools. Three variations in topic patterns were distinguished: 1. where religious education is incidental to a topic in which some other discipline is central; 2. where religious education is one of a number of contributing disciplines; 3. there religious education is the main discipline in a topic. A process model of planning is advocated involving the clear delineation of objectives leading to appropriate activities. 'It is necessary to provide learning experiences through which ideas can be explored, capacities developed and attitudes fostered.' It may be that working with objectives will provide a corrective to the difficulties associated with an integrated approach, namely, imbalance and lack of progression.

It is certainly the case that there is considerable consensus on the need for religious education in the Junior age-range to be concerned with the exploration of ideas and practices, the development of skills and capacities, and with the fostering of attitudes. These are particularly important for continuity of interest and of learning, but essential in their own right for children of the Junior school years.

Geva M. Blenkin and A. V. Kelly, *The Primary Curriculum*, Harper & Row 1981; Department of Education and Science, *Primary Education in England*, HMSO 1978; Hampshire Education Authority, *Paths to Understanding*, 1980; Jean Holm, *Teaching Religion in School*, Oxford University Press 1975; Schools Council, *Religious Education in Primary Schools: Discovering an Approach*, Macmillan Educational 1977.

GWEN PALMER

Knowledge

Distinctions are often made between types of knowing: e.g. knowing that and knowing how (Ryle); knowledge by acquaintance and knowledge by description (Russell). For the purposes of RE with the current interest in concepts, skills and attitudes, a new classification must be attempted.

1. *Propositional knowledge*. Factual knowledge which can be learnt, arranged on a syllabus and tested in examinations is central to any academic discipline. What was called Religious Knowledge was mainly learning about scripture, OT and Christian history and teachings. Church festivals could be added, but the Cowper-Temple clause*, by insisting that religious teaching be non-denominational, effectively cut RE off from any church, although the statutory act of school worship partly compensated. This division by timetable, however, has produced intolerable strains for RE.

When other world religions are added to the syllabus, the bogy of an authoritarian church mediating truths natural and revealed disappears, but the chronic search for facts about other faiths reduces the phenomenological* approach to knowledge by description, unless some direct participation can be organized.

2. *Knowledge by experience*. This is existential or first-hand knowledge and goes far deeper than finding out facts for onself. Experience is the basis of religion for many people, a sense of mystery, of wonder, or a presentiment which it is impossible fully to express. Hick calls it 'a sheer given reality'. But it is more than the formation of attitude. Because concepts fail, this field of knowledge is indicated indirectly in all faiths by expressive arts, poetry, myth, parable, analogy and negative language. Its centrality for faith prompted Ramsey's famous sentence, 'We can be sure in religion, but only tentative in theology.' Yet there is factual knowledge here too which emerges (if it does) but slowly and partially. Rudolf Otto gives us information about the numinous obliquely by studying the human consciousness of it. A powerful

religious experience breaks into the conceptual field and can be recalled, even re-enacted.

3. *Knowledge as recognition.* Insofar as recognition grows from experience, this is a development from both previous sections and relates especially to Ramsey's 'disclosure situations'. All religions stress seeing with fresh understanding (conversion), and seeing the wood and not just trees. Here is the doctrine of the heart, not merely the eye. While integral for all understanding, it is especially so for RE

4. *The ability to respond.* Skills and attitudes may be conscious or unconscious. Thus reverence shown to a holy person or sacred place may derive from learning, or it may be intuitive (i.e. as yet unaccountable). This is like being able to use and understand language in context yet unable to recall it on demand. Of course it can in part be analysed and conceptualized later, albeit losing some of its spontaneity. This practical knowledge is similar to the sense in which animals are said to know things untrained, and performance is the only guide.

—————

P. Donovan, *Interpreting Religious Experience,* Sheldon Press 1979; J. Hick, *The Centre of Christianity,* SCM Press 1977; M. Polanyi, *Tacit Dimension,* Routledge & Kegan Paul 1967; I. T. Ramsey, *Freedom and Immortality,* SCM Press 1971.

ROBIN MINNEY

Koran, The   *see Qur'ān, al-*

Lambeth Diploma

The Archbishop's Examination in Theology, designated by the letters STh (Student in Theology) and known generally as the Lambeth Diploma, was founded by Archbishop Randall Davidson in 1906 for women. Since 1947 men have been allowed to take it and now they outnumber the women. The Diploma can be taken either by written examination (in January each year) or by a thesis of 30,000 to 60,000 words, or by a combination of essays and written examinations. Successful candidates are personally presented with their Diplomas by the Archbishop of Canterbury in Lambeth Palace Chapel at a service held in April or May. New Testament Greek is a compulsory requirement and the examination is very much Bible-orientated. The Diploma

is of Honours Degree standard. It is organized by a Director and Secretary and a committee of scholars and is open to people of all denominations.

ALAN M. G. STEPHENSON

Language, Religious, and Use of Language in RE

Since most religions possess written traditions and express themselves in words, it is through language that we usually learn about them. Even their significant experiences and emotions may be explored and communicated to some extent verbally. First in importance, then, in teaching about the use of religious language is to show its wide range of possible functions. For instance, myths* and legends may portray other times and realms, parables* and allegories* offer examples and warnings, sermons and arguments persuade, law-books list rules and precepts, prayers and chants release spiritual powers, theologies and creeds formulate beliefs. To teach an awareness of this diversity is enriching in itself and is a valuable safeguard against over-simple views of what people are doing when they speak religiously.

Religious language is commonly *affective*, i.e. intended to arouse emotion, inspire action, or evoke certain kinds of experience or insight. Like poetry, it uses figurative words and phrases to help create the kinds of subjectivity (emotions, states of mind, imagery, etc.) which go with belief and behaviour of a personally involving, religious kind. Language used in religion also has many *performative* functions, achieving certain desired ends in ritual and ceremonial contexts. Examples are, consecrating marriages, absolving from sins, offering praise and worship, uttering blessings, praying prayers. The practitioner of a religion thus operates within an elaborate language-game, a network linking what is said in worship with beliefs and behaviour forming a comprehensive worldview and way of life.

Besides these functions, followers of religions generally consider their statements of belief to be *informative*, expressing truths about supernatural realities with profound significance for human life. A major debate has taken place in modern philosophy of religion* over the possibility of such 'metaphysical' assertions. The problem arises from the fact that statements about the objects of religious belief (gods, spiritual powers, supernatural realms) are typically made without general agreement existing as to ways of finally verifying their truth or demonstrating their falsity. If this is so, it is asked, what grounds are there for accepting them as factually, or 'cognitively', meaningful at all? (Such a critique of metaphysical statements was popularized in British philosophy by A. J. Ayer's *Language, Truth and Logic,* published in 1936, and has been developed by many writers since then.)

Defenders of the traditional view, in reply, have either questioned the so-called 'verificationist challenge' itself, or described ways in which religious claims can meet its demands through appeals to divine revelation or to possible verification by experiences in this or a future life. Others have suggested that the meaning of religious utterances lies less in their informativeness than in their evoking certain interpretative viewpoints, expressing profound commitments or, according to a logic of their own, fulfilling some other function peculiar to the following of a religious way of life.

Because it is closely related to broad questions about the rationality and plausibility of religion in a scientifically-educated age, the recent philosophical debate about religious language is one with which any teacher of religion would do well to be familiar.

___

M. J. Charlesworth, *The Problem of Religious Language,* Prentice-Hall, 1974; Peter Donovan, *Religious Language*, Sheldon Press 1976; John Macquarrie, *God-Talk,* SCM Press 1967; Basil Mitchell, (ed.), *The Philosophy of Religion,* Oxford University Press 1971.

PETER DONOVAN

Latin/Central America

Central America is a tropical, fertile and volcanic isthmus comprising the Republics of Belize, Costa Rica, El Salvador, Guatemala, Honduras, Nicaragua and Panama. The population of 24.5 millions includes many tribes and cultures, American, Afro-Indian and indigenous. Thirty per cent are illiterate. Eighty per cent are Catholics, eighteen per cent Evangelicals and the remaining two per cent are of other persuasions or are uncom-

mitted. The principal language is Spanish, in addition to which there are more than fifty native dialects, as well as English and to a lesser extent Asiatic languages.

Just under fifty per cent of Central America's economy is agricultural. The population is composed mostly of workers, artesans, poor country folk and students – all contributing to the enrichment of the region but impoverished and oppressed. Low export prices have caused growing dependence and underdevelopment. Basically this problem is one of chronic stagnation, however the process of transformation may be said to have begun, giving rise to revolution. The struggle of the poor to create a new life-style is based on the search for liberty, following their leader, Diriangen, and his Caribbean Indians, who refused to bow to what they regarded as slavery and colonization. Pilgrims of the resistance movement, they count on divine help.

The people are profoundly religious. Today in Latin America the social phenomenon of their religious sense is as much an object of study and discussion by sociologists, anthropologists and theologians as it is a source of ferment and inspiration for the people. Their religion is composed of prayer, vows, pilgrimages and devotions, fasts and worship, baptism, holy communion, novenas and Bible reading. Their cult centres around the Virgin Mary, Christ and his saints. They think of themselves as children of God and of Mary. God does not appear as a philosophical figure or as an expression to be associated with moral doctrines, nor as an idea. God is all-pervading, he sends rain which causes crops to germinate, he protects his people while they sleep. He is companion, brother, 'tayacan'.

Starting from the religion of the people, it is evident that they have a 'praxiological' concept of God, as had the peoples of the ot, a God guiding them to liberation, a God who puts words into the prophet's mouth, gives his people health and upholds them, exhorts and puts them sternly to the test when they are unfaithful to him. The Central American people, it may be claimed, listen to the Spirit and come by way of experience, to a more profound understanding of their relationship with God, their neighbour and the world. In their religious mind they know there are problems such as oppression, hunger, unemployment, disunity, falsehood and injustice, and that these have existed from all time, but they believe that God will help them to overcome these difficulties and that therefore they are not alone in shouldering these tasks.

The religion of the people has been the object of study from a variety of perspectives, social, regional, cultural, ideological. The sympathetic educator would say that when the people speak for themselves they become conscious of their situation and so can more easily voice their thoughts. So there is rebellion in El Salvador and Guatemala, the democracy of the rich is at a crossroads in Costa Rica, Belize is seeking its own identity, in Nicaragua there has been a revolution. Central America is facing an indigenous revolution.

The church provides for contextualized reading and reflection on the gospel. This is breaking up the traditional 'elitist' church structures and deepening the people's participation in biblical, pastoral and educational affairs. Basic Christian communities flourish, creating their own methods of Christian education, their own hymns, liturgy and theology. From these communities spring evangelizing ministries which teach the way in which the Bible should be read; priests, pastors, theologians and Christian education teachers are nourished by their experience of contemporary, social realities, church utterances and theological and gospel documents.

In central America the people feel themselves to be living amidst oppression, suffering and hope. The church, counting itself born of the people and the Spirit, serves and evangelizes. It also contributes to unification and ferment in popular movements.

For Latin American Christians, education is cultural action for freedom. Paulo Freire, a distinguished Latin-American teacher, says that all education should start from a study of people and a series analysis of the true situation of the people looking to educate themselves. If this study of people is absent, there is the great danger of reducing them to being mere 'objects'. The human vocation is to be a subject of history, not an object. As a human being reflects on the human situation, he becomes more disposed to shoulder and transform the reality under which he lives. The education of the people is a priority in the movement towards political and social freedom for all. Carrying it out has contri-

buted to the conscientization of organized movements aiming at brotherhood, love, justice and hope. As a result, people are learning to 'speak up' and have gained the ability to free themselves from oppression and exploitation. The expression 'new man' is part of the vocabulary of the people and the words 'darkness', 'light', 'dawn', words common in the Bible, are used by the people in their 'living' education.

From this point of view education is not 'neutral'. It either frees or alienates. It demands new and efficient educational procedures and presupposes a change in the methods of those who plan and produce programmes of Christian education, which are seen as being required to make an important contribution to the development of a critical sense, and responsible participation in every sphere. It is a process aimed at contributing to the development of faculties and attitudes through realizing social and community ends.

The two methods most used in Latin America are, on the one hand the systematic syllabus, institutional, confessional and conservative, studying domestic theology in cycles, and emphasizing learning dates and the acquisition of information. This is vertical and inflexible in the face of daily reality. It dominates most educational institutions.

On the other hand, there is education based on relationships between word and context. The syllabus is formulated and re-elaborated on the foundations of social and ecclesiastical reality – dynamic, dialogical, dialectical, allowing for participation. The programme is not looked upon as static but as progressing according to developments in church life and historical contingencies. Christian education is centred on the kingdom of God, not only on a theoretical and moralistic plane, but concretely in daily events. It is the new confronting the old, and implies and demands radical choices. This is why it is called a 'theology of praxis'.

Traditionally there has been preoccupation with conversion, evangelization, increase in membership of congregations, but very little preoccupation with education. Christian education has remained on the periphery of the church's magisterium. For this reason, there is need not only for a new methodology and curriculum but also a new conception of Christian education as one of the ministries through which the gospel is shared, reflected upon and proclaimed. It has been said on many occasions that Christian education should be at the service of the masses, that it should be democratic and popular. It should cease to be a myth for the majority of believers. The people are characterized by global vision; for them there is no dichotomy between faith and daily life. Their wisdom lies in inter-relating the real world with their faith.

Recently students from rural areas at a Bible course in the Matalgalpa mountains related most appositely their biblical knowledge and theology with work on the land, the harvest, and family and community life. They did not deny their faith, their theology, or their humanity.

Ernesto Cardenal founded a kind of lay monastry, a community of country folk and fishermen, in a remote archipelago at the western end of Lake Nicaragua. There, instead of a Sunday sermon, the gospel is read followed by dialogue and discussion on a gospel passage. The reflections of the country-folk and fishermen are often more profound than those of many theologians and are evangelical in their simplicity.

Thus Christian education in Central America, as well as being Bible-based and popular, which is essential, must continue to be experiential, contextual and autochthonic. This requires experimentation and the search for, and development of, appopriate methods which will be effective and liberating. The people's search for a more effective and liberating Christian education must be based on critical and gospel-based reflection, on their faith and on their own situation.

BENJAMÍN CORTÉS

Latin/South America

Background. Latin America is a vast territory extending from Mexico in the north to the Argentine Republic in the south. Its autochthons have created important civilizations: Aztec (Mexico), Mayan (Mexico and Central America) and Incan (Peru). These peoples and others less numerous and weaker, endured the sweeping advance of the Spanish conquerors and colonizers whose domination in politics, economy and culture was all-pervading.

Several centuries of Spanish and Portuguese government gave place to the emancipation of America (fifteenth century). During this period of intense struggle, the liberation achieved was political only. The continent knew a new form of oppression: economical and cultural. The colonized peoples were transformed into 'Independent' nations, owning their own land and its natural and human richness. British imperialism in the previous century and North American in this, have conditioned the Latin-American life style, which has not yet acquired its own identity.

Within this general framework religious education has played a determining role.

During the Luso-Spanish domination, the conquistadors opened the way with arms while the priests who accompanied them imposed the (Roman) Catholic faith. There were a few exceptions such as Fr Bartolomé de las Casas who struggled to obtain recognition of the Indians as human beings to be respected.

Generally speaking the autochthons were obliged to abandon their traditions, culture and original beliefs. Nevertheless, their symbols and liturgy remain latent in Latin-American Christianity giving rise to a phenomenon of creative and original popular religion. In the countries with an African imigration, black culture was added to existing influences.

On the other hand, during the nineteenth century Protestant missionaries arrived in Latin America. This new faith accompanied a cultural and economic invasion from England and the United States. By means of extensive evangelical campaigns among the middle and lower classes they succeeded in creating an active minority which confronted the Catholic Church. Schools, hospitals, social security centres, reinforced the liberal tendency, masking the political omissions of the Protestants and Evangelicals and succeeding in confirming the Anglo-Saxon influence. Those known as 'Protestant' were national groups (Anglican, Presbyterian, German): others were called 'missionary churches' (Lutheran, Methodist, Disciples of Christ); fundamentalist groups were known as 'Evangelical' (Baptist, Free Brothers, Nazarenes, etc.).

Religious education thus became a political instrument whose agents, Catholic priests and Protestant missionaries, were seldom conscious of their role.

South American Christians feel deeply that God's action in history is never thwarted by human influences. The action of the Holy Spirit continually transforms the practice of the churches and supports the Latin-American people in their struggle for liberation. There are many Christians who in working for 'preferential rights for the poor and oppressed', according to Puebla, are giving their energy and lives for their less fortunate brothers. In the Catholic sphere have arisen the proposals of Medellin (1968) and Puebla (1980) which affirm what is currently called 'liberation theology'. For twenty years in the Protestant sphere CELADEC (the Latin-American Evangelical Commission for Christian Education) has created and fostered the practice of 'popular education' and 'popular communication' from a Christian perspective.

Ecumenical action (Catholic-Protestant joined with other popular organizations) today constitutes a concrete alternative to religious education which presents alienist forms in the continent (religion as 'the refuge for the masses').

Basic Principles. Latin America is a region which calls itself 'Western and Christian'. The strong indigenous influence is no obstacle to the fact that the best and worst of the classical and Judaeo-Christian traditions are found in Latin-American culture. Thus it is that the general education which children and adolescents receive is impregnated with the tradition and values emanating from Europe and the United States.

The challenge to religious educators is now that of how to teach Christianity living in a world of deteriorating values.

From the theological point of view, religious education is orientated into different channels. Among Roman Catholics there are traditionalist groups, neo-Thomist and others, deeply involved in the theology of liberation. Among Protestants there are liberal groups and groups which are also orientated towards the theology of liberation. Furthermore there are many Evangelical groups with a fundamentalist theology. These various groups face the psychopedagogical problem: 'How do we teach the faith?'

The majority understand faith as a gift from God; education can tackle the task of deepening it. This affirmation raises the difficult problem of deciding when and where to begin. To this question there are various responses but one type of action: children of Christian parents receive a religious formation from an early age.

Objectives. In Latin America the objectives of religious education are varied and depend on the ultimate ends proposed by the different groups. In the Catholic and Protestant churches there are sectors seeking to give the faithful a deeply Christian formation in the faith, while others incorporate the task of conscientization in terms of the Latin-American reality. In this case, religious education in church, community and school is forever meeting the challenge of the Gospels and the obligation to the weak and oppressed.

On the other hand, religious educators in the Evangelical churches set themselves a task in which deepening of faith and concrete obligations do not appear. The world is a perilous place to which believers belong and accept only if their objective is to convert others.

Teaching related to participation in the liturgy and seeking to arouse devotion is an explicit objective in the Roman Catholic Church. Religious education in Jewish communities (very numerous in Argentina but less so elsewhere) seeks to conserve a cultural tradition.

Strategy. Religious education in Latin America is directed to various types of students and takes place within various frameworks. In terms of age, while the Roman Catholic Church works basically with children, the Protestant and Evangelical Churches usually deal with all ages. That is why non-Catholic Christians know the fundamentals of their faith well and can polemize from a minority position with Catholics, the apathetic and atheists. Jewish religious education is directed to children and adolescents.

In terms of social standing, Catholic religious education is directed to all the social classes, whilst Protestants work almost entirely with the middle and lower classes. Jews work in closed, mainly middle-class, groups.

Religious education is based in the churches and in confessional schools. In the Catholic Church practising Catholics send their children to Catholic schools where they receive a general and religious education. Nominal Catholics usually send their children to

Catechism classes up to their first Holy Communion. These classes are held in church. In Protestant and Evangelical churches religious education takes place in church at Sunday Schools or in Bible classes.

Basic communities and other informal groups constitute a new option for religious education in which children and adults read a passage from the Bible which is then related to everyday reality. These groups are found as much in Catholic as Protestant churches.

Mass media is little used in religious education. There are a few programmes from time to time, mostly for those of a markedly evangelical tradition. Some of the programmes of the so-called 'electronic church' reach the northern areas and to a lesser extent, the southern. Radio and television programmes more relevant to Latin America are just beginning.

The methods used in religious education are generally very traditional, but material now exists which permits students to take an active part in the learning process. The teachers are both priests and lay people. There are no mainstream educational courses offering specific qualifications for this work. Throughout the continent there are short courses but these are far from adequate.

There are good catechetical publications for Catholics and Protestants and there have been various attempts to produce material for use throughout the region. These have come up against the problem of diversity of cultures. There is a preponderance of Spanish material for Catholics and North-American material for Protestants. In Portuguese-speaking Brazil materials are in, or adapted from, Portuguese.

Ruben Alves, *et al.*, *De la Iglesia y la Sociedad*, Ed. Tierra Nueva, Montevideo, Uruguay 1971; Christian Lalive d'Epinay, *El refugio de las masas*, Santiago de Editorial del Pacifico, Chile 1968; Waldo Villelpando (ed.), *Las iglesias del transplante*, Buenos Aires Argentina CEC, 1970; II Conferencia del Episcopal Latinoamericano, *Documentos finales*, Ediciones Paulinas, Buenos Aires, 1969; III Conferencia del Episcopal Latinoamericano, *Documento de Puebla*, Ediciones Paulinas, Buenos Aires 1979.

ELVIRA ROMERA DE ARCAUTE

Lebanon   *see* **Middle East, Christian Education in the**

Life Cycle

The life cycle is a powerful and influential element in human experience and there is value in teaching the ways in which it is interpreted and celebrated in various traditions.

Pupils will be enabled to understand themselves and their environment better as they reflect on family and social events and experience a sense of wonder at the natural world and the changing seasons. Rites of passage with their attendant ceremonies offer useful areas for study and the ways in which different religious traditions cope with issues of birth, initiation, marriage and death are significant. Death and bereavement are themes in which past neglect may be remedied and rich veins of religious understanding can be explored in conjunction with biology, literature, music and art.

The teacher dealing with the subject will be able to draw from personal experience and interest and invite children to reflect constructively on their own lives. All may be grist to the mill and religion will not be isolated. Published materials which bear on the life cycle illustrate modes of working. A soundstrip set, designed for teenagers, describes and comments on the ways in which various groups deal with critical moments in the cycle (*Rites of Passage,* Mary Glasgow Publications). Sets of photographs in which a tree is taken from the same point at different items of the year illustrate change (*Trees of Europe Through the Four Seasons,* Argus). A Radio-vision filmstrip, *Behold I make all things new* (BBC), ties in new life in spring with the celebration of Easter.

Religious traditions are strongly influenced by the life cycle both in terms of explanation, e.g. teachings on creation and death, and of ritual and attempted control, e.g. marriage requirements. This is one of the fundamental areas of human experience and the teacher faces a challenge to ensure that the young are enabled to understand life and its context in a personal and positive way.

R. Carson, *The Sense of Wonder,* Harper & Row 1965; C. Herbert, *The Edge of Wonder,* CIO 1981; J. Prickett (ed.), *Initiation Rites,*

Lutterworth 1978; J. Prickett (ed.), *Death*, Lutterworth 1980; D. Taylor, *Exploring Red Letter Days,* Lutterworth 1981.

PAUL TURTON

Life Stance

A term used to describe the style and content of an individual's or a community's relationship with ultimate reality, and the consequences for life which flow from it. A life stance finds expression in values and convictions which should inform and guide life, in experience, in ceremonies, in worship (in many religions), and in community life. The users of the term value its impartiality since it encompasses the beliefs of everyone – religious or naturalistic – without discrimination.

H. STOPES-ROE

Life Themes   *see* Child-Centred RE

Literature

The extension of RE in schools beyond its traditionally Bible-centred curriculum has led some teachers to explore the value for RE of the wealth of 'secular' literature available today. A secondary school headmaster claims that 'the most fruitful discussions on religion took place when I was teaching English or Classics', and he adds: 'A class seldom fails to respond with deep interest and liveliness' when 'some fundamental human problem is raised by some great writer with no particular axe to grind' (Evans). The novels of such writers as William Golding, Graham Greene and Albert Camus; the plays of Beckett, Whiting and Ionesco; the poetry of Eliot, Auden and Hughes – all can be strained for their relevance to the themes of religion. Children's literature in the primary school can also spark off enthusiastic arguments about good and bad, innocence and guilt, suffering and death, etc., and not a few children have gained a sense of religion through the reading of Tolkien and C. S. Lewis.

Literature operates at a number of psychological levels, and some educationists feel that its use in RE may tend towards an undue concentration on its conceptual at the expense of its figurative and imaginative content. This can lead to a misuse of literature as a quarry for 'human questions' abstracted to serve the hidden purpose of religious didacticism. Such a 'cerebral' approach is a disservice to both literature and religion in the sense that it devalues the basic patterns of story*, myth* and poetry* through which both literature and religion appropriate and interpret reality. The value of literature for RE may therefore lie not so much in the questions raised as in the imaginative experience shared, and in the recovery for RE of the figurative-poetic quality of religious language itself.

This latter point leads to discussion of the Bible and to the contention that, whatever *else* it may be, the Bible is certainly 'literature'. The disqualification of the Bible from the classroom on the ground that it is not a children's book was based, says J. G. Priestley, on a view which saw the Bible 'essentially as a course-book for theological propositions'. But to approach the Bible as literature is first and foremost to attend to it as *story*, in which 'communication takes place through symbols, signs, tokens and images' rather than through concepts and propositions. Children who have developed the skill of responding to 'secular' literature will be better able to respond at the level of imagination and feeling to the language of the Bible. Questions about the *conceptual* meaning of the claims of religion will arise out of this experience; but that is not the point at which understanding actually *begins*.

This approach to the Bible through its 'literary' dimension has a counterpart in modern christology. We are urged by e.g. Pannenberg and Küng to seek an understanding of Jesus 'from below' – that is, to begin at his reality as *man* and *then* to ask how he is Son of God within and beyond that reality. Here again non-biblical literature can be of help in the classroom by intensifying awareness of the representative humanity which the incarnate Word assumed. The literature of tragedy, for example, in which many of the best novels of our century must be included, may provide for senior pupils a pattern of experience in terms of which the tragic structure of Jesus' life and death can be more deeply appropriated. An understanding of Jesus 'from below' in terms of the common humanity in which he shared may then lead to a further understanding of him as Son of God in whom that humanity is reshaped for man's salvation.

D. Anderson, *The Passion of Man in Gospel*

and Literature, Bible Reading Fellowship 1981; J. J. Evans, *Guard our Unbelief*, Oxford University Press 1971; T. R. Henn, *The Bible as Literature*, Lutterworth 1970; Jean Holm, *Teaching Religion in School: A Practical Approach*, Oxford University Press 1975; J. G. Priestley, 'Religious Story and the Literary Imagination', *British Journal of Religious Education*, Autumn 1981; Ulrich Simon, *Story and Faith*, SPCK 1975.

DAVID ANDERSON

Local Education Authorities

Since 1974, England and Wales have had three types of Local Education Authority (LEA): 1. forty-seven non-metropolitan counties, including eight in Wales, 2. in six metropolitan counties, separate districts are the LEAs: and 3. Greater London, under an Act of 1963, retains a unique system with outer boroughs as LEAs as well as the Inner London Education Authority. Scotland* has ten regions, in three of which divisions administer education, while Northern Ireland* has five Education and Library Boards. For England and Wales the 1944 Education Act, having specified the three stages of primary, secondary and further education, imposes on LEAs 'the duty . . . to contribute towards the spiritual, moral, mental and physical development of the community' (section 7). In practice LEAs must ensure adequate school and college places and sufficient teachers, books and equipment.

All schools maintained by LEAs must offer religious education (Education Act, 1944, section 25). This comprises: 1. collective worship at the start of the school day with all pupils attending 'a single act' unless premises make this impracticable or a parent requests any pupil to be excused; and 2. religious instruction, again recognizing the right of parents to withdraw their children.

Thus RE became the only *compulsory* subject required by statute and the only *voluntary* subject from which parents could withdraw their children. More recent requirements for sex education and for LEA curriculum policy statements have modified the uniqueness of this position. The principle of freedom of religion enshrined in this clause allows pupils withdrawn by their parents 'to receive religious instruction during school hours elsewhere . . . at the beginning or end of the school session'.

Section 26 adds that in county schools RE must be non-denominational with agreed syllabuses excluding any distinctive 'catechism or formulary' – a phrase originating from the Cowper-Temple clause* of the 1870 Act (the ten commandments, Lord's Prayer and Apostles' Creed have been ruled not 'distinctive' – unlike sections of the catechism). The same applies in controlled schools where, however, parents may request during 'not more than two periods in each week' religious instruction in accordance with the school's trust deed (usually Church of England). For this purpose staff of voluntary controlled schools include 'reserved teachers'*.

In aided and special agreement schools, RE is determined by the governors and any trust deed and may not be inspected by HMI or LEA officers. But as an alternative, parents may request agreed syllabus RE. Teachers in county and controlled schools cannot be required to participate in RE nor be allowed to benefit or suffer professionally by reason of religious opinions (section 30).

The fifth schedule of the 1944 Acts lists procedures for preparing, adopting and re-considering agreed syllabuses*. The LEA must convene a conference comprising four committees representing the authority, teachers' associations, the Church of England and other denominations in the area. Their duty is to seek unanimous agreement on a syllabus to be recommended for adoption by the LEA; more than one syllabus may be adopted to meet differing needs. Conference sub-committees must contain at least one member from each of the four committees, and voting involves one vote from each committee. If the LEA reports failure to reach unanimous agreement (or if it fails to adopt a syllabus unanimously recommended), the Secretary of State must appoint a body to prepare a syllabus: in no case has this procedure yet been implemented.

In addition to the statutory conference, an LEA may constitute a standing advisory council for RE* to consider 'in particular . . . methods of teaching, the choice of books, and the provision of lectures for teachers' (section 29). Despite anomalies over worship as schools have become larger and society more plural, and over withdrawal of pupils who now remain at school beyond sixteen or even eighteen, the fundamental intentions of this act have stood the test of time. Certainly they have helped to defend freedom of religion and conscience and retained local syllabus autonomy.

More recently, government circulars outlining the duties of LEAs have included the following: 1. information which should normally be made available to parents in written form includes 'arrangements for religious education and for exemption from it' (*DES Circular 15/77*, 1977); and 2. LEA policy statements on the school curriculum should be issued to all maintained schools who are asked to monitor their provision accordingly (*DES Circular 6/81*, 1981).

G. R. Barrell, *Teachers and the Law*, Methuen [5]1978; George Taylor and John B. Saunders, *The New Law of Education*, Butterworth [7]1971.

D. PAUL KING

Luther, Educational Work of

Martin Luther (1483–1546) is honoured as one of the foremost leaders of the Reformation of the sixteenth century and as the spiritual father of one of the largest of the Protestant communions. From 1511 until his death he taught in the University of Wittenberg, lecturing regularly on both the OT and NT. At the same time he was a parish pastor and preacher. Out of these two fields of activity grew both his understanding that man is justified by grace through faith and his conviction that there were serious doctrinal and practical abuses within the contemporary church.

From the beginning Luther's concern for church reform was linked with a recognition of the need for education. He spoke out frequently against the widespread ignorance of both clergy and laity, whether among Catholics or Protestants. In two treatises written in 1520, *An Open Letter to the Christian Nobility of the German Nation* and *The Freedom of a Christian*, he emphasized the need for educating people for service to God in church, state and society, and advocated that the basis for all levels of education should be the study of the holy scriptures. When the continuing ignorance of the people in the Protestant congregations was revealed by the

Saxon Church Visitation of 1528 he urged the secular authorities, who had taken over much church property, to use the revenues from it to establish schools.

Luther's two most important writings about education are an open letter of 1524 *To the Councilmen of All Cities of Germany That They Establish Christian Schools* and a sermon of 1530 *On Keeping Children at School*. In the former he drew attention to the large amounts of money spent on securing temporal peace and prosperity in the cities and argued that equal amounts be devoted to education. In both writings he argued that it was a Christian responsibility to train the coming generations for service to God and their fellow men.

Fundamentally, Luther believed that the responsibility for the Christian training and instruction of the young lay in the home. In a sermon preached in 1519 *On the Estate of Marriage* he drew attention to the duty of parents to educate children for God's service: 'Parents must know that they please God, Christendom, the entire world, themselves and their children in no better way than by educating their children.' In order to assist parents to fulfil their educational obligations he wrote his *Large Catechism* and *Small Catechism* in 1529, in which he outlined the main teachings of the church: 'In the plain form in which the head of the family should teach them in his household.' Both catechisms were based on earlier catechetical sermons preached by Luther on the Ten Commandments, the Creeds and the Lord's Prayer, and they reflect his concern for education as an integral part of the Christian life. For Luther, the Fall of Adam and its consequences was a real evil in a human being, a power to which every person was subject from birth to death. The Christian life, begun in the sacrament of baptism, was to be lived out in the daily dying to sin through repentance and the resurrection to life in the assurance of God's forgiveness. Luther insisted, therefore, that it was the responsibility of every Christian congregation to support the education given in the home by providing opportunities for instruction, the main objective of which was to strengthen faith among Christians and so help them to fight against the world, the flesh and the devil. The two catechisms, which have achieved the virtual status of educational textbooks in the

Lutheran churches, today have an honourable place as the two oldest parts of the corpus of Lutheran confessional writings.

Luther was rather suspicious of the institutional character of the church and he frequently prefers to use the words 'assembly' (*Sammlung*) or 'community' (*Gemeinde*), emphasizing thereby that the church is a worshipping and learning community rather than an institutional structure. The purpose of the church, which is the body of Christ, is that of Christ himself: it is an instrument through which God seeks to bring people into a right relationship to him and his creation. The church seeks to do this through witness, nurture, worship and service. These are the 'ministries' of the church and they share an equal importance: a neglect of any one of them is bound to lead to a weakening of the others. A fundamental principle of Luther was that the church should live in a constant awareness of its failings and be prepared to allow itself to be reformed by the Word of God (*ecclesia semper reformanda*): this renewal was intimately intertwined with the need for appropriate education, penitence and desire for reform on the part of the individual Christian.

Luther's doctrine of the priesthood of all believers highlighted the role of the laity in the life of the congregation and the mission of the church in the world. It also meant that education was no longer the prerogative of the clergy or of the wealthy laity. Luther was convinced that Christians should be literate, so that they could read and study the scriptures for themselves, but although he saw education primarily in such Christian terms, he nevertheless shared with the humanists a concern for literature, history, music and language, as is shown by his reforms at the University of Wittenberg and in the schools that he helped to establish. In this work he had the important assistance of Philip Melanchthon (1497–1560), the 'Praeceptor Germaniae' who gave organizational form to many of Luther's ideas.

Since Luther's time, Lutheran churches have followed his example by a continued concern for education. This frequently finds practical expression in extensive Sunday School programmes for people of all ages, lengthy and detailed instruction for confirmands, usually on the basis of the *Small Catechism*, and by a thorough training for the ministry. In countries with a Lutheran 'state church' pastors may be involved in Christian education in schools; elsewhere, e.g. in the USA or Australia, Lutheran churches have their own extensive school systems.

William H. Lazareth, *Luther on the Christian Home,* Muhlenberg Press, Philadelphia 1960; F. V. N. Painter, *Luther on Education,* Concordia Publishing House, St Louis 1889; Gerald Strauss, *Luther's House of Learning,* The Hopkins University Press, Baltimore and London 1978.

ROY LONG

Lutheran Church: Involvement in Education

An essential prerequisite for understanding the educational assumptions on which educational programmes in Lutheran churches are based is a knowledge of the ministry and teaching of Luther*.

Most Lutheran churches around the world take both religious and secular education seriously. They are aware of the vital role that education can play in strengthening and deepening the life of the church. As Luther tried to do in his time, Lutheran churches have always worked towards provision of education for the ordinary church member. They hold the view that education is very much a religious enterprise. It can be designed and used to serve religious ends.

Even where the provision of general education is regarded as the prerogative of the state, the purpose and underlying values, the organization and curriculum of general education continue to be matters of vital concern to the churches. The provision of basic education is, therefore, one of many social services, that Lutheran churches continue to engage in and administer in various parts of the world. Where churches as institutions are excluded in educational structures, they urge Christian parents and teachers to be involved in the day-to-day life of the schools and uphold Christian moral values in the community.

In some parts of the world, the way is open for individual Lutheran churches to take the initiative in making a significant contribution to education by sponsoring experimental programmes based on fundamental Christian beliefs and values. In such places, churches are encouraged to discover how they can fulfil their educational ministry by looking for untouched areas of need in their society. Thus the use of churches' resources to awaken public conscience, to use an example, and press for more humane conditions in society, has been part of the educational ministry of the Lutheran churches in many countries.

In many fields, old and new, educational work has always been made a vital part of the mission work. It is seen as a means of gaining more direct contact with the people. Through organized educational programmes non-Christians are exposed to the basic principles of the Christian faith. Furthermore, it has been the view of many a missionary that basic general education such as learning to read and write is rather essential for Christian nurture. The importance of being able to read the Bible is cited as one important reason why teaching how to read is a vital task in the missionary enterprise. It must, however, be pointed out that provision of education on the mission field has sometimes been used in a manner that is abusive. It has been used as a bait to make converts. Furthermore, in most non-Western cultures the educational programme introduced by some missionaries has left a lasting and far-reaching negative impact on the traditional life of the people.

The rite of confirmation. Martin Luther was a prolific writer, but he did not write much about confirmation*. This fact has bothered many a Lutheran theologian. Some do believe that Luther saw no importance in the medieval 'confirmatio'. Others maintain that he had no misgiving about confirmation as a rite, but he was opposed to the sacramental character it has acquired. He was against it because he felt that it tended to weaken the more important rite of baptism*. And yet he did not write a long commentary on his objections to this sacramental character of confirmation as he had done on other church teachings. He did not bother to provide 'a new concept for the reform of the rite of confirmation'.

The little that he said about it seems to imply that he accepted what has been called 'evangelical confirmation' without the sacramental character. Luther stood for complete freedom in those rites of the church which for him were not necessary for salvation.

The practice of 'evangelical confirmation' was adopted in many congregations during his own time. He even approved the laying on of hands on confirmands because it gave the ceremony a solemn character. Luther's teaching about the laying on of hands was that it means a personal witness to the power of God's word. It was an affirmation that God's promise of grace was upon the confirmand. Furthermore, it was an assurance of the forgiveness of sins.

Another of his objections to the medieval confirmation as the tendency for people to regard the rite as being a supplement to baptism. He was uncompromising on that. In his assessment, the importance of confirmation was basically the preparatory opportunity it provided for admission to Holy Communion. It is understood in this same way in many Lutheran churches today; but not in all of them. There is a growing number of Lutheran churches that admit children to Holy Communion before confirmation. By the same token, there are many others, especially in Africa and Asia, which insist on confirmation before admission to Holy Communion. However, regardless of what comes first, all Lutheran churches seem to practise the rite of confirmation. Through it, as through other means of grace, God saves, gathers and preserves his people. Thus the focal point of confirmation is the divine service rather than the instruction or pastoral care provided – the means of grace which is freely given by God.

Although confirmation is no longer regarded as being a supplement to the sacrament of baptism, it is nevertheless closely related to it; for one thing confirmation assumes that baptism has been administered. Thus in the Lutheran churches the rite of confirmation is connected with infant baptism. It is a rite of the church whose objective is to provide catechetical instruction for children; in other words, to enable those who were admitted into infant baptism to become full and active members of the congregation and learn about the good use of the means of grace. The preparation involves the pastoral office which provides instruction and pastoral care; the congregation which offers intercessions and witnesses the examination; the confirmands who actively participate in what the pastor and congregation do.

Educational courses used within the community of faith. It should be mentioned here that the Office of Christian Education of the Lutheran World Federation works under certain specific terms of reference with regard to its consultative services for Christian education programmes of member churches. In the first place, consultative services can only be given in response to requests received from churches. Secondly, the services are directed towards self-help, that is, towards assisting the churches to rethink and restructure their educational ministries. Finally, the services endeavour to encourage close contact between Lutheran and other churches.

In various places in Africa, it is normal for member churches to organize house meetings, worship services and Sunday Schools in an informal way. Such activities are encouraged by the Lutheran World Federation because they offer good opportunities for the children and adults to worship the Lord together in their own setting. In other churches, children's choirs play an active role in the sharing and worshipping life of the community. Many church leaders are sufficiently aware of the fact that conversion alone cannot make a church an active, living and witnessing community. They are thus convinced that structured Christian education programmes play an essential role in church life. The church has the responsibility for nurturing, equipping and edifying her members.

The Lutheran World Federation, therefore, has been providing assistance to some member churches to prepare different kinds of educational materials for religious instruction in schools, for theological education, youth work, adult education, Sunday School, confirmation, baptism and other programmes.

Nothing is imposed on churches by the Lutheran World Federation. It is the churches which identify their educational needs or problems and make decisions as to what should be done about them. The LWF consultative services have no responsibility for making decisions on behalf of the churches. This is not based merely on pedagogical and practical understandings and convictions. It is understood to be at the centre of partnership in mission.

Eric W Gritsch and Robert W. Jenson (eds), *Lutheranism: The Theological Movement and its Confessional Writings,* Fortress Press, Philadelphia 1978; Bjarne Hareide, *Document No. 16,* report of the Commission on Educa-

tion given at the Assembly of the Lutheran World Federation held in Helsinki, Finland 1963; Anza A Lema, *Pedagogical and Theological Presuppositions of Education,* Lutheran South East Asian Christian Education Curricula Committee, Hong Kong 1977.

ANZA A. LEMA

Magic in Religion

Magic is a particular type of ritual found in most religions, especially ancient and tribal religions. Magical rites are concerned with directing or warding off hidden power(s) for specific purposes. These rites normally involve four basic elements: the spell, the 'medicine', the hidden power, and the particular object toward which the power is directed.

The spell involves a formula (often secret) including the precise words and actions to be used. Any deviation from the exact formula may render the spell ineffective. The formula itself may consist of traditional stereotype sounds and noises, rather than intelligible words. The formula, however, has the inherent power to move the hidden forces or spirits in the direction intended.

The 'medicine' or material stuff of the magical act is the tangible medium of contact with hidden forces. This stuff may be any object or material which has been traditionally used to attract the forces or spirits involved. Roots, herbs, hair, claws, blood, spittle, rocks and the like, are typical items used in the rite. Normally each item has a significant connection with the object of the rite and is therefore meaningful within the symbol system of the community performing the rite.

The hidden forces which the rite seeks to direct or control may be impersonal psychical powers, bush spirits, ancestral spirits, or other supernatural powers. By performing the rite correctly, the hidden power is set in motion for good or ill.

The object toward which the magical act is directed is specific and concrete. Magical acts are not prayers for the general good of a community, but directed to specific objects or persons to be improved or destroyed. Typical examples include ensuring the fertility of a particular garden for a given crop, warding off spirits from a specific hut, killing a particular enemy in another tribe, or improving the efficiency of a musical instrument. Any area of life where danger or need exist can be the target of magical acts.

Four major categories of magic are increase rites, decrease rites (or sorcery), atropaic rites and healing rites. Increase rites are those in which the performer seeks to attract, direct or increase life power in a given situation. Such rites are believed to increase the fertility of a field, the hunting capacity of a warrior or the skill of an artisan. Love magic can attract a member of the opposite sex. Body magic can increase an individual's beauty, health or life span. Sorcery is magic directed to negative ends where the life force of an enemy or his property is decreased or destroyed. This magic directs or controls negative powers for the benefit of the one performing the ritual. Atropaic magic is designed to ward off negative forces, especially the sorcery of enemies, angry ancestors or evil spirits. Magic healing rites are employed to overcome the negative forces or spirits which have affected a person or situation.

Degrees of power and danger are involved in the performance of magical rites. Some forms of magic seem to be available to all, and the formula readily accessible. In many cases, however, the magic rite is the possession of the professional magician or 'medicine man'. By owning the secret formula the magician has personal control over the forces or spirits to be influenced by the rite. The ritual expert in negative magic is a sorcerer. Such experts are paid for their services or their expensive medicine, and may need to prepare themselves with fasts or ablutions in order to perform the ritual faithfully. In tribal societies such experts played roles similar to doctors, lawyers and counsellors in Western societies. Magic in tribal societies was integral to the pattern of life. To perform magic was to express a common faith in the hidden forces at work in the world, to demonstrate a concern for the welfare of the community, and to participate in the processes of discerning or directing the unseen forces at work in society. The rite was thus a means of focussing hidden power directly on a particular target in a way that was in harmony with the cosmology of the community.

In teaching about magic in the classroom the teacher will need to guard against a number of pitfalls. The first of these is glibly to compare magic with techniques of modern science. Much of the literature available still reflects the famous interpretation of Sir James Frazer who claimed that magic is of two kinds; homeopathic and contagious. Homeopathic magic, he argues, makes the mistake of assuming that things which resemble each other are the same; contagious magic makes the mistake of assuming that things which have been in contact with each other are always in contact. Frazer judges magic rites by criteria derived from contemporary Western logic and science. To understand magic as a living reality, the teacher must set aside such value judgments and attempt to interpret particular magical rites within the symbol system of the tribe or community involved. Within that system the rite is meaningful; it is a currency acceptable to guarantee success. The tribal gardener does not merely perform a magic rite; he or she will first dig, plant and fence the field. The magic rite performed in the field will make the work of garden preparation part of the rhythm of natural, social and supernatural forces operating in the life of the garden.

A second temptation of the teacher, will be to contrast magic with religion as some early scholars have done. The assumption of these scholars is that magic belongs to a lower order of human development. Religion is identified with the supposedly superior forms associated with major world religions, especially Christianity. It is suggested in this contrast, that magic is manipulative while religion is persuasive, magic coercive and religion supplicative. In magic one controls impersonal powers by set formulas; in religion one pleads for favours from personal divine beings. A close analysis of both world and tribal religions reveals that this distinction is not valid. Magical rites are best recognized as a particular kind of ritual which may appear in any religious system. To assume that one kind of ritual is superior to another is quite gratuitous. Each rite must be interpreted in terms of the logic of the religion or cosmology where it operates.

A third temptation is to identify magical rites with what Westerners tend to call 'superstition'. In many cases the magic rites which survive in the Western world, such as placing dill under the doormat to ward off spirits, are relics of past belief systems which are now regarded as superstitions because the meaning system associated with the rite has been rejected by the majority of the society. These relics once had a vital context in which they were integral elements.

To do justice in the classroom to magical rites they need to be placed within the framework of their belief systems. In most cases, however, because of the pejorative connotations of 'magic' it would be better to deal with such phenomena under less value-laden concepts such as healing rites, protection rites, destructive rites or fertility rites.

A *Dictionary of Comparative Religion,* ed. S.G.F. Brandon, Weidenfeld and Nicholson 1970; *Powers, Plumes and Piglets*, ed. Norman Habel, AASR 1979; Ian Hogbin, *The Island of Menstruating Men*, Chandler 1970; William Howells, *The Heathens*, Doubleday 1962; W. Lessa and E. Vogt, *Reader in Comparative Religion*, Harper & Row 1958; *Magic, Witchcraft and Curing*, ed. John Middleton, University of Texas 1967; Basil Moore and Norman Habel, *When Religion Goes to School*: *Typology of Religion for the Classroom*, SACAE, Adelaide 1982.

NORMAN HABEL

Management of RE in the Secondary School

The organization of the RE department varies according to whether the head of department is the sole specialist or is supported by other staff who may or may not be specialists themselves. In the single-specialist department professional isolation can be a problem. Non-specialists may also not be able to teach exactly as the specialist would like. Sensitivity and tact are needed here.

It is important for RE staff to be known to colleagues and for them to articulate positively the educational value of RE. Relations with the head and staff responsible for timetable and curriculum planning are particularly important. As well as talking to sympathetic staff in one's own school, membership of a professional organization for RE and attendance at courses where one meets other colleagues in the area and LEA advisers responsible for RE will be important.

A departmental team has great advantages. To share ideas is enriching. The head of department has a crucial role, but if assistant RE teachers also have specific departmental responsibilities, this will both benefit their professional development and help to spread the duties.

RE staff should be aware of the concepts, skills and attitudes developed by other areas of the curriculum so that RE can be correlated or integrated with them. Within the life of the school as a whole, RE staff are well placed to contribute to the planning of assemblies, to community service and to the development of policies for moral education and a multi-cultural curriculum.

Neither a departmental nor an LEA agreed syllabus should constrict the teaching. It is only a guide and can be regularly modified. It can take into account work done in the schools from which pupils are received and to which they will go. The syllabus can include schemes of work which suggest resources and teaching approaches. Older pupils in particular can profitably contribute to the planning of their own courses.

Resources need to be built up, both in the department and in any central school library or resource centre. A projector, video-cassettes, a tape recorder, record player and computer are assets. It may be advantageous to buy collections of a variety of books in smaller quantities rather than a limited number of full sets. Work sheets with extensions according to the ability of pupils can be built up and carefully indexed. All this makes permanent teaching rooms and storage space including a departmental filing cabinet highly desirable.

For adequate resources RE should receive a fair share of the school's capitation. An initial extra allowance may be necessary for the large items mentioned above. In general, assuming similar time allocation, one might expect RE to receive funding comparable to that for history or geography.

A good department needs time – not less than two periods a week in years one to three and where possible, in fourth and fifth year examination course option groups RE should not be blocked against subjects which are self-selecting.

There are different possibilities for non-examination RE in years four and five. If only one period is likely to be timetabled for this, it may be possible to consider a modular arrangement. This could allow areas such as RE, social education, health education and careers each to have more time in the week for a portion of the year.

The need for evaluation of the curriculum should lead to consideration of examining or testing all pupils in RE. For those with severe learning difficulties this will have to be less formal than conventional examinations. The head of department should monitor the teaching and the quality of work done by pupils in the department.

Outside the school, links with local churches and any other faith communities may give the head of department an opportunity to draw the attention of young people in those communities to examination courses in religious studies. Their adherents may be resources for the department's teaching programme.

Through personal contacts, exhibitions of RE work and brochures giving a carefully-worded and attractive presentation of RE, parents, governors and careers teachers and officers can be informed about the value of both examination and general courses in RE.

Christian Education Movement, *Is RE your Special Responsibility?* 1982; *The Management of Religious Education in the Secondary School*, 1979 and *The Total Curriculum in Relation to RE*, 1980; Brian Gates (ed.), *Religious Education Directory*, Religious Education Council of England and Wales 1982; Michael Marland, *Head of Department*, Heinemann Educational 1971.

GEOFFREY CHORLEY

Marx, Marxism

Marxism is an ideology based on the social theories of Karl Marx. Ideology and religion have many similarities, superficial and profound, and those familiar with the deep divisions and mutual hostilities found among Christians, especially before the modern ecumenical movement, will recognize some of the attitudes which divide Marxism into various camps. Orthodox Marxism, developing from Engels, through Lenin and Stalin to find expression in the Soviet Union is a dialectical materialism in which the stress falls on nature, evolution and determination. The modern Western Marxism of George Lukács and the Frankfurt School has concentrated on the sphere of history and the deliverance of man from economic determinism. This ideal-

ist tradition claims that orthodox Marxism owes little to Marx and distorts his views. Religion is a case in point. While it is completely rejected by orthodox Marxism and public policy is to eradicate it from social and individual lives, modern Western Marxism does not take such a negative view of religion and has even engaged with religious institutions and groups at both theoretical and practical levels.

Karl Marx (1818–83) was born in Trier in the Rhineland. His parents both came from distinguished Jewish families, but when Trier was taken back into Prussia the family became officially Christian, to avoid the disadvantages imposed by anti-semitic legislation. His schoolboy essays exhibit a humanistic idealism which guided his whole life and which is derived from biblical religion and not from philosophy. In his final school report he was deemed satisfactory in religion, but weak in history. In certain respects this was true of his life as a whole.

After a rather self-indulgent year at the University of Bonn, during which he came under the influence of the Romantic movement, he transferred in October 1836 to Berlin. It was five years since the death of Hegel, but although Feuerbach and Strauss had already begun the attack on Absolute Idealism, the influence of Hegel was still strong. It was through the critical use of Hegel's philosophy that Marx was introduced to radical views on the nature of the state, politics and economics. So involved did he become in this intellectual fervour that his health broke down. During his convalescence he read the entire works of Hegel – which might be regarded as mistaking the illness for the cure – and was converted to Hegel's position. However, through the influences of the critics of Hegel, when he came to present his doctoral dissertation in 1841, the subject was materialism, not idealism. One of these Young Hegelians was Bruno Bauer and Marx hoped that through Bauer he might enter an academic career. But when Bauer was dismissed from university teaching because of his radical views, not least his criticism of religion, Marx saw that that door was closed. At Bonn Marx wished to be a poet, at Berlin, a philosopher: how the history of the world might have been different had he succeeded in either career. And yet, it might be argued that religion has in the long term benefitted from facing up to the criticism mounted by Marx.

In 1844 Marx wrote an 'Introduction' to his essay entitled, 'Critique of Hegel's Philosophy of Right'. In it the twenty-five-year-old makes three powerful and memorable criticisms of religion. The first is that 'Man makes religion, religion does not make man.' He takes over Feuerbach's view that the basis of religion is man's projection of his self-consciousness into objectivity. He then turned to Feuerbach's second theory, the reversal of subject and predicate, the reduction of theology to anthropology. But whereas Feuerbach wished to disclose the value of religious statements, Marx wished only to show them to be false. Religion is 'an inverted world-consciousness'. In religion God creates man, God is more real than man. But for Marx this was 'an inverted world'.

Marx's second criticism of religion arises from this and marks the first signs of a departure from Feuerbach and 'the Holy Family', i.e. the Bauer brothers and other critics who still wished to maintain religion in some form. Feuerbach traced the origins and function of religion to the psychological level, to consciousness. But even at this stage we see the element of 'suspicion', as Mannheim was to describe it, entering the thought of Marx. Because religion is an inverted world view, it is in a position to legitimize the world as it is. Thus wherever evil exists in the political, social or economic spheres, religion is able to explain why things are as they are, indeed should be as they are. 'The struggle against religion is therefore indirectly a fight against the world of which religion is the spiritual aroma.' This was written in Paris and indicates the merging of German critical philosophy and French revolutionary socialism.

A third criticism follows from this. In the appalling conditions of the industrial revolution no comfort or support was offered by employers or by the state, but at least religion was there to help. 'Religion is the sigh of the oppressed creature, the heart of a heartless world, and the soul of soulless conditions. It is the opium of the people.' In the nineteenth century opium was taken by those who flinched from a reality they could not change. Marx does not claim that religion is ineffective: his criticism is of the very real effectiveness of religion. It makes intolerable conditions tolerable. It drains the strength from those who should rise up and insist that the world be changed. 'To abolish religion as the illusory happiness of the people is to demand their real happiness. The demand to give up illusions about the existing state of affairs is the demand to give up a state of affairs which needs illusions.' For Marx the abolition of religion will not make the world perfect at a stroke, but it will uncover the world as it is and make it possible to bring about the necessary changes. In this 'the criticism of heaven is transformed into the criticism of earth'.

The 'Introduction' begins with the confident assertion that 'For Germany the criticism of religion is in the main complete, and criticism of religion is the premise of all criticism.' This was a prescriptive rather than a descriptive statement. Marx meant that he had dealt with religion and could then go on to his criticism of the state, philosophy, politics, economics and all other aspects of social life. He did not feel it necessary to continually return to the criticism of religion as did some of his followers. Yet an important issue remains. Did Marx turn away from religion and idealism towards materialism as expounded by orthodox Marxism? Or did he reject materialism and construct a new form of idealism which was not so much a rejection of biblical religion as a secular version of it?

Even in the 'Introduction' we find a passage which raises this question. What is the hope of emancipation in Germany at that time? Certainly not in any of the social classes which existed. But rather in a new class which will emancipate all other classes as it emancipates itself, which is 'a total loss of humanity and which can only redeem itself by a total redemption of humanity. This dissolution of society, as a particular class, is the proletariat.' What is the origin of this vision, a vision of a group oppressed without oppressing, which through its suffering brings salvation to all? Certainly not what Marx was to describe that same year as 'crude and unreflective communism', materialism without a soul.

But apart from odd references and images to be found throughout his writings, the same question has to be asked concerning his final system, historical materialism. In the 'Paris Manuscripts' Marx speaks of his own version of communism as being different from idealism and materialism, claiming 'communism is not itself the goal of human development'. This utopian language has resonances with biblical eschatology. Man seems to be moving towards an end which is not even prefigured in the world as it is. Marx's own system begins with his critique of Feuerbach in the programmatic 'Theses on Feuerbach'. Feuerbach wishes to transform society by transforming man's consciousness, but Marx objects that this only leads to a new interpretation of society not a new society. In the materialism of the Theses Engels was to see 'the brilliant germ of the new world outlook'. Social history is not guided by ideas, whether from religion or philosophy, but by material forces, from which arise certain ideas. Marx set out to provide a brief history of the world to illustrate this thesis, a thesis which Engels predicted 'is destined to do for history what Darwin's theory had done for biology. . .' Although Engel's own dialectical materialism was significantly different, the analogy is instructive. In his essay 'A Contribution to the Critique of Political Economy' Marx claims that history is constituted by a series of epochs, each characterized by its own mode of production. The mode of production determines social relations, and is the real foundation of the legal and political superstructure of society and indeed determines also social consciousness. This appears to be thoroughgoing materialism, excluding not only philosophical idealism, that trusty servant of the ruling class, but also religion, its obedient lap dog. And yet Marx did not believe that history was constituted by a random series of discrete epochs. He believed that there was a progression and that the series was reaching its fulfilment. The new bourgeois mode of production would be replaced by communism, capitalism by socialism. Two points arise here. The first is the resonances once again with biblical religion. Man is called on to align himself with the will of God, but the kingdom will come regardless of man. In this predestination we see prefigured the historical inevitability of Marx's assurance that the new age is near. Man may join the new class and work for the new age, but it will come by necessity whether he joins or not. The second point is that going far beyond Darwin, Marx is claiming that there is here a historical process which actually serves moral ends. History is not simply a series of epochs, but is actually leading to that last great epoch in which justice and freedom will prevail. This would mean that the material world is unknowingly determined by the necessity of achieving certain ideals. But this is the essence of both religion and idealism. At the end Marx seems to be guided by motifs which are derived not from a 'scientific' examination of history, but from the secularizing of biblical religion. Ironically, Marx wrote thus although he had read David Strauss's foundation work demythologizing biblical religion. He and his followers espoused an eschatological mythology from which many Christians have withdrawn. History confounds predictions about the coming of the new age, whether these are biblical or Marxist.

It is possible to distinguish between Marx's philosophy and his metaphysics. The former has become the basis of modern critical social theory. It is quite independent of the latter and is widely used by those who reject historical materialism. This social theory has exposed ways in which religion has unconsciously served values, orders and institutions which are fundamentally irreligious and anti-Christian. By contrast historical materialism has been discredited by subsequent developments and has itself been exposed as an ideology.

K. Marx and F. Engels, *On Religion*, Lawrence & Wishart n.d.; N. Lash, *A Matter of Hope: A Theologian's Reflections on the Thought of Karl Marx*, Darton, Longman & Todd 1981; A. Th. van Leeuwen, *Critique of Heaven*, Lutterworth 1972; T. Ling, *Karl Marx and Religion: In Europe and India*, Macmillan 1980; D. McLellan, *Marx before Marxism*, Penguin 1972; J. P. Miranda, *Marx against the Marxists*, SCM Press 1980.

ALISTAIR KEE

Meaning, Quest for

Within religious education the quest for meaning may be considered within three broad categories. These may be termed: traditional, existential, empathic.

The traditional quest reflects the body of tradition handed down by each religion to subsequent generations. It is a cumulative form of quest whereby varied experiences of individuals and communities are passed on to each new generation. The quest is thereby continued within the accepted parameters of each religion through knowledge, experience, interpretation in addition to growth and development. The means by which each religion searches for meaning and purpose is of central significance if the religion is to develop, using tradition as a necessary complement to change.

The existential quest is one in which each individual may recognize the importance of trying to make sense of the human situation. RE will not require such a personal quest to take place but it will help identify the relevance and role of religion in the formulation of many people's quest. The existential quest may be developed with the framework of the traditional quest, for the latter can provide material through which the existential quest finds a validating authority. To a certain extent every quest for meaning is an existential quest: some remain independent of any formulated religious tradition but many find their place within the practices and beliefs of one religious tradition or another. RE will encourage a quest for meaning to enable the student to identify concepts* and attitudes* which will encourage the creation of a deeper personal awareness of the contribution of religion to the quest for meaning.

The empathic category is a less clearly defined area because it seeks to identify the importance of such a quest within a variety of religious and non-religious traditions. It does not rely upon the traditional or existential categories but regards them as both a complement and a contribution to the appreciation of the value and importance of such a quest. A quest for meaning may not take place either personally or within a particular religious tradition, it may be deemed to be an unnecessary activity: religious education, however, will encourage the recognition of the significance of such a quest in the lives of some people. It may be that the quest will be engaged through recognized religious beliefs and practices but it will normally be extended through the arts and sciences, through all kinds of literature* and other examples of human achievement and creativity.

It would be important for any complete treatment to encourage reflection upon the importance of a search for meaning; it would

act as a counterweight to the information provided by the other areas of RE. It provides the philosophical and personal emphasis required by all effective religious education.

ALAN BROWN

Media, Use of in RE

One of the reasons why teachers involved in RE today are faced with a new and crucial challenge is because education is sometimes regarded as being unduly cerebral while religion is seen as too abstract and remote. Effective communication in RE depends on addressing the pupil as a total person involving mind and imagination, heart and will. In fact the discerning use of media can act as a catalyst which affects traditional ways of teaching, requiring an approach which is more conformable with creativity, exploration and research than with ready-made syntheses. This is because such media immerse people in the world of the senses so that teacher and pupil can react to religious and ultimate questions*, not only with the mind, but also with the feelings and the emotions. What the subject needs is to maintain a balance between the cognitive* and affective* elements in the learning process.

No longer can RE rely on the simplistic use of audio-visual aids as a panacea for arbitrary or indifferent teaching. What is required is an appreciation of the importance attached to religious language which seeks to grapple with disclosure situations or moments of vision of which certain images and symbols form an integral part. From primitive times man has recognized the power of artistic expression as a vehicle for communicating religious experience. For this reason it is recommended that pupils should be introduced to evocative and imaginative modes of language as well as literal and scientific vocabulary.

What is common to almost every religion is the use of symbolism* – the language of myth* and parable*, metaphor and analogy – to point to those areas of personal and community experience which are at the limits of understanding. The essential value of audio-visual media lies in the fact that transcendental or numinous experiences cannot be taught directly. They can only be evoked through art*, poetry*, music* and the rituals of mime and the dance*. Not to be eclipsed by such expressive means of communication will be the influence of story*, which can with graphic power, stir the imagination* and sharpen the perception of young and old alike. The sensitive teacher can draw on a vast repertoire of story redolent of religious insight, produced truth and a distillation of human wisdom and spiritual awareness.

Various art forms tell the story of how in every age man has sought to celebrate his beliefs and values whether in early cave paintings, sculpture, icon*, artefact* or sacred building. In our time, photography – the vernacular of the arts – enables us to savour such artistic treasures through the medium of print, poster, filmstrip, slide, film and video. The marvels of modern educational technology should not be allowed to engender in the teacher a sense of uncritical abandon or false expectation. Pupils brought up on an unprecedented diet of sensory stimulation should be protected from an over-exposure to media in RE. Restraint in the use of visual resources should serve as an antidote to visualism, emotionalism and externalism. In recognizing the tremendous richness and diversity of the communication arts it will be imperative for the teacher to recognize the distinctive characteristics of each medium so that pupils may respond to them in different ways, according to their individual skills, capacities and intuitions. Aesthetic appreciation of impressive resources is best achieved by encouraging pupils to engage in expressive classroom activities at the personal or group level.

For successful RE lessons there are no short cuts for they will demand greater teacher preparation involving content, method, the selection of published resources and the origination of home-made materials. Verbal explanations will be enlivened by the skilful use of the chalkboard or overhead projector. Recruiting material from the vast range of colourful posters, photographs and artwork may also quicken the interest of pupils who in turn should be encouraged to contribute examples quarried from our print culture. Illustrated reference books on RE can be a source of fascination in exploring religious traditions and customs while work cards, project schemes and educational games* can also introduce a recreative element into a subject not helped by sombre connotations. Music, both instrumental and vocal, has also served religion well in worship, ceremonial

and festivity and this medium is widely represented in recorded format. In addition to drama, simulation and role play pupils will derive benefit from a host of pursuits in the sphere of arts and crafts. A sense of sympathy can be enhanced through 'dressing up' in religious apparel and ethnic costume while the tactile sense can be experienced by way of handling religious artefacts and ritual objects. The provision of planned visits involving people and places of worship, museums and cultural centres can also be a valuable dimension.

In short, audio-visual media in RE can prevent the rational and the non-rational from straying too far apart. In this way academic rigour can be sustained but not at the expense of that mystery which is at the core of religious experience.

See also **Art; Poetry and RE**.

DESMOND F. BRENNAN

Meditation, Use of in RE

Most religions use a variety of approaches to training in meditation. This training should lead to the development of a special kind of awareness which encourages receptivity to another dimension of reality. It should promote feelings of awe and humility, offering the individual the possibility of personal growth.

Bodily posture is important in meditation: indeed the body is a symbol. Ritualized movement, bowing, kneeling, standing and sitting may be done in such a way as to encourage religious awareness. In the teaching of the use of the body the attitude of the teacher is of key importance. Symbols are of particular significance in meditation as they provide a focus for the imagination. They release the emotions and transform the energy locked up in the subconscious into action. Jung points to two understandings of the symbol. The first is as the centre through which God* makes his presence known; this type of symbol relates particularly to a mystical understanding of the area between subject and object. The second is the visible symbol which moves us and shifts our centre of awareness; it speaks to our depths, changes our values and relates to the individual's 'I-Thou' experience of God. Symbols of the centre have their roots in the psyche. 'I-Thou' symbols relate to things other than man which have independent existence unaltered by man. Symbols of the centre are more suited to the inward contemplation of God. 'I-Thou' symbols involve a turning outwards rather than inwards. In meditation there is a need to use both kinds of symbols. In the first, God is all in all and 'I' am lost. In the second, there is a dialogue between the Creator and the creature.

To grasp the significance of a symbol the individual must develop the awareness which places him on the right wavelength to understand it. To achieve this positive training is necessary. Teachers of religion should introduce their students to the techniques of meditation. Most religions recommend the practice of silence and encourage an attitude or awareness which proceeds from bodily control of the senses. Christian masters of the spiritual life recommend custody of the ears and eyes as preliminaries to progress in the spiritual life. Teachers should use a variety of approaches in devising patterns of training in meditation. These patterns should foster awareness by using silence, movement and posture, and should include guidance which relates either to the symbolism of the centre or to the 'I-Thou' approach.

The awakening to a different level of awareness should call the individual to make a response. If this response evokes a motion of love it is creative, for the visible symbol speaks to the individual's depth and can change his values. It has the potential for encouraging spiritual growth and developing moral attitudes, but such growth is dependent for its effectiveness on the response of love which can lead to the fuller development of the individual personality.

Mircea Eliade, *Images and Symbols*, Harvill Press 1961; C. J. Jung, *Psyche and Symbol,* ed. Violet S. de Laszlo, Doubleday 1958; *Psychological Types,* trs. H. Godwin Baynes, Routledge & Kegan Paul 1923.

RONWYN GOODSIR THOMAS

Methodist Church

1. *Policy of the Methodist Church concerning education*

Methodism inherited from its founder, John Wesley, a deep practical concern for Christian education understood as a broad education for life based on a Christian understanding of God and man. It has been an abiding concern, sustained through ever-changing social circumstances. It expressed itself by early and vigorous involvement in the Sunday School Movement*, with its commitment to general education, in a Christian context, of poor and deprived children. It was the same concern that later led Methodism into providing voluntary schools; and still later into active participation with central and local government in state-provided schools.

The policy of the Methodist Church during this century, therefore, with regard to day schools, of seeking to co-operate in and contribute to the state system rather than of continuing or promoting voluntary schools, is directly in line with its basic Christian commitment in education. Indeed it was moving in this direction before the turn of the century, between the 1870 and 1902 Acts, not as a turning away from a policy of promoting Christian education, but expressive of a hope and belief that in schools provided by the state, whether under School Boards, or after 1902, under county education authorities, a non-sectarian but Christian education could be accessible to all. 'The primary object in Methodist Policy in the matter of Elementary Education is the establishment of School Boards everywhere, and the placing of a Christian unsectarian school within reasonable distance of every family' (Methodist Conference 1891). In common with other free churches, Methodism remained deeply concerned about the many locations, mainly rural, where the only school was of Anglican foundation. Though the bitterness of the end of the nineteenth and the beginning of the twentieth centuries faded, some tension remained down to the time of the 1944 Act, and beyond.

Since 1944 there has been a growing feeling that the Methodist Church had perhaps been unwise to follow a policy of gradually closing or transferring so many of its schools. A 1961 statement, for example, affirmed 'that where any of its remaining primary schools can make a valuable contribution to the educational provision in an area, such schools should be retained'. The same statement noted and encouraged the recent trend of uniting an Anglican and a Methodist school into one joint voluntary school, a trend that has continued and has extended to the founding in some areas of new joint Anglican-Methodist schools. In 1982 Methodism had sixty day schools, of which twenty three were joint Anglican-Methodist.

Westminster (founded 1851) and Southlands (1872) colleges were established as a consequence of the same concern. While they were established to provide teachers for Methodist schools, it was also intended that 'a large proportion of the students trained in (them) will . . . be employed in School Board schools' (Conference 1871). The policy has been, and still is, to provide teachers with a training based in a Christian understanding both of human life and of education, in the context of a college community firmly rooted in the Christian tradition. Since diversification, following the James Report, Southlands in particular, now one of four corporate members of the federal Roehampton Institute of Higher Education, offers varied courses, but both still provide a steady flow of teachers into the state system.

The Methodist Church welcomed the 1944 Act and its clauses on religious instruction and school assembly. Subsequently it has shared fully in debate and consultation about the meaning and implementation (or lack of it) of those clauses. It has in general welcomed the developments that have taken place, as to both method and content, in RE in the curriculum. The Church recognizes that these changes are not inherently a weakening of commitment to Christian education (though they can become that), but are a proper embodiment of such an education in the light of developments in educational philosophy and psychology, across the whole curriculum not merely in relation to religious education; of the changing nature of British society with growing numbers of adherents of faiths other than Christian; and of developments in an understanding of what is effective catechesis.

John Wesley himself founded a residential school (Kingswood School): currently there are fifteen residential schools of Methodist foundation, representative of all traditions uniting in the Methodist Church in 1932. Opinion in the church is divided about the theological and moral validity of the church continuing to sponsor these schools, all of them independent since the cessation of Direct Grant. Through the 1970s, Conference almost annually considered resolutions chal-

lenging the continuing of the schools as Methodist Institutions: each time, sometimes overwhelmingly, Conference declared in favour of their continuing. As well as providing a Christian education in its widest sense, they have a wider influence in the education system of the country. For example, one outcome of the creative educational theory and practice of A. B. Sackett, while he was Headmaster of Kingswood School, was the many future headmasters whom he trained.

Through the Division of Education and Youth, the Church maintains a consultative relationship with the DES at political level as well as with permanent officials, and co-operates with other churches and agencies.

The concern for Christian education informing Methodism's concern with schools also informed its policy in relation to universities, polytechnics and colleges during the post-1945 expansion of higher education, and in particular following the Robbins Report. The Methodist Church was the first to appoint a full-time secretary as national co-ordinator of its developing work through chaplaincies and in other ways.

2. Church education and resources used within the Methodist Church.

Much of the pedagogical, cultural, and theological development that has transformed RE in day schools has also found expression in the policies of those agencies of the Methodist Church responsible for its teaching ministry. Moreover, Christian education is promoted as more than a conceptual exercise: it involves all aspects of the personality, and action as well as reflection; and it involves the whole life of the local church and its involvement in the community. Worship, teaching and service are seen to be essentially interdependent.

The Division of Education and Youth has responsibility for policy for work with children, young people, and young adults, and in higher and further education; and for providing services and resources for circuits and churches in this work. The policies it pursues and the resources it provides seek always to take account of contemporary understanding of the processes of human maturation and the implications for the learning process.

It publishes annually and promotes, in partnership with the National Christian Education Council*, *Partners in Learning*, an all-age programme for Christian education in the context of worship on Sunday. It provides programme resources for weekday children's groups, and study and training resources for youth clubs and fellowships, including Bible study, social questions, and preparation for discipleship and church membership, and emphasis on community aspects that cut across age-groupings. Through the World Affairs (Youth) programme (WAY), a joint project with the Overseas Division, education in world affairs is built into the normal resources referred to, and into the normal programmes of the relevant groups.

All these resources commend related audio-visual and other materials from many other sources, religious and secular.

In support of the Christian education of children and young people the Conference approves a 'Preparation for Service' programme of study and action to be undertaken by all new workers in the local church, with children and young people, planned and promoted by the Division. The course includes modules on the personal life of the new worker and on biblical and doctrinal knowledge, as well as on the learning process and teaching methods. The Division also promotes a range of further training courses, some leading to the award of diplomas. This whole programme is sustained by voluntary part-time training staff in every district, and by regionally deployed full-time professionally trained field staff who also serve to enhance the quality of work with children and young people locally, to stimulate new forms of service, and work in new areas.

Most other divisions and agencies of the Methodist Church produce Christian education material related to their own remits or to specific groups. The National Children's Home provides literature that seeks to increase awareness of the needs of children at risk or handicapped, and of the vital place of the family in society. The major historic sites – Epworth Rectory; Wesley's Chapel, City Road; and the 'New Room', Bristol – produce educational literature including packs for use in day-school religious education, or to support school visits. The Overseas Division pursues a vigorous policy of education throughout the church on international understanding, and the theology and nature of world mission, its major publication being the monthly magazine *Now*. The Home Mission Division produces a range of literature and audio-visual resources for education in mission and evangelism; through Luton Industrial College it provides courses on a Christian view of industry and technology for ministers, students, trade unionists, and managers; and through Cliff College it offers Christian education and training in mission for lay people. The Division of Ministries is responsible for ministerial training through theological colleges and non-residential courses; for initial and continuing education of local (lay) preachers, for whom study books on the Bible, theology and worship are specially written and frequently revised; for a wide range of correspondence courses on the Bible, theology, church history and social questions through the Methodist Study Centre; and for a project for theological education for the whole church. The Division of Social Responsibility publishes a regular news-sheet as well as a range of study materials on social questions.

3. Confirmation preparation

Confirmation preparation is understood in the context of the total education programme and the total life of the church. Formal preparation begins in the active experience of the young person or adult of the whole life and worship of the Christian community in which he or she is placed.

Confirmation, or reception into membership, is based in discipleship: the Church seeks and expects of candidates for confirmation commitment to Christ, and therefore to his Church as the medium of his continuing life and action in his world.

Preparation for confirmation includes emphasis on ecumenical development and on commitment to the mission of the church in the immediate neighbourhood and in the world, as well as on the corporate life of the church in worship and fellowship, on the importance of personal piety, and on an understanding and acceptance of the faith of the church.

The wide variety of local churches, in respect for example of size and cultural context, precludes rigid regulations as to age of confirmation, or a single prescribed programme of preparation.

The Church Membership Committee, within the Division of Ministries, produces materials for the prospective church member and for those who conduct preparation classes, which are increasingly led jointly by minister and lay people, or by lay people only. It co-ordinates the contributions of other interests within Methodism, in particular of the Home Mission Division and the Division of Education and Youth. The latter produces a range of resources, for differing young people and contexts, to educate young people and children in the meaning of discipleship and of belonging to the church, and to encourage commitment. These resources are focussed in elements in *Partners in Learning* and in literature made available to every local church for the first Sunday in May each year, which is designated by the Conference as Young People's Day.

The Faith and Order Committee, along with these agencies, seeks to promote continuing reflection throughout the Church as a whole on the nature of the Christian initiation.

DOUGLAS A. BROWN

Methods in RE: A Survey

As in other areas of the curriculum, methods are affected by changes in aims and objectives and in the understanding of the learning process.

When the aim was to teach the Christian faith to children by giving them knowledge of the Christian scriptures, the method most widely used was for Bible stories to be told to or read by the class, who then reproduced them in written form or by drawing or acting them. More imaginative teachers asked their pupils to write 'diary accounts' or 'newspaper reports' of biblical events.

In the experience-based RE of the sixties, when many teachers saw their aim as helping pupils to 'find a faith to live by', class discussion was the method most usually employed in the secondary school for handling the personal and social issues which were considered to be the best means of demonstrating the relevance of the Christian faith to the lives of the pupils. Teachers of younger children, on the other hand, adopted for the explora-

tion of life themes the variety of methods normally used in primary school topic work.

When the aim of the subject came to be seen as helping pupils to understand the nature of religion a still wider range of methods was needed. The focus on living religions makes it much more possible to use the resources of the local community, e.g., to visit places of worship and to receive visits from adherents of religions, and to see and handle religious objects. It can also make homework more interesting: secondary pupils learning about Christian denominations can visit ministers and members of congregations, collect parish magazines and perhaps attend some of the churches' activities. The interest of the media, especially television, in religions makes it easier for pupils to contribute in class the knowledge which they have gained at home.

One of the objectives of the study of religion is that pupils should, as far as possible, learn to 'stand in other people's shoes'. In addition to the essential factual knowledge, therefore, they need the imaginative stimulus that can be provided by the expressive arts. They are more likely to be able to appreciate what a religion feels like to its adherents if they have some experience of its music and literature and art. Equally important is the opportunity for pupils to express through dance*, art*, music* and poetry* their understanding of such topics as festivals* and mythology*, which lose much of their significance if they are merely described in words. The preparation of food associated with a festival or the acting out of a marriage ceremony can also help to bring a religion to life.

Primary schools have long used the project method, but the introduction of mixed ability classes in the secondary school has made traditional formal class teaching even more inappropriate. The difficulties at secondary level – the vast numbers of pupils many teachers have to teach in a week, and the restricted timetable time – are outweighed by the advantages: the stimulus which adolescents receive from their more active role in learning and from the variety of activities being undertaken, the higher standard of work which they are willing to produce when there is to be an end-product which is to be seen by others, the value of being able to see the parts contributing to the whole, the opportunity the teacher has to move round the class and talk with individuals, and the optimum use which can be made of scarce resources when pupils are engaged on different tasks.

Some sort of cumulative activity, whether it takes the form of a wall display, a class book, a tape or a video or television programme, not only gives continuity to a scheme of work but makes comprehension easier through the attempt to communicate to others what is being learnt.

Discussion still has a place in RE, though not necessarily in its conventional 'spokes of a wheel' form, where the teacher responds to each contribution from the class and individual pupils have very few opportunities to speak. Variations include: pupils discussing in pairs at the beginning of a lesson, perhaps as a prelude to compiling a class list (e.g. of symbols or customs associated with Easter), or arguments for and against a particular course of action; small discussion groups dealing with a question arising out of a story the class is reading; groups of pupils working out the most appropriate way to present a topic in assembly, or mount a display, or plan what questions to ask a visitor to the class.

There has tended to be less innovation in the methods used in preparing pupils for examinations than in general RE courses. However, the revision of many 'A' level syllabuses in the seventies and of some of the 'O' level and CSE syllabuses more recently, has encouraged a more imaginative approach. Pupils can more easily handle issues in philosophy and ethics papers, for instance, if they have considerable experience in producing arguments both for and against a position. Those who take papers in the study of religion are better able to show understanding of the subject if their course includes the methods described earlier. Even the traditional biblical syllabuses can be tackled more effectively if, instead of just working through the set texts, the pupils learn about the nature of the literature and the themes it deals with, e.g., before studying a gospel looking at a variety of pictures illustrating different ways in which artists have portrayed Jesus, learning about the parable form and its use by Jewish teachers, etc. Whatever the syllabus, if pupils take an active part in the lessons and assume some responsibility for their study, they find it easier to articulate what they have learnt

when they come to answer the questions on the examination paper.

See also **Media, Use of in RE**.

JEAN HOLM

Middle East, Christian Education in the

In most countries of the Middle East, Christians are relatively few compared to their Muslim compatriots. Their percentage differs from one country to another. Christian children attend government schools as well as church-related schools (schools established and operated by different churches and Christian organizations).

In Egypt, Christian Education is one of the school subjects in both government and church-related schools. It aims at developing effective knowledge of the basic facts of Christianity as expressed in the Bible, in church history and in liturgy and worship. Such knowledge implies basic Christian concepts and values that are necessary for helping personal growth towards maturity, taking into account the basic characteristics of the successive stages of growth and the values and needs of society.

The curriculum of Christian Education in Egypt has been divided into three levels. The first six years of the basic school (previously known as primary school) aims at 1. developing faith in God as Creator of nature, plant and animal; 2. God's care for man whom God created after his image; 3. giving examples of prophets and saints, from both the OT and NT, in order to serve as models of virtuous life and moral values, such as love, co-operation, forgiveness, honesty, truthfulness, obedience and friendship; 4. acquainting men with the teachings, parables and miracles of Jesus Christ; 5. helping them to understand the importance of the Bible and memorize portions of it; 6. deep-rooting them in Christian faith and love for prayer; and 7. implanting social and behavioural values in their lives.

Christian education for the following three years of the basic school (previously called preparatory school) is focussed on 1. developing the students' understanding of basic facts, concepts and principles of the Christian faith; 2. increasing the students' awareness of themselves as being created after the image of God and God's plan for their salvation; 3. practising the Christian virtues and experiencing the inner conscience and spiritual growth; 4. offering examples of commitment to family life and social concerns through analysing some behavioural situations of personalities in the life of the church and through basic study of church history.

In the secondary school (three years following the nine years of the basic school), Christian education emphasizes the study of the Bible as the basis for Christian life, giving examples of organized study of some parts of it. The students at this level are encouraged to examine what they have accepted without discussion during the previous stages of their development. They need help to understand the role that religion may perform in helping them find healthy solutions to their personal psychological problems. The students' personality finds new avenues of growth by analysing their relationship to family, church and society.

In addition, there are more advanced courses for students of Christianity in the teacher training institutes, as well as a book on *Methods in Teaching Christian Education*; a Teacher's Guide for the teachers of the first two years of the primary school; and a book of pictures for the children in the pre-primary (nursery) classes.

The course of Christian Education in Egyptian schools takes three class periods per week in the first six years of the basic school and two class periods for the higher levels.

In each school, the Christian teachers of different subjects (such as English, Mathematics, Sciences or Social Studies) would be assigned to teach Christian Education to Christian students in their schools as part of their schedule. Christian students take their Christian Education periods at the same time as the periods of Islamic Education. Both Muslim and Christian students take examinations in their respective religions.

Christian inspectors of different school subjects in all the educational zones are commissioned to follow-up the operations of Christian Education in the schools along with their respective special subjects. In some zones, there are specialized inspectors assigned uniquely for Christian Education.

In the Department of Religious Education of the Ministry of Education, an expert on Christian Education is responsible for the operation of Christian Education in Egypt. A Ministerial Committee on Christian Education, comprised of specialized representatives of all the churches in Egypt (Orthodox, Protestant and Catholic) develops the objectives and outlines of the Christian Education courses and shares in writing the materials for the students and the guides for the teachers.

In the Sudan, similar to Egypt, Christian Education is one of the school subjects. It focusses on biblical texts chosen for the successive school years. The texts deal with worship, sacred history, religious facts and beliefs, the church, biblical personalities. The teachers are asked to read the assigned texts with the students and explain them clearly using simple expressions, full of life and movement. The basic Christian beliefs are being derived from the biblical texts.

The courses of Christian Education in Sudan take four class periods per week for both primary and general high schools and three periods per week for higher secondary schools. Christian Education is taught by qualified teachers appointed for this purpose. Priests and ministers share in teaching where there is a lack of teachers for this subject.

The Department on Christian Education of the Ministry of Education in Sudan is responsible for all aspects of Christian Education in all the schools. The Department co-operates with all the churches in Sudan in reviewing the curriculum materials. In South Sudan a counterpart is responsible for the operations of Christian Education in that region.

In Lebanon, each denomination has its own curriculum for Christian Education in its schools. Nevertheless, there have been attempts to develop a unified outline for one curriculum to be used by all the schools of the different denominations. A basic course will be developed including the outline and some basic ideas. This course will be used by the different denominations as a guideline for developing their own materials, adding their own liturgical tradition and forms of worship.

However, the Catholic Committee on Christian Education worked out a unified curriculum for all the Catholic schools in Lebanon (Maronite, Greek, Latin and other Catholic churches and orders). This curriculum used as a frame of reference the *Catechesi Tradendae* issued by Pope John Paul II in 1979, including the studies of the General Synod *On Christian Instruction* in 1977, as well as the *General Catechetical Directory* issued by the Clerical Council in 1971 after Vatican II. The Committee worked for several years and received the approval on this curriculum of the Synod of the Catholic Patriarchs and Bishops in Lebanon in 1980.

This curriculum is based on the principles of modern education. It follows the specific needs and capabilities at every age level:

1. Ages five and six, creating the appropriate atmosphere for the child's adaptation to the daily events through simple prayers, words, movement and picture.

2. Ages seven to ten, organized initiation into the mystery of Jesus and the basic mysteries, into personal and communal prayers, and into basic Christian virtues.

3. Ages eleven to thirteen, simple explication of basic elements of the faith as the young begins to develop objective and abstract ideas of the world and of time (history).

4. Ages fourteen and fifteen, personalization of instruction to cope with the adolescent's egocentrism and developing his faith along two demensions: the *koinonia* and salvation.

5. Ages sixteen to eighteen, orientation towards mature and responsible adult life.

In Syria, similar to both Egypt and the Sudan, RE is one of the school subjects in government and church-related schools. It begins in the third year of the primary school which lasts for six years. The curriculum of Christian Education for the primary level includes stories derived from the OT and the NT. For example, the curriculum for the third year primary includes: the creation of man, the first sin, the birth of Christ and his life, the mystery of salvation, Pentecost, the church, and examples of OT personalities.

In the secondary level (three years) the curriculum deals with the issues that relate to the life of the adolescents. In the first year the curriculum deals with the Trinity, the existence of God, the incarnation, salvation and the kingdom of God.

The curriculum for the second years examines issues of Christian social ethics, such as the Christian and the church, marriage, relationship with the authorities, responsibility in society. In addition to the official curriculum, each church adds what relates to its specific tradition, liturgy and language (such as Armenian and Syriac).

In Jordan, Christian Education is permitted only in church-related schools on the condition that the different denominations agree on one curriculum to be used by all of them in their schools.

The churches in Jordan adopted the curriculum of Christian Education in Syria and the Jordanian government authorized them to use it in their schools. However, each denomination adds the topics that relate to its own tradition and liturgical life. In government schools no teaching of Christian Education is allowed for Christian students.

The question of RE in the schools has been one of the basic principles of the Middle East Council of Churches, Department on Christian Education (DCE) since 1976. In 1977, it held a consultation on 'The Role of Middle East Churches in Education'. It held another consultation on 'Christian Education in Schools' in 1981. Both consultations emphasized the role of Christian education in developing the students' faith and commitment to practising Christian life and worship. It was felt that the teacher of Christian education in all the Middle East countries needs further training because of the lack of the specialized teachers in the subject.

The Department on Christian Education co-operated with the churches in different Middle East countries in developing teacher training programmes, exchange of materials, reviewing existing materials, developing and locating basic audio-visual materials and exchanging experiences among the churches and the countries of the Middle East.

MAURICE ASSAD

Middle Schools, RE in

Children in the middle years are in a process of transition from the small intimate world of family and first school to a more complex world where family, friends, larger school, trends in fashion and culture and the complicated organization of a wider world all jostle for attention. The middle years provide opportunity for an unhurried transition, laying foundations for what is to follow and building on what has already been done.

The society in which the children are growing up is one which would seem to be characterized by secular materialism, but it is also increasingly multi-cultural. The reality of a global village comes nearer each day.

Children in the middle years are interested in gathering information. They enjoy learning and are eager to discover new things about the world in which they live. They are anxious to discover the meaning behind things and to understand why things are as they are. The ultimate questions* about existence interest them and they will speculate about death and suffering and other such issues. They love story* and are capable of sensing the truth in myth*. They learn a lot from story which creates a world into which they enter imaginatively and where they can learn about situations they encounter in reality later. Story is a means of coming to terms with some of their deeper fears.

It is important that RE in the middle years is organized in such a way that the children will be interested in it and explore it with the same enthusiasm that they show for other areas of the curriculum.

Most of the more recent agreed syllabuses* of RE would have as the aim of the subject 'to enable pupils to understand the nature of religious beliefs and practices and the importance and influence of these in the lives of believers' (Hampshire 1978). Such an aim demands acquaintance with more than one religion, but it would seem appropriate that the religion which features most largely in the majority of schools is Christianity. A child would not be adequately educated if he was unaware that other religions existed. Some acquaintance with certain aspects of one or two other religions would seem appropriate in the middle years.

RE in the middle years seeks to extend the objectives for religious education found in the first school and to introduce a more explicitly religious element and a more structured style of presentation as the children progress through the school. Throughout, the emphasis is on a religious education which is open and related to the children's own interests and experience. The exploration of experiences, feelings and questions about themselves and themselves in relation to others, and the natural world continue to form an important part of RE. This leads to a greater self knowledge without which a mature understanding of religion is impossible and without which the individual will be less than whole. Such an exploration will bring the children face to face with some of the ultimate questions which

human beings ask and to which religions seek to provide answers; Is there purpose to life? Is death the end? Why is there suffering? *I am David* by Anne Holm (Puffin Books) is just one of many children's novels which open up these issues. This aspect of religious education cannot be confined to a set lesson. The sensitive teacher will see opportunities for it right across the curriculum and will help children to see the complementary nature of their own questioning and man's religious belief.

Children vary widely in their knowledge of and attitudes to religion. This diversity can enrich the scope of religious education, particularly if the teacher allows discussion. The exploration of religion in the middle years should begin with what is in, or close to, the children's own experience. Information about people and events far away and long ago will make little sense to them. A visit to a religious building can make a useful starting point, and will enable further study of aspects of that religion to be put into a meaningful context. It is important to encourage children to search out the meaning of the things they see and hear. Otherwise religion may seem to them to be about strange people doing strange things. As well as learning the names and uses of the parts of the building and the objects found there, the pupils can try to discover why they are there and what meaning they have for the people who use it. They can learn about the community which the particular building serves and how it functions.

Festivals* are another aspect of religions that most children meet at some time, either at school or at home*, or both. The major festivals of the main world religions, many of which are celebrated with special plays, food and music, make a valuable contribution to RE. Multi-cultural schools are especially fortunate in having ready resources but material is increasingly available.

A further aspect of religion familiar to some children are the rites of passage. The rituals associated with birth, coming of age, marriage and death can be the focus of interesting work at the top end of the middle school.

At the same time as pupils are exploring religion they need to be developing certain skills, sensitivities and attitudes without which they will not reach a mature understanding of religion. The skills are related to religious language, and how ritual, symbol, music and art convey meaning. Experience of different uses of language and of different types of literature form a useful foundation for a developing understanding of imagery, simile and metaphor, allegory, myth, fable and parable. The sensitivities are related to being able to stand in another's shoes without which it is impossible to appreciate another's religion. The attitudes are to do with thinking that religion is worthy of investigation.

RE will share some insights and skills with other areas of the curriculum, such as history, geography, social studies, language and literature, and the expressive arts, art, drama, music. In some schools RE takes place in one period per week. This has the advantage of ensuring that it happens but means that it is isolated. If it is integrated, opportunities for developing links across the curriculum are increased and so are the possibilities of what can be done in terms of learning experiences and follow-up.

If RE in the middle years can keep alive the children's interest in religion as a genuine and important part of human life and send them to the next stage of education eager to discover more, it will have succeeded in its task. It is not an easy subject to teach and many are daunted at the task, but it is a subject that should not be avoided and is endlessly fascinating.

HEATHER MOORE

Millar Report

In 1968 the Secretary of State for Scotland formed a Committee under Professor W. Malcolm Millar of Aberdeen University, to review 'the current practice of Scottish Schools (other than Roman Catholic schools) with regard to moral and religious education and to make recommendations for its improvement'. The remit was to be undertaken within the Scottish statutory provisions. The report 'Moral and Religious Education in Scottish Schools' (HMSO) 1972 adds an appendix with extracts from the Education (Scotland) Act 1962.

The report begins with a survey of the provision and continues with an outline of evidence submitted to the committee. The main findings include the statement; 'We take the view that the place of moral and religious education (particularly the latter) must be

justified on educational grounds and that the nature of moral and religious education must be determined by educational considerations.' A section on a developmental approach follows. Practical implications for schools are reviewed. Questions for the future are identified.

The report is notable for the way in which practical recommendations, subsequently adopted, have ensured progress. The General Teaching Council for Scotland obtained approval for a secondary teaching qualification. The Scottish Central Committee for Religious Education, established in 1974, issued curriculum bulletins in 1978 and 1981. Several local authorities appointed Advisers in Religious Education and a number of local working party reports have appeared.

J. J. LAIDLAW

Ministry: Informal/Auxiliary Courses

Training for ministers and others, e.g. teachers in religious education, is provided on a large scale in ways other than through residential theological colleges, in Britain and other countries. Indeed such training predates the foundation of most theological colleges.

Since the Second World War informal courses in various patterns, some including short periods of residence have grown in many dioceses of the Church of England and in other churches. Frequently they are ecumenical in character. The general content of the courses is similar to the ordination courses carried on in colleges. Since the students continue in their existing 'secular' occupation, the courses are spread over a longer period than those in college and the requirements are demanding.

These courses are usually designed to help prepare for ministries of various forms. They are useful too for a more highly educated laity in church life.

International Review of Missions April 1982, LXXI, 282, pp. 213.

PHILIP LEE-WOOLF

Miracle

Miracle may be described as a 'divine act transcending the normal order of things'. By their nature, miracles may tend to be spectacular or even bizarre, and can attract attention which heightens difficulties in understanding. Much debate surrounds the phenomenon of miracle and frequent attempts have been made to 'rationalize' the events. Nevertheless, miracle remains an important element in religious traditions, especially the Judaeo-Christian tradition.

The difficulties in presenting miracle in RE arise on two levels. 1. Those linked to the children's stage of conceptual development; research in the field of children's religious thinking has shown that young children are frequently unable to think of miracle in any other way than as 'magic' (Goldman). 2. Difficulties can exist for anyone in the late twentieth century, child or adult. A major problem is the apparent conflict between the world-view of the societies in which miracle-stories originated and contemporary world-views. Our world has been 'desacralized'; it is not seen as populated with demons and spirits; for the most part, modern man does not see himself as being at the mercy of nature and unable to control it. This shift in thinking about the world leads to a change in our view of miracle. Greater understanding of the world means that many events at one time thought of as miracle can now be explained as natural phenomena. However, as defined in terms of modern presuppositions, the concept of miracle takes on a greatly heightened meaning, as, in the light of present understandings of nature, 'a miracle would entail an exercise of divine power on a far greater scale than previous periods envisaged' (Nineham). In dealing with miracle a number of critical problems also exist; in any religious tradition it is necessary to distinguish between miracles which seem to be an integral part of the theology and those which seem to represent elements of folk-tale or to be embellishments.

The majority of miracle material encountered in school is likely to be biblical, but the approaches suggested may also prove appropriate for dealing with both later Christian miracles and examples from non-Christian traditions. In first school it seems best to tell miracle stories very sparingly, and only when justified by some other aspect of the story. Presentation should be such that it does not serve to heighten the 'magic'. In middle school, children may already have some familiarity with miracle stories, perhaps from earlier years at school, or from outside sources. By this stage, other areas of the curriculum and the media are already fostering in children an emphasis on the scientifically verifiable. It is important to encourage intellectual reflection upon the miracle stories, rather than merely narrating stories which they may reject as impossible, or tend to see as childish. Questions of the significance of the stories, the impact of the events on those present, and why they were passed into the tradition can begin to be raised. This process can be continued in the secondary school, where miracle may be examined more closely, looking both at the belief systems which would see an event as miracle, as well as considering the possibility of 'natural' explanations. (OT miracles provide a useful field of study here.) In the sixth-form, the concept of miracle itself may be examined. In any of these situations, it is important to help the pupil to set miracles in their essential context – the faith-systems of believers.

Geoffrey Ashe, *Miracles*, Routledge & Kegan Paul 1978; Ronald Goldman, *Religious Thinking from Childhood to Adolescence*. Routledge & Kegan Paul 1964; Dennis Nineham, *The Use and Abuse of the Bible*, Macmillan 1976; Richard Swinburne, *The Concept of Miracle*, Macmillan 1970.

CAROL FRY

Mission Schools

Missionaries started schools in many continents for basically the same reason. The 'Word-made-flesh' story is recorded in the written Bible of the Christian church. To read the written word of holy scripture became an envied skill. It gave knowledge, understanding, and power to enter another culture and faith system. Mission schools became vectors of mission and they multiplied in every continent.

They began as very small, amateur enterprises and were sometimes multi-racial. The best pupils became the first indigenous teachers. Even with minimal skills and knowledge these were used to lead rapidly proliferating units, in scattered areas around central mission stations. As the curriculum expanded they concentrated on all primary education subjects. Gradually they accepted grants from colonial governments for teachers' pay and equipment, because they served national growth. Only after 1945 (in Africa) did they begin seriously to teach secondary education. One example from Africa (Nigeria) must suffice to illustrate their size and influence.

In 1912 Government and Native Administration in Nigeria (except Northern Provinces) had 58 primary schools with 3,984 pupils. The mission-assisted schools numbered 91 with 11,732 pupils. The mission-unassisted schools could not be numbered: they had an estimate of 20,000 pupils. By 1947 the Government and Native Administration had 183 primary schools (26,040 pupils): there were 473 mission-assisted schools (153,759 pupils); and 4,328 mission-unassisted schools (358,592 pupils). These figures illustrate the major dependence of former colonial countries on the voluntary mission school system. These figures also refer to twenty four denominational churches/missions, but of these six mainline churches dominated ninety-five per cent of the enterprise.

In assessing the educational contribution of mission schools the following factors are significant: 1. They pioneered the eventual national systems of education. 2. The first national political leaders, unifying the emergent nations, owed their early education to mission enterprise. 3. They gave to many nations a *lingua franca*. 4. They created the first reservoirs of persons able to administer in the Western tradition. 5. They perpetuated denominational divisions, but also contributed to an understanding of belonging to a world family. wider than tribe or nation. 6. In many places :hey failed to come to terms with cultural indigenization, particularly at social, family, rural and agricultural levels. Their products became torn between two conflicting worlds of experience. 7. They produced high levels of stress in later years for the sponsoring churches and agencies, particularly as they became rapidly secularized and dependent on scarce personal and financial resources from the missions themselves.

It is probably true to say that in what is now called the Third World, the administrative sub-structure of nation states has the mission school as one of its principal foundations. The content, form and method of religious education in mission schools varied enormously with the period in history, the ecclesiastical denomination, the principal instructor, the languages, and the indigenous religious context.

Its earliest character was Bible-centred, making the bridge between an oral and storytelling tradition and the literary records. But there would be big differences in emphasis in a place where proselytizing was forbidden and a place where a more neutral expectation prevailed. The other simple vehicle was that of hymns and spiritual songs, coupled with prayer and worship, closely integrated with the general curriculum. Both these modes led directly to participation in public worship and prepared everyone for that kind of celebration. In missions where incorporation into the church was of paramount significance, much of the primary school curriculum in RE was geared to the learning of promises, creeds, prayers, etc. by rote learning methods.

As the years passed the dominance of the expatriate in teaching waned and the filtered dilution of teaching became inevitable. The other factor here was the use of the vernacular as an instrument of faith and theological insight. Exact translation was always difficult. The visual aids used in primary schools naturally tended to be very Western in style and it was only slowly that indigenous art began to enrich the learning process. Syllabuses were usually generated by Western educationalists and had strong denominational flavours. These were taught to indigenous teachers on a refresher course plus notes basis, and only regular school visiting, testing, helping and criticizing prevented rapid deterioration in content and range. The concept of grading material by year and class was not highly developed. At these levels there was little evidence of a capacity to use indigenous religious experience as the entry point into understanding.

As ecumenical co-operation grew in missionary conferences and embryonic Christian councils (particularly after 1945) many attempts were made at joint inter-denominational syllabus compilation, but curiously this coincided (in Africa at least) with the assertion by the state of leadership in the national school systems which led to the demise of the mission schools.

It was probably in teacher training colleges and in the central mission station schools that the best RE was achieved among a relatively small number of students. However, insofar as literacy was achieved, the personal capacity to read the scriptures was the most important gift of the mission school system.

JAMES ROBERTSON

Missionary Societies

For two hundred years, missionary societies in Britain have been among the pioneers of education in the countries to which they have sent missionaries. Many state institutions of learning in Asia, Africa and Latin America owe their origins to the work of missionary teachers of past generations. Even today, missionary societies and overseas divisions of churches regard this work as one of their priorities. This article does not attempt to cover this aspect of the work of missionary societies and orders, but to give a general view of the educational work of these agencies in the UK.

The educational ethos, methods and resources of these agencies vary enormously. Some appoint a team of specialists with a variety of skills and experience in primary, secondary, higher and adult education, to act as advisers at these levels in the supporting churches and congregations. They edit periodicals, produce occasional study packs and project materials, devise simulation games, organize conferences and seminars, respond to enquiries, and visit churches, schools and colleges, besides relating to aid and development agencies. Other missions operate with a much smaller 'home' budget, and one person may have to assume a variety of educational roles. In all cases, missionary personnel are in constant demand for deputation work, but increasingly local congregations are encouraged to develop their own programmes in education for mission.

Education for mission has been defined as 'the process of animation of a Christian community, in order that it might widen its vision and invest its strength in discovering and facing the missionary challenges surrounding it'. It cannot be taken for granted that this process is genuinely taking place through the activities outlined in the previous paragraph. The pressures of relating to a constituency which provides the financial resources for the continuing life and work of a society are such that the need to 'drum up support' in money and personnel often conflicts with the need to educate people in the 'sending' churches about the realities of the life of the 'receiving' churches in their socio-political context. Education for mission involves the education of missions; and the first steps of this process takes place when churches eschew the dissemination and use of materials and concepts loaded with paternalism, triumphalism, and an attitude towards the traditional receiving countries and churches that exhibits scant regard for indigenous cultures and values. The process of education continues with an awareness of the wealth of cultural variety in which Christian faith can take root and flourish, an understanding of the vocation of the world-wide church to multi-directional mission, and a perception that the real ecumenical task for the world church is the struggle for a genuine 'oikoumene' for the whole human family.

From this it follows that educational programmes increasingly have as their objective, not only to present the needs of the churches and peoples of developing countries, but also to interpret insights derived from the life and work of these churches for the task of mission in the secularized West. Interchange programmes bring representatives of these churches to Britain and Europe as 'Partners in Mission', whose role it is to hold up a mirror to the traditional sending churches, and to help them to see their life as local congregations in the context of the world church. In the last two decades of this century, this process of education will raise sharp questions about dialogue with peoples of other faiths, the meaning and cost of being a church of the poor, the appropriate social location for doing theology, and for the inter-relation of Bible study and worship to the proclamation of Good News and the social and political action demanded by Christian love.

DEREK G. WINTER

Mixed Ability Teaching
see **Grouping of Pupils**

Monasticism

From the beginning of Western monasticism each community was responsible for the education of its own members to fit them for the religious life. This, in the archetypal Benedictine order, required sufficient Latin to know the Rule and the liturgical texts of the *Opus Dei* and to study the scriptures and the Fathers. To this end the oblates and young monks were taught in the cloister school by an older monk as novice master. Some Benedictine monasteries in the Dark Ages accumulated large libraries and became famous centres of literary and theological scholarship.

This Benedictine pre-eminence passed with the rise of cathedral schools* and universities in the twelfth century. Thereafter, the Benedictines and the newer orders, mostly Cistercian monks and Augustinian canons, concerned themselves primarily with the vocational training of their own novices and juniors, sending a few of their ablest members to read theology or canon law at the university, where some of the larger monasteries maintained houses of study, as Canterbury and Durham did at Oxford.

Teaching outside the community formed no part of the monks' profession and their contribution to medieval education was much less than used to be supposed. Nevertheless, some monasteries – mainly Benedictine and Augustinian – often provided schools of two kinds for outsiders as a work of charity, but both were taught by hired masters, seculars or laymen, not by monks. The song school trained boys for the choir; the almonry school taught grammar to boys who might serve the convent as altarists and choristers and eventually enter the cloister as novices or become secular priests. Additionally, some abbots might receive a few gentlemen's sons, as boarders in their households, for a training that combined book learning, religious instruction and social accomplishments, but this too would be given by secular masters not monks.

A greater contribution to lay education was perhaps made by nunneries, many of which boarded and taught small numbers of well-born girls and sometimes young boys, not as a charity but for fees. In some houses the children seem to have shared the nuns' conventual life in choir, refectory and dormitory, in spite of episcopal disapproval. The teaching would be limited by the nuns' own modest educational attainments – perhaps reading, religious knowledge and polite refinements.

Friars, unlike monks and nuns, provided no schools for the laity but educated their own recruits and developed in certain of their convents a highly organized system of philosophical and theological training which enabled

them in the thirteenth and fourteenth centuries to dominate university teaching. Their chief contribution to popular religious education was made as missioners, preachers and confessors.

Monasticism disappeared in protestant countries at the Reformation, and although it continued in Catholic Europe until the Napoleonic era the work of educating the laity was taken up by the Jesuits and teaching congregations such as the Piarists, Oratorians and Ursulines. A Catholic monastic revival in the nineteenth century touched the Anglican Communion after the Oxford Movement, creating new religious communities, Catholic and Anglican, some combining a quasi-monastic life with social and educational service. In England the Benedictine educational tradition continues, but differently, in the schools at Ampleforth, Belmont and Downside.

See also **Communities in Education, Religious**.

F. L. Cross (ed.), *The Oxford Dictionary of the Christian Church*, Oxford University Press [2]1974; David Knowles, *The Monastic Order in England*, Cambridge University Press [2]1963 and, *The Religious Orders in England*, 3 vols, Cambridge University Press 1948–1959; Nicholas Orme, *English Schools in the Middle Ages*, Methuen 1973.

                                            JOHN LAWSON

Montgomery Trust   *see* **Christian Education Movement**

Moral Development

There are broadly speaking two traditions of theory and research in moral development. The first is represented by psychoanalysis and social learning theory; the second is best represented by Piaget, Kohlberg and other cognitive developmental theorists. There is a genuine tension between these two approaches, and a synthesis between them has proved very difficult to attain. At the end of the day any decision between them must rest upon an understanding of the nature of morality and the moral life.

Within the first perspective there are a number of conditions which are held to be essential for moral development. Adults have power and authority over children and they exercise these in certain ways. They mediate the moral code to children through instruction, sanction departure from it by disapproval and blame, reward conformity through approval and serve as models of the morally mature person. Within psychoanalysis the central process whereby these conditions bring about moral development is identification. The child introjects the parental rules and obeys them through inturned aggression (the conscience) and self love displaced on to the ego ideal (the desire to do good). In social learning theory the processes involved are anxiety conditioning (the conscience) and patterns of behaviour learned through positive reinforcement (the desire to be good) while parental instruction and modelling serve a generalizing and discriminating function. Thus, though the processes said to occur differ, the basic conditions for moral development are the same for both kinds of theory. Both assume that morality is learned by the child from others, and primarily from adults who have authority and power over them.

A great deal of research shows that at least the processes claimed by social learning theory do occur under the conditions described (see Wright 1971). The central question is whether the acquisition of patterns of behaviour in this way constitutes *moral* development. There are reasons for thinking it does not.

1. These perspectives do not enable us to discriminate between the learning of moral rules, and the learning of conformity to conventions, laws, religious rules and other forms of social regulation. Yet moral philosophers have repeatedly made clear that the moral domain is distinctively different from these other forms of regulation in that it is universally applicable whereas the other forms can vary from situation to situation and are always relevant only for a limited number of people, and that it is the basis for evaluating these other forms of rule and not the other way round. It is worth noting that it has been found that from an early age children recognize that moral rules cannot be changed but that conventions can.

2. Morality cannot be derived in any logical sense from the edicts of authority, whether human or divine, since morality is the basis for evaluating such authorities. We obey authorities because their commands are right; we are not good because we obey them. For an act to be judged worthy of moral praise it is not enough that it conforms to what is morally prescribed; it must be done *because* it is the right thing to do. To act out of fear of punishment or desire for approval is not to act in a way that is morally praiseworthy.

What, then, is morality? It is the primary form of regulation of relationships between persons. It is primary in the sense that without it relationships tend to disintegrate and in the sense that it provides the optimal conditions for the creative development of persons in relationship. It is the application to human relationships of a limited number of principles, in particular those of respect for persons as persons, of equal generic rights of persons as persons, of caring for the welfare of persons as persons, of fairness and justice, of promise keeping, and of truthfulness. We can distinguish six types of relationship in which these principles apply. They are: 1. close personal relationships based on preference such as friendships and relationships within the family; 2. the contractual relationship the individual has with his own society and the institutions in it; 3. the individual's relationship to all persons everywhere. Then as derivatives of these there are 4. the individual's relationship to himself, and 5. his relationship to the rest of the organic and inorganic environment. Finally, 6. there is a form of relationship which may not be experienced by many people but certainly is by some. It might be defined as the relationship between the individual and all that is not himself, implicitly or explicitly understood as a unity and addressed as personal. For the theist this is his relationship to God*; but the nontheist may yet experience the existential quality of this relationship without invoking religious language. It may be, and of course may not be, the case that this relationship is only fully experienced in mature adulthood; but it is likely that the moral structure the individual perceives in this relationship will have fundamental consequences for the rest of his moral life.

We can define the mature moral person as one who understands the basic principles of morality and their application to the kinds of relationship described, who makes specific moral judgments, and who is motivated by moral obligation and aspiration to act in accordance with them. The moral person is necessarily autonomous in at least two senses. He originates his moral judgments, and though he experiences his moral obligations and aspirations as being commanded, he is not obeying the commands of any particular authority, human or divine.

The question then is how the moral person in this sense develops. The development is twofold. One aspect is the development of moral understanding and judgment and the other is the development of moral obligation and aspiration. Both are aspects of the one process. There has been a great deal of research into the former and virtually none into the latter.

The main stimulus for research into the development of moral reasoning has come from Kohlberg. A large number of studies from many countries have so far confirmed that the framework of salient considerations within which the child justifies his moral judgments develops through a sequence of stages. Morality is understood: at stage 1 as a function of authority, rewards and punishment; at stage 2 as co-operation with others in the interests of the self; at stage 3 as conformity to the expectations of the social group; at stage 4 as the maintenance of rules and laws; and at stage 5 and 6 as a matter of contract, rights and principles. Though we can have some confidence in the empirical fact that these stages occur, we have much less confidence in the theoretical scheme within which Kohlberg interprets it. Many people do not reach the later stages, and only a relatively small minority are found at stages 5 and 6.

It should be noted that the interpretation of morality given above is essentially a stage 5/6 interpretation. Those who understand morality in terms of earlier stages would be more likely to endorse the first psychological perspective on moral development outlined at the beginning of this article. Kohlberg's claim that the last stages are the best and 'true' understanding of morality is accepted here, but there is no space to defend it. However it appears that most contemporary moral philosophers would agree.

Very little attention has been given to the development of moral obligation and aspiration. The only viable theoretical account appears to be that presented by Piaget though his account is somewhat confused and contradictory. On this view, the essential condition

for the emergence of moral obligation and aspiration is the continued experience of relations of mutual respect, as between equals, based on mutual sympathy and love. The child should find himself 'in the presence, not of a system of commands requiring ritualistic and external obedience, but of a system of social relations such that everyone does his best to obey the same obligations and does so out of mutual respect' (Piaget). Speaking as an adult Piaget says 'one must place oneself on the child's own level, and give him a feeling of equality by laying stress on one's own obligations and one's own deficiencies'.

Religious education can both foster or retard moral development. Insofar as morality is presented as deriving from the commands of God and backed up by rewards and punishments its effects will be negative. Moreover any emphasis placed upon being a 'true believer', and therefore somehow better than those who are not, will tend to undermine that mutual respect between persons which is the heart of morality. If, on the other hand, it is stressed that God too is under the moral law and has obligations to man and that all people are equal in his love, then it will endorse and support moral growth. Moreover religion can offer a framework for understanding the whole context of living which is confirming of the moral element within it, and which it is difficult to find in non-religious terms.

L. Kohlberg, *Essays on Moral Development*, vol. 1, Harper & Row 1981; J. Piaget, *The Moral Judgment of the Child*, Routledge & Kegan Paul 1932; J. Rest, *Development in Judging Moral Issues*, University of Minnesota Press 1979; D. Wright, *The Psychology of Moral Behaviour*, Penguin Books 1971; D. Wright, 'Piaget's Theory of Practical Morality', *British Journal of Psychology*, vol. 73, 1982, pp. 279–83.

D. S. WRIGHT

Moral Education

Formerly it was assumed that moral education was a product of religious education. Children were taught religion and became moral by obeying its behavioural injunctions. Moral education cannot be conducted in that way in a religiously pluralistic society, where RE is usually seen, not as an induction into any particular religion, but as an objective study of all reputable religions and their moral systems. So taught, RE gives little direct explicit moral training. This has led in Britain to a demand, vocal but perhaps not widespread, for moral education apart from RE.

This demand for secular, belief-free moral education has had the active support of those who dislike and distrust religion but who are deeply concerned with moral values. They maintain, with some truth, that public support from RE is less a desire that children should be doctrinally instructed than that they should be made good, and that if adequate ME is provided then RE is not needed in schools. Consequently the two subjects are sometimes presented as rival alternatives.

The principle under debate is whether or not moral criteria can be discovered without reference to any underlying belief system. Those who maintain that they can, argue that, when religious believers say that morality is obedience to the will of a good god, they imply a concept of good that is prior to that god and against which he is being measured. The idea of a good god is a motivating factor impelling religious people to live up to ideals that originate elsewhere – either in the structure of the universe or in the logic of thinking. Reflection on what is ultimately important to humankind ought to reveal moral criteria, which all can accept, irrespective of their beliefs or lack of beliefs.

Religious people, on the other hand, point out that it is surprising that after over 2,500 years of moral philosophizing those criteria have not been described and accepted. The diversity of moral opinions suggests that people's moral systems depend on their unanalysed perceptions of what is ultimately real, on their theory of the nature of humankind and of what sort of life they think people ought to strive to achieve. These are matters of belief, which may or may not be conceived of in religious terms. Behind morality is this belief system, and ME and RE are, therefore, neither identical nor distinct but related.

Recent attempts to provide programmes of moral education, such as those of the Farmington Trust and the Lifeline and Startline material in Britain and the theories of Kohlberg and others in America, have illustrated the intractability of the problem. They have attempted to help children realize that

choices have to be made which are important for themselves and others, explained what psychological characteristics should be brought to those problems and insisted that they should be made in a free autonomous manner; but they have not yet faced the question of what criteria should be employed in those autonomous choices. The issue is far from decided.

N. Bull, *Moral Education*, Routledge & Kegan Paul 1969; E. Cox, *Problems and Possibilities for Religious Education*, Hodder & Stoughton 1982; R. M. Hare, *The Language of Morals*, Oxford University Press 1952; P. H. Hirst, *Moral Education in a Secular Society*, Routledge & Kegan Paul 1973; E. Lord and C. Bailey, *A Reader in Religious and Moral Education*, SCM Press 1973; C. Macy, *Let's Teach Them Right*, Pemberton Books 1969; R. S. Peters, *Ethics and Education*, Allen & Unwin 1966; R. S. Peters, 'Reason and Habit; the Paradox of Moral Education', in W. R. Niblett (ed.), *Moral Education in a Changing Society*, Faber & Faber 1963; J. Wilson, N. Williams and B. Sugarman, *Introduction to Moral Education*, Pelican Books 1967.

EDWIN COX

'Mormons' *see* **Church of Jesus Christ of Latter-day Saints, The**

Muhammed *see* **Islam**

Multi-Faith Schools

Multi-faith is defined as relating to several faiths or to an institution where several faiths or cultural backgrounds are represented. Multi-faith schools are often found in or near city centres where Hindu, Muslim and Sikh youngsters work and play alongside white children whose background may be Christian or secular and/or black children of African or Caribbean origin, who, in many cases, have been born in Britain. Sometimes each faith or tradition is represented equally; in other cases one community (e.g. Asian or white) may be in a large majority. In certain areas the mixtures of groups may be extended with, e.g., Jewish, Cypriot, Maltese, Egyptian, Iranian, Chinese, Vietnamese, or Canadian children being present in small numbers alongside a larger group or groups who predominate. Technically the term applies only where three or more faiths are clearly represented, but it is used loosely 1. when two faiths are present in significant numbers, and 2. when two or more culture groups are present within the same faith (e.g. Irish Catholic, Birmingham Protestant white, and black Caribbean Pentecostalist). Asian children are often regarded as a single culture group, but they may also be distinguished by faith as Hindu, Muslim, Sikh, Chinese or Japanese; frequently it is the presence of Asian children which triggers usage of the term 'multi-faith'.

The presence of different religious communities within a single college or school presents both opportunities and problems. It provides scope to learn by exploration and discovery methods, with pupils and parents contributing information on subjects of religious significance, and allows for visits to places of worship and community involvement (e.g. Eid Parties or Divali Celebrations or Mardi Gras Carnivals). It also encourages staff to avoid the perils of seeming to promulgate a single 'official' religious view. On the other hand, the presence of such different communities can lead to suspicion, prejudice, abuse, or even to violence, especially when one or more of the communities is present only in small numbers.

On the positive side the multi-faith mixture has led to a curriculum for RE which avoids a traditional preoccupation with (Christian) biblical content and explores instead the livelier aspects of religious ceremonial and worship, pilgrimage and the use of scriptures, with attention also to practical features such as dress and food, rites of passage and family life. Belief and theology are by no means excluded, but have tended to develop out of a study of concrete aspects of religions rather than by a systematic analysis of creeds or systems.

This type of wide-ranging study of world religions, where each faith is studied in breadth first, and only then in depth, and where the study embraces background and history, cult practice and ritual, places of worship and festival, ethic and myth, people and geographical spread, has led in turn to the study of Christianity as a world religion. This is not essential in a multi-faith school, but it has become so general a practice as to be nearly universal in such schools, and the advent of a multi-faith curriculum has often led to a stimulation of Christian studies rather than their diminution, albeit of a different nature from that of earlier models.

At the same time it must be said that the curriculum for RE offered in a multi-faith school need be no different *per se* because the school services a multi-faith community. The need for a multi-faith curriculum is as great – and in some respects greater – in a school where the indigenous community predominates if effective RE is to be taught in preparation for life in today's world. The local community may affect the choice of faiths or topics covered and the style of teaching offered, but a world religions option is in no way to be restricted to schools with a multi-faith catchment area.

School assembly* is a complex and difficult issue in multi-faith schools. Some schools make ambitious plans for each assembly to contain elements from various faiths; others attempt to relate each assembly to a particular faith or festival while using a calendar of festivals to ensure even coverage of different traditions. A few fight shy of the challenge or see in it a pretext for avoiding religious aspects altogether and concentrate instead on moral or social issues. Various experiments are taking place in this area, mostly at a seminal stage. There is however widespread agreement that it is inappropriate to limit assembly to the coverage of a single faith in a multi-faith school and that it is unethical to invite children to express a commitment they do not hold.

See also **Multi-Racial Society**.

W. O. Cole, (ed.), *Religion in the Multi-Faith School*, Yorkshire Committee for Community Relations 1975; W. O. Cole, (ed.), *World Religions: a handbook for teachers*, Shap Working Party/Commission for Racial Equality, 1977 and 1980; W. O. Cole, (ed.), *World Faiths in Education*, Allen & Unwin 1978; C. Collinson and C. Miller, *Believers: Worship in a Multi-Faith Community,* Edward Arnold 1981; J. M. Hull, *School Worship: An Obituary,* SCM Press 1975; Shap Working Party, *Calendar of Religious Festivals,* Shap Working Party/Commission for Racial Equality; N. Smart, *The Phenomenon of Christianity*, Collins 1979.

PETER WOODWARD

Multi-Racial Society

A multi-racial society is one in which the existence of a variety of cultures and races is recognized. Educationally it may be argued, therefore, that Britain as a multi-racial society dates from the 1970s. Earlier than this distinctive ethnic and cultural groups existed in Britain but although, for example, the 1966 West Riding agreed syllabus was aware of 'Jewish Children and their Religion' and the presence of other faiths these did not prompt its authors to include Judaism* or Islam* in the syllabus. The ILEA Syllabus Conference 1965–68 had a Jewish and a Muslim representative but the body of the syllabus was not permeated by the insights contained in the introductory essay, 'Religious Education in a Multi-racial Society' (*Learning for Life*, 1968). In fact it was the world religions/religious studies movement associated with Lancaster university and the Shap* Working Party rather than the presence of religious minorities that provided curriculum change.

Gradually members of religions which are represented by minorities in Britain followed the path pioneered by Myer Domnitz, a prolific Jewish writer, and began to produce textbooks for use in schools. However, it is still rare to find religious studies specialists who are not from a Christian background and as long as RE is considered to be an exercise in nurture or the transmission of a cultural heritage or traditional values this situation is likely to persist.

The Birmingham LEA teachers' handbook, *Living Together* (1975), was the first comprehensive volume published by a local authority to suggest ways in which schools might respond to the diverse cultural needs of all their pupils. Since that publication it has become customary to write sections on multi-racial RE into official documents but often with the caveat that Britain is predominantly Christian and that the syllabus will reflect this heritage. In the classroom practice still varies considerably. Even in schools with Christian minorities it is possible to find white teachers disregarding not only the cultural composition of their classes but apparently oblivious of all the curriculum development that has taken place since 1960 as they teach Bible-based RE. Educationalists are no more aware of the multi-racial nature of Britain than is society as a whole.

See also **Multi-Faith Schools**.

Birmingham LEA, *Living Together*, 1975; W. Owen Cole (ed.). *Religion in the Multi-Faith School*, Hulton 1983 and *World Faiths in Education*, Allen & Unwin 1978; B. Gates (ed.), *Afro-Caribbean Religions,* Ward Lock Educational 1980; ILEA, *Learning for Life*, 1968; James Lynch, *Teaching in a Multi-Cultural School*, Ward Lock Educational 1981.

W. OWEN COLE

Music

Music has long been associated with worship. Because of its emotional power and appeal to the imagination, music has been an important teaching medium in many religions. It should not therefore be undervalued or used without scrutiny. Music is used in three main ways; in songs to be sung, in creative music making and for listening.

A great variety of material for singing is now available, for instance, old and new hymns and songs intended to be sung corporately in worship and songs intended for singing solo or by a small group. Some are composed specifically to provoke thought. Since people tend to remember best what they have sung, the contemporary relevance of the words is important. The use of tunes from a variety of traditions is now common and, as well as being musically satisfying, contributes to multicultural education. Accompaniments can be provided by a wide variety of instruments from organ, piano and guitar to combinations involving percussion and recorders. It is generally true that the more people can be involved actively in accompanying hymns and songs, the better.

Creative music making means using music as a medium for giving expression to pupils' thoughts and feelings; for example, on themes such as death, light and darkness. Pupils use simple or sophisticated instruments and/or voices and compose music to express themselves. In such activities the roles of the teacher are those of adviser and organizer. The pieces thus created need not be written down, although tape recording is helpful. Such compositions can be used to highlight the emotional peaks in a story. This can be a powerful non-verbal means of communication and is the most natural medium for some pupils. Because it involves the emotions of those concerned, sensitivity and imagination are required on the part of the teacher and pupils.

Listening material can come from a wide variety of styles, traditions and countries and can include jazz, classical, contemporary classical, folk, pop, progressive pop, Indian classical, African, and so on.

JUNE B. TILLMAN

Folk song

Traditional folk songs are concerned with the fundamental questions of life – love, children, death, suffering and injustice, crime and punishment, war and peace. Early English ritual songs such as 'The Souling Song', 'Pace-Egging Song', and 'Padstow May Day Song', accompany rites and ceremonies which have their origins in the pre-Christian fertility rites of ancient Britain. Later ballads of the fifteenth and sixteenth century tell love stories with a delicate symbolism which evaded the bowdlerism of a later age.

By the seventeenth and eighteenth centuries, the enclosure of farming land and the rise of the industrial revolution had changed the conditions of the working classes and this was reflected in the folk songs of the period. This is the time of the sheep-stealing songs, the songs of poaching, of transportation, press gangs and the cruel sea. Similarly, in the nineteenth century we find a wave of folk-songs about strikes, lockouts, pit disasters and industrial strife.

Traditional folk songs are readily available on gramophone records, particularly from specialist record companies such as Topic Records Ltd. They can be used in RE to stimulate discussion of the fundamental questions of life. Records, tapes and folk song books can also provide material for further research into a problem, and pupils may well be interested in singing some of the songs themselves, perhaps in school assembly. They may also begin writing their own contemporary 'folk songs' about the problems and joys of life today.

JOHN BAILEY

Hymns

The study of Christianity in RE would clearly be incomplete without some consideration of the place of hymns in Christian worship. This could include early hymns which both reflected and influenced the development of Christian doctrine, such as those of Bishop Synesius of Cyrene (fourth century), Prodentius (fifth century) and Sedulius (sixth century). The theology of pre-reformation hymn writers such as St Thomas Aquinas (1227–74) and Thomas à Kempis (1379–1471) may be compared with that of post-reformation writers such as Martin Luther, John Bunyan, or George Herbert.

The great hymn writers of the eighteenth century, such as Coffin, Cowper and Watts, repay careful study and the development of Methodism can scarcely be understood without reference to the hymns of Charles Wesley. Similarly, the controversies of the nineteenth century are reflected in the hymns of Sir Henry Baker, W. Chatterton Dix, Bishop Walsham How, John Keble, Cardinal Newman, Bishop Christopher Wordsworth and others.

Many recently published hymn books show contemporary hymn writers such as Brian Wren and Fred Kaan grappling with the problem of Christianity in a post-industrial society, for example in 'God of Concrete, God of Steel'.

The choice of hymns for school assembly is more difficult because the students will not all be committed Christians. It may be possible to invite them to sing a hymn of praise to God, but hymns of explicit Christian commitment, such as 'O Jesus I have promised' are surely inappropriate except perhaps in church schools. In a situation where many young people are uncommitted, a contemporary folk song such as 'Family of Man' or 'Son of Man' by Sydney Carter may be more generally acceptable.

See also **'Pop' Music**.

JOHN BAILEY

Mystery

Mystery has been thought of as that element of doctrinal propositions that is not fully comprehensible to reason. But, mystery is more; it is at the very heart of religion. Religion is man's response to mystery: in poetry and art he celebrates it, in theology he attempts to articulate and interpret it.

Mysteries are to be distinguished from problems. A problem can be solved, or at least we can specify what would count as a solution; the problem then ceases to be a problem. Mysteries (e.g. death) cannot be solved; they can only be recognized and contemplated. 'Mystery is not an eternal riddle. . . . It is the natural unity which lies at the centre of man, the corrective to his fragmentedness . . . the "pulse" of creation permeating all life. . . . It is . . . "An inexhaustible depth of meaning" which leads us to ever richer syntheses of all that we know and experience' (O'Leary and Sallnow). If RE is to be true to this mystery, to point to an awareness of it as the true focus of all religion, what are the implications?

There is a place in RE for the descriptive, critical study, across major religions, of the notions of mystery and of unknowing. In the Christian tradition the *via negativa* has emphasized the positive value of 'unknowing' as a form of knowledge. Language is inadequate; we cannot describe God or know him in himself. 'Why does thou prate of God? Whatever though sayest of Him is untrue' (Eckhart). 'Neither does anything that is, know Him as He is . . . neither can the reason attain to Him, nor name Him, nor know Him; neither is He darkness nor light. . . .' (Pseudo-Dionysius). Other examples can be found in the spiritual classics *The Cloud of Unknowing* and the writings of St John of the Cross.

The *advaita* tradition of Hinduism, from the Vedanta school of thought which has its roots in the Upanishads, emphasizes that all exists within the ultimate Mystery which cannot, therefore, be known as an object. In the end, there is no knowing, only awareness of, and joy of being – *saccidananda*.

The non-representational art of Islam, seen in the arabesque which carries the eye further and further on, points to the ultimate unknown.

There is, also, the need for a method of RE which opens up the way to apprehension of mystery (it cannot be comprehended) and to awareness that the unknown, which is known as mystery, can only be suggested, hinted at, in metaphor, paradox, parable, the work of art.

The natural response to mystery is awe. Awe has been described by Rudolf Otto as an awareness of the numinous. Awe comes at those moments of disclosure when mystery reveals itself as mystery. RE does not create such moments, but it should provoke appreciation of them and should alert to those fragile moments of wholeness, to the sensing of the strange within the familiar (and, where this is concerned, to the value of close perception and quiet reflection); it should alert to the element of mystery in all human relationships in so far as they reach any personal depth; and alert to the significance of the old Arab saying that there are two types of men: those who accept the horizon as a limit to their world, and those for whom, as they move towards it, there is always something beyond it to be discovered – some deeper mystery to be disclosed.

B. Lealman and E. Robinson, *Knowing and Unknowing*, CEM 1981; D. J. O'Leary and T. Sallnow, *Love and Meaning in Religious Education,* Oxford University Press 1982.

BRENDA LEALMAN

Mysticism

Mysticism has been variously defined. Often described as a fundamentally unitive experience of love and communion with God (in theistic religions) or intuitive, contemplative approach to Ultimate Reality (in non-theistic traditions), it is beyond ordinary human experience and reason but not antagonistic to them.

To most people mystical experience is only accessible through mystical literature, found worldwide. Common to it is the insistence on an experience of fundamental unity or oneness transcending the diversity of everyday life. Mystics also maintain the basic ineffability of their experience; this does in no way preclude its describability to which the rich mystical literature bears ample witness.

The comparative study of mystical phenomena dates mainly from the twentieth century. Classical works on mysticism were largely descriptive, often assuming that mystical experience is always the same. More recent writers distinguish between different types of experience, notably Zaehner (theistic; non-theistic; naturalistic) and Stace (introvertive; extrovertive). Others argue that whilst the basic experience may be the same, its interpretation varies according to religio-cultural conditions. Today attention focusses on the philosophical analysis of mystical language and experience, their inherent truth-claims, specific characteristics of women's mystical writings, and also on the psychological analysis of ecstatic 'peak' experiences and consciousness expansion, especially in relation to drugs.

Mysticism is both a historical and contemporary phenomenon. As the experiential matrix of all religion it is especially important for the transformation of religious awareness and spiritual practice in modern society. The varieties of mysticism provide a focal point for the comparative study of world religions as mystical literature contains ample documentation for the persistence of the human quest for transcendence, holiness and perfection and points to the continuing disclosure of the divine Spirit among men. In RE the study of mysticism can help to discover and explore the human religious dimension and its focus of transcendence*.

M. A. Bowman, *Western Mysticism: A Guide to the Basic Works,* American Library Association 1980; J. Ferguson, *An Illustrated Encyclopaedia of Mysticism and the Mystery Religions,* Thames & Hudson 1976; S. T. Katz (ed.), *Mysticism and Philosophical Analysis,* Sheldon Press 1978; U. King, *Towards a New Mysticism: Teilhard de Chardin and Eastern Religions,* Collins 1980; E. G. Parrinder, *Mysticism in the World's Religions,* Sheldon Press 1976; R. Woods (ed.), *Understanding Mysticism,* Athlone 1981.

URSULA KING

Myth

Myth is a word capable of a variety of interpretations. For many teachers and pupils it may carry connotations of fantasy or even falsity. For others, myths are stories which belong to the ancient past, and which emerged from a mode of thinking and understanding outgrown by modern scientific man. However, the characteristics of myth which have been explored and expounded by theorists over recent decades have been more to do with the meaning, language and structure of myths than with problems of definition. In broad general terms there is agreement that myths are often closely related to expression of the kind of meaning for which man searches

amidst the apparent paradoxes and contradictions of human experience. Myths are stories which express profound beliefs and are essential vehicles of communicating the faith of religious traditions. Unfortunately, the use of the term 'myth' in connection with world religions tends to give rise to controversy, particularly when applied to the Christian stories of the life, death and resurrection of Jesus. However, the word myth, if understood in terms of function rather than of implied value-judgments, can provide a useful label for a distinctive type of story.

The functions performed by the myths of the major world religions are many and varied. They can act with a cohesive power for a particular culture or society as well as for the individual believer. Their re-presentation in worship, in ritual or in ceremonial, offer a meaning to life and a framework for a way of living. The power of the myths of the major world religions operates through symbolic language and dramatic structure; the stories and their associated rituals stimulate the imagination and evoke a response. Despite a Western tendency to 'de-mythologize' they are not lightly to be cast aside, even in a so-called scientific age.

The Christian myth is no longer the sole provider of meaning and purpose in a pluralist society. It is socially inappropriate therefore for RE to be concerned only with the stories of Jesus*, though these stories clearly continue to function as the myth for Christians. The stories in and by which men live are now many and varied, religious and non-religious. If the promotion of genuine understanding and mutual respect between people and the development of the inner or spiritual well-being of the individual is held to be part of the task of education today, then some consideration of these stories becomes essential.

Encounter with religious myths can therefore be argued to be an important aspect of RE. An educational encounter involves developing the child's ability to recognize the characteristics and functions of the stories but as Bruner said, 'It is also necessary that the children "feel" myth as well as understand it – for it is different from "explanation" or "narrative".' For the development of understanding of the part that myth plays within religion certain conditions may be argued to be necessary. These are that children should:

1. be able to recognize myth and its significance; 2. have religious myths presented to them in the context of belief and behaviour; 3. experience the effect of myth on the emotions; 4. be enabled to compare religious myths with the myths offered to them by modern society.

Approaches to myth have been structured developmentally and using a variety of media. Whatever method or methods of exploration are chosen the myths of mankind present a tremendous challenge. To restrict their use to public or private reading, or to read merely in order to rationalize, is to misunderstand the power and significance of myth and its continuing role in the quest of mankind. The challenge of myth, met with imagination and thought, may lead both teacher and taught to learn a great deal about man and his vision of the ultimate.

Christian Education Movement, *Myth,* 1978; Raymond Johnston, 'The Language of Myth', *New Movements in Religious Education*, ed., Ninian Smart and Donald Horder, Temple Smith 1975; G. S. Kirk, *Myth, its Meaning and Function,* Cambridge University Press 1970; *New Larousse Encyclopedia of Mythology*, ed. Guirand, Hamlyn 1969.

GWEN PALMER

National Christian Education Council

The Council is made up of over 3000 member churches linked either through a local branch council or by direct membership. From 1803, as the National Sunday School Union, it directed its attention to work with children and young people but has latterly addressed itself to the educational needs of the total church community. The Council offers training opportunities mainly through conferences. It publishes material for Christian education in churches and RE in schools. It shares with the Methodist Church in the production of *Partners in Learning**.

The Council maintains the International Bible Reading Assocation which provides Bible reading notes for all age-groups in English and other languages. Benefactions allow limited financial support for churches extending their premises, and grants are available to groups of those under twenty five years

of age attending residential conferences. The related Robert Raikes Historical Society, so named because Robert Raikes (1736–1811) is seen as the principal founder of the movement out of which the Council sprang, provides help to those researching the Sunday School Movement. The Council is ecumenical and works alongside the education departments of the major churches.

DONALD HILTON

National Society for Religious Education

Founded in 1811, the National Society for Promoting Religious Education is a voluntary Church of England body whose primary concern is with the provision and support of Anglican schools in England and Wales. Historical documents relating to church schools are to be found in the Society's archives at Church House, Westminster. In the 1970s the Society developed its work with the setting up of religious education centres in London and York. These centres are designed to support all those working in religious education, whether in church, school or college, and offer comprehensive resource collections, courses and advice.

The Society is linked to the General Synod of the Church of England through the General Secretary, but its independence facilitates the taking of initiatives in educational matters.

H. J. Burgess, *Enterprise in Education*, National Society/SPCK 1958; Durham Report on Religious Education, *The Fourth R*, National Society/SPCK 1970; P. and H. Silver, *The Education of the Poor (The History of a National School 1824–1974)*, Routledge & Kegan Paul 1974.

PAUL TURTON

Neo-confessional

The attempt to make dogmatic RE more acceptable and effective by improving methods, by using the findings of educational research, and by constructing syllabuses based on the capacities and interests of the pupil. While this is an 'open-ended' approach within a given religion, usually Christianity, religions other than the central one are recommended to be taught only as tolerated extras rather than as a fundamental element in RE. Usually used in reference to Christianity, it assumes that the basic objective of RE is to engage the pupil in the Christian religion.

ALAN BROWN

Netherlands

In order to understand the situation and background of RE in the Netherlands, some historical information is necessary. Since the Reformation, the Republic of the United Netherlands has had an established church, the Dutch Reformed Church. Other communities (e.g. Lutherans, Mennonites, Roman Catholics) had freedom to practise their religion aside from public life but had no influence at all in the schools. The Reformed Church, on the contrary, was able to use the schools for the catechetical instruction of children. During the period of French influence and occupation (1795–1813), church and state were separated and the privileges of the Reformed Church ended. School education still sought to promote 'Christian and social virtues' according to the 1806 Education Act, but 'Christian' should not be narrowed to the particular view and doctrine of one specific church. All this resulted in a twofold development, which has marked the Dutch climate of religious education.

In the first place, the Reformed Church found itself obliged to arrange its catechetical instruction separately from RE in schools. The other Protestant churches – rather small groups – were already used to this situation. At the beginning of this development, coming of age in society still coincided with the school leaving age, that is around thirteen or fourteen years of age. But by the middle of the nineteenth century, one had to be around eighteen years old to be accepted as an adult. Because the instruction of the Protestant churches was no longer connected with the school-leaving age – as was usual in most churches in Europe – the churches were able to follow this trend in society. The age for 'confession of the faith' (or confirmation according to the Lutheran Church), was around eighteen by the end of the century, and in some regions even higher.

The advantage of this development is clear: the period for catechetical instruction could be longer, that is between the age of twelve and eighteen years. As the young people taking this instruction were older, 'confession

of the faith' could be a more personally experienced decision, even though the age of joining the church was either partly or entirely fixed by tradition. Consequently the religious education of the churches could not stick to 'instruction' only. In the last hundred years there has been an increasing attempt to widen this instruction into guidance of the young in their relations with, and experiences of, the world of Bible, faith and church life. More recently, more and more adult lay-people are participating in this process of guiding and teaching. Also in many church communities young people can now join in celebrating the Lord's Supper before confessing their faith in public.

Secondly, according to the 1806 Education Act, RE in schools had to be a Christian education which would not offend anyone's religious feelings. The Roman Catholics and Protestants (from rather traditionally Calvinistic to liberal) had to attend the same schools. This ideal turned out to be an illusion. In the middle of the nineteenth century, state schools became more and more neutral and uncommitted. Roman Catholic leaders and several groups of Protestants, who were protesting against 'the spirit of the century', joined forces and sought freedom to have schools in agreement with their convictions. Basically this political struggle was an emancipatory movement. (The political system in the Netherlands is incomprehensible without knowing this context.) After a long fight, an agreement followed in 1920.

Within a joint national system of state schools there are voluntary schools, founded by institutions or associations of parents, and county-schools, managed by the local authorities. The voluntary schools are 'aided' for all of their normal costs. Of all the pupils attending primary education in 1900, 69% went to county schools and 31% to voluntary schools. The 1920 agreement resulted in a switch: by 1940 these figures were 31% and 69%, and in 1971 28% and 72%. The 72% includes 42% for RC schools and 28% for Protestant schools. Figures for secondary schools are almost the same.

County schools in this system usually do not include RE in the curriculum. Churches, however, have a legal right to claim one lesson within the timetable to teach those pupils whose parents allow them to attend these lessons. In voluntary schools the managers or governors are free to organize RE – and morning assemblies if they wish – according to their views. In primary schools there is an increasing tendency to include religious education in an integrated approach to education. In secondary schools RE has much in common with developments in England and Wales. The status of RE in the curriculum (one, or sometimes two, hours a week) and the shifting in subjects (more about non-Christian religions and less about church history) can be cited as examples. Also the discussion about the aims of RE can be compared with these developments. Lately the accent on liberation theology has attracted special attention.

This comparison also shows that RE in these voluntary schools must take into account the different social and religious backgrounds of pupils. Secularization has been a significant modern development. The Netherlands no longer is a traditionally Christian country, since – as research in 1979 revealed – 43% of all males and 40% of all females declared that they did not (wish to) belong to any religious community. In this research 31% of the respondents said they belonged to the RC church and 25% to a Protestant church.

The RC church has a reasonably direct control of its voluntary schools. Therefore, in primary education close co-operation between parish and school was possible, for example in receiving first Holy Communion, in preparing for confirmation, and in renewal of the baptismal vows. It was a co-operation of teachers and priests. Lately parents and other members of the church community have become actively engaged in projects to introduce children to confirmation and its meaning. This development agrees with the policy of the bishops since 1964 when it was decided that the catechism should no longer be the guide-line for RE in schools. A catechism has to appeal not to children but to adults. Therefore the 'New Catechism' was written. The schools had to develop their own courses for RE, according to the 'Grondlijnen voor een vernieuwde schoolkatechese' (1964). The Higher Catechetical Institute aided the teachers in developing new aims and materials for RE. Through their reviews, 'School en godsdienst' (for primary education) and 'Verbum' (secondary), they have outlined and

influenced the discussion about RE in the Netherlands.

The Protestant groups did not have such an impetus. However, in the present situation the problems of RE in all voluntary schools have much in common. The basic question is how, in a society that is becoming more and more multi-cultural, RE in schools can be an attractive and appealing subject for pupils from various religious and social backgrounds? In addition to this, churches should have their own possibilities for religious education which have as a frame of reference the actual church life.

W. Goddijn (ed.), *Opnieuw: God in Nederland, Onderzoek naar godsdienst en kerkelijkheid*, Amsterdam 1979; F. H. Kuiper, *Op zoek naar beter bijbels onderwijs*, Amsterdam 1980; N. F. Noordam, *Historische pedagogiek van Nederland, Een inleiding*, Nijkerk 1979; J. A. van der Ven, *Kritische godsdienstdidactiek*, Kampen 1982.

F. H. KUIPER

Neutrality

In recent years changes have been advocated in the content of RE, and in the manner of its presentation. In theory, if not always in practice, the range of the subject has been extended. The emergence of a pluralist society has exposed the limitations of any approach which appears to favour one religious tradition at the expense of others. The importance of the Judaeo-Christian tradition for an understanding of Western culture is undeniable, but there are different religious traditions which require description and interpretation.

The inclusion of world religions* has presented teachers with two tasks: 1. to acquire an acceptable level of knowledge of the new material; 2. to find ways of presenting the material with fairness and impartiality. It is with regard to the second that the concept of neutrality has been useful. Neutrality presupposes that teachers are capable of distinguishing their personal convictions from their professional obligation to present data as objectively as possible, thus enabling children to make up their own minds. In some ways this is a counsel of perfection, because a genuinely neutral approach is impossible. But the concept is useful in that it reminds teachers of the need to avoid exerting influence on behalf of their personal opinions.

The case for a non-directive approach to RE is attractive, but if neutrality is too studiously applied in the classroom it can easily pass from being an instrument of *method* to being a fixed *commitment* in its own right, where the cultivation of impartiality becomes an end in itself. If this should happen in RE the pupil is effectively deprived of opportunities to choose (or to reject) a faith for himself, in which case his religious *education* will have been defective.

Jerome Bruner, *The Process of Education*, New York 1963; Edward Hulmes, *Commitment and Neutrality in Religious Education*, Chapman 1979; Basil Mitchell, *Neutrality and Commitment*, Oxford University Press 1968; Lawrence Stenhouse, 'Neutrality as a Criterion in Teaching' in *Progress and Problems in Moral Education*, ed., Monica J. Taylor, NFER 1975; M. Warnock, 'Teaching and Neutrality' in *Progress and Problems in Moral Education;* Simone Weil, *Waiting on God*, Collins 1959.

EDWARD HULMES

Newsom Report

The report *Half Our Future* (HMSO 1963) was published two and a half years after an enquiry was set up under the chairmanship of Sir John Newsom to advise on the education of pupils in England and Wales aged thirteen to sixteen of average and less than average ability. Thus the report was concerned almost exclusively with older pupils of the then widespread system of secondary modern schools. It was issued when there was still a shortage of teachers and most secondary modern pupils left school at fifteen. The general direction of the report was towards encouraging an education which could be practical, realistic, vocational and provide choice.

The report's main references to RE occur in the chapter entitled 'Spiritual and Moral Development', which outlined first the way in which schools were a reflection of society as a whole, inasmuch as even teachers differed amongst themselves in their philosophical and religious allegiances. There was also possible confrontation between the views of staffroom and classroom and between the standards of school and home. Secondly, it examined

moral education. The variety of possible views was apparent especially with regard to sexual morality: '. . . it would be stupid to deny that there are profound differences in society about pre-marital intercourse and about the permanence of marriage . . .'. However, acknowledgment of this did not prevent the report from making a prescriptive recommendation: 'For our part we are agreed that boys and girls should be offered firm guidance on sexual morality based on chastity before marriage and fidelity within it.' Yet despite the contentiousness of this issue the report assumed there was still a good measure of agreement on such ethical issues as the colour bar and the needs of the hungry and the lonely.

Thirdly, the report detected an anomaly on specifically religious instruction whereby the 1944 Education Act required instruction in the Christian (sic) religion, although not all parents or teachers were Christians. Another difficulty lay in the fact that RI was still often a non-specialist subject taught, with English and Mathematics, by form teachers. Thus, the report encouraged the growing trend towards more specialist teachers. Such an RI specialist needed to know 'the Bible and its teaching', and 'he must have thought about the relation of religion, and religious knowledge, to other fields of human activity and ways of knowing . . . his scholarship must be up-to-date, and he must move on the Christian frontiers of today'. But in addition to this factual knowledge teachers should also have the experience of a personal religious commitment.

Teachers should be able to get to know their classes. It was pointless to take six hundred pupils a week. Similarly it was problematic for someone such as a minister of religion to come into school only for one session a week, as often happened, to help with the teaching of RI.

Of schools surveyed in the report eighty per cent devoted between fifty and ninety minutes per week to RI. The corresponding figures for history and geography were sixty one per cent and fifty eight per cent respectively.

The Report rejected various ways out of the dilemma about the nature of RI: 1. to identify Christianity with moral instruction; 2. to make use of simple Bible reading without comment; and 3. to use an approach which amounted to little more than ancient history.

On the content of RI the chapter's third recommendation called for LEAS to review their agreed syllabusses and move from a content-based to a pupil-centred approach which would show by case studies how the Bible related to contemporary problems.

There is no recommendation to incorporate RI into a formal integrated scheme, but the report notes '. . . it may be possible to bring the school's religious instruction into close association with . . . social studies . . .' If in history, for example, the pupils encountered the strong and various faiths by which some men lived, there was a need for straightforward teaching of Christianity to show the difference being a Christian made and should make to the questions of human existence.

Fourthly, the single paragraph on corporate worship betrayed no awareness that this was a problem. Corporate worship was described as a potent instrument in the spiritual development of pupils and, despite the earlier recognition in the chapter that school staff and pupils would represent a variety of religious outlooks, the report affirmed 'corporate worship is not to be thought of as an instrument of education – though it is that – but as a time in which pupils and teachers seek help in prayer, express awe and gratitude and joy, and pause to recollect the presence of God'.

The report seems to be speaking with two voices. It accurately sensed the changing mood of society towards religion since 1944 and appeared to accept a degree of necessary openness. 'We believe that (religious instruction) can be, and usually is, given in a way which does justice to the mixed society in which we live, recognizing the range and degrees of religious belief and practice to be found in it, and respecting the right of the individual conscience to be provided with the material on which freely to decide its path.' Yet the report's recommendations still seem designed to initiate pupils into a Christian-based morality and to instruct them in exclusively Christian beliefs and attitudes.

GEOFFREY CHORLEY

New Zealand

New Zealand has an explicitly secular education system. The famous 'secular clause' – 'teaching shall be entirely of a secular character' – was part of an Education Act which, in 1877, established a national system of primary schools, so ending the variety of practices which had obtained when education was the responsibility of the provincial governments. It did not, however, end the controversy about the place of religion in schools. The situation was complicated because the issue of religious teaching in state schools was linked with the issue of state aid to denominational schools. For about a century little progress was made because of lack of agreement among three sections of society: those who wanted state aid for church schools (mainly Roman Catholic) but opposed 'Protestant' teaching in state schools; those who wanted religious teaching in state schools but opposed the use of public funds for denominational schools; and those who were determined to prevent both developments. It is only recently that a more ecumenical spirit has enabled Roman Catholics and the other major churches to co-operate at an official level.

Religious teaching has not, however, been entirely absent from state schools. Ironically it was made possible by the 'secular clause' itself. This had stated that schools must be kept open for at least two consecutive hours in each half day. It was therefore possible to declare a school 'closed' for a period at the beginning or end of a session and for voluntary teachers to come into the school. In 1897 Nelson Province introduced a scheme with an interdenominationally agreed syllabus of Bible readings, and the 'Nelson System' gradually spread to other parts of the country.

The ecumenical Churches Education Commission (formerly the Council for Christian Education) has provided syllabuses, handbooks and training schemes for what was inevitably a haphazard system, dependent as it was on local volunteers. The teachers' organization, the NZ Educational Institute, has consistently opposed teachers taking part in 'religious instruction', though since 1962 teachers have been allowed by law to act as voluntary religious instruction teachers.

The most significant development has been the passing of the 1975 *Private Schools Conditional Integration Act*. Although the Act is primarily about financial support for denominational schools which integrate with the state system, it has implications for religious education. 1. State schools may, with the approval of the Minister of Education, offer religious instruction additional to the legally permitted thirty minutes per week of the Nelson System, unless a majority of parents object. 2. Teachers' colleges must provide 'additional options' for students preparing to teach in integrated schools. Because the Roman Catholic hierarchy would not accept as adequate the Religious Studies courses proposed by the colleges, a two-tier system has developed: the general Religious Studies options are available to all students, and students preparing to teach in Roman Catholic integrated schools attend special courses given by voluntary lecturers.

None of the legal provisions has ever applied to secondary schools, but in spite of this freedom there is very little religious education in state schools and only a minority have any form of worship in assembly. However, in 1983 the Churches Education Commission sponsored a conference on proposals for a Religious Studies paper in School Certificate.

What kind of RE? For many decades religious instruction under the Nelson System consisted of Christian instruction based on Bible readings, in a form agreed by members of the main Protestant denominations. This co-operation was organized in a more structured way through the Bible in Schools League, which flourished for about twenty years from 1912, and later through the Council for Christian Education. In the sixties the CCE developed syllabuses along the lines of the post-1944 agreed syllabuses* in Britain.

By the end of the sixties developments in Britain began to be reflected in the CCE's advocacy of experience-based RE: life themes and the discussion of personal and social issues, but as American influence on NZ society grew, so British influence declined, and developments in the seventies and eighties in Britain have attracted far less attention. Many liberal Christians support a type of RE similar to the 'open-ended' approach of the sixties, and in fact the CEC had adopted for use in the Nelson System the syllabus of the State of Victoria (Australia), 'Religion in Life', which includes the aim that children 'will be awakened to the religious dimension of their experience'. Vigorous opposition to this kind of RE has come from two quarters: conservative Christians who demand definite Bible-based Christian teaching, and people who reject any attempt to make RE part of the school curriculum. An opinion poll in 1980 showed that fifty-two percent of the population opposed 'formal religious education in schools', thirty-five per cent supported it, and thirteen per cent were neutral.

All three positions described assume that RE is necessarily confessional. In the seventies, lecturers in the relatively new university religious studies departments (the secular university system had been established without departments of theology) took a lead in explaining that the study of religion, being distinct from instruction in a religion, was appropriate in state schools, but their voice was largely unheard by the main protagonists in the debate.

Two little-discussed factors, however, may affect the development of RE in New Zealand. Through Social Studies and Liberal Studies pupils are already learning about many of the aspects of people's cultures, especially those of the Pacific, which are part of the study of religion, and through their Religious Studies courses at university and teachers college, and particularly through the extra-mural courses mounted by Massey University, a small but increasing number of teachers are being equipped to teach religion in school. This 'objective' approach would not contravene the 'secular clause'. As a government commission report in 1962 noted, the law does not preclude teaching *about* religion.

C. McGeorge and I. Snook, *Church, State and New Zealand Education*, Price Milburn, Wellington, NZ 1981; B. Turley and M. Reid Martin, *Religion in Education*, Churches Education Commission, Wellington, NZ 1981.

JEAN HOLM

Northern Ireland   *see* Ireland, Northern

Norway

The following basic facts about Norway have to be taken into consideration:

1. Religious life is – nominally – very homogeneous: ninety-five per cent of the population belong to the Established Church of Norway (CN).

2. Paragraph 2 in the Constitution of 1814 reads: 'The evangelic-Lutheran religion

remains the official religion of the state. The parents who belong to this religion are obliged to bring up their children in the same religion.' In 1964 the following was added as the opening clause: 'All inhabitants have the right to choose their own religious life.'

3. There is comprehensive schooling throughout the nine years of compulsory school attendance (from seven to sixteen). There are very few private primary and secondary schools.

RE in the compulsory school system. Since 1739 most of the organized RE has traditionally taken place here.

1. All children who belong to CN have to attend RE classes (the subject is called *Christianity*) for two lessons a week throughout all the nine years. Children who are not members of CN can be exempted from RE classes. Teaching about non-Christian religions is given in the social science classes, from which it is not possible to be exempted.

2. Both the whole school and the RE curriculum have an explicit Christian confessional (Lutheran) aim. The Compulsory School Act of 1969 states: 'The aim of the school is to give the pupils a Christian and moral upbringing in understanding and cooperation with the home. . .'; and the Syllabus of 1974 states: '. . . what the pupils are learning in this subject shall be the basis for their beliefs and guidance for their lives'. On the other hand: 'The lessons must be given in a way which makes it possible for children from different homes, irrespective of church membership, to participate when the parents want it.' The traditional very close link between CN, the school and RE as instruction in Christianity, is being challenged by the growing secularization of society as a whole and the fact that society is more pluralistic than the statistics indicate. The tension between these two trends is – as the Syllabus of 1974 clearly demonstrates – not yet clarified. Consequences for RE are: officially the children are being given instruction in Christianity; in practice teachers tend to avoid what is really controversial in the subject and to concentrate on what everybody can more or less agree to.

The argument in favour of the Christian confessional aim of the whole school and of its RE classes used to be based on the fact that Norway has an established church. Now, however, the view is gaining strength that parents should have priority in choosing the kind of education that is given to their children. By baptizing their children (eighty-seven per cent of all children born were baptized in CN in 1980), the parents have an obligation to give them a Christian upbringing, and the school is supposed to help the parents to fulfil that task.

3. Teachers of RE in the compulsory school system do not have to be specially trained in RE and do not have to be members of CN themselves, but they are obliged to teach according to the Lutheran faith.

4. Even if, since 1969, RE is no longer understood as teaching given by the school on behalf of CN, there is still some residual influence of the church's direct influence on RE in schools: the bishop concerned and the local vicar still have the right to attend the RE classes and to 'give advice in cases concerning this teaching'.

RE in secondary general school upper stage (three years). 1. Thirty-two per cent of each generation stay on for this stage. RE is a compulsory subject (called *Religion*) of one lesson a week. It is also possible to choose RE as a non-compulsory subject in addition to the compulsory RE classes. The subject comprises Christianity, non-Christian religions, and secular views of life. Nevertheless, it is possible for pupils who belong to non-Christian religions to be exempted from RE classes.

2. In the 1974 Act the subject RE is regarded as a general knowledge subject, though Christianity is mentioned as one of the three basic values which it is important for the school to transfer to the pupils. And a law from 1971 remains saying that RE teachers are obliged to teach according to the Lutheran understanding of the Christian faith. Both the fact that it is possible to be exempted from RE lessons and the 1971 Act reflect unclarified influences from the previous confessional tradition.

3. Only teachers specially trained in RE are supposed to teach the subject.

RE in the kindergarten. The kindergarten is the only part of the educational system where private bodies play a significant role. Thirteen and a half per cent (1979) of kindergarten are owned by local parishes or Christian organizations. Twenty per cent (1981) of all children up to seven years of age go to kindergarten.

Specific subjects are not taught. In addition to Christian-based kindergarten, fifty-seven per cent (1979) of council-owned kindergarten also have a Christian aim. The local owner may choose whether he wants a Christian aim or not. Political pressure may cause Parliament in the near future to decide that all kindergarten shall have a Christian aim.

Training of RE teachers. 1. Teachers for the compulsory school system and for the kindergarten are trained in state-owned colleges of education (three years). RE is compulsory and can be studied on two levels.

2. RE teachers for the secondary general school upper stage have to be graduates in Christianity or theology from universities or from private colleges.

RE within CN. Mainly because of the traditionally strong links between CN and the school, CN has not built up an RE programme of its own apart from traditional Sunday Schools for children (which exist in most of the parishes but with highly varying levels of participation) and the teaching of the candidates for confirmation (normally an eight-month course). It is now being realized in the Church of Norway that RE in the compulsory school system can be only a part of the catechetical education of its members and is now trying to build up an RE programme of its own as a supplement (not an alternative) to RE in the school. This programme concentrates on the production and distribution of materials to parents in order to assist them in the Christian upbringing of their children.

Two bodies within CN have specialized in RE: *Norsk Sœndagsskoleforbund* (Association of Norwegian Sunday Schools) and, above all, *Institutt for kristen oppseding* (Institute for Christian Upbringing), which since its founding in 1946 has played a principal role in the RE debate. Its policy has been mainly to strengthen the confessional RE in the compulsory school system. The institute publishes the only journal for RE in Norway, *Prismet*.

Grunnskolen i Norden 1976. Compulsory School system in the Nordic countries 1976 (with an English summary), NU B 1977:5, Kœbenhavn 1977; *Skolelover* (a collection of the most important laws concerning schools), Oslo 1979; Bibliography of articles on the current debate about RE 1979–81, mainly published in *Prismet*, 1981. See also *Kirke og Kultur*, 1979 and 1981.

TROND ENGER

Nursery Schools, RE in

Before 1960 few openly questioned the appropriateness of a biblical approach to RE from the age of three years. Individual teachers may have wondered what the children made of the stories they heard, but in general it was accepted.

In the 1960s questioning came into the open. What was the long-term effect of such teaching? Investigators were concerned to discover how young children think about religious ideas and what kind of attitudes are engendered by early religious teaching based on the Bible. Ronald Goldman focussed attention on frequent misunderstandings arising from the limited experience of life and the limited thinking abilities of young children. His findings suggested that Christian teaching taken literally by young children often results in stunted understanding of what that religion has to say, and may impair or totally inhibit growth towards mature insight. Kenneth Hyde found that attempts to give biblical and doctrinal teaching at too early a stage might set up attitudes which would work against later willingness to think about these things with interest and seriousness. Especially was this a danger where children had no contact with Christianity as a living, life-influencing factor in the home, and no experience of church worship. The long-term result could be to create apathy, even hostility to religion, to lead young people to reject religious ideas, even though they have no understanding of what is being rejected. On all counts it would seem better to leave such teaching until later.

The resultant confusion among teachers of young children was acute. Such thinking seemed to be wholly destructive of what they had been accustomed to regard as RE. What should they be doing in the classroom?

During the 1970s there was much concern about the purpose of RE with young children. The task of teachers is now understood as being much wider in scope than introducing children to the Christian faith. Current suggestions for practice aim at helping pupils to grow in awareness of religion as a universal human experience, a basic dimension in the make-up of human beings. Recent agreed syllabuses recognize that teaching about Christianity should have a special place in schools because of the way in which it has influenced life and culture in our Western civilization. But this is now to be set in a much wider context. Christianity is being seen as a world religion alongside other religions of mankind. What are the implications of this emphasis for the nursery school?

Perhaps for the first time since RE became compulsory, teachers of young children will find that what is now being commended as a right and proper way into religious education coincides with what their classroom experience has long told them is sound. The 1960s saw changes of method advocated and the 1970s changes in content. New agreed syllabuses produced in the 1980s suggest a workable pattern of religious education that takes these changes into account and makes excellent sense in terms of what we know about children.

Little children come to a nursery class and join, perhaps for the first time, a group of children and adults who are strange to them and outside the familiar surroundings of home. It is not always easy for them to adapt to other people. Arguably the most important task of the nursery teacher is to help children to handle their emotions and responses, to grow through their fears and frustrations, their joys and delights, their sadnesses and disappointments. As life broadens out children are constantly coming up against the unknown and their questions are often disconcertingly profound – questions about birth, death, pleasure, pain, beauty, ugliness, feeling safe, feeling afraid etc. Until recently it was not recognized that in helping children to find 'answers' to these questions that life itself poses, teachers of young children were contributing to their religious education. Ruth Batten was ahead of her time in urging that not only was this in itself religious education, but it was the only appropriate religious education for nursery children: 'What has not been accepted is that at nursery and infant level it is the experiences themselves that are the basis of religious education'.

Violet Madge was another sensitive teacher whose work led her to the conviction that in respect of religion little children have the root of the matter in them, and that the task of the nursery/infant teacher is to help children to become articulate about their awareness.

There is now general agreement that it is right to start with the lives and experiences of the children. It is acccepted that some of the penetrating questions which young children ask about life's mysteries are questions that have been asked from time immemorial. They underlie the religious quest of mankind. In helping children to face these *at their own level in daily experience,* teachers are educating religiously as well as in other ways, and are laying good foundations for later appreciation of the religious dimension in human experience.

Ruth Batten, 'The Primary School: Experience and Tradition', *Learning for Living,* vol. 8, no. 5, May 1969; 'The Grass Roots of Religion', *Learning for Living,* vol. 10, no. 3, January 1971; R. J. Goldman, *Religious Thinking from Childhood to Adolescence,* Routledge & Kegan Paul 1964; K. E. Hyde, *Religious Learning in Adolescence,* Oliver & Boyd 1965; Carol Mumford, *Young Children and Religion,* Edward Arnold 1982; Schools Council, *Working Paper 44: Religious Education in Primary Schools,* Evans/Methuen Educational 1972.

CAROL MUMFORD

Nurture

Nurture means feeding. In psychology it means giving love to a young child for the sake of his or her mental health and personal development. Religious nurture has been generally assumed for children in the church on account of Eph. 6.4. The classic statement is given in Bushnell's *Christian Nurture*: 'the child is to grow up a Christian, and never know himself as being otherwise', in contrast to those Calvinists who would treat him as a sinner until converted. Recently Christian nurture has been defended as the *middle-way* of rearing the child in church and home, avoiding both indoctrination and a completely open-ended secular religious education. The nurturer assumes the child is already a Christian who should be confirmed in his faith. Yet the nurturer also proceeds in a spirit of enquiry claiming that this is intrinsic to Christianity. Without the former assumption, nurture collapses into religious education; without the latter claim, into indoctrination.

Horace Bushnell, *Christian Nurture*, 1861, revised edition Scribner 1919; P. H. Mussen, J. J. Congar and J. Kagan, *Child Development and Personality*, Harper 1969; Michael Rutter, *Maternal Deprivation Reassessed*, Penguin 1972; *The Child in the Church*, British Council of Churches Report on Ministry among Children, 1976; *Understanding Christian Nurture*, British Council of Churches Report 1981.

DAVID ATTFIELD

Objectives in RE

RE has been as open as any subject to the impact of curriculum development* theory, and various attempts have been made to translate the general aims of the subject (variously defined) into specific operational objectives. The Schools Council RE Committee was active in this area, especially during the 1970s, prompted by work called for in connection with the Council's enquiry into *The Whole Curriculum* (1975). The most widely used of these Schools Council documents was *Discovering an Approach* (1977), but this was produced in tandem with *A Groundplan for the Study of Religion* (1977). This led in turn to work done in connection with the projected N and F level examinations which sought to develop a method of examining in which the choice of content could be left entirely to each individual school, because the assessment was to be based on the extent to which pre-identified objectives were being achieved and not on the extent to which pre-identified content was being satisfactorily handled.

It is, however, in more general contexts than examinations that 'objectives-led' (or 'skills-based') curriculum planning has become popular in RE. Michael Grimmitt had done some detailed work on this in *What Can I do in RE?* (1973, rev. 1978), but it was the Avon Agreed Syllabus (1976), quickly followed by the Cheshire (1976) and Hampshire (1978) Agreed Syllabuses which really brought this approach to fruition.

Crucial to a satisfactory identification of objectives is the establishment of a sound framework on which specific objectives can be hung. The Schools Council *Groundplan* suggested the three-fold structure of Knowledge, Understanding and Evaluation, each related to three inter-related aspects of the

subject matter – Ideas, Actions ad Feelings. Later documents developed this into a five-fold structure of Knowledge, Understanding, Communication, Reflection and Evaluation, with an acknowledgment that there are certain contributory skills, not specific to RE, but crucial to its success, such as 'being able to enter imaginatively into other people's experiences through day-to-day situations and relationships' (*Avon*: 3–9 year olds). It is too early to say whether the 'objectives approach' can establish itself permanently as the basis for syllabus building in RE. The attraction of the old content-listing syllabuses has by no means been entirely overcome, and there is a constant temptation among many teachers to use the handbooks and 'illustrative schemes of work' which have accompanied all the new style syllabuses as a substitute for the syllabuses themselves. But that is not a problem confined to RE.

COLIN ALVES

Openness in RE

This first became an important concept in RE in the 1960s when questions were being raised about whether the subject could be educationally justified if it was understood as initiation into the Christian faith. An open-ended approach was advocated which respected the pupil's autonomy and avoided presenting beliefs and value judgments as if they were agreed truths. Inevitably there was some tension between those who supported openness and those who stressed the importance of commitment and the need to be faithful to the truth claims of religion. In the 1970s 'openness' was largely replaced by talk of the phenomenological* approach to RE which preserved the same concern for educational neutrality* but grounded methodology in a recognizable academic discipline.

Edward Hulmes, *Commitment and Neutrality in Religious Education*, Chapman 1979.

JUDITH OLLINGTON

Orders, Religious   *see* **Communities in Education, Religious**

Orthodox Church

Church and state. A policy of Christian education naturally goes back to Christ's commandment to his disciples to be 'witnesses of these things' (Luke 24.48) and to go and 'teach all nations' (Matt. 28.19). Within this universal imperative the particular problem of teaching the Christian faith in schools rests for its solution on the opportunities offered, or the limitations, imposed on the teaching Christian community in the various countries of the world by their political, social and legal institutions. In its past, the Orthodox Church has known long periods of patronage by the state (e.g. over a millenium in Byzantium before the Turkish power finally destroyed the Empire in the fifteenth century, and in Russia before the communist accession to power in 1917) when, in the context of a Christian world, the church was able to influence a sympathetic and receptive society and nurture it with the values of the gospel. But it has also known, and still does know, extensive periods of persecution and harassment, in which the blood of its martyrs and the witness of its confessors are living expressions and a leaven of its faith; under such adverse conditions, the Christian stance may perforce retreat into silent witnessing, an absence of public educational policy, since in Christ's words the kingdom which is preached 'Is not of this world' (John 18.36). Unlike the realm of the papacy in centuries past, the Orthodox Church has never grown identical with the state, but remained conscious of a radical tension between the two, which Christ outlined in his life and teaching: 'I came not to send peace (on earth), but a sword' (Matt. 10.34).

The Orthodox Church today. The present constituency of the worldwide Orthodox Church includes a family of diverse local churches, united by a common faith, creed and apostolic tradition: 1. *Historical churches,* of which the four oldest are in a minority situation in Islam- or Israel-dominated areas: the patriarchates of Constantinople, Antioch, Jerusalem, and Alexandria. Other churches are to be found in the Soviet block: in Russia, Bulgaria, Yugoslavia, Romania, Czeckoslovakia, Poland, and outside of these bounds, in Greece, Cyprus, Crete, Finland, Japan. 2. An important diaspora of immigrants have migrated to the Western hemisphere to settle amidst a cultural and religious diversity, the liberal secular, pluralistic Western society, giving them a fair opportunity to survive and grow, and to bear their public witness accor-

ding to the measure of their vitality and unity of purpose. Canonically they depend on their mother churches. 3. A small number of *young and growing native churches*, in previously non-Christian areas: in Alaska and East Africa; here the local missionary field is open and the educational task boundless.

Theological premises. These historical premises for an educational policy have their theological counterpart in the liturgy, the pronouncements of the church, the teaching of the Fathers and present day theological writings. Christian faith and man's salvation are rooted in the facts centred on the incarnation of the Son of God and his death and resurrection. These divine deeds become the substance of faith through revelation by the understanding of scripture. From the day of Pentecost, the fruit of this relevation, the truth, is contained in the one, holy, catholic and apostolic church, which the Orthodox Church believes itself to be. The truth, however, is not a static abstraction, but the divine person of the Son of God who, revealed by the third person of the Holy Trinity, the 'Spirit of truth' (John 16.13), is the Lord of history.

The life of the church. The fundamental tension between the kingdom of God and the world is reflected in the church, whose essence is to be a living symbol, and icon of both: the redeemed image of the fallen world into which the Lord Christ came in order to announce and inaugurate the kingdom, and on the other hand the true image of the kingdom which is to come. This tension, being eschatological in nature and which the saints have assumed, also postulates a Christian evangelical ethic for all times, grounded in God's commandments to man: it will be resolved at the second coming of Christ. The gift of divine life to man is experienced in the church, first and foremost in the Lord's Supper, the Eucharist. The other sacraments, instituted by Christ and the church, highlight significant moments in the life of individual Christians and the life of the community as a whole. The Orthodox view of the sacraments, as mysteries of the kingdom already apparent and operative, witnesses to an essential acceptance of the world which never loses its first destiny of being good. This, in principle, postulates the theological worth of human activity and personal life: human life, labour, marriage, family, is transfigured as reflecting total communion with God. This view places infinite confidence in man as a living person in the exercise of repentance and forgiveness, the avoidance of evil and the furtherance of good, to become, like the disciples on the eve of Christ's crucifixion, a friend of God.

The stature of man. The patristic distinction between the two biblical terms *image* and *resemblance* (Gen. 1.26) characterized God's last creature: as an *image* of God, man is endowed with the natural capacity to recognize God as his Creator and to become on earth his prophet, king, and priest; as a *likeness*, he is called to grow towards God in his lifetime, towards the likeness of his holiness. Patristic thought defines the goal of man's life as *deification* after the pattern of Christ's humanity seen transfigured. In the light of this theology, Christian education is formulated within the complementary dimensions of personal and corporate life.

The infant and his parents. In the early stages a child's whole existence is coloured by its family, it learns fundamental lessons of life and its spirit first awakes to the realm of religious experience. What will in later life become man's longing for the Father's house, is already offered vicariously to the child, from the early days of his life on earth, by the wonderful, all-pervading presence of his mother and father. In the words of Saint John Chrysostom, the Christian family is a 'little church', an *ecclesioula.*

The child and the church. The parents' prayers need to be their own genuine communication with God, not a lesson intended for the child. The central task of the Christian educator is to instil the sense of God's loving presence into the child. The Orthodox tradition offers a variety of means and allows the child to exercise all his senses: kissing the icons* over his cot and his baptismal cross; singing prayers, noticing the living flame throwing light on to the saints represented on the ikons; kissing these saints as he kisses his mother; tasting the bread and wine of holy communion, the Body and Blood of Christ, the food of God.

The specifically Christian ingredient in the life of the home depends on parental faith and worship in and membership of the church. Early exposure to the worship and activity of the church prepares the child for personal and corporate lifelong membership. The child will first express his internal perceptions and needs in the midst of the community, and in order to share them he will then learn the accepted, historical language of the group, its symbols and customs; he will finally reabsorb the experience which will bring him to enter conscious, personal membership of the church. This integration into the church relies on the involvement of the senses of the growing child, interacting as it does with the world of symbols of the church tradition, word, ikon and sacraments. Having been admitted into the sacramental body of the church in baptism, the baby, growing, developing child is a full communicant member.

The adolescent. The spiritual growth of a child into manhood or womanhood is not given a particular sanction in Orthodoxy at the age of adolescence, as it usually is in the Western confessions in the form of confirmation. Christmation is given early by the baptizing priest, and no subsequent commitment by the adolescent is prescribed. Expressions of a conscious faith occur at 'sundry times and in divers manners', in the liturgy and elsewhere, throughout the person's conscious life, when the divine gift of faith is rekindled.

Forgiveness and grace. Contemporary with the beginning of the child's schooling between the ages of seven and nine, the sacrament of repentance is added to the spiritual life of the young Christian, to continue throughout his lifetime. Divine healing and personal forgiveness are of the essence of this sacrament. A 'more excellent' way to maturity than fairness or justice is revealed in the gospel in the practice of love, mercy and forgiveness, a notion infinitely more difficult to grasp and share with others, and which may be seen as God's redemptive gift to man.

The field of ethics. For the young adult an inner and radical love for Christ allows the true Christian to be grounded in an ascetical life-endeavour and yet lovingly to accept the world in its goodness and beauty through a balance of abstinence and creativity. As there is one gospel, so there is but one morality: there cannot be two moralities, one discretionary for the initiated, and another, imperative and authoritarian for ordinary believers.

The domain of economics. In the field of economic life, the true Christian considers the world and its resources as God's gift. The created world of matter and spirit, 'heaven and earth', must be re-dedicated in the spirit of God's philanthropy and of man's balanced asceticism by each Christian to the service of God. The world should remember its own limitations, but also its true destination: at the end time to become the kingdom of God.

The political realm. In the realm of political life, the young adult will discover the same distinction, between Law and Grace, in the institution of the state versus God's kingdom which is not of this world. The Christian conscience everywhere has always endeavoured to bring the laws of the state closer to the commandments of God; and today, in our largely disestablished world, this charismatic ministry falls on the shoulders of the Christian public too, transcending party political limitations, are called to be witnesses of the gospel in the world.

Education and the teacher. Religious education is concerned with the core of the human person – not merely his intellect – and the task of the teacher is, for that reason, the more demanding and responsible. Reduced to being an academic subject, religion misses its destiny to lead to the knowledge of God. Here for the Orthodox lies the weakness of the comparative method, or of the teaching of religion purely as history, or as literature.

Parish schools. The parish school system is relatively recent and does not belong to the nature of the Orthodox Church. Other forms of education are equally useful: youth movements, family associations, choirs, etc. The school can provide knowledge about God, the church alone gives the knowledge of God. The school system risks becoming an alternative to the liturgy and ultimately a substitute for the church itself, as well as for the parents. The religious teacher must be a member of his church and endowed with the will to learn more. He is himself an example of the disciple, aspiring to grow 'unto perfect man into the stature of the fullness of Christ' (Eph. 4.13).

MICHAEL FORTOUNATTO

Overseas Appointments
Bureau   *see* **Christians Abroad; Christian Education Movement**

Pakistan   *see* **Asia**

Parable

Hebrew *mashal*, to set side by side; Greek *parabolē*, a placing beside, a comparison. While parables, like fables, allegories, and myths, are stories with hidden significance, they are clearly distinguished from these other kinds of stories due to their peculiar characteristics. These characteristics have been identified only during the last hundred years, when, beginning with the work of A. Jülicher, parables were rescued from the centuries-old tradition of interpreting them as allegories or, alternatively, as moral tales. The parable form is rare; a careful classification limits them to a few in the OT, those of Jesus and of Franz Kafka, and perhaps some from Eastern religious writings.

A now classic definition of the parables of Jesus by C. H. Dodd suggests their characteristics: 'At its simplest the parable is a metaphor or simile drawn from nature or common life, arresting the hearer by its vividness or strangeness and leaving the mind in sufficient doubt about its precise application to tease it into active thought'. In this definition, a parable emerges as a *metaphor* which implies its significance by *mundanity*, *extravagance*, and *indirection*. As a metaphor – and many NT exegetes would say an 'extended metaphor' to underscore the *narrative* quality – a parable is or exemplifies what it signifies. That is, as metaphor, a parable is unsubstitutable; it does not illustrate an idea, but embodies it. In order to interpret Jesus' parables, one must add two other widely-accepted points, namely, that the principal mode of Jesus' teaching was in parables and that the content of this teaching is the kingdom of God. Thus, the conclusion emerges that Jesus taught about the kingdom of God through metaphorical stories which are mundane, extravagant, and indirect.

As mundane, the parables imply that the rule of God applies to secular, ordinary, and in many instances, relational life, both personal and public; as extravagant or extreme, the parables imply – through tension in their plots – that the ways of the conventional world are not the ways of God (what Robert Funk calls the tension between a 'logic of merit' and a 'logic of grace'); as indirect, the parables imply that their significance must be grasped in a 'shock of recognition' as listeners apply the stories to themselves.

For some NT exegetes, these characteristics of parables are epitomized in seeing Jesus as 'parable of God'. In the life and especially the death of Jesus – at one level a mundane, secular story – the listener sees an 'enacted parable' of extravagant action which upsets the conventions of life as suffering love sides with the oppressed, the outcast, the sinner. As an illustration of Jesus' life as enacted parable, see Matt. 11.19: his practice of eating with 'sinners and tax collectors', the outcasts of society.

Parables are powerful teaching devices because as stories they stay in the memory in a way that concepts and precepts do not. In addition, these stories persuade listeners to 'teach themselves' as they apply them to their own situations. Jesus' parables are also *disorienting* teaching devices, embodying the reversal of expectations which is at the heart of the gospel, the scandal of Jesus' identification – in his table-fellowship as on the cross – with outcasts and sinners.

John Dominic Crossan, *In Parables: The Challenge of the Historical Jesus*, Harper 1973; C. H. Dodd, *The Parables of the Kingdom*, Fontana 1961; Robert Funk, *Language, Hermeneutic, and the Word of God,* Harper 1967; Joachim Jeremias, *The Parables of Jesus*, SCM Press 1947/1972; Paul Ricoeur, 'Biblical Hermeneutics', *Semeia*, 4, 1975; Mary Ann Tolbert, *Perspectives on the Parables: An Approach to Multiple Interpretations*, Fortress 1979; Amos Wilder, *Early Christian Rhetoric: The Language of the Gospel*, SCM Press 1964.

SALLIE MCFAGUE

Partners in Learning

Since early this century the British Lessons Council had prepared outlines on which the various Free Churches, with some inter-church co-operation, based weekly lesson material for use with children and young people. In the 1960s, responding to major developments within religious education, the Council produced a new syllabus, *Experience and Faith*. It held together four main emphases affecting Christian education, i.e. the Bible, the church, the Christian calendar, and everyday human experience.

Three publishing groups (National Christian Education Council*, Religious Education Press, and the Methodist Youth Department) which had previously produced separate volumes of weekly material, co-operated in 1968 to produce *Partners in Learning*, based on the new syllabus. A new awareness of the needs of adult education suggested the production of material for adult groups alongside that for children. Thus six parallel annual volumes emerged for different age-groups: 3–4, 5–6, 7–10, 11–12, 13–15, and adult. Since 1975 one volume, presented in three parts, has been published thus offering a total church community education programme. In any given week the theme for each age-group is the same; emphasis, depth of interpretation, and method vary appropriately. This format allows flexibility of use; leaders can draw material from adjacent age-groups where it better suits the local situation. Suggestions for family church worship are also given. The material can be adapted by those churches who plan a programme of worship and education in which the total church community stays together.

Beginning with the syllabus *Experience and Faith* the programme was subsequently based for a brief period on the less satisfactory *The Story of the People of God*, and more recently on the work of an annual syllabus group promoted by the publishers (currently NCEC and the Methodist Division of Education and Youth). The major emphases remain those of the initial syllabus together with an attempt to link the weekly material with the lections produced by the Joint Liturgical Group, whilst recognizing that the liturgical and educational approaches do not always coincide. The present annual syllabus thus focusses on the major peaks of the church year – Christmas, Easter, Pentecost – with additional themes arising from human experience and the biblical record.

DONALD HILTON

Pastoral Care

Pastoral care is concerned with providing an environment in which pupils can learn. This means a concern with the way in which relationships outside and within the school develop and affect learning as well as with the provision of a suitable curriculum. In denominational schools the pastoral system and the tenets of the denomination concerned are strongly linked.

Teachers of RE share with all teachers some degree of responsibility for pastoral care, whether in building up good relationships and a learning environment in the classroom, or as form tutors or year or house heads.

More particularly RE teachers may feel that their responsibility to pastoral care lies in the curriculum content of their subject, in the contribution they make to the ethos* of the institution and the quality of life it encourages and in acting as counsellor to pupils and colleagues in need.

In the curriculum area many RE teachers deal with subject matter which examines relationships between friends, in the family and the community and the moral and religious questions which underlie them. Great sensitivity is needed in timing and in the examples used, for some pupils may be living in daily life the situations under discussion in the classroom. On the other hand an opportunity to think carefully about such issues as marriage, attitudes to authority, causes of stress, prejudice, different life styles in the community, may be helpful to pupils and supportive to work being done in the pastoral care teams.

As far as the ethos of the institution is concerned RE teachers can make a major contribution. For example, because of their specialized knowledge of the needs of pupils of different religious faiths they can ensure that these needs are understood by the school.

RE teachers may be expected to act as counsellors to pupils and colleagues at times of emotional stress. This can involve either dealing directly with pupils concerned or with supporting colleagues in pastoral work with pupils and sometimes parents.

JILL DAVIES

Peace Studies

Peace Studies has become a viable teaching prospect for two reasons: 1. it fits into the pattern of topic studies that emerged in the era of expansion and experiment as an alternative to the subject based approach and 2. the intensity of political confrontation coupled with rapid development of weapons technology in the nuclear, electronic, chemical and biological fields has produced a new level of consciousness about the urgency that permeates issues of peace and conflict. At the same time it is ironic that it is this very sense of urgency that makes Peace Studies a controversial item in schools and colleges since it can be used as a cover for manipulation by devotees of any part of the political spectrum. Total academic integrity that demonstrably seeks to equip pupils with the capacity to analyse both existing and potential alternative values in the topic are a teacher's only defence when such accusations fly.

Peace Studies cannot be soundly built on a revulsion from War/Conflict Studies. The topic is as inexorably bound to these as Feminist Studies are to the doctrine of man. Indeed, analysis of conflict helps to define aspects of Peace Studies from inner mental conflict of the individual, through family tensions to neighbourhood animosities, on through class and ethnic antipathies to terrorism and to conflicting interests and ideologies at international level. Each level of conflict has a corresponding 'peace' with distinctive features that deserve close study. In each case there is also the recurring issue of whether one is talking of containing conflict as a form of peace or is reserving the word 'peace' for a genuine resolution and removal of conflict.

RE may relate to Peace Studies in two ways. 1. Peace Studies may be included as a topic within an RE syllabus, considering the relationship of religion to society and the various belief systems as they interpret the human situation. The need for and capacity of religious groups to challenge society is important although often lost within the context of state or civic* religions. 2. RE can make a contribution to a peace studies programme. An important stage in this is to overcome common misconceptions and even prejudices about the involvement of religion in war and its causes throughout history. It is profitable in contrast to consider religious resources for peace. In both approaches to the relationship of RE and Peace Studies the contribution of major religious figures to the cause of peace will play a significant part.

JAMES GREEN

Pentecostal Churches

This is one of the most diverse identifiable groups within the Christian churches. But within the English-speaking world there are common features concerning their approach to religious education. These arise from their shared understanding of salvation and sanctification. Most Pentecostals hold to the notion of the 'three stage way of salvation' – salvation at the moment of conversion, subsequently to be followed by baptism through total immersion, which may lead to baptism of the Holy Spirit manifesting itself through 'gifts of tongues' (see Acts 2.4; 10.46; 9,17; 19.6). The overall aim of the Christian education of the unconverted is to bring them to the point of conversion. The overall aim of the Christian education of those who have been converted is their sanctification such that they might receive the gifts of the Spirit and grow in grace. The growth in grace involves, on the one hand, a deepening of insight and understanding about the purposes of God for mankind revealed in Holy Scripture (the Word of God), and an associated purging of sinful attitudes and actions on the part of the Christian leading to a purer and more moral life in anticipation of the final manifestation of the kingdom of God. The role of scripture as the revealed Word of God is regarded as integral in the process of Christian discipleship.

Within this path towards discipleship a number of ingredients can be identified:

1. *The policy of Pentecostal churches concerning public education*. Pentecostal Christians accept the scriptural affirmation that the state's provisions (e.g. public education) are to be accepted and its laws obeyed. Therefore it is appropriate for children of Pentecostal parents to attend state schools and receive instruction in all the curriculum subjects on the timetable. Children will not normally be withdrawn from classes to do with religious education. In fact a biblically-based RE programme will be supported in that it may help to develop a pupil's familiarity with the Bible. However, no assumption will be made that there is anything particularly Christian happening in the classroom unless the subject is being taught by a committed Christian, and even then the neutral intention of the state education system will make it impossible for the teacher to teach in a way that intends as an outcome the conversion of his pupils. So, many Pentecostal teachers will run a variety of voluntary group activities during lunch periods and after school in which more direct evangelism will occur.

2. *Church membership preparation*. There are few specific training programmes for young adults preparing for church membership, although many Pentecostal churches do provide short series of teaching sessions for prospective members. Most churches provide youth meetings, usually on a weekly basis, at which much of the basic teaching is covered in matters spiritual, as indeed it is in the 'teens' section of the Sunday Schools. Groups like Campaigners (an inter-denominational uniformed organization) have been established in some congregations and they are regarded as providing a useful midweek base from which to teach and train young people. Many Pentecostal churches use their Sunday evening services as evangelistic occasions in which the uncommitted will be invited to make a decision of faith. The 'liturgical style' of these services can be regarded as contributing towards membership preparation.

3. *Religious education within the community of faith*. As can be seen from most Pentecostal church notice boards, the on-going Christian education of the faithful is a prime concern. From earliest days, Sunday Schools and midweek children's meetings have been a prominent feature of church programmes. But in recent years large numbers of churches have introduced all-age Christian education programmes, so that the further education of adults can be given as much prominence as the training of new members. In these programmes it is possible for the whole family to go to church together on a Sunday morning, and each member of the family to receive Christian education at what is regarded as a level appropriate to his particular age and stage of discipleship. The material used is generally that provided by the Scripture Union or the Scripture Press, (e.g. the Gospel Light All Age Christian Education Programme).

Since the educational aim within the Pentecostal churches is directed towards induction into a religious tradition with clear beliefs and ethical standpoints, the educational style adopted will usually be greatly concerned with the transmission of the received tradition. In Pentecostalism, the preacher has had an important role in this process. He has been at once the hander-on of the tradition and the vehicle through which faith has been called forth in the penitent. This underlying approach is now reinforced by the use of published material which uses the highest quality of printing and photography to pass on the received truths of the gospel to a generation of people powerfully influenced by the mass media. Much of the language of the material will be traditional in its evangelical orientation on the assumption that that language will itself convey the truths to which it gives expression. This will be the case also with regard to the Pentecostal churches' broadcast material on their own special radio programmes. There is an unfailing commitment to the truth as it is perceived to be enshrined in the received tradition, and a committed urgency in conveying this truth by using the most up to date communication tools available.

Walter J. Hollenweger, *The Pentecostals*, SCM Press 1972.

KRISTER OTTOSSON

Personal Belief of Pupils

The place of the personal beliefs of pupils in RE raises such questions as: can such belief be seen as a resource in RE? is RE concerned with promoting a search for personal belief, for a 'faith to live by' as the Crowther* report claimed? These questions sound a little dated in the contemporary debate about RE. What has come to be called the 'Lancaster' approach to Religious Studies has had undoubted influence on attitudes to and concepts of RE. The move away from the 'human experience at depth' notion of religion, fostered most notably by Loukes, has given way to a phenomenological study of religion which can, if dogmatically interpreted, lead to arid irrelevance. In an understandable desire to avoid any hint of proseletysing, religious studies presents the phenomena of various traditions for pupils to study.

A number of recent syllabuses do see RE, however, as helping pupils in their 'personal search for meaning, purpose and values' (Hampshire). That syllabus has as one of its objectives (for the 13+ age group) 'to enable pupils to recognize relationships between behaviour and belief and to examine their own behaviour and beliefs – so that they could, for example, discuss some of the experiences and reasons which may lead people to adopt religious or non-religious interpretations of life'.

If this is accepted as a legitimate objective for RE then the personal belief of the pupils would appear to have an important role. This amounts to far more than using, for example, the experience of a Muslim or Jewish child in the class to illustrate in a personal way, some aspect of that tradition. Rather it is concerned with providing an existential framework within which the pupil's own experiences play an important part.

The thrust of the newer syllabuses, such as Avon and Hampshire, comes from their starting point with human beings and their reflections on questions of meaning and mystery. *Curriculum 11–16* also sees RE as seeking 'to encourage this reflective activity' and holds it as a reasonable expectation that a sixteen-year-old should be able to be articulate about 'a self-chosen theme in the realm of belief or behaviour which is of serious concern to him'.

It would seem, therefore, that the personal belief of pupils is a factor which the wise teacher will be aware of and will hope to draw on and to stimulate. It is, however, a delicate area where great sensitivity is required so that proper respect is paid to the autonomy* of the pupil.

HMI, *Curriculum 11–16*, DES 1977.

DONALD C. G. WHITTLE

Personal Relationships: Development of Teaching about in RE

When research in the early 1960s led to increasing disquiet about the appropriateness of much biblically based religious education it was writers such as J. W. D. Smith and Harold Loukes who suggested that the real questions and sources of vision could be found in reflection on the significance of personal relationships. The basis of such a view was suggested in much of the theology of the time, particularly in works deriving inspiration from Martin Buber. The main aim was to provide content in RE which was more relevant to the pupil's own experience. At the primary level, themes on homes, families and friends continue to provide an important foundation for later religious understandings. At secondary level the many books on sex, prejudice, family life, work and leisure produced in the sixties and early seventies are being replaced by works on more explicitly religious themes. Within the context of specifically Christian education many helpful books are still appearing.

The difficulty of this approach at the secondary level lies in the fact that without theological insight it can become vague and superficial discussion and can trivialize what is of utmost significance. Often the best way of approaching this subject is through exploration of works of art which are the result of profound reflection on the meaning and complexity of relationships. For this reason English literature often provides the best source material for this kind of religious education.

JUDITH OLLINGTON

Personal Relationships: Teaching about in RE

Relationships have always been important to pupils as they cope with the expectations of parents, teachers and society, and with the realities of the playground and street and their own feelings of failure and achievement. These feelings become more complex as they move to secondary school, to the physical, emotional and social demands of adolescence, to the prospect of leaving school, developing a career, creating their own family unit and taking part in the community. Young people learn willy-nilly through experience that relationships begin, develop – or not – mature and inevitably end, that they are influenced by change, emotion, by their own sense of identity and their own and others' values and beliefs.

The importance of helping pupils develop good relationships is recognized in all phases of education. Work in many disciplines aims to develop knowledge, to increase skills* and build motivation for improving relationships. Unfortunately attention is often focussed on 'problems' and, particularly in the secondary school, material is aimed mainly at lower ability ranges. Future architects, doctors, lawyers and politicians also need to understand human relationships.

What of RE in this work? The principles of valuing oneself and others, of developing sensitive communication skills not only between individuals but between different groups in the community and of making decisions in the light of beliefs and values, are

central to RE and to education in personal relationships.

There are three areas in which RE makes an important contribution. 1. Study of the expectations which the major religions have of the life styles of adherents and how their central beliefs may help individuals seeking answers to the questions: Who am I? Why am I here? Where am I going? 2. Consideration of the major experiences of life around which the great religious festivals and rituals centre – birth, initiation, marriage, death, renewal – occasions when relationships and religious beliefs are tested and often enriched. 3. The emotions. RE may be one of the few areas of the curriculum which dare to acknowledge and explore the powerful emotions of anger, jealousy and guilt which can underlie and corrode relationships. Pupils may need the reassurance that they are not alone in experiencing or provoking these emotions.

The demands on the teacher's personal resources are great. The quality of relationships built up with pupils teaches as much as, if not more than, the resource material used. Many LEAs and other agencies offer training opportunities and support for teachers wishing to develop their own skills in teaching Personal Relationships.

JILL DAVIES

Phenomenology of Religion

This represents basically two approaches to the study of religion: 1. it refers to the attempt to examine religious phenomena in ways that do not bring in one's own theological or ideological presuppositions; 2. it refers to methods of thematic comparison in the study of religion aimed at uncovering and presenting types of phenomena. The second of these approaches roughly coincides with the comparative study of religion as understood in Britain, in so far as the latter is concerned with cross-cultural themes. The most important writers in the field of phenomenology of religion in the typology sense are Rudolf Otto (1860–1937), with his work on the numinous, Gerardus van der Leeuw (1890–1950) and Mircea Eliade (b. 1907).

The first sense of the phrase 'phenomenology of religion' looks to one aspect of the work of Edmund Husserl (1859–1938). He thought of the examination of human experience as being a descriptive science in which one cleanses oneself of the presuppositions and interpretations which we bring to bear in judging experience. The method used is a kind of 'standing back' or 'distancing', known as *epoché* or bracketing. The importance of this for religion is that religious commitment and passion sometimes seem to come in the way of the understanding of the religious activities, feelings and beliefs of others – for example if we think of certain forms of worship involving images as being idolatry. This is a value judgment which presupposes a view about what true worship is, but it fails to bring out the nature of the experience and attitudes of the people involved.

The phenomenological approach, in the sense of putting the emphasis on understanding and engaging in a kind of self-transcendence in entering into the thoughts and feelings of others, was advocated as a major ingredient in RE in *Working Paper 36* of the Schools Council (1971). It is also central to the modern approach to the study of religion and religions in higher education; but it does not of course at the same time preclude, but may help to stimulate, the open exploration of truth and value judgments about the varying religions and ideologies under consideration. But it provides a formal framework for what is put more concretely in a native American proverb: 'Never judge a man until you have walked a mile in his moccasins.'

There is argument as to how far such 'moccasin-walking' is in reality possible. Clearly the phenomenological approach implies a mixture of standing back and warmth – in brief, empathy. It also requires informational structure. Thus if we think of what it is for a Roman Catholic to attend Mass we need not only to get something of the feel of it but also to know a fair amount about the web of ideas in his or her mind, relating to doctrine and the meanings of various parts of the ritual.

Phenomenology in this sense can perhaps best be put into English as 'structured empathy'. It is obviously involved in anthropological work and various other fields. Its educational application suggests ties with literature, art and music as helping to give the feel of other people's worlds, and our own. It relates too to the documentary mode practised in some contemporary television presentations of religion, and to inter-religious dialogue.

John Hinnells (ed.), *World Religions in Education*, Oriel Press 1969; E. J. Sharpe, *Comparative Religion – a history*, Duckworth 1975; Ninian Smart, *The Phenomenon of Religion*, Mowbray 1973; G. Van der Leeuw, *Religion in Essence and Manifestation*, Allen & Unwin ²1964.

NINIAN SMART

Phenomenological Approach in RE

The phenomenological approach, whilst deriving from the philosophy of Edmund Husserl, only utilizes certain elements of his thought. One essential feature used is that of treating religion as a phenomenon. Associated with this is the attempt to approach a religion in a presuppositionless way, namely through the procedure of bracketing-out possible distorting pre-conceptions. Also there is the intention to set aside those assumptions often strongly held by students as to what is true, which come from the British empirical/positivist philosophical tradition.

In the preparation of curricula for secondary school RE in the English speaking world, the conceptual framework adopted in this approach is largely based on Ninian Smart's multidimensional typology of doctrines, myths, ethics, rituals, experiences, institutions and symbolism. There are variations on this which may include different labels such as stories, festivals, sacred places, sacred literature, etc.

This approach can also be applied to what may be termed quasi-religions or alternative stances for living. A well known example of this is the 1975 *Birmingham Agreed Syllabus*. Within the adolescence section of the handbook of suggestions for religious education, units on communism and humanism are included.

The approach can be used in the study of Christianity. In the Australian context, to overcome student stereotypes of this religion, research work on Christianity has been undertaken by students interviewing Christians using a structured interview. This has taken the form of a questionnaire on Christianity explicitly based on the dimensions of a phenomenological typology.

The phenomenological approach can also be used as a way of helping students in their own quest for meaning. This involves students looking at personal life experiences through the various dimensions. Using this method there can be discussion about the stories, beliefs, ethics, etc., that are of personal significance to them.

Whilst various criticisms are made of this approach, its value lies in the depiction of religion as multifaceted. It is a movement beyond types of religious education which over-emphasize beliefs. At its best it brings together understanding and empathy in RE.

Birmingham District Council Education Committee, *Living Together: A Teacher's Handbook of Suggestions for Religious Education*, 1975; Dorothy Hansen *et al.*, *A New Look at the Fourth R*, Methodist Ladies College Press 1981; Edmund Husserl, *Cartesian Meditations*, Martinus Nijhoff Press 1960; Ninian Smart, *The Phenomenon of Religion*, Mowbray 1973.

IAN L. HIGGINS

Philosophy of Education

Since the early 1960s British philosophy of education has been marked by a sustained effort to employ the methods and achievements of contemporary analytical philosophy to the elucidation of educational principles. This approach to philosophy, which swept the English speaking academic world in the early fifties, was rooted in the work of Bertrand Russell, G. E. Moore, and above all Ludwig Wittgenstein. It took from logical positivism a dominant concern for language, truth and logic but rejected tying meaningfulness to verification by the senses. Logical positivism pronounced religious claims, like moral and aesthetic claims, to be nothing more than expressions of emotion. The ensuing analytical approach took a much wider view, seeing different domains of meaning arising with different uses of language with different criteria for truth in these domains. Mental, moral and religious discourse, for instance, were each seen to employ language for distinct, if related, purposes in relation to man's wide-ranging social, personal and empirical circumstances. Preoccupation with the internal structures of these forms of discourse, their applications and their interrelationships led to a reconsideration of many traditional philosophical problems, shedding new light, if only to underline the intractability of such

issues as the nature of personal identity, the foundations of ethics, or the existence of God.

The use of the methods and results of this philosophical work to illuminate educational issues began in earnest in the early sixties. At that time the most significant influences in British philosophy of education were three. 1. The traditional, 'classical' view of education, derived from Greek philosophy stressing the development of reason as the means to grasping the truth about nature, man and ultimate reality. Jacques Maritain, a prominent neo-Thomist philosopher, articulated well this approach in a form which saw religious truth complementing the achievements of reason and religious education as the crowning element in a comprehensive educational programme. 2. The 'pragmatism' of John Dewey was dominant because of its emphasis on the development of the individual child as a being learning to realize himself in adaptation to his evolving social and material environment. In this the continuous development of experience according to one's context and interests by the use of a scientific method of thinking was the key. All notions of a supernatural reality were rejected, 'religion' being concerned with pursuing an imaginative ideal of the unification of the self with the universe. 3. A Christian 'existentialist' view of education drawing heavily on the ideas of Martin Buber and certain Christian existentialists. M. V. C. Jeffreys in particular developed a philosophy of education which stressed the importance of personal growth through the exercise of free and responsible choice. He sought to encourage this through the pupils' understanding of the world they live in, direct experience of community living and 'the Vision of Greatness'. He saw Christian revelation as presenting man with a call to faith that would lead to personal and social life in keeping with his true nature. Education he saw as 'the religious re-education of our world', with the school as a Christian community seeking to present all it undertakes within a Christian perspective.

In contrast to these comprehensive thinkers, analytical philosophers of education have concerned themselves with more piecemeal issues. They have sought to elucidate by careful conceptual distinctions just what we mean by important terms such as 'education', 'teaching', indoctrination', 'discipline' and 'authority'. They have drawn on recent studies in general philosophy to characterize 'knowledge', 'emotion', 'imagination' and other attributes of mind that are important for understanding educational objectives. They have looked to the philosophy of science, of history, and other subjects to illuminate the teaching of these areas. A re-appraisal of the nature and foundation of moral judgments has led to a careful consideration of the value judgments made in educational decisions and to a systematic analysis of the demands of moral education*.

The significance of this work for ideas about RE in particular has centred round three considerations:

1. The domain of religious discourse, beliefs, activities and experience has come to be seen as one of many domains in which we make sense of ourselves and our context. It is characterized, like other domains, primarily by the distinctive concepts it has developed in which to capture its particular concerns which are considered distinct from, if not unrelated to, those of other domains such as the sciences, the arts and morality. RE is thus viewed as being concerned with the initiation of pupils into this already existing public world of concepts, beliefs and practices, seeking to do justice to their significance in the complex changing pattern of human life, personal and social. Personal development in this as in any other area is seen as achieved by the individual only through entering into, exploring, and perhaps modifying, what is of its nature a socially constructed and deposited world. Meaning in religion, it is held, cannot be an individual, private construction any more than meaning in science or in any other area.

2. Though religious claims are in general very closely related to moral claims, there has been much concern to distinguish and then properly relate these two. Any justification there may be for such major moral principles as respect for persons, freedom and equality, is now widely held to be independent of particular religious doctrines and indeed likely to be presupposed by any justification of these doctrines. As a result, though RE must include concern for the moral elements that are built into religious traditions, moral education is generally seen as legitimate in its own right, and as being seriously miscon-

strued if seen only within a religious framework.

3. Philosophers of education have come to see religious education as aiming at pupils' understanding of the claims and significance of one or more religions, not their acceptance and commitment to the beliefs and practices of any one faith. There has been developed a concept of education that no longer sees education as concerned with bodies of knowledge and belief which pupils are expected to accept. Instead beliefs in all areas, including religion, are presented as acceptable only when they are justifiable by appropriate publicly agreed canons. In areas like religion where no such canons exist for truth claims that are made, education cannot be concerned with pupils coming to know or believe the claims themselves. But it can properly concern itself with pupils coming to know what religious people believe and the proper grounds for our knowing that they believe these things. Education is here sharply distinguished from indoctrination*, evangelism, or catechesis*. Where radically controversial claims are concerned it aims at an understanding of their character. It rejects all concern to achieve personal commitments to any such claims. RE is in these terms a matter of religious studies governed by appropriate canons of scholarly objectivity. It includes imaginatively entering into the minds of religious believers, seeking to understand their doctrines, worship, practices and moral point of view. Whether or not the pupil accepts that point of view is irrelevant to the study. Properly conducted, however, it must include a serious study of the foundations of various religious claims and their controversial character. In that sense it prepares the way for personal commitment. It is religious education in these terms that most contemporary British philosophers of education have advocated for publicly maintained schools, other more personal objectives being considered inappropriate in this context.

John Dewey, *Democracy and Education*, Macmillan, New York 1916; P. H. Hirst, *Knowledge and the Curriculum*, Routledge & Kegan Paul 1974; P. H. Hirst, *Moral Education in a Secular Society*, Hodder & Stoughton 1974; M. V. C. Jeffreys, *Glaucon*, Pitman 1950; Jacques Maritain, *Education at the*

Cross Roads, Yale University Press 1943; R. S. Peters, *Ethics and Education*, Allen & Unwin 1966; I. A. Snook (ed.), *Concepts of Indoctrination*, Routledge & Kegan Paul 1972.

PAUL H. HIRST

Philosophy of Religion

Any application of philosophical thought to religious understanding may be described as philosophy of religion. In practice four forms of philosophical enquiry have played a significant part in the study of religious belief and its theological expressions. *Logic*, as the study of the reasoning process itself, investigates the validity of the arguments used to support beliefs. It considers both the status of the evidence or premises and the reasoning processes employed in such arguments. Not all valid forms of reasoning follow the formal modes of syllogistic deduction: as Newman pointed out in *The Grammar of Assent* (1870), various more flexible and sensitive ways of reaching conclusions from evidence may be appropriate to certain subject-areas, including religion. Among the theologically important issues raised by logic is the question of the justifiability of attempting to reach theistic understanding from reports about essentially contingent events in the natural and historical orders of reality. *Epistemology*, as the study of the possible contents, limits and methods of understanding, when applied to religion, considers the warrantability of claims to religious knowledge and the significance of references to religious experience. It probes, for example, the possibility of claims to apprehend God* when God is conceived as ultimate, transcendent, eternal and infinite. *Metaphysics* is the attempt to determine the ultimate constitution of reality. It includes the development and examination of those arguments which purport to show that the contingent world of experience is derived from and finally dependent upon an ontologically necessary reality that is personally purposive and valuatively ultimate, i.e. on 'God'. *Analytical* philosophy, which has dominated British philosophy for much of the twentieth century, is the detailed examination of how language is used. By often minute investigations of concepts as they are actually employed, philosophical analysts seek to clarify what is expressed by means of them,

thereby resolving confusions arising from their misunderstanding and also revealing the large number of different functions which language performs. The application of this approach to religious utterances has exposed their complexity and led to considerable controversy about their reference.

The different conclusions which have been reached as a result of philosophical studies of religious belief have led to four main ways of perceiving the relationship between philosophy and religion and hence of appreciating the nature and role of philosophy of religion.

According to the first of these the proper content of religious understanding is provided by metaphysical enquiries alone. The highest goal of philosophical reflection is held to be that of determining the ultimate character of reality and of a corresponding pattern of behaviour. Authentic religion is to understand and act according to those metaphysical insights. Philosophy of religion is thus seen as both a critical and a constructive discipline. On the one hand it exposes the rationally unsupportable nature of the stories, superstitutions and practices which are to be found in popular religion. On the other it replaces them by rationally established metaphysical insights which are to constitute the doctrines and standards of future genuine religion.

The view that the highest form of philosophical understanding is found in metaphysical insights which are to be identified with true religious understanding finds its classical sources in Plato's treatment of 'the Form of the Good', Aristotle's conception of 'the Unmoved Mover' and Plotinus' neo-Platonic notion of 'the One'. Plato, for example, holds that purely intellectual reflection leads to the perception of 'the Good' as not only 'the end of all endeavour' but also the source of the existence, reality and intelligibility of the objects of knowledge. It is both knowable as 'the cause of knowledge and truth' and yet itself as beyond reality, knowledge and truth. Life is properly regulated when it is governed according to this knowledge. Plotinus goes further than Plato in developing a rationalistic form of mysticism. He considers that the contemplative vision of and unity with 'the One', which is the consummation of our being, is only achieved by means of a self-transcending form of intellectual reflection which uses philosophy to get to what is beyond thought.

In modern thought the major exponents of philosophical systems which can be regarded as providing a religiously sufficient view of reality include Spinoza, Leibniz, Hegel, Fechner, Whitehead and Hartshorne as well as some of the eighteenth-century advocates of the adequacy of natural religion and natural theology. Whitehead himself not only regarded 'rational religion' as a metaphysical product of 'the supernormal experience of mankind at its moments of finest insight' but also held that it is theoretically independent of any 'social religions of ritual and mythical belief'. Religion, in his view, is a matter of applying 'the general ideas' established by philosophy to the particular thoughts, emotions and purposes that belong to 'existence in a particular society'.

A second form of philosophy of religion regards its role as that of contributing to a complete religious understanding rather than as that of being able to provide all the contents of such understanding by philosophical reflection alone. The activity of philosophical thought in this approach is generally perceived as twofold. On the one hand rational reflection is held to be able to reach a number of basic religious doctrines, particularly about the existence and nature of God and about the destiny of human life. These, however, do not provide a religiously complete system of understanding. What reason cannot determine has to be provided by divine revelation. The other task of philosophy of religion, therefore, is that of formulating and applying rational tests whereby the authenticity of purportedly revealed truths can be established.

The classical view of the complementary character of truths discernible by reason and others which are divinely given and of the role of philosophy of religion as educing the former and validating the latter is often attributed to Thomas Aquinas. According to his *Summa Contra Gentiles*, 'There is a twofold mode of truth in what we profess about God. Some truths about God exceed all the ability of the human reason. Such is that God is triune.' These doctrines can only be known by being revealed to humanity by God. 'But there are some truths which the natural reason also is able to reach. Such are that God exists,

that he is one, and the like.' These truths can be and have been 'proved demonstratively' by philosophical reasoning. It is important to note, however, that for Aquinas revealed truths provide the criteria by which the conclusions of human reasoning are confirmed to be correct. The view that it is reason which is finally authoritative and that revealed truths are acceptable as such only if they are compatible with reason's findings was not generally accepted until much later. It is a view that Locke formulated in his *Essay Concerning Human Understanding* when he laid down that 'he governs his assent right, and places it as he should, who in any case or matter whatsoever, believes or disbelieves, according as reason directs him'. Only so, according to Locke, does a person act as God intends.

In order to show that it is reasonable to hold that God exists and that he has certain attributes, philosophers of religion have turned to one or more of the arguments for the existence of God: the ontological (which maintains that the concept of God requires us to hold that a perfect being exists), the cosmological (which argues from the existence of contingent things to the necessary existence of a being which lacks no quality), the teleological (which holds that the marks of order and design in the world point to a transcendent creator), the moral (which finds in the sense of moral duty evidence of a supreme moral orderer) and the experiential (which argues that God's reality is shown by the sense of his presence). They have also had to provide arguments which show that the existence of evil, whether natural, moral, intellectual or aesthetic, does not provide an overwhelming counter-argument to the theistic case. Once the basic truths of theism have been established, other arguments are advanced to justify the acceptance of further truths as divinely revealed. Traditionally the strongest forms of these arguments have been held to be those based on reports of miraculous deeds performed by the person presenting the revelation, of the fulfilment of prophecies by that person, and of the humanly unexpected acceptance of his message.

The third form of philosophy of religion sees the role of philosophical reasoning in relation to religion as that of investigating the scope of human reason in order to show that fundamentally religious understanding is beyond its competence. Philosophy is not to show that certain doctrines are either true or false but that all such judgments are properly beyond it. This view of the role of philosophy in religious matters is classically expressed in Kant's judgment on the religious implications of his critical philosophy: 'I have therefore found it necessary to deny *knowledge*, in order to make room for *faith*'. It is a view, however, which has a number of important antecedents. The medieval Muslim thinker, Al Ghazzali, held that the limitations of reason revealed by philosophy show that religious understanding is a quite separate matter. Pascal contrasted the God of religion and the 'God' of the philosophers, holding that human finitude renders human reason incapable of grasping the Infinite by its own powers. Since the time of Locke a number of thinkers have argued that human reason, reflecting on the principles of human understanding and the contents of human experience of the world, can never get beyond the human to the genuinely divine. Hume was almost certainly being ironic when he suggested that the conclusion of his refutations of the arguments for the reality of God is to show that religious belief is a matter of faith, not of reason: 'to be a philosophical sceptic is . . . the first and most essential step towards being a sound, believing Christian'. Others, like Hume's contemporary John Ellis and Mansel in the following century, have positively endorsed this position. During the present century it has appealed to those who have wished to affirm a religious position but have despaired of finding a convincing rational justification for it. In various ways, then, the philosophical examination of the proper limits of human reason is held to show that no aspect of religious belief should be regarded as a matter of rational inferences. Philosophy of religion is only legitimate to the extent that it recognizes and upholds the proper significance of faith as the basis of religious understanding.

The fourth form of philosophy of religion adopts the Wittgensteinian view that philosophy is an analytical discipline which is not attempting to establish the truth or falsity of statements but is concerned with elucidating their meaning in practice. It thus devotes itself to studying the grammatical and conceptual structures of religious utterances and their theological counterparts. The results of these analyses have been as controversial as the conclusions of other forms of philosophy of religion. Critics have sometimes complained that some of the supposed analyses have in fact been reductionist attempts to interpret religious statements in ways that omit the essentially religious elements in them. As a result of these analyses, however, it has become apparent that religious language is highly complex. It not only includes affirmations about what is necessarily the case in any possible world and others about what is ultimately the case in this world but need not necessarily have been so; it also includes moral, interpretative, convictional and attitudinal elements and employs mythical, metaphorical and symbolic modes of expression. It would be a mistake, however, to consider that this form of philosophy of religion is a wholly post-Wittgensteinian phenomenon. It has basic parallels with earlier philosophical attempts to identify the essential reference of religious claims. Feuerbach, for example, suggested that talk about God is to be understood as talk about the objectification and personification of human ideals, Schleiermacher that it derives from the feeling of absolute dependence, and Otto that it refers to the sense of the numinous. In their way these too were attempts to identify the contents of religious language.

M. J. Charlesworth, *Philosophy of Religion: The Historic Approaches,* Macmillan 1972; Brian Davies, *An Introduction to the Philosophy of Religion,* Oxford University Press 1982; John Hick, *Philosophy of Religion,* Prentice-Hall 1963; N. Smart, *Historical Selections in the Philosophy of Religion,* SCM Press 1962.

DAVID A. PAILIN

Pilgrimage

The idea of making a special journey or pilgrimage to a particular place grew out of what was the original motive for worship – the desire to return to a place of religious power. In the OT, Bethel (Gen. 12.8; Amos 4.4) and Shiloh (I Sam. 1.3) were religious centres for the Jews even before Jerusalem assumed prime significance (II Sam. 6.12). Other religions also have important religious centres. For Hindus the most important is Benares and for Muslims, Mecca. The faithful are expected to make at least one journey in a lifetime and in the OT we find the ideal of a yearly visit (Ps. 122.7). In many cases pilgrimage centres were associated with visions and healings and were often to be found near springs (John 5.7). A building on such a site turned a shrine into a temple.

The first Christian centres were Jerusalem and the tombs of Peter and Paul in Rome. There is evidence for the veneration of martyrs in the catacombs and under St Peter's basilica. The conversion of the empire under Constantine led to the visit of the Empress Helena to Palestine in 326 and the 'discovery' of the true cross and the holy places. Rapid expansion of pilgrimage sites followed. Some pilgrims, like the wandering Irish monks and the Saxons Willibald, Wilfred and King Ine, made their journeys in search of knowledge. Others went in search of healing, and the test of a shrine eventually came to be its power to heal.

Traditionally, the power of a holy place could be transferred through a piece of earth, water or bone. Such relics were much sought after and churches sought to hold relics of their patron and the stations of the cross so becoming centres of pilgrimage. The Reformation stemmed from a criticism of this proliferation of relics and the sale of indulgences.

In Europe the most famous shrines were Santiago de Compostela, where St James's body was said to have been rescued from the Atlantic in 816, the tombs of St Martin of Tours, the Magi at Cologne and St Francis at Assisi. The most popular in England was the tomb of St Thomas a Becket, martyred at Canterbury in 1170. The well-known inns on the route and the stories in Chaucer's *Canterbury Tales* show that for many such a journey was a holiday.

In the eighteenth century the idea of pilgrimages to holy places for religious reasons was gradually replaced for many by tourism. In the nineteenth century a desire to popularize religion produced new centres at Lourdes, Fatima and Lisieux. Methodists held rallies at famous preaching sites like Mow Cop and Gwennap Pit, and in the twentieth century Anglicans and Catholics revived the shrines at Walsingham, instituting an annual pilgrimage. Many also walk the ancient routes to cathedrals, such as the Pilgrims' Way to Canterbury.

John Bunyan's famous allegory *Pilgrim's Progress* illustrates a broader view of the idea of pilgrimage, presenting life itself as a journey to the world to come.

In school the idea of pilgrimage in all religions provides scope for exploration through local studies and drama.

John Adair, *The Pilgrims' Way*, Thames and Hudson 1978; Peter Brown, *The Cult of the Saints,* SCM Press 1981.

DAVID KEEP

Plowden Report

The report *Children and their Primary Schools* (HMSO 1967) was produced under the chairmanship of Lady Plowden. Its brief was 'to consider primary education in all its aspects, and the transition to secondary education'. The general approach was child-centred; the child was not an empty vessel to be filled from the teacher's own store of knowledge, but was an active agent in its own learning.

The report appeared at a time of widespread debate on the nature of religious education. The importance of RE in the report is reflected in the length of the section devoted to it. Its six and a half pages are more than those for mathematics and exceeded only by English and science.

It has to be said at the outset that the committee was divided on RE. Like the Newsom report*, the Plowden report reflected a time of diverse views about religion. A minority of the members believed that RE should not be included in the primary curriculum, although it was apparently RE as initiation into Christian belief which they were rejecting. The difficulty here was that the majority report argued for a confessional approach to RE with most of the children in primary schools: ' . . . young children need a simple and positive introduction to religion. They should be taught to know and love God and to practise in the school community the virtues appropriate to their age and environment . . . they should not be confused by being taught to doubt before faith is established.' Yet the report also recognized that older children needed to come to their own conclusions about religious beliefs and that this might begin in the later junior years.

The committee recognized certain difficulties with RE. An integrated curriculum made it awkward to respect the legal requirement to allow withdrawal from RE.

The report also recognized the difficulties of the agnostic teacher taking RE. Such teachers were recommended to be honest about their own beliefs in their teaching. However, it was found that teachers were generally willing to teach RE. Parents too were overwhelmingly in favour with some eighty per cent reported as desiring RE for their children.

Agreed syllabuses gave the committee cause for concern. Teachers should be freer in adapting the recommendations of the syllabuses. Existing syllabuses were also considered too factual and, if RE was to deal with children's needs, it would be necessary to determine what subject matter and concepts were relevant to the children. Care should be taken in introducing some of the more difficult Christian stories or else children from non-Christian homes might form distorted concepts. Teachers of RE 'should be able to relate the background and facts of the Christian revelation to situations which are within children's experience, and so give their teaching vitality and greater relevance to the problems of life'. Systematic study of the life and teaching of Jesus* should be left until the later junior years. OT material should not be given excessive prominence. Non-Christian historical characters such as Saladin could also be studied.

In addition to any kind of formal RE there would be opportunities at all times for experiences with a religious dimension: children learn from their relationship with their teachers and with each other and from observing the way the adults in the school behave with one another and with children. By example at first hand children can learn to love and to care for others, to be generous, kind and courageous. Good experiences in personal relationships in early life will make a most important contribution to an understanding of spiritual and moral values when children are older.'

The act of worship* was valued as a focus of unity in the school, although unlike the Newsom report the religious aspect was played down. The report called for more freedom in the interpretation of the requirements of the 1944 Education Act. It should not necessarily involve the whole school or begin the day. The needs of minority groups should be considered and non-Christian material included. Parents should be told when their children were admitted to school of their rights of withdrawal from the act of worship and from RE. The act of worship should not necessarily be conducted by the headteacher.

The report included two other specific recommendations on RE. 1. Further enquiry should be made into the aspects of religious faith which could be presented to young children. 2. Further in-service training should be provided to familiarize teachers with modern thinking on religious education.

Two notes of reservation on religious education were appended to the report. The first argued that RE must involve theology and theological instruction and this was too recondite and controversial for the primary curriculum. However, for cultural reasons younger children could be told Bible stories. Religious belief might promote moral education* by providing children with models for them to imitate. So Christ for this purpose could be represented as an exceptional human being rather than as an incarnate deity. The note is critical of the way in which some teachers might have felt inveigled into teaching RE for fear of being considered unsuitable for headships. As with the conscience clause* permitting parents to withdraw their children from RE, so too for the teachers it should be the rule to opt in rather than opt out.

The second called for a programme of ethical non-religious education to be drawn up for the children of parents who wished to withdraw their children from RE.

GEOFFREY CHORLEY

Plural Society

Pluralism may be applied as a term to any system which recognizes more than one set of ultimate principles. To describe Britain as a plural society has become common practice with the increasing secularism of public life and with the settlement here of people from a wider range of cultures. Every society, however, depends for its coherence upon the general acceptance of certain principles, which in this case might include freedom of speech within the law and tolerance of a variety of religious beliefs and practices. For centuries British society has contained diversity of Christian denominations and minority racial groups: it is the increase in religious and non-religious as well as racial diversity which has produced a more plural society.

Until 1966 at least, RE agreed syllabuses* presented a picture of 'Britannia nurturing her children in the family faith' and 'during assembly the school expressed its truest nature as an alleged Christian community' (Hull, 1975). One effect of pluralization is that previously uncontroversial questions become controversial. The response, not least from Christian teachers, has been to encourage sympathetic appreciation of other positions and faiths alongside Christianity, and agreed syllabus conferences have been broadened accordingly (notably Birmingham, 1975). The basis of this response is that 'the best interests of both Christians and non-Christians are served by the same aims' (Smart).

The debate about values within a plural society has proceeded alongside the secularization of RE and focussed on moral education as a distinct if related aspect of schooling. In 1968 the British Humanist Association* initiated a campaign to shift the acknowledged basis of values in schools away from traditional religion. At the same time the Schools' Council Moral Education Project (13–16) developed classroom methods and materials to help young people to adopt 'a considerate style of life' which takes account of others' needs, feelings and interests as well as their own. The early rivalry between ME and RE soon gave way to a complementary view of their relationship as expressed in a report from the Social Morality Council in 1970 (*Moral and Religious Education in County Schools*). The same body drew together religious, humanist and professional interests to support *A Plan for Moral Education in Schools* (1977) which seeks to develop and extend earlier Schools Council contributions to the continuing debate.

———

John M. Hull, *School Worship – An Obituary*, SCM Press 1975; Ninian Smart, *Secular Education and the Logic of Religion*, Faber & Faber 1968.

D. PAUL KING

Poetry and RE

Poetry is used in RE as an experience of imaginative sensitivity which widens the horizons of pupils. It evokes an awareness of another dimension where existence prompts reflection and questioning. Because this dimension is at the farthest limits of apprehension and also at its centre as a ground and condition of knowing, it is susceptible to the more oblique approaches offered by paradox, myth*, imagination* and poetry.

What poetry does in RE is to express the Absolute Mystery in the mystery of man. It achieves this in several ways. It may encourage pupils towards an openness of experience which enables them to capture the dynamics of what it is to be human. Such an exploration is made in the poetry of William Blake and T. S. Eliot. Poetry can also help in the quest for a pattern which unifies experiences and reveals the oneness within creation. It offers symbols and images which integrate the fragments of life and reveals the extent to which human beings deeply interact with each other and the universe. Much of R. Tagore's poetry in *Gitanjali* is of this kind.

Poetry exercises a critical negativity with respect to all human constructions of thought and feeling. It calls them into question judging them all to be unworthy, provisional and ultimately fragile. In doing this it attempts to point beyond to the hope for a vision of the ultimacy of incomprehensible love and holiness. This is a recurring theme in the work of Edwin Muir and R. S. Thomas. Finally, in attempting to call men to a self-transcendence, poetry reminds them of the darkness and pain linked with the transience and contingency of life as well as the joy and radical wonder of a nature grounded in God. The first of these is profoundly explored by Gerard Manley Hopkins and the second beautifully suggested in the *Spiritual Canticle* of St John of the Cross. Thus where poetry preserves its own integrity it is inevitably an aspect of religious education.

D. H. WEBSTER

Poland   *see* **Eastern Europe**

Political Education and RE

Political education is compulsory in most Western democracies but until recently it has either been neglected in British schools or felt to be implicit in the whole character of a school. But of recent years this *laisser faire* attitude has been challenged and found wanting. Now about forty per cent of secondary schools have some significant political education, under whatever synonym or guise. There are no national guidelines, although in 1978 the DES published an advisory paper, 'Political Competence', about the time that an HMI was appointed for political education. In the 1960s the Politics Association was founded for teachers and successive Secretaries of State have given it a guarded blessing.

The method and content most followed has been that of a working party whose report was published by the Hansard Society as 'Political Education and Political Literacy'. Political literacy was defined as something that young people need for entering the world: the values, knowledge and skills needed to be an effective citizen. For instance, toleration can be carried too far, can become permissiveness, but it must be a formal value of any educational political education for it creates a stipulation to understand the plausibility of other points of view, and what is involved in holding them or attempting to influence them, without surrendering one's own. This view of political education has something in common with moral education*: it argues that mankind is moved to action by both values and interests, and that before action one has an educational and moral duty to understand the values of others and how they will be affected. It does not say that democratic values must be defined and then imposed; this is held to be no better than teaching 'the constitution' by rote or a vague respect for 'the rule of law', when both traditional political and moral philosophy require the laws to be worthy of obedience by rational judgment and conscience. Just as in moral education, there is debate between those who see education as preserving a known and good order and those who see education as inevitably critical or questioning. The Hansard report strove to make a bridge by saying that any good curriculum must start from a knowledge of how society works as it is before applying moral criteria; but those criteria must be applied.

Tom Brennan, *Political Education and Democracy*, Cambridge University Press 1981; Bernard Crick and Alex Porter (eds) *Political Education and Political Literacy*, Longman 1978, for the Hansard Society; Bernard Crick and Derek Heater, *Essays on*

Political Education, Falmer Press 1977; Fred Milson, *Political Education: a practical guide for Christian Youth Workers*, Paternoster Press 1980.

BERNARD CRICK

'Pop' Music

After an uncertain start in the mid-1950s the pop phenomenon has spread across the nations of the non-communist world with the zeal of missionary causes of old.

At first 'pop' was the name applied to a 'popular' cultural movement and it referred solely to a certain kind of music, but soon the term was being applied to a whole life-style. This life-style was to some extent the product of a multi-million entertainment industry which seemed to be influenced mainly by profit motives rather than guided by an underlying disposition toward basic human values and ideals. In its early days the phenomenon centred around teenagers and single people in their early twenties.

Out of all the forms of mass media in the new and ever growing electronic age young people chose music as the primary way in which they experienced themselves and searched for identity and meaning. They saw the potential influence of music and many maximized it for their own use. So 'pop' became to some degree an attempt by certain people to set up a culture and a frame of reference which were apart and often in conflict with the culture offered by those born before the Second World War, most of whom had known war and who had undergone the rigours and discipline of compulsory national service and had a greater familiarity with print-type communication.

The pop phenomenon has been varied and diffuse with conflicting loyalties and attachments and it has attracted considerable hostility from some educational and religious quarters. American social analyst Kenneth Keniston said of the 1960s youth culture that human qualities such as control, planning, waiting, saving and postponing on the one hand, and revering, recalling, remembering and respecting on the other, were equally de-emphasized. In contrast, there were the experimental values of activity, adventure, genuineness, spontaneity and sentience (*Background Papers on Student Drug Involvement*). The pop phenomenon enshrined these values – a fact which worried many people. Yet in educational and religious circles there were those of a more positive disposition. The late H. R. Rookmaaker – a leading conservative evangelical – has commented: 'Anyone who thinks this is all cheap and no more than entertainment has never used his ears.' The British Council of Churches* in a special report on pop culture said if there was 'salvation' wrapped up in it then it lay in the movement's emphasis on celebration and joy; in its cry for revolution towards a better life and justice for all; in its insistence on genuine personal and communal experiences, and on instant and direct action and living.

During the 1970s, partly through two volumes, *Today's Sound* and *Sound Seventies*, many teachers became aware of the depth of theme material located in much of the pop world. There are those who think that using rock material is merely a device to gain attention for 'greater things'. But its proponents claimed that it requires teachers to see teaching as a dialogue. Alternatively, American Christian educationalist Ross Snyder, in what became termed the 'sensitizing' approach, believed that the major enterprise of this time is judging and choosing fundamental myth. He said: 'Only a pattern of ideas rather than an isolated idea, a totalizing feeling and mind image myth, rather than an abstract intellectualism can move us, can hold together the total complexity which the world is and which we are.'

Contemporary music was seen as helping this process since it provided a fund of stories, events, experiences and people in its general catalogue that can be explored from a starting point which is warm and familiar to young people. Such an approach can be used with so-called unchurched youth and in an increasingly pluralistic society. So from the late 1960s there was a flurry of experimental collections of hymns and songs which were far removed from the conventional school assembly books. This in itself ran parallel with a ferment of prayer, praise and protest within sections of the British Christian community in the early 1970s. Hymns joined pop and folk songs in describing such themes as ecology, industrialization, urban living, war, famine, inequality and mis-use of resources.

All of this need not be seen in 'Christian'

terms yet the Christian can find justification in some words of Norman Pittenger who said: 'The Christian job is to point to the places in human experience where people find the authenticity of life.' The contemporary music phenomenon is one such area – some would say the most important in the lives of many young and even a few older people. In education terms this means travelling from a ministry to young people to a ministry of young people.

See also **Music**.

Charles Hollander (ed.), *Background Papers on Student Drug Involvements*, USNSA Publications, Washington DC 1968; Tony Jasper, *Today's Sound*, Galliard 1970; *Sound Seventies*, Galliard 1972; H. R. Rookmaaker, *Modern Art and the Death of a Culture*, Intervarsity Press 1970; Ross Snyder, *Young People and their Culture*, Abingdon Press 1969.

TONY JASPER

Prayer: Children's Concepts of

There are four significant contributions made by psychologists to an understanding of children's concepts of prayer. One by Reik is a theoretical study. The others are empirical.

Theodore Reik, drawing on psychoanalytic theory, discusses three stages of development: 1. magic, 'my will be done'; 2. transition; 3. religious, 'God's will be done'.

Ronald Goldman, using a projective test of a child praying with children aged between six and seventeen, discusses four stages: 1. magical, involving direct causation and material benefits, until 9.4 years; 2. semi-magical, involving other causative factors alongside magic, with personal and material benefits, until 12.3 years; 3. non-magical, with benefit more in change of attitude of the person praying; 4. advanced, reached by some sixth-formers, arguing that no certain knowledge is available about the efficacy of prayer since it is a matter of faith.

Diane Long, David Elkind and Bernard Spilka, using semi-structured interview, incomplete sentences and direct questions with children aged between five and twelve, discuss five stages: 1. global undifferentiated, where the concept is vague and external, age five years; 2. transition, ages six to seven years; 3. concrete differentiated, where the prayer is still external, age eight years; 4. transition, ages nine to eleven years; 5. differentiated abstract, where prayer is internal and deriving from personal conviction, age twelve years.

Laurence Brown, using problem stories and choices between set prayers with children between twelve and seventeen, concludes that during adolescence belief in the causal efficacy of prayer decreases with age, while belief in its appropriateness and the actual form of prayer used depend on religious teaching and the situation to which prayer is related.

Andre Godin (ed.), *From Cry to Word: Contributions Towards a Psychology of Prayer*, Lumen Vitae Press 1968; Ronald Goldman, *Religious Thinking from Childhood to Adolescence*, Routledge & Kegan Paul 1964; Johanna Klink, *Your Child and Religion*, SCM Press 1972; Diane Long, David Elkind and Bernard Spilka, 'The child's concept of prayer', *Journal for the Scientific Study of Religion* 6, 1967, pp. 101–109; Theodore Reik, 'From spell to prayer', *Psychoanalysis* 3 (4), 1955, pp. 3–26; R. H. Thouless and L. B. Brown, 'Petitionary prayer: belief in its appropriateness and causal efficacy among adolescent girls', *Lumen Vitae* 19, 1964, pp. 297–310.

LESLIE FRANCIS

Prayer, Use of in School

The 1944 Education Act guaranteed the place of collective worship in state schools. The underlying assumption was that Christianity was the norm into which children were to be initiated. For example, the 1949 Agreed Syllabus of Cambridgeshire includes an analysis of the Christian theology of prayer and practical suggestions to help the child 'to feel that he is really praying the prayers which he speaks'.

During the 1960s and the 1970s the place of Christian prayer in the secular school has been criticized on psychological, social, educational and theological grounds. The psychological research of Ronald Goldman in 1964 into the child's developing understanding of prayer has been thought by some to caveat the propriety of praying with young children. The social analysis of documents like the Inner London Agreed Syllabus of 1968 argues that Christian prayer is inappropriate in the context of immigrant communities adhering to other world faiths, the secularization of the home background of many pupils, and the intellectual doubts of staff and pupils about the validity of worship. The educational arguments of philosophers like Paul Hirst emphasize a sharp distinction between the educational activity of schools in initiating the young into distinctive forms of knowledge, and the catechetical activity of churches in initiating into practices of the believing community. Bonhoeffer's theological problem about the place of prayer in a post-religious society is brought into the debate by the 1963 City of Oxford Handbook on Religious Education.

While the debate continues regarding the weight of these criticisms, the actual practice in state schools now varies greatly from one situation to another.

See also **Worship**.

Paul H. Hirst, 'Christian Education: a contradiction in terms', *Learning for Living* 11(4), 1972, pp.6–11; John M. Hull, *School Worship: an Obituary*, SCM Press 1975.

LESLIE FRANCIS

Prejudice

All teachers have the duty to recognize the personal prejudices which they bring to their teaching. The problem is more acute in some areas of the curriculum than others. It is particularly obvious in subject areas such as social studies or history where controversial issues, both current and past, have to be dealt with. There is the possibility in such areas that the selection and presentation of material can be influenced by the teacher's own political and sociological views. However, the most sensitive area is that concerned with religious belief. Often teachers bring to the classroom a deep conviction on ultimate questions*, which is the foundation of their personal morality. This individual commitment posed no problem when the teacher was a committed Christian and when the subject was seen as solely dedicated to a process of induction and nurture in the Christian faith. The modern perspective on RE as a subject helping pupils towards their own informed acceptance, or rejection, of a personal creed and towards sympathetically encountering the major world faiths has fundamentally changed the teacher's position.

It is perhaps helpful here to make an analogy to the teaching of literature. In one lesson a teacher may be dealing with a poem by Gerard Manley Hopkins and, in the next, with one by Thomas Hardy. The educational objective is clear – to help the pupils enter with imagination and empathy into the inner convictions of each poet. On the one hand, this involves an understanding of the religious passion that informed all of Hopkins' sensibility; on the other, an appreciation of the delicate insights into human experience that grew from Hardy's agnostic probing of the mysteries of the universe. The teacher would hope that, if either poet had been alive, and sitting at the back of the class, he would have approved the teacher's imaginative, but objective, presentation. This concept of the imaginary observer, sensitive to any manifestation of personal prejudice in the teacher's attitude, can be particularly relevant to the teaching of RE.

W. Owen Cole, 'Approaching Someone Else's Beliefs – Some Criteria', *World Faiths in Education,* Allen & Unwin 1978.

JOHN WHITE

Presbyterian Churches, Church of Scotland

Ever since the Scottish Reformation, formally dated at 1560, Scotland has been predominantly Presbyterian. Apart from short periods in the seventeenth century the Church of Scotland has been the established church whose influence on the people and institutions of the country has been profound. The involvement of ministers, Kirk Sessions, Presbyteries and the General Assembly has formed an integral part of the educational history of Scotland. The permeating influence of the church was such that it did not need to depend on its own institutions for its effectiveness and indeed only ran its own schools for about fifty years in the mid-nineteenth century. With changing attitudes, the general impact of the church has diminished but in education it retains an influence deriving from that history.

The Reformation and the First Book of Discipline. At the Reformation the privilege and clerical hold of the church which had been almost the sole agent of education was challenged and broken. A broadly-based popular system was envisaged and outlined in the *First Book of Discipline* (1560). At its heart was the desire for a continuum from primary school to university available to all. The Book of Discipline never passed into law but its educational standpoint was representative of the aims of the country's leaders and was reflected in the ensuing educational system.

A dominant feature was the local base for all education except at university level. Children of ability had access to higher education no matter how humble their origins. Local funding, a feature of the system, extended in some cases to support of students at university. Local schoolmasters, themselves the product of the universities, could tutor a child through to university entrance. A developed form of secondary schooling evolved much later. However the provision of schools was patchy. A great many parishes lacked schools. The land owners, successors to the church in wealth and possession, rarely took the initiative in establishing and funding schools, a position that only changed with legislation.

Statutory Enactments. From the first Education Act of 1496 and through a series of Acts in the century following the Reformation, attempts were made to develop a system of parish schools. The Act for Settling Schools of 1696 involved the church directly by naming the minister together with the heritors (landowners) as being required to establish a school and schoolhouse and appoint a schoolmaster is every parish. In the absence of other local and effective bodies, Kirk sessions commonly shared in the running of the local schools with the minister, whose major concern was the regular instruction of pupils in the scriptures and the catechism. The heritors, also responsible for church properties, often participated in Kirk sessions. Such a close association meant that the schools, though not belonging to the church, could not be regarded as secular institutions. It became standard practice for ministers to be responsible for superintendance of parish schools, a relationship which was statutorily acknowledged in the Education Act of 1803. This also stipulated that schoolmasters were to be examined and approved by the presbytery, being required to subscribe to the Westminster Confession and sign the formula of the

Church of Scotland. The period that followed marked the apex in official control by the church. Gradually Burgh Schools increased in numbers and status and central government began to establish its own structures and control. By the Education Act of 1861, the powers to examine schoolmasters were transferred from presbyteries to groups of professors from each of the universities, of whom half were to be professors of Divinity. The Education Act of 1872 inaugurated direct involvement of government and there followed the transfer of most church schools to local school Boards.

Church Schools. By the early nineteenth century the lack of schools in many parishes, especially in the North West, became a matter of concern. An Act of Parliament of 1824 permitted the building of additional places of worship in the highlands and islands. The Church of Scotland, having established an Education Committee in the same year and with powers to increase the means of education, immediately set up Assembly schools. Meanwhile, in the lowlands, Sessional schools were appearing as the result of initiatives by Kirk sessions. At the Disruption of 1843, when a major split within the Church of Scotland saw the formation of the Free Church, many teachers left their schools unable to continue to accept the authority of the Church of Scotland. The Free Church with a most remarkable effort developed a parallel system of schools that far outnumbered those of the established church.

Teacher Training. Initially model schools were designated, where experienced teachers demonstrated their skills. Then followed the formation of Normal institutions which were the precursors of the Training Colleges, now Colleges of Education. The Education Committee of the Church of Scotland initiated training in 1826 in an Edinburgh school. Church colleges were subsequently established in Glasgow, Edinburgh and Aberdeen. The total training of teachers in Scotland was undertaken by the churches until 1906 when the Church of Scotland and Free Church (then United Free Church) colleges were transferred to the state. That the state accepted the monopoly of the churches in teacher training for so long after the transfer of the great majority of schools is tribute

to the progressive nature and quality of the training provided.

The church has had a continuous though diminishing involvement in the Colleges of Education. At first it was responsible for the appointment and maintenance of lecturers in religious instruction, who also carried pastoral responsibilities. The church had representation on Provincial Committees (1905) replaced by Boards of Governors (1958).

Transition to a state system of education. The church welcomed the 1872 Education Act establishing School Boards, the antecedents of the Education Authorities and the present Education Committees of the Regional and Islands Authorities. With the steady transfer of schools and colleges to the state, the role of the church became increasingly advisory and consultative except in the sphere of RE. Co-operation with other churches and with the teachers' main professional assocation, the Educational Institute of Scotland, was considered appropriate. The Scottish Joint Committee on Religious Education*, formed in 1918, has a reputable record of publishing syllabus materials for RE in schools. With the increased assumption by the Scottish Education Department of responsibility for the provision for RE, including the curriculum, since the publication of the Millar Report* on Religious and Moral Education in 1972, the Joint Committee, extended over the years by representation from other professional associations, now provides a forum for consideration of matters pertaining to RE and for making representations or taking other appropriate joint action.

Church and state in education. Three church representatives have places on each Education Committee of whom at least one is from the Church of Scotland. The Church of Scotland has a representative on the General Teaching Council for Scotland and is recognized as an Official Correspondent by the Scottish Education Department of the Scottish Office. The Committee on Education of the General Assembly of the Church of Scotland maintains a constant scrutiny of educational affairs and responds to government reports and memoranda as appropriate.

Educational issues and the church. Of concern to the churches are the quality and provision of RE in schools and the need for staff who are as competent professionally as staff in other subjects. The churches exert pressure at national and regional levels for the improvements they seek. Representations have been made by individual churches, by the Scottish Joint Committee, by church leaders in a series of meetings with the Secretary of State for Scotland at his invitation in the late 1970s, by the Church of Scotland and the Roman Catholic Church conjointly. The concern has been both to be faithful to the strong Christian traditions of Scotland and to allow pupils an appreciation and understanding of what religion is about with Christianity as the main referent.

The Church of Scotland's Education Committee has offered comment on curriculum development in primary and secondary education, teacher training, the deployment of teachers and of the national resource, school accommodation, examinations and assessment, discipline, tertiary education, the handicapped, school and college councils, school chaplains. It attempts to provide progressive, yet realistic, critical and independent appraisal of current issues. Church of Scotland Assembly Reports contribute to the educational debate. 'The Aims of Scottish Education' (General Assembly Reports 1980 and 1982) notes the growth of pluralism and the advance of technology. It questions the validity of the Protestant work ethic in the face of unemployment and the popular assumption that the main objective of education is to obtain qualifications rather than a preparation for life. The report states that education is 'for the establishment of a society in which the maximum individual and general happiness exists, because all its members have been encouraged to develop their own talents, to derive satisfaction in exercising them, but at the same time to understand why checks and balances are necessary.'

'Moral Education in School' (General Assembly Report 1982) proposes ways in which moral education may feature in schools. It has a necessary and important place in RE but not as a subject on its own. It should be a mark of both a school's hidden curriculum* and its extra-curricular activities. Account is also given of various theological and philosophical stances and the implications for educational theory and practice.

Education within the church and courses

used. The minister is regarded as a teaching as well as a ruling elder. This has occasioned the high educational standards expected of the ministry, and also assigned to the minister the main educational functions within the church. Courses for members, other than those with specially designated functions, have been slow to develop and are extremely limited in scope.

Training for the ministry has a dominant position. The Church of Scotland has always depended on the universities. Recent years have seen considerable development of church-organized practical training alongside the divinity course. Other churches welcome graduates but provide training; the Free Church in its own college, the United Free Church, Free Presbyterian Church and Reformed Presbyterian Church under supervision and instruction of specially designated tutors. Since 1970 the Church of Scotland has developed a programme of residential in-service course for ministers and in 1981 it inaugurated a home-based, tutor-supervised training course for the non-stipendiary auxiliary ministry. Readers (the Presbyterian form of local preacher) are the only other group with Assembly-prescribed training procedures.

A variety of other training procedures and courses exists. For the Church of Scotland, St Colm's College in Edinburgh provides residential training for deaconesses, missionaries for home or overseas work and church members wishing to take particular course units. St Ninians, Crieff and Carberry Tower, Musselburgh, provide a variety of shorter courses for elders, youth leaders, and various congregational office bearers, and courses on evangelism, church growth, congregational programming, and stewardship.

Residential summer schools for Sunday School teachers and later for Bible class and youth leaders were run on an inter-church basis from 1919 until 1966. Teaching materials were also produced conjointly, first by the Scottish National Sabbath School Union then from 1926 to 1975 by the Scottish Sunday School Union for Christian Education. The Church of Scotland now publishes its own undated but regularly appearing Sunday School materials. In the years following the Second World War, youth houses were established in the cities as bases for youth work. In the same period, diploma courses in adult Christian Education were developed at university centres and local authorities included some adult courses in their programmes. Present policy is to promote locally based education and training through the deployment of part-time advisers in presbyteries and the promotion of group learning and short courses in congregations. Extension principles are being adopted increasingly using insights from adult psychology and adult education techniques, although the traditional minister centred approach persists strongly. Flexible teaching units, demanding a short and defined commitment, have proved effective and popular. Current course materials reflect these trends.

Preparation for confirmation. In the Presbyterian tradition admission to full communion has marked the entry to all the rights and responsibilities of church membership including admission to the sacrament of the Lord's Supper. Confirmation is not part of the Presbyterian tradition and does not feature in any of its standards. For those desiring admission 'it is the duty of the Kirk Session to satisfy itself as to their profession of faith in Christ, their knowledge of the cardinal doctrines of Christian belief, and the nature and significance of church ordinances; also to make proper inquiry to ascertain that, so far as known, their outward life is consistent with their profession. The instruction and preparation of first communicants is the special duty of the minister' (*Practice and Procedure in the Church of Scotland*).

In previous generations, little additional instruction was required when children had been subjected to rigorous instruction and examination in the Bible and the Catechism in school and to regular catechizing in church. Following the transfer of the schools to public bodies after the 1872 Education Act, the rapid development of Sunday Schools and Bible classes was notable. Examinations which were based on syllabuses that covered in considerable detail the contents of the Bible and the Shorter Catechism were introduced.

The period between the World Wars saw changes in educational methods. Sunday School and Bible-class materials had new and more attractive styles and were more closely suited to the child's stages of development. In the Church of Scotland there was a strong

concern to provide a continuous programme right through to admission to full communion. This was achieved in 1934 by the publication of George S. Stewart's *The Minister and his Communicants' Class* as a follow on to the previously published four-volume four-years Bible-class course. Although the General Assembly commended the use of this book, at no time has a course of preparation been prescribed. Of many books that have been published since, J. R. H. Paterson's *A Faith for the 1980s* has proved popular.

Issues are being raised by the consideration of admitting children to the Lord's Supper, the implications of which have yet to be fully developed. These impinge on the nature of membership of the church and the stages and form of initiation to membership.

See also **Scotland.**

Andrew M. Douglas, *Church and School in Scotland from the Reformation,* 1982 Chalmers Lectures; James Scotland, *The History of Scottish Education,* 2 vols., University of London Press 1969.

ALASDAIR MORTON

Primary School, RE in

This consists in laying foundations for an informed and sensitive awareness of the different perspectives on truth and meaning shared, first, by the people in the child's immediate environment and, later, by those in the wider world. This involves much more than learning about the externals of a religious tradition, though this may be an important element. Primary school RE is concerned with engaging children actively and imaginatively in a process of exploring and responding to the questions of life, death, purpose and value which human existence poses and which lie at the heart of all religion.

Religious doctrines incorporate the formulated responses of man's search for ultimacy. Young children need to be engaged in the search before they can attempt to look with understanding at the formulations. This is consistent both with the educational aim of providing opportunities for each child to grow and realize his full potential as a human being and with the dynamic nature of religion itself. The process successfully fostered in the primary school will continue throughout life.

Children are continuously exploring and

redefining the limits of their world, finding new patterns, discovering fresh insights: 'I sometimes lie in bed and think of life going on for ever – and you can't really think of it because living for ever – well, does for ever stop really .. . .? You can't take it in really' (Stephen aged 10). Their religious education will create opportunities to wrestle with and to enjoy the mystery of life, exploring the uniqueness of the individual, the qualities of relationship and the patterns and paradoxes implicit in the world around them.

Starting points will often arise through discussion in which the teacher is prepared to explore alongside the children, encouraging them to question and probe ever deeper, taking care not to destroy the mystery by imposing adult explanations inappropriately. Discussions and further exploration might be based on such questions as: What is precious/important? Why? What do I care about most? What makes me me and you you? What matters to other people? Why are people prepared to risk their own lives? What makes me sad/happy/frightened, etc.?

Finding words to describe the feelings involved in considerations of this kind highlights the nature and function of language. To convey meaning adequately, metaphor and symbol are crucial. An appreciation of something of the power of metaphor and symbol is therefore an essential element of primary RE. The development of the appropriate skills entails the fostering of the sensitivities needed to explore the fringes of human experience.

The primary school teacher who has clear aims for RE can assess the contribution of the whole curriculum. Effective RE cannot take place in isolation from other educational activities. Children will be encouraged to find and express meaning through the whole spectrum of the creative arts. Artistic expression and communication does not only provide creative ways of responding to questions of meaning – it is a personal involvement in those mysteries.

Story*, for example has particular power to create the special involvement needed to consider 'religious' questions. Elizabeth Cook puts the case strongly when she asserts that these days the story may be the only key to opening the door on the mysterious. Henry Treece's book *The Dream Time* unlocks a whole world of imagination as well as providing concrete starting points for discus-

sion about meaning, value and choice. 'Spear-sticks will save no man . . .', Twilight concludes at the end of the story. 'But his dream will, if he can only find the courage to hold it when the wolves glare into his eyes.'

The rich diet of stories shared in the primary school is a vital part of the process of entering the world of sacred literature. An ability to respond to the power of story to convey meaning at a variety of levels is an essential corollary to familiarity with, for example, the stories of the Bible. Without it, children will find it difficult to appreciate the complexities of the literature which deals with man's relationship with man and man's attempts to respond to experiences which challenge the limits of his humanity. Teachers will wish to consider very carefully the kind of picture of Jesus* given by the stories they choose to tell and to ask themselves 'Would anyone have bothered to crucify this Jesus?'

Children from minority ethnic and religious groups are usually keen to be assimilated with their peers and can be unwilling to share experiences which emphasize their differences. Creative drama work is important for exploring concepts such as friendship, trust, interdependence, reconciliation through, for example, problem solving exercises. Role play can help to develop the capacity to step into another person's shoes. An informed understanding and respect for different points of view can be gained by children from a variety of backgrounds exploring together themes such as 'Happy/sad times', or 'What is important to me?' The emphasis is then on shared experiences, and individuals, feeling the security of what is shared, may feel able to risk revealing what is not shared. Here again, story can provide the framework for exploration. Stories like Henry Lefevre's collection *One Man and His Dog* are excellent adaptations from the Hindu and Buddhist scriptures.

To summarize, RE in the primary school is concerned so to develop pupils' awareness of themselves as human beings, of themselves in relation to others and in relation to the world around them that they gradually become more open to and capable of responding sensitively to the thoughts, feelings and aspirations of others. The specifically religious will be explored in ways which take account of pupils' developing capacities and attitudes. Before children can step into a particular religious tradition and explore it through the ideas, feelings and activities of those belonging to that tradition, they will need to have explored their own experience of life at depths and developed the capacity to enter into the experience of others.

Liaison between primary and secondary schools is important and follow-through is obviously essential. However, RE in the primary school is not simply a preparation for RE in the secondary school or even for some later more sophisticated perception of religion, though that may come. Some of the most exciting and sensitive research in RE emphasizes the importance of the primary school years as a time when children may be especially capable of exploring and responding to the mysteries and joys of what it is to be human. It is therefore a time when RE will be giving opportunities for them to reach out tentatively and creatively to discover new patterns and levels of truth and meaning.

Elizabeth Cook, *The Ordinary and the Fabulous*, Cambridge University Press 1969; Michael Grimmitt, *What can I do in RE?* Mayhew McCrimmon, revd edn. 1980; Jean Holm, *Teaching Religion in School*, Oxford University Press 1975; Henry Lefevre, *One Man and His Dog*, Lutterworth Press 1973; Violet Madge, *Children in Search of Meaning*, SCM Press 1965; Edward Robinson, *The Original Vision*, (and other titles) published by the Religious Experience Research Unit, Manchester College, Oxford 1977; Peter Slater, *The Dynamics of Religion,* SCM Press 1979; Ninian Smart and Donald Horder (eds), *New Movements in Religious Education*, Temple Smith 1975; Henry Treece, *The Dream Time*, Heinemann 1974; Schools Council Project on RE in Primary School, *Discovering an Approach*, Macmillan 1977.

ELIZABETH RAMSEY

Professional Council for Religious Education

Formed on 1 January 1984. It brought together the Association for Religious Education* and the Professional Committee for Religious Education, one of the professional services of the Christian Education Movement*.

Associateship is open to all teachers of reli-gion in primary and secondary schools and higher education, the advisory service and inspectorate.

The Professional Council meets regularly and keeps under constant review the place of religion in education; the provision of resources and support services for teaching RE; the place of RE in the curriculum and in the national system of examinations; the role of the teacher of RE in the school and in the community; recruitment of teachers of RE and their training through initial and in-service courses; liaison with other bodies and individuals concerned; conditions of employment of teachers of RE. The Professional Council for Religious Education uses the facilities of the Christian Education Movement.

JOHN M. SUTCLIFFE

Professionalism: Its Meaning and Growth in RE

'Professionalism' is a term commonly used to honour certain attitudes and performances in a work activity which might or might not itself be afforded the status of a profession. So applied it nevertheless reflects the meanings and values enshrined in the terms 'profession' and 'professional'. Thus individual teachers may be said to exhibit professionalism by their attachment to ethical standards, by their reliance on a systematic body of knowledge, and by their readiness to submit practices and assumptions to informed scrutiny. In a broader context the term 'professionalism' may serve to regulate the attribution of honour to RE as a distinct activity. It will be asked how far RE is meeting acknowledged social needs, how far its practitioners exercise professional autonomy, and how far it depends on respected levels of training and expertise.

The practice of religious education roots its standards firmly in the professionalism of the educational community generally. Ethical standards require the avoidance of indoctrination. Pedagogic principles commend methods which invite exploration, imagination and evaluative judgment on the part of pupils rather than rote factual learning or moralizing didacticism. Over the past decade more teachers have become convinced that an understanding of any single religion cannot satisfactorily be based on the treatment of only one religion in the classroom – a conclusion which reflects the fact of global and historical interactions and encounters between the major world faiths. It recognizes also the multicultural character of the global village and of our own national community. To the extent that it gains ground this conviction will shift the body of knowledge on which RE depends. Insights afforded by the pedagogic disciplines and by theology will be joined by the range of insights afforded by the disciplines of Religious Studies and so modify our understanding of the teacher's professionalism.

A certain primacy was given to the importance of pupils' 'spiritual development'* by the Education Act of 1944. Public interest in RE has been ratified by pupils and parents in numerous surveys and opinion polls. The Act's machinery for achieving agreed syllabuses in (mainly) the county schools has been challenged on professional grounds (*What Future for the Agreed Syllabus?* and *What Future for the Agreed Syllabus Now?*); but essentially it continues to accommodate professional autonomy to a broad spectrum of public opinion, while professional opinion is shaped by a proliferation of journals and agencies. Provision of optional courses in RE within training establishments increased after 1944 and served the cause of professionalism well, though it has been seriously threatened by the impact of college closures in the late 1970s and by the impact of financial stringency on the provision of in-service courses. Professionalism may be threatened also by a failure on the part of some LEAs to appoint specialist advisers, by too common a reliance on non-specialist teachers in secondary schools, and by a lack of specialist team-leaders in primary schools.

DENNIS STARKINGS

Project Method in RE   *see* **Methods in RE: A Survey**

Proselytism

In the NT proselytes were Gentiles who had been converted to Judaism. Jesus is alleged to have criticized the Pharisees for their excessive (and improper?) zeal in proselytism (Matt. 23.15). In modern times Christian missionaries have been condemned for proselytism in the context of their schools and hospitals or when they are accused of making

converts by improper inducements. In particular, teachers in mission schools and the staff of mission hospitals are denounced for proselytizing when a pupil or patient of another faith enters their institution and emerges a Christian. It is alleged that missionaries have abused and taken advantage of their professional position of authority over a client who has come to them for a non-religious purpose.

By analogy 'proselytism' has recently entered the terminology of RE to mean the attempt by a teacher, probably but not always through RE, to convert pupils to his own faith. This is held to be professionally improper for him as the representative of a secular society, put in a position of authority in his school and trained as an expert with authoritative knowledge of his subject. He may attempt to convert children by indoctrination* or by proper teaching procedures but backed by his professional position or by the power of his personality.

Such proselytism, whether successful or not, whether intentional or not, is thought objectionable because it fails to respect the open-ended aim that alone makes RE truly defensible and educational in a plural society*. It may, however, perhaps be questioned whether every case in which a child becomes a Christian through RE is an example of proselytism in a pejorative sense: perfectly impartial and open teaching of any faith can influence a pupil to adopt it and it is unclear why this is not a possible outcome of a properly professional approach on the part of the educator.

Edwin Cox, *Changing Aims in Religious Education*, Routledge & Kegan Paul 1966; R. J. Hammer, 'Proselytism', *Concise Dictionary of the Christian World Mission*, ed. S. Neil, G. H. Anderson, and J. Goodwin, United Society for Christian Literature/Lutterworth Press 1970; F. H. Hilliard, *The Teacher and Religion*, James Clarke 1963.

DAVID ATTFIELD

Provision for RE

In maintained schools in England and Wales it is governed by the Education Act of 1944. Schools are bound to provide lessons of RE throughout the school career of every pupil, except where parents declare in writing to the head teacher that they do not wish their child to take part. In county and controlled church schools the scheme of work for the subject must accord with the LEA syllabus which is agreed by the churches, teachers' organizations and the LEA itself. In aided church schools RE is the responsibility of the foundation managers or governors. In practice this has meant that head teachers have had a considerable amount of discretion in the style and amount of RE taught in their schools. LEA agreed syllabuses have in general become less prescriptive over the years as it has been realized that the personal style of staff and local resources must be taken into account when a detailed scheme of work is drawn up within a school.

Many of the aided church schools too are now offered a diocesan syllabus to help with their work. In earlier days it was not uncommon for local clergy to take RE in their local church school. It is now more usual for the need for specialist training for RE teachers to be recognized, especially in secondary schools. However, in too high a proportion of secondary schools and in most primary schools, staff with specialist training in RE are not to be found. There are many teachers without specialist training who have gradually equipped themselves to make a useful contribution to RE by experience and occasional part-time study.

In 1944 there was a consensus that religious instruction, incorporating much of the underlying *raison d'etre* of our culture, was necessary for all pupils. Since then the motivation has changed radically. The consensus has melted away and society has become multicultural, not only by the arrival of numbers of new commonwealth citizens but also by the wide variation of believers and unbelievers among the indigenous population. Increasingly teachers of RE are required to contribute to broadly based studies in the humanities, and in social, health and moral education. Teachers therefore have access to an everwidening selection of resources both more particularly on the various religions now current in Britain and with regard to the broader issues. Thus RE can be seen as contributing an important element to the core of personal education which is seen as a vital component in the curriculum.

Provision for RE has been strengthened by the appointment of specialist LEA advisory staff and by the establishment of specialist departments for RE in the teacher training institutions, who offer not only initial training but a pool of expertise for in-service work. Perhaps the greatest problem is to match the increasing expectation of RE to the limited and perhaps diminishing financial provision.

RODNEY COCKS

Psychology of Religion

The early 1980s has witnessed an increasing interest in the psychology of religion both in Britain and America. This has been reflected in the number of books published and the conferences held in the UK at Lancaster, Oxford, Birmingham and in Europe. The British Psychological Society has published in its bulletins various articles and letters on religion including an exchange of views on the extent, scope and relevance of a psychology of religion. The renewed interest in the psychology of religion is encouraging to those committed to the subject.

The social psychology of religion. There has been a tendency by researchers in the psychology of religion to focus almost exclusively on the individual, his beliefs, practices and experiences. The limitations of such an approach has led to the demand for a social psychology of religion in which the importance of group factors are fully recognized. There are, however, those (Giles et al.,) who think a more dynamic, interactionalist consideration of religion is essential. In this context the interest lies not so much in the religion of individual or group but how religious factors affect the interaction between individuals and groups in different social environments. Such a widening of the scope of the psychology of religion is to be welcomed as it offers a more realistic evaluation of religious belief and behaviour in its appropriate cultural context.

The structure of religious attitudes. If progress, beyond the simple accumulation of data, is to be made then some kind of theoretical framework must be developed. One attempt to provide a suitable framework is that offered by Scobie. His system is essentially an extension of Eysenck's hierarchical structure of attitudes. The emphasis on Scobie's formulation is at the ideological level. Ideologies are described as ways of thinking or general approaches to problems or topics and conservatism, tender-mindedness, authoritarianism and dogmatism are cited as examples. The ideologies then express themselves in different socially significant areas to form attitudes. For example, the individual who is conservative at the ideological level will be conservative in his religious and political beliefs, and will accept traditional norms in sexual attitudes, child-rearing, patriotism, etc. While such a framework obviously needs thorough testing, it has the advantage of not being 'religion bound'. It can be applied to politics, work or any other social attitude area (Scobie).

*The scope of religious experience**. Implicit in our understanding of religion is the assumption that religious people have religious experiences or religious experiences make people religious. This may not necessarily be the case. It seems that problems of labelling may be underestimating the incidence of religious/paranormal experiences in the general population. Hay has found that many people have experiences which are similar in nature and yet they do not all label them as religious. They may not attach the same degree of importance to them or respond to them in the same way. So the researcher is faced not only with a number of different religious experiences but also different ways of describing or responding to these experiences.

Cross-cultural psychology of religion. The psychology of religion has often been criticized for its almost exclusive preoccupation with Christianity. While there is some evidence of an increase in the amount of research done on other world religions, a more fundamental problem still remains. It is not simply the content of religion that may be different but the whole psychology of man underpinning that religion or the whole culture may be quite distinct. This can have a profound effect on the research conducted and on the sort of questions the investigator asks (Giorgi). It is therefore important to recognize the value not only of a comparative but of a cross-cultural psychology of religion.

Psychology of religion and RE. Over the years religious educators have seemed to be inhibited by a recognition that their subject was derived from Christian instruction from the parish priest. The independence of religious education meant that many teachers were still reluctant about dealing with religious commitment in case they were accused of preaching and reverting back to religious instruction. This structure was reinforced by a number of books dealing with religious conversion (Sargant). It is only with the continuing focus of the psychology of religion on commitment and experience that teachers have been encouraged to recognize that to concentrate on only the content of religious beliefs is to miss the fundamental significance and importance of any religion. The religious educator's dilemma serves to highlight a significant problem for teachers of religion (or any other social-attitude area). Teaching religion and politics is very different from teaching mathematics or music. There are a number of unique problems that are related to the personality and attitudes* of the pupil and not to the content of the subject (Scobie). To be effective in religious education a teacher must be aware of the child's attitude to religion. This demands more effective methods of measurement (Francis). There have been a number of large scale studies (Peatling, Francis) using these methods. They have attempted to examine the development of religious thinking and attitude with age. Investigations of this kind are of considerable value because they help our understanding of the place and importance of religion in the development of the child's personality. There appears to be a significant fall in positive attitude to religion as the child grows older. Whether this change is a simple consequence of the ageing process or is caused by the school or home environment has yet to be clearly established.

Although progress is slow, there are hopeful signs of development in the psychology of religion having a positive value in RE.

Michael Argyle and Benjamin Beit-Hallahmi, *The Social Psychology of Religion*, Routledge & Kegan Paul 1975; Laurence B. Brown, *Psychology and Religion*, Penguin 1977; David Capps, Lewis Rambo and Paul Ransohoff, *Psychology of Religion: A Guide to Information Sources*, Gale Research Co., Detroit 1976; Hans J. Eysenck, *Psychology of Politics*, Routledge & Kegan Paul 1954; Heije Faber, *Psychology of Religion*, SCM Press 1975; Leslie J. Francis, 'The psychology of religion: revived not yet reborn', *Bulletin of the British Psychological Society* 31, 1978, pp. 44–5; The psychology of religion beyond revival', *Bulletin of British Psychological Society* 32, 1979, pp. 141–2; 'Developments in the psychology of religion', *Bulletin of British Psychological Society* 34, 1981, pp. 387–8; Howard Giles, Susan Jones, Martin Horton and John Lay, 'Towards a more dynamic social psychology of religion', *Bulletin of British Psychological Society* 28, 1975, pp. 47–50; Bruno Giorgi, 'A cross-cultural psychology of religion', *Bulletin of British Psychological Society* 35, 1982, pp. 63–4; H. Newton Malony, *Current Perspectives in the Psychology of Religion*, Eerdmans 1977; Eamonn F. O'Doherty, *Religion and Psychology*, Alba House, New York, 1978; John H. Peatling, 'Cognitive development in pupils in grades four through twelve', *Character Potential: A Record of Research*' Vo. 7 1974; William Sargant, *Battle for the Mind*, Heinemann 1957; Geoffrey E. W. Scobie, *Psychology of Religion*, Batsford 1975; 'The psychology of religion: a religious revival', *Bulletin of British Psychological Society* 30 1977, pp. 142–4; 'Teaching in social attitude areas', *Association of Educational Psychologists' Journal* 4 (8) 1978, pp. 13–20; Also volumes in *Bulletin of British Psychological Society* 1977–81.

G. E. W. SCOBIE

Public School Education
see **Independent Schools**

Quakers   *see* **Religious Society of Friends**

Quiet Rooms in Schools

Medieval colleges and schools were built on the monastic pattern with life centred on the chapel and hall. Early post-reformation grammar schools were usually associated with the parish church and often used a secularized chapel, as at Crediton. Many of the new public schools of the nineteenth century were religious foundations with the chapel at the centre of community life.

With the founding of county secondary schools after 1902 and the rebuilding of older foundations, problems arose. Some of the old charities, like the Harpur Trust in Bedford had been declared secular. Nonconformists would not allow Anglican worship places in state schools. A few chapels were built by private funds. Some War Memorial areas were treated with deference and silence observed. In the fifties and sixties there was a movement to introduce an undenominational worship area into state schools. Leicestershire was one Authority which did this. A room would be designated with some hint of an altar table and provision for sitting or kneeling in prayer. Such rooms were intended for private devotion and were available for small groups but were not intended for corporate worship. Its rationale is similar to the chapel at Heathrow Airport but as it had no regular function and was expensive space, it has not been maintained or widely adopted.

DAVID KEEP

Qumran Scrolls

A series of scrolls, written mostly in Hebrew, which were discovered in the Dead Sea desert between 1946 and 1957, though occasional discoveries are still made. They prove to have belonged to a Jewish sectarian community whose headquarters was Khirbet Qumran on the west shore of the Dead Sea. They consist of the following classes of literature: 1. Copies of the text of the OT, mostly in Hebrew. These have proved immensely valuable, since they carry our knowledge of the OT text in Hebrew a thousand years back towards the autographs. 2. Copies of already known Jewish literature belonging to the inter-testamental period. 3. Original works, probably all by members of the community. Of these the most remarkable are the *Manual of Discipline* outlining the constitution and intention of the sect; the *Thanksgiving Hymns*, hymns of high devotional value addressed by the leader of the sect to God; the *Damascus Fragment* (or *Zadokite Document*, already partly known) giving obscurely the history of the sect. There are also commentaries on scripture, an angelic liturgy, a symbolical vision of a harlot, and many others. The sect seems to have come into existence about 140 BC as a protest against the assumption of the high-priesthood by the Hasmonean Simon. It was destroyed by Roman troops in AD 68.

Apart from the light which these discoveries have thrown on the text of the OT, the main significance of the Qumran Community lies in the light it throws on the religious background of the Judaism of the last century BC and the first AD. The aim of the sect was to obey the law more perfectly by the methods taught by its original founder, 'the teacher of righteousness' (better 'the official teacher'). The members of the sect looked forward to the end-time as an imminent event, when the last great battle with evil would take place and God would finally intervene in favour of the righteous. Its links with Christianity consist in the fact that, like Christianity, it began as a nonconformist Jewish sect with a strong eschatological flavour. Its interpretation of scripture has much in common with that of the NT writers: both sets of believers interpreted the OT primarily in terms of the history of their own community, the Qumran members in terms of the vicissitudes of their sect, Christians in terms of the life, death and resurrection of Jesus Christ. In the *Thanksgiving Hymns* we find a doctrine of justification by faith which, *mutatis mutandis*, is very reminiscent of that set out by Paul in Galatians and Romans. Of all the books in the NT, probably the Fourth Gospel has most links with the Qumran sect's outlook: emphasis on light and darkness; a strong element of predestinarianism; the Qumran attitude towards the angelic 'Prince of Light' recalls the Johannine concept of the Paraclete. But Qumran is still completely centred on the Law and has no room for Gentiles, nor has the all-important breaking-in of the kingdom yet taken place in Qumran belief, as it has in Christian.

The well-informed teacher of RE will esteem the scrolls chiefly as invaluable aids towards introducing us to the thought-world in which Christianity was born. They are also very useful as they illustrate the history of the tradition of the texts of the OT.

M. Burrows, *More Light on the Dead Sea Scrolls*, Sacker 1958; K. Schubert, *The Dead Sea Community*, Harper 1959; K. Stendaal (ed.), *The Scrolls and the New Testament*, SCM Press 1958; E. F. Sutcliff, *The Monks of Qumran*, Burns & Oates 1960; R. de Vaux, *Archaeology and the Dead Sea Scrolls*, British Academy 1973; G. Vermes, *The Dead Sea Scrolls in English*, Penguin Books 1968; G. Vermes, *The Dead Sea Scrolls: Qumran in Perspective*, SCM Press 1982; G. Vermes, *Discovery in the Judean Desert*, Desclee, New York 1956.

ANTHONY HANSON

Qur'ān, al– (the Koran)

The *Qur'ān* is the sacred Book of Islam*. It is not only a book to be read, but a book to be read aloud, as the Arabic word indicates. During its recital, in the original Arabic, the Word of God (which Muslims hold the *Qur'ān* to be) becomes a living voice.

Muslims believe that God (*Allāh*) caused the *Qur'ān* to be revealed to the Prophet Muhammad in a series of Revelations from AD 610 (the year of his call to be the Messenger of God) to his death in AD 632 (AH 10). This period is divided into two halves by Muhammad's move from Mecca to Medina in AD 621. The move (*hijra*) brought changes in the style and content of the Revelations. In the Meccan period the Revelations are characterized by fervent prophetic exhortations. In the Medinan period the Revelations are more measured, and concerned with the formation of an Islamic community.

The *Qur'ān* is divided into 114 chapters, each of which is called a *sūrah*. This Arabic word is not best translated 'chapter', because the original expresses the indispensability and structural unity of each *sūrah*, which is not conveyed by the English word. The *sūrah*s do not appear in the order in which they were originally revealed. The first to be revealed is numbered 96 in the *Qur'ān*. It is an oversimplification to say that the *sūrah*s appear in an order which places them in a sequence of diminishing length. The present (and final) canonical text was completed a few years after the death of Muhammad, during the reign of the third Caliph, *ʿUthmān*.

The *Qur'ān* is a guide to belief and action. It is the basis of Islamic Law (*sharīʿa*). Its central doctrine is that of *tawḥīd*, the oneness of God. All created things are dependent upon God. True religion consists of submission to the Will of God. This is the significance of the Arabic word *islām*. The *Qur'ān* prescribes and regulates the relationship which should properly exist between God and his creatures, between members of the Islamic community (*umma*), and between Muslims and non-Muslims. It describes the rewards that attend submission to God in this world and the next, as well as the judgment which awaits unbelievers. It enjoins Muslims to pray, to give alms, to fast during *Ramaḍān*, and to make the pilgrimage to Mecca. It calls for belief in God, in his angels, in holy books (of which the *Qur'ān* is the last), in the prophets (of whom Muhammad is the Seal), and in Predestination.

The *Qur'ān* has long been the subject of detailed exegesis in the Islamic science of *tafsīr*, but because of their belief in its divine origin, and in its unchangeable form, Muslims hold that it is inappropriate to subject its contents to Western (non-Islamic) historical/critical scrutiny. The stylistic felicity of the original is recognized by Arabic speakers who insist that although vernacular versions may be necessary, they can never compare with the original, which must always be used in public worship.

A. Y. Ali, *The Holy Qur'ān*, Arabic text, English translation and commentary, Lahore 1976; A. J. Arberry, *The Koran Interpreted*, Oxford University Press 1964; M. M. Pickthall, *The Meaning of the Glorious Koran*, New English Library 1960.

EDWARD HULMES

Rastafarianism

A black, Afro-Zionist religious movement which originated in Jamaica during the 1930s. Moulded out of the island's traditions of slave rebellion and revival religion, the movement thrived initially among working-class blacks in the poorer areas of Kingston. Its original leaders took their inspiration from Marcus Garvey (1887–1940), a charismatic political figure with a vision of black redemption through return to Africa.

In November 1930, Hailie Selassie (Ras Tafari) was crowned Emperor of Ethiopia. Subsequently, a number of Jamaican preachers, noting the event, read in it the fulfilment of Garvey's prophecy 'look to Africa, when a black king shall be crowned, for the day of deliverance is near'. Their reading of the scriptures convinced them that Ras Tafari, Hailie Selassie of Ethiopia, was an incarnation of the living God, embodying the divinity as Moses and Jesus had before him.

Selected biblical passages such as these words of the Bride in the Song of Songs – 'I am black but lovely, daughters of Jerusalem' – suggest to Rastafarians that not only the Queen of Sheba, but Solomon, Moses, Jesus and the people of Israel as a whole were black.

The Rasta brethren, exiled in Jamaica, are a remnant of the black tribes of Israel; and Ethiopia (which stands for all of Africa) is the true Zion – both the original homeland and final destination of Rastafarians and of the black race as a whole.

Rastafarian belief, based on a selective but careful reading of the Bible, refined by lengthy discussion ('reasoning'), and communicated through the medium of reggae music, has much in common with the Judaeo-Christian tradition. In some places, the movement has been closely associated with the Ethiopian Orthodox Church, one of the oldest Christian churches, which broke away from the Eastern Orthodox and Western churches at the Council of Chalcedon in AD 451.

Rastafarian morality is rooted in the OT commandments and the two 'great' commandments of the NT. In additon, Rastafarians pursue a 'natural' way of life, which is embodied in uncut hair ('dreadlocks'), a preference for vegetarian food, and the use of cannabis ('ganja'), seen both as medicinal and as an aid to 'reasoning'. Rastafarian belief includes a critique of Western capitalist civilization ('Babylon'). Based on slavery and colonialism, Western civilization is seen as a reincarnation of the Roman Empire. 'Babylon' is destined to be destroyed ('burned') by God ('Jah') in a final conflagration which will mark the day of repatriation when black people return to Africa and all other peoples are restored to their original homelands.

Since the 1950s the Rastafarian movement has grown rapidly in Britain, especially among young working-class blacks, providing them with a sense of identity and destiny that makes sense of the rejection and alientation they experience in a predominantly white society. One cannot now fully understand the experience of British-born black youth without understanding Rastafarians. Moreover, the Rastafarian movement is in itself a rich field for study, combining as it does theological, political, sociological and psychological elements. The movement also has an educational immediacy not only because of the contemporary significance of race relations and the international popularity of reggae, but also because it holds up a mirror to Western civilization, in which white Christians are able to assess themselves and their society as they come to understand Rastafari.

RICHARD ZIPFEL

Rationality

Undeterred by accusations of wanton indoctrination and irrationality, advocates of RE maintain both that there are good reasons for retaining and advancing their subject, and that the subject can be taught in a reasoned and reasonable way.

The Piaget-influenced work of R. Goldman and others aims to foster rationality in RE by taking due note of the way in which an individual's degree of conceptual competence is governed by the psycho-developmental stage he has reached. Some, to whom this approach is unduly intellectualistic, argue for greater emphasis upon the affective, and point out that excessive concentration upon thought leads to a narrow definition of 'relevance' as 'that which is intellectually assimilable'. Others seek to show that those in the Piaget-Goldman line underestimate the rational capabilities of young children.

However they stand on this issue, few RE specialists – even those most influenced by the more extreme varieties of existentialism – would defend their subject on the ground that it is *ir*rational. Well aware of the charge of coercive indoctrination* they recognize the need for reasoned discussion of beliefs, attitudes and practices. Some have been heard to say that rational debate in RE should be 'open ended' – thereby raising the unhappy possibility that everything of importance will drop out! This is by no means a facetious remark, for the question, 'How far can the RE teacher be 'neutral'?' presses hard.

Those who advocate neutrality* are sensitive to the need of children to come by their own convictions in their own time and in their own way. Others, who are equally opposed to coercion, have replied on psychological grounds that a teacher cannot and ought not to try to opt out of his cherished convictions – indeed, that the more successful he is in the attempt the more likely it is that the pupils will draw the inference that something as 'neutral' as religion hardly merits serious attention; on philosophical grounds that there can be no going behind one's presuppositions to an Olympian vantage point from which all religious – not to mention humanism and

communism – may be viewed objectively; and on educational grounds that if truth is to be prized, and if religion places its adherents in contact with truth, then it would be perverse to encourage pupils to distance themselves from it.

The upshot is that reasoning about religion is never presuppositionless, but is always within the context of a world view. In RE the implications of this should frankly be faced. Clarity in the spirit of charity is the goal. Certainly no self-respecting educationalist, and no society which values relative stability, will encourage the initiation of pupils into patterns of thought and ways of life for which no good reasons can be given. Equally, no Christian teacher will so emphasize things cerebral as to overlook the place of (a reasonable) *faith*, or the need of divine revelation. Nor should it be forgotten that one of the candidates for redemption is man's reason.

G. H. Clark, *A Christian Philosophy of Education*, Eerdmans 1946; W. D. Hudson, 'Is religious education possible?', *New Essays in the Philosophy of Education*, ed. Glenn Langford and D. J. O'Connor, Routledge & Kegan Paul 1973; M. V. C. Jeffreys, *Truth is Not Neutral*, Religious Education Press 1969.

ALAN P. F. SELL

Religion

A satisfactory definition of religion has proved to be singularly elusive. Some definitions have excluded Buddhism*, others have included Marxism* and Nationalism. In the late nineteenth and early twentieth century there were two main approaches: through an explanation of the origin of religion, and through the isolation of its essence. In recent decades the attempt to define religion has been largely abandoned and replaced by a description of what characterizes it.

RE has been influenced by the work of scholars in the field of religion, though the debt is often unrecognized, and sometimes theories which have long been discarded in the world of scholarship live on in books written for use in schools. An obvious example is the evolutionary approach which characterized much of nineteenth-century anthropology. It was assumed that simple societies belonged to the early stages of man's development and that the more complex societies of 'advanced' civilizations were a later and therefore 'better' stage of development. Widely-used textbooks for RE start with 'primitive' religions, with the frequent use of words like 'fear' and 'superstition', and with the juxtaposition of such things as animism and totemism – which would have astonished scholars like E. B. Tylor and Andrew Lang for whom these represented competing theories of the origin of religion. Similarly, in such religious education textbooks, as for many nineteenth-century scholars, Christianity is seen as the crown and climax of the evolutionary process.

The attempt to define religion in terms of its essence has tended to follow a line which stretches back to Friedrich Schleiermacher at the beginning of the nineteenth century. Schleiermacher reacted against the eighteenth-century emphasis on doctrines as constituting religious knowledge; he said that religion was a dimension of human life, and its essence was a consciousness of absolute dependence. A century later *The Idea of the Holy*, by Rudolf Otto, had a more direct influence on RE. For Otto it was a sense of the numinous, experienced as both *mysterium tremendum* and *mysterium fascinans*, that lay at the heart of religion. The implication for RE of this understanding of religion was worked out by John Wilson in *Education in Religion and the Emotions*. Wilson defined religion as an 'emotion-based activity', directed to the object of worship, and said that the central task of RE was therefore education in the emotions.

Another influential writer whose starting point was the human situation was the existentialist theologian Paul Tillich. He defined religion as 'ultimate concern', that which we take with ultimate seriousness – a definition broad enough to embrace everyone.

The suggestion that the essence of religion was located not in some external object but in human faculties shared by all people was welcomed by many RE teachers who found themselves trying to convince reluctant adolescents of the relevance of religion. 'The religious dimension of life' became a widely used expression.

The word 'dimension' has, however, also been used in quite a different sense. In *Secular Education and the Logic of Religion* Ninian Smart described religion as a 'complex object', having six dimensions: doctrinal, mythological, ethical, ritual, experiential and social. Smart stands in that tradition of the study of religion which describes religions as they are rather than trying to explain their origin or isolate their essence, and which takes seriously what religious people do as well as what they believe.

Smart's analysis of religion reached a wider audience in the religious education world through Working Paper 36, *Religious Education in Secondary Schools*, produced by the Schools Council Project on Religious Education for the 11–16 age group. The six dimensions were used as a framework for developing a syllabus by Michael Grimmitt in *What Can I Do in RE?*, in which he suggested that there were appropriate stages in a pupil's schooling for the introduction of the various dimensions. A rather different approach was taken in Jean Holm's *Teaching Religion in School*, in which the framework was the way in which people actually experience and practise their religion: aspects such as worship, rites and customs, festivals, sacred writings, codes of ethics, institutions and communities and their traditions.

In the second half of the seventies many new agreed syllabuses expressed the aim of RE as helping pupils 'to understand the nature of religion' or 'to understand religious beliefs and practices'. However, although in theory the description of religion as multi-dimensional was accepted, in practice some of the dimensions or aspects of religion tended to be treated much more seriously than others. There are a number of reasons for this.

Western Protestantism has emphasized beliefs and values, and has regarded rituals, customs, symbols, etc. as 'externals'. The emphasis on beliefs has been reinforced by the philosophers' attack on Christian theology, and many secondary teachers have felt that their pupils' attitude to religion was dependent on their belief about the existence of God* and the problem of evil. The emphasis on values has been reinforced both by the popular belief that to be moral is to be religious and by the fact that for many decades RE was considered to be the main means of children's moral education. And the strong strand of individualism in Western Protestantism has encouraged a concentration on pupils' own 'search for meaning', to the relative neglect of corporate activites and the significance of traditions.

Two factors have helped to redress the balance. The study of religions such as Judaism* and Hinduism*, in which beliefs are less important, has focussed attention on other dimensions, and the broadening of the study of Christianity to include Roman Catholicism and the Orthodox Church, and their significant use of ritual and symbolism, has provided a stimulus to seeing religion in a new perspective.

M. Grimmitt, *What Can I Do in RE?*, Mayhew McCrimmon 1973; Jean Holm, *Teaching Religion in School*, Oxford University Press 1975; R. Otto, *The Idea of the Holy*, Oxford University Press 1923; Schools Council, *Religious Education in Secondary Schools,* Evans/Methuen Educational 1971; N. Smart, *Secular Education and the Logic of Religion,* Faber & Faber 1968; J. Wilson, *Education in Religion and the Emotions,* Heinemann 1971.

JEAN HOLM

Religious Communities
see Communities in Education, Religious

Religious Education Council of England and Wales

Founded in 1973, it provides at national level a forum for discussion and a vehicle for joint action whilst respecting the right of any constituent member body to act individually or to record a dissenting view. It also exists to explore and clarify the aims of RE in schools and colleges, to promote the professional aspects of RE teaching, and to explore the relationship between RE and related areas of the curriculum.

Currently forty-two national organizations form the membership, which for purposes of election is divided into two categories: 1. professional – bodies wholly or substantially concerned with RE in county schools and higher education; 2. confessional – bodies whose main focus is the educational work of their own organizations (the educational organizations of the churches and other religions being members within this category). The Council, financed by member bodies' subscriptions, meets twice a year, appoints a chairman, secretaries and executive committee, and organizes occasional conferences.

In addition to making representations to the Secretary of State and to Parliament, it has published: *What Future for the Agreed Syllabus?* (1976); *What Future for the Agreed Syllabus – Now?* (1977); *The Development of RE: A Report on the recruitment and training of teachers* (1978); *RE and the Training of Primary Teachers: Report of a Survey* (1979); *Views on : Statements from 23 National Bodies* (1981); *Religious Education Directory for England and Wales* (1982).

HOWARD MARRATT

RE, Nature of

Conceptions of the nature of RE may be divided into those which emphasize religious education as a religious activity and those which emphasize it as an educational activity. The former is the traditional view, and it is probably safe to say that in all past societies and in most present day societies religious education has been understood as that process of teaching and learning by means of which religions have sought for their transmission and self-perpetuation. This would always be specific to a particular religion, and thus we may speak of a Jewish religious education, a Christian religious education and so on. In this accepted, traditional sense, religious education would proceed through a convergent teaching procedure, in which the personal religious commitment of the teacher, the content of his teaching, and his intentions for his pupils would converge. Traditionally, it was the nature of religious education to speak from faith to faith.

This conception of RE as essentially a religious activity has led to the exclusion of religion from the curriculum in the state or public educational systems of many countries (e.g. India*, France,* USA*) or to administrative arrangements whereby its distinctively religious character was protected (e.g. Ireland,* Western Germany,* Greece, Australia*). This often takes the form of public maintenance of denominational schools, in which case it is not merely a matter of RE being conceived of as a religious activity, but the whole of education being so understood. Another popular arrangement which expresses this view of the nature of religious education is that whereby religious education is imparted by accredited representatives of the religion or religions in question to their adherents, this taking place in the state schools but not being carried out by the normal staff, nor perhaps in official school hours. It is the rise of the modern systems of national education in the last century or two which has created the tension between the religious and the educational aspects of RE and with it a wide range of administrative, philosophical and theological problems. The distinction was often seen as implying a struggle for church or state control of education, as may be seen in nineteenth-century England in the writings of such men as Frederick Denison Maurice and John Stuart Mill.

If RE is understood as an educational activity rather than as a religious activity, its nature (i.e. its essential characteristics and purpose) will be different. Although the two views may be traced in British religious education for more than a century, the view that the nature of the subject should be determined by its educational characteristics did not achieve real prominence or become generally persuasive to RE teachers in state-related schools until the late 1960s, under the influence of writers such as Edwin Cox, J. W. D. Smith and Ninian Smart. The Birmingham Agreed Syllabus (1975) was the first new official syllabus in which the religious nature of RE was explicitly replaced by a self-conscious and an articulated educational understanding. The change in the nature of RE was often expressed by claiming that the subject must be justified on educational grounds rather than on theological grounds and, although this distinction is an over-simplification, there is an important sense in which contemporary British RE in county (state) schools should be thought of as a new subject in the curriculum, having its roots in the philosophy and sociology of education and in the theories of curriculum development. It is not a natural development of the old RE, which was a domestic activity of the church, but represents a radical break with past traditions, which can be seen as the secularization, the professionalization, or the liberation of the subject, depending upon one's point of view.

During the 1970s and early 1980s the theory and practice of RE as a branch of education have become so well established that it has become increasingly necessary to use different expressions to describe that religious education which is a branch of religious activity.

These expressions include catechesis, Christian nurture, religious upbringing and so on. The expressions 'Islamic education', 'Christian education' and so on are also used to distinguish the religious nature of religious education from its secular, educational sense, but such expressions are rather misleading, because it is the very nature of the educational process which is in question.

The situation is further complicated by the fact that when RE is conceived of as an educational activity, and its study as a branch of educational studies, there will still be room for a wide range of views about the nature of the subject. Some of these will flow from conceptions of the nature of education itself, and so we will have one view of the nature of RE which will emphasize its role in the transmission of culture, another which will see it as primarily an experiential, child-centred activity, another which will see itself mainly in cognitive* terms as imparting knowledge of religion as a form of human understanding, another which will emphasize the affective and imaginative role of RE in changing young people's attitudes*, another which will emphasize RE as imparting certain skills* and techniques, and so on. In so far as the content-matter of RE is religion, the nature of the subject will similarly be affected by different understandings of the nature of religion itself. One view will emphasize a close connection between religion and morality, another will see religion as being primarily a matter of having certain emotions or feelings, a third view of religion will emphasize it as comprising the ultimate concerns of mankind, a fourth view is that religion is to be identified by studying the explicit phenomena of the world religions, while a final example of these views of religion, all of which are influential in British RE today, regards it as divine revelation which can only be truly appreciated from within. These differences in understanding religion itself will issue in different approaches to curriculum and teaching in the classroom. Thus we see that redefining the nature of RE as being determined principally by the requirements of education, while it solves many problems and prepares the way for the progress of the subject in the public curriculum, opens up many new enquiries.

The transformation of the subject has also created a number of vocational and theological crises. The vocational problems arise when teachers whose main motivation was religious, and who thought of this in religious nurture* or evangelistic terms, found professional opinion turning against them and found themselves unable or unwilling to rethink a vocation in the new, educational terms. From the theological point of view, it can be argued that the secular, educational nature of RE does not place it beyond a theological interpretation, in which such education would be seen (for example) as contributing to the building up of personhood and so having a place in the divine education of mankind. But whereas the theological basis for RE when conceived of as being explicitly religious was an explicit and direct theology, any theological basis for RE conceived of as an educational subject will be implicit and indirect, and will take its place alongside the other disciplines (philosophy, sociology, psychology etc.) which constitute a possible rationale for the subject.

Is there something about the nature of each school subject such that the teaching of that subject should exhibit characteristics of the subject? Should the teaching of geography itself be geographical in some sense? Should the teaching of history itself be historical and the teaching of music musical? Should the teaching of religion itself be religious? Or do all these teaching areas have something in common which enables us to speak of a logic of education? There is a sense in which the nature of RE will continue to be religious in so far as it will deal with religion as a subject matter, and there is a related sense in which it will continue to be religious in that it will seek to offer pupils at least some of the values and challenges which religions offer mankind. But it will continue to be vital for RE in the state school that these senses in which the nature of the subject may still be conceived of as being religious should be qualified and limited by the nature of education. This seems to suggest that distinctions between RE on the one hand and other teaching processes involving religion such as religious nurture, religious indoctrination*, and religious evangelism* will continue to be important because they will indicate different conceptions of the nature of RE.

J. E. Greer, 'The Nature of Religious Education', *British Journal of Religious Education*, 5, 1, Autumn 1982; J. M. Hull (ed.), *New Directions in Religious Education,* Falmer Press 1982; D. C. Meakin, 'The Justification of Religious Education', *British Journal of Religious Education* 2, Winter 1979; R. M. Rummery, *Catechesis and Religious Education in a Pluralist Society,* T. Shand 1975.

JOHN M. HULL

RE Room

The need for specialist accommodation in secondary schools – self-evident for physical education, science and craft subjects – has only relatively recently become a requirement for English, history and RE. The latter were taught traditionally in general classrooms furnished with desks and chairs but often lacking visual stimulus or anyone delegated to ensure their attractive appearance. With 'talk and chalk' the predominant methods, little more was needed than a blackboard, books and seating.

Spaces designated for RE teaching have been developed as methods have been extended, as more varied classroom materials have become available and as pupils have been grouped in classes containing wider ranges of academic ability. A further factor has been the growth of subject matter from which lesson content is selected. In larger schools, RE rooms may be located together and in the same area as those for English, humanities and social education.

The content and arrangement of RE rooms are intended to provide the greatest possible variety of stimuli, including audio-visual media, and to create a humane and relaxed environment for learning. Much classroom activity in RE, in common with English, is concerned with human relationships, the work produced by pupils often being intended to communicate with an audience other than the teacher. The main features of provision may be listed as follows, although priorities will vary from school to school: 1. Permanent display facilities covering much of the wall space; for much of the time the rear wall remains hidden from pupils so front and side walls merit priority. 2. The front wall retains a chalk board and screen for overhead, film or slide projection. 3. Windows fitted with black-out blinds or curtains. 4. Storage facilities for easy access to resources: open book shelving within the room; filing cabinet for worksheets, catalogues, posters and slides; a shelved area, preferably 'walk-in' and lockable, for stock and equipment. This last area services adjoining RE rooms in many schools. 5. Stocks of books and materials to support the RE programme need to be constantly brought up-to-date as well as being readily accessible within the room unless this is adjacent to a library or resources area. The same is true of audio-visual equipment (e.g. slide projector and radio/cassette recorder) although more expensive items will probably be shared within the school (e.g. video TV, film projector, reprographic machinery). 6. Power points at both the front and back of the room and a TV aerial point. 7. A fitted work surface along one side of a room, and a water supply, will facilitate painting, art and three-dimensional work. 8. Soft floor covering (except around a sink) reduces the noise level and contributes to a more humane environment.

The arrangement of furniture is related to the area available. The standard classroom of some fifty square metres assumed one teacher working with thirty or so pupils with desks or tables in rows to allow circulation space. Such a pattern is frequently retained for formal teaching and examination courses. When pupils are operating in small groups, tables can be arranged in blocks, and for class discussions the U-shaped arrangement of furniture encourages more natural communication. Some recent school buildings provide flexibility for groups both larger and smaller than thirty: double units of about one hundred square metres are fitted with folding screens. These allow several classes to share a film or illustrated talk and also, on occasion, a screened area for discussion with up to fifteen participants.

A much broader conception lies behind 'Focus rooms in secondary schools' as described in the Hampshire LEA Handbook, *Approaches to Religious Education,* 1970, secondary section A, unit 5. While designated as the centre of the RE department, the focus room is intended 'for reflection and discovery' based upon any aspect of the school's life and work. Specifically not a chapel, it attempts 'to create a setting where the majority can feel at ease and be stimulated to deeper thought about the fundamental questions concerning man's existence, purpose and destiny, in a secular world'. In one such room the central feature was an oval craftsman-made table; other furniture was contemporary, the floor carpeted and windows curtained. Whilst a baby grand piano offered opportunities for recitals, wall panels and shelving provided space for representative art and craft.

D. PAUL KING

Religious Experience

If religion is to be understood as man's response to his experience of the transcendent, religious experience cannot be defined in terms of religion but is to be seen rather as an awareness, however momentary or imperfect, of an order of reality both beyond and yet capable of permeating the rest of life. Such experience will always have a strong element of subjectivity. First-hand descriptions of it, however, regularly insist on the reality of that which is experienced, compared with which it is often the normal experience of everyday life that is said to appear unreal.

The study of religious experience in modern times was pioneered by William James, who however gave popular currency to the concept of a religious experience as something striking, unmistakable and often sensational. More recent research, e.g. that of Hardy and Hay, has emphasized the universality of the capacity for such experience which, though often weakened or inhibited by social or psychological factors, appears to be a basic part of the human make-up. Thus the image of religious experience as a meteorite coming from outer space and hitting the individual with a scientifically measurable frequency and impact has given way to the idea of man as a being naturally equipped with a spiritual radar system with which he can regularly become aware of, and so participate in, what Schleiermacher called 'a life in the infinite nature of the Whole'. Such an experience, once regarded as the preserve of specially gifted individuals ('the mystics'), is now recognized as being more or less universally available to those who will submit to the appropriate spiritual disciplines. The fast-spreading study (or cult) of altered states of consciousness has also greatly widened, as well as complicated, the idea of religious experience, and the same is true of the writings of Maslow, whose concept of the 'peak experience', while in itself too promiscuous, has nevertheless enriched the notion of the religious by relating to it many forms of life-enhancing experience which previously were not generally thought of as relevant to or even compatible with the more traditional categories of spirituality.

A common tendency in recent times has been to treat religious experience as an individual phenomenon. As a reaction to claims sometimes made in the past by the churches (e.g. *Nulla salus extra ecclesiam* – no salvation outside the church), the concept of religion as that which a man does with his solitariness (Whitehead) has been liberating. Nevertheless there is today a growing recognition, both within the established churches and in less orthodox movements, that it is only within a community and within a living tradition that religious experience can have its full flowering, and that the cultivation of such experience as an end in itself can only achieve a limited degree of spiritual growth.

While there are obvious dangers in any attempt to promote religious experience in the classroom, a religious education that becomes unduly concerned with an objective and (so-called) phenomenological* study of religion may well fail to convey any immediate sense of what religion itself is all about, or to link up with the first-hand experience of children or young people, such a link being essential if the subject is to remain alive. Experimental work both in this country and overseas has shown that there can be a place for, e.g., meditation* and silence within the RE framework, and that opportunities for such experience are valued where there is no sense of an invasion of privacy.

Recent research (e.g. Lomas, Robinson) suggests that the developmental theories of psychologists such as Piaget, Goldman and Kohlberg, concentrating as they do on cognitive growth, fail to do justice to a spiritual sensitivity which may appear in children from a very early age. The inability of young children to communicate the insights of such experience has at times led educational theorists and some teachers to conclude that religious understanding of any kind cannot occur before the age at which appropriate powers of expression begin to emerge. However if childhood in its fullest sense is to be understood as not just that period of years between infancy and adolescence but as a potentially enduring capacity for a particular kind of comprehension of the world and man's place

in it, then it may well be that religious experience is something that children are better at than some adults, however superior the latter may be in co-ordinating the verbal concepts necessary for a systematic understanding of religious truths (see O'Leary and Sallnow). Further, there is a certain unreality in any contrast drawn between the inarticulateness of children and the supposedly superior expressive abilities of adults, since it is commonly said by those who have had religious experience that the essence of it is beyond description. That they then often go on to describe it at great length points to an important distinction: between the language of the exchange of information and that of imaginative communication. Such descriptions can in fact convey a most powerful and convincing impression of the reality of spiritual experience because the language they use is such as to appeal to our own, possibly very different, experience. This kind of communication, called 'indirect' by Kierkegaard, is of the greatest importance in RE. If teachers are to be aware of the religious experience of their pupils it is thus necessary for them to be sensitive to a wide range of forms of imaginative expression, verbal and non-verbal, and at the same time to be aware of the great variety of media by which this indirect communication can be achieved. The absolutely central place of poetry* and the arts* in religion has of course been recognized in all cultures, except possibly our own in recent years. Attempts have recently been made, e.g. by Herbert and Lealman and Robinson, to provide material which will enable both teachers and pupils to explore through the arts new and creative interpretations of personal experience in relation to traditional forms of religion.

Alister Hardy, *The Spiritual Nature of Man,* Oxford University Press 1980; David Hay, *Exploring Inner Space,* Penguin 1982; Christopher Herbert, *A Place to Dream,* CIO 1976; William James, *The Varieties of Religious Experience,* Longman 1903; Brenda Lealman and Edward Robinson, *The Image of Life,* CEM 1980; *Knowing and Unknowing,* CEM 1981; Peter Lomas, *True and False Experience,* Allen Lane 1973; Abraham Maslow, *The Farther Reaches of Human Nature,* Penguin 1973; Karl Nipkow, 'Religious Education in Germany: Developments and

Problems', *British Journal of Religious Education*, 1, 4, Summer 1979: Donald O'Leary and Teresa Sallnow, *Love and Meaning in Religious Education,* Oxford University Press 1982; Edward Robinson, *The Original Vision* and *Living the Questions,* Studies in Religious Experience, Manchester College, Oxford 1977, 1978; F. Schleiermacher, *On Religion: Speeches to its Cultured Despisers,* Harper 1958.

EDWARD ROBINSON

Religious Experience Research Unit

Founded in 1969 at Manchester College, Oxford, by Sir Alister Hardy, the eminent Darwinian, in the conviction that the biological study of man was incomplete without an understanding of the spiritual dimension of his nature. A public appeal for accounts of personal experience brought in some 4,000. The Unit also initiated sociological surveys at Nottingham University under David Hay and Ann Morisy, the results of which suggest that religious experience in some form is characteristic of the majority of the population of Britain. Among the publications of the Unit have been two on the religious experience of childhood. In recent years its work has concentrated on the relationship between religious experience and the visual arts, a field in which it has co-operated with the Christian Education Movement*.

Alister Hardy, *The Spiritual Nature of Man,* Oxford University Press 1980; David Hay, *Exploring Inner Space,* Penguin 1982; Brenda Lealman and Edward Robinson; *The Image of Life,* CEM 1980; *Knowing and Unknowing,* CEM 1981; Edward Robinson, *The Original Vision* and *Living the Questions,* Studies in Religious Experience, Manchester College, Oxford, 1977, 1978.

EDWARD ROBINSON

Religious Society of Friends (Quakers)

You will say, Christ saith this and the Apostles say this: but what canst thou say? Art thou a child of Light and hast thou walked in the Light, and what thou speakest, is it inwardly from God?

These words of George Fox (1624–91), the founder of the Religious Society of Friends well express the central Quaker affirmation of the indwelling of God in every person – the light of Christ enlightening everyone, the inner light or that of God in everyone. But God is not only at work within the soul; he is also at work without, in the world. Quakerism expresses something of the seventeenth-century interest and confidence in the natural order: observation and experiment reveal the handiwork of God in and through the world he has made. Fox and William Penn planned a 'garden schoolhouse' and Thomas Lawson who was associated with it made the point, 'His works within and His works without, even the least of plants, preaches forth the power and wisdom of the Creator, and eyed in the spaces of eternity, humbles man.'

Mankind as creature and the world as creation both reveal God the Creator who is available any and everywhere. Unlike most of his contemporaries, Fox believed that God was still speaking to people and that Christ, who had come to teach his people himself, was both alive and present. The first Friends rediscovered the contemporary inspiration of the Holy Spirit. Quakerism, flowering in the middle of the seventeenth-century, is the culmination of the Reformation, of the movement away from the authority of the church, beyond the authority of the Bible to the authority of the individual guided by the Holy Spirit discerned in the gathered group.

From these insights, a number of Quaker 'testimonies' flow. The indwelling light of Christ in all leads to 1. an emphasis on the basic dignity and equality of all men and women, both inside and outside the church, as children of God irrespective of race or religion; 2. an attempt always to try to reach and answer that of God in everyone, which leads to certain ethical insights, one of which is the refusal to take human life – the Quaker peace testimony, and 3. a view of the priesthood of all believers that makes a special priesthood or separated ministry unnecessary. The indwelling of God in nature leads to an understanding of the world as sacramental, which means that the sacraments themselves are seen to be non-essential. This awareness of God revealed both in man and nature has meant in practice an emphasis on: 1. Personal relationships with God rather than on defining him, on experience rather than dogma. Friends have no credal statements. 2. Silence.

Whilst God is available at any time and place, Friends have particularly found that he reveals himself to those who listen and wait quietly upon him. Silence has therefore been the medium of Quaker worship in which anyone may speak, read or pray as led by the Spirit. 3. Quiet waiting for the presence and guidance of the Spirit in reaching decisions about business affairs and outward concerns, all Friends being eligible to participate. 4. A response of loving obedience to the ever present God who comes to meet man over the whole of life's relationships.

Broadly speaking, Friends, with their stress on firsthand immediate experience of God, have tended to undervalue other sources of inspiration, e.g. the importance of history, particularly biblical history, and the value of human learning in the religious sphere. In their emphasis on the inward, they have tended to neglect the outward and an early criticism levelled against them was that they so stressed Christ living in us as to forgot his dying for us. Further, the final authority of the individual apart from the gathered group has sometimes been taken to extremes. Yet Friends have come to see the importance of the intellect in religious growth. Also the searching query of Fox 'but what canst thou say?' needs to be balanced by Paul's question 'What have you that you have not received?' and the authority of the individual needs to be tested by the leadings of the gathered group.

Membership. For many years the Society of Friends had only an informal membership: a Friend was one who kept the Quaker testimonies – a costly thing in the early days of persecution. But it became increasingly necessary in matters, e.g. of care for the poor or the education of children, to have a clearer Statement of Membership, which gradually emerged during the eighteenth century.

Adults who wished to join, having attended a Meeting for Worship for some time and shown themselves to be in sympathy with Friends' views, applied for membership to an appropriate local group. The ensuing procedure has remained virtually unchanged for well over 200 years and is stated below.

From the early days, children whose parents were considered to be members also belonged to the Society and enjoyed membership from birth. The Society of Friends was a group of worshipping families; and, as in Judaism*, the family was not regarded as a collection of individuals but as corporate personality or entity in which children were as much members as parents, according to their measure of the light of Christ. Children were part of the covenant of grace stretching back to Abraham, whereby with their parents they were admitted into fellowship with God and became his people and he their God.

This system has had its critics all down the years on a variety of grounds, e.g. it denies free choice, under-emphasizes the importance of personal decision and conviction and public witness, and leads to the formation of a society which is as much a family social club as a dedicated religious community. Several different forms have been put foward such as junior, temporary and associate membership but the present position is that there are two ways in which membership may be acquired: 1. by personal application; 2. by admission on the application of parents or guardians. For the former any person aged sixteen years or over may apply: application from persons under sixteen should be accompanied by parents' consent. Applications should be sent to the local Monthly Meeting, (primary meeting for local suggestions) which appoints two Friends to visit the applicant and report back and a decision is then made. Moral and spiritual achievement in an applicant is not asked for; sincerity of purpose is. The chief conditions to be looked for in applicants are that they are humble learners in the school of Christ; that their faces are set towards the light, that the Quaker way of worship helps them forward in their spiritual pilgrimage and that their desire for membership arises from an understanding of Quaker faith and practice as a whole. It should be made clear that the Society is essentially Christian in its inspiration even though it asks for no specific affirmation of faith and understands Christianity primarily in terms of discipleship.

Parents or guardians intending to bring up their child while under sixteen in accordance with Quaker principles may apply for his or her admission into membership. Monthly Meetings may appoint Friends to visit the parents before reaching a decision. No initiation ceremonies are held but new members are often welcomed into membership at a Meeting for Worship. If after reaching the age of sixteen such a member wishes to indicate his personal acceptance of that membership, the Monthly Meeting shall take the course it feels appropriate to acknowledge it.

Religious education and worship. For Quakers religious education is a matter of silence, words and deeds and their inter-relationship. It is concerned with man's response to God who listens, speaks and acts and is therefore closely bound up with worship. Friends come together in quiet waiting on God in which the mind is stilled and the outward silence becomes an inward stillness in the presence of the God who listens. But this God who listens is also a God who speaks, and the worshipping group also listens, open and ready to receive his message. In fact the whole period of worship may pass in silence although more often those present may feel called to read, speak or pray aloud. The God who listens and speaks is also a God who acts, so that worship comes from the world and flows back into it through the lives of those who participate in worship. So worship is central to the Quaker view of reli-gious education.

Indoctrination and openness. A main way of maintaining the continuity of a religious body is by the passing on of its faith, order and practice from parents to children. Historically this has been done in the Society of Friends by means of a 'guarded' education, which provided a maximum of Quaker influence and a minimum of worldly influence, which meant the isolation of a 'peculiar' people from the 'world's people'. This process of conditioning amounted almost to indoctrination and any who refused to conform were liable to be disowned from the Society. Down the years there has been a growing awareness that this is inconsistent with the Quaker understanding of the Inward Light and today there is a clear recognition that no one can determine the religion of another. It is one thing to share faith with children or others; it is quite a different thing to try to impose it. The emphasis is on growth from within, on personal search and discovery to find meaning and purpose in life for oneself.

Truth – experience, words and deeds. It is easy to give an over-intellectual apprehension of God, to teach children religious ideas, 'notions' as Fox called them, before they are ready to receive them. Initially more of a 'wordless witness' is required where religion

is acted as well as spoken, where people do things together as part of the order and natural rhythms of life – a devotional pause at meals, quiet reflection after a story, a talking with God before bed, a growing into the mystery and wonder of existence and of the God behind it. And all this is mediated within an environment of security and belonging which gives an experience of love-offering the experience of being loved, not in a possessive selfish way, but in a way which liberates a child, releases him, frees him to become the best he has it in him to be. Experiences are mediated by words which help with under-standing but which should not hurry the young into traditional formulas of the faith, words which express doubt and rebellion as well as positive affirmation, which balance certainties and uncertainties.

In the end, truth cannot be fully enshrined in words and being open to new truth is very important. From the first, Friends recognized spiritual truth direct from Christ and natural truth revealed in the world: they have only more recently come to see the importance of artistic, aesthetic truth and the place of the imagination in finding and relating different aspects of truth into a unity. Equally important is 'doing the truth' to be found in the experienced relationships over the whole of life.

Growth. Another term used by Friends for the Light is the Seed; as a result the idea of growth has always been important – tending, feeding, watering, weeding and pruning to provide a healthy environment and produce a healthy plant. Of course, educational growth has all kinds of possibilities as against largely pre-determined growth in nature, and choice of direction is central. Growth is from within, is often gradual, unpredictable and myster-ious. Friends have not, therefore, been concerned with applying pressure for spiritual decisions which cannot be forced at only one particular time. In fact turning points or affirmations of faith are sometimes barely recognizable at any one moment and only become conscious on looking back in time.

From what has been said so far, it will be clear that the *home* and *Meeting* are essential elements in religious education. If it is hard to find a sense of God in the home, it will not be easy to find God in Meeting or in life. Parents must provide both a framework of security, yet nurture for independence and in so far as they reveal a love which cannot be earned and show a forgiveness always extended, they point to the character of God.

The Quaker way of life and an interpretation of it is reinforced by contact with like-minded families and with the Meeting for Worship in which children take an increasing part as they grow up.

The smallness of the number of children in a small Society brings particular problems as far as nurture is concerned. It is often difficult to form a group of children of the same age-range within a Meeting. Isolation is often a problem although Meetings within a defined area are sometimes able to join together in making provision for their children. The Society of Friends has a closely knit structure which makes it possible to arrange local, regional and national gatherings of camps, summer schools, visits to historic Quaker places, etc., for children and young Friends.

The fact that Friends have no full time ministers and have often undervalued the importance of a teaching ministry, means that nurture in the Quaker faith for adults tends in general to be rather sketchy and unsystematic and depends on local initiative and enthusiasm. A lay Society particularly needs a centre which provides for community living, worship, study and fellowship; and Woodbrooke, the first of the Selly Oak Colleges in Birmingham, founded in 1903, is designed to meet this need. It provides a wide range of courses in Quaker, biblical and theological studies as well as in social, political and international affairs. In order to enable Friends to go there, courses vary in length to suit different needs; some last only a few days or weeks, others for a term or a year.

Besides home and Meeting, the third most important factor in religious education, historically at any rate, is the Quaker school.

Quaker education. There is a widespread personal involvement of Friends in education as teachers, administrators, advisers, inspectors or as lay members of committees or councils, boards of governors or managers.

Some of the educational insights which stem from basic quaker affirmations are: 1. *The Inner Light*: the emphasis on the Light is both personal and corporate – the worth and uniqueness of the individual along with the way individuals relate to each other. (a) *The importance of the individual:* this will mean such things as the organization of an institution's life to serve the individual's needs and to develop the great variety of individual talents: the quality of personal relationships, an unconditional, positive regard for pupils and students, a warm acceptance and open understanding without shame of their situation; no corporal punishment in schools – a non-judgmental approach which helps the pupil to judge himself or herself leading to change and development from within; each individual consciously or unconsciously may be in direct relationship with God. (b) *The way in which individuals relate to each other:* an equality of status but difference of function of all who make up the educational community; an ordered community reflecting a peaceable spirit through its network of reciprocal amicable relationships; an emphasis on cooperation rather than competition – judging one's progress against oneself rather than others; some form of service within the community and its neighbourhood, widening to include national and international concerns. 2. *A Sacramental Universe.* There are no special religious places or persons; God may be known in all places at all times through any or all of life's relationships. Classes, lectures, seminars, private study, games, hobbies – all the formal and informal activities, the planned and unplanned events that make up the total life of an institution are important: they will be of different significance to different people, but play their part in the building up of wholeness and fullness of life. 3. *Silence.* Silence has always found a place in specifically Quaker education: in a pluralist society where students are often uncertain about the formulation of their faith it may be specially useful. Friends emphasize the importance of corporate silent waiting upon God but along with this go the capacity to be quiet and receptive, to listen and to be sensitive and open to the promptings of the Spirit. 4. *Government.* The Quaker method of reaching decisions corporately in worshipful dependence upon God has never really been attempted in the running of Quaker Schools and is often not practicable. Yet it is increasingly recognized that people have the right to be consulted about matters that affect them and that there should be wide consultation between governors, heads, teachers, administrators, parents and students.

Quaker Schools. From the earliest days Friends have run Schools and at present various groups of Friends are responsible for nine secondary boarding schools in England, the oldest of which dates back to 1779. Six are co-educational, one is for girls and two for boys (one admitting girls into the sixth form). Today only a minority of Quaker children attend Quaker Schools, most attending those in the maintained system. The schools have a Joint Bursaries Scheme which enables the great majority of Quaker parents to send their children to them if they so wish. Yet they may be regarded as exclusive although they accept a fair proportion of children, for example, in boarding need or whose parents are working abroad.

Since Quakerism is expressed in life rather than formulas, the schools stress the importance of an educative community. The most important thing about a school is the kind of community it is, the kind of corporate life it leads through the Spirit which sustains it and 'bloweth where it listeth'. The qualities which the school community tries to foster are those of an open, seeking, undogmatic friendship which yet stems from an underlying moral, spiritual and peaceable foundation of quiet waiting, the readiness to listen to and be receptive to the promptings of the Spirit, and of a homely community where mutual tolerance, confidence and respect are important, and where a sense of individual responsibility and a sense of responsibility for others reaches out into the wider world. This kind of approach is reflected as far as possible in and through the school curriculum. Study for examinations, the acquisition of skills and the appreciation of the arts also take their rightful place in the wider growth towards truth, maturity and wholeness which all must find for themselves as they face the challenge of becoming humble learners in the school of Christ.

Much of what has been said cannot be regarded as peculiar to Friends, but when it is all taken together as a whole, it perhaps does make for a particular ethos in education.

The Maintained System. Most Quaker children are in fact educated within the maintained system and therefore receive such religious education as is given under the 1944 Education Act. In general Quaker parents welcome this as an opportunity for a broad religious education as distinct from a Quaker and Christian one more appropriate to home and Meeting. They support RE as a separate subject in its own right, believing that religion has always been an important phenomenon and can provide a coherent interpetation of the whole of human life and experience. A well balanced RE syllabus adequately taught may help pupils to recognize and respond to religious phenomena, to explore the dimension of mystery undergirding all experience – birth, life, death, etc. and to discover meaning and purpose in life. It will draw on a pupil's own situation and background and use a multi-cultural and world-faiths approach including non-theistic life stances; and Christianity will hold a special place, though not a 'confessional', one, in view of its importance in British culture.

Christian Faith and Practice in the Experience of the Society of Friends, London Yearly Meeting 1960; *Church Government,* London Yearly Meering 1968, reprinted with amendments 1980; A. Neave Brayshaw, *The Quakers, Their Story and Message,* [3]1938, reprinted Quaker Home Service 1970; W. A. Campbell-Stewart, *Quakers and Education as Seen in their Schools in England,* Epworth 1953; Edgar B. Castle, *Approach to Quakerism,* 1961, reprinted Quaker Home Service 1973.

PHILIP WRAGGE

Research in RE

Research in religious education has generally been sporadic, haphazard and unsystematic. It tends to be highly derivative and much of it is poor in quality. There is very little of any significance which is empirically sound, which employs large stratified samples and a rigorous research design, which uses sophisticated analyses or objective assessment procedures. Since the mid-1970s the picture has begun to improve slowly, though there remain many one-off studies which suffer from serious conceptual inadequacies and which fail to control important variables.

There are, however a few major pieces of research of distinction which have influenced deeply the thought and practice of teachers of RE. They can be grouped under four headings.

1. *Child development.* One of the most important pieces of work was that of R. J. Goldman. He utilized Piaget's findings concerning the development of concepts to a study of the development of the religious thinking in children and young people. He conducted clinical interviews with a small, non-random sample of pupils using three Bible stories. Despite its methodological and psychometric weaknesses, his research demonstrated that religious thinking developed in ways similar to all other thinking. It went through a series of stages of increasing complexity. He concluded that abstract religious concepts should not be included as part of religious education until children had attained a mental age of thirteen years. The effect of this was to render suspect much of the traditional biblical work of the first half-dozen years of schooling and to encourage a wider use of the thematic approach to RE.

J. H. Peatling's research was closely related to Goldman's work in that he too adopted a Piagetian framework and used the same biblical stories. Yet methodologically his investigation was stronger and more sophisticated. He overcame Goldman's sampling problems by using an objective questionnaire, thus securing the powers of inference offered by proper randomization. His results confirmed that religious thinking passes through stages. The boundaries of these stages are significant for they show that between a departure from the concrete operational stage at a mental age of ten years to an entry into abstract thinking at a mental age of sixteen years there is a five year intermediate stage unaccounted for by previous researchers. Thus the real growth in abstract thinking occurs in the middle and late teens and continues into adulthood.

Changes in the attitudes*, involvement and behaviour of children and young people in relation to religion were the focus for L. J. Francis' research. This well-planned, lucid and empirically secure study showed that between eight years and sixteen years children were progressively less favourably disposed to religion. The decline is consistent through the age levels to fifteen, but becomes markedly accelerated during the fifteenth and sixteenth years. It is not associated with any specific developmental or environmental changes. These results suggest an urgent need

for schools and churches to re-examine the RE curriculum they offer.

2. *Religious experience.* A research unit set up in 1969 by A. Hardy in Oxford initiated studies into religious experience using scientific methods. In the initial stages personal experiences were collected as a result of newspaper appeals though later work used a questionnaire technique on a random sampling basis (Hay and Morisy). The analysis of this material yielded a classificatory scheme of the elements found in religious experiences (Hardy). It included sensory, cognitive* and affective* elements as well as those which fostered the experiences. The results of the research are provisional though it is clear that a significant proportion of people have religious feelings and that these fundamentally influence their lives. Hardy believes that this work shows the reality of the spiritual nature of man.

During this research E. Robinson was impressed by the fact that many people referred to the importance of childhood experience for their later development. A detailed and rigorous questionnaire confirmed the authority and significance of this experience and questioned some of the conclusions of developmental psychologists. Further work has traced the growth of religious experience during life.

The educational implications of this research have not been fully established. It does, however, point to the importance of the expressive arts in the understanding of religious ideas; it suggests that the capacity for formal operational thought is not a requirement for the apprehension of the holy; and that the meaning of the religious and moral is not easily restricted by time, place or age.

3. *Moral growth and faith development.* The research of L. Kohlberg on moral development* and moral education* has sparked interest among religious educationalists. This is because, despite maintaining the autonomy of morality, he suggests that religious development and moral development parallel each other, that the attainment of a particular moral stage both precedes and makes possible the attainment of the equivalent religious stage and that to live according to moral principles ultimately requires what in some sense, amounts to faith. The faith orientation which acceptance of his universal moral principles

requires, he calls stage 7, and this stands at the apex of moral development.

The research has achieved a high level of technical sophistication and there is a consensus that Kohlberg is right to affirm that there is a cognitive-developmental dimension to thought about social relationships. However it remains arguable that he has offered a sufficiently theoretical and empirical account of specifically moral development.

J. W. Fowler's research into faith stages offers a structure with considerable heuristic power. It is derived from lengthy semi-clinical, open-ended interviews interpreted according to models provided by Erikson, Selman, Piaget and Kohlberg. Fowler understands faith as a way of construing and interpreting experiences. And he charts its growth through six stages. These include parallel levels of moral and cognitive development as well as levels of competence in symbolic understanding, social awareness and role-taking. The stages are invariant and sequential; they are dependent on age and maturation. Fowler's structure offers religious educators practical ways to identify the faith stage of their pupils and makes possible sensitive intervention to prompt further growth. There is much within this research which is still provisional. Before it is finally established it will require more secure cross-sectional and cross-cultural work as well as a longitudinal analysis.

4. *The curriculum.* Two pieces of research undertaken by H. Loukes were influential in changing classroom teaching in the 1960s. The first was an enquiry carried out for the Institute of Christian Education which analysed religious beliefs, attitudes and practice of adolescent pupils. The second examined RE in schools where it was being well taught. Both pieces showed that for the most part traditional biblical religious education was viewed by pupils as boring, irrelevant and immature. Evidence pointed to the need of young people to use their own experience of living as a basis for RE. Loukes argued these conclusions in a persuasive manner urging teachers to achieve a meaning and depth in their teaching by establishing it on a basis which touched the problems of life. This work was beset by difficulties of method and definition which could not be disguised by attractive writing. It has generally been felt that the implicit* approach argued for is in fact a covertly Christian one.

The Schools Council Projects on RE under the direction of Ninian Smart and based at Lancaster University, have offered teachers a means of teaching this subject which is at once both open and educational. The Secondary Project guided by D. Horder fostered an approach to RE which was largely thematic in character, which isolated objectives carefully and which widened its content to include major world religions. It showed what an initiation into the understanding of religion required and further charged each teacher to be an agent in the curriculum development of his own subject. It envisaged pupils leaving school with a minimum body of knowledge and the ability to demonstrate perception, sensitivity and skill in handling religious questions. The materials for the new curriculum were developed in association with a large number of teachers drawn from a wide variety of schools. Part of the success of the project is due to the high degree of teacher involvement in the initial discussions as well as the testing stages. The Primary Project, led by J. Frost, suggested that RE for younger children should take seriously the existence of the plurality of traditions in the world and should be open in approach and exploratory in spirit (*Discovering an Approach*). Its aim was to develop those capacities and attitudes which facilitate an understanding of religious ideas. Although it recommended the learning of some explicit and factual religious material, it was particularly concerned to help teachers to encourage their children to explore and reflect on their experiences of life in a particular environment. Like the Secondary Project this research produced its materials in very close co-operation with teachers in a wide sample of schools, LEA advisers and HMIS. Its emphasis on the educational nature of RE gave it a wide acceptance among non-specialist teachers of younger children.

Conclusion. Despite the authority of this research it does ignore significant areas. One of the most important of these concerns the sense of mystery or awe at the heart of religious education, though there are foundations for its investigation in the available research. At a theological level they appear in K. Rahner's attempt to formulate an anthropocentric theology. At a psychological level they occur in J. E. Loder's understanding of the paradigm of creativity. At a philosophical level they are evident in R. Holley's arguments for a spiritual dimension to personhood. If these studies can be utilized in a sympathetic way they will offer an approach which affirms the value of the expressive and imaginative arts in RE.

J. W. Fowler, *Stages of Faith: The Psychology of Human Development and the Quest for Meaning,* Harper 1981; R. J. Goldman, *Religious Thinking from Childhood to Adolescence,* Routledge & Kegan Paul 1964; D. Hay and A. Morisy, 'Reports of ecstatic paranormal or religious experience in Great Britain and the United States – a comparison of trends', *Journal for the Scientific Study of Religion* 17, 1978; A. Hardy, *The Spiritual Nature of Man,* Oxford University Press 1980; R. Holley, *Religious Education and Religious Understanding,* Routledge & Kegan Paul 1978; L. Kohlberg, 'Education, moral development and faith', *Journal of Moral Education* 4, 1, 1974; J. E. Loder, *Religious Pathology and the Christian Faith,* Westminster Press 1966; *The Transforming Moment: Understanding Convictional Experiences,* Harper 1981; H. Loukes, *New Ground in Christian Education,* SCM Press 1965; *Teenage Religion,* SCM Press 1961; J. H. Peatling, *Annual Review of Research, Religious Education,* Character Research Press 1980; K. Rahner, *Theological Investigations,* vols 1–20, Darton, Longman & Todd 1961ff.; E. A. Robinson, *Living the Questions,* RERU 1978; *The Original Vision,* RERU 1977; Schools Council, *Discovering an Approach,* Macmillan 1977; *Journeys into Religion,* Teacher's Handbook A, B, Hart-Davies 1979; *Religious Education in Secondary Schools,* Evans/Methuen 1971: M. P. Strommen (ed.), *Research on Religious Development,* Hawthorn Books 1979; D. H. Webster, 'American research in Religious Education: a review of selected doctoral theses', *Learning for Living,* 14, 5, 1975; *Playing Hide and Seek with God: Some Themes in Contemporary Research in Religious Education,* CEM 1981.

DEREK WEBSTER

Reserved Teachers

In a voluntary controlled school containing more than three teachers, the LEA has a duty under Section 27 of the Education Act 1944 to appoint 'reserved' teachers, that is teachers selected as competent to give religious instruction according to the trust deed of the school, or in accordance with whatever practice was observed in the school before it became controlled. Such religious instruction is provided for those children whose parents specifically request it.

The number of reserved teachers appointed is in proportion to the total number of staff (e.g. one reserved teacher in a total staff of three to five, four in a staff of sixteen to thirty). There is no obligation upon the LEA to appoint a reserved teacher in schools with less than three teachers. The governors of such schools remain obliged, however, to provide religious instruction according to the trust deed where it is requested. The head teacher, a non-reserved teacher, or a visiting clergyman, may, subject to their willingness, provide such instruction.

A head teacher may not be a reserved teacher. The governors of a secondary school must, and in a primary school may, be consulted by the LEA before any reserved teacher is appointed and they may request the dismissal of a teacher from his reserved status on the grounds of failure to provide the required religious instruction.

Although no statistics are available for England and Wales as a whole, current practice suggests that there are relatively few withdrawal classes taken by reserved teachers.

See also **Voluntary Schools**.

Sir William P. Alexander and F. Barraclough, *County and Voluntary Schools,* Councils & Education Press 1967; G. Taylor and J. B. Saunders, *The Law of Education,* Butterworths.

ROBERT WADDINGTON

Resource Centres

Religious Education Centres have been described as a growth industry in a declining educational market. In general terms such centres seek as their primary aim to assist the serving teacher so that ultimately the quality of RE is enhanced at the classroom level. Formerly educationalists, once qualified, might have assumed adequate professional competence to last them for a lifetime; today even veteran teachers acknowledge the need to engage in post-experience training and this need is especially acute with a subject like RE which involves a considerable number of non-specialists at both primary and secondary level. Teachers' Centres, whether for RE or general subjects, are not an end in themselves. Used creatively they can be seen as points of departure – a springboard from which teachers can come to terms both personally and professionally with the contingent demands of their subject, and this in turn can engender a new sense of confidence leading to purposeful curriculum innovation and development.

The passing of more than forty years since the 1944 Education Act becomes all too apparent when one applies to RE today the relevant clauses of the Act to the very altered circumstances of our contemporary world. The pattern of in-service programmes provided by centres reflects the preoccupying needs of the teacher-consumer. These might be summarized as follows: 1. The educational validity of RE in a pluralist society. 2. The relationship between religious and moral education. 3. The distinctive role of RE in county schools and 'education in faith' or nurture* in credal communities. Major considerations also focus throughout on curriculum development*, the importance of multi-cultural education involving world faiths, the vital role of religious studies in public examination not to mention the vexed questions of assembly* in county schools. These and many other issues are a source of concern and not infrequently of controversy. Fortunately a great number of agencies exist which are helping teachers to cope nationwide.

The first of the modern RE centres was established as a national audio-visual bureau in 1963. Since then a wide variety of local and regional counterparts have been set up by Roman Catholic and Anglican dioceses and Free Church bodies. An ecumenical dimension is also to be discerned in the co-operative endeavours of centres funded by local councils of churches with the material assistance in some intances of LEAS. Almost 400 general purpose teachers' centres come under the aegis of the latter and in not a few cases a substantial input for RE is maintained through the dynamic influence of the local inspectorate and resident wardens sympathetic to the subject. In 1973 the DES initiated two major in-service centres specially for RE and these are situated in Birmingham and outer London respectively. An added impetus was subsequently provided by the National Society for RE* with notable foundations in London and York. Many colleges, institutes and schools have emerged as centres of excellence bringing the current number of such agencies to an impressive figure. Thus it can be seen that in a relatively short space of time a network of support establishments has ensued catering for a wide variety of constituents and their respective needs. Smaller centres are ministering to the interests best determined by local groups of teachers, whereas national and regional centres with a more comprehensive brief are also developing distinctive contributions or strengths to complement the work of their satellite counterparts.

The work of each centre will vary considerably according to personnel, expertise, premises, resources and locations. All will be involved in courses, whether residential or part-time, evening, day release or weekend. Such courses may take the form of lectures, seminars, workshops or tutorials. Considerable emphasis is now placed on courses which involve group activity where the probationer can work alongside a more experienced colleague in the production of class projects and curricular schemes. Opportunity will also be provided so that teachers operating together can originate essential resource material geared to their own pupils' requirements. Considerable attention will also be given to commercially produced resources housed in a centre thus ensuring that such collections – often available on loan – are fully utilized and not regarded as museum pieces.

Mention must also be made of the significant contribution of other national bodies like the Christian Education Movement*, the Association for Religious Education*, the SHAP Working Party*, all of whom have greatly assisted teachers in terms of in-service support and resource provision. One of the prime factors in mobilizing and motivating RE teachers has been the widespread attention given to agreed syllabuses. Such enterprises have encouraged teachers, advisers, inspectors as well as SACRE* and LEAS to explore in depth the rationale and implementation of a religious education programme accommodated to present and future requirements. It is here that RE centres have been able to offer a signal service functioning either on the home base or through outreach activities at national or regional conferences. Distance learning facilities have also been recruited through the dissemination of media evaluation, resource lists, teaching manuals, newsletters and information broadsheets.

DESMOND F. BRENNAN

Revelation

1. *Meaning of revelation.* As used with regard to religious experience revelation always implies divine grace and human understanding and the term is used to refer to both the means whereby God* makes himself known to man and to the form of that knowledge. It refers to those processes of disclosure whereby what was previously hidden is made apparent and intelligible but the known content is never entirely understood and remains mysterious. The revealed knowledge acquired by man is categorized as salvific rather than merely informative and is necessarily other than that knowledge acquired by means of research and reflection.

A distinction is often drawn between 'general' and 'special' revelation. The former is the revelatory value of all human experience: the latter is that present in particular events, objects and persons.

Three theological interpretations of revelation may be identified: (a) the handing down of propositional truths about God resulting in an objective body of knowledge expressed in scriptural and doctrinal statements which can be added to as time passes; (b) the self-manifestation of absolutely mysterious God as Subject and Person (not as the philosophical Absolute) by means of a person or persons whereby new life is offered to man and not mere intensification of present life; (c) a subjective, interactive relationship of an individual person with God within the community of God's people whereby that person's life is enriched, fulfilled and saved. This interpretation emphasizes 'the God of the depths' who is graciously present but often hidden in human experience.

2. *Treatment of revelation in RE.* The teaching of a revealed religion as part of a series of religiously educational activities will necessarily reflect the theological interpretation of revelation espoused by the teacher.

In terms of the above identified theological interpretations of revelation the following emphases in approaches to the children's learning are familiar: (a) the study of scriptures and doctrine so that children may learn dogmatic truths about God and themselves; (b) the encouragement of empathy with a person or persons through whom God may become known to man; (c) the study of life-themes and the provocation of religious understanding of the depth and richness of everyday life. As it is possible to adopt each of the three academic theological interpretations of revelation at different times, and as many religious educators insist on the professional importance of theological neutrality* in their work, so syllabuses of RE may be devised whereby each of the three approaches is adopted at different stages.

With older children revelation itself becomes a topic of study raising questions about the means of distinguishing spurious from genuine revelation, the particularity or universality of a revelation, the status of sacred writings, the relationship between means and content in revelation, the logical priority of religious belief, and the cultural status of revelation as a means of acquiring knowledge in the modern world. The epistemological, cosmic and evaluative questions raised by the topic of revelation make it a fruitful vehicle for inter-disciplinary work and integrated work with children at the tertiary stage of schooling.

J. Baillie, *The Idea of Revelation in Recent Throught,* Oxford University Press 1956; Emil Brunner, *Revelation and Reason,* Westminster Press 1946; H. D. McDonald, *Theories of Revelation,* Allen & Unwin 1963; G. Moran, *Theology of Revelation,* Burns & Oates 1966; G. Moran, *Vision and Tactics,* Burns & Oates 1968; H. R. Niebuhr, *The Meaning of Revelation,* Macmillan 1941; D. J. O'Leary and T. Sallnow, *Love and Meaning in Religious Education,* Oxford University Press 1982; R. Pearce, *Ideas,* H. E. Walter 1974.

RAYMOND HOLLEY

Ritual

Within the faith community, ritual acts as a focal point, giving shape and coherence to history and belief, dramatically concretizing that to which the believer is committed, giving him that confidence which stems from belonging to a group. Word, action and symbolism open the door of belief for the young. Participation is the point at which the committed believer is strengthened to bear witness to his faith. The value of ritual in RE is that its concrete expression illustrates information and concepts taught orally or through literature. These are given life as one meets the believer as well as the belief. In sound and movement ritual proclaims possible answers to the universal questions of life and death, meaning and purpose, which religious education explores in the classroom. It captures that which *can* be expressed yet reaches out, in its imaginative dimension, to that which is unseen and unknown.

Within the various traditions the Mass, Eucharist, or Lord's Supper points to God's control *of* and purpose *in* history, to man's sinfulness, to God's power and *wish* to forgive. It celebrates a belief in the reality of the relationship between God and man. It gives value to the individual, and an opportunity to make an ordered response to God's actions, a response which can later be translated into responses throughout his daily life. In the classroom the student can assess the possible truth and relevance of this particular ritual affirmation within the context of his own search for personal understanding of himself, others and life.

Mere description will not act as a growth point for the student. Actual observation, partial participation in a Shabbat or Passover meal (though imitative exercises, e.g. re Muslim prayer positions, can be insensitive and counterproductive), thoughtful conversation with a believer, vicarious experience through literature all help the student 'rise up and walk' along his own road. What are the implications for the daily life of the Muslim who recites *salat*, having made the right intention? This act of submission is more than an ordered duty. In constant remembrance, man is shown God's care and guidance for each individual. In *salat* man responds in love and gratitude, aware of the reality of the precious gift, relationship with his Creator. That response should be reflected in his relationship with the earth and with his brother.

Ritual helps the student concentrate, understand, remember. The Seder meal gives order, clarity and visual expression to the events of the Exodus. The student finds relevance in thoughtful discussion as wine is spilt when the plagues are recited, an action calling men to affirm their own – and God's – grief when evil leads to suffering, whether of the innocent or the guilty. And when God frees man, it is *for* a purpose, not merely *from* an evil. Thus God is affirmed to have a purposeful relation with man.

Likewise the actions and words of the Hindu cremation service offer a concrete basis for discussion as the student meditates on life, death, immortality.

Through ritual, the student explores universal questions in a specific situation and is then freed to rethink his own already formulated responses.

VIDA BARNETT

Roman Catholic Church

1. General education policy

The RC church has always seen formal education as an important part of its mission. The first schools and universities were established and run by the church. In penal times RCS were forbidden to run educational establishments in Britain and, although there were a handful of clandestine schools, most of those who wanted an RC education went overseas. In the late eighteenth century, as the Penal Laws were gradually relaxed, a few schools and seminaries were opened in Britain. During the first half of the nineteenth century, following the influx of religious who had fled from France after the Revolution, many schools both parochial and private were founded. It was expected that the laity should have an education in faith commensurate with their secular education, and that such an education was best guaranteed by establishing RC schools.

At first these institutions were wholly independent of the state. But by 1870 the number of parochial church schools was such that they were acknowledged to be an important part of the total educational provision in the country. The Education Act of 1902 set up a dual system of education, which recognized that church and other voluntary schools had a function and status parallel to that of state schools and that the state should therefore in some way support them. This unique system has, over the past hundred years, and especially since the 1944 Education Act, enabled the RC church to provide catholic schools for most of those who desire them for their children. In addition a system of independent schools, ranging from small nursery schools to large boarding schools for older pupils, has also flourished.

Given the substantial involvement in schools a parallel involvement in teacher training has been inevitable, in order to ensure a supply of teachers able to teach the catholic faith in these schools. Although the numbers of RC Colleges of Higher Education has been reduced in line with the national cut-back in provision for teacher training, they still make a significant contribution to the higher education scene. Currently (1983) they cater for about 6000 students, though by no means all of these are preparing for a career in teaching.

Other RC formal educational establishments include seminaries for the training of priests, of which there are four in England and three overseas for English students; University Colleges in London and Cambridge (Heythrop and St Edmund's House); Plater College near Oxford which specializes in social studies; the Franciscan Study Centre in Canterbury, which is a theological institute associated with the University of Kent. Apart from these there are numerous institutes established by the church which offer less structured opportunities for education in faith; e.g. a number of dioceses have pastoral centres which arrange part-time courses in various aspects of theology, scripture, liturgy, spirituality etc.

The underlying motive in the considerable allocation of resources by the RC church to these ventures has been the belief that religious teaching and worship within an RC community is among the best ways to ensure a lifelong commitment to the faith. In 1981 a Report commissioned by the RC bishops of England and Wales was published (*Signposts and Homecomings: The Educative Task of the Catholic Community*). Its brief was to 'review the principles of Catholic Education and to make recommendations'. Its first conclusion is: 'The total activity of the Church is educative. Its purpose under the guidance of the Holy Spirit is to communicate Christ to mankind and to elucidate the meaning and significance of this communication to each

successive age.' In the practical implications of this basic statement it sees a shift from children to adults. It speaks of 'the absolute centrality of sustained adult Christian education . . . as the single most important educational activity of the Church', on which all other educational initiatives depend. The catholic school is stated to be of continued importance through the experience it gives of Christian community and through the provision of a systematic catechesis, but it is seen to attend to only one stage (however important) in a person's continuing growth in faith.

The phrase sometimes used to describe the relationship between the RC educational system and the state's is 'critical solidarity'. The church must be involved with human concerns and hence with education itself. Christians, like all others, have a duty to work for the true progress of mankind. This is the meaning of the word 'solidarity' in this context. But human progress is not an inevitable process; it has to be judged in the light of faith. Hence the necessity for a 'critical' approach, which may offer its own distinctive contribution to the common work.

2. Education within the church

The traditional way adult enquirers have been prepared for reception into the RC church has been through individual instruction, usually for a period of about six months, given by a priest or nun. The initial approach would have been prompted in a variety of ways, through personal contact, through response to an advertisement (the Catholic Enquiry Centre was founded in the mid-1950s to explore means of using the media to provoke interest and enquiry into the church), through having attended Enquiry Classes. After reception into the church little further was done in any formal way to continue the education in faith of the new member. It was assumed that adequate instruction was given to adult members of the church through the weekly sermon, and through their taking part in the day-to-day activities of the local parish. Recently, however, there has been a considerable change of attitude, with regard to both the education in faith of enquirers and the continuing Christian education of adult members of the church.

The Second Vatican Council called for a

revision of the rite of baptism* of adults and decreed that the catechumenate (the formal period of preparation for baptism) for adults should be restored. The *Rite of Christian Initiation for Adults* (RCIA) was published in 1972. The key feature of the RCIA is that the catechumenate is a journey of faith towards baptism undertaken in the company of members of the local church who themselves 'renew their own conversion, and by their example lead the catechumens to obey the Holy Spirit more generously'. It is thus seen as a formative process during which the individual is gradually initiated into the full Christian life.

The journey is mapped into four periods, which are marked by distinct liturgical rites. The first period is the awakening of faith in the individual by his own enquiry and by evangelization. Its purpose is to give the candidate time and opportunity to reflect on his beliefs and hopes and to begin to develop a relationship with God and with the Christian community. In time the enquirer is invited to take a first formal step into the church by enrolment as a catechumen.

The second period, the catechumenate itself, may be of short or long duration (perhaps even several years), dependent on the growth in faith of the candidate. During this period he gains an experience of the life of the Christian community and takes part in a thorough catechesis. An essential element of this part of the journey is the sharing of faith and experience between the catechumen and those members of the local church who accompany him. The climax is the rite of election which formally admits the catechumen to an immediate preparation for the sacraments of initiation.

This marks the beginning of the third period, usually during Lent, when, supported by the local community, the candidate enters a pre-baptismal retreat, culminating with the Easter Vigil during which he receives the sacraments of baptism, confirmation and the eucharist.

The final period lasts through the Easter season and is a time for the newly baptized (the neophyte) to deepen his faith and experience of belonging to the church, and for the local church to discover its own responsibility towards its new member.

The principal features of the RCIA are thus as follows: it is a process rather than an event; it involves a gradual insertion into the life of the local Christian community and is concerned with far more than instruction; it is a community responsibility involving lay people as well as clergy; it is bound up with the renewal of faith of the community itself.

Alongside this changing attitude towards the education in faith of enquirers there is also a growing acceptance of the importance of the continuing Christian education and formation of adult members of the church. This is voiced in many church documents: e.g., *General Catechetical Directory, Catechesis in Our Time, The Easter People.*

Some form of adult Christian education takes place in many, if not most, parishes: study groups, prayer groups, retreats, courses, conferences, etc. These attempt to take as their starting point the felt needs of the participants, e.g., anxiety about change in the church, about RE in school, about social justice; a desire to be better prepared for marriage, for spiritual growth, or simply to be better informed about the faith of the church.

It is generally recognized that the Christian education of adults ought to take place in a community setting. There is consequently an emphasis on fostering small groups of believers in the parish, which will provide their members with that support and friendship which is necessary to sustain growth in faith. It has been suggested that the pattern proposed by the RCIA for catechumens can be adapted for the continuing education in faith of all adults (see *The Easter People*), perhaps especially those who though baptized are largely uncatechized.

What is described above is at this stage no more than an indication of changing emphases and attitudes. The RCIA has not yet been officially adopted in England and Wales, although its use is gradually becoming more widespread. Likewise, although there are numerous initiatives in adult Christian education, there is still a long way to go before a coherent pattern will have developed. Nonetheless progress along the lines sketched out above seems assured.

3. Confirmation preparation

The theology of confirmation* as a sacrament distinct from baptism is somewhat confused, and this lack of clarity is reflected in the varying practice of its administration and preparation.

In apostolic times there is little evidence of a separate sacrament of confirmation. But by the middle of the third century it seems that an anointing by the bishop, distinct from the baptismal anointing, was the norm. A person was initiated into full communion in the church by a single rite which included baptism, confirmation and the eucharist, administered by the bishop, usually at the Easter Vigil. As the church grew, and particularly following the Edict of Milan (312) after which infant baptism became more common, the bishop could not baptize all those seeking admission to the church. In the Eastern church the priest was allowed to perform the rite of anointing if the bishop was not available. But in the Western church the rite of anointing was reserved to the bishop, and confirmation was therefore deferred until an opportunity arose of presenting the baptized candidates to the bishop.

While for a number of centuries parents were urged to present children to be confirmed in infancy, by the time of the Council of Trent (1545–63) the then established practice in the RC church of confirming around the age of seven years was reaffirmed. In 1971 following the Second Vatican Council the revised *Rite of Confirmation* was published. This requires the candidates to renew their baptismal promises, which suggests a degree of maturity on the part of the candidates and implies the appropriateness of a later age for confirmation. The pattern is therefore changing and distinct practices are emerging: some are confirmed at primary school age (between eight and eleven); others are confirmed while of secondary school age (twelve plus). The type of preparation may vary somewhat according to the age and maturity of the candidate. For those in the younger age-bracket the preparation will tend to concentrate on the instructional element; for older candidates there will be a greater emphasis on personal response to the gift of the Holy Spirit.

A typical programme of preparation includes the following theological instruction: Spirit in Creation; Spirit in the Old Testament; Baptism/Death/Resurrection; Eucharist; Jesus: the Individual, the Community; Growing Up and Change; In the Likeness of Christ; The Trinity: Prayer as Relationship; the Spirit: Reconciler, Unifier, Welder; Service, Anointing and Witness; the Spirit and the Church; the Rite of Confirmation. (See *Growth in the Holy Spirit: Education for Confirmation*.)

Allied elements of the preparation will be moments of celebration and encouragement to undertake service projects. The celebrations serve a twofold purpose: to emphasize that confirmation is part of the process of becoming inserted into the public life of the church, and to associate the period of preparation with prayer. The service projects are a practical reminder that confirmed Christians are 'obliged to spread and defend the faith both by word and deed as true witnesses to Christ' (Constitution on the church, Second Vatican Council). In the process of preparation it is envisaged that the candidate's home, school and parish should work together, each with its distinct role to play. The home provides the basic support for faith by the example and love of the parents; the RC school ensures appropriate instruction and an experience of an educative Christian community; the parish is the local church wherein the candidate finds the wider community, scope for service, experience of liturgical worship, instruction and celebration.

---

1. General education policy
A.C.F. Beales, *Education Under Penalty*, University of London Press 1963; M. Hornsby-Smith, *Catholic Education: The Unobtrusive Partner*, Sheed & Ward 1978; RC Bishops of England and Wales, *The Easter People*, St Paul Publications 1980; Sacred Congregation of the Clergy, *The Catholic School*, Catholic Truth Society 1977; *Signposts and Homecomings: The Educative Task of the Catholic Community: A Report to the Bishops of England and Wales*, St Paul Publications 1981.

2. Education within the church
M. Dujarier, *The Rites of Christian Initiation*, William H. Sadlier 1979; James B. Dunning, *New Wine: New Wineskins: Exploring the RCIA*, William H. Sadlier 1981; *Liverpool 1980*, St Paul Publications 1981; K. Nichols and J. Cummins, *Into His Fulness: Christian Adult Education Today*, St Paul Publications 1980; Pope John Paul II, *Catechesis in Our*

Time, Catholic Truth Society 1979; Sacred Congregation for the Clergy, *General Catechetical Directory*, Catholic Truth Society 1971; Sacred Congregation for Divine Worship, *Rite of Christian Initiation of Adults*, Catholic Truth Society 1981; W. Saris, *Towards a Living Church*, Collins 1980.

3. Confirmation preparation
Instructions on the Revised Roman Rites, Collins 1979; W. J. Koplik and J. E. Brady, *We Celebrate Confirmation*, Silver Burdett 1978; A. J. McCallen, *More Like Christ*, Collins 1978; K. Rahner, *A New Baptism in the Spirit: Confirmation Today*, Dimension Books 1974; M. Searle, *Christening, the Making of Christians*, Kevin Mayhew 1977; Westminster RE Centre, *Growth in the Holy Spirit: Education for Confirmation*, Anthony Clarke Books 1981.

DAVID KONSTANT

Rousseau, Jean-Jacques

Jean-Jacques Rousseau (1712–78) has had such a marked influence on educational thought that his seminal work, *Émile*, seems commonplace today. In 1762 it seemed revolutionary, not least in the conviction with which it presents the child as free of all innate tendencies toward evil. 'God makes all things good; man meddles with them and they become evil.' Society, with its unnatural affectations, corrupts. This is the key to his educational thought.

From birth to five, the child develops his senses. Rousseau commends the nurturing style of the peasant family. The child is seen, not as a potential citizen, or anything predetermined, but as a human being with unbounded natural possibilities. Religion would be an inhibiting and inappropriate element at this stage. The present enjoyment of life must never be sacrificed for future possibilities.

From five to twelve, deliberately avoiding the use of reason, which is not yet available (another reason for postponing religious education), the educator is to concentrate on the physical potential of the child, so that he may become confident and capable. 'The education of the earliest years should be merely negative. It consists, not in teaching virtue or truth, but in preserving the heart from vice and from the spirit of error.' Rous-

seau is a developmentalist, 'childhood is the sleep of reason', and as such he anticipates Piaget's 'readiness' theory.

From twelve to fifteen years, the powers of the mind are to be encouraged through exposure, in a carefully controlled way, to the phenomena of nature, building on the child's natural curiosity. Here he anticipates 'discovery learning'.

Eventually between fifteen and twenty years, the youth, who has already built relationships with the natural world, may be introduced to human relationships through carefully chosen biography. His moral concern should be encouraged through acts of kindness and charity to those in need, a precursor, perhaps, of 'community service'*. Religion may now be confronted. As he thinks about man and the universe the young man is moved by conscience, the voice of nature within him, to worship their divine originator. There is no room for the several 'dimensions' of religion here. Religion, Rousseau conceives, is not sectarian but rather purely 'spiritual', with no room for such irrelevancies as ritual or vestments. Gradually, selected companions extend Émile's experience of human nature, until, armed against the vices and excesses of society he is ready to meet his partner, conveniently trained to be a meek, domestic wife.

Women do not develop reason sufficiently to decide religious issues, therefore they must accept religion on authority. We cannot speak of religion too soon for little girls 'for if we wait till they are ready for a serious discussion of these deep subjects we should be in danger of never speaking of religion at all'.

Rousseau's religion is a form of deistic naturalism. Whatever the religion adopted by the state in which we live, we accept it as citizens, but true religion is a natural relationship with the God we meet in our solitariness.

Jean Jacques Rousseau, *Émile*, trans. Barbara Foxley, Everyman, Dent 1911; Karl Barth, *Protestant Theology in the Nineteenth Century*, SCM Press 1972; Ronald Grimsley, *Rousseau and the Religious Quest*, Oxford University Press 1968; Robert R. Rusk, *Doctrines of the Great Educators*, Macmillan ³1965.

KENNETH MULLIS

Russia   *see* **Eastern Europe**

SACRE   *see* **Standing Advisory Councils for Religious Education**

Sacred Books

Each of the world's major religions has emphasized its revelation in a sacred book or books, to which it accords a measure of respect different in kind and degree from that offered to other literature. In many faiths the sacred scriptures are the focus of daily devotion and repetition (Guru Granth Sahib, Qur'an*, Pali Canon, etc.). In at least three cases (Torah, Bible and Qur'an) the basic, orthodox scriptural emphasis on monotheistic faith is occasionally tempered by a mystical identification of some aspects of the scriptures with the divine Spirit, as occurs with the Shekinah, the Logos, and, in a different way, with the Ummul Kitab.

In most faiths the scriptures have been assembled over a protracted period of time and then handed down from generation to generation; they usually contain writings in a wide variety of different categories such as myth, legend, history, poetry, biography, epistle, prayers, spells, laws, etc.

Some scriptures include scriptural material from other traditions, and Islam (from Jews and Christians) and Christianity (from Jews) in particular have 'borrowed' in this way. In certain cases the canon of what is to be included and the accepted text have emerged with remarkable ease and without undue dispute (e.g. in Islam), whereas in other cases there has been lengthy confusion and fierce argument.

The scriptures are used in many different ways by the faithful, sometimes for devotional reading, in other cases for specific guidance or decision making. Muslims and Christians take the oath in courts of law with the Qur'an or the Bible as their witness, and Sikhs use the Guru Granth Sahib to help choose the names of their young children.

Frequently, the scriptures are a source of authority in matters of doctrine, law or practice, and rank alongside or sometimes above, the voices of history, tradition, or the community, in determining the viewpoints that are accepted as authoritative. In many religions this combines with a view of the scriptures as the revealed word of God which accepts their message in a literalistic way and rejects any questioning of their accuracy or authenticity. Alongside this there sometimes emerges a series of views, arising from recent scholarship, which emphasize the roles of archaeology and history, modern criticism and textual study, in determining the historicity of the documents as we have them today. The outcome is often a questioning of their literal accuracy and an emphasis on the scriptures as functional documents, set within the communities that composed them.

In British RE much of the content taught has traditionally been biblical, and the LEA agreed syllabuses* that boomed in the 1940s and 1950s largely followed this tradition. Public examination syllabuses have focussed more on scripture than on religion, though the recent emphasis on religious studies has broadened the scope of these examinations considerably, and papers based on the study of religions, philosophy, beliefs, history and ethics all have their place now. With this development has emerged a fresh study of biblical material which is less content based and aimed rather at exploring the role and function of biblical material in the light of modern criticism and scholarship.

The inclusion of non-Christian religions in RE today has also introduced the study of non-Christian scriptures, and the Torah, the Qur'an, the Guru Granth Sahib, and the sacred texts of Hinduism and Buddhism all feature to some degree. Certain courses are thematic, with, e.g., the role of the scriptures or their use in worship as the common link; other studies are historical or analytical, and some look at content, though rarely from a devotional viewpoint. The role of such study in a multi-cultural setting, where the scriptures studied may include those of a majority of the school community whose home attitude could be one of literalist devotion, poses problems for schools which they are only recently learning to resolve.

J. B. Alphonso-Karkala, *An Anthology of Indian Literature*, Penguin 1971; A. J. Arberry, *The Koran Interpreted,* Oxford University Press 1964; R. O. Ballou, *The Pocket World Bible,* Routledge & Kegan Paul 1948; E. Conze (ed.), *Buddhist Scriptures,* Penguin 1959; R. Davies, *Holy Books*, Longman 1981; M. Eliade, *From Primitives* to Zen: A Thematic Sourcebook of the History of Religions, Collins 1967; W. Foy (ed.), Man's Religious Quest: A Reader, Croom Helm/Open University Press 1978; G. Lanoczkowski, Sacred Writings: A Guide to the Literature of Religions, Collins 1961; R. C. Musaph-Andriesse, From Torah to Kabbalah: A Basic Introduction to the Writings of Judaism, SCM Press 1981; Trilochan Singh et al., Selections from the Sacred Writings of the Sikhs, Allen & Unwin 1960.

PETER WOODWARD

Sacred Places

A place is held to be sacred when it is believed that the divine has been manifested there or the divine power has been felt there. A classic example is the place near Horeb where Moses saw and heard the angel of God (Ex. 3.1–6). Such places are often marked by buildings or other artefacts.

The manifestation of God may have been a theophany or a natural phenomenon explained as a demonstration of divine power. The black stone set in the corner of the Ka'ba in Mecca, for instance, was probably a meteorite once venerated by the pre-Islamic community and now sacred to Muslims.

The sacredness of a site once acknowledged may be recognized by different succeeding traditions. Celtic temples, for example, were often converted into Christian churches and holy springs, stones and trees were sometimes incorporated into the later sanctuary. The Christian dedication to the angel Michael usually indicates that the church, often on a hill-top, was built on a pagan site.

The structure which marks a holy place may be functional or it may be a deeper expression of the awareness which has registered in the human consciousness in that place. As such it might evoke a similar consciousness in someone today. Even a pillar of stone marking a sacred place can impress the visitor. At the other end of the scale, the splendour of a cathedral often evokes some sense of the greatness of God.

Sacred places can be considered at a number of levels: they might be presented descriptively merely as a place; or be seen as an expression of man's belief about himself or his place in the world or his relationship with the divine; or be examined as places where men and women in the past had an encounter with God and where pupils themselves might have a similar encounter.

See also **Pilgrimage**.

———

Mircea Eliade, Patterns in Comparative Religion, Sheed & Ward 1958.

ROBIN T. PEARCE

Salvation Army

Founded in the East End of London in 1865 when the Rev. William Booth was invited to lead evangelistic meetings there, although this name was not adopted by the Movement until 1878. The aim was to bring the gospel message to the poor and depressed who were largely untouched by the ministrations of the existing churches. Initially there was no thought of bringing into being a separate body of people, but this followed logically as the new converts did not feel at home in the churches and William Booth began to need their services for his expanding work.

Although some able, talented and even a few educated people were attracted, it was largely a movement of needy people with few pretensions to wealth or learning. However, the Christian teaching that was given and the sober and industrious ways that were engendered led inevitably to the raising of the material standards of life of Salvationists and the provision of better opportunities for their children. Hence eventually many took full advantage of secondary and further education, some to the highest levels.

Extensive and variegated social services in Britain and overseas continue to meet the needs of the under-privileged and disadvantaged, with rehabilitation and re-education programmes wherever possible.

1. Policy on public education. In the UK the Salvation Army has not participated as a body in the school system. However, many Salvationists have entered the teaching profession and Salvation Army officers have locally been invited to give religious instruction. In some places 'holiday clubs' have been found. With the introduction into schools of some studies relating to the Army, information material for both teachers and pupils has been made available from International Headquarters.

A far more active involvement has been undertaken in some other parts of the world, the Salvation Army being an international movement operating in eighty-six countries.

In Newfoundland* the church was the pioneer in education and the denominational system became the rule. Accordingly in 1892 the Salvation Army was recognized as a religious denomination eligible for educational grants and over the years became one of five major religious bodies on the island, having in 1964 ninety schools with 10,000 pupils. From 1969 many church schools were absorbed into an integrated system but the Army continues to share with other denominations a measure of real responsibility for ensuring that education harmonizes with the principles of the Christian faith. Further education is provided on an international basis in Norway* at the Jelhœy Folk High School.

In conformity with the general pattern of the development of missionary work in the Indian sub-continent and in Africa*, the Salvation Army became extensively involved in educational work, first at primary level and later in teacher training, other forms of vocational training and the secondary fields. In due time governments assumed responsibility for much of this work but Salvation Army secondary and high schools continue to function in Zimbabwe, Zambia, Zaire and in parts of India. Teacher training is still undertaken in Zaire. A very reduced involvement in primary education remains.

Other scattered elements of educational work persist in South East Asia (e.g. Indonesia) and in Hong Kong a large secondary school is operated as well as primary schools and vocational training centres. Similar schools are maintained in the Caribbean; in Haiti to secondary level. Other countries with kindergartens and schools include Chile and Peru. Vocational training centres include, for example, a training farm in Argentina and projects for handicapped people in many lands, notably Kenya.

2. *Membership preparation.* Salvationist parents are encouraged to dedicate their children at an early age to God and his service, being invited to take part in a dedication ceremony. A slightly differing commitment is made by non-Salvationist parents who wish to bring their children for dedication. Following this the children's names are placed on the Cradle Roll and in due course a welcome is given to the children's activities. It is believed that children can give their lives to God and begin to experience his salvation and when

this happens they have the opportunity of becoming junior soldiers in the Salvation Army. For this there are five preparation classes and after enrolment a training class and the junior soldiers' training and award scheme. The first Sunday in April is usually set aside as the junior soldiers' day of renewal. From the age of fourteen years a young person can be considered for senior soldiership, the requirements of which are taught in eight preparatory lessons. The Articles of War, setting out the Army's eleven articles of faith and promises to be made, have to be signed before the public swearing-in ceremony takes place. Local officers to carry special responsibilities in various aspects of Army work are selected as necessary from the ranks of those who have become senior soldiers. These enter into specific undertakings and are guided in their duties by appropriate sets of orders and regulations. Efforts are made to provide training facilities, e.g. a weekend house party for young people's sergeant-majors (Sunday School superintendents) or a 'Brengle' institute for instruction in the living of a holy life.

The needs of the Army for full time officers is regularly brought before soldiers and local officers and specially emphasized in Annual Councils conducted for young people. Those who are too young to be considered can join the Link fellowship and those of the right age (eighteen years is the earliest age at which training can begin) can begin to be processed through recommendations, interviews, correspondence lessons and attendance at an assessment conference when all aspects of the applicant's call and suitability can be examined.

Those finally accepted for training are obliged to complete their candidates' correspondence course and then report for a two year training course. In the UK this training is given at the William Booth Memorial Training College. General William Booth envisaged such training colleges as 'universities of humanity' and every effort is made to train cadets (students) spiritually, academically and practically so that they can carry out a sustained ministry and rise to the call of any emergency demanding practical leadership and succour. As well as following internal courses of instruction some cadets are given the opportunity of preparing for public examinations. At the end of the training period cadets are commissioned as officers and then obliged to undertake further studies as part of their total training.

3. *Courses (internal) for children and adults.* The Salvation Army has produced its own Sunday-school lesson material since 1905. Today this comprises *Living and Believing* for primary children (a three-year cycle of books), *Living and Believing* for junior, intermediate and Bible classes (a five-year syllabus) and *Army Beliefs and Characteristics* in two volumes.

When junior soldiers reach the age of twelve years they can be enrolled as corps cadets for the purpose of training them for Salvation Army service. A six-year programme of studies on the Bible, Christian doctrine and Army history and activities is supplemented by devotional periods and practical Christian witness and service.

Baden-Powell groups of cub-scouts, scouts, brownies and guides operate at some Army centres. A distinctive group is the Salvation Army Boys' Adventure Corps which is designed to provide an outreach programme for boys aged six to fourteen years.

Musical interests are very well catered for through young people's bands, singing companies and timbrel brigades. A number of well-attended summer music schools and camps provide expert instruction as well as spiritual and moral training.

Salvationists (and others) can take advantage of a series of study pamphlets and a whole range of correspondence courses in biblical, doctrinal and related studies is available. International Headquarters houses the Editorial and Literary Departments. The Editorial Department produces *The War Cry* (the largest selling weekly religious paper in Britain), *The Young Soldier* (of comparable circulation), *The Musician, The Deliverer* (featuring the social services) and *All the World* (an international public relations production). The Literary Department is responsible for producing a flow of books and pamphlets including *The Salvation Army Year Book,* Sunday School teaching material, *The Soldier's Armoury* (a Bible-reading plan with daily commentary), special material for use in overseas territories, a magazine for private circulation among English speaking officers throughout the world and the *Home League Exchange* for those directing the work of

the Home League, the Army's women's organization.

Situated in London, is the International College for Officers to which centre come officers from many lands for further fellowship and training. This college plays an important role in maintaining the international spirit and nature of the Army.

LYNDON TAYLOR

School Boards

By the 1860s public elementary schooling in England and Wales had become a competitive denominational enterprise assisted by government grant. The object of the Liberal Education Act of 1870 was to supplement voluntary schools based on sectarian religion by predominantly secular schools provided by local school boards elected triennially by the ratepayers and financed by local rate in addition to parliamentary grant. Liberals thus hoped to make good a deficiency of school places and also ease the 'religious difficulty' by making available disinterested religious teaching in areas where only denominational schools existed. In the board schools Religious Instruction was optional at each board's discretion, but if provided it must contain 'no religious catechism or religious formulary which is distinctive of any particular denomination' (the Cowper-Temple* clause), and withdrawal from this, as from sectarian instruction in voluntary schools*, was protected by a timetable conscience clause*.

This continued the policy of secularization begun in 1862 by new government regulations linking grant to the teaching of prescribed subjects, excluding religion. Although school boards had thus no financial inducement to teach religion, the vast majority of the 2,545 boards eventually established did so. Anglicans and Catholics condemned the principle of unsectarian schooling; nonconformists generally accepted it, and some now surrendered their schools to the local board. Sectarian controversy dominated elections and each board's policy hinged on its membership, or in small rural boards on its chairman. Where radicals or nonconformists had control, Religious Instruction might be confined to Bible reading; where churchmen ruled there might be a detailed syllabus embracing distinctive doctrines.

Denied rate aid, the voluntary schools –

over eighty per cent of them Anglican – suffered increasingly from board school competition. This became an acute political issue in the 1890s. Liberals, closely identified with nonconformity, stood by their 1870 settlement; Conservatives, representing the Anglican interest, planned to put denominational schools on the rates and replace school boards by all-purpose county and borough councils. This they did by their Education Act of 1902.

Marjorie Cruickshank, *Church and State in English Education*, Macmillan 1963; James Murphy, *Church, State and Schools in Britain 1800–1970*, Routledge & Kegan Paul 1971.

JOHN LAWSON

Schools Council

The considerable influence of the Schools Council on recent changes in county school RE can be traced back to the Schools Council's RE project at Lancaster University from 1969–73. The newly inaugurated Religious Studies Department had already excited interest and comment for its non-confessional descriptive approach and for its strong emphasis upon the teaching of world religions. Under the chairmanship of Professor Ninian Smart, the project team applied this approach to the teaching of RE in county schools.

From 1944 until the late 1960s county school RE had been dominated by a 'Scripture Knowledge' approach which presupposed some kind of Christian allegiance among most of the citizens of the UK. This approach corresponded less and less to the secular, largely post-Christian, reality and some local authorities had adopted teaching programmes which were thematic, centred on the experience of the child or the problems of adolescents. These syllabuses were less 'confessional' in tone even if they remained largely Christian in their terms of reference. The Lancaster team continued with many of the insights of this earlier work but took account of the greater pluralism of a society which now included significantly increased non-Christian religious communities. Accordingly they maintained the experience and child-based approach but broadened the scope of RE to include objective treatment of the major world religions.

For historical reasons Christianity still received most emphasis but the new RE could be taught by teachers with any religious belief or none and set out to treat religion 'phenomenologically' through an examination of its six dimensions: the doctrinal, the mythological, the ethical, the critical or experiential, the ritual and finally the social. No religious faith was presupposed in the pupil and each faith was to be examined objectively through the experience based approach.

World religions material was considered suitable for school children of all ages. The work of the Lancaster Project gave rise to two important publications: Working Paper 36 (*Religious Education in Secondary Schools*, 1971) and Working Paper 44 (*Religious Education in Primary Schools*, 1972). These were followed by a series of Schools Council books and resources for teachers and pupils at both primary and secondary schools, with impartial treatment of the different faiths through an experience-based approach.

This emphasis on experience is given greater importance still in the School Councils Occasional Paper, *A Groundplan for the Study of Religion*, published in 1977. The 'Groundplan' attempts to provide an exhaustive list of all the items which should be covered or considered in the treatment of religion or (although this is not clear) of any individual religion. Abandoning the earlier sixfold classification, these items are divided under three broad headings: factual knowledge; understanding ('as from the point of view of an adherent'); and evaluation ('as from the point of view of an observer'). Perhaps due to the opaque highly technical language in which it is written, the Groundplan has not been published commercially and has not had anything like the influence of the earlier Lancaster Project.

See also **History of RE in England**.

Working Paper 44: *Religious Education in Primary Schools*, Evans Methuen 1977; *Discovering an Approach* Macmillan Educational 1977; Working Paper 36: *Religious Education in Secondary Schools*, Evans Methuen 1971; *Journeys into Religion* (Series and two vol. teacher's handbook), Granada Publishing 1977 and 1981 including: *The Man from Nazareth as They Saw Him*; *The Muslim Way of Life*, *Pilgrimages*, *Religion in Britain Today*,

Signs and Symbols, Exploring Belief, How Others See Us, The Life of Man: The Family, Science and Religion, The Hindu Way, Religion through Culture: Judaism, Why do Men Suffer?; *A Groundplan for the Study of Religion*, Schools Council 1977.

DUNCAN M. MACPHERSON

Science and Religion

Aims. The aims of science and religion are distinctive. Scientists believe in cause and effect in the material world and investigate the 'how' of these interactions. Religious thinkers are concerned with purpose and investigate the 'why' of life.

Methods. The methods of science and religion are also distinctive. Following Karl Popper it may be said that a theory is a 'scientific theory' if predictions can be deduced from it which can be tested against observation with the possibility of the refutation of the theory. Each current 'scientific theory' is a hypothesis which has stood up to a number of such tests, but any such theory may fail on further testing. Present 'scientific theories' have the same status now as old theories (such as the caloric theory of heat, the phlogiston theory of burning or the non-interchangeability of mass and energy) had when they were the accepted 'scientific theories' of their day. This hypothetico-deductive method as well as testing new hypotheses also continually tests the scientists' belief in cause and effect.

On the other hand 'religious belief' rests on certain revelations and/or traditional doctrines. A 'religious belief' cannot be tested in the same way as a 'scientific theory' because, first, it does not make predictions (for this life!) which, if not occurring, would make everyone drop the belief; for example an answered and an unanswered intercessory prayer can both be interpreted as God's will. Secondly, paradoxes are acceptable in 'religious beliefs' in a way that they are not acceptable in 'scientific theories'. A 'scientific theory' of light cannot treat light as exclusively waves at one place and as exclusively particles in another place whereas Jesus can be accepted as fully God and as fully man.

It should be acknowledged, though, that once a number of 'scientific theories' or a number of 'religious beliefs' have been accepted then the modes by which they are filled out and their interrelationships delineated are much the same in science and religion. For science, T. S. Kuhn calls this normal science within a paradigm.

Apparent Conflict. Science and religion may appear to be in conflict when: 1. Science or religion tries to answer questions in the other's sphere, e.g. astronauts saying that they have found no God in space or theologians arguing about the age of the earth. 2. One side misunderstands the other, perhaps due to different usage of terms, e.g. a scientific 'law' is descriptive whilst a religious 'law' is prescriptive. 3. Commonly held (but inaccurate) world views are invested with the authority of science or of religion, e.g. that scientific theories (supposedly found by induction) are certain or that religious dogma can disprove scientific theory. 4. Religion fails to recognize that a scientific theory has changed, e.g. the change first from an earth-centred universe to a heliocentric one and then the change to our present concept of an expanding universe.

Interactions. Whenever new ideas are being formulated, the language used draws upon concepts already in current usage. Religion and science have both drawn upon the concepts of the other, sometimes in conscious analogy and sometimes by the passive acceptance of prevailing thought. Problems arise for religion when concepts that have been used in articulating religious thought are rejected by scientists when new scientific theories are accepted. The problems of this kind for science are mostly in the past as science has now largely divested its language of religious overtones.

For Christianity it is the difference in thought between the time of Jesus (which indeed prevailed largely unchanged right through to the Reformation and beyond) and today that is significant. Major changes include:

1. The view of the universe: then the earth at the centre, the stars on spheres encircling the earth, heaven above the stars and hell in the bowels of the earth; now the earth an insignificant (in material terms) planet of one sun in one galaxy in a vast universe. Then the ascent of Jesus corresponded to the physical direction of heaven, now it does not.

2. The view of time: then a short past history with man living through nearly all of it, a present of decline and a very limited future;

now a past time of thousands of millions of years with man present for less than a thousandth of the time, a present of evident progress in many ways and a future for the universe stretching away beyond comprehension. Even if the Apocalypse is fulfilled in nuclear holocaust, it would, in a material sense, hardly ruffle the time-scale of the universe.

3. The view of the past: then a certainty about the authority of holy writings and about the events of the past; now an uncertainty about meanings, motivations and happenings. Parallels to this historical uncertainty are the uncertainty principle in physics, the statistics of random events in chemistry and mutations in biology.

4. The view of miracles: then an acceptance of one-off interventions by God in the world and an attribution of many events, from drought or plague down to lesser things, to the intervention of supernatural forces; now an acceptance of cause and effect so strong that the inexplicable are left as unproven. The explosion of Mount St Helens is explained by, and adds to, the scientific study of volcanoes whilst a UFO sighting is left unproven.

5. The norms of argument: then an acceptance of myth, parable and allegory in their own right; now the dominance of logical arguments with other forms seen only as an alternative form of expression. So nowadays myth, like Genesis chapter 1, has to be explained, otherwise it will be interpreted literally and usually rejected.

Implications. If we assume that our present religious tradition has arisen from: (*a*) the nature of God and of mankind that we believe to be constant; (*b*) the essence of the religious thought or revelation which writers and thinkers endeavoured to put into words; (*c*) the words used by the original writers; (*d*) the translation of the original writings into the language of the reader; then we observe that some religious people believe in the infallibility of the last translation, others believe in the infallibility of the original writings, whilst yet others endeavour to go back through the original writings to the original thought and to rewrite that thought in the language of the reader. The argument so far would certainly lead us not to rely upon the final translation nor upon the original words. But what about the original thought? Following our line of

analysis the answer must be no. For example, it seems hardly conceivable that the doctrine of original sin would have developed, to explain the propensity of men and women to do that which they know to be wrong, if there had already been (*a*) a theory of evolution, implying a gradual development of the faculties rather than of decay from original perfection; (*b*) the present debate on the relative effects of heredity and environment; and (*c*) the present emphasis on the individual, and on the psychology of the individual, rather than on group consciousness.

So perhaps we have to endeavour to go right back to the nature of God* and of mankind and only then to rewrite in the language of the reader. This requires a belief in the possibility of continuing revelation. And it is inevitable that each further step backwards that we probe the less certain our picture will appear to others. Yet is not this the only route towards a valid answer?

————

D. Cupitt, *The Debate about Christ*, SCM Press 1979; D. Cupitt, *The Worlds of Science and Religion*, Sheldon 1979; T. S. Kuhn, *The Structure of Scientific Revolution*, University of Chicago Press 1972; K. Popper, *Conjectures and Refutations*, Routledge & Kegan Paul 1963; M. Richardson and C. Boyle, *What is Science?* Association of Scientific Education 1979; Russell Stannard, *Science and the Renewal of Belief*, SCM Press 1982.

JOHN BAKER

Scotland

John Knox and his fellow-reformers were the founding fathers of Scottish education and their impulse was the true teaching of Christ and his gospel. They spelled out their plans for kirk and school in *The Scots Confession*, 1560, which was read in the face of Parliament and ratified, and *The First Book of Discipline*. Schools and schoolmasters were to be provided throughout the land and the Bible and catechism were to have the central place in the curriculum.

The terms Bible, scripture, religious instruction, religious knowledge have had a long life in the Scottish classroom. They involved memorizing and verbalizing, the hallmark of religious worth in a land where catechizing was the rule and the sermon was the main course in the Sunday 'diet of worship'.

The term religious education only came into common use with the appointment of a committee by the Secretary of State for Scotland in 1968 with the remit: 'Within the existing framework of the statutory provisions governing the obligation to continue religious instruction, the responsibility for its content and the question of inspection, to review the current practice of Scottish schools (other than Roman Catholic schools) with regard to moral and religious education and to make recommendations for its improvement.'

The outcome was *Moral and Religious Education in Scottish Schools* (HMSO 1972), usually known as the Millar report*. It assessed the current practice of primary and secondary schools in Scotland, taking evidence from education authorities, head teachers, classroom teachers and from pupils. Particular issues under review were: the possibility of examinations in RE, the training of student-teachers, worship in school, the place of the school chaplain, the appointment of advisers in RE and a programme of curriculum development in RE. The Millar report recognized in pupils an increasing alienation from Christian beliefs and the traditional pattern of Christian values. In this it was ahead of unreflecting church opinion in Scotland. The educationists noted that 'the styles and forms of the Church, particularly the social forms, have little appeal to the young people'.

The educational outcome of the Millar report was considerable. In 1974 the Secretary of State set up the Scottish Central Committee on Religious Education (SCCORE) with responsibility for RE in the primary and secondary school. All its members were appointed on educational grounds and, for the first time since the Reformation, six were Roman Catholic teachers. SCCORE is a sub-committee of the Consultative Committee on the Curriculum, an open recognition by the state that RE has its proper educational place in the school and within the national structure for curriculum development. SCCORE's particular task was to prepare a curricular framework which could be developed to meet the varying needs of pupils in both denominational and non-denominational schools in different parts of Scotland. The committee recognized that the old-style Bible-centred syllabus produced

for national use largely under church auspices was no longer adequate. They noted, on the one hand, that if education is education for living, it is still education within a local community. On the other hand, they recognized that there is no one theology or ideology which commands widespread assent even in traditionally Calvinist and Presbyterian Scotland.

In *Bulletin 7: A Curricular Approach to Religious Education* (HMSO 1978), SCCORE saw its task: 'to suggest guidelines, highlight the issues, provide material and stimulate groups of teachers to experiment in their own situations'. It started from the premise that school and teacher have a duty, arising from their professional commitment, to meet pupils' needs, to provide for those pupils an opportunity to explore the non-material and religious aspect of life, accepting that they come to religious education from different standpoints and should be helped to arrive at their own answers. *Bulletin 1* also took account of RE and slow learners, handicapped children, the supply of specialist teachers and, in particular, the introduction of certificate examinations.

A re-assembled SCCORE has gone on to produce *Bulletin 2: Curriculum Guidelines for Religious Education* (CCC 1981). It builds on the groundwork of *Bulletin 1* and is a specific working document to supply a structure for RE in the secondary school. It offers a rationale for religious education in these terms: 'Religious education in schools is concerned with understanding the experience of man in his search for meaning, value and purpose in life. The religions of the world are the classic expressions of this search and, for many people, provide the context of meaning, value and purpose within which experience is to be understood. Through his understanding of this search the pupil is helped towards a deeper awareness of his identity, enabling him to grow and develop freely in a world of divergent beliefs and values.'

The pupil should be helped to become aware of his own feelings and commitments and actions and to test them in the light of reason and experience and the evidence of the great traditions of the religions of the world. Naturally it is recognized that in the Scottish tradition Christianity will hold the central place in the RE curriculum. Even today, and allowing for the right of the 'conscience clause'* and the variety of a multi-cultural urban community, it is clear that parents, teachers and voters generally still give their approval to this principle. Denomi-national schools, on the other hand, must assume that teachers, parents and pupils have a personal and responsible commitment to the faith which is the *raison d'etre* of their schools.

Further bulletins will follow from SCCORE. Two major tasks in RE in the final decades of this millenium will be to supply more qualified specialist RE teachers and an adequately time-tabled programme of RE throughout the school in accordance with successive Educa-tion (Scotland) Acts, and the provision of certificate examinations in RE, for which there are already published proposals. These proposals for the introduction of a syllabus and examinations in religious studies have been welcomed by the Church of Scotland and the Roman Catholic Church and have already received the approval of the Secretary of State for Scotland. The Munn Report on *The Structure of the Curriculum* (HMSO 1977) sees religious education as a vital element in the core curriculum for secondary pupils as well as an elective leading to a certificate examination. At a later stage the universities provide courses to honours degree standard in Religious Studies.

See also **Presbyterian Churches, Church of Scotland.**

DONALD M. MCFARLAN

Scottish Joint Committee on Religious Education

In 1918 the Educational Institute of Scotland, the Church of Scotland and the United Free Church of Scotland formed a joint committee to produce a Syllabus of Religious Instruction for use in Scottish Schools. This led to the formation of the Scottish Joint Committee on Religious Education. Its membership now includes representatives of the Educational Institute of Scotland, the Churches, the Convention of Scottish Local Authorities and teachers' professional organizations concern-ed with RE.

The aim of the Joint Committee is to promote the development of RE and to foster co-operation between church and school. It seeks to fulfil this in three significant ways:

1. Preparation and publication of syllabus material for nursery, primary and secondary schools. The Joint Committee was the chief source of RE resource material until the setting up of the Scottish Central Committee on Reli-gious Education under the aegis of the Secre-tary of State in 1974. 2. Considerations of Reports and representation to the Secretary of State and appropriate bodies on develop-ment of RE. 3. Annual conferences for teachers and others interested in RE. The summer conference in St Andrews and the regional conference held in a different area each year give consideration to the latest developments in educational methods and religious studies, and are recognized by Local Authorities as in-service courses.

JOAN H. CRAIG

Secondary Schools, RE in

Until the 1960s use of the term 'instruction' in relation to the teaching of 'religion' in secon-dary schools implied that there were skills which with appropriate guidance and sufficient practice could be acquired to an acceptable level of competency. But RI teachers in the early 1960s were beginning to discuss the contribution their subject made to the total education of young people. It then became common for teachers to refer to the subject as Religious Education and for RE to replace RI on school timetables. It is now generally accepted that RE in school is prop-erly concerned to develop informed critical awareness about religion in all young people; it is not about induction into a faith.

A particular legacy of the 1944 Act derives from the protection of at least one period a week of denominational religious instruction in voluntary aided schools. This notion of 'one period' was transferred from its original context and became the accepted norm for RE in the mind of most timetablers. A one-period-a-week subject automatically finds itself of low status in a secondary school and so a major concern for RE teachers has been to raise the status of their subject and win acceptable recognition in terms of timetable periods and resource allocation. There has been significant expansion in the numbers of trained specialist RE teachers and professional associations who publish journals, run courses and produce teaching materials. Universities and colleges offer in-service courses at all levels for those wishing to pursue their specialism in teaching RE. In schools where courses leading to public examinations are offered RE has a timetable allowance equal to other subjects, in addition to the 'statutory RE' period, but its place in an options scheme may not always make large numbers possible. In these ways the status of RE is being slowly enhanced.

In the quest for educational respectability among colleagues and classroom acceptability among adolescent pupils, RE teachers have often stressed the subject's relevance to life and issues such as war, sex, drugs and pollution have figured in schemes of work. Recognizing the value of relevance as a criterion, other subject areas took up similar themes and this led to new subjects such as humanities* and social studies* appearing on timetables. In some schools specialist RE teachers have been fully involved in these integrated schemes to produce educationally worthwhile courses, though in other schools the proper concerns of RE are no longer taught. A consequence of this has been a radical reappraisal of the role of RE whereby some advocate that other subject areas be left to explore the issues of contemporary social morality formerly regarded as an integral part of RE, while RE itself becomes more theological.

A common starting point in secondary schools is now some introduction to the nature and language of religion. This may move on to a consideration of the denominations and sects of Christianity and that, for example, religion touches family life in quite different but equally significant ways in a whole range of contemporary world faiths. The aim of such a syllabus is sympathetic understanding and also a degree of critical evaluation. In the 1960s neutrality* and objectivity were important concerns in secondary schooling; a teacher of RE whose pupils were not able to tell if he were a practising Christian or not was considered a success. Extreme neutrality and objectivity can easily be seen by adolescents as indifference and irrelevance, so the contemporary move is towards a kind of parliamentary 'declaration of interest' or to 'the explicit phenomenological approach'. This requires teachers to be clear and confident about their own beliefs and how they affect their lives both in and out of school. This is neither hidden from nor imposed upon the pupils but drawn upon by

both teacher and pupil to give concrete examples in open and exploratory dialogue.

At one time an important aim of RE was that pupils should be able to comprehend the biblical stories in terms of being able to follow the language and relate them to geographical and historical contexts in the Ancient Middle East. Modern translations, paraphrases and strip cartoon versions have made the Bible immediately accessible to nearly all: the television news, comment and documentaries have rendered much of the geographical context and contemporary issues a matter of general knowledge. RE can provide some of the historical and theological background necessary for a more complete appreciation of attitudes held and events which occur. In this way RE has been leading the way in a curricular response to an increasingly multicultural society. RE is now able to embark on a period in its history when at secondary school level, liberated from peripheral matters, it can make a significant contribution to the development in every young person of a genuine and practical philosophy of life and an informed, sympathetic understanding of those of his or her fellow human beings.

See also **Sixth Form.**

Edwin Cox, *Changing Aims in Religious Education,* Routledge & Kegan Paul 1966; Durham Report on Religious Education, *The Fourth R,* SPCK 1970; Ronald Goldman, *Religious Thinking from Childhood to Adolescence,* Routledge & Kegan Paul 1964; Harold Loukes, *Teenage Religion,* SCM Press 1961; Schools Council, *Journeys into Religion: Teachers' Handbook A,* Hart-Davis 1977; Schools Council Working Paper 36, *Religious Education in Secondary Schools,* Evans/ Methuen 1971.

DAVID SELLICK

Secularism

Writers like Paul Van Buren have drawn attention to the difficulty of providing a definition adequate to all this word has come to mean. For the purpose of this article, the following definition has been selected: 'the withdrawal of areas of thought and life from religious – and finally also from metaphysical – control, and the attempt to live and understand in these areas in the terms which they alone offer'. Secularism then is a process of change. How and when it originated and the extent of its influence on different societies have been variously argued, but its presence and power in present day Britain are not in dispute. As a social phenomenon, it can be discerned in the declining figures of membership of the major churches, the shrinking and aging congregations at public worship and a growing disuse of Christian rites to mark the solemn occasions of personal or public life. God – even the 'God of the gaps' – for many has no reality or perhaps, more accurately, no usefulness. The problems and mysteries of life are solved without other worldly reference. Many are ambivalent in this situation, holding sentimentally to some religious belief or practice, yet bringing nothing of this into their everyday concerns. There they share the common belief in scientific progress as the key to the good life and measure goodness itself in terms of personal material benefit. Yet such attitudes are seldom adopted as a result of intellectual or reasoned choice but rather through unconscious assimilation of a climate of opinion and a way of doing things which have gradually superseded other teaching and attitudes – some with a religious base – equally unconsciously accepted.

Inevitably, challenges to religion will affect RE. The 1944 Act in its religious provision envisaged a kind of Christendom, an essential equation of morality with the Christian ethic, and differed little from church catechesis. Such assumptions are no longer credible in the changed society, as some religious educators recognize. The school, itself is changing or subtly being changed, so that training for success in this life seems the hidden assumption of the curriculum rather than the church's expectation of an education for eternity. Yet, secularism produces no mass efforts to dislodge religion from the school and two of its aspects, pluralism and tolerance ('the children of secularism') help to strengthen its position in a new form. Tolerance means that different opinions have a right to co-exist. Pluralism recognizes diversity in society, and this latter principle finds religious support in the settlement in cities of immigrants whose religion is not Christian. So a religious education which can take account of these principles, rather than being authoritative and based on a single religion, can claim a place in the school and avoid the charges of indoctrina-

tion and proselytizing. The result has been new experiments with varied approaches, 'teaching that', 'education in', 'teaching how', 'teaching about', as detailed by Rummery in his *Catechetics and Religious Education*. Each approach is an honest endeavour to meet the pupils of a changing society with a religious education appropriate to a secular setting. Church education equally cannot be unmindful of secularism's challenge and of the need to produce an adequate response, as some churches are already trying to do.

M. Jarrett-Kerr, *The Secular Promise*, SCM Press 1964; R. M. Rummery, *Catechetics and Religious Education*, E. J. Dwyer, Sydney 1975; N. Smart, *Secular Education and The Logic of Religion*, Faber & Faber 1968; J. W. D. Smith, *Religious Education in a Secular Setting*, SCM Press 1969; R. Tucker, (ed). *Catholic Education in a Secular Society*, Sheed & Ward 1968.

JOHN GRAY

Sensitivity

'Sensitivity' is not used here in a technical, psychological sense but rather to suggest, on the one hand, the extent to which children and adolescents may be receptive to transcendental experiences all or some of which might be construed as religious and, on the other hand, the importance of religious educators in particular being alert to the existence of this dimension in the lives of young people. 'Transcendental' is a convenient word for all those experiences which transcend to a memorable extent *for the individual concerned* ordinary modes of thought, feeling, consciousness or perception so that they are felt to be on another plane. Some may be extravertive (Stace) and involve heightening to an extra-ordinary vividness ordinary sensory perceptions; others may be introvertive, even trance-like or ecsomatic states which are in Wordsworth's phrase, 'by form or image unprofaned'. Transcendental experiences are likely to be described by believers and, *faute de mieux*, by unbelievers in language highly charged with religious associations, though aesthetic overbeliefs are frequent as well as religious ones. Common triggers may include an impressive ceremony (not necessarily religious), a work of art such as a symphony or a natural phenomenon with no man-made expressive intention such as a sunset. Relatively *objective* considerations, the quality of performance of the symphony or the splendour of the sunset, seem less significant than the readiness of the *subject*; relaxation of mind and body either induced or resulting from tiredness or in convalescence may be conducive. Frequently, however, such experiences occur in the course of humdrum activities in ordinary surroundings. They are significantly more commonly described in both the published autobiographies and the questionnaire responses of people with well-developed creative interests and abilities and are often felt by them to be importantly associated with their creativity. Research suggests that among intelligent young people just under half the males and more than half the females (giving fifty-six per cent overall) will admit to and describe transcendental experiences which may occur at any age but are commonest around puberty.

For the religious educator the importance of transcendental experience is that it frequently represents the young person's deepest experiences of joy, awe, reverence, his most powerful intuitions of value and of meaningfulness in the universe, feelings which may have been absent from or only weakly present in religious observances. (Secular conversions to a Wordsworthian type of nature-mysticism were not a nineteenth-century phenomenon only.) It seems, then, that they could represent for many an essential germ from which moral and aesthetic as well as religious life begins to grow. Often they may have been repressed or forgotten for lack of a language in which they can be expressed and Maslow has found that they can be released beneficially into consciousness by simply talking approvingly about them. Reading with the young or putting in their way the work of those artists (in all media) who reach out beyond 'the loquacious level that rationalism inhabits' (William James) should be an equally obvious strategy.

See also **Transcendence**.

David Hay, *Exploring Inner Space*, Penguin Books 1982; Abraham H. Maslow, *Towards a Psychology of Being*, Van Nostrand 1962; *Religions, Values and Peak Experiences*, Ohio State University Press 1964; Michael Paffard, *Inglorious Wordsworths*, Hodder 1973; *The Unattended Moment*, SCM Press 1976; W. T. Stace, *Mysticism and Philosophy*, J. B. Lippincott, Philadelphia 1960.

MICHAEL PAFFARD

Shap Working Party on World Religions in Education

The Working Party is a registered charity which was founded in 1969 during a conference held at Shap Wells in the Lake District. One of the speakers at the original Shap conference was Professor Ninian Smart, who is now its president. His 'Lancaster approach' to religious studies had a considerable influence on the Working Party.

'Shap' encourages the sound teaching of world religions and religious studies at all levels of RE. Working Party sub-groups have concerned themselves with such areas as primary schools, secondary schools, examinations at 16+ and higher education, but its major impact has probably been upon individual teachers through in-service courses which it organizes, its information service, and its impact on the secondary school syllabus.

The Working Party has produced a number of books itself and publishes an annual *Mailing*. Its members have served as members of and consultants to agreed syllabus conferences and to the Open University, Schools Council and other bodies.

Working Party publications: W. Owen Cole (ed.), *World Religions, A Handbook for Teachers*, Commission for Racial Equality 1976; John Finel (ed.), *World Religions for CSE or 16 plus*, Shap 1974; John Hinnells (ed.), *Comparative Religion in Education*, Oriel Press 1972; J. Hinnells and E. Sharpe, *Hinduism*, Oriel Press 1972.

W. OWEN COLE

Sheffield Report

Sponsored by the University of Sheffield Institute of Education in 1956 and published in 1961. It sought to answer four questions: 1. What difference has been made in Religious Instruction by the introduction and revision of agreed syllabuses? 2. Was the effect of having to follow an agreed syllabus wholly beneficial? 3. What variations (i.e. selections) from agreed syllabuses happened in practice? 4. What happened to the doctrinal content of agreed syllabuses?

The report was prepared by 'practising teachers and others concerned with the conduct of schools' and by means of a survey focussed attention on the middle forms of secondary schools in various parts of the Institute's area. Preliminary discussion established the need for the survey to be thorough, and this was accomplished by means of a very carefully prepared set of questions addressed to 1,233 pupils aged fourteen and fifteen in all types of secondary school. The answers given showed that the standard of Religious Knowledge in the schools was very poor and that the wide spread which might have been expected across the whole ability range was not to be found. The report established also that very few teachers chose to take enough training in Religious Education to fit them for specialist posts and that agreed syllabuses were frequently no more than elaborate schemes of work.

In their recommendations the authors included improved initial training of specialist teachers, the encouragement of students to specialize in the teaching of RE courses organized by LEAs for non-specialist teachers, the appointment of more specialist inspectors and advisers, and increased research into the content and methods of RE.

KENNETH D. EXLEY

Sikhism

1. Philosophy of Education

The purpose of education is to impart knowledge and also to bring about changes in the attitudes of the people. Sikhism agrees with this twofold purpose of education, but does not however, favour the development of material or sectarian attitudes which divide man from man and nation from nation. It stands for world fellowship, peace and happiness. With Sikhism perfection of man, physical, moral and spiritual, is the goal and this can be achieved by the practise of certain religious and moral truths. Learning devoid of religious thought limits man to material things and consequently the Sikh Gurus encouraged spiritual orientation to education in order to check the unbalanced development of the human personality. 'An educated person, a scholar, or a seer is one, who puts the garland of God-remembrance round his neck,' said Guru Nanak (*Adi Granth* 938).

Etymologically the word 'Sikh' means a learner, i.e. one who endeavours to educate himself throughout his life. Illiteracy and ignorance are the social evils while education and knowledge are the source of illumination: 'the man of unenlightened mind is blind, groping in the dark like worms crawling in offal' (AG 116) and only 'through enlightenment the mind loves truth' (AG 128).

Guru Nanak enkindled the spirit of inquiry among his followers and encouraged critical analysis of traditional ideas. 'God is served through wisdom and through wisdom alone one attains honour' (AG 1245) was his advice to the people groaning under the weight of indolent priestcraft and meaningless religious ceremonies. He created a new class of people with a rational outlook on life and its problems. The state that led people to accept stereotype knowledge and age-old conventions unquestioningly had no part to play in the concept of education propagated by Guru Nanak and his successors.

The Sikh Gurus stressed the importance of knowledge together with truth and wisdom. This could be achieved by a threefold process of observation, listening and reading: 'When the lamp is lit darkness is dispelled. Similarly by reading the religious books evil-mindedness is destroyed' (AG 791). Learning and enlightenment must go together hand in hand, knowledge is rightly called power, but this power has to be harnessed for productive purposes with the aid of reason and wisdom. The man who can yoke them together is really the wise man: 'One realizes what one reads, only through wisdom' (AG 1245). Book learning is therefore not synonymous with wisdom. Mere acquisition of knowledge or storage of factual data sometimes makes one proud and an egotist:

The scholars study more and more to gain knowledge.

But they use it for vain discussions (AG 152) and 'He who wastes his wisdom in strife is not to be called wise.' (AG 1245). Hence reading for reading's sake without practical realization of knowledge seems to be a meaningless venture. As a matter of fact,

The more one reads and writes

The more agitated one becomes (AG 467). There is no dearth of learned men, but there are 'very few who contemplate on what they learn' (AG 413). 'He who reflects upon himself is truly learned' (AG 152). Learning depends not upon the amount or variety of one's reading but on the capacity for reflection while reading. A Gyani or a learned person is therefore one who has realized himself and practises what he preaches and, on the other hand, 'An educated person who is greedy, avaricious and vain is to be termed a fool' (AG 140).

The role of a teacher therefore, should be to awaken the spiritual depths in man; 'That teacher alone is educated who enlightens his mind with divine knowledge and gives such instruction to his disciples,' (AG 937) said Guru Nanak. Man is blessed with the light of reason and endowed with power to change his mental state and physical environments. The education that fails to make him into a civilized human being, conscious of his moral and social responsibilities then has no meaning for mankind. 'The literate and the illiterate will be judged hereafter by their deeds' (AG 469). It should not stop short of training of the mind but should include the refinement of character as well. An educated person is expected to be honest in dealings, humble of speech and full of compassion for the needy and naked. For Guru Nanak 'sweetness and humility are the essence of all virtues' (AG 470). 'It is the ethical living of a Sikh that is dear to me and not his being a Sikh' said Guru Gobind Singh. 'He alone is really learned who does good to others' (AG 356).

Righteousness, justice, compassion for the weak and other virtues are not only to be practised in private but should be a feature of society. If learning is a process by which a person through his own activity changes his behaviour then the inculcation of moral and spiritual truths is sure to save him from falling into the snares of evil. 'Truth is higher than everything but higher still is truthful living' (AG 62).

2. Teaching of Sikhism in schools

Religion has been an important factor in the development of human culture and civilization. It is the source of moral insight and ethical action of the individual. Its teachings lend stability to the communal life and its institutions and to the development of individual personality. The exclusion of religion from the school curriculum would therefore amount to neglecting a significant area of human thought and activity. Public education has an obligation to fulfil the vital cultural, intellectual and spiritual aspirations of the people.

In a country having a plurality of faiths national unity requires that RE must include the study of Judaism, Islam, Hinduism, Buddhism and Sikhism along with Christianity. In most multi-racial areas some of the suspicion and misunderstanding which exists between the various sections of the community is perhaps due to their ignorance of the religious and cultural heritage of the people who have made Britain their home. If racial harmony is to be achieved, religious and cultural differences have to be known, for knowing is halfway to understanding.

Each tradition has its distinctive features which should not be concealed. The teacher's aim should be to promote a spirit of understanding and mutual respect among pupils who recognize that differences exist, and to enable the pupils to live with them. Much racism stems from religion. The school should be one of the places where accurate, unbiased learning can take place. Sikhism is a popular subject in schools and colleges of higher education, but has still to find a significant place in British universities. Syllabus content is usually related to two areas of Sikhism. The first is tangible, the Gurdwara and its worship, the lives of the Gurus, the Sikh way of life including diet and clothing. The second must be left for the later years of a child's education but should not be neglected, for it is the essence of Sikhism. It is Sikh belief about God, the nature of man, and the way of liberation. It should also include a study of Sikh ethics.

Where a school includes Sikh children their parents would want the religion to be taught for reasons of self esteem. If a child never hears his own culture mentioned he may be inclined to conclude that it is not worth knowing about. Elsewhere Sikhs would ask for its inclusion because it is a world religion, the fourth most numerous faith in Britain, after Christianity, Judaism and Islam. Its concept of Guruship way of worship and the place of the scripture in Sikhism are distinctive features requiring examination in any course of religious studies.

3. Teaching within the Sikh Community

There are about a quarter of a million Sikhs scattered in the various industrial towns in the UK. This is perhaps their biggest concentration in any country outside India. They are now well settled and have little thought of ever going back to India or migrating elsewhere. Basically the Sikhs are very devout and have now established Gurdwaras (communal places of worship) in most large towns. Sikh families attend Gurdwara services on Sunday mornings. Some Sikhs go daily to the evening services held in the Gurdwaras. The Sikh community has therefore more than enough opportunities of listening to the sermons and Kirtan (hymn singing). The Gurdwara is also more a social centre in the UK than in India and East Africa where social functions such as weddings, are not arranged in Gurdwaras. In spite of a higher incidence of Gurdwara attendance and greater number of religious cum social functions, there is a danger of Gurdwara services losing their appeal and becoming stereotyped. More emphasis is laid on hymn singing than on the exposition of the scripture or the serious discussion of the relevance of Sikhism to the life in twentieth-century Britain. The custom of opening the scripture at random and preaching extemporarily persists. Rarely will an expositor choose his text beforehand and then build round it a sermon for the edification of his congregation. Outward symbols of faith often seem more important than inward purity and at a time of crisis their lack of inner conviction and hollow piety often leads to the abandonment of the very faith of which the outward forms are only the emblems. Any apostasy among the British Sikhs perhaps stems from their ignorance of their religion and culture. Gurdwaras might be criticized for serving more as places of social gatherings and less for the dissemination of the religious principles and ethics on which the Sikh way of life is based.

Home is the cradle of the children's religious education. Attitudes within the home and society at large influence the unformed minds of the young. Life in the highly industrialized Western society is extremely fast and poses peculiar hardships for settlers from Asia. Manual jobs, awkward hours of work, coupled with the need for overtime earnings leave no time for many to relax and exchange ideas with children. Keeping to the Indian ideals of early rising and meditation becomes difficult.

In the Punjab where most of the activities of everyday life take place in the open, children imbibe religious habit by watching their parents and others going about their religious observances. Their actual participation in the routine activities of life at home and in the community enables them to pick up the rudiments of their cultural behaviour as they grow up. In a joint family system children spend most of their time under the care of their grandparents and as such the chances of their going astray or acquiring bad habits are minimized. All these factors which influence the formation of habit and character in the early stages of life are conspicuous by their absence in the new setting. Under the changed situation the option left with the community is to revive the ancient role of the Gurdwara for instructing the religion to the younger generation. Most of the Gurdwaras have already started weekend classes for the teaching of the Gurmukhi language in which the Sikh scriptures are written. Occasionally groups of young Sikhs are also seen performing kirtan in the Gurdwaras. The process could be speeded up if English were the medium adopted for teaching Sikhism to the young for whom it has become a second mother tongue.

Gurdwaras naturally have a responsibility for meeting the needs of those who first came to Britain and established them. However, the unchanged services are becoming linguistically and culturally remote from young people whose orientation and interests are British not Indian, and contemporary rather than the issues which faced the Sikhs three centuries ago. Concern for the younger generation must include the application of Sikh theology and ideals to the world in which they are growing up.

W. Owen Cole, *Thinking about Sikhism,* Lutterworth 1980; W. Owen Cole and Piara Singh Sambhi, *The Sikhs,* Routledge & Kegan Paul 1978; Piara Singh Sambhi, *Understanding your Sikh Neighbour,* Lutterworth 1980.

P. S. SAMBHI

Simulation   *see* **Games**

Sixth-Form

This is the description given to the final stage of secondary education in England and Wales for pupils over sixteen years of age who wish to continue in full-time general education for a further period of between one and three years. Many sixth-forms operate an open-access admissions procedure offering a variety of courses leading to 'A' level, 'O' level, CSE, or certification by examining bodies like the City and Guilds of London Institute and the Royal Society of Arts. The main criteria of entry into such sixth-forms is the suitability of courses offered to the requirements of the student rather than a general entry requirement based on a specified number of 'O' levels.

Provision for sixth-form education is extremely varied, ranging from the traditional pattern in secondary schools to sixth-form colleges and tertiary colleges but also including 'mushroom' sixth-forms, sixth-form centres and consortia of local schools. The most notable recent development has been the emergence of the sixth-form college where all sixth-form work in a given area is concentrated. In some localities provision remains more traditional, the sixth-form being the upper forms of the secondary schools. A sixth-form centre, providing teaching and social facilities, is often a feature of such schools and it may well cater for sixth-formers from a number of local schools, but without the independence and control over the curriculum exercised by a sixth-form college. 'Mushroom' sixth-forms concentrate all sixth-form work in one school, students from other schools joining it at sixteen. Where individual schools wish to retain sixth-forms but are unable to offer a full range of courses a local consortium may be set up to ensure adequate provision for sixth-form education in a given area. The tertiary college caters for all students over the age of sixteen whether following vocational or general education courses on a full-time or part-time basis. Students in the sixteen to nineteen age group are not usually referred to as sixth-formers in such colleges.

The sixth-form curriculum has become more varied in recent years, in part due to the requirements of students who are not following the traditional route through the sixth-form to university. RE at this level reflects these changes and other developments in the subject. Examination syllabuses now include world religions options and many sixth-forms offer courses in the major world religions at examination and non-examination level. Some have taken the opportunity under the examination boards' mode three provision to design courses which have a particular relevance in their own locality where there may be a substantial ethnic minority representing one of the major faiths. New interest has thus been generated in Islam* and Sikhism*, though a study of world religions in the sixth-form is not confined to such areas. Many sixth-forms continue to offer courses based on biblical studies and church history with the possibility of running a variety of options where numbers permit.

In an attempt to avoid over-specialization at this level (a constant criticism over the years) most sixth-forms have a general studies programme offering a variety of courses, usually non-examined, designed to broaden the education of students. RE may contribute to such a programme either as a discrete discipline or in combination with others to present an integrated general studies programme which may cover religion, the arts, literature, history and the sciences and thus enable students to gain some understanding of religion within a broad framework of study.

Moral education may form part of a general studies programme or of a course specifically designed to consider beliefs and values in contemporary society, the aim being to give mature consideration to moral issues rather than to impose any one view on students. RE staff often play a major part in planning and presenting such courses.

Teaching styles at sixth-form level can be adapted to the greater maturity and commitment of students so that less emphasis need be given to expository teaching and students are encouraged to learn through wider reading, research and discussion. The general aim of RE at this level is to give to students a more detailed knowledge based upon the intellectual disciplines required in the study of the subject, to encourage a more mature understanding of the place of religion in human culture and contemporary life and to contribute to their own personal search for meaning.

Frank Earl (ed.), *Aims and Objectives in Religious Education,* Schools Council 1977; Rupert King, *The English Sixth-Form College,* Pergamon Press 1968; Eric Macfarlane, *Sixth-Form Colleges,* Heinemann 1971; Schools Council Working Paper 36, *Religious Education in Secondary Schools,* Evans/Methuen 1971.

FRANK EARL

Skills

RE involves pupils not only in the attainment of knowledge and understanding, but also in the acquisition and deployment of skills and attitudes*. Indeed one of the distinctive features of RE is the wide range of skills deployed, some basic to all learning, some required elsewhere in the curriculum, while a few are peculiar to RE. An 'O' or 'A' Level pass in RE can therefore be presented to employers as a useful qualification.

Whatever else may be involved, integral to a skill is the notion of an ability or aptitude acquired through training and practice: but there is no consensus on the classification and description of skills, which may be manual, cognitive, affective and social *inter alia*. Skills cannot be grouped into tidy and watertight compartments: some skills may belong to more than one category, depending on the perspectives from which they are viewed. 'Social skills' is a phrase to which a number of different meanings may be given. The following analysis of skills makes no claims to be definitive. It implies a wide variety of teaching and learning methods, backed by ample resources.

1. *Heuristic skills.* These are the ability to (*a*) make observations and calculations; (*b*) read and find references; (*c*) listen carefully to information and procedures to be followed, when these are given orally; (*d*) classify, i.e. gather observations/data into appropriate classes; (*e*) appreciate sequences; (*f*) form a hypothesis that can be tested in experience or against previous (supposed) knowledge or understanding; (*g*) ask questions for a variety of heuristic reasons (e.g. to obtain (more) information; to clarify information or procedures already given; to help classify or appreciate sequences).

These skills are widely used in the acquisition of knowledge (e.g. in the natural and social sciences) and without them other skills (e.g. interpretative, communicative and critical skills) cannot be deployed. To acquire these skills in RE, or any subject, the use of primary sources and discovery methods is required. In RE they are necessary for understanding a faith that is unfamiliar.

2. *Interpretative skills.* These are used in the attempt to understand the meaning of data, however presented, for example, in documents, maps, photographs, graphs, charts or diagrams. They include the ability to: (*a*) arrange information (1(*d*), 1(*e*)), construct a hypothesis (which may involve the use of the imagination) cf. 1(*f*) and avoid the confusion of classes or class-concepts (this skill is basic to the two which follow).

(*b*) To grasp that all data are presented, not raw or neutral, but already arranged or ordered in a particular way (i.e. are already to some extent 'interpreted'): in consequence to realize that there is no simple distinction between raw, uninterpreted data and subjective interpretation, for all data tend to be presented from, or to support, a point of view, or both: this cognitive skill is compatible with the continual striving of the interpreter to reach a view nearer the truth.

(*c*) To reflect on one's experience at depth in order to understand/appreciate others' experience and how they interpret it (i.e. their concepts and symbols) (this skill is basic to the next).

(*d*) To appreciate the pre-conceptions, perspectives, points of view, interpretative-categories and techniques of others, including a perspective etc. that one does not share.

(*e*) To distinguish between a sign, which usually stands for one concrete idea and a symbol, which stands for several ideas, some of which are abstract, and to appreciate that what in some contexts is a sign (e.g. the cross as a sign of Christianity) may in others be a symbol (e.g. the cross as a symbol of what Christians believe about the death and resurrection of Jesus).

These skills are among the most difficult to acquire, and may not be acquired until college or university level, yet some attempt must be made to develop them in pupils, since all religions are interpretations of life and experience. Within every living religion there tends to be a range of interpretation, which it would be wise to communicate to senior pupils.

3. *Communicative skills.* This is the ability to present information in a lucid, sequential and intelligible manner, for example by (*a*) drawing, painting or modelling as in plasticine; (*b*) mapping, making charts, diagrams, graphs, collages and scale-models; (*c*) speaking or joining in discussion, including asking questions to communicate something; (*d*) role-play (which can also be an interpretative and an evaluative skill); (*e*) factual or imaginative writing.

To acquire these skills is for the pupil to 'participate in his own learning processes': the attempt to communicate often improves one's heuristic and interpretative skills, however much communicative skills are logically dependent on them. In RE these skills are used when, for example, in project work, drama, music, pupils make concrete the actions, customs and places associated with religions, or when, by the use of work-sheets or any of the above means, pupils attempt to communicate some aspect of a religion and so grasp its meaning more clearly.

4. *Critical skills.* These are the ability to: (*a*) weigh evidence and assess arguments (cf.2(a)); (*b*) allow for prejudice and detect stereotyped descriptions; (*c*) appreciate the distinctions made by others; (*d*) make valid distinctions oneself; (*e*) form reasoned opinions based on evidence weighed and sifted (beliefs); (*f*) distinguish such a belief from both mathematical proof and 'blind' belief; (*g*) recognize conceptual confusion (e.g. 'squaring the circle' or when the same term is used with different meanings but without that fact being recognized), and the difference between a puzzle (where concepts need clarification) and a problem (where further knowledge is required).

Such skills are associated with science and philosophy in the universities, but they are no less applicable to RE in school. Pupils continually ask for religious beliefs to be proved when they are failing to make the distinction in 4(*f*) above. There is conceptual confusion when it is assumed – too readily at least – that when Buddhists teach the *anatta*-doctrine, they are denying the same self or ego which Western psychologists describe and discuss, or when there is failure to appreciate that in Hinduism the way of escape from the wheel of rebirths, the way known as *karma*, is quite different

from the law of *karma*, which binds one to that same wheel.

5. *Affective and social skills.* Different groups identify different social skills, for example, to the home economics teacher, it may be making a meal, in health education, brushing one's teeth and taking a bath, to employers, it may be the ability to relate to others and to get on with them, or it may be the ability to fit into a group, including the appreciation of how groups function, that is quite differently from individuals acting on their own.

To these, RE adds its own list of desirable social skills and attitudes, among which are: (*a*) the ability to exercise empathy, that is to make an imaginative identification with the points of view, actions and needs of other individuals and groups, including the adherents of different religions (cf.2(*d*)); (*b*) this ability implies the *attitude* of respect for the person, that is the acceptance of others for what they are in themselves as persons, and not for their attainments, beliefs or goodness; (*c*) this in turn implies the *attitude* of tolerance and the ability to exercise it: that is, being prepared to struggle for the right of others to hold and express an opinion/view one does not share, an attitude consonant with being committed oneself to one's own view and with being willing to subject that view and the views of others to critical scrutiny (are there limits to what even a liberal society can deem acceptable, e.g. the National Front, Scientology, the Moonies?).

If the kind of RE assumed here implies respect for the person, it must imply at least the quest for self-respect and self-esteem, that is the acceptance of oneself as having a worth or value which is not dependent on how others value oneself.

6. *Evaluative and moral skills.* The ability to: (*a*) make value judgments backed by appropriate reasons (i.e. appropriate e.g. to aesthetics, economics, morality and religion) cf.4(*e*); (*b*) distinguish between a moral rule (e.g. 'Do no murder') and a moral principle (e.g. justice as fairness, consideration for others); (*c*) act on moral judgments made in the light of values held; (*d*) take the initiative and exercise responsible choice, without waiting to be told either to take action or what action to take.

It is assumed that we cannot engage in RE

without also engaging in moral education* and that the affective, social and moral skills are learned as pupils grapple with many human situations where it may be difficult to decide what is the right course of action.

The same is true, *mutatis mutandis,* of all these skills: difficult they may be to acquire and practise, but they can be acquired only as pupils engage with a vast amount of material, not all of it in the RE classroom, where to gain knowledge and understanding calls for their deployment.

See also **Affectivity; Cognitive Education in RE.**

IAN C. M. FAIRWEATHER

Slow Learners

Slow learners are the fifteen to twenty per cent of pupils making least satisfactory progress in their school work. Percentages will vary from school to school. Such pupils are to be found in all schools, not simply in special schools.

For too long slow learners have been treated as a problem in RE. Kenneth Hyde's 1969 research study *Religion and Slow Learners* has not been followed up as the author might have hoped. Difficulties in understanding abstract religious concepts and linguistic problems in coping with religious language have been overstressed. Some narrow differentiated programmes for slow learners have excluded them from vital aspects of religion.

A more positive approach begins by acknowledging that different overall aims in RE are not needed for slow learners. An understanding of religion does not depend upon high intellectual capacity. There is a wealth of experience through which religion can be conveyed, so that slow learners need not be at a disadvantage.

To seize this opportunity teachers need to re-examine relationships and attitudes. Meaningful relationships and encouraging but non-sentimental expectation by the teacher of pupil performance are essential. More time and imagination must be given to distinguishing the core of knowledge, skills and attitudes from those aspects of religious understanding which will remain on the periphery of awareness.

The quality of the environment in which slow learners are taught reflects the value placed on learner and subject. Drab classrooms or display boards monopolized by work from more able pupils speak for themselves. Readiness to listen to and accept the pupils' contribution in a colloquial style can encourage self esteem and lead to modest advances in using and understanding religious language.

A rich variety of experiences can be introduced at a concrete level of operations if teachers pay more than lip service to the value of a learning situation which is as multi-sensory as possible. Story and myth, ritual and symbolism, mime and role play, movement and music, painting and puppetry, poster and photography, artwork and artefact, visits and visitors offer enriching entries into religious meaning. No teacher of RE is equally at home with such a variety of teaching styles, but an approach which uses all the senses can lead to profound pupil insights. Teacher colleagues with other skills have much to offer, especially those who have been trained to teach slow learners.

Mixed ability classes are common in primary schools and are often presumed appropriate for slow learners taking RE in secondary schools. After visiting over five hundred schools, the Schools Council project team which produced *Curricular Needs of Slow Learning Pupils* acknowledged the merits of mixed ability teaching for pupils making normal progress, but 'they had not observed the curricular needs of slow learners being satisfactorily met within this kind of school organisation'. They found that successful departments in primary and secondary schools 'were invariably marked by a high proportion of class teaching providing prolonged pupil-teacher contact with continuity of curriculum and teaching methods'. If the individual slow learner is not to be lost in the group every RE teacher requires careful organization, interesting presentation and adequate contact time.

Wilfred K. Brennan, *Shaping the Education of Slow Learners*, Kegan Paul 1974; Violet R. Bruce, *Awakening the Slower Mind*, Pergamon 1969; Kenneth E. Hyde, *Religion and Slow Learners*, SCM Press 1969; Schools Council, Working Paper 63, *Curricular Needs of Slow Learners* Evans/Methuen Educational 1979.

IAN WRAGG

Social Education

In traditional societies social education was accomplished through religion. Such societies functioned on an agreed religious basis. The answers to life's fundamental questions, the nature of the universe, man and society were delineated through the religion of the community and universally accepted. The prevailing culture rested on this base. All the many matters in the cycles of personal and social life were worked out accordingly.

The child's earliest socialization was through participation in family life which, as time passed, broadened into sharing in the life of the wider society. To be a member of a family and society meant sharing its faith. Where formal education existed this articulated, in intellectual categories, both the religious beliefs and social values derived from these beliefs.

Presuppositions of this nature underlie the provisions in the 1944 Education Act for religious instruction. The school was to continue the child's socialization into Protestant Christianity already begun by home and church. Provision was made for those coming from homes and communities not sharing these beliefs to withdraw from this part of the curriculum.

In recent decades many Western societies have undergone change towards secularization. In such societies considerable personal autonomy is possible. Roles in such societies tend to be achieved rather than ascribed. There is freedom of public and private lifestyle. Preparation for entry to adult society has altered accordingly. In schools, social education is replacing RE as the means used to prepare children for life in society. Schools have introduced courses with titles such as 'Personal and social development' and 'Life skills' in order to achieve this. The task of socialization has, therefore, become widely based in schools.

RE, however, still has a key role in ensuring that the ultimate questions in life are dealt with, that the place of personal religious commitment is understood and that an open attitude to other life-styles, cultures and religions is fostered.

T. Luckman, *The Invisible Religion*, Macmillan 1967; J. Marvell, 'Durkheim and the transformation of religious education', *Journal of Beliefs and Values*, 1, 4, 1980.

JOHN MARVELL

Social Issues

One of the most frequently stated aims of the *whole* curriculum is that pupils should, as a consequence of the experience of education, develop a mature understanding of the world in which they are living. In seeking to justify the place of RE in such a curriculum it is argued rightly that pupils will achieve no such understanding if prevented from seriously studying the religious sources of so much that is problematic to man in society. In our own time a pupil cannot begin to understand events in Ireland, Poland, the Middle East, Central Africa and Latin America unless an attempt is made to give him access to the religious dimension of individual and communal life.

The Crowther Report* used a phrase about the concerns of education as a whole which is sometimes quoted to support RE in schools, 'The teenagers with whom we are concerned need, perhaps above all else, to find a faith to live by.' RE has a distinctive contribution to make here in examining the consequences of finding a faith by which to live. The action in society of persons and groups who are adherents of the major world faiths is properly the concern of the religious educator. It is for these main reasons that social issues have always featured in RE syllabuses.

The approach through social issues is frequently associated with the name of Harold Loukes and sometimes described as a methodology which was tried and failed during the 1960s. This is an unfortunate criticism which fails to acknowledge the weight of the research carried out by Loukes and published in his book *Teenage Religion*. Loukes sought the views of pupils receiving RE and found them severely critical of much that syllabuses contained. The pupils argued that the subject should relate to those aims we have mentioned in particular taking up issues of personal relations, personal responsibility and problems of meaning. Such topics as, authority, friendship, sex, marriage and divorce, money, work, leisure, suffering and death, were repeatedly mentioned by pupils as being vital.

To suggest that this approach has been tried

and found wanting is not supported by evidence recruited from classroom practice. Certain agreed syllabuses produced in the late 1960s, for example those of Lancashire, *Religion and Life*, and the Inner London Education Authority, *Learning for Life*, attempted to digest the work of Loukes. But this trend was very much in its infancy when the phenomenological approach* of the Schools Council began to be the predominant influence in syllabus making. The popularity of syllabuses at CSE and 'O' Level dealing with 'Christian Responsibility' is perhaps the most significant echo of the work begun by Loukes.

It is of interest that the 1980s seem likely to generate a renewed interest in the place of theology as opposed to religious studies in teaching RE. A weakness of the work attempted in the wake of Harold Loukes work was that most teachers of the subject had a training which was predominantly historical or doctrinal. The task of introducing pupils to the distinctive skills and concepts involved in theologizing about life remains to be undertaken. Unless and until pupils acquire some of these skills it is difficult to grasp how empathy with one who has found a faith by which to live might be achieved.

Harold Loukes, *Teenage Religion*, SCM Press 1961.

IAN H. BIRNIE

Social Morality Council

Established in 1966 to provide a forum for joint study and action on moral issues by religious believers and non-believers. A registered charity, it states its object in the following terms: 'to promote morality in all aspects of the life of the community'. To do so it aims to bring a broad cross section of opinion to bear on controversial issues of our time. Membership is drawn from the major Christian denominations, other world faiths present in Britain and from humanists.

In 1970, United Nations International Education Year, the Council published a significant report entitled, *Moral and Religious Education in County Schools*. More recently and with support from the DES it has worked to develop moral education in primary and secondary schools. In 1980 a resource and information centre was established at St Martin's College, Lancaster and a

regional adviser was appointed to pioneer work with a number of education authorities. The *Journal of Moral Education* is published under the auspices of the Council.

IAN H. BIRNIE

Social Studies

In the school curriculum in England and Wales, social studies has gone through a process of development and change since World War II. In the 1940s social studies took the form of civics; in the 1950s the emphasis on child-centred teaching saw a shift towards Local Studies; in the 1960s social studies appeared as a title in its own right, with a focus of interest upon 'life' issues; in the 1970s it gave way to an approach better described as social science. 'The new social studies' therefore refers to the relatively recent attempt to distil and amalgamate the insights of sociology, economics, anthropology, psychology, social psychology and politics and to apply these to topics for classroom study.

It should be noted that in the 1960s a special opportunity occurred for RE and social studies to integrate if not to merge, but since that time both disciplines have become more distinct and have moved some distance apart.

Comparison with the situation in the USA is useful. There, social studies has had a long and accredited place in the curriculum and features a simplified sociological core. RE is not allowed in American public schools and therefore social studies has tended to avoid religious issues.

In England and Wales, the social science teacher will introduce pupils to the application of social science principles across a wide spectrum of social life in different societies. So far as religious issues are concerned, the teacher will be concerned to do three things: 1. to encourage awareness of the religious factor as a significant element in human life; 2. to encourage the responsible analysis of statistics relating to those who express or otherwise demonstrate religious commitment or association; 3. to encourage a fair and balanced study of such critiques of the religious factor by well-known social scientists, such as Freud and Marx, together with contrary opinions, such as those of Jung and Durkheim.

The social science teacher will expect the subject of RE to be dealt with from a qualitatively different point of view – including, for example, more room for the affective dimension. Religious literature concerned with a responsible life-style and the concern among teachers of RE for 'critical openness' forms a natural bridge for curriculum co-operation between RE and SS.

ATSS submission in *Views on RE*, Religious Education Council of England and Wales 1981; J. Bradford, 'Religious Education and Social Science', *The Social Science Teacher* 7, 1, October 1977; 'Teaching the Sociology of Religion – A Sequential Approach', *The Social Science Teacher* 11, 1, Autumn 1981; D. Gleeson and G. Whitty, *Developments in Social Studies Teaching*, Open Books 1976; D. Lawton and B. Dufour, *The New Social Studies*, Heinemann 1973.

JOHN BRADFORD

Socialization

The process by which someone learns the patterns of a group of which he is a member. Applied to the child, it includes learning the expectations of behaviour, thought, and sentiments appropriate to his culture. Although these patterns vary considerably both among and within societies, we assume the basic learning processes for the child are everywhere the same. Socialization occurs in interaction with others who define for the child what they consider right and proper. The child learns skills, identifies with role models, establishes emotionally significant relationships, and develops an image of and feelings towards himself. The agents of socialization invariably include the immediate family members and, depending on the context, other relatives, teachers, peers, literary and television heroes, clergy, and others. In learning such patterns as language, the skills of a job, the expected behaviour in given roles, and feelings appropriate for given occasions, the child is not a passive recipient; rather, from his very infancy, he initiates activities, and subsequently he comes to define and interpret both his own behaviour and the behaviour of others. Socialization is a developmental process, building upon a biological inheritance and the patterns that have already developed. Some socialization is anticipatory, preparing for roles to be played later in life; some in later years, as in conversions, involves

resocialization, the surrender of previous roles and the learning of new ones.

Religious socialization, in the broad sense of education in morals and values, is part of every child's socialization. Kohlberg, following Piaget, describes three idealized hierarchical and sequential levels in moral development, from an early egocentric concern with punishment, to a concern with approval and adaptation to a conventional order, to the development of conscience and a set of universal principles over and above any immediate ordained social rules. In a narrower sense, religious socialization refers to those patterns learned within particular religions and churches. Children are given the religious affiliation of their parents and usually, under the direction of the family, are exposed to a single set of beliefs and practices which offer affinity within their own religious group and set them apart from others. The beliefs and practices which the child learns extend beyond the religious doctrine of the church itself and may include attitudes and behaviours associated with work, political questions, child-rearing, sex, money and social relationships. The religious influence on both personality and attitudes is likely to last beyond childhood, especially when it is strongly supported by a close solidarity group and other institutions in the community. Critical social experiences in a person's daily life, however, may bring about a readiness to change, leading to new forms of religious participation. Religious socialization always includes an emphasis on feelings and sentiments and, accordingly, all churches, to one degree or another, employ rituals and ceremonies imbued with emotional and symbolic meanings. For the child, no other device is likely to be as meaningful.

John A. Clausen, (ed.) *Socialization and Society*, Little Brown 1968; James E. Dittes, 'Psychology of Religion', *Handbook of Social Psychology*, vol. 5, Addison-Wesley [2]1969; Frederick Elkin and Gerald Handel, *Child and Society*, Random House [3]1978; Lawrence Kohlberg, 'Development of Moral Character and Moral Ideology,' *Review of Child Development Research* 1, ed. Martin L. Hoffman and Lois W. Hoffman, Russell Sage Foundation 1964; 'Education, Moral Development and Faith', *Journal of Moral Education* 4,

1974; Gerhard Lenski, *The Religious Factor*, Doubleday 1961; *Religious Education*, 75, 2, March-April 1980.

F. ELKIN

Society of Friends   *see* **Religious Society of Friends**

Sociology of Religion

The study of religions provided a dominant interest for the fathers of modern sociology. A classic among their writings was Emile Durkheim's encyclopaedic *Les Formes Elémentaires de la Vie Religieuse* (1912), an anthropological treatise of non-European religions which proceeded from the Darwinian assumption that the evaluation of religion can be traced in the practice of contemporary primitive societies. Durkheim stands within the positivist tradition and his interpretations do not admit supernatural accounts except as sociological phenomena. This tradition has caused many believers to view with suspicion the contribution of sociology as a discipline liable to weaken the foundations of religious faith. But Durkheim also offered an appreciation of religious practice in its provision of the symbols of cultural integration within a society.

The contribution of Karl Marx* is more explicitly polemical though less systematic in his application. Like Durkheim after him. Marx conducted his studies within an evolutionary frame and had occasion to examine the political features of ancient societies as manifest in contemporary examples. He concluded that religion was an illusory happiness and that religious hope had the function of dissipating action for social change in the present world: in a celebrated phrase in his 'Critique of Hegel's Philosophy of Right', he dismissed religion as 'the opium of the people'. The effects of religion upon revolutionary consciousness and zeal were explored further by Lenin and survive in neo-marxist thought in the analysis of the state. Louis Althusser, for example, classifies 'the system of different churches' and 'the system of different public and private "Schools" ' as 'ideological state apparatuses'.

A further seminal contribution in the analysis of religion in terms of its effect or function is the thesis developed by the German sociologist Max Weber (1864–1920) that protestantism – particularly its Calvinistic variants – substituted a major factor in the development of a capitalist ethic characterized by economic rationality, thrift, deferred gratification, taboos upon personal indulgence and so on.

In the twentieth century the work of the early positivists and functionalists has been subjected to scrutiny, criticism and empirical testing. Weber is widely thought to have overstated his case. Much work has been preoccupied with the variable of social class. There have been diligent studies of particular religious organizations, noteworthy among which is the work of the British sociologist Bryan Wilson. More recently, the attentions of sociologists have been turned to new religious movements such as Scientology and the Unification Church. However, the overriding theme in recent years has been secularization: this has been a preoccupation not only in the West, where it has culminated in David Martin's *General Theory,* but also in communist societies such as Poland where discrepant findings have been published within the respective communist and Catholic schools.

A significant current among sociologists applying themselves to religious affairs is the tradition of *sociologie religieuse* formerly dominant (but now unfashionable) in France, where it is associated principally with the work of Gabriel le Bras. As distinct from the sociology of religion, religious sociology operates in the service of a religious community and its agenda is directed by the religious hierarchy. Latterly, sociologists have departed from this tradition by asserting independence to define problems and investigate them sociologically.

The potential contribution of sociology to religious education is twofold. First, the methods, concepts and insights of sociologists have a role to play in enhancing an understanding of the effectiveness and functions of RE and in locating these within a broader social context. Second, some of the concerns of sociologists are transferable with varying degrees of adaptation as contents in the school curriculum.

The first of these contributions has doubtless been under employed, not least because latent sociologists of RE have not had a Piaget to write a clear agenda of scientific investigations. A scholarly exception is the survey reported in Harold Loukes' *New Ground in*

Christian Education (1965). The role played by religous institutions in the general process of socialization, whether independently or through the provision of opportunities in schools, lends itself to a careful sociological examination that has barely been undertaken. In the comparable field of political socialization and political education, there has been extensive research on the relative efficiency of primary agencies, the roles of voluntary organizations, the sources of awareness and the intensity of commitment. Much of this work has been done in the USA where Herbert Hyman, Easton and Dennis, Hess and Torney, and Fred Greenstein have provided leading studies. As a consequence of this neglect, the observations of Marx are simplified in Althusser and so they remain: in the analyses of 'schooling' which currently dominate the sociology of education in the Western world and which are generated in Great Britain by the Open University, RE is too commonly overlooked.

As subject matter and method in the study of religion, however, sociology has made rather more impact, both in schools and in higher education.

In recent years a number of factors have favoured the adoption of sociology and cognate disciplines in the school curriculum. The variety of religious alternatives in such pluralist societies as post-war Britain affords a detached view of religions as sociological phenomena. Sociological perceptions of religious behaviour lend themselves with ease to the increasingly favoured activity methods of classroom discussion and drama and to survey and fieldwork practice. At the same time, educationists have been wanting to explore the special opportunities of interdisciplinary approaches: RE in schools has frequently been integrated with other humanities subjects and the topics that have been chosen for co-operative study have been those in which each of the contributory subjects have shared an interest: accordingly, the ancient myths of the Judaeo-Christian tradition, which featured prominently in the early agreed syllabuses of RE have tended to give way to themes drawn from the modern world. The notions of 'interest' and 'relevance', which John Dewey established as desiderata in the educational process, have also engendered an emphasis upon the immediacy of content to the social milieu of the learner. In an age in which television is a reliable stimulus to student-interest, its agenda of current affairs and simulated family life has been a fruitful source of starting-points for the classroom teacher. At all levels, sociological observation suffers from its epistemological proximity to common sense: and particularly at the school level sociology translates with ease into everyday language.

Themes like friendship, snobbery, money, work, leisure and suffering were commended to the teacher by Harold Loukes whose *Teenage Religion* (1961) represents a turning-point for RE in the secondary school. In the subsequent fifteen years, schools publishers provided for the market numerous resources of the 'stimulus-starter' kind which took topics from the contemporary world to be studied in the context of RE: many of these new contents represented the traditional concerns of sociology – such as the family, social class, industrial society and aspects of social disorganization.

Whereas at school level sociological content found its way into the classroom for consideration by the methods conventional to RE, in universities it was sociological method that penetrated religious content. At the University of Sussex, for example, theology was complemented by courses in the sociology of religion, the psychology of religion, a history option on the Reformation and so on. The conception of such 'religious studies' courses at university and college level owes much to Ninian Smart's identification of the various dimensions of religious practice.

Simultaneously, theologians like Karl Rahner and Hans Küng, have expressed themselves open to sociological evidence in their own activities and have rejected the notion that theology enjoys any monopoly of religious insight. Whether in the school curriculum or in the domain of scholarship, there has been in recent years an increasing appreciation of the complementarity of sociological and conventional approaches to the study of religions.

Gabriel le Bras, *Etudes de Sociologie Religieuse,* Paris 1955; Emile Durkheim, *The Elementary Forms of the Religious Life,* Allen & Unwin 1915; Harold Loukes, *Teenage Religion,* SCM Press 1961; Thomas

Luckmann, *The Invisible Religion*, Macmillan 1967; David Martin, *A General Theory of Secularization*, Blackwell 1978; Max Weber, *The Protestant Ethic and the Spirit of Capitalism*, Unwin 1938; Bryan Wilson, *Religious Sects*, Weidenfeld & Nicolson 1970.

ROGER HOMAN

South America *see* Latin/South America

Special Education, Special Schools

It is impossible to generalize about the place of RE in Special Education because 'Special Education' is in itself a general term. Even if restricted in meaning to that education which takes place within special schools, the range of disabilities to be found within such setting in diverse – physical, sensory, emotional and intellectual. The hallmark of current trends in Special Education is the emphasis on providing individuals with educational programmes to meet their specific needs. Often these will concentrate on measurable or demonstrable behaviour. RE may suffer neglect because it is often viewed in terms of values, attitudes and morals for which it is more difficult to prescribe. Debate is required, not only about the formulation of criteria for these areas but about what should be taught in them.

In addition to the problem of fitting RE into individually tailored curricula in Special Schools, there is a further difficulty. Special School pupils are all, to some extent, set apart from their peers. One of the tenets of religious education is to place the individual in relationship to the world. This should be the starting point for constructive RE teaching in the special sector, because research has shown that Special School pupils may have more problems in establishing positive self-concepts than their counterparts in the mainstream.

Many pupils in Special Schools are in a special group in relation to religious faiths. For example, within the Christian stories, the handicapped are often healed. This can reinforce an outdated concept that the handicapped are lesser humans and in need of special 'caring'. Similarly, the handicapped may be denied the privilege of caring for their neighbour because of being forced into the role of those who are cared for. There may also be a danger in the notion of 'miracle' when paralleled with 'cure'.

Within the Islamic tradition, the handicapped are given exemption from most religious obligations. A handicapped Muslim child is set apart from his peers by such ruling. This 'apartness' is evident in the allowances made for the handicapped in other major religions and is a major problem which should be confronted by RE in Special Schools.

The population in Special Schools is wide in terms of age, ability and religious affiliation. The teacher must use all the resources available to mainstream teaching while not neglecting the special problems of these special children. The content of RE in Special Schools will not be dissimilar to that in the mainstream but must be as tailor-made to individual needs as are the other curricular areas. In this matter RE will itself be special because it must grapple with the 'special needs' of the children so designated.

PAULA HALLIDAY

Spens Report

The Spens Committee, convened in October 1933 and reporting in 1938, was charged to investigate secondary schools other than 'modern' schools, looking especially at the framework and education provided for pupils between the ages of eleven plus and sixteen.

In its conclusions it anticipated many developments in secondary education which have since become established practice. It recommended radical changes in the position and teaching of scripture, English, Latin, mathematics and science, later rather than earlier specialization, a more prominent place for aesthetic subjects and the creation of posts of special responsibility linked to advanced work and specialist teaching.

In the chapter on 'Scripture' (a term used as a synonym for Religious Instruction) the authors start from the premise that 'no boy or girl can be counted as properly educated unless he or she has been made aware of the fact of the existence of a religious interpretation of life'. Scripture should be taught primarily with a view to understanding what the books of the Bible were intended to mean by their authors. Further, whereas 'scripture' is examinable, 'religion' is not, and Religious Instruction is only a part of Religious Education. This latter takes place both in the class-room in scripture lessons and also elsewhere at other times. The report calls for the appointment of a specialist teacher of scrip-ture in all schools except the smallest, but notes the problem of securing a supply of teachers adequately prepared to teach the subject. The time allocation for scripture must be sufficient and instruction in the subject should not be discontinued at the approach of a public examination.

KENNETH D. EXLEY

Spiritual Area of Experience

The unseen reality which permeates the human scene is referred to as the spiritual dimension of existence. The term 'spiritual experience', usually refers to an awareness of divine presence, though such awareness takes many forms. Thus a spiritual experience can be felt in a time of prayer or worship, but can also be felt in a burst of enthusiasm for an event, person, place, or thing that evokes a special response in awe and wonder.

The word 'enthusiasm' literally means 'filled with the spirit of God', so that a zest for life is a spiritual or at least a spirited approach. Sam Keen in *Apology for Wonder* stated that 'Wonder and awe are closely associated with the experience of the holy.' Rabbi Abraham J. Heschel in *Between God and Man* pointed out that 'Wonder and radical amazement is the chief characteristic of the religious man's attitude toward history and nature.' The Hebrew word for spirit, *ruach*, also means wind and breath. Thus a spirited experience is likely to be one in which the breath rushes and the person feels a sense of elation or exhilaration.

Frequently the spiritual experience is felt at both a conscious and an unconscious level. There is both that which can be described and an intuitive apprehension that defies descrip-tion. The fullness of the spiritual experience reaches deeply into the innermost self or the soul of the participant.

The spiritual area of experience ranges from the sensing of divine presence to the recogni-tion of a heightened quality in an event or an encounter, and a response of awe and wonder.

See also **Religious Experience**.

Abraham Heschel, *Between God and Man*,

Harper 1959; Sam Keen, *Apology for Wonder,* Harper 1969.

DOROTHY A. DIXON

Spiritual Development

The spiritual development of the individual and of the human species has been mapped out by numerous theorists in a number of different ways, yet a channel of commonality can be discerned along the mainstream of these various writers. If we define spiritual development as growth in awareness of unseen reality (including the vast unconscious realms of the human psyche), and the way the individual relates to these ineffable dimen-sions of existence, we have a working field for exploration.

Studies of individual spiritual development tend to follow the same three-fold pattern. Intellectually, according to Jean Piaget, a human being grows from the 'preoperational' or intuitive thought patterns of early child-hood through the 'concrete operational' patterns of middle childhood into finally an area of thinking where abstract reasoning is possible. This third phase Piaget calls 'formal operations', and it includes the kind of expen-sive thinking whereby a person not only pictures the whole world but the whole range of possibilities in mental and word operations.

Bringing the individual stage development more into focus on moral reasoning abilities, Lawrence Kohlberg of Harvard University cites three areas of progressive development which he calls, respectively, pre-conventional morality which is based on external rewards and punishments; conventional morality, the norm of the middle-grade children, based on rigid legalism; and mature post-conventional thinking which deals with universalizing ethics such as the categorical imperative of Kant or the golden rule of many of the world's religions.

Faith development levels are under investi-gation by James Fowler of Emory University, paralleling the levels of Piaget and Kohlberg. Fowler cites stage levels of faith development that can be summarized into three categories: the 'intuitive-projective' level of early child-hood, the 'mythic-literal' of middle grades; and the 'universalizing' of mature years. It is in the 'intuitive-projective' level that the small child relates to unseen reality with a kind of subconscious awareness that is like sensing the splendour of unseen presence, indefinable, ineffable, yet wondrous, and awe-inspiring.

This intuitive awareness then gives way, in middle childhood, to a 'concretizing' of the 'presence' – so that biblical references are taken rigidly and literally, and the child's concept of God is quite anthropomorphic. This level of faith development parallels, somewhat (though not always chronologically), the Piaget stage of concrete operations and the Kohlberg stage of conventional morality. Most persons do not grow beyond these stages, according to the developmental theorists. Yet for those who do, there is, according to Fowler, the higher realm of faith development of spiritual growth that is universalizing. It is grounded in one's own faith tradition, whatever that may be, but it sees a universal sweep of value in each person's own relatedness to God, or ultimate reality, and the concurrent relatedness to others and the whole universe in harmony and reconciliation.

Spiritual development can then be seen in unfolding patterns that are both individual and corporate, and that grow along a continuum of early unconscious and unformed feelings through the discipline of rigid adherence to mutually respected rules and laws, to an eventual level of relatedness with God and man that is universalizing and as infinitely expansive as the human mind can fathom.

DOROTHY A. DIXON

Spiritual Rights

A spiritual right may be taken to refer both to the freedom to belong to a religion which provides a creed, code and cult, etc., and to the freedom of being open to have and to reflect upon such experiences as a sense of wonder, joy, relatedness, or of the numinous, a moment of 'encounter', a state of serenity etc. A spiritual right is thus a basic human right in the sense that it is necessary for a minimum quality of human life.

The United Nations *Declaration of the Rights of the Child* (1959) is unique in referring to the spiritual rights of children; this provision is in the context of a requirement for normal and healthy development.

In an International Year of the Child discussion paper (J. Bradford, 1979), five spiritual rights were postulated for those under the age of majority: 1. the right to the best of the spiritual heritage of the culture into which he or she is born; 2. the right to express his or her spiritual belief in private and/or public without discrimination; 3. the right to deepen, doubt or alter the spiritual commitment into which he or she is being nurtured or educated; 4. the right to schooling, family life and other institutional support complimentary to his or her spiritual development; 5. the right, especially in early life, to such protection from spiritual damage and handicap as is reasonable and appropriate. These spiritual rights are of course 'moral' rights and not legal rights, though in Federal Germany, for example, a child can decide its religious training from the age of twelve and about its faith from the age of fourteen.

As a general rule, human rights statements about religion refer to the rights of adults and underscore the parental right to bring up children in accordance with their convictions, *vide* the United Nations *Declaration of Human Rights* (1948), Article 18, and the March 1952 Protocol to the *European Convention*, Article 2.

Noting the distinction of D. D. Raphael between rights of recipience and rights of action, it should be observed that during adolescence there is a complex period of negotiation in which parents gradually hand over supervisory responsibilities to their young people who correspondingly develop in spiritual autonomy.

J. Bradford, *The Spiritual Rights of the Child – A Discussion Paper*, Church of England Children's Society for UK IYC 1979; Ian Brownlie (ed.), *Basic Documents on Human Rights*, Clarendon Press ²1981; C. Glenn Cupit, 'Children's Rights in the International Year of the Child', *Journal of Christian Education* 64, Australian Teachers' Christian Fellowship, Sydney, June 1979; David Jenkins, 'Theological Inquiry Concerning Human Rights', *Ecumenical Review*, XXVII, 2, April 1975, World Council of Churches; D. D. Raphael, *Moral Judgements*, Greenwood 1977; *United Nations Declaration on the Elimination of All Forms of Intolerance and Discrimination Based on Religion or Belief*, November 1981; Victor L. Worsfold, 'A Philosophical Justification for Children's Rights', *Harvard Educational Review*, 44, 1, February 1974; C. A. Wringe, 'Pupils'

Rights', in *Proceedings of the Philosophy of Education Society of Great Britain*, VII, 1, Jan. 1973; C. A. Wringe, *Children's Rights*, Routledge & Kegan Paul 1981.

JOHN BRADFORD

Sri Lanka *see* Asia

Standing Advisory Councils for Religious Education

A Local Education Authority in England and Wales may have a Standing Advisory Council for Religious Education (SACRE). Section 29 (i) of the 1944 Education Act gives the details for the composition, responsibilities and functions of such a body.

The membership of a SACRE is at the discretion of the LEA, both with regard to its size and as to which interested parties should serve on it. In practice, the composition of any SACRE reflects the local situation, so that if an LEA decides to create such a council it invites those parties having most interest in, and professional understanding of, RE to be represented.

Once established a SACRE becomes a permanent official body within the Local Authority's structure. It meets at regular intervals, at its own discretion. The internal organization and method of working is determined by a SACRE to enable it best to discharge the responsibilities indicated in the 1944 Education Act.

These responsibilities are to offer what help, advice and support it can provide, according to the resources available, both to teachers in the Authority's schools engaged in RE, and to the Education Committee of the Authority in matters concerning RE. The Education Committee is required by the 1944 Education Act to respond to any matters brought to its attention by the council.

One major responsibility of an LEA with regard to RE cannot be discharged by a SACRE. A SACRE cannot provide a new agreed syllabus. That is the function of an agreed syllabus conference for which Schedule 95 of the Education Act makes detailed provision. There is no reason, however, why the membership of a council should not be the same as that of a conference, or contain within its membership such representatives as will enable it to function

both as a council and as a conference for agreed syllabus purposes.

A SACRE is a way in which an LEA may provide support for RE in its schools. The following example is not intended as a model, but serves to illustrate how a SACRE, created by following the general provisions made in the Act, has been realized in one particular situation.

The membership is approximately forty. For the most part the members are teachers from schools and colleges in the Authority, together with representatives of the churches and other religious, national organizations such as the Christian Education Movement* and Inter-school Christian Fellowship*, members of the Education Committee and officials of the Authority. Most of the teachers are leaders of local teachers' groups in their own part of the Authority's area.

This SACRE meets once each term. It acts as a forum for all parties interested in, and responsible for, RE, and especially to support local teachers' groups. Through working parties and individual members' efforts, it maintains five levels of support for schools – by making provision for courses and meetings, producing papers on all aspects of RE, publishing a termly newsletter, maintaining collections of resources, and carrying out surveys from time to time. Reports are made to the Education Committee.

The value, function and style of any SACRE must derive from the local situation. That described here represents one response among many.

PETER STREET

Standing Conference on Inter-Faith Dialogue in Education

Formed at a multi-faith conference at Westhill College, Birmingham, in September 1973, SCIFDE seeks to convene the type of inter-faith conference where effective dialogue between different faiths and stances may take place. From its early days it has been serviced by the World Congress of Faiths, with which it retains close links. Members meet in committee three times a year and organize an annual conference, usually in a large city with a multi-ethnic population. These conferences have featured topics such as Initiation Rites, Death in the World's Faiths, Marriage and the Family, the place of Women and the place of Youth in Society today. The conferences have produced material for publication on 'Living Faiths' and have also passed motions seeking to exert pressure on LEAS and other bodies to implement sensitive policies on multi-faith/multi-cultural issues in education.

John Prickett (ed.), *Initiation Rites*, Lutterworth 1978 and *Death*, Lutterworth 1980.

VIDA BARNETT

Story

An examination of the entry for 'story' in the full *Oxford English Dictionary* reveals immediately why an understanding of the nature of story is of central importance to those who wish to communicate religious ideas and why that communication has become increasingly difficult. Early medieval usage assumed story to be 'a narrative, true or presumed to be true, relating to important events'. By the twentieth century the same word can, in certain contexts, be defined as synonymous with a lie, as in the scolding phrase 'you story-teller'.

Nevertheless, human experience of all types still seems to demand a narrative form. Story remains the basis of communication of human events and relationships in theatre, television and gossip. The answer to the question, 'What happened?' is never clear cut. A degree of subjectivity and hence of evaluation must necessarily accompany the answer. The problem would seem to be that Western society has become so obsessed with external observation and the critical method that ancient story, like modern chemistry, is assumed to be comprehended (and frequently rejected) on the basis of objective analysis.

In story the action takes place inside the actors as well as outside. The hearer is therefore asked for a holistic response, not just a cognitive appreciation. Interpretation is a matter for the feelings and the emotions as well as the intellect, and participation comes through the imagination. Story is an art form. As such it is capable of interpretation at different levels depending upon the age and background of the hearer. The only difference between an adult story and a child's story is the range of experience referred to.

Some experiences are universal and appear unrelated to age and culture. These often form the basis of religious story and/or myth.

These would always seem to contain potential for further growth and insight by containing a reference point which is always beyond.

Story is a major means of communication in all religions. All religious 'founders' appear to have used it extensively. At the same time their own significance has been communicated by their followers in story form. Thus, for example, Christians can talk of the stories of Jesus and the Christ story as two distinct notions.

More recently it has become traditional to distinguish between different types of story (e.g. folk, fairy, saga, biography, myth etc.) but these distinctions become increasingly difficult to sustain. Tolkien, for example, has argued that the gospel embraces the essence of fairy story – it is the good catastrophe, the sudden joyous turn.

Navonne argues that one of the most common forms of the religious story is the travel narrative – the journeying and the homecoming (e.g. Abraham, Joseph, Moses, Rama and Sita, *Pilgrim's Progress*) where the journey, actual or imagined, corresponds with the passage of life itself and its ultimate destiny.

To arrive at dwelling is as crucial as journeying. It is this ability of story to establish self identity and to help in the discovery of one's place in the whole created order of things which makes it a significant educational tool in the task of transforming external cognition into self knowledge. Entering into the stories of others (biography*) is the surest means of discovering our own story (autobiography).

J. Crossan, *The Dark Interval: Towards a Theology of Story*, Argus 1975; Ted Hughes, 'Myth and Education', *Writers, Critics and Children*, ed. G. Fox *et al.*, Heinemann 1976; J. Navonne, *Towards a Theology of Story*, St Paul's Press 1977.

JACK PRIESTLEY

Student Christian Movement

The Student Christian Movement (SCM) has played a major role in Christian education for nearly a century as an ecumenical organization of Christian students in colleges, polytechnics and universities in Britain. The SCM's primary objective is defined as 'the advancement of the Christian religion' but the movement is not committed to the doctrinal basis of any section of the church. It is part of the international World Student Christian Federation.

Most of scm educational activity takes place in autonomous local groups, of which there were more than fifty on British campuses in 1982. Typically, scm groups arrange a termly programme of weekly meetings at which a wide range of topics related to the Christian faith are discussed. Most groups invite 'expert' speakers to introduce discussion, but increasingly alternative methods are being used; role plays, films, videos and drama. Each group elects a committee which is free to decide which topics to address, but they are encouraged to link these to the national movement's two year long study themes. Two overall characteristics underlie all scm activity: the aim of developing a lively and critical understanding of the Christian faith, and the exploration of the application of that faith to contemporary social and political issues.

Regional and national conferences are an important part of scm educational work, giving students the experience of concentrated experience together. National conferences have taken as their themes: 'Facing the Deep', a reappraisal of central Christian doctrines; 'Voice in the Wilderness', contemporary Christian discipleship; 'Prophecy and Utopia'. The scm produces a wide range of educational material for students and a journal, *Movement*.

PETER GEE

Student Christian Movement in Schools *see* Christian Education Movement

Sudan *see* Middle East, Christian Education in the

Sunday School Movement

Whilst many men and women opened schools on Sunday in the latter half of the eighteenth century, Robert Raikes of Gloucester is recognized as the founder of the movement. From 1783, through his paper, *The Gloucester Journal*, he commended what he called, 'an experiment, harmless and innocent'.

As the industrial revolution developed, men and women in many parts of Britain progressed from his negative aim of preventing the growth of juvenile delinquency on Sundays to the positive concern to teach children how to read. Many teachers were paid to instruct their charges not only to read, but how to write as well. The movement grew rapidly. Both churchmen and dissenters commended it, and many parents took advantage of the teaching provided. Other educational agencies were at a low ebb. These schools welcomed all children and transformed bored idlers into willing learners.

The outbreak of the French revolution led to the schools being regarded with suspicion by politicians and opposition from those who feared they were creating rebels against established society. Religious leaders disliked the teaching of writing in Sunday Schools. Nevertheless the movement exposed the need for schools for all children. As others opened day schools, Sunday School teachers concentrated more on teaching Bible studies. Hymn books and lesson notes became widely used, and the Sunday School Union claimed it provided the movement with a 'federal unity, an organization and a literature'.

Numbers grew steadily throughout the nineteenth century and gradually links between the schools and the congregations promoting them were formed. Anniversaries, often called 'charity sermons', demonstrated to parents and others how much the children had benefited from regular attendance and teaching.

The universal movement stimulated the provision of day school education for all. Consequently Sunday School leaders began to re-think the purpose and content of their teaching. Casual instruction by well-intentioned amateurs was replaced gradually by the desire to develop competent Christian education.

Early in the twentieth century this concern to make Sunday School teaching more effective was stimulated by pioneers like Hamilton Archibald. Arguing that education begins with the child, not with a book nor lesson, Sunday Schools were graded into departments to cater for various age-groups. The earliest divisions had been between the 'ignorant' and the 'instructed' (those able to read). Many denominations gave new support to the movement and the British Lessons Council assumed responsibility for planning lesson courses from 1920.

Against the background of two world wars and rapidly accelerating social change, the new vision of 'The Child in the Midst', classic of the modern movement, found a focus in the establishment of Westhill Training College, Birmingham. This has provided training in Christian education for men and women from many lands and has stimulated pioneering experiments in teaching the Christian faith.

A former principal of Westhill, H. A. Hamilton, showed the need to think in 'family church' concepts. The vast majority of Sunday School scholars came from homes with no close church associations. All too often they met in a different building and at a different time from the worshipping congregation. With the increase of leisure, modern transport and entertainment proving attractive, attendances fell dramatically unless the parent congregation became a vital force in the lives of those in their pastoral care.

So from baptism a child was given a 'church friend', families were encouraged to sit together in worship and to share together in planning for and celebrating the great Christian festivals. 'Family church' courses made great demands on those using them. As Hamilton recognized, many saw this development as only a new form of organization rather than a challenge to explore in depth its purpose and work.

Influenced by 'family church' thinking, there has been an almost universal change from Sunday afternoon to Sunday morning activity, enabling children to share in some part of church morning worship. Some churches have encouraged adults and children to explore the same themes, following the Christian year*.

As the movement has grown the need for deeply committed Christian teachers has become more and more obvious. It is strange to read in an early Sunday School Union report that 'more teachers than hitherto are religious persons'. Payment of Sunday School teachers soon gave way to the recruiting and training of volunteers eager to communicate so much more than simply the knowledge of Bible stories.

Whilst the movement had its origin in Britain, men and women quick to see its potential for good were eager to commend it to others in Europe and beyond. A Sunday School was opened in India in 1803, the same

year as the English Sunday School Union was formed.

Soon there were Sunday School Unions in America, and denominational bodies, as in Britain, took increasing share in the promotion and development of the movement. The centenary was celebrated by raising a special fund for European Sunday School teaching. In 1913 the first World Sunday School Convention was held and the nine hundred delegates pledged support for a missionary to India. From 1907 the world movement functioned through two committees, one for North America and the 'British', which sought to promote the work in Europe, Australia, South Africa and India.

Conventions and assemblies have been held in this century in Jerusalem, Tokyo, Washington, Belfast, Nairobi and Lima. Member units have helped struggling groups by special gifts.

In due course the World Sunday School Association changed its name to indicate a widening interest and became in 1948 the World Council of Christian Education and in 1971 united with the World Council of Churches*.

_____

J. Kenneth Meir, *Labour of Love*, Methodist Youth Dept 1971.

J. KENNETH MEIR

Sweden

The growth of the Swedish school was a sign of the church's care for its members. When the state, through the School Decree of 1842, formally was made the new head of the school, that was a sign of a state that was positive towards religion. Schooling thus continued to rest on a Christian ideology. This corresponded to what had long been natural for a people with a uniform Lutheran creed and view of society. It characterized the teaching of Christianity in compulsory grade (primary) school, which turned into a Church of Sweden school with an ecclesiastical confessional Christian education, where the catechism was central.

Around the turn of the century in Sweden, as well as in many other countries, changes took place within society which had consequences for the formation of Christian teaching in school. The old agrarian class society was succeeded by a demographically mobile society. Political parties grew up, some of which were opposed to the prevailing order of society. The liberal social democratic demands for religious freedom were confronted with the confessional form of Christian education in grade (primary) school. On the religious level, the biblical revival movements as well as religious liberalists questioned the catechism teaching of the school. Psychological and pedagogical objections were voiced: the catechism of Luther certainly was not adjusted to the developmental stages of children; cramming the catechism was an out-of-date method.

The pluralism of Swedish society grew stronger. In comparison with many other European countries, there was a difference: unity of ideology and religion was stressed in Sweden. The solutions concerning RE found in the time between the wars and in the post-war period should be seen in the light of the state's attempts to find an education which was acceptable to all citizens.

The solution from the period between the wars made the Bible central, rather than Luther's catechism. Christian ethics were stressed, since they were seen as compatible with the unitarian values of the modern democratic society, into which Sweden was growing. Christianity was taught as a non-confessional, ethical Bible education. The Ten Commandments and the Sermon on the Mount were the new textbook.

The between-wars solution was never fully accepted. The post-war period brought with it demands of a more radical change of education as a whole and thus also of the contents of religious education. RE should be the same for all Swedish citizens, and thus it had to be formed in a way to guarantee full religious freedom and tolerance. Teaching of *Christianity* was turned into teaching of *religion* and in school this covered different religions and philosophies. The change was principally initiated in the 1940s but was effected only during the 1960s. In the 1964 curriculum for high (secondary) school and the 1969 curriculum for grade (primary) school it can be clearly seen how the teaching of Christianity changed its position and its content in Swedish schools: the subject changed its name from 'Christianity' to 'Religion'; the total number of teaching hours was lessened to give more space to more societally oriented subjects; the

subject was moved down from a number one position on the grade card to a place among other social and nature oriented subjects; morning prayers with Christian contents were replaced by gatherings of a more secular kind; objectivity of education was stressed, especially concerning the subject of religion.

The curricula now in use, from 1978 and 1980 respectively, do not differ principally from their predecessors from the 1960s. However, these curricula have tried to correct a development where objectivity sometimes became neutral and disengaged. Objectivity in RE ought to allow for involvement on the side of the students. It should give the student a possibility to choose freely between different alternatives, without the influence of any authority. One leading pedagogical principle is thus to put the student, not the subject, or the teacher, or the textbook, in the centre. This centring is motivated by two big investigations (*The Teenager and the Questions of Life*, 1969, and *The Teenager and Life*, 1979, Liber, Stockholm), where students in the last year of grade school were asked about their interest in different religions and other existential questions. Both investigations showed that teenagers are very interested in existential questions but not so apt to look for these in traditional religious material. Putting the student in the centre of education thus demands that religions and philosophies are taught in a way which allows the student to meet his own existential questions in what is taught.

From 1978 onwards the high school curriculum for religion officially contained certain main elements: Christianity, other religions, philosophies and ethics. Christianity thus is given a special status as one main element. This is motivated by the fact that, seen globally, Christianity is the largest religion, and that it is the foundation of European and Swedish cultures.

In the curriculum for grade school from 1980, integration of subjects became a leading principle. That implies that religion no longer is taught as a separate subject but is integrated with other societally oriented subjects. The Bible is central for education in Christianity. At the same time all possibilities for integration with other societal subjects should be used.

Much freedom is given to the particular

school or teacher when it comes to forming education, and at the same time student influence on education is stressed. The guideline in RE is that objectivity should be observed, while student involvement is stressed. To solve the tension built into this, the curriculum stresses the possibility for associations and churches to take part in school activities: visiting lecturers, study tours, and using 'free activity time', i.e. having students take part in different activities in the association and/or church. This is financially supported by the school.

The development of RE in Swedish schools has actualized both for the Church of Sweden and for the free denominations the need for complementary education in Christianity. It is obvious that the position of Christianity in school has been weakened by having less teaching hours and the competition of other religions and philosophies. The students' knowledge of the Bible and Christianity has lessened. Therefore, both in the Church of Sweden (with its traditional form of preparation for confirmation) and in the free denominations (where this kind of preparation either has been given earlier or is just being developed), the interest in preparation for confirmation has grown. Thus, for example, in the Swedish Covenant Church preparation for confirmation is met with a renewed interest, shown in the production of new material and initiatives taken to create an ecumenical educational programme for teachers in confirmation classes. Within the pentecostal movement, a tradition which has not shown much interest in this kind of preparation, the interest also has been awakened.

While the school and the churches have separated concerning religious education, there are signs of a rapprochement beginning between the two. The school has seen the danger of objective religious education: it might become meaningless for the students. And therefore the churches are offered a new position in school. In order to reach the growing youth with the gospel, the churches need to know which conditions are prevailing among that group. The churches and the school could meet again. The future will show the result.

CARL-EBER OLIVESTAM

Switzerland

It is very difficult to give an overall view of RE in a country like Switzerland which is composed of twenty three small states (cantons) speaking four different languages, each having their own systems of education adapted in principle to their different mentalities, influenced by the predominating denomination (Roman Catholic or Protestant Reformed) and their own relationship with the state. To this is added the country's mixture of confessions (for historical reasons some cantons adopted the Reform of the sixteenth century, others did not), in practically equal numbers. The systems of education and of RE vary according to church traditions.

However, it is possible to find many points in common which allow cantons speaking the same language, and churches, deeply committed to ecumenism, to collaborate among themselves.

Today it is customary for religious education to take place in the family, the church and school. The spiritual awakening of infants up to five years devolves entirely, at least in principle, on the family; the church provides parents, through ad hoc meetings, with the means of giving their children an authentic Christian witness. Later, when the churches intervene actively in the educational process, parents are associated with this effort through specific meetings and liturgies or masses more particularly oriented towards the family. From six to sixteen or seventeen years, when the school takes over their education, young people take part in Christian instruction in their parishes and schools. Catholic parishes celebrate family masses, hold catechism classes in preparation for First Holy Communion, run groups of pre-adolescents directed by lay catechists, groups for adolescents to prepare for confirmation*, and sometimes children's clubs and holiday camps, as well as groups and camps for older adolescents.

The Reformed Church offers the children Sunday Schools as well as liturgies for parents and children; catechism properly so called, preparatory to confirmation, lasting two years, is for young people from fourteen to sixteen or fifteen to seventeen years according to the regions. The most dynamic of the churches offer pre-adolescents (twelve to fourteen years) catechetical groups usually run by lay people. Here and there, there are groups of adolescents of over seventeen years who continue to deepen their faith through active research.

RE in schools differs according to the relationship of the churches with the state. In the Catholic cantons RE is integrated into the school timetable and given by teachers in primary schools, and by priests in post-primary schools and colleges, where it is obligatory up to school-leaving age in German-speaking Switzerland. This is also true of private Catholic colleges. In the pre-dominantly Protestant cantons, where the church is allied to the state, RE is integrated in the curriculum in primary schools and given mainly by the teacher; in post-primary schools courses of Christian culture are organized in first studies for twelve to fifteen year olds. These courses are obligatory in German-speaking Swiss schools, optional in French-speaking Swiss schools. From sixteen to twenty years in German Switzerland, facult-ative courses are offered to pupils. The teachers are churchmen or religious specialists trained by the churches.

Where church and state are separated, instruction takes place in or out of the ordin-ary timetable; it is not taught by the resident staff but by lay or ordained persons from outside the school staff. There are also chaplaincies in the colleges.

Religious instruction is generally comple-mented by well-known international youth movements such as Scouting and the YMCAS, which organize activities in the parishes, or by Bible groups, which work on the school premises. The established churches are some-times also the administrative centres for organizing children's holiday-camps or camps for young people of different ages.

Generally speaking catechetical research has developed greatly during the past twenty years, as the attitudes of young people to traditional religion have modified. Various works of catechetical theology, as well as a vast amount of pedagogical material (catech-etical pamphlets, books and workcards for children, adolescents and parents, and audio-visual materials) have been published or are in the process of publication. This development will continue since offices for research and publishing are very active. Research in the Catholic Church is co-ordinated around direc-tives ('Zielfelderpläne' inspired by German research) carefully studied by the best diocesan specialists. In the Reformed Church research aims at finding pastoral and catechet-ical methods most likely to touch the hearts of the young, and is inspired by the theological renewal in the churches. This research is bearing fruit: in many places the catechetical movement is very lively and new sectors of activity have come into being during recent years. The Reformed Church in the canton of Vaud, for example, has found 1000 lay catechists to furnish catechism for pre-adoles-cents (something which did not before exist); the Catholic Church has set thousands of volunteer catechists to work (more than 1000 for the town of Geneva alone, with its popula-tion of 200,000 Catholics). Many of them receive pre-adolescents into their homes in order to talk with them about their life and faith. Pastors and priests are trained in prac-tical catechetics following their theological studies. Professional catechists or priests wishing to take a degree in RE, are trained in catechist schools or catechetical institutes, more or less linked with faculties of theology, at Fribourg, Lucerne or Zürich. The churches in the cantons provide ad hoc courses for lay volunteers.

Ecumenical collaboration is very strong in the cantons of mixed confessions. In Geneva and Neuchâtel ecumenical catechetical centres produce catechetical material and common training courses for their volunteer catechists. In Geneva schooling itself is in many areas ecumenical so that Catholic and Protestant children receive the same instruc-tion. These ecumenical contacts profoundly enrich the churches. Quite recently the Reformed Churches in almost all Switzerland have begun to offer children participation in the Lord's Supper, following the Catholic custom. The Catholic Church has tended to delay the age of confirmation so that often young Catholics are confirmed at the same age as young Protestants.

The Catholic and Reformed Churches are similarly oriented: catechizing is a *continuous* process and the contents of programmes and the methods used develop with the psycho-logical development of the young people; it is also '*global*' in the sense that the teaching seeks to embrace the whole person, affec-tions, intellect, activities and social life; it is church-based in that it is rooted in the Christian community and it is prayerful. However, this does not necessarily mean that the churches succeed in realizing these objectives in spite of all their efforts. Many young people – maybe the majority – from the age of twelve become indifferent to Christian instruction and lose any living link with the church. The more profound insights of the churches' Christian education programmes are very seldom put into practice and new efforts must be made as a matter of urgency.

Pierre Bovet, *Le sentiment religieux et la psychologie de l'enfant*, Delachaux et Niestlé ²1951; K. Frör, *Grundriss der Religionspädagogik*, Konstanz 1975; K. E. Nipkow, *Grundfragen der Religionspädagogik*, Gütersloh 1975; Fritz Oser, *Handbuch der Religionspädagogik*, vols 1–3, ed. E. Feifel, R. Leuenberger, G. Stachel and K. Wegenast, Gütersloh 1973; *Theologisch denken lernen: Ein Buch für Pädagogen*, Walterverlag 1975; Claude Pantillon, *Une philosophie de l'Education, pour quoi faire*? L'âge d'homme, Lausanne 1981; G. Stachel and W. C. Esser, *Was ist Religionspädogogik*? Einsiedeln 1975; K. Wegenast, *Orientierungsrahmen Religion*, Gütersloh 1979; Alain Wyler, *L'éducateur au service de la foi*, Le Centurion, Paris 1978; *Evangile et Adolescence*, Bureau Protestant de Recherche Catéchétique, Geneva 1970; *Recherche sur la Communication de l'Evangile*, Peter Lang, Berne 1980.

ALAIN WYLER

Syllabuses   *see* **Agreed Syllabuses**

Symbolism

The subject of symbolism is one of interest to scholars from a wide variety of disciplines. Its complexity is heightened by the lack of consensus over when 'symbol' should be used and when it is more appropriate to refer to signs, signals, images or emblems. Paul Tillich has argued that a symbol may be identified in that it 'represents something which is not itself, for which it stands and in the power and meaning of which it participates . . . it opens up reality and it opens up the soul' (*Theology of Culture*).

John Macquarrie said of religious symbols: 'there is a wide range of religious symbols and while the degree of affinity between the symbol and what is symbolized varies, it would seem that there is always some affinity, and that religious symbols are never just extrinsic or accidental' (*God-Talk*). Through symbolism, belief finds a means of spontaneous expression and the believer a means of affective as well as cognitive response.

Religious symbols occur in many forms. They vary from the icon* of the Eastern Orthodox Christian, which functions as 'a window into heaven', to the crucifix of Catholicism, and mystical syllable *Om* of Hinduism to the *tefillin* of the Jew. On considering the 'penny-dropping' model of religious language put forward by Ian Ramsey it can be seen that much of the language of religion is also symbolic. The power of the ultimate or the transcendent breaks through the image, the credal statement or the confession of faith; another level of reality is disclosed.

The significance of religious symbolism, by its very nature, is best grasped within the faith-community for which the symbols express meaning. Nevertheless, one of the concerns of RE in a pluralist society must be to develop as far as possible a sensitive understanding of the nature and role of symbols in world religions. Imagination and empathy are capacities which are vital in the approach of RE to symbolism. The task of the religious educator is to enable children to develop understanding without destroying the power of the symbols which some of them may have encountered in a religious and/or cultural context.

Most of the schemes that have been suggested for teaching about symbolism are child-related and structured developmentally, but also endeavour to take into account the complex nature of symbolism. Thus Jean Holm advocates experience of a variety of ways of communicating feelings (including non-verbal means of communication) as well as visits to places of worship to precede a unit of work on Signs and Symbols for nines to elevens. A foundation is then built from which real understanding of the nature of symbolism can later follow. Others suggest a progression from the development of the language and emotional experiences of early childhood through to the explicit introduction of the pictorial language of signs followed by the imagery of visual and verbal symbolism. Most would agree that explicit reference to symbolism should begin in the middle years of schooling (nine to thirteen), but should continue to be deepened throughout the secondary years.

Thomas Fawcett, *The Symbolic Language of Religion*, SCM Press 1970; John Macquarrie, *God-Talk*, SCM Press 1967; Albert C. Moore, *Iconography of Religions*, SCM Press 1977; Ian T. Ramsey, *Religious Language*, SCM Press 1957; Paul Tillich, *Theology of Culture*, Oxford University Press 1959.

GWEN PALMER

Syria   *see* **Middle East, Christian Education in the**

Teachers

In Britain teachers of RE, whether secondary specialists or primary teachers with resource responsibilities, may be trained by one of two routes: concurrent training on an RE course providing specialism in both Religious Studies and Religious Education; consecutive training (the usual secondary schooling route) whereby a degree course is followed by the Post-Graduate Certificate in Education with RE as a specialism. Because of the nature of the RE curriculum and the desirability of teaching another subject, many RE teachers take a two-subject degree (including Theology or Religious Studies) or a degree in a relevant discipline, prior to their PGCE course. Whereas most courses in RE have a standard curriculum, different degree courses in Religious Studies reflect the interests of their institutions and may, like all degree courses, be self-standing and not totally relevant to the needs of the school curriculum. Although a match between degree and professional studies is not essential, intending teachers ought to consider the relationship between its contents and their future professional needs. The major elements of Religious Studies degrees will include biblical studies (texts and/or history and/or theology); church history and theology; philosophy and/or ethics and/or sociology of religion; the nature of religion or of world religions, including Christianity; a range of options, either in the foregoing elements or in language(s), liturgy etc. The extent to which the syllabus is orientated towards Christianity may reflect the college's religious foundation or the university depart-

ment's interests, but such orientation does not necessarily imply a biased approach to the material studied, any more than open-mindedness need be practised within or developed by a course studying more than one religion. The aims, intentions and methods of the course are more significant as a preparation for RE; respect, sympathy and tolerance, creative thinking, critical insight and disciplined study, combined with commitment*, personal enthusiasm and intent are essential qualities for the academic study of religion as much as for schoolteachers and pupils. Such qualities are often more highly regarded for admission to higher education than the possession of GCE 'O' and 'A' level passes in Religious Studies (though the latter are increasingly valued). Similarly the exacting responsibilities for RE (either formatively of primary pupils or of the whole ability and age ranges of a secondary school) require commitment, broad and deep knowledge (especially as agreed syllabuses become less particular and prescriptive), a range of technical skills and an interest in persons and life in general. These are the more necessary when RE is related to, or integrated with, other subject areas such as art or history, or linked with the needs of moral, multicultural or social education. For such reasons the teacher must be not only committed to the importance of RE but also sympathetic to its aims and intentions.

The diverse professional requirements for RE cannot be met solely within initial courses of training. In-service courses nationally or locally provide for academic or curriculum study at degree, diploma or sub-diploma level and for the personal development of the teacher at his or her own level of need.

An increase in the numbers of trained RE teachers in secondary schools depends on two factors: 1. proper timetable provision, with a general objective being two periods per week minimum for every secondary school pupil; 2. expansion in the number of periods taught by teachers actually trained in RE. Between 1965 and 1977 the proportion of such periods only improved by five per cent and the percentage of RE teachers who were unqualified in the subject was as high as fifty-eight per cent. If all primary schools and all upper classes (fourth year upwards) of secondary schools made adequate provision for RE (apart from the need to provide feasible options in Religious Studies at GCE 'O' and 'A' level) there would still be a need for an increase in the number of RE teachers of one hundred per cent. This is in spite of a fall in the birth rate and does not take into account the replacement of secondary teachers unqualified in the subject, which would require a further increase in numbers.

It is clear, however, that all competent teachers of RE have good prospects, not only in promotion to the headship of their subject but also in wider academic and pastoral responsibilities in schools or further service as head teachers, advisers, inspectors or lecturers in higher education.

HOWARD MARRATT

Textbooks

Following the establishments of RE in the 1944 Education Act, the early years were somewhat unproductive of textbooks. The agreed syllabuses of the early 1950s were confessional in approach and relied almost entirely on biblical material. Textbooks reflected this: the most widely used books were Bible commentaries. Among these one of the most popular was the Cambridge Bible Commentaries series. This position lasted into the 1960s, and was only remedied after the appearance of the work of Ronald Goldman, Harold Loukes and Ninian Smart.

RE textbook production has always lagged behind thinking and practice in RE. Therefore it was several years before a new generation of textbooks began to appear reflecting the thinking of the researchers. The first major breakthrough in RE textbooks was the series 'New Outlook Scriptures', by Bernard Youngman. The series presented the OT, NT, Christianity through the Ages and Christianity Today, as a series of challenges to be faced by the pupils. The series was produced in a modern format, with numerous photographs and quotations, each page being subdivided by the use of different typefaces. Each chapter ended with a series of tasks for the pupils to perform; these reflected the modern thinking by not always demanding a written response. This work reflected the general theme of the series, 'challenge', and pupils were asked to place themselves in the situations presented, rather than simply comment on them. Book Five for instance, written against a background of social upheaval and a breakdown

of accepted norms, asked the following question, 'In what ways is Bingo a social menace?'

This series helped to encourage a much more questioning attitude in RE although the series was very much a Christian response to questions about life. By contrast the series, 'Encounter' by Ian Birnie treated the upper age range to a similar set of questions, but with a much more open-ended approach. The book was a collection of extracts, some real, some fictional, posing life situations, asking questions, without expecting Christian answers. This book was the forerunner of a wide range of books which have been produced to fill the 'Personal and Social Education' side of RE.

In the 1970s the emphasis in RE shifted away from the neo-confessional approach put forward by Goldman, towards an approach which looked at both the experience and the phenomena of religion, and not simply at the practice of Christianity. RE textbook publishing blossomed with this change in emphasis. Two major contributions during this period were, 'People with a Purpose' and 'Faith in Action'. These series have taken various characters, both historical and living, and shown their abilities to cope with diverse conditions. A major criticism of such series has been that they expose adolescents to 'super Christians', the danger being that the pupils dismiss the beliefs because of their lack of connection with their own experiences.

A major emphasis in RE for the past ten years has been the teaching of world religions*. Again the published material has lagged behind the practice, early works simply attempted to describe a range of religions with their founders and a few of their practices. Geoffrey Parrinder's *A Book of World Religions* was of this style. His later work, however, was more related to the thinking of the time, as shown in *Worship in the World's Religions*. The setting up of the SHAP Working Party* on World Religions has led to numerous excellent books, each dealing with a specific religion. W. Owen Cole's *A Sikh Family in Britain* is an excellent example of the attempt to come to terms with the differing lifestyles experienced by faith groups in Britain. Alongside this is *A Hindu Family in Britain* by P. Bridger, *Understanding your Jewish Neighbour*, by M. Domnitz, and *Who Am I?'* by M. Ballard. The teaching of world religions has caused heart-searching, but the need to present other major religions, largely unknown to teachers and pupils alike, has produced some fine and critical work on the teaching of Christianity in the classroom. *Five Religions in the Twentieth Century* (ed. Owen Cole) is an example of this sort of work. Christianity is treated as a world religion and not simply as a Western phenomenon. The Schools Council series 'Journeys into Religion', is one of the first attempts to present an integrated secondary course, where the phenomena of religion are presented in both a historical and a living context. The series also accepts the challenge of the debate about 'non religions' by presenting aspects of science and humanism in the texts for older pupils.

In the light of the work on world religions, modern textbooks dealing with the traditional RE subjects have reflected these changes in emphases. A recent example of this has been *What Manner of Man?* by M. A. Chignall. Many series of books not originally intended for the RE teacher have been used to good effect. The series 'Connexions' and more recently the 'World Studies Series' are notable examples.

The most glaring omission in the publishing of RE textbooks is the lack of material for slow learners, although this is not simply confined to RE. For many years perceived wisdom has been to simplify other courses or to use materials written for younger children. Most syllabuses do not take account of the specific needs of this group of pupils. Recently however, two books have appeared that begin to redress the balance. *Jesus, His Story in Pictures*, and *The Apostles* by Peter Mullen and Martin Pitts.

M. Ballard, *Who Am I?*, Hutchinson 1971; Ian Birnie, 'Encounter' series, McGraw Hill 1967; (ed.) 'People with a Purpose' series, SCM Press 1973: D. Brickett (ed.). 'Faith in Action' series, REP 1974; P. Bridger, *A Hindu Family in Britain*, REP 1969; M. A. Chignall, *What Manner of Man?*, Edward Arnold 1979; W. Owen Cole, *A Sikh Family in Britain*, REP 1973; (ed.), *Five Religions in the Twentieth Century*, Hulton 1981; 'Connexions' series, Penguin 1968; M. Domnitz, *Understanding Your Jewish Neighbour*, Lutterworth 1974; Peter Mullen and Martin Pitts, *Jesus, His Story in Pictures*, Edward Arnold 1979; *The Apostles*, Edward Arnold 1980; G. Parrinder, *A Book of World Religions*, Hulton 1965; *Worship in the World's Religions*, Sheldon Press 1974; Schools Council, 'Journeys into Religion' series, Granada 1975: 'World Studies Series', Nelson 1978; Bernard Youngman, 'New Outlook Scriptures' series, Hamish Hamilton 1967.

CHRISTOPHER HALLIDAY

Themes

Wherever education is seen in terms of the growth of persons the basic problems is that of relating what Whitehead termed 'inert knowledge' to the age-old Socratic question of how should men live. Missionary literature provides many extreme examples of how cognitive knowledge of a faith can seemingly be held over long periods only for time to reveal that there was no application to behaviour or life style.

Thematic teaching denotes the various attempts by religious educators to forge links between what is learned and what is acted upon. 'Life themes relate religion to life by emphasizing the total unity of experience' (Goldman). In recent years, however, the term 'theme' has been widely used of two separate trends which, although they may have one overall end in mind, nevertheless are quite distinctive in their approaches.

Experientialists such as Hubery have sought to make Christianity meaningful by the process of re-arranging syllabus material so that the biblical literature is taught, not according to a chronological order of events, or according to doctrinal development, but rather as illustrative material to a syllabus structured according to the stages of child development. Thus, for example, a theme on 'home life in Jesus' time' is felt to be appropriate for early childhood, whereas the story of David and Jonathan would be introduced in early adolescence to illustrate a theme on 'Friendship'.

Jean Holm also lays emphasis on the developmental nature of thematic teaching but links it with what she has termed 'implicit religion' and rejects any idea that the Bible must of necessity be introduced. 'A theme is not made religious by the addition of biblical material. It is not even made more religious'. This is perhaps the main defining characteristic of the second type of thematic teaching, associated with the work of Ronald Goldman. Its rationale is summed up by Norman Bull when he comments, 'it is in the actual expression of *daily* life, not what is usually thought of as a religious life that the encounter between God and children will take place'.

Ironically Goldman's own examples, seen in his publications on 'Bread' and 'Shepherds and Sheep', actually represent a half-way stage between Hubery's approach and the life theme proper as defined by Jean Holm. As John Hull has pointed out, the question really is whether the problem with which Goldman was dealing was the religious significance of ordinary life or the problem of the meaning of religious language in a secular society.

Nevertheless, beginning with the West Riding *Handbook of Suggestions* in 1964 all subsequent agreed syllabuses have assumed a thematic approach for young children and there is an obvious connection between this approach and notions of integrated RE in the secondary school.

The experiential* and life theme approaches were necessary rebellions against Bible-based syllabuses which were often conceptually detached from the lives of pupils. It must, however, be questioned whether ultimately they have made religion seem closer to or even more remote from the everyday life of children. There is undoubtedly a need to show that religion is implicit is ordinary day-to-day living, that religion is not theology. But it might also be necessary to reveal the ordinariness of explicit religious material at the same time. For example Alan Dale held that his biblical translations for young people were essentially thematic in that supposedly sacred themes such as kingship and salvation were shown to arise from ordinary life and language.

It may well be that in our attempts to link the cognitive and the affective we need to push both towards the centre rather than concentrate on either one to the detriment of the other. What is religious literature but a case book of the ordinary experiences of others interpreted religiously, against which we can measure our own?

N. J. Bull, *Symbols*, Rupert Hart-Davies 1966; Ronald Goldman, *Readiness for Religion*, Routledge & Kegan Paul 1964; Jean Holm, *Teaching Religion in School,* Oxford University Press 1975; John Hull, 'Theme Teaching as a Method of Religious Education', *Lumen Vitae*, 30, 1, 1975.

JACK PRIESTLEY

Theological Colleges

Theological colleges provide professional training for ministers. Traditionally, candidates for ordination in Oxford and Cambridge received a classical education, with some additional tuition in theology. When this was denied to Dissenters they set up dissenting academies*, thereby pioneering the professional training of the ministry in England and Wales.

Free Church colleges often developed out of academies, e.g. Homerton, Airedale and Rotherham. Others, like the Bristol Baptist College, the oldest surviving Free Church College (1679), were built specifically for training ministers. Some colleges, like Trevecca (1768) and Hoxton (1791), were the result of the Evangelical Revival. The growing interest in education in all its forms in the early nineteenth century provided a new impetus to those dedicated to an educated ministry. The Wesleyan Methodists began training at Hoxton in 1835 and Didsbury in 1842. Congregationalists began in Manchester in 1843, building upon earlier work in the city and county. Presbyterians built a college in London in 1844. In time, some churches had a number of colleges serving different parts of the country. Some of these undertook to provide a general education in addition to ministerial training. As educational opportunities generally increased, some colleges expected their candidates to obtain general educational qualifications first. The opening of Oxford and Cambridge to Dissenters in 1871 created an opportunity which was quickly seized. Mansfield College was erected in Oxford (1886) and Westminster in Cambridge (1899).

In the Church of England the first colleges were founded by cathedrals: Durham (1831), Wells (1838), Chichester (1840), Salisbury and Exeter (1841). Cuddesdon, founded in 1854 to train ordinands dissatisfied with Oxford and Cambridge, was an episcopal foundation, modelled on Catholic and monastic lines. Other colleges were formed to promote the interests of other types of churchmanship. The introduction of ordination training to King's College, London (1843) heralded the use which the churches were to make of universities in the years to come.

Roman Catholic colleges began on the continent. The dispersal of Douai College (1568) by the French Revolution resulted in the founding of St Edmond's College, Ware (1793) and St Cuthbert's, Ushaw (1808). Oscott College began as a distinctively English foundation (1794). Priests are still trained abroad at the Venerable English College and Beda College in Rome and at the English College in Spain. Pre-college training, once widely done at 'minor' seminaries, is done now only at St Joseph's College, Upholland. Some colleges like Ushaw, Durham, are participating actively in the faculties of theology in the universities, i.e. ecumenically, while Heythrop College now functions as a School of Theology within the University of London seeking to make a Roman Catholic contribution to the study of theology in the university.

Among the colleges generally, ecumenical co-operation has been fostered by the Cambridge Federation of Theological Colleges, the Oxford Certificate in Theology, the joint training schemes at Manchester, and the creation of The Queen's College, Birmingham (1970).

Today the training given by the colleges is complemented to an increasing degree by agencies outside the colleges. Many colleges use faculties of theology in the universities. Local churches, hospitals, the Probation and Aftercare Service, and industrial chaplaincies are widely used for practical training. At Manchester and elsewhere residential colleges are assisting in training for auxiliary and lay ministries by extension methods. The Northern Baptist College in Manchester began an alternative pattern of training in 1978 in which students of more mature years are put in charge of churches and trained in part on the job and in part at the college.

Spiritual formation continues to form an important part of training. Nowadays with many ordinands married and living out of college the role played by daily worship in the college chapel is supplemented by worship in local churches, group activities in the homes of students, retreats and help from lay groups, as often off campus as on campus.

Experiments in the Third World to make theological education more contextual are being studied by colleges in this country. Theological educators are challenged to broaden their context to include world as well as church and make their work a running dialogue not only with scripture and tradition but also with contemporary issues.

Alternative Patterns of Training, ACCM 1975; W. Bardsley Brash, *The Story of Our Colleges, 1835–1935,* Epworth 1935; F. W. B. Bullock, *A History of Training for the Ministry of England in England and Wales,* vols 1–2, 1955, 1959; *The Cherwell Report,* The Commission for Priestley Formation, Roman Catholic Episcopal Conference of England and Wales 1979; *Ministerial Formation: Report of the Consultation on Ministerial Formation,* Manila 1979, Geneva 1980; N. Moon, *Education for Ministry, 1679–1979,* Bristol Baptist College 1979; Geoffrey F. Nuttall, *The Significance of Trevecca College 1768–91,* Epworth 1969; J. Stein (ed.), *Ministers for the 1980s,* Handsel Press 1979; *Theological Colleges for Tomorrow,* CIO 1968.

R. J. MCKELVEY

Theology

1. Definitions

'Theology' comes from two Greek words *theos* ('god') and *logos* ('word,' 'measure', 'reason'). Literally therefore theology is the practice of reasoning applied to the divine; organized thinking and speaking about God. The use of 'theology' as the name for a field of study with its own special tradition and disciplines emerged in the twelfth century AD when the medieval universities were developing. 'Theology' was an academic discipline, distinct from the 'liberal arts' (like grammar and rhetoric), taking up in a more methodical and consciously organized way the age-long study of scripture in the church and also the study of doctrinal questions. It had to be developed in relation to the increasingly critical 'arts' (which less and less took Christian faith for granted) and to take account of both heretical Christian views and the views of unbelievers. As an academic discipline therefore theology has always had to live with the connections and tensions between faith and reason, devotion and criticism, deepening the awareness of believers and clarifying understanding in the face of unbelievers. As its history indicates, 'theology' referring to an academic discipline means *Christian* theology. Obviously other faiths can and do develop organized and critical reflections on their understanding of and claims about God. In an increasingly pluralistic world it will presumably become increasingly necessary to add the adjective. In any case it is necessary to *understand* an adjective with 'theology' (i.e. theology is Christian or Jewish or Islamic, etc.). This is so because theology is disciplined and responsible reflection and argument on the beliefs and traditions of a faith considered from within. In principle, theology is the activity of a believer carried on on behalf of and with responsibility to the community of believers ('faith seeking understanding'). In this it is distinguished from, e.g. Philosophy of Religion, History of Religions, Sociology of Religion, etc. (all of which are disciplines which theology has to take fully into account). Christian theology has developed many interrelating sub-disciplines because the Christian understanding of God grows out of the experiences, practices and history of a community or communities widely extended throughout space and time. The sub-divisions include biblical studies (OT and NT with supporting archaeological, linguistic and textual studies); church history; Christian doctrine (studied historically – how did it grow?– systematically – how does it fit together?; philosophically and practically – what does it mean?); liturgy (practices and forms of worship); Christian ethics and various branches of applied and pastoral theology. A creative and responsible relationship between theology as an academic subject and theology as a necessary contribution to the perennial task of the Christian churches to criticize and renew their understanding and practice of Christian faith in relation both to the historical tradition and to the discoveries and demands of the contemporary world is difficult to maintain. Theology in this sense cannot be done by theologians alone. But it cannot be done without theologians, as Christianity without its tradition and history is irresponsible sectarianism. Collaborative theology is essential.

John Coulson (ed.), *Theology and the University,* Darton, Longman & Todd 1964; G. R. Evans, *Old Arts and New Theology,* Clarendon Press 1980; John Macquarrie, *Principles of Christian Theology,* SCM Press 1966; David Tracy, *The Analogical Imagination,* SCM Press 1981; Maurice Wiles, *What is Theology?,* Oxford University Press 1975.

DAVID E. JENKINS

2. Theology and RE

Theology impinges upon RE in two ways. 1. Insofar as pupils are taught the doctrines of the religions and may study the various ways in which religious people understand these doctrines, theology will be part of the content of classroom teaching. One cannot teach the Gospel of Mark to children of any age without at the same time teaching them something of the theology held by Jesus, the early church, the modern church and the teacher. 2. Theological implications may be found in any aspect of the theory, content and method of RE. A certain syllabus may suggest a particular theological outlook, although that theology will not be taught as an explicit part of that syllabus. Similarly, particular methods may rest upon or imply certain theologies. A teacher may teach religion through art with greater understanding if he has studied the theology of the icon*; one may scrutinize the theological assumptions of the life-theme, or ask how theology would evaluate the view of religion which the phenomenological method of teaching seems to require. Some of the theological questions of this second type will be peculiar to RE. Other theological questions will relate to RE insofar as it is part of education as a whole, and thus theology may ask questions about the teacher-pupil relationship, the nature and goals of learning, the purpose of the school itself and so on.

The problems raised by this theological scrutiny of RE may be tackled in two ways. First, the theologian may attempt to make explicit* the theology hidden within the process. This may be thought of as a sort of theological criticism, in which the theologian points out that what is done or how or why it is being done is not neutral, but is suggesting to both pupils and teachers certain views about God, man, history and so on, views which are relevant to the concerns of religious faith. But the theologian cannot stop with this exposure of theological implications. Let us suppose that it was possible to show that a certain RE syllabus proceeded from an assumption about the nature of religion which was theologically unacceptable, but which presented certain compensating advantages, such as offering better possibilities for integration, or falling more neatly into a certain curriculum theory, or meeting certain philosophical objections to the teaching of religion. What should happen next? Why should the religious educator as educator take seriously the comments of the theologians? Would it be right to modify on theological grounds an educational practice which seemed to have the support of all the educational disciplines? Does not the coherence of RE in a plural society depend upon professional practice being legitimated only by widely acceptable professional norms? If theology can also validate the professional practice, so much the better for those practitioners who are adherents of that theology, but if theology is critical of the professional practice then either professional practice is to be changed, in which case practitioners who are not adherents of that theology might have something to say about it, or professional practice remains unchanged, in which case the whole business of theological criticism seems to be little more than an exercise in diagnosis carried out by doctors who have no licence to heal.

The relations between theology and RE therefore move into a deeper and more systematic stage, in which an attempt will be made to consider the possibilities and the limits of theology as forming part of the rationale for religious education, and ultimately for educational theory and practice as a whole. In this sense, we may speak of a theology of RE, which will form part of a theology of education as a whole. The problems become extremely complex. One has a kind of Chinese doll puzzle. Just as the problem of how theology might relate to RE is only a special case of the problem about relating theology to education as a whole, so the latter is only a special case of relating theology to the social sciences as a whole, and this, in turn, is part of the problem of relating theology to any of the other human enterprises, and ultimately, of how theology might relate to anything at all. What does it *mean* for theology to *relate*? What does it mean for theology to contribute?

Theology of RE must be placed within the theological disciplines. Here, it is presumably

part of practical theology, and Frederick Schleiermacher, Gerhard Ebeling, Bernard Lonergan or any other leading writer in the area of theological method may be consulted in order to discover what possibilities there may be. There will be as many theologies of RE as there are theologies and theological methods.

Theology of RE must also be located as one of the disciplines by means of which education is studied. It will co-exist with the philosophy, psychology, sociology and curriculum theory of RE. It will deal not only with theological problems raised by Christian faith but also with the theological problems raised in RE by Islam, Judaism and the great world faiths which have the intellectual vigour and the social relevance necessary for the task. An additional set of theological problems, one step further back, will be presented by the need to make sense of this theological variety of rationales. The problems of creating a theology of world religions are comparable to those presented by the attempt to create a theology of RE in a plural and secular society.

The vital methodological step is taken when one conceives of a relation between theology and RE which is midway between the view that theology is a necessary part of any theory of RE, and, on the other hand, the view that theology cannot contribute anything to such theory and that it would be impossible and illegitimate for theology to make the attempt. If the latter is the case, then there is no way for the teacher with an articulate theology to make sense of his professional calling. If the former is the case, then teachers and educationalists who do not participate in a theology are in some serious sense professionally defective. A theology of RE will honour the secularity of RE and will not attempt to domesticate it. Theology of RE must show that it is a possible and a partial contribution to the creation of a theory which will undergird RE. This is a modest relationship, but one which can be realistically attempted, and which will serve the purpose of maintaining theology and RE in a relationship of mutually critical dialogue.

John M. Hull, *Studies in Religion and Education*, Falmer Press 1984; Karl Ernst Nipkow, 'Theological and Educational Concepts, Problems of Integration and Differentiation',

British Journal of Religious Education, 1, 1, Autumn 1978, pp. 3–13; Arthur Rowe 'Theological Stance and Religious Education' *British Journal of Religious Education* 4, 1, Autumn 1981 pp. 36–38; Derek Webster, 'Creativity Within Religious Education: A Note Towards the Significance for Religious Education of a Dialogue Between Christian Theology and Humanistic Psychology', *British Journal of Religious Education*, 2, 4, Summer 1980, pp. 129–135.

JOHN M. HULL

Tolerance

Its importance and basis. Education is concerned with the growth and development of the individual and the community. In a pluralistic society this constructive relationship of mutual growth and development is not possible without the existence and nurturing of tolerance. In essence, tolerance permits the other to be present in their particular identity, veraciously and responsibly. Ethically tolerance is based on the right of each individual to be him/herself, and of each community to be itself. Theologically, tolerance has its basis in the awareness that the divine cannot be controlled by man, nor adequately contained in any system of doctrine or practice. Consequently one must acknowledge the possibility that the conviction, faith and culture of the other may derive from genuine encounters with the sacred. This is further reinforced by the perception that the divine demands a *free* response from man. Thus the voluntariness of faith rules out the forced imposition of one's own faith or practice upon one's neighbour.

Its nature. Tolerance essentially characterizes a relationship: 1. between individuals; and 2. between communities; and may exist in one of two identifiable forms – formal tolerance and positive tolerance.

Formal Tolerance is essentially the absence of a relationship to the other as other. It is marked by an attitude of indifference and unconcern. This may manifest itself in different degrees according to the extent to which the other threatens to impinge.

1. The other is simply not acknowledged as of such significance that a particular relationship to the other needs to be devised. In RE this frequently takes the form of minimizing the apparent contradictions of conflicting claims of the various religions from an established perspective. Through a supposed benevolent and gratuitous acceptance of them all as equally valid, the distinctiveness of the other is ignored in a faint relativism which regards all belief systems as not only equal but similar. In the end, genuine encounter is prevented. Cultural and religious imperialism is both implicit in, and a consequence of, this perspective.

2. Where the other's impingement is perceived to be significant, one may cope by avoiding the unpleasantness which may arise out of close contact through a degree of withdrawal into self-containment. This is the apparent reaction of many people (to each other) in the urban environment.

3. The self-containment may involve further self-restriction which eventually leads to self-destruction either through total isolation or a dissolution of the self where no distinctive element remains to be asserted. Of the latter instance one might cite the merging of an immigrant community into the indigenous society where no distinctive contributions of the immigrant survives. Of the former, ghettoes and apartheid are social phenomena which approximate to this condition. All are rooted in the formal tolerance of a refusal to relate to the other. It might be pointed out that this formal tolerance readily transmutes into that intolerance which denies the right of the other fully and freely to exist as the other; in which case a rebellion occurs against the self-restriction occasioned by the impinging of the other.

Positive Tolerance – this does not consist in the building of self-protective barriers, nor in the willingness to regard the other as no more than a potential image and replica of the self. In contrast it is genuine openness which is prepared to see the other as both different and significant so that the self may be challenged, and possibly wounded, in the dynamism of the relationship. By taking a positive attitude one is fostering a joint history such that a mutually transforming relationship is created. In this respect tolerance forbids the politics of isolationism on the one hand, and confrontation on the other, and confirms instead the relevance and validity of dialogue between individuals and faith, which in RE is the mutual exploration and conversation of those diversely committed.

Are there limits to tolerance? Although

tolerance must be enjoined wherever differing faiths, cultures or ideologies meet, the common humanity in which all universally partake lays certain constraints. Whatever is deemed to be dehumanizing of any particular person or group of persons, is to be resisted because no genuine human existence is possible without the acknowledgment of the common humanity of all. In RE this excludes the consideration of Nazism or Fascism as a life-stance with a legitimate claim on the loyalty of men. Arguably it would exclude also oppressively authoritarian religious movements like the Unification Church (the Moonies), but would definitely include the great religious traditions whose disciplines, if authoritarian, are none the less purposed to enrich human social existence.

Tolerance and commitment. Tolerance and commitment are not mutually exclusive, indeed a confident, self-critical, commitment prevents the insecurity which so readily leads to intolerance. A person with no clear commitment is no more objective in his/her thinking because of this; on the contrary, those most uncertain and most easily threatened respond to others most irrationally and intolerantly. Commitment is not, therefore, a defect to be avoided, but through education commitment is to be tested and deepened.

G. Mensching, *Tolerance and Truth,* University of Alabama Press 1971.

                    W. S. CAMPBELL/M. C. FELDERHOF

Traditional or Tribal Religions

The religions of developing peoples, often relating to simple forms of tribal animism or polytheistic faith, but also referring to more highly structured patterns of belief in a Supreme Being, among, e.g., certain sections of African society. In addition to African traditional religions the term encompasses Australasian Aboriginal faiths, Polynesian customs and beliefs, American Indian religion and some South American faiths, Cargo Cults, and a variety of minority tribal groups among the hill tribes of India, the peoples of South East Asia and the Arctic regions, etc. In total there are probably between two and three hundred million such people in the world today – more if those who combine a tribal faith with a major religion such as Islam or Christianity are included.

A key factor in identifying such tribal religions is their lack of written scriptures or historical records – the place of these is often occupied by local myths – and it is only in this century that their existence and value has been uncovered by anthropologists, traders and missionaries. For the most part each tribe or community enjoys its own exclusive customs, though certain elements or divinities may be 'borrowed' from neighbouring tribes. There is little attempt to convert others or to expand the influence of any one tribe, which is often seen as purely local, but the syncretistic mixing of traditions is not uncommon.

Traditional religions are not to be identified with pre-historic religion, for they often take a complex and sophisticated form in which ritual, sacrifice and dance may occur in a highly developed and stylized presentation. Rites of passage are generally observed amidst intricate ceremonial, and the power of spirits, divinities and ancestors is regarded with awe and reverence. In many cases a Supreme Being is honoured in addition to the minor local gods, though often the latter have temples and priests in a way that the more august and remote Supreme Being may not. Priests and mediums abound to conduct the ritual, and to care for the temples and holy places where carved images are enshrined as the focus of man's worship and intercession.

Teachers of RE have often ignored such traditional religions in schools as being 'heathen' or 'primitive', and have consequently discarded an area rich in valuable resources. The emphasis on rites of passage is natural and healthy and the exploration of ritual, sacrifice and dance makes an exciting opening to the study of religion with twelve-year-old children. The combination of worship before polytheistic images with reverence for a Supreme Being or Sky God opens up perspectives that can be pursued either in OT developmental theology or in relation to the study of Hinduism and Sikhism, or Hinduism and Islam. The treatment of myth* as living truth, handed down with purpose from generation to generation, and capable of being moulded and rewritten today, is ideal as an introduction to the topic with late juniors or in the early secondary years, and may prevent their rejecting scriptural material as 'disproven' when they find a clash in Genesis between scientific 'fact' and religious affirmation. If an appropriate specific community can be selected (as opposed to a broad, superficial survey) there is excellent material here for the foundations – or even for a more advanced study – of what religion is.

V. Barnett and P. Woodward, 'The Novel and Multi-Faith Education', in W. O. Cole, *World Religions – A Handbook for Teachers*, Shap Working Party/Commission for Racial Equality 1977 and 1980; D. A. Brown, *A Guide to Religions*, SPCK 1975; V. Brown, *Voices of Earth and Sky*, Stackpole 1974; R. Bruce and J. Wallbank, *Beginning Religion*, Edward Arnold 1982; M. Eliade, *Patterns in Comparative Religion*, Sheed & Ward 1958; S. L. Fahs and D. T. Spoerl, *Beginnings: Earth, Sky, Life, Death: Stories, Ancient and Modern*, Beacon Press 1958; E. B. Idowu, *African Traditional Religion*, SCM Press 1969; J. S. Mbiti, *African Religions and Philosophy*, Heinemann 1969; R. C. Mitchell, *African Primal Religions*, Argus Communications 1977; Open University, *Man's Religious Quest*, AD 208, Course Notes for Units 24 and 25 – Aspects of African Religion, Open University Press 1977; E. G. Parrinder, *African Traditional Religion*, SPCK 1954; E. G. Parrinder (ed.), *Man and his Gods: An Encyclopaedia of the World's Religions*, Hamlyn 1971; J. V. Taylor, *The Primal Vision*, SCM Press 1969; E. Tooker, *Native North American Spirituality of the Eastern Woodlands*, SPCK 1979; H. W. Turner, 'A bibliographical essay on Tribal ("Primal") Religions' in W. O. Cole (ed.) *World Religions – A Handbook for Teachers*; H. W. Turner, *Living Tribal Religions*, Ward Lock Educational 1971.

PETER WOODWARD

Transcendence

This refers to an extending beyond the bounds of the universe, understanding or human experience. Transcendence has two common uses related to 1. the divine and 2. personal experience.

1. Attributes of the divine exceed all limits of human understanding. God transcends space and time: he is non-spatial and eternal. He transcends the universe and is independent of it, yet the universe is an expression of his nature through which he mediates his presence. He transcends the limits of knowledge, power and personhood, yet allows humans awareness of him without definite knowledge. Divine transcendence is over the world but manifest in the world.

2. 'Transcendental experience' has three referents. (*a*) The phrase may refer to experiences 'in another dimension', nature mysticism, personal ecstasy or peak experiences. All such experiences have personal significance, are regarded as natural, and may be interpreted from a secular or religious perspective. (*b*) The phrase may refer to religious experience. If so, it can be understood in two different ways. (i) Some talk of 'religious experience' to indicate specific and identifiable experiences. A distinction is frequently made between religious experience and religious mysticism. Religious experience refers to experiences of 'another presence' which 'exists' outside the individual; religious mysticism indicates the process and goal of mystical union between the worshipper and the divine, or in non-theistic mysticism the goal of 'spiritual maturity', e.g. nirvana. (ii) 'Religious experience' is sometimes used as an interpretative concept to indicate the religious interpretation of all experience. The first usage is preferable. The second usage is better described as 'religious faith' or 'religious outlook'. (*c*) Transcendental experience may refer to 'the way of transcendence', a way of life, especially of allegiance to Jesus.

RE has passed through three phases since 1944.

Up until about 1961 RE was confessional: it set out to help pupils become Christian. Concern with the transcendent focussed on teaching about God and Jesus. Religious experience was used as an interpretative concept for normal experience understood at full depth. In the following decade (1961–71), RE focussed on the Christian faith and human problems, subtly advocating Christianity: a neo-confessional* approach. Since about 1971, the aim of RE has been to help pupils understand the nature of religion: an educational aim. During the decade 1971–81 attention began to be focussed on the education of the emotions and on transcendental experience as elements in RE, and the Religious Experience Research Unit* (RERU) at Oxford has offered analyses of the experiences of many people, stimulating interest in its educational importance. Surveys have shown that between a third and a half of the population of Great Britain and the USA report that they have had a significant 'religious experience'.

See also **God**; **Religious Experience**.

C. Davis, *Body as Spirit: the Nature of Religious Feeling*, Hodder & Stoughton 1976; P. Donovan, *Interpreting Religious Experience*, Sheldon 1979; A. Hardy, *The Spiritual Nature of Man*, Oxford University Press 1979; D. Hay, *Exploring Inner Space*, Penguin 1982; D. Hay and A. Morisy, *Reports of Ecstatic, Paranormal or Religious Experience*, RERU 1977; G. B. Miles 'Some Aspects of the Religious Experience of Sixth Formers' in *Journal of Beliefs and Values*, 1, 4, 1980 and *Transcendental and Religious Experiences of Sixth Form Pupils: An Analytic Model*, Winterbourne Rectory, Bristol 1981; M. Paffard, *Inglorious Wordsworth*, Hodder & Stoughton 1973 and *The Unattended Moment*, SCM Press 1976; R. J. Pearce, 'Religious Education and Emotion', *British Journal of Religious Education*, Summer 1979; R. S. Peters, *Reason and Compassion*, Routledge & Kegan Paul 1973; E. Robinson, *The Original Vision*, RERU 1977; K. Ward, *The Concept of God*, Blackwell 1974; J. Wilson, *Education in Religion and the Emotions*, Heinemann 1971.

GRAHAM B. MILES

Typology of Religion

As the general phenomenological approach* to the study of religion has developed and matured during this century a number of distinguishable strands have appeared within it. One such strand is typology, the comparison of religious phenomena across space and time. In the recent study of Moore and Habel typology has been used as a technical term to identify their approach and method in the study of religion with particular reference to the school context. Their approach has drawn heavily on the insights of such phenomenologists as Kristensen, van der Leeuw and Eliade, who have not used typology as a self-designation. Typology is best described as a method of study of the phenomenon of religion. Like any method, however, it rests on a number of key perspectives. These include the following:

1. In common with phenomenology of religion in general, typology lays stress on the attitude of empathy in the study of religion. Whatever our final reflective judgments on the nature and significance of religion might be, an essential starting point is to try to come to terms with the phenomenon as it is experienced, believed and valued by the believers. To help us stand alongside the believer we need to become aware of our own attitudes, values, prejudices, biases and theories and, at least for a while, hold these in suspension.

2. The purpose of cultivating this empathetic stance is to try to describe the phenomena of religion from the perspective of the believer. If we are to reach any serious understanding of religion, even if this serious understanding takes the form of a negative judgment, it needs to take the believers seriously.

3. The purpose of this empathetic description is to provide the student with basic data on which to reflect in order to understand the nature and significance of the phenomenon so described. How do we achieve this understanding?

4. The typologists argue that we have to begin to use larger constructs in which we locate and integrate the particular description. These wider constructs are at three levels of inclusiveness: (*a*) the construct of the particular religious tradition; (*b*) the constructs of the phenomenon across cultures and religious traditions; (*c*) the construct of humanity and society.

It is best to illustrate this through an example. Let us assume that we have achieved an adequate empathetic description of the Gikuyu *irua* or rite of initiation into adulthood. How do we make sense of this ritual? (*a*) It is important to attempt to locate this ritual within the fabric of Gikuyu religious life. This involves constructing a more or less ideal or typical portrait of the Gikuyu system of belief, and practice, and discerning how the *irua* is informed by other Gikuyu beliefs and practices. (*b*) But, while the *irua* is specific to the Gikuyu, as a rite of passage into adulthood it bears remarkable structural and symbolic similarities to initiation rites in other cultures. Typologists attempt to discern some of the typical and recurring characteristics of rites of passage (and other component phenomena) as they occur across cultures and use these generalizations to interpret particular rites (such as the *irua*). (*c*) If, despite all their differences in specific detail, there are family resemblances between religions and between the component phenomena of religions, how do we interpret these structural and symbolic similarities? Why, for example, do rites of passage such as the Gikuyu *irua* reflect such recurring structures in religions? Are they grounded in some fundamental personal or social characteristic or need? At this level of questioning in search of understanding we begin to draw on the insights of such disciplines as philosophy, psychology and sociology. At this level we are dealing with religion at an extraordinarily high level of abstraction and generalization. Thus typology begins with the concrete and specific data of religious phenomena, but moves through more complex levels of abstraction in search of integrating understanding.

In the primary school it is probably impossible for most students to grasp the complex internal relations of religious traditions. But they can handle, albeit without abstract sophistication, some of the more concrete component phenomena of religions such as sacred persons, places, dress, stories, dances, rituals, and so on. At this stage of their growth it is likely that the younger students will treat each phenomenon in relative isolation and not integrate it into the wider context of its particular tradition or the cross-cultural patterns. Here, however, a necessary foundation is being laid for an ongoing process.

With the greater maturity that comes in the lower secondary school, students need to be encouraged to begin integrating the more or less isolated phenomena into both their particular traditions and the cross-cultural patterns. It is important that students begin to discern that religions are not loose collections of bits and pieces but systems of belief and practice which provide an integrative framework within which people live their lives. It is equally important, however, to discern that despite the highly distinctive character of particular religions there are patterns and themes which run across the various religions.

In the upper secondary school, with the students' increasing capacity for abstract and conceptual thinking, it is possible to begin exploring the hot questions concerning reli-

gion as such within the larger frames of reference of psychology, sociology and philosophy.

M. Eliade, *Patterns in Comparative Religion*, Sheed & Ward 1979; M. Eliade, *Rites and Symbols of Initiation*, Harper & Row 1965; A. van Gennup, *Rites of Passage*, Chicago University Press 1960; W. B. Kristensen, *The Meaning of Religion*, Nijoff 1960; B. S. Moore and N. C. Habel, *When Religion Goes to School: Typology of Religion for the Classroom*, Texts in Humanities, South Australian College of Advanced Education 1982; J. Waardenburg, *Reflections on the Study of Religion*, Mouton 1978.

BASIL MOORE

Ultimate Questions

In RE these are of two kinds, 1. practical, and 2. academic.

1. Practical questions concern the conduct of religiously educational activities and arise by way of inferences drawn from theoretical studies in fields such as philosophy, theology, psychology, sociology and ethics. These questions are concerned with (i) the instantiation of norms implicit in the concept of education; (ii) the professional concept of religion adopted by the religious educator; (iii) the appropriateness of aims of religiously educational activities; (iv) the efficacy of approaches and methods employed; (v) the optimum conditions of children's learning; (vi) the formal structure and substantive content of both the agreed syllabus of RE and that of each school relative to its type and locale; (vii) the place of RE in the total curriculum; and (viii) the training and professional status of religious educators. Reference to such questions is necessary for the efficient promotion of religiously educational activities and for distinguishing such activities from other nurturing activities such as training, socializing, indoctrinating, edifying and converting.

2. Ultimate academic questions in RE concern the content of religiously educational activities and whilst these are logically distinct from practical questions in appealing to objective criteria of theoretical scholarship they are necessarily dependent upon answers given to the latter in terms of selection and use of material. As all educational activities benefit persons by provoking depth and breadth of self-understanding, and as religious under-

standing is primarily concerned with spiritual insight, so the ultimate academic questions in RE concern the nature of the spiritual dimension of personal life. All such questions contribute to the all-pervading question central to religiously educational activities, namely that concerning the cosmic character of each person as a subject.

These ultimate questions posed by personal life focus attention upon the non-rational mystery of life which is characteristic of the spiritual and in order that religious understanding may be provoked to tussle with such mystery subsidiary academic questions arise concerning the child's (i) direct experience of sensible religious objects; (ii) mastery of religious discourse; (iii) use of the powers of the imagination; (iv) acquisition of information about the religions of the world, and of religious information about personal spirituality; and (v) mastery of skills*, both intellectual and religious.

E. Cox, *Changing Aims in Religious Education*, Routledge & Kegan Paul 1966; M. Grimmitt, *What Can I Do in RE?* Mayhew-McCrimmon 1973; R. Holley, *Religious Education and Religious Understanding*, Routledge & Kegan Paul 1978; E. Hulmes, *Commitment and Neutrality in Religious Education*, Chapman 1979; D. J. O'Leary and T. Sallnow, *Love and Meaning in Religious Education*, Oxford University Press 1982.

RAYMOND HOLLEY

Unions

Among the unions, the National Union of Teachers has had the longest history of involvement in discussions about RE during which it has maintained its position that the RE teacher should be a professional educator, rather than a propagator of religion.

When the new Education Act was contemplated the NUT issued its proposals for dealing with religious instruction in state schools. Although these had some influence, the union was by no means satisifed with the situation created by the 1944 Act. The union was particularly concerned that teachers should be free to exercise initiative in planning schemes of work, and that church membership should not be made a criterion of ability to give religious instruction.

One of the union's proposals had been the

formulation of a national agreed syllabus. Although this suggestion was not adopted, the NUT, in conjunction with the Joint Conference of Anglicans and Free Churchmen and the Association of Education Committees, did produce *A National Basic Outline of Religious Instruction* (1945), a document intended to counter regimentation in the content and methods of religious instruction which, it was feared, was likely to result from the operation of the new Act. The outline encouraged teachers to help children to find their own honest answers to religious questions.

In the early 1950s the NUT and the Joint Four contributed to a major inquiry made by the Institute of Christian Education into the working of the 1944 Education Act (*Religious Education in Schools*). A smaller-scale study was conducted in 1963–4 by the NUT and the British Council of Churches* which highlighted the low number of specialist teachers in the secondary schools studied, together with the lack of a conscious attempt by many teachers to encourage a critical approach among pupils (*Some Aspects of Religious Education in Secondary Schools*).

A more recent piece of research was conducted by the Assistant Masters' Association in the mid 1970s (*Religious Education*, 1978). Less than two-thirds of the schools surveyed included RE as a subject on the timetable for all pupils to sixteen-plus and schools generally attached little significance to an agreed syllabus*.

Since the 1960s the general trend among the unions has been to support strongly the place of RE in the curriculum on educational grounds, while arguing that the relevant sections of the 1944 Education Act are in need of revision. Most unions hold the view that RE should no longer be supported by the compulsory provisions of an Act of Parliament, but that its position in the curriculum should be strengthened by the appointment of more specialist teachers in all types of school and of more advisers in RE. The broadening of the subject to include, for example, the study of religions other than Christianity, is welcomed by the Assistant Masters' Association, while the Professional Association of Teachers takes a narrower view of RE below sixth-form level.

Of the further and higher education unions, the Association of Teachers in Colleges and

Departments of Education (which in 1976 became part of the newly-formed National Association of Teachers in Further and Higher Education) has made a significant contribution to thinking about RE through its Religious Studies Section's annual conference and its journal (currently entitled *Journal of Beliefs and Values*). The ATCDE also published a report recommending that teacher-training institutions should help to promote in all students an awareness that they live and will teach in a multi-cultural society, and urging that all students should have some knowledge of the religions of minority communities (*Teacher Education for a Multi-Cultural Society* 1974).

Religious Education in Schools, National Society/SPCK 1954; *Religious Education in State Schools,* Professional Association of Teachers 1976; *Some Aspects of Religious Education in Secondary Schools,* inquiry by the British Council of Churches and the NUT, 1964.

ROBERT JACKSON

United Reformed Church

The United Reformed Church in the UK came into being in its present form in 1981 when the Re-formed Association of Churches of Christ and the United Reformed Church in England and Wales united. It was in 1972 that the earlier union of the Congregational Church* in England and Wales and the Presbyterian Church of England had resulted in the formation of the United Reformed Church in England and Wales. The present church has therefore inherited attitudes and policies of its three constituent denominations towards public education and has had to develop its thinking and define its policies with regard to Christian initiation, nurture and education.

1. Public education

The URC shares with the other Free Churches in England and Wales a policy towards public education which cannot be fully understood without reference to history. In the early years of Nonconformity academies were established to offer an alternative education particularly for those preparing for Christian ministry. Later, in the early part of the nineteenth century, under the influence of the Sunday School Movement* with its emphasis on literacy, it began to be recognized that a more sustained approach to the education of children was necessary. Congregationalists and Presbyterians supported the formation of the British and Foreign School Society* to provide non-sectarian voluntary education. While the Society's schools were largely in urban areas the rival National Society*, almost exclusively Anglican, provided schools throughout the country in urban and rural areas.

With the introduction of state funds to support the voluntary schools the National Society soon attracted more state aid than the British and Foreign School Society and the gap between what they could offer widened annually to the disadvantage of the Nonconformists. Throughout the century the state played an increasingly central role in the development of education and as standards and provision increased, and as the population growth outstripped the capacity of the voluntary societies to provide schooling for all children, Nonconformists began to press for a national system of education, publicly funded and enforced. They feared the power of the Church of England and the growing involvement of Roman Catholics in education. While the majority pressed for non-sectarian RE in schools there were some, like the leading Congregationalist R. W. Dale, who advocated the exclusion of religion from the public education provision. The 1870 and 1902 Education Acts which played such an important role in shaping the education system in England and Wales marked the peak of Nonconformist involvement in educational controversy. During these political developments in which Congregationalists were particularly prominent there evolved a consensus that the churches should no longer seek to safeguard their privileged position but should rather press for a state system of education available for all children.

It was with great reluctance that Nonconformists came to accept a state system which allowed voluntary schools to receive state funds and to co-exist alongside the schools provided by the state. By the time the 1944 Education Act came into force the earlier antagonism towards the voluntary schools supported by Anglicans and Roman Catholics had lost its force. Instead the Free Churches were satisfied with the religious clauses in the Act safeguarding non-sectarian RE in the county schools. This has meant that much of the debate about public education in the churches that formed the URC has been pre-occupied, since 1944, with RE rather than with education as a whole.

In accordance with the position it inherited from its parent churches, the URC places its emphasis on the provision by the state of a full public education system paid for through taxation. It is primarily concerned with the improvement of that system and to that end is represented on the Joint Education Policy Committee* through the Free Church Federal Council*, which makes representations to government on educational matters. From time to time there are debates about aspects of public education at the URC General Assembly. The quality of RE in schools and the extent of its provision have formed the basis for resolutions in the General Assembly and representatives of the church have shared in the production of documents on education in the Free Church Federal Council. Multi-cultural education in a pluralist society is another subject that has commanded attention. Responsibility for advising the church on public education is entrusted to its Church and Society Department.

With the growth in the provision of higher education* in the second half of the twentieth century the URC, in common with other denominations, has deployed some of its ministers as chaplains to students in institutions of higher education. It has direct responsibility for Westminster College Cambridge in which some of its ministers are trained, but also recognizes the training offered in independent colleges with long associations with Congregationalism, at Mansfield College, Oxford, the Manchester Congregational College, and colleges at Swansea and Bala Bangor in Wales.

2. Confirmation preparation

The processes of negotiation leading to the formation of the URC in 1972 and again in 1981 placed considerable emphasis on Christian initiation and nurture. In 1972 in its Basis of Union the church acknowledged the importance of the gospel sacrament of baptism* administered in infancy or at an age of responsibility. It stated that 'baptism is the sacrament of entry into the Church and its corporate ministry'. Although the Basis of Union made provision for the baptism of persons 'at an age of responsibility; upon profession of faith', the Congregational and Presbyterian Churches were predominantly paedobaptists and the URC remained thus, baptizing infants and then receiving them in due course, upon profession of faith in Christ, to 'enter upon the full privileges and responsibilities of membership'.

In the negotiations with the Re-formed Association of Churches of Christ the doctrine of baptism was one of the major issues. Churches of Christ expected personal faith as a pre-requisite of baptism and therefore practised the baptism of believers. Over a long period of discussion and negotiation the way was found for a union of the Re-formed Association with the URC with full recognition of both forms of baptism. In the statements made during the negotiations some emphasis was placed on enhancing the importance of the service of confirmation*.

In practice the preparation for confirmation or believer's baptism is the responsibility of the Elders' Meeting in which ministers and elders elected by the Church Meeting exercise oversight of the spiritual life of the local church. The candidates are usually prepared by means of a series of meetings in which they consider the nature of Christian discipleship, the mission, ministry and organization of the church, the history of their church and its place in the ecumenical movement and their personal faith. Some Elders' Meetings devise their own courses of preparation but most use the courses and guidelines published from time to time by the URC.

3. Christian education

Christian education of the children and adults in each local congregation is also the responsibility of the Elders' Meeting together with the Church Meeting. Each local congregation develops its own programmes of education in the light of its own circumstances and convictions. Nevertheless there are some common patterns discernible within the URC as a whole.

While all denominations have been developing new ways of involving adults and children together in programmes of Christian education and in the worship of the local church, it was in Congregationalism that much of the pioneering work was done in response to the inspiration of H. A. Hamilton. His concept of Family Church challenged the earlier patterns of church life which largely separated children and adults in both worship and education. His work led to a growing relationship between the worship and the education offered in the local church. At first the change involved a modification of the principal act of worship so that adults and children could worship together for at least part of the service, but it led eventually to a complete reappraisal of the relationship between adults and children within the Christian fellowship.

Prior to the formation of the URC, the Congregational Church had published a series of Christian Education Handbooks largely based on Hamilton's concept and reflecting a growing emphasis on the importance of experience in the educational process. In 1968 the Congregational and Presbyterian Churches shared with other Free Churches in commending a new series of annual volumes entitled *Partners in Learning**. The URC now regards *Partners in Learning* as the principal publication for use in the regular Christian education programmes for adults and children. Although the volumes are jointly published by the National Christian Education Council and the Methodist Church Division of Education and Youth many of the writers are members of the URC. Support for these volumes in preference to other courses derives from the fact that their educational approach is based on the importance of the Bible, Christian history, personal experience, the community of the church and the celebration of the Christian year*. They provide material for worship and education for the whole church on parallel themes to facilitate co-operation between adults and children.

The Church Life Department of the URC, which is primarily responsible for advising the church on Christian education, has consistently sought to develop an understanding of the church as a learning and worshipping community of people of all ages. It issues reports, produces educational publications, organizes training conferences for leaders and co-operates with other denominations in a training course for leaders and teachers. The main emphasis is to encourage churches to develop all-age programmes of Christian

education. Other departments of the URC also publish educational courses, from time to time, on particular themes and aspects of Christian responsibility.

See also **Congregationalism**; **Presbyterian Churches, Church of Scotland**.

D. W. Bebbinton, *The Nonconformist Conscience,* Allen & Unwin 1982; H. A. Hamilton, *The Family Church in Principle and Practice,* Independent Press 1941; John M. Sutcliffe, *Learning and Teaching Together*, Chester House Publications 1980; Wilfred Tooley (ed.), *Partners in Learning*, Methodist Church Division of Education and Youth and The National Christian Education Council, annual volumes.

JOHN REARDON

United States of America

Religious education in the USA is strongly influenced by the dream or the ideal called America. This dream of success, wealth and happiness attracted the first settlers and the waves of immigrants that followed them. The Puritans immediately set up schools so that every child could read the scriptures. The church, family and school were to work together for a perfect society, the realization of the kingdom of God on earth.

The Puritan version of the dream did not survive the seventeenth century. The open land to the West was the crucial factor in the development of the United States. Religious life was strongly affected by the frontier experience and the intense revivalistic movements that spread from the frontier. The 'Great Awakenings' of the eighteenth and nineteenth centuries had less interest in education than had seventeenth-century Puritan society.

The US Constitution separated the government from any 'establishment of religion'. Education in religious matters was to be left to religious organizations. Protestant denominations, through Bible societies and missionary work, tried to create a 'Christian America' with a mission to the whole world. The Sunday School became the chief vehicle of Protestant education.

Despite the supposed wall of separation between church and state, the government supported schools incorporated much of the culture's religiosity. These public schools, beginning in the 1840s, were conceived to be places of moral training that would avoid religion's divisiveness. Bible reading and prescribed prayers were part of the daily routine and assumed to be non-denominational. The fast growing Catholic population objected to these religious practices and the Catholic Church set out to create its own school system. The Jewish immigrants came in large numbers after 1890. They too had problems with the public schools but they made extensive use of these schools and accompanied that education with their own instruction and observances.

At the turn of the twentieth century the Sunday School was well organized but intellectually thin. The Religious Education Association was founded in 1903 to overcome the deficiencies of the Sunday School. The REA sought to create an education ideal in all the religious groups and to work with the public schools. It had some success with liberal Protestant churches in the first decades of the century. It continues today to strive for conversation among Jewish, Catholic and Protestant education.

The 1940s represented a shift in Protestant education. The neo-orthodox theology of the time was critical of liberal theology and progressive education. A greater emphasis upon the Bible and doctrine can be found in the curricula developed during that period. The notion of a separate profession of religious educator gave way to an understanding of education as part of church ministry.

In the early 1960s the US Supreme Court declared unconstitutional both state imposed prayer and Bible reading in the public school. The court did allow and encourage the study of religion. Departments of religious study expanded in colleges and universities. A similar movement in elementary and secondary schools has been less successful. The difficulty of devising curricula and some remaining distrust from the past make the issue politically volatile.

The Roman Catholic Church, now about twenty-five per cent of the population, has undergone widespread change since the 1960s. With a shrinking percentage of Catholic children in the church schools, increased attention has been given to parish-based programmes. Catholicism has taken over the earlier Protestant ideal of one or several professionally trained educators to direct parish education.

Jews constitute less than three per cent of US population but their presence is strongly felt, especially in many of the major cities. As one of the 'three American faiths', Jewish religion exists with only slight antagonism in the culture. The freedom which Jews have experienced in the USA has been accompanied by fears of assimilation. Education is emphasized in family and synagogue and through observance of the Sabbath and great holy days.

The Sunday School still bears the main burden of Protestant education, supplemented by adult education programmes and a great diversity of socially oriented activities. The Sunday School remains especially prominent in the southern United States. From its beginning the Sunday School kept some distance from the clerical organization of the church. It prides itself on the laity's involvement in teaching the Bible to children. The churches and their educational programme were an important vehicle for black people throughout the nineteenth century and into the twentieth century.

The 1970s produced a powerful revival of evangelism and a stress on being 'born again'. Television became a major instrument of evangelical religion. Some of this movement rejected modern education, attempting, for example, to reinstate biblical fundamentalism in public school science curricula. More broadly, the religious movement helped to revitalize the piety of Protestant and Catholic churches creating new interest in the study of the Bible, Eastern meditation and spirituality.

The three main religious traditions seem likely to co-operate further in educational ventures. Other religions – less than one per cent of the population – receive little attention. An increase in Muslim influence will perhaps change the established patterns. Catholic schools though fewer in number remain important. The number of Protestant evangelical schools (usually called Christian) is growing rapidly.

Robert Lyn, and Elliot Wright, (eds.) *The Big Little School: 200 Years of the Sunday School,* Religious Education Press 1980; Neil McCluskey (ed.), *Catholic Education in America: A Documentary History,* Teachers College 1964;

Merton Strommen, (ed.), *Research on Religious Development,* Hawthorn 1971; Marvin Taylor (ed.), *Foundations for Christian Education in an Era of Change,* Abingdon 1976; John Westerhoff (ed.), *Who Are We? The Quest for a Religious Education,* Religious Education Press 1978.

GABRIEL MORAN

University Departments of RE
see **Higher Education**

USSR *see* **Eastern Europe**

Vacation Term for Biblical Study

The Vacation Term for Biblical Study, held annually for two weeks, provides courses at a high academic level on biblical and related subjects. Scholars who are experts in their field are invited, without regard to their personal religious standpoint. The Term was inaugurated in 1903 through the initiative of Margaret Benson and was a branch of a larger movement which procured the admission of women students to theological courses at King's College, London, and led to the institution of the Lambeth Diploma* and the Archbishop's Licence to teach Theology. A permanent lending library is maintained in London from which relevant books are brought to the course. In addition to readings from selected Hebrew and Greek texts, daily classes in both languages are provided. Though the original intention was to hold the course alternately at Oxford and Cambridge its venue for over twenty years has been St Anne's College, Oxford.

E. M. STAMPER

Values Education

Values Education is an inescapable part of any educational system though it may not always be openly acknowledged as such. Its presence may be observed in anthropological accounts of young people growing up in primal societies, e.g. Samoa or the early colonial period in Africa, through to the sophisticated system of modern states, e.g. France, China, USA or USSR. Primal and sophisticated alike have a common expectation that young people will take their place as responsible adults to their own benefit and that of their community.

The relevant learning situations are as diverse as the cultures named above. They range from the initiation into adult life of a tribal warrior/hunter/herder, through the home/family trade/late entry to schooling of rural Denmark to the extended period of subject-based formal education met in industrialized countries. In addition to a central theme of appropriate skills and the physical development they require, attention is always paid to the growth of cultural and personal consciousness. Some accomplish this by exposure of the young to folk-lore, community history, selected material from philosophy or religion, or to a dominant political philosophy or religious tradition.

Acknowledging that all elements of any learning system become wittingly or unwittingly vehicles of transmitting values, the term 'values education' is used for a part of a curriculum in which the matter of values is consciously addressed. In both the atmosphere of learning and any specific VE element two issues have to be faced. One is the aim of the educator or the community on whose behalf he/she is acting. The other is the divergence between the school's VE efforts and the values of the sub-cultures from which the pupils come.

Aims. There are three aims that mark off polarities in VE: 1. to produce conformity to existing values; 2. to produce dedication to radical change; 3. to foster a capacity for critical appraisal of both existing and potential values. Historically one is unlikely to find a pure example of any one of these so they are best used as 'types' or markers by which to review and assess one's own work in VE. One has to keep in mind that the capacity for critical appraisal needs to be applied to alternative as well as existing values for it is not difficult to show that radical change is often demanded on the basis of views which their exponents cannot or do not critically examine. Indeed today's radical critics have often become tomorrow's tyrants enforcing a new conformity. Where all adults are able to take part in the political process and even more where there is a variety of cultures and interest-groups in one society the most appropriate aim is where the capacity for critical appraisal of all existing and alternative values is maximized and there is openness to existing and alternative values that survive such appraisal.

Sectors and topics. The sectors that make

up VE may be defined by beginning with the individual's sense of identity and pass through the individual's relationships in kinship, peer group, friendships at work or in leisure to the formation of opinion and the exercise of responsibility in issues of local, national and international concern. Topics within these sectors emerge from their key aspects: 1. In the matter of the sense of identity, these are a basic outlook of trust, confidence and hopefulness, the capacity for self-control, for intimacy rather than isolation and for taking into one's own personality attitudes and ideals one has admired and sought to imitate. 2. In the relationships group, key aspects are a balance of openness to others with a capacity to discern their strengths and weaknesses, a capacity to make new beginnings through forgiveness and, often more difficult, being forgiven, the quality of relationships with peers, with younger and older people, with those for whom one is responsible and those to whom one is responsible. 3. In the group concerned with opinion formation and the exercise of a citizen's responsibilities, key aspects are the degree of access to accurate information, the nature of the world-view held, the opportunities and limitations in one's contemporary society for sharing opinions and exercising responsibility.

Related curriculum components. There are many contenders for the Values Education function, each with its own group of enthusiasts: health, sex, political* and moral* education, social, philosophical, environmental*, or religious studies – the list seems endless. Between these there is a great deal of overlap and those interested in VE should make good use of the books and other resources published in each area. When they are regarded as resources for a VE which is clear about its aim and objectives, any sense of confusion and contention disappears.

RE as a resource for Values Education. Where RE is given a place in a Humanities or Moral Education programme of VE one is likely to find an empirical/rational framework and an emphasis being laid on education for decision-making. This tends to have three phases: 1. accurate observation; 2. setting out alternative choices; and 3. imaginative exploration of likely consequences for each possible choice (the Futuristics of American VE).

RE has three distinct roles in such a programme: 1. to see that long term aspects of the issues are not evaded or ignored; 2. to focus attention on any religious or political beliefs underlying motivation; and 3. to provide a monitoring system that transcends personal, group, ethnic or national interests and that will operate throughout the decision-making and the actions that flow from it.

Values Education as an aspect of RE. The approach and roles outlined above can also be used here where it is judged best to begin with the pupils' own experience. However, there are times when there is advantage in distancing the discussion, at least at first, from a controversial issue. In this case a look at the evidence of the moral impact of one or more religions can form a basis for examining a contemporary issue. The evidence is to be found in the historical accounts of the practices of a religion as well as its sacred literature (if any) and in the lives of those who have reflected its meaning in different ages. The range and nature of religious concern with ethics can be well illustrated through the contrasts to be found between Buddhism, Christianity and Islam not least in the way each belief system makes use of the concept of time dominant in the culture in which it originated.

The late Ian Ramsey, Bishop of Durham, echoing Isaiah directed our attention to 'knowledge', 'discernment' and 'commitment' as vital aspects of religious language. He could with no less validity have presented them as the key links of RE to Values Education.

JAMES GREEN

Voluntary Schools

Under the terms of the Education Act 1944 voluntary schools are primary, middle or secondary schools which are maintained by the LEA but which were established by a voluntary providing body. Before the Act most voluntary schools were provided and maintained by charitable trusts, most of which were religious foundations linked with a major religious denomination (of which the Established Church of England provided the largest number). After the passing of the 1944 Act those voluntary schools which formed part of the newly established maintained sector became either Voluntary *Aided* schools or Voluntary *Controlled* schools. Voluntary *Special Agreement* schools form a minor category of secondary schools. Their features are largely those of *Aided* status.

1. *Voluntary Aided Schools*. Under the Education Act 1944, the governors or managers of an aided school must provide fifty per cent of all capital costs of external maintenance (the figure has been reduced several times and is now fifteen per cent). Those governors or managers who represented the voluntary providing body or religious trust (called foundation governors or managers) hold a majority in the governing or managing body. This majority was two or three under the 1944 Act; under the Education Act 1980 the majority is two but three in schools of more than three hundred pupils. This Act also abolishes the use of the term managers in primary schools. The foundation governors have a duty to preserve the voluntary nature of the school in accordance with a trust deed. The governing body appoints the staff of the school, controls the use of the premises out of school hours and establishes the admissions policy (which, under the 1980 Act, it is required to publish). The Articles of Government usually state that the governors control the general direction of the curriculum and in an aided school both the secondary secular instruction (see Section 23 of the 1944 Act) and the religious education (under Section 25 of the Act) are clearly matters to be determined by the governors (see 3 below). It cannot be a condition of admission to a voluntary aided school that a pupil does or does not attend a particular place of worship or any Sunday School.

2. *Voluntary Controlled Schools*. Though remaining in most circumstances the property of the trustees or foundation, these are wholly maintained by the LEA. The governors who represent the foundation are in a minority on the governing body. The admissions policy is established by the LEA which is obliged to state the arrangements by which parents can express a preference in the choice of schools. Though the governors are likely under the Articles of Government to control 'the general direction of the curriculum', the provisions of Section 25 of the 1944 Act (see 3 below) regarding religious education must be adhered to. The staff in a controlled school are appointed by the LEA though some of the arrangements for such appointments may be delegated to or include the governors.

'Reserved teachers'* are appointed by the LEA but the foundation governors must be satisfied as to the competency of those appointed.

The governors control the use of the school premises on Saturdays, the foundation governors alone control the use on Sundays. Virtually all voluntary controlled schools are Church of England schools.

3. *Religious Education* in voluntary schools, as in county schools, is governed by Section 25 of the Education Act 1944. RE in all schools is to consist of (*a*) an act of collective worship on the part of all pupils and (*b*) religious instruction (each LEA being obliged to produce an agreed syllabus for the instruction that takes place in county or controlled schools). In a voluntary aided school RE must normally take place on the school premises, though Section 7 of the Education Act 1944 allows for worship in church on special occasions. Details of such occasions must be kept in school records and parents given notice so that they may withdraw their children if they wish. The worship in an aided school is controlled by the governors and will conform to the provision of a trust deed. Religious instruction will also be in accordance with such a deed or, if no such document exists, in accordance with the teaching practice that existed in the school before it became a voluntary aided school. Parents who desire their children to receive religious instruction of a different kind may withdraw their children for such instruction. Under certain well-defined conditions pupils whose parents wish it must be provided in the aided school with instruction according to the LEA's agreed syllabus. Inspection of religious instruction according to the trust deed must be arranged by the governors. Most of the major governing bodies (mainly religious denominations) provide, locally, authorized inspectors. Should any religious instruction in an aided school be according to an agreed syllabus*, the inspection* of such teaching may only be carried out by an HMI or person duly authorized by the Secretary of State or the LEA.

In a voluntary controlled school the act of collective worship for all pupils (except those withdrawn by their parents) takes place on the school premises and its character is in accordance with the trust deed. If the latter makes no provision for worship then the governors decide whether worship shall conform to the practice existing before the school became voluntary controlled or shall be undenominational in character. Religious instruction is given in accordance with the LEA's agreed syllabus, but the pupil whose parents express a wish for denominational teaching in accordance with the trust deed shall receive such teaching in a withdrawal class (for not more than two periods each week). The teaching shall be carried out by one of the 'Reserved Teachers'. The inspection of the teaching in such withdrawal classes is to be arranged by the foundation governors. Arrangements for the inspection of teaching in accordance with the agreed syllabus shall be those that exist for county schools. It should be noted that many church authorities (dioceses for example) have, through Boards or Councils of Education, produced syllabus material or notes for the guidance of teachers of RE in aided schools.

ROBERT WADDINGTON

Wales

Classical writers, like Julius Caesar and Cicero, comment favourably on the Celtic commitment to education. This commitment was to be continued by Celtic Christianity. In Wales the Age of the Saints (sixth century) was witness to the conversion of the people to the new faith and to the birth of the Welsh language. There is evidence that during this period there were centres of educational excellence, furthering in a Christian context the Romano-British tradition of learning and scholarship. Since the Bible demanded a degree of literacy from some, at least, of Welsh Christians it is not unexpected to find evidence of early translations into Welsh.

Continental and Irish influences were to provide an enrichment of Welsh religious life during the early centuries. Later, the establishment of monastic schools, especially those of the Cistercians, maintained the emphasis on an educated Christianity during the mediaeval period. It is significant that 'Welsh as an already established literary language held a higher position than did English in the monastic schools of England. Centuries later, however, when the grammar schools eventually threw off the total domination of Latin, the means of communication in the grammar schools of Wales became English, not Welsh'

(*The Fourth R**). Succeeding centuries were to see these schools play an important role in the life of Wales, and they were to be found, despite fluctuating fortunes, in many Welsh market towns. Their language was English, their ethos Anglican and their emphasis classical, but this did not prevent them from educating young men who were to contribute greatly to Welsh life, often through the medium of the Welsh language. From the seventeenth to the twentieth century the nonconformist academies, with a wider curriculum, provided a significant complementary development.

It is impossible to minimize the influence of the translation of the Bible into Welsh. This task was mostly accomplished by Bishop William Morgan, and the Bible was published in 1588. It is somewhat ironic that a 1563 Act of Parliament argues that 'by conferring both tongues together the sooner (those reading them) attain to the knowledge of the English tongue' since it transpired that it was this translation that assured the survival of the language as a literary and spoken language. The passionate plea of John Penry, the Elizabethan Puritan martyr, for such a task to be undertaken and for an adequate supply of preachers to communicate the gospel in the language of the people did not go unfulfilled.

Between 1671 and 1681 three hundred Welsh Trust schools were established as a result of co-operation between moderate Puritans and Anglicans, and in the early eighteenth century the Society for the Propagation of Christian Knowledge established ninety-six charity schools in Wales. All these schools were religious in intention and English in language. But between 1731 and 1761 a pattern of circulating schools was established which was to achieve for the Welsh people an exceptional degree of literacy in their own language and was to attract the favourable attention even of the representative of the Czarina of Russia. The founder of this system of schooling was Griffith Jones, an Anglican parson of Llanddowror in Dyfed. He was an exceptional administrator and organizer. He established a 'college' to train his itinerant teachers. They were despatched, after due training, throughout Wales between September and May to establish schools for both children and adults. They remained at one location for a period of three or four months before moving on. Griffith Jones's aim was quite simply to enable everyone to read the Bible, and the measure of his success was the phenomenal degree of literacy achieved throughout Wales. He succeeded because he took his schools to the people and insisted on using the Welsh language, since English was to most people a foreign language. 'To Jones more than any man the Welsh owed a massive break-through to literacy. It was this which sealed the success of the Methodist Revival and the triumph of Nonconformity, with all their attendant consequences for Welsh life. It did more than anything else to preserve and fortify the Welsh language and literature, of which the Bible was the corner-stone. . . . He . . . remains one of the prime makers of modern Wales and one of Britain's most notable educational pioneers' (*Pioneers of Welsh Education*).

The Methodist Revival, different in character and theology from its English counterpart, benefited from Jones's pioneering work and in turn inspired the majority of the population to further their biblical and Christian education. The flowering of a folk culture in the nineteenth century, rich in hymnody, theology, preaching, poetry and music, leading eventually to heightened educational and political demands and their realization, owes an immense debt to the Christian passion for education, and in particular to the central concern for Bible teaching and understanding. In this context it is important to acknowledge the role of the Sunday Schools (which were for over a century schools for adults as well as for children, and at their best centres of intellectual discipline), while not forgetting the many other church-based educational and cultural activities.

This resumé suggests that education and religion in Wales, whilst being influenced by developments in England and elsewhere, were nevertheless different in tangible ways. The Welsh language provided the most obvious difference – a difference which still bears significantly on educational, religious, political and media concerns. But another difference was that the denominational 'mix' in Wales was more evenly balanced than elsewhere in the UK – a factor which was further underlined by the Disestablishment of the Anglican Church in Wales in 1920. A third difference was that when, according to the 1944 Act, all education authorities were to prepare agreed syllabuses of RE, a tradition was established in Wales of a syllabus being prepared on a national basis and then offered to every authority. The Welsh Society of the Institute of Christian Education facilitated the work which continued with the revision of this syllabus undertaken in 1963. When the Christian Education Movement* in Wales came into being in 1968 it inherited the mantle of the Welsh Society as well as the pupil-orientated activity of the Student Christian Movement* in schools. In 1978 the CEM in Wales prepared a new syllabus with attendant guidelines and a discussion document on school worship which were accepted, with minor changes, by all but one of the new authorities. This syllabus reflects the comprehensive developments in RE since 1963 and has provided a new impetus for the subject in many schools.

The CEM has successfully established a close working relationship with every LEA and its schools, with the university, and the institutes and colleges of higher education, and with the Welsh Joint Education Committee and the Welsh Office, as well as with all the churches in Wales, and has attempted to meet the special needs of Wales. Other organizations with a distinct interest in Christian education in schools, such as the Inter-School Christian Fellowship*, have also been actively involved with school groups, mostly on an extra-curricular basis.

In common with many European countries, Wales has become extensively secularized during the last forty years. One consequence is that most children and young people now in the schools have only the most tenuous of church allegiance. (It is worth noting that church schools are a far smaller percentage of the whole than in England.) This factor, above all others, has focussed attention on the need for a different kind of religious education from that which assumed the existence of Christian homes and a Christian society. Educational considerations have therefore become paramount, and these are reflected in many of the developments in RE and discussed in a number of reports. Research undertaken in Wales since the 1960s has revealed a comparable lag between the religious thinking of children and their conceptual thinking in general as that noted by Goldman and others, namely a lag of three or more years. In addition it has been found that attitudes to RE in secondary schools on average were moderately favourable in the 1960s and 70s, regardless of the strength of pupils' religious allegiance, and that there was a homogeneity of attitudes among rural and urban pupils as well as among Welsh-speaking and non Welsh-speaking children.

Efforts are being made, with financial assistance by the Welsh Office, to prepare and publish a considerable range of materials in RE through the medium of Welsh to meet the needs of examinees and of more general RE classes from infant to sixth-form level. The Schools Council in Wales has published a substantial volume of material for worship in the secondary schools, also in Welsh. A national centre for RE based at the University College of North Wales, Bangor is serving both schools and churches throughout Wales. Most LEAS are supporting in-service courses in RE in both languages, and preparing materials for their schools. The Welsh Joint Education Committee is also involved in publishing books in Welsh for both junior and secondary schools. This last organization has produced a number of exciting options to the traditional 'A' level syllabuses which enable schools to introduce aspects of religious studies other than the biblical in their sixth-forms.

Durham Report on Religious Education, *The Fourth R*, National Society/SPCK 1970; *Primary Education in Wales,* Central Advisory Council for Education (Wales), HMSO 1967; *Welsh Education Survey No. 3,* The Welsh Office 1976; Glanmor Williams, *Pioneers of Welsh Education*, Faculty of Education, University College, Swansea, (n.d.).

HERBERT HUGHES

Wesley, John, Educational Work of

The education of all and sundry was an integral part of John Wesley's plan for 'the reform of the nation, and in particular of the church'. Within the context of his endeavour to 'spread scriptural holiness throughout the land' he sought to 'unite the pair, so long disjoined, knowledge and vital piety' (C. Wesley). For him, the grace of God in the justification and sanctification of sinners was available to all;

so also should be the benefits of sound learning. He held that the minds of children could be formed 'to wisdom and holiness by instilling the principles of true religion, speculative and practical, and training them up in the ancient way, that they might be rational, scriptural Christians' (*A Plain Account of Kingswood School*).

Thus he trained his 'helpers', often unlettered men and women, to be local and itinerant preachers; he wrote and disseminated many pamphlets for the widest possible consumption; he founded several schools in Bristol, Newcastle and elsewhere; he encouraged both those who ran small day schools in various parts of the country, and pioneers of Sunday School work such as Hannah Ball.

To Kingswood School (founded on the outskirts of Bristol in 1748; transferred to Bath in 1851) he gave his closest attention, and there he developed his basic ideas in theory and practice. He was disgusted with the looseness and irreligion of the public schools of his day, even those of the highest reputation, and Kingswood was to be a direct contrast to them in life-style and curriculum, though he took from them the notion of a boarding school as the right setting for Christian education.

Before founding the school he studied the writings of the Moravian Comenius (1592–1670) and visited the schools of the later Moravians in Herrnhut, as well as the Pietist A. H. Francke's (1663–1727) orphan house in Halle. The works of the French Protestant mystic P. Poiret (1646–1719) and the French Catholic (with Quietist tendencies) C. Fleury (1640–1723) became standard texts for teachers at Kingswood, and Fleury seemed to him in his description of the early church to have given a model for life at Kingswood. He was aware of the teachings of John Locke (1632–1704) though he did not approve of all of them, and took over from him many of his *Thoughts Concerning Education*. Philip Doddridge's (1702–51) Dissenting Academy in Northampton also influenced his ideas and practices.

Life in the 'Christian family' of Kingswood was strictly ordered; idleness and effeminacy were the chief enemies, and games and holidays were excluded (this comes directly from Locke). Religious exercises were frequent every day, and on Sundays virtually continuous. There were regular fast days, and the diet on the other days was simple and nourishing. Boys always worked by day and slept at night in the presence of a master, and parents were not allowed to withdraw their sons even for a day until their course of studies was complete.

This at first lasted for two years. In its original form it began with the basic subjects, and proceeded to Latin grammar and literature (mostly Terence, Sallust, Caesar, Cicero, Cornelius Nepos, Velleius Paterculus and Erasmus), and later to Greek (part of the New Testament and one book of the Iliad were read) and Hebrew. Geography, chronology, rhetoric, logic, ethics and church history had their place, and English authors included Bunyan, Milton and Law. Work in the garden was prescribed and music was taught to some.

Wesley's successors came to realize that his basic principles did not necessarily involve so harsh a régime or so crowded a time-table. But they did not forsake his ideal of a 'Christian family', and it was from this, together with his concept of the relation between Christianity and human knowledge, that A. B. Sackett (headmaster 1928–59) was able to develop his programme of liberalization. He wrote: 'Christian education is not character training, nor the indoctrination of an ecclesiastical creed, nor biblical instruction. It is determined by allegiance to Jesus of Nazareth as the living principle and Lord of human life, and by what his incarnation implies about the nature of God, and man, and the universe in which man is set.'

J. Wesley, *A Plain Account of Kingswood School*, 1768, in *Works*, ed. Jackson, London 1831; A. H. Body, *John Wesley and Education,* Epworth 1936; Rupert E. Davies (ed.), *An Approach to Christian Education.* Epworth ²1957; A. G. Ives, *Kingswood School in Wesley's Day and Since,* Epworth 1970; F. C. Pritchard, *Methodist Secondary Education,* Epworth 1949; P. E. Sangster, *Pity My Simplicity,* Epworth 1963; John Walsh, *A. B. Sackett: A Memoir*, Epworth 1979.

RUPERT DAVIES

West Germany

In the Federal Republic of Germany (FRG) the major domain of institutional RE since the Reformation is religious instruction ('Religionsunterricht') in schools (usually two lessons a week). Whereas it is the state's, not the churches' responsibility to provide for RE as a regular subject the attendance is principally free. Under the age of fourteen, the child's parents decide on it, afterwards the young people make the decision for themselves.

The reason for these regulations is that, notwithstanding the state's supervision, RE has to be profiled 'in accordance with the principles of the religious communities' (Constitution 1949, Art. 7.). This compromise expresses on the one hand the implementation of the article on religious freedom (Art. 4), on the other hand the lasting historical influence of the two Christian churches. The state is neutral but not indifferent, serving the idea of religious freedom not by excluding but by including adequate facilities for the exercise of a so-called 'positive religious freedom' – a typical German solution. In more recent years 'Ersatzunterricht' (substitutive instruction) has been instituted in most parts of the FRG for those who do not want to attend RE. This new subject is called either 'Ethikunterricht' (Ethics) or 'Werte und Normen' (Values and Norms) – the rationale being the educational interest of having every student come into contact with issues concerning the meaning of life.

The system described is practically based on forms of close co-operation between state and churches. Curricula and materials are developed in church educational centres; they are published, however, by the governments of the 'Bundesländer'. The training of teachers lies with state universities or similar institutions. If the churches want to add personnel trained in their own institutions (e.g. catechists), they have to be of equivalent standards. The in-service training is organized by decentralized RE centres belonging to the churches (the Comenius Institute in Muenster/W is responsible for centralized research and development) and by RE teachers' organizations. The recruitment of teachers could be improved. Because of a shortage of specialist RE teachers it is not always possible to provide lessons in RE. This is particularly true in vocational schools.

The history of RE in Germany in this century shows on the Protestant side two major shifts, one since 1930, the second since the 1950s. From the eighteenth century ('Enlightenment') onward RE has played an integral role in school and society by assimilating Christian tradition and values to the spirit of cultural progress ('Kulturprotestantismus'), to the aims of individual formation ('Bildung'), and to collective nation-building. State and church mutually used Christian education as instruments on the basis of overlapping interests.

Because of Karl Barth and the new 'Theology of Crisis' or 'Dialectical Theology' after World War I, the way of ideological (not institutional) integration was abruptly stopped. RE was re-defined and now seen as 'the great irritation' based on the non-assimilable 'scandalous' gospel which demands a personal 'decision'. The spiritual renewal of the churches during the Nazi-regime and the 'Kirchenkampf' added a strong rooting in congregational life. RE (now named as 'Evangelische Unterweisung') won the character of a mixture of teaching and proclaiming the gospel and of instruction and worship (hymns, prayers). The teacher was seen as a witness of and the pupil as a listener to the word of God. Non-theological life themes were almost completely reduced. The Bible became the dominating content (G. Bohne, H. Kittel).

Both Protestant and Roman Catholic RE had been re-established after World War II as a form of 'church in the school'. Soon, however, this view was questioned. The second change starting in the early 1950s has led to a new integration of RE in the educational framework of the school. In some concepts since about 1970 RE is also seen in a critical distance to society, church, and even religion itself (G. Otto et al., S. Vierzig). In the curriculum the central position of the Bible was maintained until the second half of the 1960s, but the interpretation was following more and more modern historical-critical methods.

A decisive next step was the development of a second didactic type of RE: the 'thematic or problem oriented' RE ('thematischproblemorientierter Religionsunterricht') on life themes (H. B. Kaufmann) also called RE in context (K. E. Nipkow), together with a new 'child orientation' (D. Stoodt) and the rediscovery of the category of 'experience' (H. Halbfas). Waves of new instructional material

('models'), media (secular texts, audio-visual aids), and methods (discussion, drama, group work) accompanied the new ideas. The reform of the late 1960s was brought about by the influence of society-oriented theological hermeneutics (J. Moltmann, J. B. Metz) and above all by the impact of modern theories of general education, socialization and interaction.

The phase since 1975 has been marked by a new balance between 'present reality', 'biblical tradition' and the 'Wirkungsgeschichte' of the Bible (U. Früchtel). Altogether, RE has become open-ended in aims, content, and methods with a sharpening awareness of the challenges of other world religions and encouraging forms of ecumenical co-operation.

RE in West Germany comprises not only religious instruction in schools but RE in church Kindergärten (age 3–5), Kindergottesdienst ('children's service', 6–12; the term 'Sunday School' is not used), confirmation classes (12–14), church youth work and adult work. In all these areas the conceptual transformations have moved in directions very similar to those of RE in schools, and the work is done more or less on Christian grounds, but with an open educational commitment to the free orientation of the students.

Very few attempts have been made to elaborate an overall theory of RE covering the issues of all fields mentioned. Where such a step has been made by K. E. Nipkow, in his three volume work Gründfragen der Religionspädagogik, his triple starting point – society (vol 1), church (vol 2), and the sharing persons, namely children, youth, and adults (vol 3) – aims at a redefinition of Christian education as 'intergenerational learning'.

Gerhard Bohne, Das Wort Gottes und der Unterricht, Berlin, Furche 1929, 1964; Erich Feifel, Robert Leuenberger, Günter Stachel, Klaus Wegenast, Handbuch der Religionspädagogik, vol. I–III, Gütersloh, Gerd Mohn, Zürich U. Köln, Benziger 1973–1975; Ursula Früchtel, Leitfaden Religionsunterricht. Arbeitsbuch zur Didaktik des Religionsunterrichts, Zürich u. Köln, Benziger 1977; Hubertus Halbfas, Theology of Catechetics, Herder and Herder 1971; Hans-Bernhard Kaufmann, Muss die Bibel im Mittelpunkt des Religionsunterrichts stehen? (1966/1968) in: Hans-Bernhard Kaufmann (ed.), Streit um *den problemorientierten Unterricht in Schule und Kirche*, Frankfurt/M. Berlin, München, Diesterweg 1973; Helmuth Kittel, *Vom Religionsunterricht zur Evangelischen Unterweisung*, Hannover, Schroedel 1947, 1957; Karl Ernst Nipkow, *Beyond the Bible in Religious Education*, Concilium vol. 3, no. 6, 1970; 'Religious Education in Germany: Development and Problems', *British Journal of Religious Education* 1, 1979; *Grundfragen der Religionspädagogik*, Gütersloh: Gerd Mohn 1975 (vols 1 and 2), 1982 (vol. 3); Gert Otto, *Religionsunterricht, Kirche, Schule*, Hamburg, Furche 1961; Gert Otto, Hans-Joachim Dörger and Jürgen Lott, *Neues Handbuch des Religionsunterrichts*, Hamburg, Furche 1972; Siegfried Vierzig, *Ideologiekriti und Religionsunterricht. Zur Theorie und Praxis eines kritischen Religionsunterrichts*, Zürich u. Köln, Benziger 1975.

K. E. NIPKOW

Wonder *see* Emotional Development

Work Camps

The Work Camp movement was inspired by the volunteers from France, Germany, the Netherlands and England who, in 1920, went to help re-build the farm homesteads destroyed on the Verdun battlefields during the First World War. The initiators in 1920 were the Service Civil International and the Society of Friends. Thus the basic principles of the Work Camp were established: 1. direct action; 2. reconciliation; and 3. international co-operation. Post-war reconstruction, including work for displaced persons and refugees, was the main concern in the early years: but, it was not until after the 1939–45 war that the Work Camp movement developed on a large scale throughout the world. In many countries in Africa and Asia the movement often took the form of Young Pioneer ventures helping in rural development and building programmes.

Characteristic features of Work Camps have lasted over the years. The volunteers have mainly been students in their late teens and early twenties using part of a vacation to help in physical tasks – starting an adventure playground, modernizing a community hall, providing temporary housing after an earthquake, building a village water tank. They live together under simple conditions and contribute all or part of their own living and travelling expenses. There are fifteen to thirty people in the average-sized project, which lasts anything from two weeks to two months or more. The sixteen to eighteen age-group has usually been treated as a junior division within the Work Camp movement, using youth workers, teachers and young clergy as leaders.

Variation and new ideas have modified the Work Camp model. Some organizations, anxious to stimulate local initiative ('prime the pump'), ask volunteers to keep a low profile. The Work 'Camp' becomes an initiative of smaller groups – twos and threes living with local families or, at least, among the people they are there to help. The skills of community development and conscientization are applied. In these and other ways the Work Camp has changed or, as some would say, has been subsumed into new techniques of social action.

The early image of 'pick-and-shovel ambassadors' has indeed changed. Teams of young volunteers are recruited to run holidays for the elderly or the handicapped: others act as staff 'relief teams' in residential homes. Also, partly because of more professionally manned and generously financed schemes; partly because of the taint of shambling amateurism associated by some with Work Camps; and, more positively, because of the volunteer's innate taste for adventure and the new challenge, there is always a pressure to move on to new styles and spheres of operation.

The amount of negotiation and planning necessary for a Work Camp has meant that most projects have been set up by agencies, usually international ones – the United Nations and the World Council of Churches, for example. The ideals of the agency colour the aims and pattern of the Camp. Philanthropy is everywhere, but for those who like to make clear distinctions, it is never easy to say that 'their venture is religious' and 'that one is just social'. Attempting, if the need be felt, to clarify the distinction is one of the many educational merits of the Work Camp.

Few who take part in a Work Camp are disappointed and nearly all acknowledge enrichment from a number of points of view: 1. Perhaps it has been the first experience of living away from home with an international group dedicated to some worthwhile social work. 2. There may be experience of different religious attitudes and practices either through the nature of the project or of the worship shared. 3. It will involve close knowledge of a particular aspect of social need. 4. There can be insight into career possibilities, not only through the project task, but by meeting professional workers and community members. Often there can be a great sense of realistic challenge about 'a life of service' and a commitment to further involvement in the future.

TIMOTHY NEWELL PRICE

World Church

The term used to describe the totality of Christian churches which exist throughout the world. This great variety of institutions is part of the phenomena to be studied in religious education and is a resource for teachers dealing with such topics as, What Christians Believe, Christianity as a World Religion, the Missionary and Ecumenical Movements, and World Development.

The World Church provides a context for the study of local church life; it reveals the wide diversity of church life, particularly in respect of church policy and worship, the ways in which Christians feel they should respond institutionally and personally to social need or emergency, the diversity of assumptions made about church life, social action, authority and theological study. Study of the World Church as such will not normally be part of the curriculum, rather the World Church provides information about Christian understanding, practice and experience which illuminates and enriches many parts of the RE curriculum. Examples of the concepts which information from the life of the World Church may illuminate are: plurality, ethnocentrism, compassion, service, interdependence, piety, mission, revolution, worship*, ritual*, et al.

The most accessible sources of information are the publications and other services of church missionary and development agencies, world confessional bodies (e.g. Lutheran, Reformed, Methodist, Anglican, Salvation Army, RC Church) and the World Council of Churches*.

JOHN M. SUTCLIFFE

World Council of Churches

Educational themes have always been on the agenda of the ecumenical movement. Even the pioneer conferences of this movement discussed 'Education in relation to the Christianization of National Life' (World Missionary Conference in Edinburgh, 1910) and 'Church, Community and State in Relation to Education' (Life and Work Conference in Oxford, 1937). In 1946, after the Second World War, the newly constituted World Council of Churches (WCC) started its Scholarships Programme, established the Ecumenical Institute of the Château de Bossey in 1948, undertook, in 1957, in its Department for Laity, youth work, together with the World Council of Christian Education, and created the Theological Education Fund in 1958.

Still, in the sixties, educational themes in an ecumenical context were directly discussed in the World Council of Christian Education (WCCE), which traced its history back even further than the Missionary movement and the Faith and Order and the Life and Work movements. Sunday School conventions, started in 1889, led in 1907 to the formation of the World Sunday School Assocation, which in 1947 changed its name to the World Council of Christian Education. At the end of the fifties and during the sixties it increasingly shared in many activities with the World Council of Churches, mainly in youth work and education. Taking up recommendations from the Third Assembly of the WCC at New Delhi in 1961, a WCC/WCCE Joint Study Commission on Christian Education was established, whose mandate was 'to work towards the formulation of a common theological understanding of education' and 'to suggest how the two organizations might be of assistance to the churches in developing new lines of approach to this task'. On the basis of this report, the 1968 Uppsala Assembly of the WCC established the Office of Education and a joint negotiating committee went to work. This led finally to the decision, taken by the WCCE in Lima 1971, to merge with the educational work of the WCC. Thus the increasing importance of the role of education in church and society all over the world, especially since the sixties, found its visible expression in the ecumenical movement.

In the wcc a new Unit on Education and Communication took shape, which with some structural adjustments has been renamed the Programme Unit on Education and Renewal of Unit III (1973). In its present form the Programme Unit includes the following sub-units and desks: 1. Education: involving General, Christian and Ecumenical Education, Family Ministries, the Church-Related Educational Institutions Programme, Biblical Studies, Adult Basic Education and Scholar-ships and Leadership Development Pro-gramme; 2. Renewal and Congregational Life; involving the concerns of the laity; 3. Youth; 4. Women in Church and Society; and (since 1981) 5. Theological Education.

The educational policy of the wcc leading up to the Fifth Assembly (1976) in Nairobi focussed primarily on working for liberating educational processes and structures not for, but with people: laity, women, youth, chil-dren, families, congregations and communi-ties. Education for liberation and community, the first priority of the unit's work, became the educational theme of the Nairobi Assembly. The Assembly itself strongly endorsed the aim of the Unit 'to enable persons, communities and institutions to participate as fully as possible in the challenges that faith in God and Christ calls for them, in the renewal of churches and in the transformation of society' (Central Committee 1976). But it asked also for a better theological clarification of the criteria of all educational activities: what is, in detail, the role of education and renewal in search of true community? Thus three main themes emerged as the context in which all programmes of the Unit should be focussed: '1. the need for a bold articulation of the Christian faith; 2. the enabling of the laity for service in the world; 3. a new emphasis on the congregation as the primary place for worship, spiritual formation and personal develop-ment' (Central Committee 1976). Since then, the Unit on Education and Renewal, through its five sub-units working together, has been trying 'to focus the WCC and its constituency on both the understanding and the practice of "ecumenical learning for fully inclusive human community"'. This involves the full range of theological and pedagogical reflec-tion and action as well as liturgical and spiri-tual life, to enable Christians in their commit-ment to be part of learning communities'

(Unit III Report for Central Committees 1981). Learning in community, the first priority of the Unit's work after Nairobi, became the educational issue of the Sixth Assembly of the wcc, 1983, in Vancouver.

See also **Sunday School Movement; Young Men's Christian Association.**

'Encuentro, New Perspectives for Christian Education', *World Christian Education* XXVI, 3 and 4, WCC 1971; Leon Howell, *Acting in Faith: The World Council of Churches since 1975*, WCC 1982; David E. Johnson (ed.), *Uppsala to Nairobi 1968–1975*, SPCK 1975; Gerald E. Knoff, *The World Sunday School Movement*, New York 1979; Karl Ernst Nipkow, 'Alientation, Liberation, Community', *Ecumenical Review* 30, 2, 1978; David M. Paton (ed.), *Breaking Barriers*, SPCK 1976; *Seeing Education Whole*, WCC 1970.

ULRICH BECKER

World Religions

Reasons why world religions have found a place in the RE curriculum are many:

1. *Theological.* There has been some move away from Christian claims to the exclusive-ness of grace, truth, revelation. A more sympathetic approach by Christians to other religions was encouraged by the Edinburgh Missionary Conference in 1910. 'The mis-sionary to the Hindu should possess, and not merely assume, a sympathetic attitude towards India's most ancient religion.' It was encouraged by theologians such as Paul Devanandan and M. M. Thomas. Others who have made a vital contribution to this area are, e.g., W. Hocking (cf. his idea of 'recon-ception', that at any stage a religion is whole and has a claim to truth but it must be able to expand, to include aspects of other religions and to broaden its understanding of the truth). Raymond Panikkar has explored the idea of Christ *incognito* in every religion. Klaus Klos-termaier has written about the real, hard experience of dialogue between Christians and Hindus. Abhishiktananda and Bede Griffiths are utterly open to Mystery in other religions and to the possibility of dialogue rooted in a lively and deep spirituality.

Dialogue amongst members of different religious traditions is now taking place in many countries and at many different levels.

Amongst Christians a variety of positions has emerged ranging from that of the absolutist (e.g. Barth – God's revelation in Christ stands over against all experience) to that of the relativist and pluralist (e.g. John Hick – the Christian experience of God in Christ is just one of mankind's ways of experiencing God).

2. *Philosophical*. Since the last century, in the West there has been a growing interest in the questions, What is religion? and, How is it to be studied? Definitions, necessarily vague and all failing, perhaps, to do justice to the complexity of the subject, cut across the religious traditions. They include reference to the experience of the transcendent (cf. Schleiermacher and 'the feeling of absolute dependence'); the distinction between sacred and profane (cf. Otto's thesis that the basis for this distinction is found in feelings of awe and wonder); the experience of ultimacy (cf. Paul Tillich's definition of religion as that which has ultimate authority and value). Some, like Durkheim, have approached the subject from a social rather than an individual perspective. In any event, as Smart argues in *The Religious Experience of Mankind*, religion seems to include ritual, mythological, doctrinal, ethical, social and experimental dimensions. Perhaps the crucial dimension is the experience of, or implicit/explicit recognition of, the reality of an unseen world.

The question of how to define religion leads on to that of how religious phenomena can best be studied. In recent years, the emphasis has been on religion as it is found now, and on observation and description of this across the whole field of religious phenomena, and across geographical spread.

3. *Changes in Society*. Increasingly in recent years, people in the West have found themselves meeting with those of faiths other than Christianity. They not only meet them but have to live alongside them. Many have felt the need for RE to be orientated to our pluralist society.

4. *Educational*. From the late 1960s the Department of Religious Studies at Lancaster University under Ninian Smart greatly influenced religious studies and teacher training courses; the descriptive study of religion was stressed. This led to work by the Schools Council (cf. *Religious Education in Secondary Schools*, Evans/Methuen), to the formation of the Shap Working Party* on World Religions in Education, and to the development of interested bodies such as SCIFDE (Standing Conference on Inter-Faith Dialogue in Education*). Smart's approach provided an educational rationale for RE within secular institutions. Religion was defined as a form of knowledge; the aim of RE was to understand the central concepts, structure, etc., of this academic discipline.

This provided the teaching method which is often known as phenomenological* and which has been associated with world religions in RE. When sensitively adapted this method can bring a degree of description to the subject which avoids indoctrination*. It can encourage a balance of objectivity and reflection which allows pupils to approach religions critically and, at the same time, to further their personal search for meaning.

The 1944 Act allows for flexibility of interpretation and the newer LEA syllabuses, representing a consensus of opinion in a particular area, encourage or allow for study of world religions.

Perhaps the chief contribution of the world religions movement is the *methodology* which it has adopted. The methodology of the phenomenology of religion (a particular discipline within the comparative study of religion at university level, only one branch of phenomenology and only loosely connected to Husserl's philosophical tradition of phenomenology) has been taken into the school situation. The essentials of this methodology are: it describes rather than explains; it starts from *observable* phenomena; it is concerned to describe *all* forms of religious expression – ritual, symbolic, mythical, doctrinal, ethical; it highlights the different cultural expressions of religious experiences, and the different conceptual frameworks within which these are interpreted, but avoids comparing religions as such; it makes use of the phenomenological concept of *epoche* i.e. objectivity, suspension of judgment, a distancing from presuppositions. *Eidetic vision* is important, that is, the search for the essence of phenomena. (Essence held to be accessible only within a particular manifestation.) This involves entering imaginatively into the inner significance of phenomena for religious believers, and endeavouring to understand the functions of the phenomena rather than attempting to evaluate them.

Very many teachers and pupils have found great delight and excitement in the world religions movement. It has opened up new areas for exploration and has provided a substance lacking in the problem-centred approach of the 1960s. It leads to a far wider context and view of Christianity than did the older Bible syllabuses and more easily includes the interests of pupils of faiths other than Christianity or of none.

Nevertheless, there are those who have reservations about including religions other than Christianity in the RE syllabus. Does their inclusion not help to undermine our cultural heritage? Perhaps less time, for instance, is spent on Bible study and the Bible provides the background to so much of our literature. Is not a theological position which some would regard as unsound easily encouraged e.g. relativist and syncretist? Is it not easy to overburden pupils with information, to concentrate on the gadgetry of religion and on irrelevant exotica without engaging pupils' experience? Is this approach too purely objective and descriptive to promote the pupils' personal growth? What is the nature and place of commitment*? These are all questions which deserve to be thought through.

Pupils' experience can be engaged through the sensitive use of evocative material and of artefacts*; the sharing of foods; visits to places of worship; making video programmes; looking at slides; simulation of e.g. a Passover meal, a Communion service; using appropriate novels, stories, visual art, drama.

There is debate about the age at which it is appropriate to teach world religions. Many agree, however, that, in some form, this approach is appropriate at all ages.

There is debate, too, about the merits of thematic teaching (e.g. sacred places, sacred books, festivals, initiation ceremonies) over against a consecutive exploration of, say, one, two or three of the major religions. It is vital to remember that Christianity can be studied as a world religion applying phenomenological method. But should Christianity occupy the major part of the syllabus? This is a question which has to be wrestled with.

General Background: Abhishiktananda, Guru and Disciple, SPCK 1974; George Appleton, On the Eightfold Path, SCM Press 1961; Marcus Braybrooke, The Undiscovered Christ, CLS, Madras 1973; Inter-Faith Organizations, 1893–1979: An Historical Directory, Mellen 1980; D. Brown, A New Threshold: Guidelines for the Churches in their Relations with Muslim Communities, Sheldon Press 1976; Bede Griffiths, Return to the Centre, Collins 1976; J. Hick and B. Hebblethwaite (eds), Christianity and Other Religions, Fount Books 1980; Jean Holm, The Study of Religions, Sheldon Press 1977; Klaus Klostermeier, Hindu and Christian in Vrindaban, SCM Press 1969; Raymond Panikkar, The Unknown Christ of Hinduism, Darton, Longman & Todd 1964; J. A. T. Robinson, Truth is Two-Eyed, SCM Press 1979; Ninian Smart, The Religious Experience of Mankind, Fontana Books 1969; Guidelines on Dialogue with People of Living Faiths and Ideologies, WCC 1979; Jewish Christian Dialogue, WCC 1975.

Curriculum Development: W. Owen Cole, World Faiths in Education, Allen & Unwin 1978; World Religions: A Handbook for Teachers, ed. W. Owen Cole, CRE 1977; Jean Holm, Teaching Religion in School, Oxford University Press 1975; Robert Jackson (ed.), Approaching World Religions; John Murray 1982; Schools Council, Discovering an Approach, Macmillan 1977.

BRENDA LEALMAN

World Studies

One of the variants of interdisciplinary and integrated enquiry emerging from curriculum innovation in the 1960s at both primary and secondary level. Though most explicitly associated with the World Studies Resources Centre at Groby College in Leicestershire, and the World Studies Project at the University of York, this approach can be more generally identified in other major curriculum initiatives such as the Integrated Studies Project, and composite concepts like 'Development Studies'* and 'Multi-cultural Education'.

Movements such as these relate to existing curriculum subjects, including RE, in at least two ways. They may bring the subject into a co-operative venture with others to form a new composite timetable unit, or they may operate within the 'traditional' subject and its discrete share of the timetable. In both cases the effect on RE has been to open it up to a broader, even global interpretation, especially through the adoption of a thematic or problem-orientated approach.

With respect to religious education, this trend has operated on the cultural side through the growing use of comparative religion whereby other world religions are studied alongside Christianity in British schools. Pupils are introduced to the basic history, philosophy and ritual of, say, Islam, Hinduism or Buddhism, and this approach has been fostered especially where multi-cultural population structures exist, such as Birmingham and Bradford. However, it is also becoming increasingly evident in majority areas of the country, where ethnic minorities are rare or diffused. It is perhaps curious that the comparative approach is less evident within the Christian spectrum itself, despite the fact that the world-wide diffusion of Christianity took place on a denominational basis through the work of their respective missions. This has influenced certain disparities and convergences across the myriad indigenous cultures of the Third World, some of which are significant in terms of contemporary problems. It is with such problems that the development studies side is concerned, and in respect of this, RE has embraced broader humanitarian themes such as the combating of poverty, malnutrition, disease, exploitation and oppression. In short, the resolution of issues of human conflict and human rights. Indeed, agencies of the various Christian denominations in Britain have been more active on this front than they have in relation to that of comparative religion. They have also combined with other, not specifically religious, agencies to produce the major effort to promote world/development studies in schools. This went under the acronym, VCOAD – Voluntary Committee on Overseas Aid and Development, which has in turn generated the Centre for World Development Education – CWDE.

Probably the most evident and distinctive contribution to world studies made by these agencies of religious education and their partners has been the generation of a wide range of well produced and inexpensive teaching materials for use at both primary and secondary level. The object of the exercise has been to release teachers from overdependence on traditional texts in the various subjects contributing to a world studies approach, especially as respected researchers have shown many such texts to be riddled with racism and other misleading images of peoples, places and problems overseas. Most notable among the avalanche of progressive materials in this field has been *The Development Puzzle*, first published by VCOAD and subsequently by CWDE. In addition to such collective publications, individual churches and religious agencies have produced teaching materials to promote and support world studies in schools.

The involvement of RE in world studies has not been without its problems. On the cultural side for example, concentration on the structure and content of individual world religions has been viewed by some critics as overlooking the problems contributed by organized religious movements to the plight of humanity. On the development studies side, the apocalyptic approach to the study of material deprivation could well have equally limiting effects in terms of perceptions of the Third World. Nonetheless, the balance of the modern interaction in British schools between 'religious education' and 'world studies' has been positive in respect of promoting wider perspectives on the human condition.

COLIN BROCK

Worship

To observe an act of worship is to observe dramatised theology. Although the interpenetration of religion, custom and culture is often most apparent within worship, the final arbiter of the forms worship can take in a particular religious tradition is what its theology permits. The study of worship, therefore, is a convenient way of encountering, through observable phenomena, those beliefs, teachings and practices which taken together constitute a religion's or a denomination's distinctive theology. Because in most religious traditions worship has a strongly representational element – it uses story, action, posture, music, dress, furniture, art and architecture – it can be studied at several different levels according to the capacities of the pupils. For example, using such a structure as, *How people worship, Where people worship* and *Why people worship*, the study can either be concerned with describing accurately what worshippers do, what words are spoken, how a holy book is used, what special clothes are worn etc., or with uncovering the doctrines and beliefs underlying such practices.

But that which is most significant in worship is not directly observable. The attention of the worshippers is not merely drawn to the observables of worship, to the stories, the actions, the music etc., but through them to the deity, the true object of worship. Worship, like the religious symbol, 'points beyond itself while participating in that to which it points' (Tillich). The phenomenon of worship which is studied in RE has a noumenal focus perceived through faith and it is to this that the pupils' attention also needs to be directed. The need for RE to 'transcend the informative' (Smart) is especially important in its treatment of worship. The learning experiences devised by the teacher must not only evoke the feelings, aspirations and intentions of the worshippers as they engage in the worship of their deity, they must also seek to disclose their sense of the divine. An imaginative use of audio-visual presentations of worship, especially those which include worshippers giving personal testimony to their faith, may go some way to meeting this need but inevitably it will fall short of providing the first-hand experience of worship which is so crucial to accurate understanding.

Provided it is voluntary and not offensive to their own religious beliefs or otherwise, older pupils making a serious study of religion might be encouraged to attend acts of worship in the places of worship of local faith communities. They would attend as *observing participants* making a conscious effort to suspend their own beliefs and enter into the religious perspective of an adherent. For pupils to relate their theoretical knowledge of a religion to its practice in this way, preferably with an opportunity for classroom evaluation later, would be a valuable and legitimate educational experience. But encouraging pupils to participate in worship in order to develop a more profound understanding of a subject of study, namely of worship itself, is very different from requiring them to engage in worship as an expression of personal faith. It does not follow, therefore, that the provision of acts of worship for pupils in school which imply that the school itself is a faith community or a reflection of one, can perform the same function or that such provision can be justified on the same educational grounds.

J. M. Hull, *School Worship: An Obituary*, SCM Press 1975; G. Parrinder, *Worship in the World's Religions*, Sheldon Press 1974; N. Smart, *The Concept of Worship*, Macmillan 1972.

MICHAEL GRIMMITT

Yoga

A religious activity and discipline within Hindu worship whereby Hindus aim to unite the Soul (Atman) with the Universal Spirit or God (Brahman). Of the eight levels of attainment, those which can most readily be taught in RE are Asana, body control; Pranayama, breathing control; and Dharana, mind control. It is through the control of these forces within a person, Hindus argue, that the soul can be freed and united with Brahman.

The teaching of yoga would most naturally fall within lessons about Hindu worship since yoga is integral to the pupil's understanding of concepts such as reincarnation, *shanti*, *karma*, *moksha*, the caste system, the symbol 'OM' and important prayers such as the Gayatri Mantra. It permeates every stage of Hindu life from birth to rebirth.

Yoga can be practised anywhere where the body is not restricted in movement and the atmosphere is congenial to peace. Pupils need room to move and should wear loose clothing. Communication of the atmosphere, discipline and appreciation of yoga requires of the teacher empathy and sensitivity rather than agility. Simplicity of posture is important. A well-planned experience, which would contribute to the pupils' affective learning, could include 1. Body Control: Surya Namaskar which could lead to the teaching of the Gayatri Mantra; Bhujang; Gomuch, Dhanur, Garadha and Bhadra. 2. Breathing Control: alternative nostril breathing; Bhastrika, bellows. 3. Mind Control: the symbol of 'OM'; simple meditation. Each session should end with the relaxation posture, Savasana.

Surami Vishnudevananda, *The Complete Illustrated Book of Yoga*, Souvenir Press 1961; Richard Hittleman, *Yoga for Health*, Hamlyn 1971.

ALTHEA DRAPER

Young Men's Christian Association

The YMCA began in London in 1844 under George Williams (1821–1905) and quickly spread throughout England, Europe, Australia and North America, prompting the formation of the World Alliance of YMCAs in 1855 on the acceptance of the Paris Basis which stated that the association was based on the confession of belief in Christ as God and Saviour. This basis was eventually passed on to the World Council of Churches*. A major figure in the development of the World Alliance was John R. Mott (1865–1955). In 1980 the YMCA was operating in eighty-six countries and had over twenty-two million members and participants.

In 1971 the British YMCA stated its purpose as 'A world-wide fellowship based on the equal value of all persons. Respect and freedom for all, tolerance and understanding between people of different opinions. Active concern for the needs of the community. United effort by Christians of different traditions.' Since each local YMCA, although affiliated to the National Council, retains its autonomy, there is a wide variety of local provision, including sports and physical education, camping, counselling, social, leisure, educational, religious and residential facilities. Many YMCAs are open to women, adults of all ages and those of all religious faiths and of none.

The British YMCA is involved in Youth and Community Work, Training through the National College, Youth Unemployment, young worker education, international exchange programmes, and world-wide refugee work. It has recently published useful reports on race relations and the ecumenical movement.

Clyde Binfield, *George Williams and the YMCA*, Heinemann 1973; Leslie J. Francis, *Youth in Transit*, Gower Publishing Company 1982; C. Howard Hopkins, *History of the YMCA in North America*, Association Press 1951; C. Howard Hopkins, *John R. Mott, 1865–1955: A Biography*, Eerdmans 1979; Jean Hutton, Colin Quine and Bruce Reed, *The Wholeness of Life*, National Council of YMCAs 1975; T. J. Massey, *The YMCA in Australia: a history*, F. W. Cheshire, Melbourne 1950; C. P. Shedd (ed.), *History of the World Alliance of YMCAs*, SPCK 1955.

LESLIE FRANCIS

Young Women's Christian Association

The YWCA began in England in 1855 with Emma Roberts' Prayer Union and Mary Jane Kinnaird's General Female Training Institute. These two groups merged to form the YWCA in 1877, leading to the organization of the World YWCA in 1894. The YWCA shares the same evangelical origins as the YMCA. In 1980 the YWCA was operating in over eighty countries.

The early YWCA groups were motivated by a Christian response to the social effects of the industrial revolution on the lives of young women. Today the YWCA describes itself as an 'Association founded on Christian ideals to serve and work with people.' As an ecumenical movement, the YWCA is open to males and females, without distinction of race, nationality, politics or religion.

The British YWCA operates accommodation, leisure centres, further education courses, advisory services, neighbourhood centres and programmes like play buses and the Duke of Edinburgh award scheme. The association works among handicapped children, disabled people, single parents, women's groups, minority cultures, widows and retired people.

Julian Duguid, *The Blue Triangle*, Hodder & Stoughton, 1955; Theodora Maclagan *et al.*, *The YWCA of Great Britain: four studies*, YWCA 1955; Anna V. Rice, *A History of the World's Young Women's Christian Association*, The Women's Press, New York 1947; Mary S. Sims, *The YWCA – an unfolding purpose*, The Women's Press, New York 1950.

LESLIE FRANCIS

Yugoslavia   *see* **Eastern Europe**

SELECT BIBLIOGRAPHY

Colin Alves, *Religion and the Secondary School*, SCM Press 1968
Ian H. Birnie (ed.), *Religious Education in Integrated Studies*, SCM Press 1972
W. Owen Cole, *Religion in the Multi-Faith School*, Hulton 1983
W. Owen Cole (ed.), *World Faiths in Education*, Allen & Unwin 1978
Terence and Gill Copley, *First School RE*, SCM Press 1978
Edwin Cox, *Changing Aims in Religious Education*, Routledge & Kegan Paul 1966
— *Problems and Possibilities for Religious Education*, Hodder 1982
Alan Dale, *The Bible in the Classroom*, Oxford University Press 1972
Ronald J. Goldman, *Readiness for Religion*, Routledge & Kegan Paul 1965
— *Religious Thinking from Childhood to Adolescence*, Routledge & Kegan Paul 1964
Michael Grimmett, *What Can I Do in RE?*, Mayhew McCrimmon (revised edition) 1980
J. Hinnells (ed.), *World Religions and Education*, Oriel Press 1969
R. Holley, *Religious Education and Religious Understanding*, Routledge & Kegan Paul 1978
Jean Holm, *Teaching Religion in School*, Oxford University Press 1975
John Hull, *School Worship: An Obituary*, SCM Press 1975
— *Studies in Religion and Education*, Falmer Press 1984
E. Hulmes, *Commitment and Neutrality in Religious Education*, Chapman 1979
Kenneth Hyde, *Religious Learning in Adolescence*, Oliver & Boyd 1965
L. Kohlberg, *Essays on Moral Development Volume 1*, Harper & Row 1981
Eric Lord and Charles Bailey (eds), *A Reader in Religious and Moral Education*, SCM Press 1973
Harold Loukes, *New Ground in Christian Education*, SCM Press 1965
— *Teenage Religion*, SCM Press 1961
Violet Madge, *Children in Search of Meaning*, SCM Press 1965
Carol Mumford, *Young Children and Religion*, Edward Arnold 1982
D. J. O'Leary and T. Sallnow, *Love and Meaning in Religious Education*, Oxford University Press 1982
Jean Piaget, *The Moral Judgment of the Child*, Routledge & Kegan Paul 1932
— *The Science and Education and the Psychology of the Child*, Grossman 1970
Schools Council, *Discovering an Approach*, Macmillan 1977
— *A Groundplan for the Study of Religion*, Schools Council 1977
— *Working Paper 36: Religious Education in Secondary Schools*, Evans/Methuen 1971
— *Working Paper 44: Religious Education in Primary Schools*, Evans/Methuen 1974

N. Smart, *The Phenomenon of Religion*, Mowbray 1973
— *Secular Education and the Logic of Religion*, Faber & Faber 1968
N. Smart and D. Horder (eds), *New Movements in Religious Education*, Temple Smith 1975
J. Wilson, *Education in Religion and the Emotions*, Heinemann 1971
The Child in the Church, British Council of Churches 1976
The Fourth R, National Society/SPCK 1970

INDEX OF NAMES